The Blitzkrieg Legend

An Association of the U.S. Army Book

The Blitzkrieg Legend

The 1940 Campaign in the West

Karl-Heinz Frieser
with
John T. Greenwood

Naval Institute Press
Annapolis, Maryland

Naval Institute Press
291 Wood Road
Annapolis, MD 21402

The original edition was published under the title
Karl-Heinz Frieser, Blitzkrieg-Legende. Der Westfeldzug 1940
Munich: Oldenbourg (2nd edition) 1996
(= Operationen des Zweiten Weltkriegs, 2)

ISBN-10: 1-59114-294-6
ISBN-13: 978-1-59114-294-2

Library of Congress Cataloging-in-Publication Data
Frieser, Karl-Heinz.
[Blitzkrieg-Legende. English]
The Blitzkrieg legend : the 1940 campaign in the West / Karl-Heinz Frieser with
John T. Greenwood.
p. cm.
Includes bibliographical references and index.
ISBN 1-59114-294-6 (alk. paper)
1. World War, 1939–1945—Campaigns—Western Front. 2. Lightning war. I. Greenwood, John T.
II. Title.
D756.3.F7513 2005
940.54´21—dc22

2005016997

Printed in the United States of America on acid-free paper ∞
12 11 10 09 08 07 06 9 8 7 6 5 4 3 2

Contents

Charts and Maps

Charts

Maps

Gallery A

Gallery B

Gallery C

Editor's Introduction

When Karl-Heinz Frieser and I began working on an English translation of his *Blitzkrieg-Legende: Der Westfeldzug, 1940* (The Blitzkrieg Legend: The 1940 Campaign in the West) back in 1996, we never expected it to take so long to see the finished book. This project began as a cooperative undertaking between the Military History Research Office of the German Armed Forces in Potsdam, Germany, and my former employer, the U.S. Army Center of Military History, where I was then the chief of the Field Programs and Historical Services Division. Since that time, I have become the chief historian for the Office of the Surgeon General, U.S. Army, and the project moved to the Association of the United States Army (AUSA) in 2000. As a result of the support of Gen. Gordon R. Sullivan, U.S. Army (Ret.), president of AUSA and former chief of staff, U.S. Army, and with the encouragement and solid backing of Lt. Col. Roger Cirillo, U.S. Army (Ret.), who heads up the AUSA book publishing program, Karl-Heinz Frieser's book is at long last appearing in English.

Mr. Gerald Lewis Geiger, a World War II and Korean War veteran who served in the U.S. Army in Europe and later in the U.S. Air Force, completed the original translation for Schreiber Translations of Rockville, Maryland. Mr. Geiger's efforts made possible the editorial work that Karl-Heinz and I then undertook over the next nine years as the project stumbled along like the French army facing Heinz Guderian and his Panzers on the Meuse River in May 1940. Karl-Heinz has been intimately involved in all aspects of the manuscript's preparation—he has read and commented on every page of every revision that I have completed. He has quickly and completely answered every question I have had. His deep, personal commitment to the completion of this work despite his heavy workload as an author and branch chief at the MGFA (Militärgeschichtlichen Forschungsamt) has been the major reason for its successful completion.

Putting Karl-Heinz's German text into publishable English text that is historically and militarily accurate in all its German, French, and English aspects has been an interesting voyage of discovery. I quickly learned that German and American footnoting and bibliographical styles were dissimilar enough to produce significant additional work. I have adopted the standard American practice of a full source citation in the initial note and an abbreviated form thereafter. With sources in German, French, English, and a few other European languages, and citations required in English for all the non-English titles, the editing workload has been significant. Again, Karl-Heinz's assistance has been critical to completing this project. In the end, I believe I was able to resolve most of the issues associated with footnotes and sources. In accordance with U.S. Naval Institute Press style, the footnotes have been converted to endnotes at the back of the book.

The editor and translator are responsible for all insertions in the text that are set off in square brackets, except those in direct quotations, which are the author's interpolations. English translations of foreign words and phrases are given in parentheses.

In the text, ranks of the German personnel are retained in German in their initial appearance while all others are in English. I have tried to minimize unneeded repetition of ranks, so the initial mention of a personality is the only time his rank appears unless subsequently a higher rank was achieved, such as with Erich von Manstein. For the reader's benefit, positions or commands held by individuals appear as they did in the original book. A table of German and U.S. Army equivalent ranks is provided.

One of the most challenging aspects of my work was to return to their original English form all quotations from English-language sources that had been published in German or translated into German in the book. This required locating all such original editions cited by Karl-Heinz, if possible, or later editions, if necessary, and replacing each quotation in German with the original English version. This took considerable time and effort. All notes referencing such citations contain both a German-language source, if cited by Karl-Heinz, and the original English source.

German military terms are used sparingly and only when they are particularly critical to the text or are commonly accepted in military history publications, such as Panzer, which is used throughout for armored units and vehicles. Only certain important German units appear in German in the initial appearance and thereafter are in English translation. All Belgian and French units appear in English translation.

All photographs maps, charts, and diagrams from the original German edition have been retained in this edition. However, the text of the maps, charts, and diagrams has not been translated into English due to associated costs that would have affected the book's final price. To assist in understanding the untranslated pages, a glossary has been prepared that includes many of the German abbreviations and words contained in the maps, charts, and diagrams.

Karl-Heinz Frieser's book is an important contribution to military history and to the twentieth century because it unravels a legend that has stood for more than sixty-five years. His research in the original documentation in the German Federal Military Archives is complemented by wide-ranging research in primary and secondary sources. As he says, his story ranges from Adolf Hitler and the army general staff at the highest strategic and national levels down to the company officers and enlisted men who actually won the victory at Sedan. While telling this multidimensional story, his primary focus remains on the operational level of war where the outcome was decided on the battlefield between the Meuse River and the English Channel in May 1940.

John T. Greenwood

Preface

In starting my research on the *Westfeldzug* 1940 (the 1940 campaign in the west), I naturally went along with the old theory that this campaign had from the very beginning been planned as a so-called blitzkrieg. The approximately fifteen hundred books and essays that I analyzed almost without exception confirmed this generally accepted idea. I was, therefore, surprised when the exact opposite began to emerge with increasing clarity during my archival research. As a member of Militärgeschichtliches Forschungsamt (MGFA, Military History Research Office of the Bundeswehr) I had the opportunity over several years to go through the pertinent files of the Bundesarchiv-Militärarchiv (Federal Military Archives) in Freiburg, specifically from the highest strategic echelon down to, in some cases (as regards the key episodes), the lowest tactical command echelon. This focus resulted in a new perspective. It became increasingly clear that the campaign in the west happened differently from the way it was planned.

Unfortunately, many of the files on the lower command echelons were destroyed during the war. Therefore I conducted interviews with numerous eyewitnesses. The German veterans' associations that I approached were able to supply duplicates of many war diaries, after-action reports, and so on, whose originals had been burned. The files of the Service Historique de l'Armée de Terre (Historical Service of the French Army) in Vincennes also provided important references.

Naturally, it was impossible to cover the campaign in the west to its fullest extent, with all of the many different events that it featured. That also appears unnecessary in view of the way in which the point of main effort had been devised, so that it derived from the planning and course of the campaign itself. The campaign was decided by a single operation, called Sichelschnitt (the sickle cut). Actually, the decision had already come with Guderian's operational breakthrough at Sedan. That battle—which featured the clash of two different concepts of war—signified a turning point in military history and will be covered in particularly great detail. The military events in the Netherlands, whose army capitulated after only five days, as well as those in northern Belgium recede into the background by comparison. The airborne troops that were dropped here were intended primarily to carry out an operational deception maneuver to divert attention from the actual point of main effort at Sedan. The second part of the campaign (Fall Rot, or Case Red) is also covered only as a brief afterword because the defeat of the Allies was already definite at that point in time.

First of all, I thank my superiors in the MGFA who allowed me to expand this monograph, which originally was planned as a purely operational history study, into a broad account. That was the only way to clear up the scintillating blitzkrieg problem with its operational-strategic ambivalence. Among the domestic and foreign historians who gave me many suggestions, I feel particularly indebted to Col. Robert Allan Doughty, the head of the Department of History of the U.S. Military Academy at West Point. A staff ride to Sedan, directed by him, first brought me into contact with the topic that has fascinated me ever since and that in recent years became the focus of my historical research. Among the very many eyewitnesses to whom I owe written and verbal acknowledgements, I emphasize above all Gen. Johann Adolf Count von Kielmansegg (Ret.), the former commander in chief of NATO's Central Army Group (CENTAG). I am especially indebted to the Drafting Section of the Military History Research Office. Mr. Ulf Balke, supported during the final phase by Mrs. Stefanie Dittel, managed to convert my rough drafts into informative sketches and to insert many creative ideas. I was also lucky that Mrs. Christa Grampe was assigned to me as editor. She reviewed my manuscript with great care and much empathy.

I especially thank Dr. John Greenwood who has devoted his time and attention to editing and preparing my book for publication in English since we first began working on this endeavor in 1996. He and I have spent countless hours reviewing and correcting the text so that it is as true as possible to my original German edition and tells the story as I intended. I believe that together we have made a significant contribution to the understanding of the entire story of the blitzkrieg.

Karl-Heinz Frieser

Abbreviations and Translations of Frequently Used Foreign Terms

Term	Translation	Abbreviation
abends	evening	
Ablauflinie	line of departure	
Abmarsch	departure	
Abteilung	battalion or detachment	Abt.
Abwehr	defense or Wehrmacht counterintelligence	Abw
Angriffsbefehl	attack order	
Ardennen	Ardennes	
Armee	army	
Armeegruppe	army group (Fr. and Brit. forces)	
Armeekorps	army corps	AK
Armeeoberkommando	army command	AOK
Artillerie	artillery	Art
Artillerieregiment	artillery regiment	ArtRgt
Aufklärung	reconnaissance	Aufkl
Aufklärungsabteilung	reconnaissance battalion (Ger.)	Aufklabt
Aufklärungsbataillon	reconnaissance battalion (Fr.)	Aufklbtl
Auftragstaktik	mission tactics	
ausser Dienst	retired	a.D.
Bataillon	battalion	Btl
Batterie	battery	Bttr
Befehlshaber	commander	Befh
Belgien	Belgium	
Belgische	Belgian	belg.
Belgische Ardennenjäger	Belgian Ardennes Light Infantry	ArdJg
Britische Armee	British Army	brit.Armee
Brücke	bridge	
Bundesarchiv-Militärarchiv	Federal Archives-Military Archives	BA-MA
Centre de Résistance	company sector (Fr.)	C.R.
Char B	French heavy tank	
Corps d'Armeé	army corps	C.A.
der Reserve	reserve	d.R.

Term	Translation	Abbreviation
des Generalstabs	of the general staff (general staff officer)	d.G.
Deutsches Reich	Germany (literally, German Empire)	
division d'infanterie	infantry division (Fr.)	D.I.
division d'infanterie motoriseé	infantry division motorized (Fr.)	D.I.M.
division légère méchanique	light mechanized division (Fr.)	D.L.M.
Dragoner	dragoon	
Dünkirchen	Dunkirk	
Durchbruch	breakthrough	
Eintreffen	arrival	
Feldwebel	sergeant	Fw
Festung	fortress	
Festungsinfanterie	fortress infantry	
Festungsinfanterie-division	fortress infantry division	FestungsInf-Div
Festungsinfanterie-regiment	fortress infantry regiment	FestungsInf Rgt
Fliegerkorps	air corps	Fl.Korps
Flugabwehr	antiaircraft	Fla
Flugabwehrkanone	antiaircraft artillery	Flak
Flugabwehr (Regiment)	antiaircraft (regiment)	Fla(Rgt)
Forges et chantiers de Le Méditerranée	French tank	FCM
Frankreich	France	
Französische Armee	French army	franz.Armee
Gefechtsgruppe	battle group	
Gefechtsstand	command post	Gef.Std
Gegenangriff	counterattack	
General der Flieger	Luftwaffe lieutenant general	Gen.d.Fl
General der Panzertruppe	Panzer lieutenant general	Gen.d.PzTr
Generalkommando	corps headquarters	Gen.Kdo
Generaloberst	general	Gen.Oberst
Generalquartiermeister	general staff officer, in charge of supply and administration	Gen.Qu
Generalstab (des Heeres)	army general staff	Genst(dH)
Geschütz	gun	Gesch
Großdeutschland	Grossdeutschland (greater Germany)	GD
Gruppe	group	Gr, Grp

Term	Translation	Abbreviation
Hauptwiderstandslinie	main line of resistance	
Heeresgruppe	army group	HrG
Heeresgruppe A	Army Group A	HrG A
Heeresgruppe B	Army Group B	HrG B
Heeresgruppe C	Army Group C	HrG C
Heeresgruppe G	Army Group G	HrG G
Heeresgruppe H	Army Group H	HrG H
Heeresgruppe O	Army Group O (Upper Rhine)	HrG O
Höhe	elevation or hill	
Hotchkiss 35	French tank	H 35
Hotchkiss 39	French tank	H 39
im Generalstab	on the general staff	i.G.
Infanterie	infantry	Inf
Infanterie Division	infantry division	InfDiv
Infanterie Division (motorisiert)	infantry division (motorized)	InfDiv(mot)
Infanteriegeschütz	infantry gun	InfG
Infanterie Korps	infantry corps	InfKorps
Infanterie Korps (motorisiert)	infantry corps (motorized)	InfKorps (mot)
Infanterie-Regiment	infantry regiment	InfRgt
Infanterieregiment Großdeutschland	Grossdeutschland Infantry Regiment (German army)	IRGD
Jäger	light infantry (army) or fighter aircraft (air force)	Jg
Kavallerie	cavalry	Kav
Kavallerie Brigade	cavalry brigade	KavBrig
Kavallerie Division	cavalry division	KavDiv
Kavallerie Regiment	cavalry regiment	KavRgt
Kolonialinfanterie-Regiment	colonial infantry division (Fr.)	Kol.InfDiv
Kommandant	commandant	Kdt
Kommandeur	commander	Kdr
Kommandierender General	commanding general	KG
Kompanie	company	Kp
Korps	corps	
Kradschütze	motorcycle rifleman	KradSchtz
Kradschützen-Bataillon	motorcycle rifle battalion	KradSchtzBtl
Kraftfahrzeug	motor vehicle	Kfz
Kriegstagebuch	war diary	KTB

Term	Translation	Abbreviation
Küraisser	curassier	
leicht	light	le
leichte Kavallerie Division	light cavalry division (Fr.)	le Kav Div
leichte mechanisierte Brigade	light mechanized brigade (Fr.)	le mech Brig
Leutnant	2d lieutenant	LT
Maas	Meuse River	
Maasübergang	crossing of Meuse River	
Maschinengewehr	machine gun	MG
Maschinengewehr-Bataillon	machine-gun battalion	MG-Bataillon
mechanisiert	mechanized	mech
Mosel	Moselle River	
motorisiert	motorized	mot
Niederlande	Netherlands	
Nordafrikanische Infanteriedivision	North African infantry division (Fr.)	Nordafrik. InfDiv
Nordsee	North Sea	
Oberbefehlshaber	commander in chief, commander	OB
Oberkommando der Kriegsmarine	navy high command	OKM
Oberkommando der Luftwaffe	Luftwaffe (air force) high command	OKL
Oberkommando der Wehrmacht	armed forces high command	OKW
Oberkommando des Heeres	army high command	OKH
Oberleutnant	1st lieutenant	Obtl, OLt
Oberstleutnant	lieutenant colonel	OTL
Operationensabteiling (des Operations Generalstafs des Heeres)	operations section, army general staff	OpAbt
Pakzüge	antitank platoons	
Panzer	armored fighting vehicle	Pz
Panzerabwehr-Kanone	antitank gun	Pak
Panzerarmee	Panzer or armored army	PzArmee
Panzeraufklärungsabteilung	Panzer or armored reconnaissance battalion	PzAufklAbt
Panzerdivision	Panzer or armored division	PzDiv

Term	Translation	Abbreviation
Panzergruppe	Panzer or armored group	PzGrp
Panzergruppe Hoepner	Panzer Group Hoepner	PzGrp Hoepner
Panzergruppe Hoth	Panzer Group Hoth	PzGrp Hoth
Panzergruppe Kleist	Panzer Group Kleist	PzGrp Kleist
Panzergruppe Reinhardt	Panzer Group Reinhardt	PzGrp Reinhardt
Panzerjägerabteilung	Panzer or armored antitank battalion	PzJgAbt
Panzerkampftwagen	Panzer or tank	Kpfw
Panzerkompanie	Panzer or armored company	PzKp
Panzerkorps	Panzer or armored corps	PzKorps
Panzerkorps Guderian	Panzer Corps Guderian	PzKorps Guderian
Panzer-Pionier-Bataillon	Panzer or armored engineer (pioneer) battalion	PzPiBtl
Panzerturm	armored cupola	
Panzerzug	armored or tank platoon	PzZug
Patrouille	patrol (Fr.)	
Pionier	engineer (pioneer)	Pi
point d'appui	platoon strongpoint (Fr.)	P.A.
Renault 35	French light tank	R35
Rhein	Rhine River	
Schützen	riflemen	Schtz
Schützenregiment	rifle regiment	SchtzRgt
Schwadron	squadron	
schwer	heavy	
Schwerpunkt	point of main effort	
Sichelschnitt	Sickle Cut	
Sous Sectuer	regimental sector (Fr.)	
Spähpanzer	armored reconnaissance vehicle	
Spähwagon	reconnaissance or scout car	Spw
Staffel	echelon	
Stoßtrupp	assault team or detachment	
Sturmpionier	assault engineer (pioneer)	
Sturmpionierbataillon	assault engineer (pioneer) battalion	SturmpionierBtl
Teile	element	
Unteroffizier	noncommissioned officer (NCO) or corporal	Uffz

Term	Translation	Abbreviation
Verbände	units	
Verbindungsoffizier	liaison officer	VerbOffz
Verfolgungsabteilung	advanced detachment	Verfol-gungsAbt
Verzögerungslinie	delaying line	VZL
Vorausabteilung	forward detachment	VorausAbt
Wasserturm	water tower	
Wehrmachtführungsstab	Wehrmacht operations staff	Wfst
Wehrwirtschafts- und Rüstungsamt (des OKW)	Defense Industry and Armament Office (Defense Industry Office)	WiRüAmt
Zitadelle	citadel	

The Blitzkrieg Legend

Introduction

The Miracle of 1940

The whole world is searching for the new methods used by the Germans—and they were not at all new—because war is always a system of expedients.[1]

General der Artillerie [Franz] Halder,
Chef des Generalstabes des Heeres
[Chief, Army General Staff],
immediately after the Campaign in the West.

General [Maxime] Weygand said in Lille on 2 July 1939: "The French Army is stronger than ever before in its history; its equipment is the best, its fortifications are first-rate, its morale is excellent, and it has an outstanding High Command. Nobody wants war but if we are forced to win a new victory then we will win it."[2]

Hitler's gambler's policy failed early in September 1939. He thought that he could crush Poland in an isolated campaign, but instead Great Britain and France declared war on him. In that way, he conjured up the specter of World War I, the two-front war. In 1939, the German Reich, poor in raw materials, was no more able than in 1914 to last through a long, drawn-out conflict with the Western sea powers. The Treaty of Versailles had caused the Wehrmacht (German Armed Forces) to shrink to dwarf size. The Wehrmacht that Hitler had been hectically building up since 1935 was still completely unprepared for another world war. In his book *Dunkirk: Anatomy of Disaster,* Patrick Turnbull described how he was surprised by the outbreak of World War II: "The news that Germany had invaded Poland was blazoned in vast headlines on the front page of the local newspaper thrust into my hands. It was 1 September 1939, and I was breakfasting on the terrace of a hotel in Fez's *Ville Nouvelle.* . . . The Germans, I was convinced, had committed an act of suicidal folly. Britain had the world's most powerful navy, France the world's finest army. . . . The end would come quickly, probably before Christmas, and with little difficulty!"[3]

Just how sure of victory the French felt behind their Maginot Line was expressed by their Supreme Commander, General [Maurice] Gamelin. In January 1940 he said that "he would be ready to give a billion to the Germans, provided they would do him the favor of taking the initiative in the attack."[4] But "the most mystifying event in the history of modern war" happened in May 1940.[5] During World War I, the German armies had tried in vain for four years to break through the French front; this time, the breakthrough at Sedan was already accomplished after four days. The German Panzers were now able to push almost unhindered through the French rear areas and on to the Channel Coast and envelope the northern wing of the Allies in a gigantic pocket. The campaign was over after a total of six weeks.

Since then, historians have outdone each other in superlatives as they tried to express in words the elemental force of this event. Liddell Hart spoke of "the most sweeping victory in modern history"[6]; Barrie Pitt, on the other hand, talked about a "military catastrophe . . . that has no equal in the history of war."[7] Cohen and Gooch equated this defeat to a "Greek tragedy."[8] The American historian William L. Langer wrote: "Modern history can point to few such stunning events as the defeat and collapse of the French Republic in June 1940. Since Napoleon's swift campaign against Prussia in 1806, no big military power had been crushed so quickly and so relentlessly. In less than 6 weeks, one of the powers that directed the world was literally swept off the international scene."[9]

At first, the international public reacted almost aghast, but a plausible explanation was soon found: It was the "blitzkrieg." Allegedly, Hitler had invented a completely revolutionary strategy, the strategy of the blitzkrieg, which his generals then implemented on the battlefield. If this had been so, then the inventors could have watched their plan materializing quite calmly and full of satisfaction. But, in view of the precipitating events, the victors were at first just about as surprised as the vanquished. When the German Panzer divisions broke through near Sedan, Hitler shouted: "This is a miracle, an absolute miracle!"[10]

The breathtaking speed of the German thrust caused the dictator to panic. He thought he could detect an insidious trap and wanted to stop the operation. The older officers and generals, who during World War I had fought bitterly for many years against the same enemy, also viewed this development with incredulous astonishment. The subsequent General der Infanterie [Günther] Blumentritt—who at that time was involved in the planning and execution of this operation in the headquarters of Army Group A—even talked of a triple "miracle." The first one happened in the Ardennes Forest where the German Panzers had become stuck in a miles-long traffic jam on the narrow roads. But, quite inexplicably, the air forces of the Allies let this big chance slip through their fingers. Blumentritt was even more mystified by the second miracle, that is, the breakthrough at Sedan that came off within just a few hours. And now the third miracle came to pass. At times, the German Panzer divisions rushed headlong to the Channel Coast, their flanks exposed. But the feared Allied counteroffensive failed to materialize.[11] Even General der Panzertruppe [Heinz] Guderian—who, like no other, was undeterred in his belief in success—was surprised by the developments at Sedan. In his *Memoirs* he writes "the success of our attack struck me as almost a miracle."[12]

The German success had not at all been planned in advance in that way. Instead, as will be shown, it sprang from the accidental coincidence of the most varied factors. But Nazi propaganda fashioned the myth that the German victory was due to a concept spelled out long before and garnished it with an as yet relatively unknown catchword blitzkrieg. At the same time, it was suggested that the inventor of these new methods was Adolf Hitler, the "greatest military genius of all times"(*größte Feldherr aller Zeiten*). The Allies were only too willing to pick up on this myth because, after all, it gave their generals, who had failed so miserably, an easy excuse.

But the *Blitzkrieg-Legende* (Blitzkrieg legend), as such, which since then has exerted considerable influence on the interpretation of more recent German history, was created by a few historians only after World War II. They came up with the fiction of a blitzkrieg strategy that aimed at nothing less than world rule. After the "grasp for world power" had failed during World War I, the Germans supposedly realized that their economic potential would not suffice for a global war against the Western sea powers.[13] Now, allegedly, the same lofty goal was to be attained step-by-step by carrying out smaller, limited expansion efforts (so-called blitzkriege, or lightning wars). As fascinating as the theory of Hitler's blitzkrieg strategy might appear in terms of its intellectual compactness, it is much too simple to be true. This study is intended to show how the miracle of 1940, the *Blitzsieg* (lightning victory) in the western campaign, came about. This study will also show how the blitzkrieg theory was embraced only *after* the campaign, and how it then led to disastrous consequences for the Germans.

1

The Blitzkrieg

Word and Concept

I never used the word Blitzkrieg *because it is a very stupid word.*[1]

Adolf Hitler, 8 November 1941

The Word "Blitzkrieg"

In sober military language, there is hardly any other word that is so strikingly full of significance and at the same time so misleading and subject to misinterpretation as the term *blitzkrieg*. Its early history is already hidden behind the fog of legends. It was asserted again and again that Hitler coined this evocative term. Some think that it was cooked up in the propaganda kitchen of Dr. [Josef] Goebbels. It is also assumed rather superficially that the word cropped up only after the surprising successes of the German Wehrmacht at the start of World War II. Allegedly, it was coined in the Anglo-Saxon language, where, as the very first piece of evidence, an article from the 25 September 1939 issue of *Time* magazine about the Campaign in Poland is quoted: "This was no war of occupation, but a war of quick penetration and obliteration—*Blitzkrieg,* lightning war."[2]

This assumption is based on an error. A more careful analysis of military publications proves that this word was already known in Germany before World War II. The word *blitzkrieg* was expressly mentioned in 1935 in an article in the military periodical *Deutsche Wehr* (German Defense). According to it, countries with a rather weak food industry and poor in raw materials should try "to finish a war quickly and suddenly by trying to force a decision right at the very beginning through the ruthless employment of their total fighting strength."[3] A more detailed analysis can be found in an essay published in 1938 in *Militär-Wochenblatt* (Military Weekly). Blitzkrieg is defined as "strategic surprise attack" carried forward by the operational employment of armor and the air force as well as airborne troops.[4] But such choice references are rare in German military literature prior to World War II.[5] The word *blitzkrieg* was also practically never used in the official military terminology of the Wehrmacht (German armed forces) during World War II. It assumed significance only through propaganda journalism. Especially after the surprisingly quick victory in France in the summer of 1940,[6] German papers were flooded with the word, as the following essay with the rather characteristic title "*Blitzkriegpsychose*" (Blitzkrieg Psychosis) shows:

> Blitzkrieg! Blitzkrieg! Blitzkrieg! That word was flashed at us everywhere during the weeks between the defeat of France and the start of major air attacks against England. Whether in the newspapers or on radio, there was not a day when our enemies did not mention that word. It became so much a part of them that they did not even take the trouble of looking around for a corresponding word in their own language; no, the "linguistically skillful" Englishmen simply took the word "Blitzkrieg" from the German language and every Englishman knows what that means, he knows what he and his country face now, once Germany starts hitting hard and fast.
>
> There is just one appropriate word for the events in Poland, Norway, Holland, Belgium, and France, and that word is "Blitzkrieg." With the speed and force of lightning, our Wehrmacht struck and destroyed every obstacle.[7]

But there was already a break at the end of 1941 after the failure of the German blitzkrieg against the Soviet Union. Henceforth, this word was frowned upon, and Hitler, of all people, energetically denied that he ever used it.[8] Instead, the German press maintained that this catchword was merely a malevolent invention of British propaganda: "It was the British who invented the term 'Blitzkrieg.' It is wrong. We never said that this mightiest of all struggles could ever take place with the speed of lightning."[9]

In the meantime, the Anglo-Saxons began to like this onomatopoeic German word and varied it in a farcical fashion. The German soldiers were referred to as "blitzers"; and there were phrases such as, for example, "out-blitz the Blitzkrieg."[10] The German air raids on London were also called "the Blitz." The vocabulary of the British tabloid press today cannot get along without the term blitzkrieg when it comes to dramatizing surprisingly quick victories in sports.

After the campaign in the west, the term blitzkrieg also showed up along with the word *Panzer* (tank or armor) in most of the major languages of the world. At the same time, an attempt was made to transfer this word into the particular language concerned.[11] This term was also used for the categorization of campaigns after World War II. For example, Iraq's failed surprise attack against Iran in 1980 was referred to in the press rather ironically as "the slowest Blitzkrieg of all time." But the epidemic spread of this word did not help clarify the concept that was presumed to be behind it.

The Concept of Blitzkrieg

In his essay "Blitzkrieg Ambiguities," George Raudzens differentiates seven different meanings of this rather scintillating term. He complains of an "anarchy in interpretation" but in the end must admit that he does not have any pat solution.[12] That shows that the blitzkrieg exegesis has gotten lost in a semantic labyrinth. Because there is obviously no way out, there is only one possibility, and that is to pick up the famous thread of Ariadne in order to find the way back to the entrance to the labyrinth.

But before we go into the confusing semantics of blitzkrieg, we first of all want to explain the triad of tactical, operational, and strategic echelons.

> *Tactics* means true command in the context of "combined arms combat." It is the responsibility of lower- and middle-echelon command.
>
> *Conduct of operations* (that is to say, far-reaching military movements and battles) is the task of the higher command echelon. According to the criteria of the Wehrmacht, the operational level of warfare commenced at the army (in exceptional cases, at the corps), whereas today a corps (in exceptional cases, also a division) can take over such command assignments. Tactical combat operations are planned and conducted at that echelon in the context of a higher-level operation; the latter, again, is aimed at strategic objectives.
>
> *Strategy* is the responsibility of the top command; that is the echelon where we encounter cooperation among political, economic, and military command agencies of a country with a view to the politically defined wartime objectives.[13]

Operational-Tactical Interpretation

> *"Blitzkrieg," this form of modern warfare, which today is discussed all over the world, is a tactic that shaped up only in the course of various German campaigns . . . but that cannot yet be expressed in fixed strategic formulas.*[14]
>
> *Weltwoche* (World Week), Zürich, 4 July 1941

An analysis of German military publications before and during World War II clearly showed that the term blitzkrieg as a rule was used in a purely military context, in other words, as an operational-tactical term. This brings us to the following brief definition: By blitzkrieg we mean the concentrated employment of armor and air forces to confuse the enemy with surprise and speed and to encircle him, after a successful breakthrough, by means of far-reaching thrusts. The objective is to defeat the enemy quickly in a decision-seeking operation.

The blitzkrieg was no political-strategic inspiration on the part of Adolf Hitler that his officers then transferred to the operational level and finally to the tactical echelons. Quite the contrary, this idea sprang up long before Hitler seized power; it was crystallized from purely tactical necessity. As will be shown later, the term was already contained in the *Stoßtrupp-Taktik* (stormtroop or assault team tactics) that were developed during World War I. In that way, the Germans wanted to put an end to rigid front lines involved in positional (trench) warfare and to return to mobile warfare. Above all the successes of the German general Oskar von Hutier drew attention to this tactic that aimed at breaking through enemy field fortifications. Somewhat exaggeratedly, Anglo-Saxon authors later referred to him as the "father of Blitzkrieg tactics."[15] At any rate, the blitzkrieg, as described later on, is nothing but the further development of the original assault team idea. Oberstleutnant Braun, for example, in an article published in 1938, already compares blitzkrieg to a "large-scale, powerful '*Stoßtrupp*' mission."[16] But *Stoßtrupp* is a term used on the lower tactical echelons and as a rule refers to a platoon or a company.

Generaloberst Heinz Guderian is also called the founder of the blitzkrieg idea.[17] He took over this *Stoßtrupp-Taktik,* whose prescription for success was based on speed and surprise, and combined it with the elements of modern technology, such as the tank and aircraft. In so doing, he was not concerned with the implementation of strategic ideas or political programs; his goal, instead, was to find a way back to mobile operations.[18] To that extent, the term blitzkrieg is extensively a synonym for the modern operational war of maneuver.

Strategic Interpretation

The phenomenon of the blitzkrieg, however, was also interpreted in a much more comprehensive fashion. Many historians used this handy term to characterize Hitler's strategy of conquest. A characteristic feature of this theory is its close tie-in with the military economy of the Third Reich that many authors referred to as a blitzkrieg economy. This assumption, which is rather hotly debated among historians, can be described as follows:

> The *German blitzkrieg strategy* was allegedly intended, in the endeavor for world rule, to bridge the deep chasm between far-reaching wartime objectives and inadequate power potential by overwhelming the enemies, one after the other, in a series of individual, successive campaigns that would last only a short time.
>
> The *foreign policy objective* was to isolate the particular opponent and thus to localize the conflict. In that way it would be possible to avoid the risk of a long, drawn-out, multifront war of attrition.
>
> The *domestic policy goal* was to motivate the population for war and to avoid long, drawn-out wars that would be too much of a strain on the endurance of the people.
>
> The *economic objective* was to mobilize the country's own power potential in the context of a quickly available armament in width (coupled with a rather risky renunciation of any armament in depth). The indispensable prerequisite for a blitzkrieg, in other words, a strategic first-strike capacity, was to be created by at least a temporary armament lead over the enemy who was to be attacked by surprise.

The *military objective* was to overrun the enemy, after exploiting the element of surprise, by using fast, mechanized forces with air support; the encirclement of the enemy's armies, in the course of broad-ranging encirclement operations, was to bring about a quick and decisive victory.

According to this theory, the blitzkrieg was a strategy of limitations and calculability of the following:

enemy
time
area
economic potential
military potential

In the view of quite a few historians, this "ingenious blitzkrieg strategy" that Hitler allegedly invented always made it possible to mobilize the country's manpower and material resources only to the extent that was believed necessary to defeat the next particular foe. The alternation between short campaigns and pauses to exploit the newly conquered territories thus determined the rhythm of blitzkrieg strategy. The objective of this stage-by-stage procedure was supposedly to broaden continually the country's own wartime economic base. Total mobilization was to be started only once the country's own potential for conducting a world war seemed adequate. But when the blitzkrieg against the Soviet Union failed at the end of 1941, it was necessary to do that which was to have been avoided at all costs—namely, the premature switch to total war.

The theory of the blitzkrieg strategy turns up as an almost ideological, tightly buttoned up model of thinking. Alan S. Milward, one of its best-known advocates, had this to say in 1975: "Today it is generally recognized that the military strategy of National Socialist Germany can adequately be described as a 'Blitzkrieg' strategy."[19] That theory had already been developed in the United States in 1945 and was formulated mainly by Burton H. Klein.[20] In the end, it also prevailed in Europe. For example, Andreas Hillgruber fell back on it and tied it in with his theory of the step-by-step plan, which he thought expressed Hitler's program in the endeavor to achieve world power: "This was to be done in two big stages in the context of a 'program' that had been spelled out conclusively during the twenties: First of all, the important thing was to erect a European continental empire via the defeat of France and, subsequently, the conquest of the European part of Russia. This was followed by another 'stage' to build up a German 'world power' position with colonial territories in Africa, oceanic bases, and a strong sea power that, during the generation after Hitler, was to build the base for a decisive struggle between the 'world power' Germany and the 'world power' the United States of America."[21]

But a number of critics criticized Hillgruber's step-by-step plan as being too deterministic and inadequately documented.[22] According to Erdmann, the step-by-step plan suggested "a system that it is doubtful can be used in adequately characterizing Hitler's visions and improvisations."[23] Hillgruber tackled the thesis of the blitzkrieg strategy rather gingerly and used it only to back up his step-by-step plan model, which Marxist historians above all increasingly exaggerated.[24] As a result, this heavily overloaded term blitzkrieg finally drifted away from its military roots and was extensively shoved into the alien atmosphere of social-economic matters.[25]

According to a more recent assumption, the idea of the blitzkrieg does not primarily go back to Hitler but was allegedly conceived in the executive suite of IG Farben, a market-dominating chemical corporation. In the stiff competition among the monopoly groups of the heavy and chemical industries, the latter prevailed in 1936. In this connection, IG Farben proposed to produce chemical substitutes to compensate for the shortage of Germany's armament-related raw materials. According to this thesis, the resultant autarky was to make it possible for Germany to pursue limited blitzkrieg campaigns. This supposedly was the objective of the four-year plan that was adopted in 1936 and bore the signature of IG Farben.[26]

In spelling out his expansion objectives, the dictator was also allegedly guided by a three-stage expansion program that reportedly had been drafted long before by industry. First of all, an economic core region in central Europe was to be created, and it was then expanded into a large-scale European region. But the traditional objective of world rule was to be the very end of this entire endeavor.[27]

The theory of blitzkrieg strategy has been subjected to increasing doubt in recent years. In this connection, it can be argued that this involves a fiction that was put together by historians only after the fact. According to Timothy Mason, the blitzkrieg successes were based on a "fatal combination of domestic policy compulsion, foreign policy accident, and extreme adventurousness on the part of Hitler. The successes then gave the whole thing the appearance of a system although it was not."[28] Hew Strachan expresses this particularly clearly: "Blitzkrieg, therefore, may have had some meaning at a purely operational level, but as an overall strategic and economic concept it was non-existent."[29]

The Campaign in the West and the Origin of Blitzkrieg

Because of Germany's unfavorable geographic position in the center of Europe, the German general officer corps was always trying to conduct so-called quick wars to force an immediate operational decision. Moltke had gained such a victory in 1870 in the Sedan encirclement battle. But, at the start of World War I, the Schlieffen plan, based on this same principle, simply failed. It gradually became clear that the nature of war had changed dramatically. On account of the enhanced effect of weapons, firepower dominated movement. Far-ranging operations were often nipped in the bud before they got started; they froze in the firestorm of machine guns and in the steel thunderstorm of the artillery. This was followed by a long, drawn-out positional war that was fought in the course of battles of attrition. Reluctantly, the generals had to admit that the significance of the art of conducting operations increasingly faded into the background because the decision had shifted from the battlefields to the factories. The struggle of hostile peoples took place in the form of a lengthy economic war in which the Western sea powers cut Germany off from its raw material sources by a blockade.

The German generals learned their lessons from the loss in World War I; they no longer believed that quick wars could be won against opponents of superior strength. In 1937, Oberst [Georg] Thomas, Chef des Wehrmachtswirtschaftsstabes (chief, War Economy Staff), made the following assertion: "The mistaken fixation upon a short war has been ruinous for us; we should therefore not be guided by the illusion of a short war in the age of air and Panzer squadrons."[30]

A scenario drafted by Großadmiral (Grand Admiral) [Erich] Raeder in 1937 indicated what ideas prevailed within the Wehrmacht high command as regards the nature of a future war: "and so, there can only be a kind of fortress warfare that boils down to alternating tactical successes and failures. In the cycle of changing fortunes arising from these tactical successes, final victory will then go to the state that has the larger population but, even more so, the state that has unlimited material and food. . . . Just exactly how this kind of warfare can affect Germany, if the missing raw materials cannot be procured continually, needs no special explanation considering our geographic location."[31] This is why he warned against the illusion of "seeking the decision in a single large operation."[32]

The general officer corps was definitely skeptical toward such military adventures. As indicated in a lecture note, General der Artillerie [Ludwig] Beck, Generalstabschef des Heeres (army chief of staff), made the following comment to Generaloberst [Walther] von Brauchitsch, Oberbefehlshaber des Heeres (commander in chief of the army), during the Czech crisis in July 1938: "The idea of a Blitzkrieg . . . is an illusion. One should really have learned from the modern history of warfare that surprise attacks have hardly ever led to lasting success."[33]

A study published in 1938 made the following categorical statement: "The possibilities of defeating an equivalent opponent by means of a 'Blitzkrieg' are zero. . . . In other words: It is not military force that is strongest; instead, it is economic power that has become the most important power in the modern world."[34] But then the miracle of Sedan happened in May 1940. The lightning victory during the campaign in the west triggered a radical change of opinions within the German general officer corps. That campaign was decided in a single operation that essentially lasted just two weeks, Operation Sichelschnitt (Sickle Cut). Like an earthquake, the campaign in the west caused numerous outdated doctrines to collapse; the nature of war was revolutionized on the battlefield. But it is such times of rapid and radical change in long-held ideas and concepts that constitute fertile soil for novel key words and slogans, as was stated so aptly by Goethe: "Where terms are lacking, a word crops up at the right time."[35]

The word that cropped up at the right time in the summer of 1940 was *blitzkrieg*. Rarely in military historiography has a term been so over-interpreted as this one. Upon closer examination, it is indeed a semantic trap. The word *Blitz-Krieg* (lightning war) promises more than it can deliver—looking at it in historical terms—because the term *Krieg* (war) suggests the presence of an overall strategic concept of war. But that concept remained mostly stuck on the lower operational echelon. It would have been semantically more correct to speak of *Blitzoperationen* (lightning operations) or *Blitzfeldzügen* (lightning campaigns). Of course, the idea was to achieve a strategic objective, in other words, to bring the war to a quick end; but the means were provided only at the operational and tactical levels.

In an exaggerated form, blitzkrieg signifies an attempt to turn strategic necessity into operational virtue against the background of shortages in economic resources. But this operationally construed strategy, with its strategically construed operations, contained an inherent contradiction. Now Hitler and some generals indeed believed they had found the secret of victory in blitzkrieg, in other words, an operational miracle weapon that could be used to defeat even an economically—and thus strategically—far superior opponent by means of quick battles of annihilation (*Schlieffen*). The enemy, superior in the long run, was to be defeated by a surprise attack, that is, a knockout in the first round. This thinking was illusionary in an age of industrialization and had a fatal effect later on when it came to designing the campaign against the Soviet Union.

2

Blitzkrieg without the Blitzkrieg Concept

The Background of the Campaign in the West

It was victory that gave Blitzkrieg the status of doctrine.[1]

Hew Strachan

Did Hitler Have a Strategic War Concept?

The German Reich had lost World War II politically even before it had really begun militarily. Paul Schmidt, Hitler's chief interpreter, reports on a ghostlike scene in the Reich Chancellery where he had to translate the British declaration of war on 3 September 1939:

> After I finished, there was total silence. . . . Hitler sat there as if petrified and stared straight ahead. He was not stunned, as was maintained later, and he did not rant and rave either, as others claimed they knew. He sat in his seat completely quiet and motionless. After a while, which seemed like an eternity to me, he turned to Ribbentrop who kept standing at the window as if frozen. "What now?" Hitler asked his Foreign Minister with a furious gaze in his eyes as if he wanted to indicate that Ribbentrop had misinformed him about the reaction of the British. Softly, Ribbentrop replied: "I assume that the French will shortly give us an identical ultimatum." . . . Göring turned to me and said: "If we lose this war, may Heaven have mercy on us!"[2]

Hitler's military advisers had warned him that the outbreak of a new world war, at this early stage, would lead to a catastrophe.[3] According to what Raeder told the officers of the submarine fleet on 22 July, Hitler noted that there must under no circumstances be a war with England because that would be tantamount to *Finis Germaniae* (the end of Germany).[4] The German officers were still in shock from what had happened in World War I. At that time, all their military skill was doomed to failure because the Royal Navy had cut off Germany from its supplies of raw materials.

This is why Hitler again and again told his worried generals and admirals that they did not need to plan for a war against Great Britain; he even assured them that he would not risk any war before 1944.[5] Generalmajor a.D. (ausser Dienst, retired) [Bernhard] von Loßberg confirmed in his memoirs just how unprepared the Wehrmacht was upon the outbreak of World War II when it came to fighting a world war. He reports "that the overall armament effort was geared toward a goal to be attained only in 1944 and that 1939 was only a phase on the way there."[6]

In a conflict with Great Britain and France, both of which were sea powers, the most important component of the armed forces would have been the navy. At the beginning of the war, however, the German navy was still being built up. Apart from the battleships and heavy cruisers that were not yet ready for combat, it had only three armored vessels (dubbed pocket battleships), a few destroyers, and fifty-seven submarines. Only two pocket battleships and twenty-three submarines were ready for swift deployment in the Atlantic early in September.[7] Raeder, the Oberbefehlshaber der Kriegsmarine (commander in chief of the navy), commented on the nearly hopeless inferiority of his naval forces upon the outbreak of the war: The navy, he noted, could demonstrate only "that it knew how to die decently."[8]

The nightmare of German military policy had always been the two-front war. But this is precisely the specter that Hitler had again conjured up. At first, the Wehrmacht concentrated only on Poland, whose army was numerically almost as strong as the German army, which was still being expanded.[9] At the same time, a new front rose up in the rear of the German army in the form of the superior fighting forces of the Western powers. Generalfeldmarschall Wilhelm Keitel, Chef des Oberkommandos der Wehrmacht (OKW) (chief of the Wehrmacht high command) since 1938, admitted after the war that "a French attack during the Polish Campaign would have encountered only a German military screen, not a real defense."[10] Later on Generaloberst a.D. [Franz] Halder [then Chef des Generalstabes des Heeres (chief, army general staff)] was particularly emphatic about this: "The success against Poland was only possible by almost completely baring our western border. If the French had seen the logic of the situation and had used the engagement of the German forces in Poland, they would have been able to cross the Rhine without our being able to prevent it and would have threatened the Ruhr area, which was the most decisive factor for the German conduct of the war."[11]

Hitler was a go-for-broke gambler who again and again challenged destiny and who did not shy away from risking everything on the throw of the dice. He was reinforced in his attitude by the yielding attitude of the victorious powers of World War I:

> In March 1935 he reintroduced compulsory military service in violation of the provisions of the Versailles Treaty—and Western powers reacted only weakly.

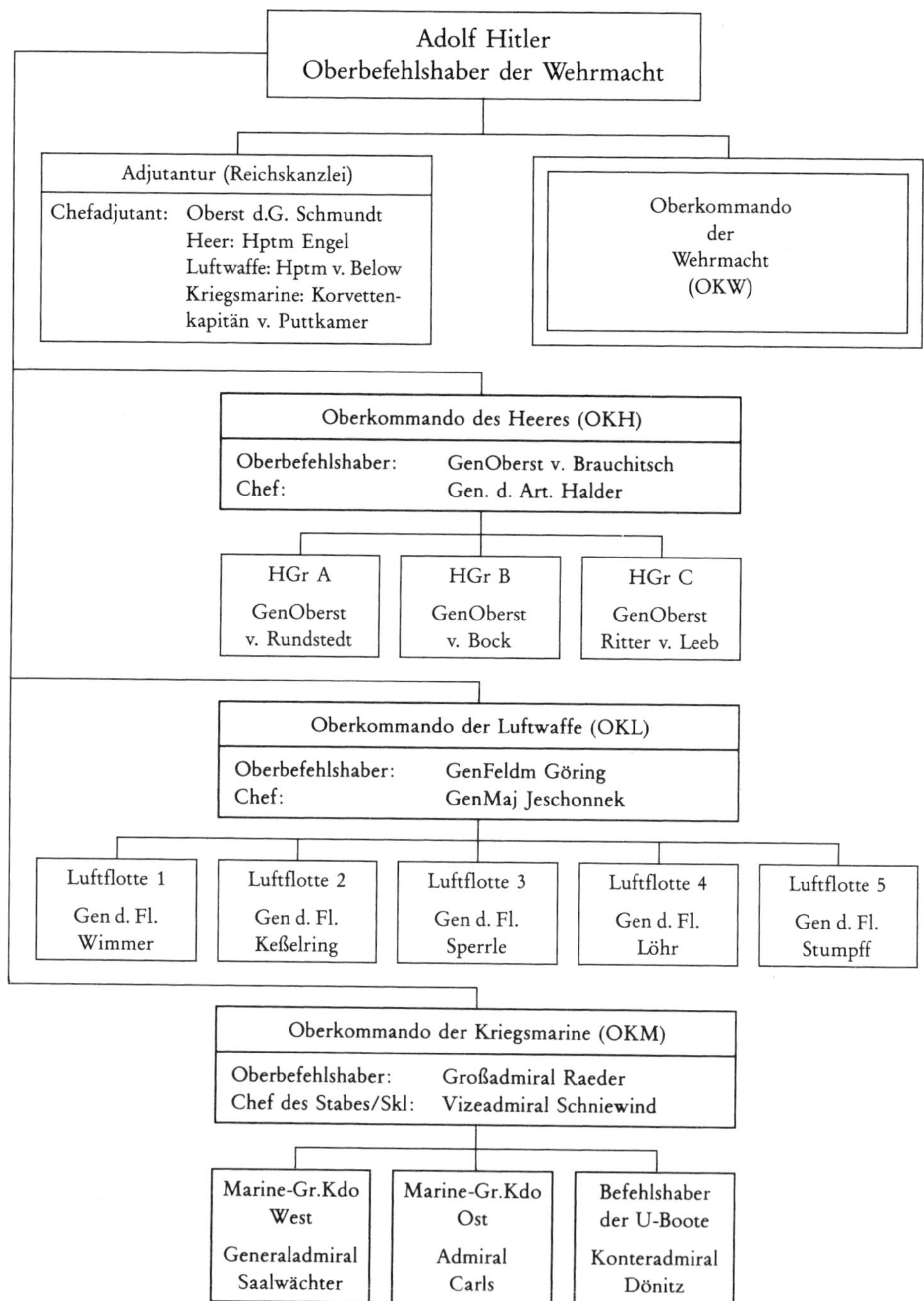
Spitzengliederung der Wehrmacht im Mai 1940
Adolf Hitler
Oberbefehlshaber der Wehrmacht
Adjutantur (Reichskanzlei)
Chefadjutant: Oberst d.G. Schmundt
Heer: Hptm Engel
Luftwaffe: Hptm v. Below
Kriegsmarine: Korvetten-kapitän v. Puttkamer
Oberkommando der Wehrmacht (OKW)
Oberkommando des Heeres (OKH)
Oberbefehlshaber: GenOberst v. Brauchitsch
Chef: Gen. d. Art. Halder
HGr A GenOberst v. Rundstedt
HGr B GenOberst v. Bock
HGr C GenOberst Ritter v. Leeb
Oberkommando der Luftwaffe (OKL)
Oberbefehlshaber: GenFeldm Göring
Chef: GenMaj Jeschonnek
Luftflotte 1 Gen d. Fl. Wimmer
Luftflotte 2 Gen d. Fl. Keßelring
Luftflotte 3 Gen d. Fl. Sperrle
Luftflotte 4 Gen d. Fl. Löhr
Luftflotte 5 Gen d. Fl. Stumpff
Oberkommando der Kriegsmarine (OKM)
Oberbefehlshaber: Großadmiral Raeder
Chef des Stabes/Skl: Vizeadmiral Schniewind
Marine-Gr.Kdo West Generaladmiral Saalwächter
Marine-Gr.Kdo Ost Admiral Carls
Befehlshaber der U-Boote Konteradmiral Dönitz

Armed Forces High Command, May 1940

Gliederung OKW/OKH im Mai 1940

Oberkommando der Wehrmacht (OKW)
Chef: Generaloberst Keitel

Wehrmachtführungsamt (Chef: Generalmajor Jodl)
Abt. Landesverteidigung (Chef: Oberst d. G. Warlimont)
— Grp I/Heer: OTL d. G. v. Loßberg
— Grp II/Marine: Korvettenkapitän Junge
— Grp III/Luftwaffe: Hptm Speck v. Sternburg
Abt. Wehrmachtnachrichtenverbindungen (Chef: Oberst d. G. Juppe)
Abt. für Wehrmachtpropaganda (Chef: OTL d. G. v. Wedel)

Amt Ausland/Abwehr (Chef: Admiral Canaris)
— Chef d. Stabes: Oberst d. G. Oster
— Verb Offz z. OKH: OTL d.G. Groscurth

Wehrwirtschaftsamt (Chef: Generalmajor Thomas)

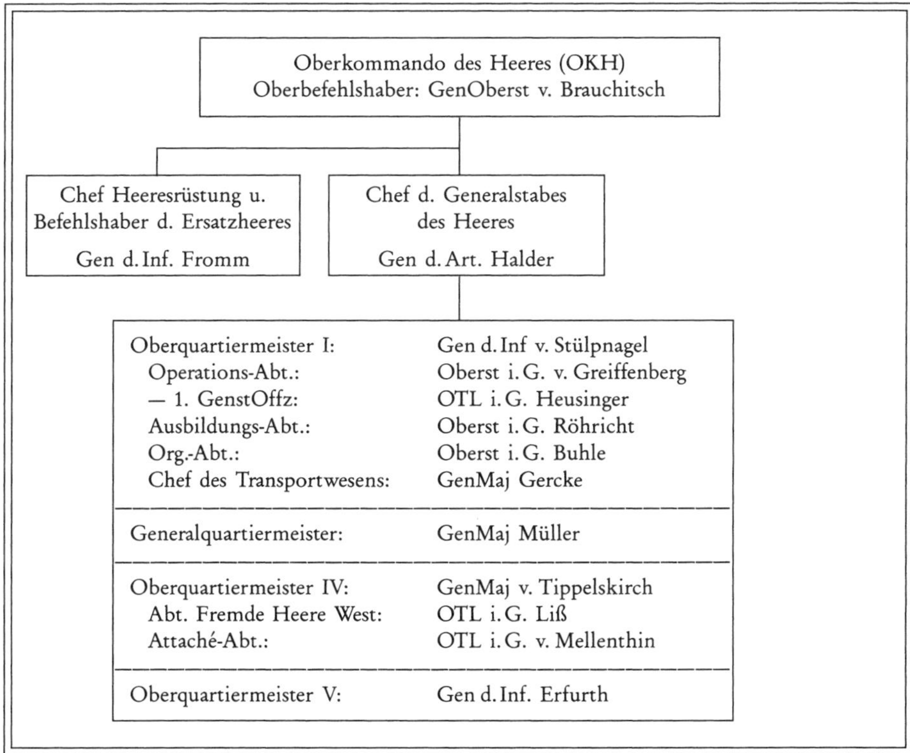

Armed Forces High Command/Army High Command Organization, May 1940

In March 1936 German troops marched into the demilitarized zone of the Rhineland—and the Western powers only protested.

In March 1938 Hitler incorporated Austria—and this time, likewise, there was only a diplomatic protest.

In September 1938 during the Munich Conference, Hitler demanded that the German-inhabited parts of Czechoslovakia be ceded—and the Western powers gave in.

In March 1939 the Wehrmacht marched into rump Czechoslovakia and occupied Bohemia and Moravia—once again, the Western powers shied away from taking military counteraction.

When Hitler decided to attack Poland, he was convinced that the Western powers would again not dare to respond by going to war. On 22 August 1939 he assembled a number of higher-ranking generals at his Berghof mountain retreat on the Obersalzberg (near Berchtesgaden). During this fateful address he stated: "England's situation in the world is very precarious. England will not accept any risk. In France, they have a manpower shortage (decline in births). Little was done for armament. The artillery is obsolete. France did not want to get into this adventure. . . . In other words, England cannot give Poland any real help. . . . A military response can be ruled out. . . . The opponents did not figure on my great power of decision. Our enemies are little worms. I saw them in Munich."[12]

Hitler commented several times to the effect that the Western powers would only be "bluffing."[13] As von Loßberg reported later, Hitler during those days acted "rather calm, considering what he was like, and gave the impression of a man who was completely sure of himself."[14] He summarized the mood as follows: "The Führer knows that London will not do anything really serious and if London stands pat, then the French will certainly take great care not to do anything either."[15]

Something that [Generalfeldmarschall Erich von] Manstein remembered is very important here: Hitler declared "that he would never be so mad as to unleash a two-front war, as German leaders of 1914. . . . Raising his coarse voice, he had explicitly assured his military advisers that he was not idiot enough to bungle his way into a world war for the sake of the City of Danzig or on account of the Polish Corridor."[16]

That introduces the key word *Danzig*. Many French war resisters simply asked: *Mourir pour Dantzig?* (Why die for Danzig?). As will be shown in a subsequent chapter on the causes of the French defeat, there were also pacifist groups that played a role here, although their importance should not be overestimated. The real tragedy of the Western peace movements took place as World War II was unleashed. Their peace demonstrations were staged with great idealism and nearly convinced the German dictator that those countries would not counter his aggression against Poland with any military resistance. Just how much Hitler had fallen for this illusion is pointed out by a comment made by Keitel. Just fourteen days before the start of the campaign in

Poland, Generalmajor [Georg] Thomas presented a memorandum that concluded Germany "could not last through a war on the grounds of its war economy." At that point, he was interrupted by Keitel, the chief of the Wehrmacht high command: "[He] told me that Germany would never fight a world war. There was no danger because, in Hitler's view, the French were a degenerate pacifist people, the English are much too decadent to render Poland any real help, and America would never again send even one man to Europe in order to fetch England's or Poland's chestnuts out of the fire."[17]

Hitler's many years of peace propaganda aimed at the Western European population had been very successful—as a matter of fact, too successful! The numerous peace demonstrations in western European cities during the Polish crisis caused him to overestimate the effect, and so he fell into the trap of his own propaganda. It is an irony of history that the code word that on 10 May 1940 triggered the attack of the Wehrmacht against the Western powers was Danzig.

Hitler's decision to launch the Polish campaign is one of the most catastrophically wrong decisions in German history. The campaign actually lasted only two days. On the third day, it became a world war following the declarations of war by Great Britain (and immediately thereafter, by the Commonwealth States) as well as France. The illusion that the Allies would only bluff had burst like a soap bubble. The go-for-broke gambler had again risked everything on one throw of the dice—and this time he lost. The reaction in Berlin was all the more dismayed. As von Loßberg reported, Oberst [Rudolf] Schmundt, Hitler's chief military aide, at first refused to believe the news because "the idea that the infallible Führer had been wrong after all seemed simply incomprehensible to him."[18]

Some generals, however, reacted with bitterness against Hitler. For example, General der Infanterie Carl-Heinrich von Stülpnagel, who later joined the 20 July Resistance Movement, said: "So, now we have the second world war! That is the bill we have to pay for the irresponsible game of the last several years. This time the gambler put his money on the wrong card!"[19] Generalmajor [Erich] Fellgiebel said: "The news of the French-English response reportedly hit Hitler and Ribbentrop like a bomb. They had always made fun of Bethmann-Hollweg [Reich chancellor in World War I], but they are not one whit better. That is how they play with the destiny of a nation. This is irresponsible!"[20]

Hitler's real strategic fiasco was that at the start of the world war he had unleashed, he had only an operations plan against Poland, which his generals had perfectly worked out, but he did not have an overall strategic war-fighting concept for a conflict with the Western powers.[21] Germany was totally unprepared for a conflict with its most dangerous opponent, the British Empire. Hitler had built neither a strategic long-range bomber fleet nor sufficient submarines and surface vessels. The navy had not even been built up to the level permitted under the Anglo-German Naval Treaty of 1935. Looking back, von Loßberg wrote: "But if Hitler had planned the war against England for 1939 or if he had only seriously considered it, then he would certainly have set naval rearmament up entirely differently. What good would the heavy ships be that were not ready until many years later and whose construction (with the exception of the subsequent battleships *Bismarck* and *Tirpitz*) had in fact been soon discontinued in this war? But how eminently important would it have been if, in 1939, we had not had just barely 30 submarines but 100 or more!"[22]

The German general staff was not even mentally prepared for this war. Hitler had rejected any precautionary advanced planning along those lines as an insult to his foreign policy skills. Some German generals, Keitel, for example, tried several times in so-called war games to "clarify the military situation in case of a war against the West."[23] Hitler rejected that categorically with the following assertion: "There must be no preparations in the west other than the occupation of the West Wall for security purposes. There cannot be and there will not be a war with the Western powers over the Polish issue. Discussion on such an impossible case quite unnecessarily endangered secrecy and thus also threatened political negotiations."[24] If, however, Hitler did not have a war plan against the Western powers, he could hardly have had a blitzkrieg plan against them.

Was the Polish Campaign a Blitzkrieg?

Techniques of Polish campaign no recipe for the west. No good against a well-knit army.[25]

Halder, Army Chief of Staff, 29 September 1939

It is interesting to note that in recent years the Polish campaign has increasingly been assessed not as a genuine blitzkrieg but only as a preliminary stage.[26] This campaign was planned on neither the strategic nor the operational levels on the basis of a completely novel concept. Once again, the military command was confronted with the problem of a two-front war on account of the Reich's unfavorable central geographic position and tried to bring about an immediate decision by means of a quick war. The Polish campaign was actually decided after just four days, and it was essentially completed after eighteen days. In contrast to the operational plans of Moltke and Schlieffen, the enemy's encirclement did not have to be brought about by complicated maneuvers; instead, it was already geographically prearranged. The German attack divisions that had also been deployed in East Prussia and Slovakia squeezed the Polish army from three sides starting with the deployment stage. Besides, the attack formations of the Red Army were ready in the east. However, the initial situation prior to the campaign in the west was entirely different. There the Wehrmacht faced the French-Belgian line of fortifications.

An essential difference with respect to the campaign in the west emerged precisely in connection with the German armored force. In contrast to the Sickle Cut Panzer operation of May 1940, during the Polish campaign German armor was not yet employed independently on the *operational* level either at the corps or army echelons. Instead, the Panzer formations on the *tactical* level usually fought in a divisional framework.[27] Some trump cards that later on became so symbolic of German blitzkrieg, such as airborne troops, were intentionally kept in reserve.

For other novel concepts, the Polish campaign was only a proving ground. For example, the combined employment of armor and air had never before been tried out on a larger scale in Germany. This is why a large-scale exercise was scheduled at the Grafenwöhr training area in northeastern Bavaria from 21 to 25 August 1939 to test tactical support for the army by dive-bomber (Stuka) and bomber units.[28] The Polish crisis, however, caused this exercise to be canceled on short notice. Instead, the new method was tested directly in actual warfare.

But the Polish army was not an equal foe. Polish officers, who were already dreaming of marching on Berlin, learned rather painfully that wars cannot be won by bravery alone. Not only was their army old-fashioned in terms of equipment and training, but its leadership style was also outmoded. Particularly symbolic is the anachronistic tragedy that Guderian reported of the troopers of the Polish Pomorska Cavalry Brigade attacking German Panzers with their sabers.[29] This time those German tanks were not the cardboard or canvas mock-ups of the Reichswehr [German army of the Weimar Republic era] of just a few years earlier; this time the Poles ran into tanks made of hard steel.

Although the general staff thoroughly analyzed the Polish campaign and immediately translated the lessons learned into a training program, it considered the campaign to be unfit as a yardstick for judging a conflict with the Western powers. Respect for the opponents of World War I was still very high. Thus, Generaloberst Ritter von Leeb, the commander in chief of Army Group C, issued this warning: "Surprise [is] not possible. Our sacrifices in blood will be tremendous, and we will still not be able to defeat the French. An attack against France can never be launched like an attack against Poland; instead, it will be protracted, and we will have extremely heavy losses."[30] The situation estimate prepared by Generalleutnant [Georg] von Sodenstern, the chief of staff of Army Group A, is equally characteristic of the pessimism that prevailed within the general officer corps: "Paying due credit to our Panzer successes in Poland, we must nevertheless note that armor has little or no chance of success against such defenses [in the west]."[31]

Interestingly enough, the general staffs of the Western powers arrived at the same conclusion.[32] For example, the French prime minister [Paul] Reynaud referred to the German attack on Poland merely as an "expedition."[33]

Did the Time Factor Work for or against the Wehrmacht?

Until the Spring of 1940, every delay of the offensive worked in favor of the German force potential.[34]

Hans-Adolf Jacobsen

Numerous historical studies maintain that the Wehrmacht at the start of World War II had a considerable armament lead over the Western powers, which supposedly enabled it to launch an immediate blitzkrieg. But this strategic first-strike capability allegedly declined month after month as a result of the rearmament effort of the Western powers. Racing against time, the Germans would have had to attack as quickly as possible to force an early decision. But here we come to a considerable difference between myth and reality. In what follows, we will show that the time factor, in long-range terms, worked against the Wehrmacht, whereas in medium-range terms worked in its favor.

The Polish campaign was not even completed when on 27 September Hitler shocked the general officer corps with his announcement that he was determined to attack the Western powers as quickly as possible. He spelled out this intention in his memo of 9 October and set 25 November as a provisional attack date. The military amateur Hitler asserted in all seriousness that an attack would be "possible in three weeks." And, rather feistily, he added, "If we can't bring that off, we will deserve to be beaten."[35]

Here is the strategic analysis on which the dictator based his 27 September statement: "'Time' will, in general, work against us when we do not use it effectively. The economic means of the other side are stronger. The enemy can purchase and transport. Time does not work for us in the military sense either."[36] It is entirely true that the German Reich was not in a position to last through many years of warfare. Of the thirty most important raw materials for the armaments industry, it had only seven in adequate quantities. Above all, it had almost no nickel, tin, tungsten, molybdenum, chrome, beryllium, platinum, or bauxite.[37] Thomas, the chief of the War Economy and Armaments Office, never tired of pointing to these shortages. If there were to be another world war, then the Western sea powers, by virtue of their raw material potential, would certainly last longer.[38] Hitler's insistence on immediately pushing ahead and, so to speak, running head-on against the wall of the French-Belgian fortifications, appeared suicidal.

By order of the commander in chief of the army, von Stülpnagel, the deputy chief of staff for Operations on the Oberkommando des Heeres (OKH, army general staff), in the middle of September drafted a memorandum that concluded that the army was not equipped for fighting "against well-prepared fortifications." There was no thought of mounting a promising breakthrough offensive against the strong French-Belgian line of fortifications before the spring of 1942.[39] But Hitler demanded an immediate attack: "It cannot begin too early. The coming months will not add to our own attack strength but it will considerably strengthen the defensive force of our enemies."[40] The dictator even wanted to predict the exact moment at which the Allied forces would catch up with the alleged lead: "In six to eight months they will be better. That time may suffice to close the deficiencies."[41]

But reality impressively refuted Hitler. It was exactly those seven months, between the Polish campaign and the campaign in the west, that represented the interval that the Wehrmacht needed so urgently to add to its armament and above all to improve the training of its only partly ready units. The dictator had to admit his mistake in the spring of 1940. He allowed that "the quiet during the winter did after all yield advantages [for the German Reich]," and he noted that the Allies on the other hand supposedly "fell behind us in the delivery of war matériel and in the organization of new units!"[42] Hitler's military advisers had managed to persuade him simply to postpone his plans. Weather conditions, which were also rather unfavorable for an offensive, again and again made it necessary to cancel the previously ordered target date. And so, fortunately for the Wehrmacht, the attack date was postponed twenty-nine times until 10 May 1940.[43] In the following sections we will show how the strength ratio shifted ever more clearly in favor of the German armies between the two campaigns, thus turning Hitler's original assertion upside down.

Weapons and Ammunition

The brilliant blitzkrieg campaign against Poland concealed the fact that the Wehrmacht at that time was also on the brink of disaster. The German forces, it so happens, would not have been able to continue fighting much longer: They had shot their bolt. Only the swift end of this campaign, which actually was completed after eighteen days, saved the Wehrmacht from logistical collapse as far as ammunition was concerned. But Hitler seemed increasingly to lose touch with reality. In the previously mentioned 9 October memorandum, he even went so far as to maintain that no country in the world "has a better ammunition supply than the German Reich."[44] Almost at the same moment, the chief of supply and administration delivered the news that the fighting forces were no longer capable of carrying out any operations for the foreseeable future due to the critical ammunition situation.

Ammunition was stockpiled only for one-third of the divisions and even that would last them only fourteen combat days. Requirements for another fourteen combat days could be covered by reserve stockpiles but that would be the end.[45] The Luftwaffe was in a similar situation—after about fourteen combat days, the pilots would have used up their bomb supplies and could then "go play cards," as Generaloberst [Erhard] Milch, the Luftwaffe inspector general, urgently warned Hitler.[46] Most alarming, however, was the somber forecast by Thomas, who had already drafted a memorandum on that point.[47] On 27 September, he once again briefed Halder about the critical situation of the German war economy. As the chief of the army general staff then confided to his diary, Germany had a monthly shortfall of six hundred thousand tons of steel and, in addition, a major increase in powder production could not be expected until 1941.[48]

What now followed was one of Hitler's typical mood swings. He slipped from one extreme to the other and worked himself into a "crisis psychosis" that caused him to overdramatize the ammunition problem.[49] His ceaseless demands for an increase in output finally led to the appointment of a special minister for munitions. General der Artillerie [Karl] Becker, the chief of the Army Weapons Bureau, rather unjustifiably felt that he was forced into the role of a scapegoat. Feeling that he had failed, he committed suicide.

As shown in the following list, the seven months between the Polish campaign and the campaign in the west were sufficient to render both the army and the Luftwaffe operational again. Using a base figure of 100 percent for the ammunition stockpiles as of 1 May 1940, the pertinent percentages show the shortages as of October 1939.[50]

Army Weapons	**Shortage as of October 1939 (%)**
Light Infantry	30
2-cm Gun	47
Light Mortar	76
Heavy Mortar	78
Light Infantry Gun	56
Heavy Infantry Gun	70
Light Field Howitzer	25
Heavy 10-cm Cannon (K 18)	38
Heavy Field Howitzer	31
15-cm Gun (K 16 and 18)	20
21-cm Heavy Mortar	86
Luftwaffe Weapons	
50-kg Fragmentation Bomb	51
250-kg Fragmentation Bomb	65
500-kg Fragmentation Bomb	48

Equipping units with weapons had also been very spotty in the autumn of 1939 because the supplies were unable to keep up with the hasty organization of new formations. Heavy artillery recorded the highest growth rate as a result of the output increase that now began. From October 1939 until May 1940 the number of 21-cm heavy mortars increased fivefold from 22 to 124.[51]

Motorization

In his 9 October memorandum, Hitler, completely mistaking reality, observed that the Polish campaign did not cause any "serious damage to the units."[52] Concerning the maintenance problems for Panzers and wheeled vehicles, he commented, "If a force cannot make these losses good in twenty days, it is a poor force."[53] In reality, most divisions had vehicle losses of up to 50 percent. The motorized formations in part took until the spring of 1940 before they were ready for a new large-scale operation after replenishing their shortages.[54] Later on, Oberst i.G. [Walter] Buhle, the then chief of the Organization Department in the army general staff, observed: "A much earlier start of operations in the west—as Hitler had intended in the beginning—would thus have been impossible in view of the motor vehicle situation alone. The discrepancy between what we wanted and what we were able to do became worse and worse during the war."[55]

The continued postponement of the offensive had the most advantageous effect on the German Panzer force. The German Panzers, which in September 1939 spread fear and terror among the weak Polish army, would have suffered a fiasco if they had been launched immediately thereafter against superior French armor. At that time, the Panzer formations of the Wehrmacht consisted mostly of the light models I and II. But they were completely unsuited for tank battles because their inadequate armament could not even penetrate the armor of French light tanks. The German Panzer force that burst out of the Ardennes woods in May 1940 differed considerably from that which Hitler had wanted to send into battle the autumn before. The number of medium and heavy models had increased between October 1939 and May 1940 as follows: Panzer III, from 151 to 785; Panzer IV, from 143 to 290; and Czech models, from 247 to 381.[56]

Personnel Replacements

The time factor during the early phase of the war worked for the Germans especially in the personnel field. At the start of the war, the French forces were able to mobilize 6.1 million men,[57] while the Wehrmacht came up with only 4.5 million men.[58] But that meant that France's manpower resources were mostly exhausted. On the other hand, the German nation of 80 million had been allowed to maintain only a professional army of 100,000 men as well as 15,000 navy personnel on the basis of the Versailles Treaty. Hitler did not introduce compulsory military service until 1935, so there was an as yet unused potential of "white age classes" (1901–13) amounting to a total of 4 million men fit for military service.[59]

Training

The personnel strength of the German fighting forces represented only a facade at the start of the war. Out of the 4.5 million (including 427,000 men in construction units), only 1.31 million men in the active duty units and 647,000 men in Reserve I could be graded as fully trained; 808,000 were classified as untrained. In addition, 1.2 million veterans of World War I had been mobilized, although it was impossible adequately to familiarize them with the weapons and techniques of a modern war.[60]

The Polish campaign was not nearly as smooth as claimed in the reports coming from National Socialist propaganda. But when von Brauchitsch, the commander in chief of the army, dared to warn Hitler and point out the serious training deficiencies in many units, Hitler went into a rage and threatened to relieve him immediately. In re-

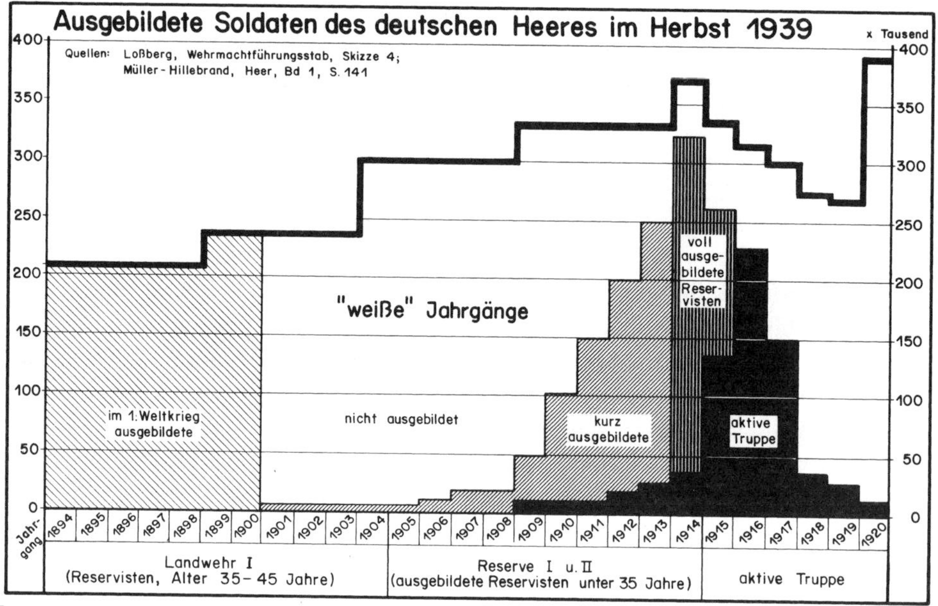

Trained Soldiers of the German Army, Autumn 1939

ality, however, his criticism was justified, especially with regard to officer training, as General der Infanterie a.D. [Edgar] Röhricht, the former chief of the Training Department of the army general staff, later confirmed: "One big worry sprang from the deficient skills of the officer corps who had been moved into commanding positions as a result of the hasty expansion of the army; that officer corps had to be considered to a great extent as being unequal to the tasks connected with its position."[61]

What now followed was a training offensive that is almost unparalleled in military history. A special training division was organized at the Königsbrück troop training area for the training of commanders. The courses, lasting three to four weeks, were used to pass three hundred commanders through each time. The units were also prepared for their subsequent assignments with extraordinary thoroughness, above all in crossing rivers and fighting against fortified positions. The training of the French army was in sharp contrast. During the eight months between the German attack on Poland and the campaign in the west, they remained in their positions, mostly without doing anything. The French units received hardly any combat training, and many were detailed to build bunker positions or assigned to help the farmers in agricultural tasks. On the other hand, the time gained until May 1940 benefited the German Wehrmacht in many different ways. There was no area in which they benefited as much as in training. The units that attacked from their assembly areas in May 1940 could hardly be compared to those that had marched into those positions in October 1939.[62]

In summary, it may be said that the time factor during the initial phase of the war definitely worked in favor of the Wehrmacht that was just beginning to be built up. Paradoxically, the Western powers should have mounted a blitzkrieg to bring about an early decision.

Was There a Blitzkrieg Economy before the Campaign in the West?

It is however criminal if the political leadership were to rely on surprise.[63]

Hitler, 23 May 1939

The German war economy revealed an astonishing development during World War II. There was never any comprehensive mobilization during the first half of the war (up to the failure of the blitzkrieg against the Soviet Union in 1941). On the other hand, the second phase of the war was marked by the so-called armament miracle created by newly appointed Minister [Albert] Speer [initially Reichsminister für Bewaffnung und Munition (Reich minister for weapons and munitions) and later Reichsminister für Rüstung und Kriegsproduktion (Reich minister for armament and war production)]. That raises the question as to why the German leadership was unable or unwilling to mobilize the unused production reserves during the first half of the war. The British economic historian Alan Milward seems to have found a convincing explanation. He developed the fascinating theory of Hitler's blitzkrieg economy.[64] The German Reich was unable to carry on any long-lasting war effort, so it deliberately refrained from strategic armament in depth to concentrate on a quickly available armament in width. In that way, presumably, it was possible to conduct a successive series of blitzkriegs that were limited in time and area.

The theory of Hitler's ingenious blitzkrieg economy has already been questioned in the introductory chapter. According to the latest research findings, this sparkling concept proved to be a crossbreed between a "peacetime war economy" and a "wartime peace economy."[65] At that time, Thomas described this mixed form rather cautiously as a "transition economy."[66] Conditions resembling peacetime continued to prevail to an astonishing extent in the German economy even after the start of the war. And so, Thomas commented rather sarcastically in November 1939: "We will never be able to beat England with radios, vacuum cleaners, and kitchen appliances."[67]

To some extent, the rather minor cutback on civilian consumption was quite in keeping with the intentions of Hitler the propagandist who was quite sensitive to the population's frame of mind. Above all, Hitler wanted to keep the arms industry workers in a good mood. "The regime acted as if one could expect German men to die a hero's death on the field of honor, whereas they could not be expected to put up with wage cuts or higher butter prices for the population as a whole."[68]

The low degree of mobilization during the war's initial phase can be traced back partly to the anarchical way in which the ruling mechanisms of the Third Reich were structured. There was an administrative Darwinism among rival courts. The effects of this confusion of jurisdictions were made worse by Hitler's fickle decisions. Only the zigzag course of economic control measures, ordered by Hitler, was like a blitz (lightning-like). To the very end of the campaign in the west, there was neither a specific blitzkrieg economy nor was there the alternative, namely, a total economic mobilization.[69] The Third Reich appeared monolithic only from the outside. During the first phase of the war, it was in any case not in a position to concentrate the potential of its strength toward a particular point. Looking back, Thomas had this to say in 1945: "There was complete leaderlessness in the economic field in Hitler's so-called Führer-state and there was an unspeakably confused parallelism because Hitler did not grasp the need for firm, far-sighted planning, because Göring knew nothing about the economy and economics, and because the responsible experts had no real authority."[70] The Reich's economy minister [Walter] Funk is reported to have put it even more forcefully: "You had to be crazy or drunk to last in this mess—and I prefer being drunk."[71]

But the most important reason why there could not have been any specific blitzkrieg economy before the campaign in the west resides simply in the fact that the German leadership just did not want that. In the end, it was the fear of the specter of 1914 that emerged victorious in the conflict of goals between armament in breadth for a hoped-for short war and armament in depth for a feared long war. Former combat soldier Hitler, like his generals, was clearly aware of the traumatic experiences of the battles of attrition during World War I. This is why the German leadership shied away from orienting the entire armament effort rather unilaterally toward the conduct of a quick war. As mentioned before, Hitler rejected as criminal the idea that "the political leadership should rely on surprise."[72] Rather he demanded: "We have to prepare for a long war along with a surprise attack."[73]

Thomas accentuated this in a similar manner on 28 March 1939 when he admitted "that a war, employing all available energies, must be pursued forcefully and must be short because we cannot last through a long war in terms of food and raw materials. It is quite natural that, considering our geopolitical position, we must always aim for a short war and lightning-like decisions." But then he added: "But whether it [the lightning-like decision] will come off . . . that is questionable. It seems dangerous to draw up a war-fighting concept solely on that basis."[74]

Economic mobilization clearly shows that the campaign in the west was not designed as a campaign of six weeks (which is what it actually turned into), but rather was a rehash of the many long years of struggle during the World War I. This is why the German military potential was not to burn out like a firework but was to be kept at a low flame for a long period. The model of the long war guided the decision-making process in the conflict of goals between armament in breadth and armament in depth. The following fact is the clearest indication of that: armament planning for the campaign in the west, in terms of the time frame, called for a noticeable increase in output only in October 1940. But the high point should have been reached only in the autumn of 1941.[75] However, everything turned out quite differently. At that point in time, the German troops were no longer before Paris but rather before Moscow.

As spelled out before, the campaign in the west, the scale of priorities within the armament effort, if anything, points to the exact opposite of a blitzkrieg concept geared toward a swift decision. First of all came requirements that clearly pointed to the prospect of a long-lasting positional war as in World War I: ammunition and powder factories, tools, and machine tools. The second priority called for the production of new submarines as well as Ju-88 aircraft. These were weapon systems that would only have a long-term effect in case of a strategic war against Great Britain. Only the third (and next to the last) priority included combat vehicles, in other words, Panzers.[76]

A particularly informative figure here is the distribution of steel within the army armament effort. Among the 445,000 tons that were allocated for the second quarter of 1940, only 25,000 tons were left over for battle tanks and armored vehicles, in other words, a mere 5 percent of the steel quota. That was less than the 26,000 tons that had been earmarked for barbed wire, obstacles, structural steel, and so on, for conducting a positional war. About twice as much steel was made available for the preparation of factories for *future* ammunition production as for the production of armored vehicles.[77]

So, the campaign in the west in 1940—quite in contrast to the campaign in the east in 1941—was not planned as a blitzkrieg from the very beginning. That is something that can be demonstrated particularly clearly by looking at the mobilization of manpower resources (for example, the practice of granting exemptions to allow men to work in industry). Before the start of the campaign in the west, the General Army Office ordered an indefinite freeze. But before the start of the campaign in the east, the freeze was limited to three months, in other words, up to September 1941.[78] Within those three months, it was believed that the Soviet Union, the "colossus on feet of clay," could be overrun in a blitzkrieg.[79] In planning the campaign in the west, the German command was still guided by the model of the long war similar to World War I. At that time, the leadership had realized that in the age of industrialized warfare military conflicts would in the last analysis be decided in the factories and workshops. This is why a considerable segment of the labor force was first of all left in the factories. A Führer order, dated 17 January 1940, even said this: "To increase the output of the armament industry, it will be necessary to make the urgently needed skilled workers *immediately* available to the armament industry even if that should cause a temporary reduction in the personnel strength of the military formations; these are the skilled workers for whom wartime exemptions, backed up by an urgency certificate, are already on file."[80]

And so it happened that quite a few Panzer soldiers had to again exchange their black uniforms for blue mechanics' overalls. Hitler and his advisers believed that it was unrealistic to tie their hopes to a single decision-seeking Panzer operation. They wanted to prepare the economy and the arms industry for many years of struggle against the Western powers.

Was the Army's Organizational Structure Geared to a Blitzkrieg?

All victories were won . . . without any Panzers, only by virtue of the infantry's spirit of attack. In that way, the infantry erected an eternal monument to itself.[81]

From the War Diary of Army Group B,
4 June, after the Fall of Dunkirk

Personnel Structure

In a generally accurate analysis of the German blitzkrieg successes, the British military author General [Sir John] Hackett writes: "True Blitzkrieg is only for bold and highly skilled professionals, and for youngish professionals at that."[82] This idealized image may have applied to individual Panzer divisions even though they contained draftees and not professionals (as in the case of the British). In reality, during the campaign in the west, 45 percent of soldiers in the army were over the age of forty and 50 percent of the men had just a few weeks of training.[83]

The problems mentioned here have already been addressed as they affected the Wehrmacht in the midst of its build-up effort. But it was the shortage of officers that turned out to be particularly critical. After the introduction of compulsory military service in 1935, Hitler managed to put together an army of 5.5 million soldiers by the start of the campaign in the west. During that same span of time, however, it was impossible to train an adequate number of company commanders, battalion commanders, and so on. The 100,000-man army of the Reichswehr could have only 4,000 officers. That figure included 450 medical officers and veterinarians and another 500 officers had to be transferred to build up the new Luftwaffe, so there were a mere 3,050 officers available as a nucleus of an army that in the end was to number several million.[84] The French army, on the other hand, was not bound by any treaty clauses and had been able to train an enormous contingent of officers since the last war. At the start of World War II, the French army had 39,000 active duty officers plus more than 90,000 reserve officers.[85] In contrast, well-trained regular officers, who really are indispensable when it comes to conducting a blitzkrieg, were rather an exception in the German formations in the spring of 1940.

Equipment

As far as weapons were concerned, the armament plans, if anything, were drawn up rather narrowly along the lines of anachronistic trench warfare thinking and not with a vision of a real blitzkrieg. It is also easy to refute the National Socialist propaganda myth that Hitler demonstrated revolutionary farsightedness in contrast to his conservative generals. One of the oddities in the dictator's leadership style was that he again and again failed to delegate and got himself bogged down in technical military details. In light of this mania, it seems rather odd how little he was interested in Panzers before the campaign in the west. Instead, heavy artillery fired his imagination as if the important thing was to fight the Battle of Verdun a second time. So he conceived the bright idea of using the guns intended for the battleships *Scharnhorst* and *Gneisenau,* the only two operational battleships, to hit the Maginot Line. That sort of suggestion naturally distressed the navy high command.[86]

The so-called ammunition crisis that deteriorated into a crisis psychosis due to Hitler's overreaction proves that the dictator and his military advisers were still thinking in terms of the positional warfare of World War I. After all, it is the movement factor and not the firepower factor that predominates in blitzkrieg. In reality, there were considerably more dramatic bottlenecks in other armament sectors. For example, the wretched condition of motorization should have provided cause for concern. The striking shortage of vehicles, above all Panzers, is typical of the alleged blitzkrieg army of 1940. By comparison, the British Expeditionary Force (BEF) was motorized in an enviable fashion. After requisitioning numerous civilian trucks, the French army could come up with about 300,000 vehicles.[87] Early in 1940, however, there were only 120,000 trucks available for the German army, which had to overextend its supply lines for an offensive into the enemy's territory.[88] Thus, the image of the fully motorized German blitzkrieg army is a figment of propaganda imagination. The primary cause of this shortage in the Wehrmacht was the lack of steel and rubber.[89] Just how problematic the situation in the motor vehicle sector was is clearly indicated by the fact that only about 1,000 new trucks were produced per month, or less than 1 percent of the inventory. But that was not even enough to cover the normal monthly wear and tear (without combat operations) of 2 percent.[90] On top of that, fuel supplies were also very modest in contrast to what the Western powers had.[91]

As a consequence of this motor vehicle mess, Halder called for a rigorous "demotorization program" that involved a "drastic and ruthless restriction of motor vehicles in existing and newly activated units."[92] Once again, the horse was to take the place of the engine. Thus, in the spring of 1940 the Wehrmacht was characterized not by Panzers and motor vehicles but by horses. During World War I, the German army used 1.4 million horses; during World War II, it used 2.7 million, almost twice as many.[93] Among the 157 divisions (including those that were still being organized) that the German army had in May 1940, only 16, about 10 percent, were fully motorized. The others mostly marched along at traditional infantry speed, followed by horse-drawn vehicles. In the campaign in the west, also, the infantry was the Queen of Battles.

Most of the German divisions were equipped rather modestly, if not skimpily. Only half of them could be classified as fully combat ready.[94] Hitler had plunged the as yet unprepared Wehrmacht into the adventure of a world war—and its equipment was correspondingly adventurous. In terms of matériel, most German divisions could cer-

The German Blitzkrieg Army 1940 propaganda . . . *Bundesarchiv Koblenz [Federal Archives]*

. . . and reality *Bundesarchiv Koblenz [Federal Archives]*

tainly not stand comparison to a standard division of the French army or even the British army. Some German divisions hardly came up to the level of World War I. Many sons carried the same machine guns that their fathers had carried during the last war. Frequently, it was even the fathers themselves who had to fight with the same machine guns they had used in World War I.[95]

Structure and Organization

In the spring of 1940 one might well describe the German army as semimodern.[96] A very small number of the best-equipped and best-trained elite divisions were offset by many second- and third-rate divisions. Thus, there were actually two armies within the Wehrmacht: on the one hand, the ten Panzer and six motorized infantry divisions, and, on the other hand, the actual army that looked rather old-fashioned and had inferior equipment. But it is only those sixteen elite divisions that can be categorized as blitzkrieg divisions. The remaining 90 percent were better suited for defense, less suited for attack missions, and not at all suited for a blitzkrieg. After all, modern mobile warfare can only be fought with motorized formations.

The political leadership decided that the Wehrmacht would keep organizing new units, although it was not even in a position to equip adequately all of the existing ones. And so, the drop in quality between the first-wave divisions and the following waves became increasingly alarming as regards armament, training, and officer strength.[97] The first wave consisted of the active duty divisions of the peacetime army that had been reinforced with reservists. The second wave consisted of mostly younger soldiers from Reserve I (fully trained). The third and fourth waves included soldiers from Reserve II, in other words, members of the white age classes who had merely gone through a brief training cycle lasting two to three months. The Landwehr (territorial forces) accounted for a similarly large percentage and included veterans of World War I, most of whom were already over the age of forty.

In addition, many Landesschützen (regional defense personnel) more than forty-five years old had already been recalled to active duty. They were assigned to guard duty and security missions in rear areas. But the personnel shortage was so serious that even Landesschützen units were put under the control of field units. The problem now was to equip those regional defense units in whatever minimum way possible. At the start of the war, many regional defense soldiers had neither steel helmets nor boots, gas masks nor mess kits. In some cases, they were not even issued a uniform, so that only an armband reading Deutsche Wehrmacht identified them as soldiers.

The Wehrmacht went to war with these four waves supported by regional defense reservists. At that time, the active duty component of the ground forces consisted of only 730,000 men, less than one-fifth of the total force. A fifth wave was organized especially for defense missions along the western front. That wave was a rather motley outfit in terms of personnel; many soldiers had only had eight weeks of training. That appeared to be all that was doable at that moment. Nevertheless, until the beginning of the campaign in the west, the Wehrmacht mobilized additional waves (sixth to ninth waves). This meant that half of all German soldiers had gone through only a few weeks of training and that one-quarter were over the age of forty.

On 8 May, just two days before the start of the campaign in the west, orders were even issued for the organization of a tenth wave (with a total of nine divisions). Unit training, if possible, was to take ten to fourteen days before the divisions were to be sent out into the field. A number of officer slots were to have been manned with officer candidates, and 50 percent of the noncommissioned officer slots were to be manned with privates first class and privates. Fortunately, however, the swift end of the campaign preserved these hardly combat-worthy divisions from being employed as cannon fodder.

The military leadership had faced a conflict between quality and quantity. After the campaign in Poland, it had been proposed that no additional, scarcely usable, divisions should be organized. Instead, numerous soldiers were to be discharged to work in the armament industry so that it would be possible at least to produce enough weapons for the already existing formations. This is expressed very clearly in a paper prepared by Army Group C and addressed to the army high command: "It is better to constantly fully replenish full-fledged divisions . . . than to leave increasingly noticeable gaps and, in turn, to establish formations of inferior value."[98] Instead, however, the basic principle of mass was given preference. The organization of more and more new divisions resulted in a weakening of the formations of the first and second waves from whom cadre personnel had to be taken for this purpose.

If a country's military leadership plans a blitzkrieg to overrun the enemy swiftly with powerful motorized formations, then it seems senseless to organize a large number of third-rate infantry divisions that are suitable only for static defense. But the leadership of the Wehrmacht was guided by the image of a long war and prepared for a rehash of positional warfare such as prevailed during World War I. This structure looked practical for that purpose. After all, manning endlessly long trenches requires a large number of infantry divisions whose combat value need suffice merely for defensive missions.

In terms of its structure, the German army resembled a lance whose point consisted of hardened steel; but the wooden shaft looked all the longer and therefore ever more brittle. This steel tip dealt the Allies the deadly thrust. It seems rather characteristic of the course of Operation Sickle Cut that this spearhead became separated from the shaft. The fast units, the Panzer divisions and the motorized infantry divisions, attacked so impetuously that, contrary to all planning, they simply took off and left the nonmotorized bulk of the army in the dust. Thus, the infantry divisions were downgraded to the extras of blitzkrieg. Often, their only mission was to march behind the Panzer divisions and to occupy the territory conquered by those divisions. So, a rather paradoxical situation arose. The Panzer divisions achieved the operational breakthrough upon the first rush and thus prepared the way for the decisive end of the campaign. The infantry divisions that were still marching through the Ardennes in

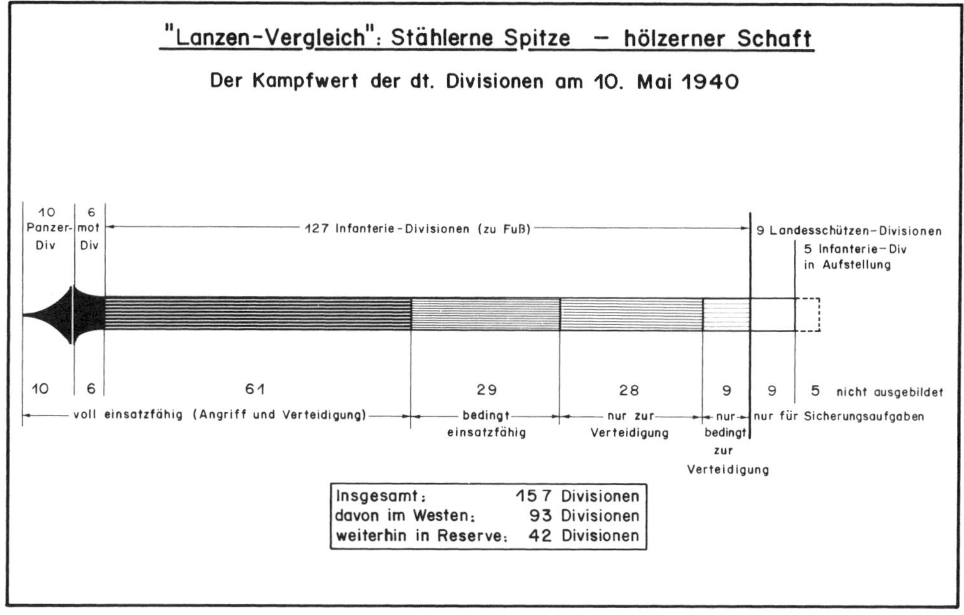

Lance Comparison: Steel Tip—Wooden Shaft

many cases neither saw any foe at all nor fired a single round from their obsolete weapons.[99]

The Allied intelligence services were later reproached for failing to recognize correctly the structure of the German blitzkrieg army in spite of voluminous information. This criticism seems unjustified because the German army, in terms of its structure, actually was not a blitzkrieg army.

Operational-Tactical Concept

One will look in vain for indications of an operational-tactical blitzkrieg doctrine in the military regulations issued prior to the campaign. The idea of the operational-level employment of German armor turns up in army regulations only starting in 1940.[100] Because they were still thinking in terms of World War I, most generals rejected precisely those methods that were initially to become so typical of blitzkrieg. Just a few, like Guderian, were already envisioning modern mobile warfare. But Guderian was far ahead of his contemporaries with his ideas. As he put it, from the very beginning he had to fight against "a barrier of reaction" in the army general staff.[101] When he was a young general staff officer in the Reichswehr, he was assigned to the Motorized Transport Department where one day he expressed the hope that "we were on the way to transforming our motorised units from supply troops into combat troops."[102] Immediately, his inspector, Oberst von Natzmer, straightened him out: "To hell with combat! They're supposed to carry flour!"[103]

Even at the start of the campaign in the west, there were two contending views in the armed forces about the future image of war: The majority of the conservatives determined the official guidelines, while the small group of progressives were waiting for the chance to prove the validity of their constantly doubted theories.

General a.D. [Johann Adolf] Graf von Kielmansegg's statement in connection with the origin of blitzkrieg appears rather characteristic. He participated in the campaign as general staff officer 2 (Ib), the chief of the Supply and Administrative Section of the 1st Panzer Division. He disputes the idea that German successes were based on "some kind of Blitzkrieg concept, whatever it was" and certainly not at all as a "complete system." Instead, he speaks of an "improvisation or, more accurately, an *ad hoc* solution that simply popped out of the prevailing situation."[104] Halder, who had monitored the preparation and implementation of German operations in his capacity as chief of the army general staff, had already come up with a correct estimate of this "blitzkrieg without the blitzkrieg concept" immediately after the end of the campaign in the west: "The whole world is searching for the new methods used by the Germans—and they were not at all new—because war is always a system of expedients."[105]

The well-known paratroop general [Kurt] Student expressed this situation particularly clearly when he said, "actually there was never any such thing as a 'Blitzkrieg.' In point of fact, this was a term—an idea that somehow was suspended in air—and that quite gradually and quite naturally emerged from the existing circumstances and the time frame."[106]

Was the Wehrmacht Superior in Terms of Strength?

In tactics, as in strategy, superiority of numbers is the most common element in victory.[107]

Carl von Clausewitz

It is obviously a basic principle of propaganda to exaggerate the enemy's strength and to downplay your own. All the more shining will victory then be and all the more excusable will defeat be. In that regard, we must point to one of the oddest inconsistencies of the campaign in the west. Why did the official reporting of the Third Reich not deny the grotesquely exaggerated data that turned up in foreign countries here and there? That would have made the victory of the Wehrmacht, which in reality was numerically inferior, look even more triumphal. Why did propaganda, so masterfully managed by Goebbels, engage in shameless exaggerations that seemed to confirm or perhaps even surpass the images of horror suggested in Western reports? The reason for this is very simple: The primary objective of German propaganda was to deter

Great Britain from continuing the war and to scare the United States away from any thoughts of entering it. What could seem more suitable for this than the myth of the invincibility of the Wehrmacht? This gave rise to the frightening image of the German blitzkrieg army that crushed any enemy like a steel avalanche.

Just how limited the possibilities of the raw material–poor German Reich were in reality already emerged in 1940. Thus, the air battle over England proved that most aircraft types were not suitable for a strategic air war, above all on account of their short range. Besides, the British were definitely able to outdo German armament in decisive areas. In 1940 the armament industry of the German Reich was able to increase its output by only 76 percent compared to the prior year, while that rate was 150 percent in the United States and 250 percent in Great Britain. Germany was strangled economically by a naval blockade and thus had no chance of winning an arms race against the two sea powers. During the following year, the German growth rate stagnated whereas the British war economy once again achieved an increase of 86 percent, while the American war industry increased 200 percent.[108] But for the United States, an economic superpower, that was just a modest beginning. The United States did not become involved in the war until after Pearl Harbor and then went into a crash armaments program.

In analyzing the campaign, a rather strange alliance emerged between authors from Germany and the Western countries, who, on the basis of different motives, tried to make the Wehrmacht appear bigger than it was in reality. The contrast was further increased because French and British publications did not exactly exaggerate the strength of their own fighting forces that had suffered an incomprehensible debacle. This is why a myth necessarily had to be formed, and that myth still exists.

German Reich. On 10 May, the Wehrmacht had a theoretical total strength of about 5.4 million men. Here is the breakdown for the individual Wehrmacht components: army, about 4.2 million; Luftwaffe, about 1 million; and navy, about 180,000. To this one can add about 100,000 men of the Waffen-SS.[109]

The total also includes the replacement army and the construction units that were earmarked only for labor assignments and that, in September 1939, already numbered 427,000 men. The personnel strength shrinks considerably if one deducts the units that remained along the eastern border and in Poland or those that were stationed in Norway and Denmark. Theoretically, 3 million men were earmarked for the army to be used in the campaign against the Western powers, including the reserves in rear areas that were still partly being organized.[110]

The Allies. At the beginning of September 1939, the French armed forces mobilized a total of 6.1 million men.[111] In the spring of 1940, the army was about 5.5 million strong (including colonial units). Of that number, about 2.24 million men manned the northeast front at the start of the German offensive.[112]

In peacetime, Great Britain maintained only a regular army. After mobilization in September 1939, the army had a personnel strength of 897,000 men, a number that grew to 1.65 million by June 1940.[113] To support France, the British army sent an expeditionary army to the Continent [the British Expeditionary Force, BEF]. In May 1940 it numbered just about 500,000 men, including the reserves who were immediately ready for embarkation to France.[114]

In view of Hitler's invasion intentions, Holland and Belgium had also mobilized their forces. Not considering the territorial army, the personnel strength of the Dutch army came to about 400,000 and that of the Belgian army to around 650,000 men.[115]

Accordingly, the German army of the west had a strength of about 3 million men, including reserves, at the start of the campaign. It faced around 4 million soldiers in the ground forces of the Allies.

Number of Divisions

On 10 May the German army had 157 divisions.[116] A total of 135 divisions were earmarked for the offensive in the west (including 42 reserve divisions).[117] Of these, several were just being newly organized and were hardly employed during that campaign. Only 93 divisions mounted the offensive after the start of the campaign.

On the other hand, France had 117 divisions, with 104 divisions (including 11 reserve divisions) manning the northeast front.[118] At the start of the campaign, the BEF consisted of 13 divisions, of which three had not yet been completely organized.[119] In addition, the 1st [British] Armored Division and the 52d [Highland] Division had been transferred to the Continent.[120] To the Allied contingent one must also add 22 Belgian and 10 Dutch divisions.[121]

In other words, in May 1940, the 135 German divisions (including 42 reserve divisions) faced a total of 151 Allied divisions.

Artillery

In terms of artillery, the Western powers were almost twice as strong. France alone had more than 10,700 artillery pieces. To that one must add 1,280 artillery pieces with the British army, 1,338 in the Belgian army, and 656 in the Dutch army. This means that the Western armies were able to employ around 14,000 artillery pieces against only 7,378 for the Wehrmacht.[122]

Tanks

Quantitative Comparison. The numbers given below appear to be rather high. Some authors deliberately took the Panzer I out of these statistics. These "curious little machines," as Len Deighton called them,[123] were equipped only with machine guns. The Panzer II was likewise not suitable for engaging enemy battle tanks because of its rather weak 2-cm gun. That means that only the 349 Panzer IIIs and 278 Panzer IVs were left as real battle tanks from German production. Three out of the 10 German Panzer divisions, including the 7th Panzer Division, commanded by Generalmajor [Erwin] Rommel, were equipped mostly with Czech models. But despite these reinforcements, the German armored force was definitely inferior to French armor. Comparative statistics can illustrate the overwhelming superiority of the French armored forces. For example, the total weight of all tanks produced in France since World War I came to 61,645 tons, whereas that of the German tanks was only 36,650 tons.[124]

German Armor Strength on 10 May 1940	
German Models	
Panzer I	523
Panzer II	955
Panzer III	349
Panzer IV	278
Czech Models	
Panzer 35 (t)	106
Panzer 38 (t)	228
Total Strength:	2,439[125]

French Armor Strength on 10 May 1940 (Northeast Front)	
AMR and AMC	450
Renault F.T. 1918 (mod.)	315
Renault 35	900
Hotchkiss 35/39	770
FCM	100
D 1	45
D 2	100
SOMUA	300
Char B	274
Total Strength	3,254[126]

These statistics relate only to the French tanks stationed along the northeast front on 10 May. At that time, the French army had a total of 4,111 tanks (not including the 250 tanks stationed in North Africa and overseas).[127]

At the start of the German offensive, the British Expeditionary Force had only 310 tanks on the Continent. But one must also count the 330 combat vehicles of the 1st

[British] Armored Division that were in the process of crossing the English Channel and that arrived in France by the end of May.[128]

Astonishingly, hardly any statistics on the campaign in the west mention the Belgian and Dutch combat vehicles, which were either equivalent to or superior to most German Panzer I and II models. That applies above all to the types armed with a 4.7-cm gun. The Belgian army had about 270 armored combat vehicles (mostly T 13 and T 15), while the Dutch army had around 40 (mostly of the Landsverk type).[129]

Here is what that means: The assertion that the armed forces of Western powers fell victim to overwhelming German armored might is only a myth. In May 1940 the 2,439 battle tanks of the Wehrmacht faced 4,204 Allied battle tanks.

Qualitative Comparison. The image of the German Panzers among the world public has been fashioned entirely too permanently by the heavy models, the Panther (Panzer Model V) and the Tiger (Panzer Model VI), which, however, were employed only during the second half of the war. It was a big shock to the U.S. Army when, at the end of 1944, the gigantic King Tigers came rolling at it out of the Ardennes woods. American projectiles bounced off the armor of those huge tanks without causing any damage. But this steel colossus, which some authors refer to as the best battle tank of World War II,[130] bore hardly any resemblance to the German Panzers that had rolled through the Ardennes in 1940, partly on the same trails and roads. With its seventy tons, a single King Tiger weighed as much as twelve Panzer I models. So, this tiny model that marked the beginning of a long development process looks almost like an embryo compared to the later Panzers V and VI. This comparison also symbolizes the rudimentary developmental stage of the German Panzer force that was still being built up and organized in the spring of 1940.

The provisions of the Versailles Treaty prohibited the German Reich from producing or owning Panzers. Surrounded by strict secrecy, some experimental models were tested deep inside Russia during the phase of cooperation with the Red Army. But, at first, it seemed that the Germans would never catch up with the Western powers. When Hitler ordered the organization of an armored force, the German designers had to skip several developmental stages all at once. According to Guderian's ideas, the Panzer I was intended only as a training vehicle and certainly not for combat employment. The inadequately armed Panzer II also was a stopgap solution at best. Because the development and production of Panzer III and IV models dragged out longer and longer due to technical problems, the two light models were produced in large numbers and accounted for almost two-thirds of the Panzers during the campaign in the west.

Furthermore, the hasty tempo of Panzer production meant that the German Panzers were technically not yet ready for use. That could be seen in 1938 during the invasion of Austria. To be sure, there was no resistance whatsoever, and the vast bulk of the population instead welcomed the incorporation into the Reich, which it had wanted back in 1918. Still, dozens of Panzers broke down due to technical reasons. In the end, not only cheering Austrians but also broken-down Panzers lined the route of advance to Vienna. That was a tremendous embarrassment for Austrian-born Hitler who had visualized the entry into his former home as being considerably more triumphal. In spite of its short duration, the Polish campaign also proved that the German Panzers were still suffering numerous childhood diseases. In the campaign in the west, the number of broken-down Panzers sometimes reached alarming levels. After barely two weeks, most of the units had only half their Panzers ready for action.

The Armor Factor. The thickness of the armor showed a decisive qualitative difference between the German and the Allied models. For the Panzer IV, it was 30 mm, whereas the French Char B had 60 mm and the British Matilda Infantry Tank had 80 mm. These two colossi became the nightmare of German soldiers because there was no German Panzer cannon or German antitank gun (*Panzerabwehr-Kanone* or Pak) that could penetrate that Allied armor. Numerous after-action reports reflect the nasty surprise represented by that situation. The 1st Panzer Division experienced such a clash on the morning of 17 May north of Laon at Crécy: "Although the southern exit had been secured, French tanks did turn up there and one of them simply ran over our security outposts and rode toward Mortiers along the advancing columns of the 1st Motorcycle Rifle Battalion. That French tank was knocked out in Mortiers only after the surprised Panzer Battalion of the 1st Panzer Regiment mounted up and hit the French tank, that was simply driving through the German positions, with several well-aimed rounds from the rear. The crew surrendered. It was found that the French tank (B 2) was just about saturated with 3.7-cm hits and also had some 7.5-cm hits without a single round having penetrated its armor."[131]

The following episode took place on the same day, not too far away: "In the evening of 17 May, the 6th Panzer Division had beaten off an attack by heavy French tanks in the Hauteville-Neuvilette bridgehead. In the process, one antitank gun in the unit of Oberleutnant Neckenauer made 25 hits on a French tank. That tank was knocked out only with the 26th round that hit the tracks."[132] Just a day before, in Stonne south of Sedan, a single Char B had attacked a German Panzer column and had knocked out thirteen Panzers and two German antitank guns. Its armor later showed 140 hits without a single projectile having penetrated.[133]

The Armament Factor. The technical backwardness of the German Panzer force that was still being organized also emerged in this area. The French had been fortunate in designing the world's best weapon of this kind with their 4.7-cm tank gun. It was used to equip not only a variant of the AMC vehicle, but also the D 2, SOMUA, and Char B tank types. The latter also had a 7.5-cm cannon. The French 3.7-cm cannon, which was developed during World War I, must be considered inadequate for tackling heavy tanks. Many armored combat vehicles had in the meantime been equipped with a mod-

Die wichtigsten Panzertypen im Vergleich

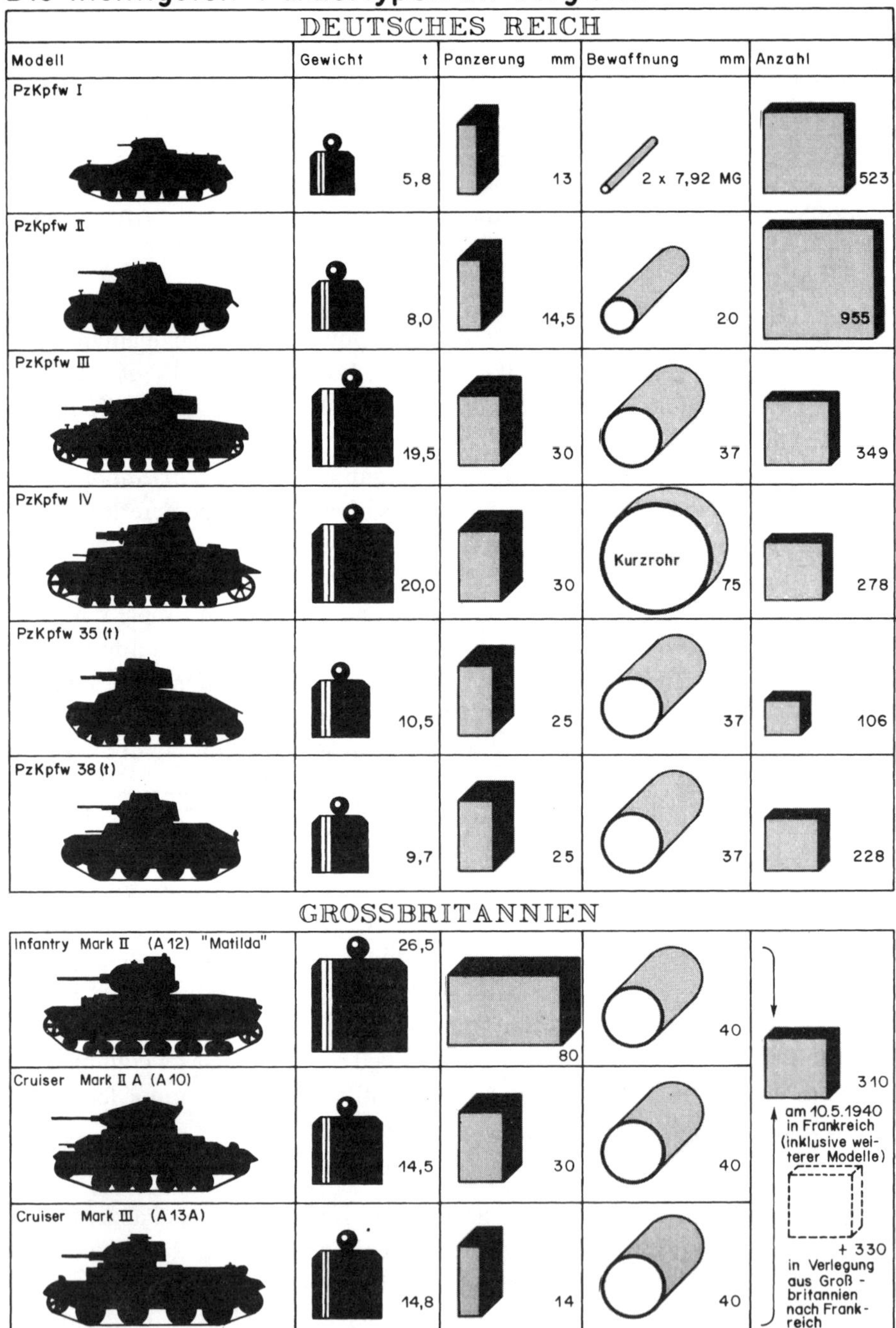

Modell	Gewicht t	Panzerung mm	Bewaffnung mm	Anzahl
DEUTSCHES REICH				
PzKpfw I	5,8	13	2 x 7,92 MG	523
PzKpfw II	8,0	14,5	20	955
PzKpfw III	19,5	30	37	349
PzKpfw IV	20,0	30	Kurzrohr 75	278
PzKpfw 35 (t)	10,5	25	37	106
PzKpfw 38 (t)	9,7	25	37	228
GROSSBRITANNIEN				
Infantry Mark II (A 12) "Matilda"	26,5	80	40	310 am 10.5.1940 in Frankreich (inklusive weiterer Modelle) + 330 in Verlegung aus Groß-britannien nach Frank-reich
Cruiser Mark II A (A 10)	14,5	30	40	
Cruiser Mark III (A 13A)	14,8	14	40	

Comparison of the Most Important Tank Types: Germany, Great Britain, and France

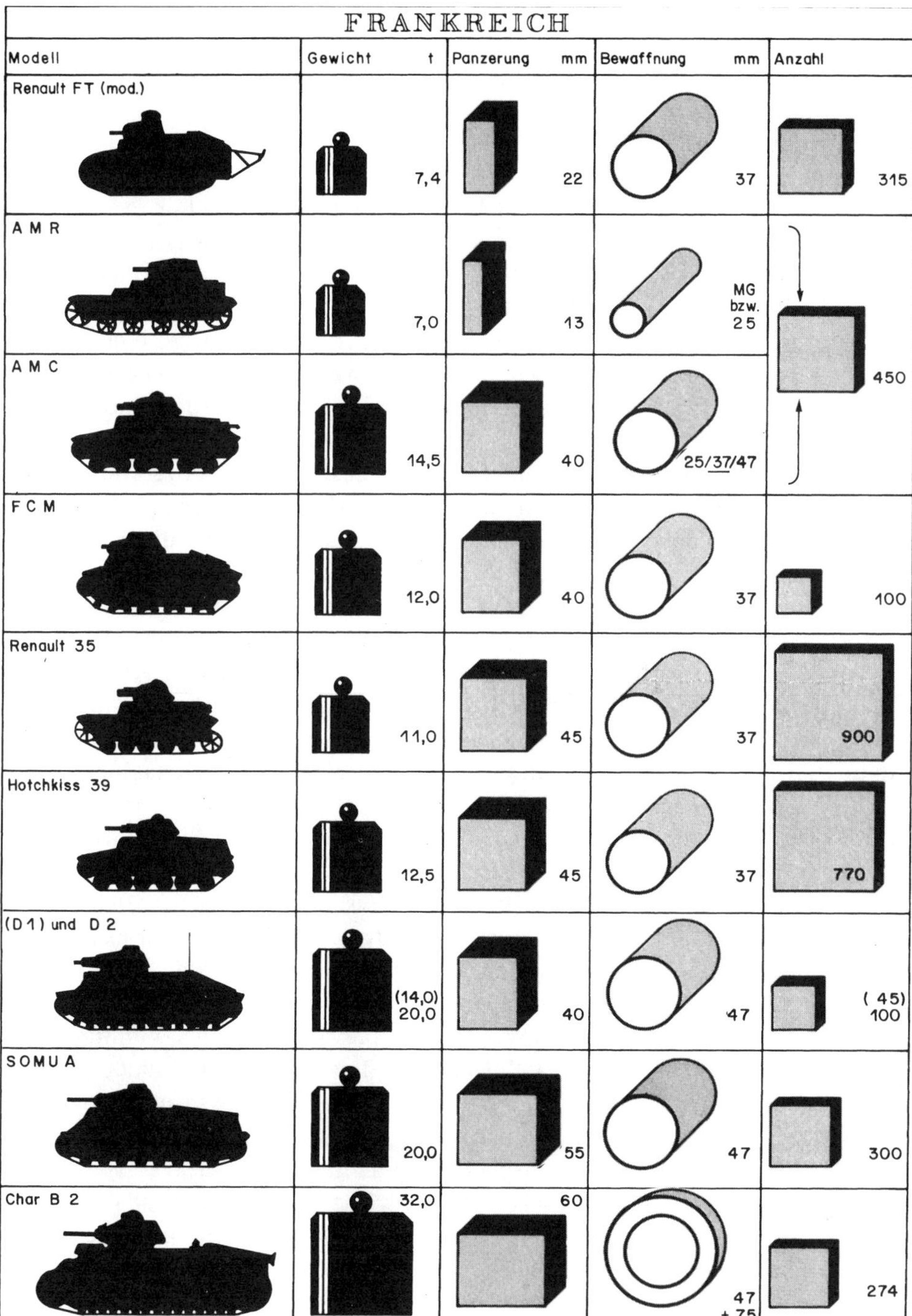

FRANKREICH

Modell	Gewicht t	Panzerung mm	Bewaffnung mm	Anzahl
Renault FT (mod.)	7,4	22	37	315
A M R	7,0	13	MG bzw. 25	450
A M C	14,5	40	25/37/47	
F C M	12,0	40	37	100
Renault 35	11,0	45	37	900
Hotchkiss 39	12,5	45	37	770
(D 1) und D 2	(14,0) 20,0	40	47	(45) 100
SOMU A	20,0	55	47	300
Char B 2	32,0	60	47 + 75	274

ern weapon of the same caliber. The standard armament of most British tanks was a 4-cm gun with a high muzzle velocity.

The light Panzer II with the 2-cm gun accounted for the bulk of German Panzer units during the campaign in the west.

In comparison, most German models seemed undergunned. For example, the Panzer I did not even have a gun; it only had two machine guns. The rather puny 2-cm gun of the Panzer II was hardly any threat to the light Allied combat vehicles. This means that almost two-thirds of the available German Panzers could not be employed against enemy tanks. The Panzer III and the two Czech models likewise only had an inadequate 3.7-cm gun. The infantry used a variant of that weapon as an antitank gun. The German *Landser*s (soldiers or GIs) rather mockingly referred to these guns as "Panzer door knockers" because of their deficient penetrating performance.

The stubby 7.5-cm short-barrel cannon of the Panzer IV symbolized the fact that German Panzer technology at that time was only half-ready and had not fully matured. When this tank was equipped with a long-barrel gun of the same caliber during the campaign in Russia, it proved entirely effective. But during the hasty buildup phase of the German Panzer force, installing such a weapon in the turret of the Panzer IV created some design problems. However, the short L/24 barrel was at best a stopgap solution as far as firing performance was concerned. The initial velocity was only 385 m/sec, whereas the projectiles of the British 4-cm tank gun left the barrel with a speed of 800 m/sec and achieved a considerably longer trajectory. As a result, the Panzer IV, with this sawed-off looking cannon, was troubled by poor accuracy and inadequate range. It was able to engage enemy tanks only at relatively close range, and it was unable to penetrate the heavy Allied models even from very close range. So it was most suitable as a supporting tank against large ground targets and to neutralize the infantry.

An episode from the actions of the 4th Panzer Division shows the tremendous problems encountered in just trying to knock out a smaller point target, for example, an enemy antitank gun. As it broke through the Dyle position on 15 May, the 1st Battalion, 35th Panzer Regiment, ran into an antitank gun blocking position south of Gembloux. Not even the heavy Panzers were able to prevail in the duel with the enemy antitank guns: "The 1st Battalion, 35th Panzer Regiment, lost almost all its heavy vehicles here. To knock out the enemy antitank guns, the tank crews partly dismounted to destroy the enemy guns in what amounted to hand-to-hand fighting. They did the job, and they even captured some prisoners, but their losses were heavy." [134]

So this is how far the situation had deteriorated! The Black Hussars had to dismount from their fighting vehicles, as if they were doing punishment exercises in the training area, and, like infantry, they had to creep up on the enemy to overcome him in close combat. This incredible incident was even proudly emphasized in the unit's war diary. Hitler had started a war and was not even able to give his elite troops, the Panzer soldiers, the right kind of Panzers. One of the most important topics of this study will be to describe how, in spite of all this, a couple of Panzer divisions, almost by themselves,

The dreaded French Char B (twin armament: 7.5-cm and 4.7-cm guns) *Bundesarchiv Koblenz [Federal Archives]*

The light Panzer II with the 2-cm gun accounted for the bulk of German Panzer units during the campaign in the west. *Bundesarchiv Koblenz [Federal Archives]*

were able to decide an entire campaign in just a few days. Here we want to show that it was not the thickness of the armor and the caliber of the gun that decided the issue but entirely different factors that determined the success of the German Panzer force.

Aircraft

Quantitative Comparison. Probably one of the most stubborn myths that almost all reports and studies stress is the superiority of the Luftwaffe. General [Joseph] Vuillemin, the commanding general of the French air force, after the campaign in the west even insisted that his pilots had to tackle "an enemy five times superior in number."[135] This distortion springs from unclear, often speculative, statistics that for a long time caused considerable problems in academic research.

German Reich. The different results derived from the calculation of the operational strength of the Luftwaffe are a perfect example of the relativity of numerical data. In looking at the assertion that the Germans attacked with more than 5,000 aircraft on 10 May 1940, at first sight the number looks correct. On paper the effective aircraft strength was exactly 5,446.[136] But that number shrinks considerably, the more precise the criteria become. The fact is that only 4,020 aircraft were operational. Another reduction results if one counts only the combat aircraft (bombers, dive-bombers, ground-attack aircraft, fighters, and destroyers).[137] Of that number only 2,756 were operational (with an actual strength of 3,864). Just how many really got into action is something that can no longer be reconstructed today. After all, a part of the fighters were always held back for home air defense in the *Luftgau* (air districts). We are left with 2,589 operational combat aircraft (actual strength 3,578), if one deducts at least the units employed against Norway.[138]

French and British reports to some extent grossly exaggerated the strength of the Luftwaffe. That was due not only to the fact that by making the enemy look bigger their defeat would be somewhat diminished, but it was also the way the Luftwaffe depicted itself that led to this inflation. This was a fatal mixture of Göring's boastfulness and propagandistic calculation. General der Flieger [Lt. Gen.] Wilhelm Speidel expressed this idea particularly aptly: "Nowhere has there been as much bluffing with statistics as in the Luftwaffe before and during the war. Not in the General Staff and not among the operations staffs of the field units. Least of all among the units themselves that were only too familiar with their own weakness and their constant efforts to increase the number of operational aircraft. But among the brass, above all in the case of the commander in chief of the Luftwaffe himself, who was only interested in the kind of strength figures he wanted to hear and he wanted to believe. . . . Certainly, Göring never clearly realized that at most 1,000 bombers were ready to take off at their airfields in the morning of 10 May 1940."[139]

Operational German Combat Aircraft as of 10 May 1940 (Western Front)

Type	Actual Strength (Total Number)	Operational
Bombers (He 111, Do 17, Ju 88)	1,563	1,090
Stuka [Dive-bombers] (Ju 87)	376	316
Ground-Attack Aircraft (Hs 123)	49	38
Fighters (Me 109)	1,279	923
Destroyers (Me 110)	311	222
Total	3,578	2,589

France. At the start of the campaign in the west, the French air force had 2,402 fighters, 1,160 bombers, and 1,464 reconnaissance aircraft, a total of 5,026 aircraft.[140] If we count only the fighters and bombers, that gives us a figure of 3,562 combat aircraft.[141]

These statistics reveal inconsistencies that were designated as "mysteries" not only by contemporaries but also by some historians.[142] The French air force had a total of 3,562 combat aircraft (2,402 fighters and 1,160 bombers) and thus had almost as many combat aircraft as did the Germans who had 3,578 (excluding the squadrons employed against Norway). On 10 May the Germans attacked with 2,589 combat aircraft, which, along the front lines, were opposed by only 879 operational French aircraft. To be sure, 465 combat aircraft were outside France (mostly in North Africa), but where were the remaining 1,528 fighters and 690 bombers? In 1942,that question was addressed to the responsible political leaders and generals in the parliamentary investigating committee in Riom. The British author Len Deighton commented on this as follows: "General Gamelin himself asked, 'Why, out of the 2,000 modern fighters on hand at the beginning of May 1940, were fewer than 500 used on the northeast front?' Perhaps the answer to that question is contained in the fact that the Commander in Chief was asking it. 'We have a right to be astonished,' added Gamelin. *We* have that right perhaps, but did Gamelin have it?"[143]

French Combat Aircraft Strength as of 10 May 1940

	Fighters	Bombers	Total
Total Number (Actual Strength)	2,402	1,160	3,562
North Africa/Colonies	237	228	465
French Rear Areas	1,176	511	1,687
Front	989	421	1,410
Operational at the Front	637	242	879

The situation seems even more mysterious in view of the testimony of Vuillemin, the commanding general of the French air force. He stated that, at the time of the armistice, he had more operational aircraft than at the start of the German offensive.[144] It must be kept in mind that the French air force lost 892 aircraft within six weeks.[145]

Pierre Cot and Guy La Chambre, who held the office of air force minister in succession after 1936, rejected that accusation and argued that the output figures of the aviation industry were extraordinarily high. Between March 1938 and June 1940, a total of 4,010 modern aircraft were delivered to the air force.[146] Here it is interesting to note the tremendous capacity increase after the beginning of the war. Between 1 September 1939 and 1 May 1940, the French air force received 1,732 aircraft[147] and another 1,131 new aircraft after the German offensive between 10 May and 12 June.[148] The great significance the French government assigned to a strong air force can also be seen by the fact that, in spite of the protests of the French aviation industry, it had purchased an additional 340 combat aircraft and 230 training aircraft in the United States in 1938–39. Of the American aircraft ordered after the start of the war, the French air force on 1 May already had 440, including 306 Curtiss fighters, and that number rose to 544 by June.[149] In this connection, Pierre Cot almost passionately countered the reproaches directed against his former ministry: "In the year 9 A.D., the Roman general Quintilius Varus stumbled into an ambush laid for him by Arminius and perished with his three legions in Teutoburg Forest. Then, historians tell us, Augustus is reported to have cried out: 'Varus! Varus! Give me my legions back!' By the same token, we could shout to the air force: 'What did you do with our aircraft?'"[150]

Those aircraft had not disappeared by any means. Most of them were at airfields in the country's interior or in depots; they just did not happen to be at the front. Shortly after the armistice, a control commission counted 4,268 aircraft in the unoccupied part of France. In addition, it became known that there were then 1,800 aircraft in North Africa.[151] But the charge of organizational failure that was leveled against the French air force general officer corps is off target. At the start of the campaign, the French air force potential was mobilized at a rather low level. That was not because the responsible generals did not know how to do the job any better but precisely because they wanted it that way. The French command assumed that the conflict with the German Reich would turn into a long, drawn-out strategic war of attrition—as in World War I. The air force that still had enough aircraft at the end would emerge victorious. This is why it appeared wrong to put everything on the table from the very beginning.

But that is precisely what the Luftwaffe did. It mobilized all reserves for the offensive to win air superiority immediately. This is why one cannot compare either the operational doctrine or the strength figures of the German and French air forces on 10 May. The few French aircraft employed at the front were merely intended to fight the first of many anticipated battles. But it was the first battle that brought the decision.

Great Britain, Belgium, the Netherlands. In estimating the strength of the Royal Air Force, we also come to the question as to which strength figure is the correct one: the limited number of aircraft that the Royal Air Force had ready at the time of the German offensive, or the number that it could have mobilized if, like the Luftwaffe, it had suddenly and immediately thrown its full potential onto the scales. The operational strength of the Royal Air Force along the French northeast front was about 500 aircraft (including 224 bombers and 160 fighters) as of 10 May 1940.[152] But these figures tell us little about the overall potential. Otherwise, how could one explain that the Royal Air Force lost 1,029 aircraft during the campaign in the west, considerably more than were at the front on 10 May?[153] For example, out of the 42 British fighter squadrons, only 14 were on the Continent in the beginning.

After the start of the German offensive, however, the British high command transferred additional squadrons to France. Numerous aircraft were also employed from airfields in England itself. The Luftwaffe noticed that fact especially over Dunkirk as it was suddenly attacked by modern Spitfire fighters. If, in addition to the squadrons already based in France, one also considers those that were held in readiness in England, then one comes up with a strength figure of at least 1,870 aircraft (including reconnaissance aircraft) as of 10 May.[154] But even this number cannot anywhere near describe the actual total strength of the Royal Air Force. The British aviation historian R. J. Overy explained that in addition to the 1,911 "first-line" aircraft ready in September 1939 there were 2,200 other aircraft (mostly older models) on standby.[155]

The strength figures for the Belgian and Dutch air forces are either given very inaccurately or completely ignored in most reports. The Luftwaffe command at that time showed considerably more interest in those statistics. During the first few hours of the campaign, it concentrated on neutralizing those aircraft in a surprise attack. Belgium had a total of 377 aircraft (including transport aircraft, liaison aircraft, etc.). Of that number, about 78 fighters and 40 bombers were operational on 10 May. The Dutch air force consisted of 124 frontline aircraft, of which 63 fighters and 9 bombers were actually employed at the start of the campaign.[156]

There are very few legends that seem so undying as the tall tale of the numerical superiority of German combat aircraft. The important thing here is to use the right yardstick.[157] Depending on which criteria one picks, one winds up with two highly differing versions of the force ratio.

Operational Combat Aircraft on the Western Front as of 10 May 1940

France	879
Great Britain	384
Belgium	118
the Netherlands	72

Allies	1,453 Bombers and Fighters
German Reich	2,589 Bombers/Dive-Bombers/Ground-Attack Aircraft/Fighters/ Destroyers

This numerical comparison creates a false image because it relates only to Allied combat aircraft that simply happened to be operational at the front when the German offensive was launched. Naturally, the degree of operational readiness was definitely higher in the case of the Luftwaffe. After all, the German generals knew the exact timing of the surprise attack and had ordered a maximum number of aircraft to be made ready for takeoff.

Another distortion of the comparative criteria resulted from the fact that a number of historians, in looking at the Allied side, considered only the few aircraft that belonged to the frontline units as of 10 May. In reality, in addition to the 1,410 combat aircraft at the front (including 879 operational), the French also had 1,176 fighters and 511 bombers in rear areas. This deployment was part of a precautionary measure so that not too many aircraft would be destroyed on the ground in case of a German surprise raid. By the same token, the Royal Air Force kept 540 fighters and 310 bombers on standby in Great Britain. They were moved to the Continent immediately after the German attack or entered the fight from their airfields on the island itself.[158] We get a completely new picture if we consider these additional units (even if we deduct miscellaneous British reserves):

Combat Aircraft Present (Actual Strength) at the Front and in Rear Areas on 10 May 1940

France	3,097
Great Britain	1,150
Belgium	140
the Netherlands	82
Allies	4,469 Bombers and Fighters
German Reich	3,578 Bombers/Dive-bombers/Ground-Attack Aircraft/Fighters/ Destroyers

These figures reflect the actual strength ratio. The Germans had been able to mobilize about three-quarters of their potential; for the French, it was a little more than one-quarter.[159] In other words, the Luftwaffe succeeded in turning the *absolute* superiority of the Western air forces into a *relative* German superiority at the moment of its surprise attack.

A comparison of production capacities shows how dramatically the relationship between the two air force potentials developed to the disadvantage of the Germans. In 1939 the British aviation industry had already surpassed the German aviation industry in terms of the monthly output rate. In 1940 British and French aircraft production was almost double that of the German output during the first five months up to the actual campaign in the west.[160] To this we must add shipments from the American armaments industry. At the end of 1939, the French had ordered a total of 4,700 aircraft,[161] whereas the British had placed orders for the delivery of 14,000 aircraft and 25,000 aircraft engines by August 1940.[162] It follows from all this that the Luftwaffe never at any time had any chance of catching up with the numerical lead of the Western powers.

Qualitative Comparison. Most authors start with the assumption that the pilots of the Allies almost throughout had to fight with inferior aircraft against the technically superior German aircraft. However, that idea must be considered after a more careful comparison (see chart pp. 50–53). After World War I, the Germans were allowed to have at least a small army and an even more modest navy; but they were completely forbidden to build up air forces. When Hitler ordered the Luftwaffe to be organized, it seemed that the technical backwardness could not possibly be overcome except in the long run. The outstanding achievements of German designers look all the more astonishing. At times, the Me 109 of professor Willy Messerschmitt was considered the world's best fighter aircraft. It proved to be definitely superior to the older Morane 406 and Potez 63 fighters of the French air force. But the difference in quality did not appear to be all too great when compared to the Bloch 152. The Dewoitine 520 and the Curtiss Hawk were entirely equal to the German aircraft. This also applied to the British Hurricane. In the Spitfire, the Royal Air Force even had an aircraft that in some ways was superior to the Me 109.

The newly introduced French bomber models had to be considered as the world's most advanced in 1940.[163] But the modern British bombers were also mostly superior to comparable German bombers—quite apart from the Ju 88. The Ju 87 dive-bomber, the Stuka, is a special case. As shown in the chart (p. 52), that aircraft actually wound up at the end of the performance scale in terms of speed, range, and bomb load. Of course, accuracy seemed rather respectable because the Stuka attacked from the dive and not horizontally. However, the actual effect of this legendary aircraft had more to do with morale than actual efficiency, as will be described later. Its greatest disadvantage was that it could be employed only in cases of German air superiority, otherwise this cumbersome aircraft would have fallen victim to enemy fighters all too easily. The enormous Stuka losses during the air battles over England later demonstrated that.

Another cliché involves the superiority of the German pilots. On average, those pilots were considerably more poorly trained than the Allied pilots. Hitler had ordered the Luftwaffe to be organized just a few years earlier, practically from scratch. The quality of pilot training was quite in keeping with the excessively hasty buildup of the Luftwaffe. During the last 31/2 months before the start of the war, 281 Luftwaffe personnel died in aircraft accidents while 287 were seriously injured.[164] Experienced pilots were

Die wichtigsten Flugzeugtypen im Vergleich

1) BOMBER	Motorleistung		Geschwindigkeit km/h	Reichweite km	Bombenlast kg
Junkers Ju 88 A 1	2 x 950 PS	DEUTSCHES REICH	450	2900	2900
Heinkel He 111 H 1/2	2 x 1200 PS	DEUTSCHES REICH	400	2360	2000
Dornier Do 17 Z 1	2 x 1050 PS	DEUTSCHES REICH	410	1115	1000
Junkers Ju 87 B 2 (Stuka)	1 x 1200 PS	DEUTSCHES REICH	360	635	500
Armstrong Whitworth "Whitley" III	2 x 920 PS	GROSSBRITANNIEN	335	2000	3175
Vickers "Wellington" I	2 x 1145 PS	GROSSBRITANNIEN	415	4100	2100

Comparison of the Most Important Aircraft Types: Bombers and Fighters

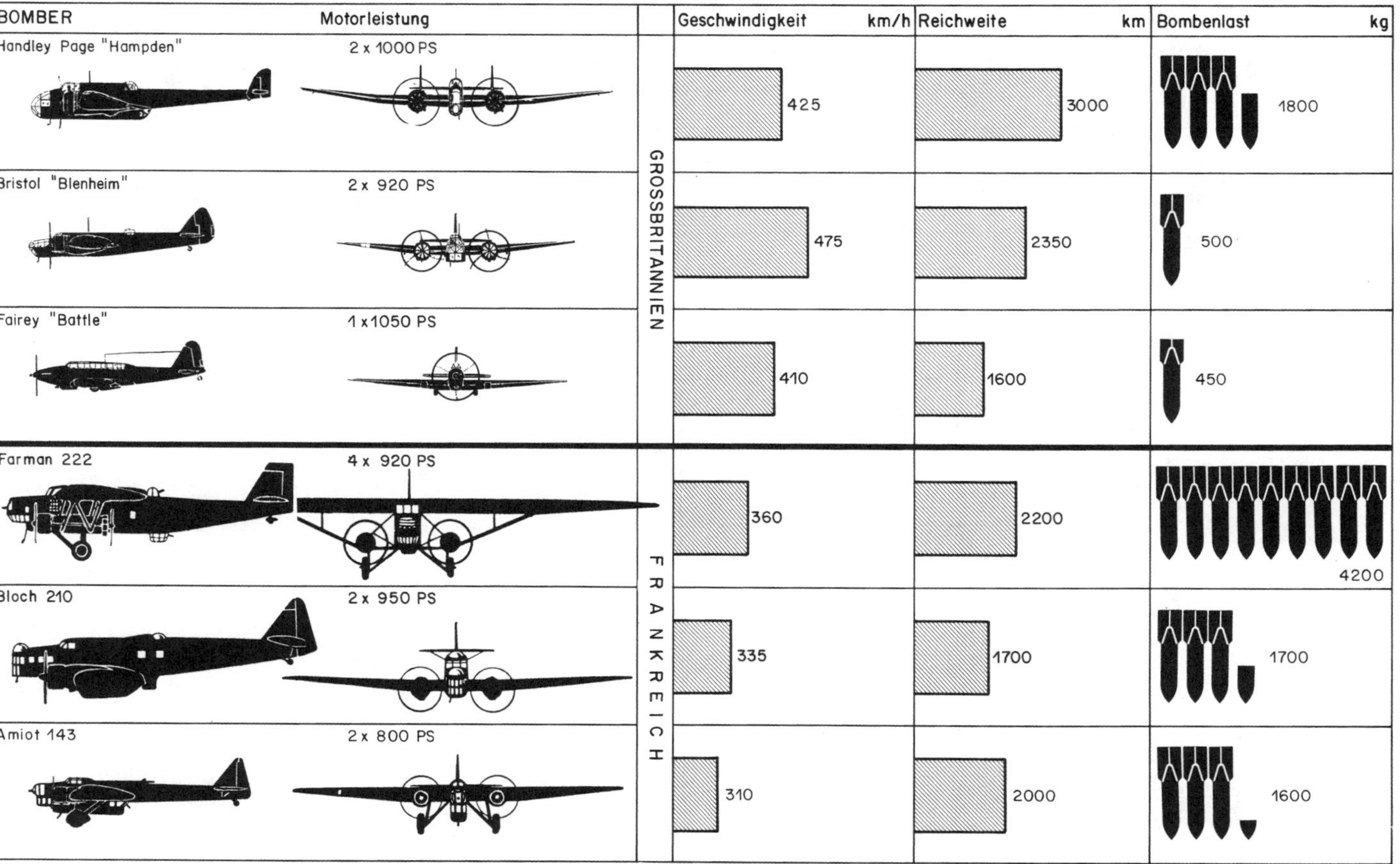

BOMBER	Motorleistung		Geschwindigkeit km/h	Reichweite km	Bombenlast kg
Handley Page "Hampden"	2 x 1000 PS	GROSSBRITANNIEN	425	3000	1800
Bristol "Blenheim"	2 x 920 PS	GROSSBRITANNIEN	475	2350	500
Fairey "Battle"	1 x 1050 PS	GROSSBRITANNIEN	410	1600	450
Farman 222	4 x 920 PS	FRANKREICH	360	2200	4200
Bloch 210	2 x 950 PS	FRANKREICH	335	1700	1700
Amiot 143	2 x 800 PS	FRANKREICH	310	2000	1600

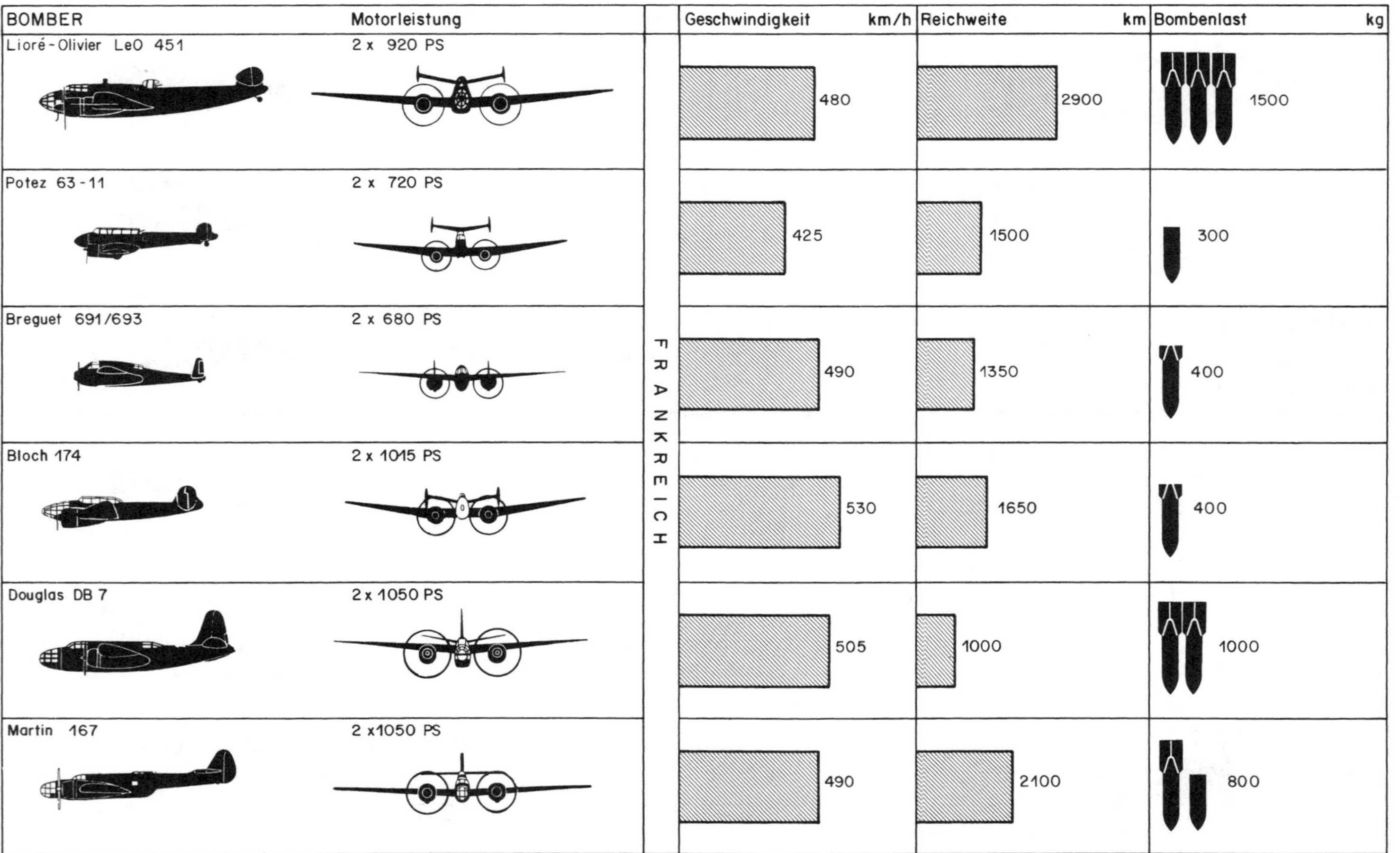

BOMBER	Motorleistung		Geschwindigkeit km/h	Reichweite km	Bombenlast kg
Lioré-Olivier LeO 451	2 x 920 PS	FRANKREICH	480	2900	1500
Potez 63-11	2 x 720 PS		425	1500	300
Breguet 691/693	2 x 680 PS		490	1350	400
Bloch 174	2 x 1015 PS		530	1650	400
Douglas DB 7	2 x 1050 PS		505	1000	1000
Martin 167	2 x1050 PS		490	2100	800

2) JÄGER

Flugzeug	Motorleistung	Land	Geschwindigkeit km/h	R.weite km	Bewaffnung	mm
Messerschmitt Bf 109 E	1 x 1100 PS	DEUTSCHES REICH	555	580	2 x MG 7,9	2 x MK 20,0
Messerschmitt Bf 110 C	2 x 1100 PS	DEUTSCHES REICH	510	910	4 x MG 7,9	2 x MK 20,0
Supermarine "Spitfire" I	1 x 1175 PS	GROSSBRITANNIEN	590	800		8 x MG 7,69
Hawker "Hurricane" II	1 x 1260 PS	GROSSBRITANNIEN	550	770		8 x MG 7,69
Dewoitine D 520	1 x 920 PS	FRANKREICH	530	990	2 x MG 7,5	1 x MK 20,0
Bloch 152	1 x 1060 PS	FRANKREICH	515	640	2 x MG 7,5	2 x MK 20,0
Curtiss "Hawk" 75	1 x 1050 PS	FRANKREICH	500	1320	2 x MG 7,61	2 x sMG 12,69
Morane-Saulnier MS 406	2 x 860 PS	FRANKREICH	490	800	2 x MG 7,5	1 x MK 20,0
Potez 630	2 x 670 PS	FRANKREICH	445	1220	6 x MG 7,5	2 x MK 20,0

in short supply and therefore had to be employed almost without interruption.

The aura of German air superiority appears questionable above all if one analyzes the loss figures during the campaign in the west. For example, the French air force lost 892 aircraft, but only 306 were lost in air combat. On the other hand, French fighters shot down 733 German aircraft.[165] The Royal Air Force lost 1,029 aircraft.[166] However, the Luftwaffe that allegedly had sovereign command of the airspace lost 1,559 aircraft during the campaign (including 323 damaged).[167]

Overview

According to a military rule of thumb, the attacker should be numerically superior to the defender at a ratio of 3:1. That ratio goes up if the defender can fight from well-developed fortifications, such as the Maginot Line. Paradoxically, in May 1940, the defenders were numerically superior to the attacker in almost all areas. This means that other rules must also have applied during the campaign.

But the Wehrmacht proved to be inferior also in qualitative terms with regard to most of the weapon systems. That appears rather astonishing at first sight because the German Reich at that time played a leading economic-technological role in the world. Between 1901 and 1933, thirty-one Nobel prizes were awarded to Germany for natural sciences whereas only six went to the United States of America. But, of all things, it was in the field of military technology that the Germans were not in the lead—and that was due to the restrictive clauses of the Versailles Treaty. So we can explain that, for example, German Panzer development initially lagged about one generation behind French and British armor development. During the second half of the war, German scientists managed to come up with some trailblazing developments in spite of the rather painful lack of strategic materials. They designed the Me 262, the first operational jet fighter; they built the V-1, the first cruise missile; and, with their V-2 rocket, they opened the gates to the space age. To that extent, it has to be an irony of history that during the war's early phase, when the Wehrmacht recorded the greatest military successes, it was lagging behind in weapons technology.

After the disaster at Sedan, the French supreme commander Gamelin gave Winston Churchill three reasons for his army's defeat: "Inferiority of numbers, inferiority of equipment, inferiority of method."[168] But today we know that only the third reason was accurate. It had to do with the tactics that were used in employing the troops.

Was the German General Officer Corps for or against the Campaign in the West?

Although the Germans started the war, they were not enthusiastic, neither the civilians, nor the soldiers, least of all the generals. Never has a general staff been so little to blame for a war as the German general staff for the

> *Second World War, and never has it approached its task with so much distaste; never have the politicians been so firmly in the saddle with the army reduced to the role of the horse. The dictatorship had made the war; it was its war.*[169]
>
> Golo Mann

Hitler had elevated Germany to a leading military power once again, and many different interests linked the general officer corps to Hitler. Nevertheless, numerous generals considered the dictator to be a people's tribune who had risen from the gutter and whose proletarian nature repelled them as much as his undisguised brutality. Hitler, the revolutionary, also expressed his profound contempt for the military elite of the German Reich whose ideas he mocked as romantic and reactionary. So he said that "he simply could not understand the German soldiers who were afraid of a passage at arms. Frederick the Great would spin in his grave if he saw today's generals."[170] With trenchant irony, he castigated the childish attitudes of the generals who headed the army and argued that one cannot fight a war with "Salvation Army methods."[171] The most frequent target of his scorn was the commander in chief of the army, von Brauchitsch: "He [Hitler] needs optimists and not pessimists. He is not ill-disposed toward the general, but he has no use for political scaredy-cats. The best thing would be to smoke the entire General Staff out from its building on Bendlerstraße and put young people in. That generals know nothing about politics is something that Frederick the Great already said, but that they are afraid of fighting a war, that is a realization that was reserved for him."[172]

During his command conference in the Reich Chancellery on 23 November 1939, Hitler revealed the obsession with which he was working toward an attack against the Western powers. Addressing the numerous generals and admirals who had lined up in formation, he said: "Some people might reproach me: Struggle and more struggle. I believe that struggle is the fate of all beings. Nobody can avoid struggle if he does not want to be vanquished. . . . My decision is unalterable. I will attack France and England at the best and soonest moment. Violating the neutrality of Belgium and Holland means nothing. Nobody will ask any questions after we have been victorious."[173] But, in this address, Hitler threatened not only his foreign policy foes; he also informed his own generals quite unmistakably: "I will stop at nothing and I will annihilate anybody who is against me."[174]

According to general staff–style calculations, Hitler's lonely decision to attack the Western powers, especially immediately after the Polish campaign, must be considered to be irrational. He disclosed this plan for the first time to Schmundt, his chief military aide, on 8 September.[175] He informed the commanders in chief of the three Wehrmacht components as to his intentions in the Reich Chancellery on 27 September, the day Warsaw capitulated.[176] They were horrified by Hitler's plan. Rarely had the attitude of the German general officer corps been so unanimous as in its rejection of the war in the west. Von Brauchitsch considered that campaign to be "insanity"[177];

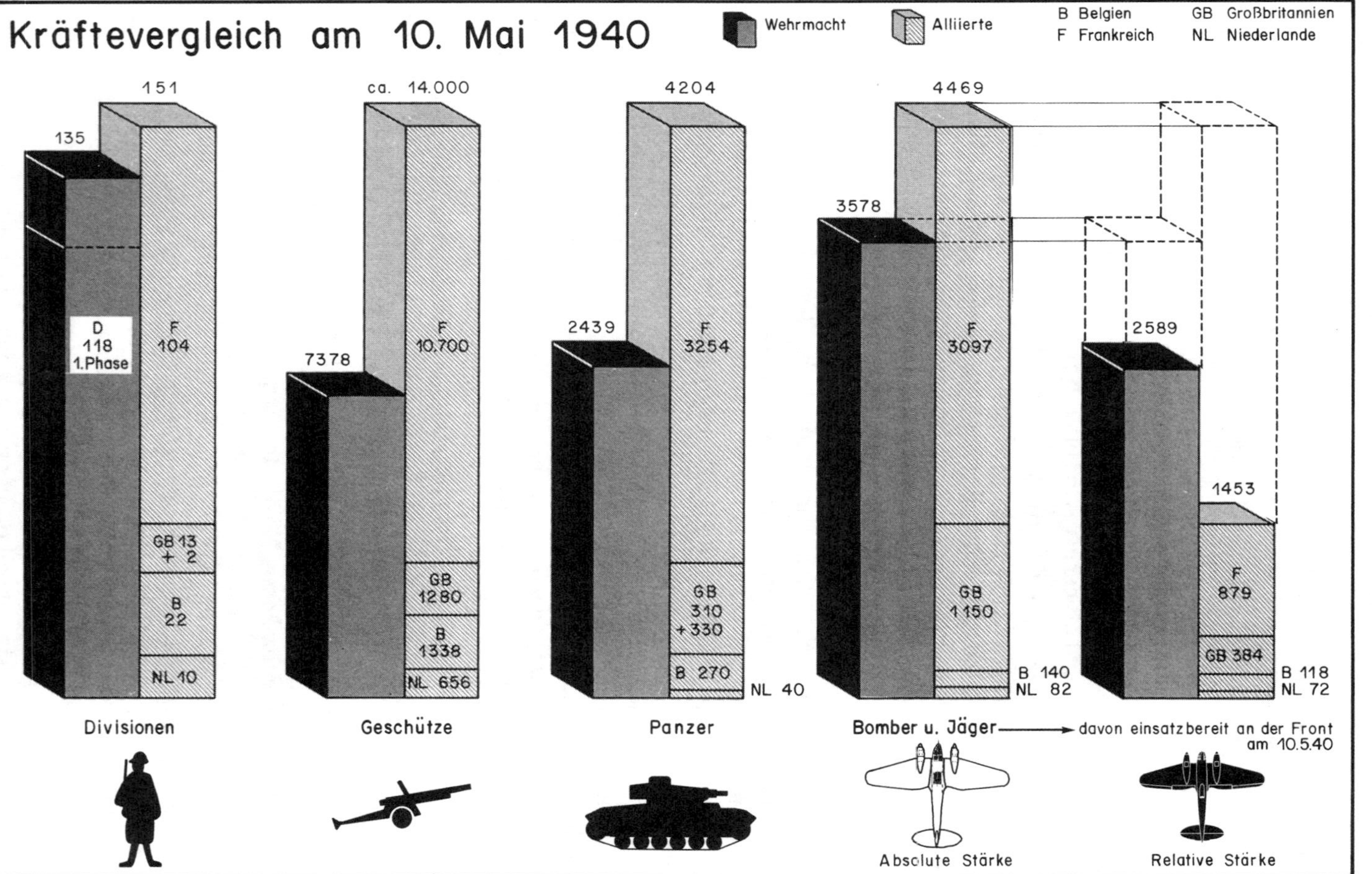

Comparison of Forces, 10 May 1940

von Leeb, commander in chief of Army Group C, talked in terms of an "insane attack."[178] There was resistance also among the echelon of the field army commanders. Generaloberst [Walter] von Reicheneau, who was notorious as a "Nazi general," was "as if thunder-struck" and termed the plan to be "just about criminal."[179]

Von Reicheneau not only dared contradict Hitler openly but even saw to it that the Dutch were warned of Hitler's planned aggression. The Dutch were urged to activate their defenses, combined with the previously prepared flooding, to show that the inevitable element of surprise had been lost. To do that, on 6 November Reicheneau met with [Dr. Carl] Goerdeler, the leader of the civic resistance, who, in turn, routed his message via a neutral foreign country.[180] Just how great the outrage was is indicated by the fact that, in private conversation, Hitler was accused of being "bloodthirsty."[181] This offensive plan was considered to be so crazy that even the otherwise very obedient Keitel, after a dispute with Hitler, offered his resignation.[182] But it was not only the generals who rejected an offensive in the west; Göring was also against it, especially at that early point in time.

Initially, an attempt was made to get Hitler to drop his insane idea through objective arguments that were spelled out in a series of memorandums. Thomas considered such a plan to be hopeless in terms of a wartime economy whereas the commanders in chief of the various army groups mostly cited the lessons learned during World War I and warned that the offensive might become bogged down early on. A study that von Stülpnagel had drafted by direction of the commander in chief of the army arrived at the conclusion that an offensive would not be possible before the spring of 1942.[183] But Hitler's mind was closed to all arguments, and he was as if possessed by the thought of employing only martial force. He sensed only defeatism behind all of these attempts to dissuade him from his plan for an offensive and stigmatized above all the Spirit of Zossen where the army high command was located.

It was von Brauchitsch who got the most vehement rejection. On 5 November in the Reich Chancellery, the commander in chief of the army tried to explain that his field armies were not militarily ready for an offensive in the west. The infantry was still inadequately trained, he argued, and therefore did not attack with sufficient impetus during the Polish campaign. Also, there had been breaches of discipline, as at the end of World War I. Hitler erupted in rage and accused Brauchitsch, in his position as commander in chief, of daring to "condemn his own Army and run it down."[184] He demanded that any court-martial files be immediately submitted to him as evidence. Then he left the room, "slamming the door hard and loud" and left the generals standing there.[185] Von Brauchitsch was not able to submit sufficient credible evidence and that made the crisis even worse. In that situation, Hitler seriously considered replacing him. But there was no alternative in terms of personnel because the higher-ranking generals made common front against the campaign. Brauchitsch offered to resign on 23 November, but the dictator had to refuse to accept his resignation.

The commander in chief of the army would not have been the right man to rebel against Hitler anyway. He admitted that he simply could not cope with Hitler's demoniacal will and that on occasion he lost his power of speech in Hitler's presence.[186] And so, Halder, the army chief of staff, became the central figure of the resistance during that phase. His plans extended all the way to the coup d'etat and to Hitler's assassination. He was guided in his approach not only by the military realization that it would hardly be possible to win a campaign against the Western powers but also by moral-religious grounds. But Halder's attempt, together with the commanders in chief of the three army groups, failed to assemble an active alliance against Hitler. To be sure, [Karl Rudolf Gerd von] Rundstedt and [Fedor von] Bock saw the situation in similar terms, but they simply could not bring themselves to engage in any active resistance. Only von Leeb would have been prepared to go all the way. Quite on his own, he tried to persuade the commanders of the other two army groups to resign together to outflank Hitler, but he was not successful.[187]

Von Stülpnagel, the deputy chief of staff for operations on the army general staff, played a particularly dynamic role. He was particularly indispensable to his boss, Halder, since he established contact with other resistance groups: with the group of conspirators in the Abwehr [Wehrmacht Counterintelligence Department] around Vizeadmiral [Wilhelm] Canaris; with the opposition group in the Foreign Office under State Secretary [Ernst] von Weizsäcker; with conspiratorial civilian circles; and, above all, around Generaloberst z.V. (zur Verfügung, Special Assignment) Ludwig von Beck and a number of frontline generals, such as [Erwin von] Witzleben and [Erich] Hoepner, who were critical of the regime.[188]

Halder described the conflict of conscience, in which he was enmeshed at the time, as a "terrible and agonizing experience."[189] He did not want to take the risk of launching a coup d'etat without adequate backup support from the commanders in chief of the army groups. In that situation, an attempt on Hitler's life seemed to be the only solution. There are several indications that he was seriously weighing such a possibility. For example, he ordered Oberstleutnant [Helmuth] Groscurth to establish contact with Hauptmann [Johannes] Marguerre, the counterintelligence explosives expert who was under Canaris.[190] The situation seemed so desperate that he even toyed with the idea of shooting Hitler himself. Groscurth made the following entry in his diary: "Amid tears, H[alder] said that he had for weeks had a pistol in his pocket every time he went to Emil [cover name for Hitler] in order possibly to gun him down."[191]

But in the end, Halder lost his nerve. On 5 November Hitler had his famous and previously mentioned fit of rage in the Reich Chancellery, which was directed against von Brauchitsch. When the latter, "pale as a ghost" and completely shaken, left the room, Halder was waiting for him. On the return trip, Brauchitsch mentioned that Hitler, in his fury, had raged against the Spirit of Zossen, which he would exterminate. Halder, who was unsure to begin with, misunderstood that comment to the effect that his coup d'etat plans, which he had hatched in Zossen, had been betrayed to Hitler. He panicked and ordered von Stülpnagel to destroy all documents. That eliminated the central figure of the opposition against Hitler, and the military resistance had in effect failed during that phase.

There has been much criticism of hesitant Halder who, like Hamlet in a general's uniform, simply could not or would not decide to take action. He himself commented as follows after the war: "The German Army did not grow up in the Balkans where regicide keeps recurring in history. We are not professional revolutionaries. . . . I would like to put the following question to my critics who are still very numerous today: What should I have done, that is to say, what should I have prevented? Starting a hopeless *coup d'etat,* whose time had not yet come, or becoming an assassin—in my capacity as German officer, as top representative of the General Staff? . . . I must say that quite honestly, I was not fit for that, I did not learn that kind of thing."[192]

The general now reversed course and became excessively involved in planning the preparations for the offensive. If this campaign could not be somehow prevented, then at least it should end in victory. At that time Halder could not yet guess that he would one day also be dragged through prisons and concentration camps as a victim of the Nazi regime and that he would escape his ordered execution only by accident.[193]

The behavior of the German general officer corps prior to the campaign in the west is not necessarily an example of resolute resistance. On the other hand, this episode is perfectly suitable for invalidating the old prejudice about the aggression-hungry and revenge-mongering German military establishment. It is certainly not true that the German general staff, as if possessed, had worked toward a war against the Western powers in order to at last have an opportunity to translate into action the secretive blitzkrieg concept—constructed after the fact by historians—with the goal of achieving world rule.

3

The Struggle over the Sickle Cut Plan

When France lay prostrate under the German heel, the men of the victorious Army would have been astonished had they known that their highest military chiefs had not believed such a victory to be possible—and that the victory had been gained by a plan which had been forced on a doubting General Staff as the result of a backstairs approach. . . . Yet those were the facts hidden behind the triumphant façade.[1]

Liddell Hart

An analogy to the blitzkrieg legend is the Sickle Cut myth. This operation had been planned completely differently from the way it actually took place. Generalleutnant [Erich] von Manstein was the inventor but also the first victim of the Sickle Cut plan because he was reassigned from his post due to this allegedly extraordinary idea. In the end, the plan was accepted, although the majority of the general officer corps rejected it. Of course, the result was a dilution of the original idea that would have boiled down to a "blitzkrieg in slow motion." Due to a series of accidents and also to the independent actions of individual generals, the operation took an entirely different course and in the end achieved precisely the success that Manstein had envisioned. The term "sickle cut" was invented only later, and not even in Germany. It comes from the descriptive language of Winston Churchill, who spoke of a "sickle cut" or, originally, of an "armored scythe stroke."[2]

The First Three Deployment Directives

At the start of World War I, all the German general staff had to do was to fetch the Schlieffen plan from the file cabinet. That plan had been designed in 1905 and revised over and over again since then. But, in September 1939, there was no operations plan for action against the Western powers. The moment the Polish campaign was over the dictator hastily ordered that a plan for an offensive be drafted. As early as 27 September, he told the commanding generals of the three Wehrmacht components that the German attack units were to advance with their main effort on the right wing via Belgium, pushing toward the Channel coast.[3] He spelled out his intention in a memorandum drafted on 9 October.[4] On that same day, he issued the following orders in his Directive No. 6 for the Conduct of the War:

> (a) An offensive will be planned on the northern flank of the Western Front, through Luxembourg, Belgium, and Holland. This offensive must be launched at the earliest possible moment and in greatest possible strength.
>
> (b) The purpose of this offensive will be to defeat as much as possible of the French Army and of the forces of the allies fighting on their side, and at the same time to win as much territory as possible in Holland, Belgium, and Northern France to serve as a base for the successful prosecution of the air and sea war against England and as a wide protective area for the economically vital Ruhr.[5]

Hitler's strategy can be interpreted in many ways, but there is no trace at all of any idea of a blitzkrieg. Instead of immediately putting all his money on one card—a decisive battle to finish the war swiftly, Hitler intended only to gain partial objectives: as many as possible of the enemy formations were to be defeated and, by the same token, as much territory as possible was to be conquered. But that was to be used only as a base for future warfare. Obviously, Feldherr (warlord) Hitler, still caught up in the thinking of World War I, was mostly concerned with gaining ports and airfields as a prerequisite for the anticipated war of attrition, especially against Great Britain.

Halder issued the first deployment directive on 19 October. The *Schwerpunkt* (point of main effort) was to be on Army Group B's right wing. With its three field armies plus the bulk of the Panzer units, that army group was to thrust on both sides of Brussels toward Bruges to seize the Belgian section of the Channel coast.[6] But the hastily conceived draft was only "the expression of a forced improvisation devoid of ideas."[7] When this plan was presented to Hitler, Keitel recalled that he commented: "That is just the old Schlieffen Plan, with the strong right flank along the Atlantic coast; you won't get away with an operation like that twice running."[8]

That reproach was bound to backfire on him because, after all, Halder had stuck closely to Hitler's requirements. Besides, this was a rehash of the Schlieffen plan only upon very superficial examination. In the view of the chief of the German general staff at that time, the formation of the main effort on the right wing was only supposed to represent the operational-level means for achieving the strategic goal of a decisive battle. While the thrust ordered by Hitler was aimed only at the Channel coast, Schlieffen's pivoting maneuver to the southeast was to be continued by swinging past Paris and heading for the Swiss border. Schlieffen had wanted to envelop all enemy armies stationed in northeastern France and decide the war swiftly and suddenly. In 1939, however, his successors planned precisely that which he had rejected most passionately, an *ordinary* victory on the operational level without any strategic decision.

In looking at the history of the German general staff, it is clear that the first deployment directive displays an utter lack of imagination. But the decisive question was this: Did Brauchitsch and Halder really want to present a workable operations plan or does this first deployment directive rather document an active resistance? The activities among the top leadership of the army high command at that time would seem to point to the second possibility. The operations draft that was submitted was only intended to show Hitler the senselessness of an offensive in the west. At that time, Halder, especially, was more heavily involved in opposition plans to prevent the campaign to begin with than in operations plans to put it over. In that case, he would be able to defeat Hitler with his own weapons, and he could always make reference to Hitler's rather uninspiring outline sketch.

The army high command's second deployment directive, dated 29 October, did not introduce any essentially new ideas either.[9] Now an additional main thrust was planned with Panzer units passing south of Liège heading to the west. At any rate, a shift of one point of main effort farther to the south indicated rather clearly a trend that was to be continued in the following operations drafts. On the other hand, the idea of trying two Schwerpunkts at the same time did not amount to much either. The first operations draft at least had one definite Schwerpunkt.

On 11 November Hitler caused even greater confusion when he ordered the creation of an additional main thrust farther to the south. An army corps consisting of armored and motorized units thrusting toward Sedan via Arlon was to spearhead it.[10] But that meant three points of main effort simultaneously; in other words, the Schwerpunkt was everywhere and nowhere. The constant postponements of the attack date that cannot be explained by the weather alone also pointed out just how unsure Hitler had become.[11]

Then an episode occurred in January that cast doubt on all the past planning. This was a typical case of friction, the way von Clausewitz had described it, one of those little grains of sand that can play havoc with the gears of a gigantic military machine. Major [Hellmuth] Reinberger, a general staff officer in the airborne forces, was to travel on official business from Münster to Cologne on 10 January. In the officers club the evening before, he met Reserve Major [Erich] Hoenmanns, a pilot who had been recalled to duty, who persuaded him to come along in his plane. In-flight visibility suddenly deteriorated. In addition, the Rhine was frozen over and could hardly be distinguished from the adjoining riverbanks. Hoenmanns realized that they had drifted off course and wanted to turn back. At that moment, the engine quit for some inexplicable reason and the aircraft made a crash landing, although nobody was injured. A farmer, who was not far from where they had crashed, told them that they were near Mechelen on Belgian territory. Reinberger was very upset to hear that because in his attaché case he carried extracts from the strictly secret deployment plan as well as operations orders for airborne missions. However, he managed to burn only some of the papers before Belgian gendarmes showed up and arrested both officers.[12]

The news about this embarrassing incident triggered a crisis mood in the Wehrmacht leadership. Furious, Hitler ordered two high-ranking Luftwaffe generals to be relieved. In reality, the Belgians did not get much, but the German operations staffs had to assume that the worst had happened. Since then, many history books mistakenly reported that this event caused an abrupt and basic change in the German operations plan, which presumably had now been revealed to the enemy. Paradoxically, however, the Mechelen Incident did not in the end lead to the exposure of the German operational intentions but rather those of the Allies—as will be explained later.

The third deployment directive of 30 January 1940 did not reveal any new ideas either. The three points of main effort that had been ordered on 11 November 1939 were still in the directive.[13] As the only essential change, the operation was now to be placed on a new basis of "secrecy and surprise." Here the important thing was to shorten the time for the assembly of the attack formations from five days down to twenty-four hours. Most Panzer divisions were moved to the left bank of the Rhine so that they could "hit the ground running."[14]

The period of bad weather that now followed provided an opportunity to once again thoroughly check out the operations plan that seemed to have wound up on a dead-end street. All past proposed solutions could only lead to tactical and, at best, operational-level partial successes. Hitler castigated the planning effort of the army high command as the "thinking of a cadet officer."[15] Above all, he missed a spark, the kind of idea that would have introduced the element of surprise. He did not conceal his disdain, but he said that his generals had indeed read their Clausewitz but not enough Karl May [the author of a series of exciting German-language tales about the American Wild West].[16] In the meantime, however, an outsider—who did not at all belong to the general staff of the army high command, which was responsible for operational planning—developed an idea as to how to make possible that which seemed impossible.

Manstein and the Development of the Sickle Cut Plan

The objective of achieving a final decision on the ground . . . can be attained only if the will to force such a decision from the very beginning dominates the direction of operations.[17]

Memo of Army Group A, 12 January 1940

Manstein's Alternate Plan and the Fourth Deployment Directive

On 21 October von Manstein, the chief of the general staff of Army Group A, received the first deployment directive from the army high command. Right away he developed an alternate plan that already contained the basic idea for what later was called the Sickle Cut plan. In his estimate, there were two serious weak points in the deployment directive:

1. An offensive with a reinforced right wing would lead to a frontal clash with the main forces of the enemy; Schwerpunkt would clash with Schwerpunkt. The

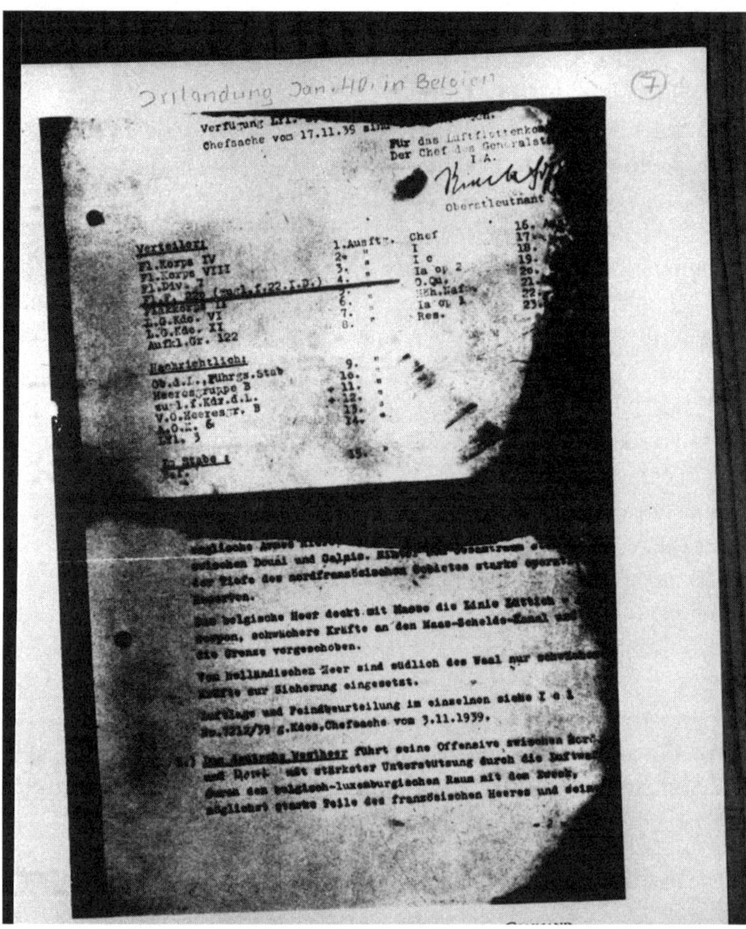

[illegible]landung Jan. 40. in Belgien (7)

Verfügung Lfl. [illegible]
Chefsache vom 17.11.39 [illegible]

Für das Luftflottenko[illegible]
Der Chef des Generalst[illegible]
I.A.
[illegible]
Oberstleutnant

Verteiler:
Fl.Korps IV — 1.Ausftg.
Fl.Korps VIII — 2. "
Fl.Div. 7 — 3. "
[illegible] (zugl.f.22.I.D.) — 4. "
[illegible] — 5. "
[illegible] — 6. "
L.G.Kdo. VI — 7. "
L.G.Kdo. XI — 8.
Aufkl.Gr. 122

Nachrichtlich:
Ob.d.L., Führgs.Stab — 9. "
Heeresgruppe B — 10. "
[illegible].d.L. — 11. "
V.O.Heeresgr. B — 12. "
A.O.K. 6 — 13. "
Lfl. 3 — 14. "

Im Stabe:
[illegible] — 15.

Chef — 16.
I — 17.
I c — 18.
Ia op 2 — 19.
O.Qu. — 20.
[illegible] — 21.
Ia op 1 — 22.
Res. — 23.

englische Armee [illegible]
zwischen Douai und Calais. [illegible]
der Tiefe des nordfranzösischen Gebietes starke operat[illegible]
Reserven.

Das belgische Heer deckt mit Masse die Linie Lüttich [illegible]
Antwerpen, schwächere Kräfte an den Maas-Schelde-Kanal und [illegible]
die Grenze vorgeschoben.

Vom holländischen Heer sind südlich des Waal nur schwäche[illegible]
Kräfte zur Sicherung eingesetzt.

Kräftelage und Feindbeurteilung im einzelnen siehe I c 1
Nr.[illegible]/39 g.Kdos.Chefsache vom 3.11.1939.

3.) Das deutsche Westheer führt seine Offensive zwischen Nor[illegible]
und Mosel mit stärkster Unterstützung durch die Luftwa[illegible]
durch den belgisch-luxemburgischen Raum mit dem Zweck,
möglichst starke Teile des französischen Heeres und sein[illegible]

- 2 -

Half-burned secret documents from the German aircraft that made an emergency landing near Mechelen on 10 January 1940. *Bundesarchiv-Militärarchiv Freidburg i.Br. [Federal Military Archives] (ZA 3/55)*

result of this struggle that was to be fought on the tactical echelon at best could lead to a partial operational-level success. But the important thing was not to force the enemy frontally behind the Somme River but rather to cut him off in his rear along the Somme and to encircle him. That was the only way one could achieve a decisive victory on a strategic level.

2. It was precisely the successive course of an offensive on the right wing that would be bound to invite the enemy to mount a counterblow. The farther Army Group B advanced along the Channel coast, the more easily the French army would be able to thrust into the ever longer exposed flank from the south.

Manstein's alternate plan seemed so astonishingly simple because both problems could be solved simultaneously with a single step. He called for the point of main effort to be shifted from Army Group B in the north to Army Group A in the center. Strong Panzer units were to attack where they would be least expected, through the presumably impassable Ardennes woods. If it were possible to cross the Meuse River at Sedan by way of a surprise attack, then the way would have been cleared to the solution of both problems in operational terms:

1. After the successful breakthrough at Sedan, fast Panzer formations were to push into the rear area of the Allied front all the way to the mouth of the Somme. In that way, the enemy's entire northern wing would be trapped along the Channel coast in one gigantic pocket.
2. The breakthrough at Sedan would at the same time provide the operational point of departure for solving the problem of providing flank protection in an offensive manner. One field army was to thrust southward into the anticipated deployment area of the enemy counterattack before the latter could get going.

It is interesting to note that later on the Panzers of Guderian quite accurately drove along the main attack axis projected by von Manstein. But that was not done by accident; the accident was that both men were stationed in the same city, Koblenz, during the preparatory phase of the war in the west. The headquarters of Army Group A, where Manstein developed the famous Sickle Cut idea, was billeted in the Kurfürstliches Schloss [prince elector's castle] on the bank of the Rhine. The headquarters of XIX Corps, later called Panzer Corps Guderian, was also in Koblenz. On top of that, the two generals were billeted in hotels that were next to each other. And so, strategist Manstein was able to conduct intensive talks about the feasibility of this bold operations draft with Panzer expert Guderian, one of the few generals who immediately understood his ideas.

Guderian was also predestined for this because of his knowledge of the terrain. He had participated in the advance through the Ardennes in 1914. In January and February 1918, he attended and graduated from a four-week general staff training course in Sedan, which the Germans occupied at that time. Manstein reports that Guderian immediately showed "unbounded enthusiasm for our plan."[18] To his "great relief," Guderian confirmed that the idea of punching through the Ardennes with Panzer divisions was not utopian. Of course, Guderian demanded that he be allowed to employ a sufficient number of Panzer and motorized divisions, "if possible all of them."[19]

With the approval of von Rundstedt, the commander in chief of Army Group A, Manstein drafted a total of seven memorandums from October 1939 through January 1940 (they were dated 31 October; 6, 21, and 30 November; 6 and 18 December; and 12 January).[20] The army high command tried to dismiss Manstein's arguments with statements that simply did not hold water. Halder made fun of this plan as an egocentric attempt to give Army Group A more importance. Von Brauchitsch praised this highly imaginative idea, although he immediately added that there were no longer any additional forces available. Above all, headquarters refused to pass the proposal on to the Wehrmacht high command for examination.

In the end, von Manstein became the first victim of the Manstein plan. Halder managed to neutralize this "bothersome eager beaver" by means of a personnel chess move. He convinced von Rundstedt that Manstein must not be skipped during the next round of promotions: Generalleutnant [Hans] Reinhardt, who was junior in terms of seniority, was soon to be appointed commanding general of a Panzer corps, and in Army Group A. Halder also hinted that Manstein might get an army corps. When the latter learned of his good luck on 27 January, he was not exactly happy. He immediately assumed that one of Halder's intrigues was behind that; he figured that Halder simply wanted to "kick him upstairs." He became the commanding general of a "phantom corps" because the XXXVIII Army Corps, which he was to take over, had yet to be organized and for the time being existed only on paper. Above all, he was once again back in Stettin, far from the western front.

Just how much Manstein must have felt sidelined is indicated by an episode reported by Generalmajor [Friedrich-Wilhelm] von Mellenthin in his memoirs. At that time, with the rank of major, he was a general staff officer of one of the divisions of the corps that was just being organized:

> A tragic-comic event is worth mentioning here. On the train trip to the East, I ran into Generalleutnant von Manstein, the Chief of Staff of Army Group A on the Western Front, at a railroad station in Berlin. In his usual brash style, he asked me: "Mellenthin, what are you doing now in Warthegau? After all, things are going to pop soon in the West." . . . To my astonishment, the commanding general, who inspected our divisions a few weeks later, was Generalleutnant von Manstein. . . . Standing alone with Manstein after the inspection, which came out just fine, I could not help but say to him: "General, things never turn out the way you figure!"[21]

Shortly before taking over his new command, Manstein was allowed to experience a moment of satisfaction. During a "war game" in Koblenz on 7 February, he found that Halder gradually moved closer to his views. But the actual decision was worked out at that time behind the scenes. Two close collaborators of Manstein, Oberst i.G. [Günther] Blumentritt and Major i.G. [Henning] von Tresckow, did not at all like the way in which their superior was to be sidelined. At the end of January, Schmundt, Hitler's chief military aide, paid an information-gathering visit to Army Group A. Blumentritt and von Tresckow used that opportunity to brief him on this alternate plan that Halder had until then prevented from being passed on to the Wehrmacht high command. One other thing that may have played a role here was that Tresckow and

Schmundt had known each other very well since both served in the 9th Infantry Regiment in Potsdam. Hitler's army aide at that time, Major [Gerhard] Engel, made the following entry in his diary on 4 February: "Schmundt was in Koblenz and . . . was very much impressed by a longer conference with von Manstein. The latter expressed strong objections to the operations plan proposed by OKH [army high command]. Schmundt was very excited and told me that, in talking to M[anstein], he encountered the same ideas regarding the main point of effort as the Führer kept expressing, but in a much more precise manner."[22]

Without any knowledge of von Manstein's thinking, Hitler had also gotten the idea of attempting the decisive breakthrough at Sedan. Although the army high command constantly tried to get him to forget about his pet idea, he nevertheless came back to it again and again. Now the important thing was to arrange a meeting, "via the backstairs," so to speak, without the especially distrustful Halder having any suspicions. In the end, Schmundt got the rather conspiratorial bright idea of scheduling a "working breakfast" in the Reich Chancellery in Berlin on 17 February with the five newly appointed corps commanders and Rommel, the new commanding general of the 7th Panzer Division, who had been ordered to attend.

When the conference was over, Hitler asked von Manstein to follow him to his office. Only Jodl and Schmundt participated in this conference, along with the two main characters. Normally, Hitler had the rather unpleasant habit of interrupting the briefings given him by his generals after a short time to embark upon one of his feared monologues. This time he listened to Manstein's briefing silently and as if transfixed.[23] Impressed by the general's captivating line of argument, he also managed to hide the personal aversion that he otherwise entertained against von Manstein.[24] Instead, he turned out to be "enthusiastic" and agreed to all of von Manstein's conclusions, even the employment of "strong Panzer forces."[25] The die was cast and the Sickle Cut plan had prevailed.

The moment had come for this idea whose boldness had initially startled almost all the generals. A few days before that, on 13 February, after Schmundt had comprehensively briefed him about Manstein's counterproposal, Hitler had decided to shift the main effort to the south.[26] Jodl passed that decision on to the army high command, with the specification that a new operations draft was to be prepared on that basis. In the meantime, Halder had also decided to go along with that very idea, which a short time ago was still off limits. He did so, last but not least, on the basis of the results of some map exercises.[27] When he was summoned to the Reich Chancellery on 18 February together with von Brauchitsch, he was already able to submit a completely new operations plan that accommodated Hitler's ideas.

The result of that conference was the fourth deployment directive, which was submitted on 24 February.[28] The most important sentence in this last and final version of the operations plan for Fall Gelb (Case Yellow) read as follows: "The Schwerpunkt of the attack to be mounted across the territory of Belgium and Luxembourg is south of the Liège-Charleroi line." Army Group B had the mission of attacking north of that line to draw as many elements of the French-British army as possible toward it:

Eighteenth Army was to push into Holland.

Sixth Army was to cross the Meuse at Liège and attack through northern Belgium.

Army Group A had the mission of crossing the line of the Meuse River between Sedan and Dinant with an operational probing attack by armored and motorized elements and of pushing toward the mouth of the Somme River.

Fourth Army was to attack south of the Liège-Namur line and cross the Meuse River on both sides of Dinant.

Twelfth Army was to advance through southern Belgium and Luxembourg and cross the Meuse River in the Sedan sector.

Second Army initially had the mission of following the offensive, echeloned in depth to take over the sector of the front that was freed after Fourth and Twelfth Armies had veered off toward the Channel coast.

Sixteenth Army was to seal off the left flank of the penetration south of Sedan.

The main effort of Army Group C in the southern sector was geared toward the defensive. It was to simulate attacks against the Maginot Line across the way and thus tie down strong enemy formations.

The Basic Question: Who Was the Author of the Sickle Cut Idea?

This question is of such central significance because it involves one of the most fateful misunderstandings in German military history. Were Hitler and Manstein really thinking the same thing as they pointed their fingers toward Sedan on the map? The subsequent course of the campaign reveals that the dictator was not at all in a position to grasp the true operational dimension of this idea. Nevertheless, after the victorious campaign, he entertained the delusion that he had created this idea and that he was a great warlord. But there were also considerable differences between Manstein's bold idea of the Sickle Cut and Halder's fourth deployment directive.

The discussion as to who played the decisive role in the birth of the Sickle Cut plan narrows down to just three persons—Halder, Hitler, and Manstein. But this means overlooking the fact that Guderian, a Panzer expert, had counseled Manstein regarding the translation of his idea into action. One might even speak of a Manstein-Guderian tandem. After the chief of staff of Army Group A had been reassigned from his post, Guderian passionately advocated this idea, which he also subscribed to. During the offensive, he again and again ignored the applicable regulations and orders and, undeterred, implemented his own ideas. And so it is last but not least due to him that the operation after all took place the way Manstein had visualized it.

The Sickle Cut Idea of Manstein and Halder

Halder was then considered one of the intellectually outstanding men among the German general officer corps. But Manstein, who was younger and very ambitious, turned into a rival whose abilities many generals definitely graded much higher. For example, [Ludwig] Beck had noticed Manstein, the operational prodigy, rather early. It was due to Beck's mentoring that Manstein was assigned as deputy chief of staff for operations on the army general staff in October 1936. This meant that Manstein, although he was relatively young, had become Beck's deputy as chief of the general staff and was also considered as Beck's future successor. But Beck, who later became one of the leading personalities of the military resistance movement, had already fallen into discredit with Hitler. In the wake of the Blomberg-Fritsch crisis, it was not Beck who became the new commander in chief of the army—something that would automatically have meant Manstein moving up into his position later—but rather the lower-rated Brauchitsch. At the same time, Manstein was ordered to Liegnitz as division commander, and Halder was put in his place. A few months later, Beck resigned in protest against Hitler's aggressive foreign policy, and Halder became his successor on 1 September 1938.[29] The rather tense relationship between the two generals can be understood only against this background.[30]

Halder, who was from Bavaria, and Manstein, the Prussian, differed not only by virtue of their very nature but also in the way their thinking was structured. Especially in English-language studies, Halder was often compared to a professor of mathematics on account of his methodical, systematic way of thinking. That was probably also due to the fact that he would, from time to time, seek relaxation by doing mathematical exercises during the few breaks he had in his duties as the chief of the general staff.[31] His relentless logic, with which he was wont to tackle operational questions, was only too well-known and feared.

Manstein's thinking was entirely different. His thinking ran along straight, logical lines only at the strategic echelon, where, in contrast to a number of other German generals, he displayed astonishing farsightedness. On the operational echelon, on the other hand, his system consisted of again and again acting quite consciously in an unsystematic fashion. For him, as a military leader, the best solution often was not the logical solution because the enemy might well be figuring the same thing. Instead, the solution had to be seemingly illogical and the thing to do was to take the enemy by surprise. The "crazy" idea of putting the main effort against the Western powers in the geographically most unfavorable spot and attacking with the bulk of the Panzer divisions, of all places through the extremely difficult Ardennes, is just one of many examples. This incalculability would later also make him dangerous to the Soviets on the Eastern front. One essential difference between Manstein and Halder emerged precisely when it came to making decisions. The latter would often sometimes ruminate night after night whenever he faced grave decisions; he would run through all possibilities and keep calling on his assistants for advice. On the other hand, Manstein

Generalleutnant Erich von Manstein. *Bundesarchiv Koblenz [Federal Archives]*

General der Artillerie Franz Halder. *Bundesarchiv Koblenz [Federal Archives]*

Generaloberst Gerd von Rundstedt. *Bundesarchiv Koblenz [Federal Archives]*

Generalleutnant Hans Reinhardt. *Bundesarchiv Koblenz [Federal Archives]*

was a man of fast, often lonely, decisions. In case of doubt, he trusted his intuition rather than mathematical calculations. In historiography he is today indisputably considered the ablest among Hitler's generals. His forte was maneuvering with large formations on the operational echelon. This is where he developed a virtuosity in which he proved to be far superior to his opponents.

Undoubtedly, a rivalry existed between the generals, and the "cautious Halder clearly evinced resentment towards the daring genius of Manstein."[32] In his capacity as army chief of staff, Halder did not forward the undoubtedly better operations draft prepared by the chief of staff of Army Group A to the Wehrmacht high command. That was certainly not due only to the fact that he did not want to give his younger competitor a chance to outshine him. Instead, he acted the way he did on the basis of fundamental considerations, including those of a moral nature. As chief of the general staff, Halder was responsible for operational-level planning. This is why he wanted to prevent Hitler's political go-for-broke mentality from spreading to the operational echelon. He immediately realized the fascination that was bound to spring from Manstein's bold idea. If the adventurer Hitler was to learn of that adventurous idea, he would inevitably catch fire, because he himself entertained the unripe idea of a thrust via Sedan.

Besides, it ran counter to Halder's systematic way of thinking to invalidate a higher-level strategic logic by means of subordinate operational-level logic. Once before, the German general staff had made that cardinal mistake when in 1914 it used the Schlieffen plan to get around the objective strength ratio. The attempt to achieve an immediate decision by way of a modern Cannae had failed against the same opponent in a similar situation. As demonstrated by the course of World War II, the skeptical chief of the German general staff turned out to be right. To that extent, it seems ironic that of all people Halder—after he had struggled in vain against this operational feasibility craze—suddenly made a radical about-face. That was to have a fateful effect during the planning of the campaign against the Soviet Union.

Later on, Halder even maintained that he was the real creator of the Sickle Cut plan. He claimed that he had already proposed at the end of September to mount a counterstroke with the point of main effort running through the Ardennes.[33] But there is no firm evidence of that.[34] Obviously, he did consider that possibility for a short time but then discarded it again because of the attendant risk. Indeed, at first he was a determined opponent of that idea when Manstein proposed it. After the war, a retired Halder exerted lasting influence on international military historiography. In the studies that were prepared [for the U.S. Army] under his supervision[35] and also in the voluminous literature about the war in the west, we encounter an assertion that can be traced back to him to the effect that he made a complete "sickle cut" out of the "sickle movement" that Manstein merely sketched.[36] According to him, the Panzer thrust to the mouth of the Somme River had not been firmed up until the fourth deployment directive that he had drafted. But that thesis is hotly disputed.[37] There are above all four aspects that must be considered when comparing the operational concepts of Halder and Manstein.

Provisional Character

It seems rather problematic to compare Manstein's preliminary operations drafts in detail to the subsequent army high command operations plan. In his memoirs, he himself commented on that by means of a classical metaphor: "Naturally I did not immediately find myself presented with a cut-and-dried operation plan in that October of 1939. Hard work and endeavour must always confront the ordinary mortal before he attains his goal. No ready-made works of art can spring from his brain as did Pallas Athene from the head of Zeus."[38]

Considering Manstein's astonishing operational creativity, we may well assume that he would have further perfected his idea if he had not been reassigned from his post precisely on account of that idea. The idea of the Sickle Cut, which Halder would like to get credit for, was in reality undoubtedly already expressed in Manstein's first memorandum. Graf von Kielmansegg commented on that score quite unmistakably: "The idea was entirely and totally Manstein's."[39]

Request for Panzer Forces

If one compared the fourth deployment directive of 24 February 1940 drafted by Halder to Manstein's provisional draft of 18 December 1939, one cannot help but note that an adequate number of Panzer divisions were earmarked for the push to the Somme only in the operations planning of the army general staff. But it must be kept in mind that Manstein's memorandums had, so to speak, a diplomatic character. As he himself put it, they were "tailored to the particular point in time, to that which at the moment might perhaps be doable."[40] That applies above all to the request for Panzer divisions. This is precisely where he conducted intensive talks with Guderian, who wanted "if possible all of them."[41]

But the word "Panzer" was at first taboo for the chief of the general staff of Army Group A. It would have been most unwise of him if he had taken the second step before the first one and if he had from the very beginning demanded almost all Panzer divisions for Army Group A. After all, the commanders in chief who would have had to surrender those Panzers jealously guarded their prestige object. At first, Manstein only wanted to make it clear that the main thrust would have to be made from the east and not from the north toward the Somme to be able to encircle the enemy.

Once that basic operational-level idea had been accepted, then the corresponding force allocations, especially in terms of Panzer divisions, would follow automatically. He was able to shed his diplomatic self-restraint only during the conference with Hitler on 17 February. As Jodl testified, Manstein's request was formulated just as a conditio sine qua non (indispensable condition) was absolutely crystal-clear. In the final analysis, it so happens, he demanded "strong Panzer [forces] or none at all."[42]

The final evidence that Manstein actually planned a Panzer operation is that on the very next day Hitler instructed the army high command to place "the bulk of the heavy Panzers" under Twelfth Army.[43]

The Time Factor

In modern military history, probably few operations depended so extensively on the speed of implementation as did Sickle Cut. Guderian, who had advised Manstein regarding the tactical feasibility of his idea and who helped fashion this plan, felt that the time factor constituted the main problem:

> Phase 1: The Meuse River had to be crossed at the latest on the fifth (!) day of the offensive, otherwise the French would be able to move reserves up to the river in time the moment they had figured out the deception maneuver represented by the Sickle Cut plan.
>
> Phase 2: After crossing the Meuse River, the Panzer divisions had to push to the mouth of the Somme River as quickly as possible, disregarding their exposed flanks, otherwise the Allies would still be able to escape the trap in time.

Indeed, it was already possible on the fourth day of the attack to cross the Meuse River at Sedan. The German Panzers were able to beat the approaching French reserves by just a few hours. When the Meuse crossing at Sedan was run through a map exercise in Koblenz on 7 February, Halder referred to Guderian's time frame as "senseless." In his opinion, an attack was possible at the earliest on the ninth, but probably only on the tenth day of the attack. He arrived at the same result on 14 February in Mayen where the map exercise was continued. Besides, he spoke up in favor of a "paced general attack," in other words, a methodical advance. To begin with, infantry divisions were to create a bridgehead in the course of a tactical engagement; only then would the Panzer divisions follow up to exploit the breakthrough in the course of an operational-level engagement. Guderian, however, believed that this way of using Panzers was wrong and, rather depressed, talked in terms of a crisis of confidence. Nor could any support be expected from Army Group A because Halder had seen to it that the latter's chief of staff was reassigned. "Now was the time when we needed Manstein!" Guderian complained in describing this situation.[44]

Of course, Guderian's arguments later persuaded Halder who also pleaded for an attack with the Panzers way out in front. But he did not want to go along with Guderian's demand that the Panzer divisions push to the Somme, heading for Amiens immediately after crossing the Meuse River. As army chief of staff he and almost the entire general officer corps considered it indispensable to first secure the bridgehead by moving up infantry divisions. The thrust was to be continued only after steps had been taken to build up an adequate screen, above all, on the left flank.[45]

This precisely underscores the difference between Halder's half-hearted 4th Deployment Directive and Manstein's bold Sickle Cut idea. Halder dared not venture the big leap to the Channel coast in one swift move. Instead, he first wanted to stop in the bridgehead along the Meuse, literally, half-way along. In that way he ran the risk of simply giving away the big opportunity of completely encircling the Allied northern wing and thus winning a strategic victory, in return gaining only an ordinary operational victory. Manstein, however, wanted a total decision that at the same time signified the acceptance of the total risk. The operation's most interesting moment was bound to come once Guderian had managed to cross the Meuse River. Now we come to the question as to whether he was to follow the directives of his superiors or his own ideas that went back to Manstein.

Simultaneous Secondary Thrust to the South

From Manstein's operations draft, Halder had taken the basic idea of a thrust to the Somme mouth, although not in every respect. He turned down outright the second basic idea of launching a secondary thrust to the south simultaneously with the main thrust to the west. This idea, which was confirmed by the subsequent course of the campaign, precisely demonstrated Manstein's farsightedness. Manstein was guided by three arguments:

1. The exposed left flank was to be defended "offensively."[46] Manstein figured on a French counterattack along the ever-longer southern flank. In view of the speed of the planned advance, it seemed problematical to him to be able to move up on schedule an adequate number of infantry divisions in order then to line them up, "like a long string of pearls," to cover the left flank.[47] Instead of this standard but passive procedure, he wanted to use one of the breakthrough armies to push south from Sedan—smack into the middle of the anticipated counterattack's deployment—even before the French were able to deploy for that counterattack.

Study P-208, prepared in 1959 under Halder's overall editorial direction, observes, full of satisfaction, that Manstein's prognosis—that setting up such a long defensive front quickly would be impossible—did not prove to be true. Instead, it was possible to build up a four-hundred-kilometer-long defensive front from Sierck (in the southeastern corner of Luxembourg) all the way to the Channel coast.[48] But that is only half the truth because Guderian, who was guided by Manstein's idea after the breakthrough at Sedan, ignored the orders given him by his superiors and ordered strong formations to swing south for the "offensive defense." In this attack directed against the Massif of Stonne, his troops punched smack into the assembly area of the French counterattack.

2. Manstein had yet another intention with his idea of an "offensive" defense of the southern flank. If the southern flank were to be sealed off only defensively in

combination with a push to the Somme River mouth, then the enemy might build up a new defensive front along the Somme and Aisne rivers between the Channel coast and the Maginot Line that began at Sedan. Manstein's pivoting movement of Twelfth Army to the southwest, into the Rethel-Reims area, therefore also had the objective of once and for all ripping the enemy front wide open.[49] When the campaign was continued after the capture of Dunkirk, the Allies had built up a strong defensive position precisely along the line predicted by Manstein. The German troops had to break through that line in a frontal attack that claimed disproportionately large casualties.

3. With his strategic farsightedness, Manstein was already contemplating the second phase of the campaign. Beating France and its allies in a single big operation is something that he considered to be illusory. That sort of thinking had already proved to be fatal in 1914 when it came to implementing the Schlieffen plan. Instead, he referred to Clausewitz, who had said that the "culmination point" must not be reached prematurely in the course of an offensive.[50] He suggested that the campaign be carried out in two immediately successive major operations, so that from Sedan, the pivot, each half of the Allied front would be encircled and annihilated. *Fall Gelb* (Case Yellow): A Panzer thrust from Sedan to the Channel coast was to encircle the northern wing of the enemy army (Sickle Cut). *Fall Rot* (Case Red)[51]: Next, the southern wing had to be enveloped from Sedan to the Swiss border. That thrust was to be made "after the pattern of the Schlieffen plan" and was to force the French into "a battle in the rear of the Maginot Line with the fronts reversed."[52]

It is interesting to note that Manstein was actually planning a double Sickle Cut with mutually opposite pivoting movements. During the first phase, the Twelfth Army was to be ready to anticipate the very turning movement that Army Groups A and B were to perform during the second phase. They were thus able to form the hinge of that mighty door that would swing toward the rear of the troops stationed behind the Maginot Line. But, the army high command rejected such far-reaching considerations and stuck with the purely defensive screening of the southern flank. On the eighth day of the offensive, however, Halder suddenly found himself in a euphoric mood and, as will be shown, in a radical about-face wanted to translate Manstein's initially discarded idea into action. But now it was too late.

Summarizing, we can say this: Halder was not the author but rather the most determined opponent of Sickle Cut. That kind of daredevil idea ran counter to his cautious way of thinking. His flexibility and intellectual framework emerged only as the campaign wore on, when the operation increasingly gained a dynamism of its own and took place with the speed of an avalanche. It was he who fully grasped the idea of the Sickle Cut that was now emerging in full force. While Hitler and most of the representatives of the higher-ranking general officer corps seemed paralyzed, he led the operation expertly and with a boldness that was astonishing considering his basic nature.

Manstein's and Hitler's Sickle Cut Idea

Hitler was not only a suggestive propagandist, but, from time to time, he himself was a victim of his own suggestions. One of the most fateful consequences of the war in the west was that the dictator increasingly worked himself into the role of the warlord and in the end was unable to distinguish between delusion and reality. So he was convinced that he had been the inventor of the Sickle Cut plan. In so doing, he stood reality on its head when, later on, he asserted in all seriousness: "Among all the generals I talked to about the new plan in the West, Manstein was the only one who understood me."[53]

At first, Hitler came out in favor of putting the point of main effort on the right wing, an idea that was expressed in the first deployment directive of 19 October. During a conference with Brauchitsch and Halder on 25 October, he suddenly asked about the possibility "of making the main attack south of the Meuse—perhaps with a secondary operation against Liège—in order to advance west and then northwest to cut off and destroy the enemy forces in and moving into Belgium."[54] The commander in chief of the army and his chief of staff were "completely surprised" and indicated little readiness to follow up seriously on this idea. Hitler, likewise, was obviously not particularly convinced as to the correctness of his spontaneous inspiration because he no longer talked about it during the weeks thereafter but developed completely other operational-level concepts.

It would be wrong to equate these scraps of thinking with the well-thought-out and exactly justified considerations that Manstein expressed in his 31 October memorandum. Instead, this was one of those abrupt impulses with which the dictator upset his advisers day after day. Halder commented: "It was a typical Hitlerian idea; one can even say a good one. . . . But how little capable he was of really thinking out its full military implications was shown later by his interventions in the course of the operation."[55] Retired Generaloberst [Hermann] Hoth also believes that this is another one of Hitler's many "leaps of intuition" and warns against upgrading "a thought that was blurted out on 25 October 1939, and that was dropped again on the next day" to the status of a real operational-level idea.[56]

The dictator, however, was dissatisfied with the drafts the army high command submitted to him and continued to pore over the maps. On 11 November, he surprised the general officer corps with the brainstorm of trying an additional push to Sedan. Guderian was to head an army corps of armored and motorized units that was to cross the Meuse at that point. As noted earlier, however, a third point of main effort was now added to the previous two points of main effort that had been laid down in the second deployment directive. Hitler obviously did not dare put all his money on one card and thus violated one of the most important basic principles of blitzkrieg, the principle of concentration. To justify himself, he stated that the point of main effort was to be formed only while the operation was in progress, depending on how the situation developed. Manstein's criticism was directed against that element of indecisiveness in operations planning. He saw the following weak point: "According to Moltke, mistakes made during the initial deployment cannot be corrected. . . . The Luftwaffe can shift its point of main effort any time but the Army, once the operation is under way, cannot do that any longer, at least it cannot do it in a short time."[57] Above all, he believed that the XIX Corps' isolated thrust toward Sedan was a half-measure, and so did Guderian who was in command of that corps. The plan was for XIV Corps (Motorized) to follow merely as a reserve instead of using it from the very beginning together with Guderian's corps for a combined attack against the Meuse River line at Sedan.

During the ensuing time, Hitler's thinking revolved increasingly around Sedan, a city that already fascinated him because of the legendary battle that was fought there in 1870. He was increasingly inclined to shift the point of main effort there without being able to express that thought in the form of a clear concept.[58] All the more eager was he to soak up every bit of information that his chief military aide, Schmundt, brought to him on 2 February after a visit to Army Group A in Koblenz. In Manstein's thinking, he found precisely those arguments, formulated in a captivating manner, that he had been missing until then. Therefore, 2 February must be considered as the day when Hitler decided to make a radical change in the old operations plan. The "conspiratorial" meeting after the so-called working breakfast on 17 February was intended rather to clarify additional questions, at which time Manstein was at last able to put his cards on the table and demand that strong Panzer forces be made available. On 13 February, via Jodl, Hitler had already instructed the army high command that the main thrust was now to be mounted toward Sedan. But, in so doing, he did not say a single word to the effect that he was initiated in Manstein's trend of thought. The same is true on 18 February, when he decidedly addressed Manstein's requirement of the day before for strong Panzer forces to the army high command.

The vast number of myths about the campaign in the west also includes the assertion—to be found in practically all history books—that Hitler's instinctive intuition led him to the same operational-level solution that Manstein derived from his general staff–style calculations. That assertion must be resolutely contradicted. Both men, of course, did say the same thing, but they did not mean the same thing. Here the misunderstanding must be seen in the accidental geographic agreement in the locality called Sedan. After the war, for example, former generals Halder and Hoth as well as Manstein pointed out that the ideas that Hitler tied in with Sedan were of a *tactical* nature.[59] As Manstein allowed, he had merely realized that "the easiest place to cross the Meuse was at Sedan."[60] But this militarily self-taught man was not in a position to think this idea through to the end. Manstein, however, was concerned with the *strategic* question as to how one could achieve a total decision. Hitler's considerations were aimed primarily at the opposite bank of the Meuse River—Manstein was thinking all the way to the Channel coast. Here, along the lower course of the Somme River, a total victory was possible, as he could anticipate, if one could push there fast enough and thus encircle all Allied troops concentrated in the north.

As for the operational translation of this strategic idea into action, the Panzers were to drive through the Ardennes and cross the Meuse River in a surprise attack. The selection of the exact site for the Meuse crossing was a tactical problem, with Manstein's adviser Guderian coming out in favor of Sedan because, on the basis of his own familiarity, he considered the terrain there to be suitable. To get to the point: Hitler tied tactical and thus purely inductive considerations to Sedan, whereas Manstein had deductive, higher-level strategic ideas. But that was an elementary difference that would emerge only during the campaign after the crossing of the Meuse River. The dictator really panicked when the Panzer divisions, after the breakthrough at Sedan—just as Manstein and Guderian had wanted—pushed to the Channel coast at top speed. But how could Hitler have so wanted and planned Operation Sickle Cut if he almost had a nervous breakdown and ordered the Panzers to stop just as success seemed around the corner?

The reason for the big misunderstanding about Sedan is that Hitler, as a military layman, was not always able to recognize the differences between tactical, operational, and strategic considerations.[61] He was like the amateur chess player who manages the same ingenious chess move, rather by accident, as a grandmaster (although the latter does this on the basis of a much more complex thinking process) and now believes that he, too, is a grandmaster. But when he tried to trip up his general staff that had already won the game and ordered the Panzers to stop before Dunkirk, he preserved the British army from checkmate. Just how little Hitler understood the idea behind the Sickle Cut will be described in detail in the analysis of the operation itself.

The Revolving Door Effect of the Schlieffen Plan and the Sickle Cut Plan

> *A perfect battle, such as at Cannae, is rare in the history of warfare. This is because it features, on the one side, a man such as Hannibal, and on the other side, a man such as [Gaius] Terentius Varro, both of whom, in their own ways, cooperate toward the attainment of the greater end.*[62]
>
> Generalfeldmarschall Graf von Schlieffen

Manstein's operational-level considerations that constituted the basis of the Sickle Cut plan can be replicated only if, as he himself emphasizes, they are contemplated against the background of the Schlieffen plan.[63] In his well-known *Drehtür-Vergleich* (revolving door comparison), Liddell Hart very clearly tied together the functional principle of the two plans. In both cases, one could successfully get into the enemy's rear only if the latter, as a result of a forward movement, triggered a "revolving door effect" without wanting to do so.[64] In 1914 the pivot was at Diedenhofen (Thionville), south of Luxembourg. The more impetuously the French pushed into Alsace-Lorraine, the more forcefully the swing wing was bound to hit them in the back from the direction of Belgium. In 1940 the pivot was exactly reversed, in other words, in the clockwise direction. The farther north the Allied intervention forces pushed into Belgium, the more easily the German Panzer divisions could get through the Ardennes and into their rear and push all the way to the Channel coast.

Schlieffen Plan and Joffre Plan in 1914

In 1870, during the war against France, Moltke had managed to achieve a decision immediately, when he was able to surround one French field army in the encirclement battle of Sedan, the "Cannae of the 19th Century." In the year 216 B.C., Hannibal, with about fifty thousand men, encircled and wiped out a Roman army of almost eighty thousand men at Cannae. The Carthaginian warlord managed to entice his Roman opponent, [Gaius] Terentius Varro, into mounting a frontal attack against his army's center that bulged provocatively forward. The lightly armed troops stationed there were pushed back farther and farther. On both wings, the closely echeloned, heavily armed troops held their positions like corner posts; therefore, the Romans pushed into the center, like into a sack. At the same time, the disproportionately reinforced cavalry of Hasdrubal, on the left wing, overran the Roman cavalry opposite and then attacked the enemy horsemen fighting on the other wing from the rear. When the latter were defeated, the entire Carthaginian cavalry was employed against the rear of the Roman army and was able to close the deadly trap.[65]

Schlieffen planned a gigantically projected repeat of this encirclement battle in northeastern France. It seemed extremely difficult frontally to break through the fortification front line along the eastern French border. That is why he proposed that this front be outflanked to the north after which one could thrust into the enemy's rear. The weak left German wing along the French border had the mission of enticing the French to stage an offensive into Alsace-Lorraine. At the same time, almost the entire German army (seven-eighths of the divisions) were to march through neutral Belgium and in a gigantic wheeling movement through northern France head toward the Swiss border to trap the French army in a gigantic pocket. This means that the weak left wing was to play the role of Hannibal's infantry while the mighty right wing would play the role of Hasdrubal's cavalry. The more deeply the French troops pushed into the trap—as the Romans did once upon a time—the more difficult would it be for them to withdraw to the rear once the German right wing that was wheeling toward it from the rear threatened encirclement. Schlieffen thus hoped that the French offensive would do him this "favor" by running smack into the trap he had laid for them in Alsace-Lorraine.

French military doctrine before World War I, like German doctrine, was unilaterally fixated on the attack. The rule proclaimed at that time by the École Supérieure de

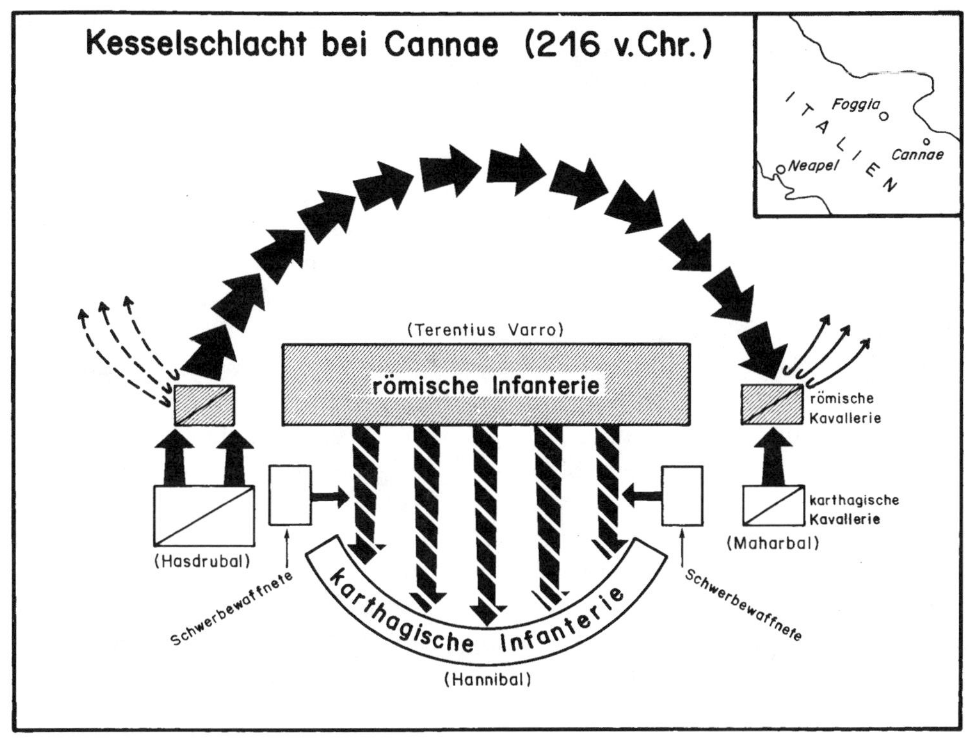

Encirclement Battle at Cannae, 216 B.C.

Guerre [War College] was: "L'attaque à l'outrance" [All-out attack].[66] The French wanted to beat the enemy to the punch. The opposite of the Schlieffen plan was the so-called Plan XVII of the French chief of staff [Joseph] Joffre. An almost "mystical belief in the offensive" marked this operations plan.[67] Joffre was eager to follow the footsteps of the Roman warlord Terentius Varro because, without wanting to, he was planning an offensive smack into the middle of the trap. The French were not only eager and anxious to reconquer Alsace-Lorraine; they even wanted to "get to Berlin by going through Mainz," as General [Ferdinand] Foch put it.[68]

World War I began with the strategic surprise of the German push through neutral Belgium. The colossal right wing marched with clockwork precision relentlessly into the rear of the French army while the latter, as expected, attacked into Alsace-Lorraine. In that way, however, it set in motion the gigantic machinery that Schlieffen had planned and that was bound to lead to its annihilation. Now, the Germans quite incomprehensibly refused to accept this "gift." One of the biggest military stupidities of this century took place along the border of Alsace-Lorraine. The French pushed into the pocket planned by Schlieffen, but the Germans on the left wing, again with all their might, kicked the attackers out after they had voluntarily plunged into the abyss of perdition. Joffre's offensive failed after just a few kilometers and his troops were forced back behind the border fortifications. In that way, the execution of the Schlieffen plan in 1914 was turned into a satire of the Battle of Cannae, with the right wing obviously not knowing what the left was doing.

Astonishingly enough, the discussion of the Schlieffen plan to this very day is fixated mostly on the right wing. Schlieffen's successor, Moltke the Younger, had reduced the force ratio between the two wings from 7:1 to 3:1.[69] In reality, however, the decisive mistake was not to weaken the right wing but rather to strengthen the left wing. The formations employed here had now become so strong that the French attackers were no longer able, as Schlieffen had wanted, to push deeply enough into Lorraine. On the contrary, the Bavarian crown prince's spontaneous counterattack on the left wing was diametrically opposed to the revolving door movement that Schlieffen had wanted. And so the operational-level logic of the Schlieffen plan was reduced to absurdity.

How could that fatal forward movement of the German left wing have come about? First of all, there were dynastic rivalries that played a role here. The Bavarians, on the left wing, did not wish to retreat voluntarily whereas the Prussians on the right wing were to be victorious. But there were also ideological motives. Schlieffen had demanded the temporary abandonment of larger parts of Alsace-Lorraine in case of a French offensive, conducted "as a favor" for the Germans. He even said: "If the French cross the Upper Rhine, then we will resist them in the Black Forest."[70] But the kaiser, as well as patriotically minded circles, resented the idea of Alsace-Lorraine soil being given up.

The so-called Schlieffen plan has caused much irritation among historians. That plan, which the outgoing chief of staff passed on to his successor in 1905, in reality was a memorandum and not a specific deployment plan.[71] Besides, there was never any such thing as *the* Schlieffen plan, but rather there were variants that differed from each other above all by virtue of the extent and scope of the wheeling movement on the right wing.[72] The best proof of this can be found in Schlieffen's statements during the last general staff ride he directed. Here, he once again went through the variant of the so-called favor and emphatically stressed that, in case of a French offensive into Lorraine, one must under no circumstances carry out that gigantic wheeling movement via Lille and Paris (later on labeled the Schlieffen plan). Instead, one would have to march farther to the west and to swing south already in the Sedan area after crossing the Meuse River in order to encircle the French attacking armies in Lorraine.[73] That is exactly the situation that materialized in August 1914. Now, why did the Younger Moltke not follow Schlieffen's pattern? As Jehuda Wallach suggested, in that situation only a "second Moltke" could have fought a "second Sedan."[74] The pivotal point for the decisive encirclement movement to the south would have been in the very area in which his uncle, Moltke the Elder, had already directed the famous encirclement battle of 1870.

Schlieffen certainly shared the responsibility for this fatal development. He had elevated the idea of encirclement to a cult; he not only dogmatized it, he almost mystified it. And thus, his epigones proved to be "more Schlieffenish . . . than Schlieffen himself."[75] Before World War I, the German general staff finally developed such an encirclement mania that it concentrated only on the grand solution, the wide wheeling movement via Lille. One of those opportunities for a modern Cannae, so rare in the history of warfare, materialized doubly in August 1914. That chance was exploited on the eastern front at Tannenberg because the objective was limited to encircling just a single Russian field army. But along the western front, Schlieffen's successors were so fixated upon the *strategic* encirclement of almost the entire French army in a monomaniacal manner that they completely lost sight of the realistic chance of an operational-level encirclement in Lorraine. Here we need only refer to Clausewitz: "the man who sacrifices the possible in search of the impossible is a fool."[76]

The Sickle Cut Plan and the Dyle Plan in 1940

The German Deception Maneuver on the Right Wing. In his memoirs, Manstein devoted astonishingly much space to the analysis of the Schlieffen plan and compared the 1939 starting position rather completely with that of 1914. At that time, the general staff could hope "that the French would do us the good turn of launching a premature offensive into Lorraine."[77] Schlieffen, therefore, "accepted the risk of initial reverses in Alsace, at the same time hoping that the enemy, by unleashing an offensive in Lorraine, would do their own bit toward making the Germans' big outflanking operation a complete success."[78] But this time, it was considerably more difficult to coax the enemy into the trap of a modern Cannae. A strategic surprise seemed almost impossible because it was Great Britain and France who had declared war on the German Reich. Until May 1940, they had eight months to prepare for the expected German offensive. An operational-level surprise was also hardly possible because the trick of 1914—that is to say, getting into the rear of the French army from the north via Belgium—had to be considered as being known ever since the Schlieffen plan had failed.

Manstein, therefore, suggested that the main effort of the attack be shifted from Army Group B on the right wing to Army Group A in the center. After the breakthrough at Sedan, there was to be a wheeling movement, not to the south as in the Schlieffen plan, but to the north toward the mouth of the Somme River to encircle the Allied northern wing along the Channel coast. But the army high command initially rejected Manstein's idea as absurd and dangerous. It seemed to represent an operational game of chance and was fatally reminiscent of the Schlieffen plan. Once again, the fate of the Reich was to depend on the success of a single operation. Above all, everything depended on the enemy making the same decisive mistake as in 1914, when he wanted to push into the Lorraine trap. This time the encirclement could come off successfully only if the Allies, as Manstein assumed, would march into the Belgian trap with their left wing. That was the only way one could set the required revolving door mechanism in motion.

Liddell Hart compared this connection to a bullfight. Accordingly, Army Group B, attacking in the north, was to represent the red cape of the bullfighter. It was to arouse the Allied intervention forces to rush forward into Belgium like a raging bull—smack into the trap. This is because now the Panzer divisions, concentrated in Army Group A like a bullfighter's sword, would be able to thrust into the exposed right flank.[79] In terms of theory, this operational chess move must appear truly brilliant. But what would happen if the French and British troops were to stop at the border? In that case, they would be able to withdraw in time behind the Somme River. But if they were able to break out to the south, the German encirclement wing was in turn threatened with a Cannae along the Channel coast. Manstein's estimate of the enemy situation, however, was to turn out correct.

Allied Operational Intentions Become Known. An incident occurred in January 1940 that normally would only be a footnote in historiography, if it had not provoked the Allies into a fateful mistake. This involves the previously described emergency landing by two German officers near Mechelen, Belgium. From the French viewpoint, the episode took place like this:

> The Germans knew exactly what movements we would make in case of an invasion of Belgium because we were kind enough to stage a "dress rehearsal" for that, before their very eyes. Here is how that happened. One fine day, a German aircraft landed in Belgium. Its passengers were general staff officers who carried with them a . . . plan for the invasion of Belgium at a certain date. Just for the sake of appearance, they tried to burn their documents but made sure that they would not be successful in doing so. We were immediately informed of the incident in detail. The British Army was placed on alert. . . . Then tremendous troop movements were carried out, all reserves were moved to the front, and, from their reconnaissance aircraft, the Germans observed all these movements and recorded them carefully, probably surprised by the success of a ruse of war that was as old as the hills and totally obvious.[80]

Of course, the story told here about the agents is pure speculation. According to German files, this was by no means the specifically mission-oriented employment of an agent provocateur but rather a highly embarrassing emergency landing. The effect was so profitable for German intelligence that this action could not have been staged better if it had been intended. Thus, the Manstein plan was accepted in the end not due to the presumed disclosure of the German operations plan but as a result of the opponent's overreaction that revealed Allied operational intentions.

The German intelligence service knew not only with a great degree of probability that the Allied intervention troops would advance into Belgium in case of a German attack, but also had a rough idea of the organization of those troops. It was even able to find out that those troops would go into position along the so-called Dyle Line. In addition, it had been possible to break the French radio code.[81] Hermann Zimmermann entitled his book on the XVI Panzer Corps' breakthrough of the Dyle Line *Der Griff ins Ungewisse* (Reaching into the Unknown). Retired Generalleutnant Walter de Beaulieu, the former chief of staff of that corps, commented with a certain degree of irony: "The Panzer battle of Hannut had been prepared like a war game! The way the enemy was supposed to occupy the Dyle Position—using his best motorized troops—had also filtered through before the start of the fighting. Talking about a 'reach into the unknown' in such a situation is impossible. Everything happened the way it had been figured out."[82]

German Deception Measures. Reconnaissance findings impressively confirmed Manstein's estimate of the enemy situation. Accordingly, a new Cannae was within the realm of possibility if his encirclement idea could be carried out consistently. But there was a double prerequisite for implementing the revolving door effect: On the one hand, the enemy's attention had to be deflected to Army Group B in the north; on the other hand, the advance of the Panzer divisions concentrated in Army Group A through the Ardennes had to be concealed as long as possible. To do that, the most varied and bizarre methods were employed even during the preparatory phase:

> There are people who go to neutral foreign countries and who, depending on their personality, are either assimilated or appear to be well-known chatterboxes, [and who] tell their business contacts indiscrete things; there are neutral attachés, etc., in the most varied places throughout the world, who can pick up one or the other piece of news from good friends; there are telephone lines tapped by the enemy on which one conducts "careless" conversations; finally, there are clubs, perhaps there might even be an elegant lady, who consciously or unconsciously can spread rumors. During the months before the offensive, the news of the German "1940 Edition of the Schlieffen Plan" was spread around again and again in the most varied form through many such channels. Indeed, these measures obviously contributed to the success.[83]

Canaris, the chief of German counterintelligence, was the coordinator of these deception actions. Radio deception played a special role here.[84] Propaganda was also employed in a specifically target-oriented fashion to conceal German operational intentions. After the start of the campaign, every success achieved within the sector of Army Group B in the north was trumpeted to the world loud and clear; the breakthrough at Sedan was mentioned only belatedly and in passing. That initially irritated even the German soldiers themselves, as shown in a 2d Panzer Division after-action report after crossing the Meuse River at Sedan: "So, we made it! Down there flows the Meuse River and all those many pillboxes, that is the legendary Maginot Line. . . . The little portable radio gives us the evening news. We hear of successes in Holland and Belgium and we are deeply disappointed that nobody reports about us. . . . Only slowly did it dawn on us that the idea is to let the enemy believe that the success along the Meuse River has not been fully grasped by us even so that he will not get to feel the thrust of the Panzer group into his rear as an iron stranglehold for as long as possible."[85]

The then Hauptmann i.G. Graf von Kielmansegg proved to be better informed:

> Since we were put under Guderian's Corps, everybody had been thoroughly familiarized with the decisive aspect of this breakthrough at Sedan. They told us: "You are the tip of the spearhead of the German attack. All Germany's eyes are upon you!" . . . In reality, that was not correct, by the way, at least at that point in time. The concealment of the true intentions of the German command was still in progress at that time. While the Wehrmacht's report commented in some detail on events in Holland and Belgium, the successes of the decisive left wing were mentioned only in short, meaningless sentences, as if this were just a sideshow. We had our fun with that, because, after all, we knew what this was really all about.[86]

However, it was on the battlefield that the operational deception actions turned out to be decisive. For example, the Luftwaffe during the first three days was quite deliberately employed away from the actual direction of the main thrust. The feared bombers and dive-bombers attacked almost only in the sector of Army Group B in Holland and Belgium as well as in French rear areas. Over the Ardennes were primarily German fighters that pounced upon every enemy reconnaissance aircraft like hawks.

A secret weapon of the Wehrmacht—the airborne force—played the most important role in this deception maneuver carried out on an operational scale. In one of the most spectacular commando missions of World War II, Fort Eben Emael, one of the world's strongest fortresses, was swiftly seized. At dawn on 10 May a detachment of about eighty elite soldiers landed in silent cargo gliders on the roof of the fortress and, using shaped charges, attacked the gun turrets and casemates. The twelve-hundred-man-strong garrison was forced to the lower floors and had to capitulate one day after the arrival of German reinforcements. But the airborne missions in Holland and northern Belgium had only a mostly *tactical* purpose, which was to support the advance of Army Group B. Their *operational-level* purpose was much more important—to simulate that the point of main effort of the German offensive was in that area.

As a result of all these diversionary maneuvers, the French and British generals during the initial phase of the campaign in the west began to take off to the north, as if hypnotized. They overlooked the deadly danger that was threatening them on the right flank. While the Allied elite forces advanced northward toward Belgium, German Panzer divisions were pushing to the southwest, running opposite and past them on the right. By the time the general staffs of the Allies recognized the real German point of main effort, it was too late; their troops were already in the trap.

In this connection, it seems rather odd that for some time Hitler planned an airborne mission against Sedan, of all things.[87] He was persuaded to drop the idea only because the terrain was rather unfavorable there. Such a mission would have been diametrically opposed to the intended operational deception behind Sickle Cut. In that way, Hitler would have provided unmistakable signs as to where the real German main effort was to be placed. Later on, propaganda asserted that Hitler was thinking of the Sickle Cut from the very beginning. This idea is convincing evidence that he did not at all understand the operational connections inherent in this idea and the revolving door mechanism that constitutes its basis. The previously mentioned thesis confirmed that Hitler merely tied tactical ideas in with Sedan.

***Schwerpunktprinzip:* The Principle of the Main Point of Effort.** The first deployment directive, dated 19 October 1939, still placed the main effort on the right wing. At that time, the strength ratio between Army Groups B and A was 37:26 divisions. But the opposing left wing of the Allies had also been enormously reinforced. This would have led precisely to the result predicted by Manstein: main effort would have clashed with main effort. In the meantime, however, following his suggestion the main effort had been shifted to the left attack wing in the Ardennes. When the offensive commenced on 10 May 1940, the original force ratio had been just about turned upside down. Now, the ratio in the distribution of divisions was 45:29 in favor of Army Group A. Above all, Army Group A had seven of the ten German Panzer divisions. In addition, most of the forty-two reserve divisions available on 10 May were earmarked as reinforcements for this army group that was attacking at the point of main effort.

The German general staff had learned from the mistakes of 1914. At that time, Schlieffen's idea was watered down and in the end was reduced to absurdity. That was to have an effect on the differing proportions between Army Groups A and B because the revolving door could be set in motion only if the strong left wing of the Allies faced a weak right German wing and if the weak right Allied wing faced a strong left wing on the German side. The dividing line between the two wings ran along the Liège-Namur line. The Meuse River, which veers off to the northeast here, subdivided the deployment area into a northern wing and a southern wing.

The force ratio on the northern attack wing was 60:29 divisions in favor of the Allies. Army Group B attacked with two field armies and a total of 29 divisions. It faced the Dutch army (10 divisions), the main body of the Belgian army (20 out of 22 divisions), and the British Expeditionary army (12 divisions, including 3 that were incomplete). The French army concentrated numerous elite units here: The First and Seventh Armies (15 divisions) and the 3 mechanized divisions of the Prioux Cavalry Corps.

On the southern attack wing, between Namur and Longwy along the border of Luxembourg, the ratio was 45:18 divisions in favor of the Wehrmacht. Army Group A attacked with the Fourth, Twelfth, and Sixteenth Armies as well as Panzer Group von Kleist [General der Kavallerie Ewald von Kleist], with a total of 45 divisions. This does not include the Second and Ninth Armies that followed behind as the second echelon. The Belgian army covered the Ardennes with only 2 divisions that were, however, supposed to fight merely a delaying action. The French had entrenched themselves behind the Meuse and Chiers rivers with the Ninth and Second Armies. On 10 May, they hastily pushed 4 cavalry divisions and 2 cavalry brigades into the Ardennes. In the actual breakthrough sector between Dinant and Sedan, the Meuse defense line consisted mostly of 7, partly second-rate, infantry divisions.

The Maginot Line had also been built to save personnel and thus to get additional forces for the defense of other frontline sectors. But, on 10 May, this extremely expensive system was "guarded," so to speak, like a prestige object by 36 divisions that were faced mostly passively on the German side by the 19 divisions of Army Group C.

In May 1940 135 German divisions (including 93 in the first wave) attacked a total of 151 Allied divisions (including 114 frontline divisions). But because the Wehrmacht, as the attacker, had the initiative and determined the point of main effort, it was possible to convert the *absolute* superiority of the Allies along the entire front line into a *relative* German superiority in the sector of the front where the operational decision was to be made. Still, this operations plan entailed an enormous risk because everything depended on whether the opponent would actually make his "contribution" to getting the revolving door going.

The Dyle-Breda Plan: Gamelin in the Role of Terentius Varro. In French military history, there is hardly a supreme commander who was exposed to such severe criticism as Gamelin after his failure in May 1940. But his decision to advance into Belgium in case of a German attack must be termed as completely correct and logical—from his viewpoint. The Maginot Line protected the right flank of the French front line. In the center, the Meuse River and the Ardennes formed a double blocking position. He was thus able to concentrate his best formations on the left wing. The Germans had previously selected the plains of Flanders for several offensives during World War I because they had so few obstacles. It seemed probable that they would try once again, following the method of the Schlieffen plan, to attack through this ideal tank terrain with the main effort on the right wing (that was precisely the original intention of the German command!). To prevent Belgium from falling into the aggressor's hands without any protection at all, British and French intervention troops were to come to the aid of the friendly although officially neutral neighbor. There were three lines along which positions prepared by the Belgian army could be taken up:

1. Scheldt Line: This minimum solution screened a narrow coastal strip and some ports to the west of the Scheldt River. It was discarded because most of Belgium would thus be unprotected.

2. Albert Canal Line: With this maximum solution, it would be possible to use almost the entire Meuse River, up to the place where it flows into the Albert Canal

at Maastricht, as a defense line and most of Belgium could thus be covered. That line was much too close to Germany and far too removed from France. The Belgian government wanted to permit the entry of French and British troops only after the German troops had first crossed the border, so it was doubtful whether this exposed line could be reached quickly enough.

3. Dyle Line: This line was a compromise solution, extending from Antwerp along the Dyle River all the way to Namur where it linked up with the Meuse River line.

The decision to advance to the Dyle Line was certainly not a gross mistake, as was asserted so often later on. Instead, it offered a series of advantages:[88]

1. The front line was definitely shortened; above all, it was possible for the northern wing of the Ninth Army to advance all the way to the Meuse between Givet and Namur.

2. By virtue of the additionally prepositioned glacis, the French defense gained more depth, something that was also important in terms of air defense.

3. The desired linkup with the Belgian army was thus achieved. Otherwise, the latter would have withdrawn prematurely to the northwest into the national redoubt around Antwerp. That would have made it possible for the Germans to march immediately all the way through to France.

4. A considerable part of Belgium, with Brussels, the capital, and important port cities could thus be included in the defense. That was, above all, bound to motivate the British so that they would fear the loss of the coastline.

5. The Belgian buffer zone could be used to prevent the northern French industrial region from once again becoming a theater of war (as in World War I).

6. A possible Allied counteroffensive against Germany could be conducted much more easily via Belgium than across the French border because the German Westwall [Siegfried Line] opposite it was particularly strong there. Besides, that would enable the Allies completely to push into the Ruhr Region, Germany's industrial heart. That idea had been considered already at the start of the war when the Allies wanted to come to the aid of Poland.[89]

7. France—whose prestige as a European hegemonic power had suffered considerably over the past several years—could not afford to leave one of its allies, Belgium, in the lurch, especially after Hitler had smashed Czechoslovakia and Poland.

Gamelin, however, added the so-called Breda variant to the Dyle plan. Accordingly, the French were to thrust via Antwerp to Breda also to establish contact with the Dutch army. The French supreme commander was completely taken by the idea of the continuous front from World War I. In that way, he kept thinking in terms of the continuous front line from the Swiss border to the North Sea. As a result of the way this plan was broadened, Gamelin's troops ran the risk of moving away from the safe

French tree trunk, as it were, and climbing farther and farther out on the Belgian limb, then also to reach for the Dutch branch. Breda was twice as far from France as it was from Germany. So, Gamelin's pet idea in the end turned out to be an illusion. The French advance forces had no chance of winning the race to Breda against the fast German formations; instead, they ran into the trap at top speed.

Gamelin's sad fate resided in the fact that in broadening the operations plan he edged farther and farther out on that limb that Sickle Cut was to cut off from the tree trunk. Originally, only ten French and five British divisions were to carry out the Dyle maneuver. On 20 March 1940, however, Gamelin came out with a new version of the plan that also took into consideration the Breda Variant. Now, the strength of the left swing wing was to amount to thirty divisions, including numerous motorized and partly mechanized elite units.

The operational-level consequence of this move can best be recognized by the new role of the French Seventh Army. Originally, it was part of the Central Reserve and was held in readiness in the area around the Reims. This is precisely the direction from which Manstein had expected an operational counterattack, and this is why he suggested that the German Twelfth Army was to push into that area to put up an offensive defense for the German left flank. Such a French counterattack never took place. The French Seventh Army had been shifted to the left wing, where, according to the original version of the Dyle plan, it was to stand by as a reserve. In the final version of that plan, however, it was supposed to be used for a push to Breda. But then Gamelin ran into resistance from General [Alphonse-Joseph] Georges, the commander in chief of the northeast front. Still, Gamelin had tied his prestige to that operation, and he was even prepared to throw the entire French Seventh Army on to the scales. In that way, he deprived Georges of his own coherent reserve, which, if necessary, he could have used to launch an operational counterattack. Georges believed that this was a dangerous mistake and protested: "That is an adventure. If the enemy should only be feigning in Belgium, then he can maneuver elsewhere. We should therefore not employ our reserves for this operation! This is nothing but a dream!"[90] Gamelin behaved like the Roman warlord Terentius Varro before the Battle at Cannae. In spite of all warnings, he ordered an advance smack into the middle of the trap and thus created the prerequisite for the encirclement.

Still, it would be an oversimplification to make the French supreme commander—as has happened so often—into the sole scapegoat. The way to disaster had already been sketched in the original version of the Dyle plan that was met with broad agreement within the French and the British general staffs.[91] Similar to the 1914 Joffre plan, it involved that kind of "big favor" that fully played into the hands of the German encirclement plan. Gamelin's tragic error, instead, is that he took a big gamble without having to do so by settling on this sole solution almost in a deterministic fashion. He managed to broaden the Dyle plan into the Dyle-Breda plan, and, in that way, he magnified the debacle that was already sketched in past planning into a monstrosity.

Around the turn of the century, the operational concept of *manoeuvre à posteriori* had been fashioned in the French army, mainly under the man who would later be Marshal Foch. Accordingly, the operations plan was to be drafted only *after* the start of the fighting, once sufficient information was available on the enemy's presumed intentions. In that way, one could respond to all eventualities at the right time. But the principle of manoeuvre à priori was discarded; it called for spelling out a precise plan even *before* the start of the operation.[92] In Gamelin's Dyle-Breda plan, the principle of manoeuvre à priori had been pushed to extremes. But it would be wrong to charge him alone with this fateful stereotyped approach. World War I had not been decided by bold operational decisions, but by battles of attrition that had been methodically planned in advance. The French and the British army high commands had remained mired in this rigid thinking habit. The Dyle-Breda plan was designed in a similar rigid and schematic fashion. At the start of the fighting, as if by way of blind automatism, the Allies triggered that fateful swing maneuver of the left wing, regardless of whether the Germans would actually attack the way the Allies presumed.

Never before had a French army been so perfectly prepared for an operation. Gamelin had planned everything in detail in advance and had written a precise script. His problem, however, was that the Germans did not go by his script. The real trouble was that the Wehrmacht in the beginning quite deliberately behaved as if they would play the role Gamelin had written for it. His preconceived notion was to be reinforced that the Germans, à la Schlieffen, would again attack with the main effort on the right wing, although this time with Panzers. On 10 May, the start of the German offensive, General Pierre Jacomet, the secretary-general in the War Ministry, stated full of satisfaction: "If you had seen, as I have done this morning, the broad smile of General Gamelin when he told me the direction of the enemy attack, you would feel no uneasiness. The Germans have provided him with just the opportunity he was awaiting."[93]

So, ironically, the French would become the victims of the Schlieffen plan, not in 1914, but in 1940. They were so transfixed by Flanders that they completely lost sight of the Ardennes. Their favorite prejudices about the German neighbor, whom they considered to be uninspired and pedantic, also tripped them up. Such a fantastic idea as attacking through the Ardennes, of all places, using the bulk of German armor, somehow reminiscent of Hannibal's war elephants crossing the Alps, in their opinion might perhaps have sprung from the head of one such as Jules Verne, but not from that of a German general. The French military historian [Pierre] Le Goyet expressed the following judgment on the campaign in the west: "Oddly enough, it must be said that the French—who are said to be continually striving for bold, revolutionary solutions on the basis of their talent for fantasy—were caught up in rigid formalism and schematism, whereas the Germans, considered to be methodical, contemplative, and dogmatic, suddenly turned out to be daring and creative in their thinking and actions. This intellectual surprise . . . was one of the factors that determined the German victory."[94]

The Opposition to the Sickle Cut Plan among the German General Officer Corps

I would like to note that the push to Sedan means creeping up on the enemy by way of an operational endeavor in whose course the God of war might just catch us unawares.[95]

[Alfred] Jodl, Chief of the Wehrmacht Operations Bureau,
talking to Hitler on 13 February 1940.

Alistair Horne, the author of one of the best-known monographs about the campaign in the west, described the Sickle Cut as one of the most "ingenious plans ever devised by a military brain."[96] At the same time, however, he noted that most German generals were not at all aware of that in the spring of 1940 and that they even rejected this "adventurous" idea. An episode that took place in the Reich Chancellery in Berlin on 15 March illustrates just how skeptically the majority of the higher-ranking general officer corps viewed the nucleus of the entire undertaking, the planned operational breakthrough at Sedan. Hitler had summoned von Rundstedt, the commander in chief of Army Group A, his individual field army commanders, and von Kleist and Guderian to a conference. Each was to present his operations plan for the first phase of the coming offensive. Guderian was the last to speak.

In response to one of Hitler's questions, Guderian explained what he would do after having successfully crossed the Meuse River. At that moment, General [Ernst] Busch, the commander in chief of the Sixteenth Army, broke in with the following remark: "Well, I don't think you'll cross the river in the first place!" Hitler was silent and eagerly waited for Guderian's reply. The latter turned to Busch and said: "There's no need for you to do so, in any case."[97] In this connection, Guderian spoke later of a "hard task ahead, in whose successful outcome nobody at that time actually believed, with the exception of Hitler, Manstein and myself."[98] However, Hitler proved to be an extremely unstable ally, Manstein had been neutralized, and along with Guderian that left only a few younger generals who were increasingly aware of the hitherto unsuspected possibilities that slumbered in the German Panzer force.

In the meantime, however, Guderian had found a mighty ally in Halder, who had gone through an astonishing change of opinion. Von Brauchitsch, the commander in chief of the army, also began to subscribe to the increasingly optimistic situation estimates of his chief of staff. A paradoxical situation developed here in which Halder, using the same arguments earlier employed by Manstein, had to defend himself against the same reproaches that he had earlier cited against Manstein's plan. Probably never before did a chief of the German general staff catch such a crossfire of criticism for an operations plan as did Halder in the spring of 1940. The later highly praised Sickle Cut plan was condemned as "crazy and foolhardy," especially by the higher-ranking members of the general officer corps.[99] Halder himself was referred to as the "gravedigger of the Panzer force."[100]

The trauma of the failed Schlieffen plan stigmatized the new operations plan. Once again, everything was obviously to be risked on one throw of the dice and a single encirclement maneuver was to decide an entire campaign. In connection with the criticism of the encirclement mania of the Schlieffen school, it had been noted rather sarcastically that it would be impossible, in the industrial age, "to trap the fighting forces of a big power like a mouse."[101] But that is precisely what was to be attempted once again. The army high command obviously believed, so it was charged, that it could coax the French-British intervention troops into the Belgian-Dutch trap like a mouse and then spring the trap quickly. In that way, something that could not be accomplished in four years of World War I was to be achieved in just a few days.

The most vehement criticism came from Generaloberst [Fedor] von Bock, the commander in chief of Army Group B. He stopped in on Halder in the latter's Berlin apartment and implored him to drop that absurd plan. In the process, he reproached Halder for playing with Germany's destiny.[102] The arguments he cited in this connection sounded entirely plausible: "You will be creeping by 10 miles from the Maginot Line with the flank of your breakthrough and hope the French will watch inertly! You are cramming the mass of the tank units together into the sparse roads of the Ardennes mountain country, as if there were no such thing as air power! And, you then hope to be able to lead an operation as far as the coast with an open southern flank 200 miles long, where stands the mass of the French Army!" He declared that this transcended "the frontiers of reason."[103]

Von Rundstedt, the commander in chief of Army Group A, also suddenly doubted that the operation would be successful. Now one could really tell that Manstein had been transferred. Only his initially disdained idea was rehabilitated, not he himself. The subsequent Generalfeldmarschall writes in his memoirs in the chapter entitled "Sentenced to Being Just a Spectator": "The reader will appreciate that I was not feeling exactly grateful to the body which had banished me into the German hinterland at the very moment when the plan for which I had struggled so long and doggedly was coming to fruition in the west."[104]

That led to the paradoxical situation where this bold plan, in whose feasibility originally only its inventor had believed, was now to be translated into action by, of all people, a general who had been one of the plan's most vehement opponents. Halder had replaced Manstein with von Sodenstern whose thinking ran along absolutely conservative lines. That was to turn into a boomerang for him because the new chief of staff of Army Group A was not willing to go along with Halder's sudden change of mind. In the coming offensive, Sodenstern was to hold a key position because the Panzer divisions, earmarked for the Sickle Cut all the way to the Channel coast, were concentrated in Army Group A. He now did everything he could to frustrate his predecessor's plan, which he considered to be impossible to execute, or at least to weaken it decisively.

Operation Sickle Cut was a jump into the unknown, a venture for which there were no models in the history of war up to that time. Now the fateful events of 1914 seemed to be repeating, when the Younger Moltke shied away from the Schlieffen plan's boldness and, as Generalfeldmarschall [Paul] von Hindenburg criticized later, dared carry it out only in a "watered-down" form.[105] The Sickle Cut could come off successfully only if all the money were placed on one card, the Panzer force. The moment Manstein had been removed from his post, headquarters, Army Group A, was scared by its own courage and, so to speak, wanted to plan "a blitzkrieg in slow motion." The decisive question now was this: Should the Panzer or infantry divisions lead the attack?

Blumentritt, the operations officer on the general staff of Army Group A, claimed that "the motorized formations were to be left behind, the infantry divisions to do the fighting, and the Panzer force to be used only after the tactical breakthrough had been made and when the German forces had gained freedom of action."[106]

Von Rundstedt also indicated to the army high command on 21 February that he believed the "spearheading of offensive by Panzers is no longer justified under present circumstances."[107] Von Sodenstern now became the central opposition figure against the Sickle Cut plan, which his predecessor planned as a Panzer operation. One of his first measures as the new chief of staff of Army Group A was to make his opposition clear in a brief memo that he submitted to von Rundstedt on 22 February. In that paper, he stated unequivocally:

> I am not convinced that even the reinforced Panzer and motorized units will manage to force the crossing over the Meuse with the kind of breadth that is necessary for operational purposes. Yes, I doubt, to begin with, that they will be in a position to cross the Meuse River even only here and there, holding the bridgeheads thus gained until the following infantry divisions would be able to make room for an operational exploitation featuring the necessary breadth and depth. . . . But even if that should come off successfully, the Panzer and motorized units by that time will be so 'exhausted' that sending them deep into the enemy rear areas will no longer offer any chances of success.[108]

Sodenstern summarized his criticism in a detailed memorandum dated 5 March.[109] The arguments cited here sound convincing even today, although we know that the operation had a successful ending:

> 1. A rapid and thus surprising thrust to the Ardennes would presumably seem to be hardly possible "even without any action by the enemy" merely because of the difficult terrain. During the advance through the Ardennes in 1914, in many cases, "not even individual horsemen were able to make headway off the road" in the thick woods. A skillful defender would find it all the more easy to block the narrow forest trails with barriers and mines to stop the *cumbersome* Panzers.

2. One would have to figure that the French army would dispatch mobile delaying units far forward of the Meuse River into the Ardennes. A first clash with those units might be expected already along the Belgian border fortifications.

3. German marching units would constitute an extraordinarily vulnerable target for enemy air raids, above all because there would again and again be long traffic jams in front of the barriers. Just a few hits would suffice to turn the long marching columns "into immobile colossi that would block all roads completely." It would take many hours, perhaps even many days, to "untangle this immobilized mass, doomed to inaction" and to clear the way so as to enable the infantry to advance.

4. The advance of the Panzer divisions would be stopped at the latest along the Meuse River, with superbly developed French fortifications behind it: "The Panzer loses its terror when it runs into a segment of the river that had long been prepared for defense. Its great effect in terms of morale lies out in the open terrain!" The river crossing itself could not be forced by Panzer divisions, having only little infantry, but only by infantry divisions as such. But, moving them up would create a huge traffic problem because all the roads would be clogged with the vehicles of the Panzer divisions.

Even if the Meuse River had been crossed successfully, the Panzer divisions would in the meantime be so worn out that they could be employed for their real mission—the operational-level push into enemy rear areas—only after thorough refitting.

Sodenstern, therefore, demanded that the Twelfth Army would have to be reinforced with one or two Panzer divisions to handle the advance through the Ardennes and the breakthrough at Sedan. The Panzer force would, first of all, have to be held back as an operational reserve that could then punch deep into enemy rear areas through the breach that the infantry knocked into the front.

Sodenstern's line of argument appears completely valid—against the background of what war was considered to be like at that time. In contrast, the Sickle Cut plan was a bold vision because it was based on the intellectual anticipation of that revolution of the operational nature of war that actually materialized in May 1940. Halder told his critics: "It would later on be impossible to justify in the history of war if one were, sometime in the future, to admit that we could have done the job quite easily with the Panzers."[110]

He felt that the outcome of several war games confirmed his opinion. There is a rather interesting statement in his detailed comments on Sodenstern's memorandum: "The mission assigned to the German Army is very difficult. With means dating from the last war, that mission cannot be accomplished in the existing terrain (Meuse) and in view of the existing reciprocal force ratio—especially also as regards artillery. We must resort to extraordinary means and bear the attendant risk."[111] Blunt though this last sentence may sound, it does contain a key concept needed to understand the campaign in the west. It is precisely those "extraordinary means" that are hinted at here and that are concealed behind the word "blitzkrieg."

Conclusion: The Sickle Cut—A Go-for-Broke Gamble

Manstein's Sickle Cut plan has again and again been misinterpreted in military historiography. Looking at it carefully, it is more than just an operations plan; it is actually the substitute for a strategic solution that the political leadership failed to develop. That also explains its astonishing similarity to the Schlieffen plan. Great Britain and France declared war, but they had remained mostly passive in spite of the German attack on Poland. They had no need for seizing the initiative on the operational echelon because, protected by mighty fortifications, they could calmly wait for the economic effects of their naval blockade. After all, they knew that time in the long run would work for them, just as it had in World War I. The image of the "fortress besieged by the world" was now conjured up again in Germany.[112] Only an attempt at an operational-level sally out of the fortress could save it from being "starved out" strategically in time.

Thus, Manstein developed his revolutionary plan. He believed he had discovered that operational gap whose exploitation could bring about an immediate strategic battle of decision, all skeptical predictions to the contrary. But that plan looked like an adventure. After all, it was connected with a tremendous risk, as the reproach was made, because the fate of the Reich was to depend on the outcome of a single operation. Because politician Hitler was playing this go-for-broke game and had thus maneuvered Germany into a catastrophic strategic situation, all the general officer corps could do was to play the operational go-for-broke game. Thus pushed to the brink, there was only one way out: flight forward.

The campaign in the west cannot be fitted into a series of Hitler's preplanned annexations and campaigns of conquest.[113] On the contrary, it was the Western powers that declared war at a most unwelcome point in time for the German leadership and thus forced it to react. The Sickle Cut plan, therefore, does not appear as the result of a long-planned, expansion-oriented blitzkrieg strategy aimed at world rule. Instead, it looks like an operational-level act of desperation to get out of a strategically desperate situation.

But Manstein was not a gambler like Hitler who trusted in his luck based on his mystical belief in providence. He did not play roulette. Instead, he put all his money on one trump card that he alone was sure would win the game on the basis of general staff–style calculation. When the operational intentions of the Allies were exposed after the Mechelen incident and when Manstein's enemy situation estimate had thus been confirmed impressively, the army high command also decided to play this card. Against the background of World War I, the war against the Western sea powers already seemed strategically lost. Therefore, any and all risks were justified on an *oper-*

ational level. Looking at it on the *tactical* level, Sodenstern's objections were indeed plausible; but he was unable to offer any alternative that contained the hope for a rapid strategic decision. Even the chief of the general staff, Halder, who was known as being rather cautious, now declared that an opportunity missed—no matter how minor it was—would be much graver than the "failure of a daring attempt."[114] He commented along these lines to von Bock: "Even if the operation only had a 10% chance of success, I would stick to it. It alone will lead to the enemy's annihilation."[115]

Bock, the commander in chief of Army Group B, was stunned when he learned of the breakthrough at Sedan on 13 May. He wrote in his diary: "The French really do appear to have taken leave of their senses, otherwise they could and must prevent it."[116] But Manstein and along with him Halder had calculated correctly: The Sickle Cut plan was successful precisely *because* it seemed so "crazy." This is why the general officer corps of the Allies failed to anticipate it, and this is why the surprise was so complete.

4

The 1940 Ardennes Offensive

Success springs from speed. The important thing is to forget about your right and left flank and to push quickly into the enemy's depth and to take the defenders again and again by surprise.[1]

From the Attack Order of Panzer Group Kleist

Panzer Group Kleist: A Disputed Operational Experiment

The revolutionary idea of the Sickle Cut could be implemented only with the help of revolutionary methods. The most important of them was the first, autonomous employment of the Panzer force on the operational level.[2] Army Group A rejected the idea of employing the Panzer force "as during the Polish campaign." The army high command, however, was thinking far beyond that and finally introduced a completely new dimension of warfare. During the Polish campaign, there was as yet no autonomous Panzer Corps, not to mention a Panzer Group. Instead, apart from a few exceptions, the Panzers were employed in division strength (according to present-day criteria, in a brigade context), mostly on the tactical echelon. They were to advance in cooperation with nonmotorized forces and merely formed the spearhead for the infantry armies that were marching on foot and whose headquarters directed the operation. Guderian, on the other hand, had emphatically demanded that the Panzer force be completely separated from its umbilical cord with the infantry. Later he criticized the employment of Panzers during the Polish campaign: "One or two [Panzer] divisions cannot yet carry out any independent operation, as could a Panzer Army."[3]

The operational echelon began in the Wehrmacht with the field army and, in special cases, with the corps. To that extent, Guderian's requirement was first realized with the creation of the Panzer Group Kleist, which consisted of five Panzer divisions supported by three motorized infantry divisions. The novel thing in the history of war was that the so-called *Schnelle Truppen* (mobile units), that is to say, the Panzer and the motorized infantry divisions, were to carry out a completely independent attack operation, far out in front of the infantry armies. Panzer Group Hoth, which was under Fourth Army, screened the right flank of Panzer Group Kleist. Army Group A was thus subdivided into two echelons: the mobile units that were to mount an operational

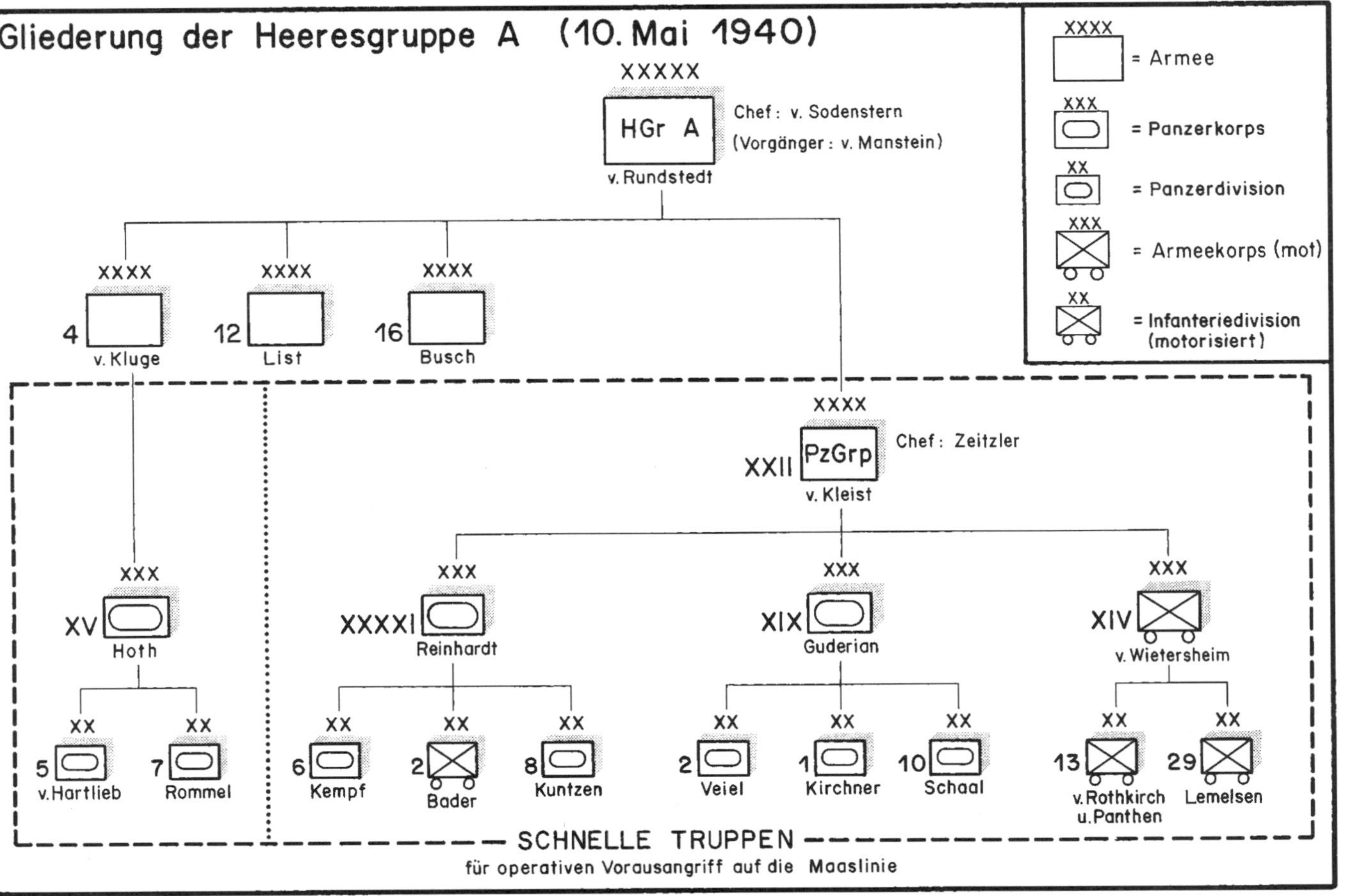
Gliederung der Heeresgruppe A (10. Mai 1940)
XXXXX
HGr A
Chef: v. Sodenstern
(Vorgänger: v. Manstein)
v. Rundstedt
XXXX
4
v. Kluge
XXXX
12
List
XXXX
16
Busch
XXXX
XXII
PzGrp
Chef: Zeitzler
v. Kleist
XXX
XV
Hoth
XXX
XXXXI
Reinhardt
XXX
XIX
Guderian
XXX
XIV
v. Wietersheim
XX
5
v. Hartlieb
XX
7
Rommel
XX
6
Kempf
XX
2
Bader
XX
8
Kuntzen
XX
2
Veiel
XX
1
Kirchner
XX
10
Schaal
XX
13
v. Rothkirch u. Panthen
XX
29
Lemelsen
SCHNELLE TRUPPEN
für operativen Vorausangriff auf die Maaslinie
XXXX = Armee
XXX = Panzerkorps
XX = Panzerdivision
XXX = Armeekorps (mot)
XX = Infanteriedivision (motorisiert)

Organization of Army Group A, 10 May 1940

probing attack, and the infantry armies that would march in their wake and were to secure the conquered territory.

According to Liddell Hart's previously mentioned bullfight comparison, Army Group B on the right wing constituted the red cape of the bullfighter that was supposed to provoke the enemy to rush into the trap. Now, Army Group A, like the bullfighter's sword, was able to thrust into the unprotected flank. Panzer Group Kleist formed the tip of that sword. It had a total of two Panzer corps plus one motorized infantry corps with a total of 41,140 vehicles, including 1,222 battle tanks, or half the German Panzer force. As for personnel, the Panzer Group had 134,370 men.[4] During the advance to the Channel coast, it was furthermore supported by numerous special units, above all by engineers and the I.Flakkorps [I.Flugabwehrkorps, antiaircraft corps] of the Luftwaffe.[5]

Commanding this huge Panzer formation, with its unheard-of dimensions, was a very tough task. Actually, only one man could do the job and that was the Panzer expert Guderian. He had always fought for the idea of employing Panzers independently on the operational level; now, at last, he had an opportunity to prove the feasibility of his idea. But, surprisingly, it was von Kleist who was appointed commanding general of the Panzer Group. The way Guderian put it, he "up to now had not shown himself particularly well-disposed to the armoured force."[6] This ambivalent behavior appears typical of the dilemma of the German general officer corps, which was subdivided into a strong conservative and a smaller progressive wing.

Panzer Group Kleist was by far the strongest motorized major formation that had ever been employed in this context up to this time. Because it comprised half of all German Panzers, it was bound to appear to be just about a "super Panzer army." But, surprisingly enough, it only held a subordinate position in the command structure of Army Group A. It was not even granted the status of a proper field army. Perhaps, for reasons of camouflage, the intention was to avoid the use of the term Panzerarmee (Panzer army). Even looking at it formally, the Gruppe von Kleist (Group von Kleist), mostly called Panzergruppe Kleist (Panzer Group Kleist), was merely something halfway between a corps and an army.[7] For example, von Kleist was entitled only to the rank of Befehlshaber (commander), not the rank of Oberbefehlshaber (commander in chief), as in the case of a "real" army. Panzer Group Kleist was tainted with the odium of something entirely provisional. It merely represented an ad hoc formation to carry out an extremely risky operational experiment.

If the surprise attack had failed along the Meuse, then this would have meant the breakup of the Panzer Group after just a few days. This is why the headquarters was not correspondingly reinforced. The general staff of Panzer Group Kleist corresponded rather to the headquarters of a corps. That meant that just a colonel had to handle one of the most demanding organizational tasks of the entire war. Oberst i.G. [Kurt] Zeitzler, the chief of staff of Panzer Group Kleist, had exactly two months to prepare this gigantic motorized formation for an operation for which

General der Panzertruppe Heinz Guderian. *Bundesarchiv Koblenz [Federal Archives]*

there were no regulations or models. Nor could something like that be practiced during maneuvers for reasons of secrecy. Zeitzler, a short, roundish man with the nickname Kugelblitz (Lightning Ball), proved to be such a hot-shot organizer that he laid the cornerstone for one of the most astonishing careers of the war. Just two years after the end of the campaign in the west, he became Halder's successor as chief of staff of the army.

During the preparations for the offensive, the formations of Panzer Group Kleist were billeted in the Daun-Bernkastel-Idar-Oberstein-Gießen-Marburg area. It had no assembly area of its own; instead, as Zeitzler put it, it was "not the landlord" but only the "guest" of the infantry armies under whose control that sector fell.[8] The commanders in chief of those infantry armies energetically demanded that the Panzer Group be placed under their command because only one headquarters could command in a particular area according to all military logic.

The actual unit employment planning for the offensive appeared to be even more complicated. Panzer Group Kleist was not assigned its own attack sector, such as the

General der Kavallerie Ewald von Kleist. *Bundesarchiv Koblenz [Federal Archives]*

Generalmajor der Infanterie Erwin Rommel (shown here with the rank of Generalfeldmarschall). *Bundesarchiv Koblenz [Federal Archives]*

Panzer armies got later during the Russian campaign. Instead, they were to carry out an operational probing attack ahead of the infantry armies. The entire supply operation necessarily ran through the sectors of those infantry armies. This is why the commanders in chief of the field armies demanded that the Panzer Group would have to be placed under the field army in whose sector it would be attacking. Von Kleist was against that. He was afraid that the infantry armies would try to subordinate and keep

General der Infanterie Hermann Hoth. *Bundesarchiv Koblenz [Federal Archives]*

the Panzer Group on a short leash, so that the infantry divisions could sweep forward in their attack on the tactical level. In that connection, he emphasized that the independent operational mission of the Panzer Group could be accomplished only if it were placed directly under an army group.[9]

But headquarters, Army Group A, was also not exactly happy either with this "cuckoo's egg" that the army high command had slipped into its nest, especially since the Panzer Group was like a foreign body within the otherwise so accustomed organizational structure. And so, von Rundstedt decided on a compromise that henceforth hovered over Panzer Group Kleist like a sword of Damocles. If the Panzer Group were indeed able to maneuver in an operational context far ahead of the infantry armies, then it would be allowed to retain its independence. However, if the attack were to falter and one of the following armies were to catch up, then it would be placed under that army. The fight for operational independence was therefore the motivation that guided von Kleist's command activities.

In the end, however, the command of Army Group A did achieve a paradoxical effect through its discordant decision: The fact that the Panzer formations rushed headlong to the Channel coast, "as if chased by a thousand devils," was not due only to its operational mission. Those Panzer units had started on their flight forward so that the infantry armies moving in their wake would not catch up with them.

The Importance of Logistics

> *If ever the success of an operation depended on supplies, that is the case with our operation.*[10]
>
> Oberst i.G. Zeitzler, Chief of Staff, Panzer Group Kleist, during preparations for Operation Sickle Cut

During the blitzkrieg against the Western powers, all combat actions took place with such tremendous speed that any mistakes during the preparatory phase could hardly be corrected, least of all in the field of logistics. Just what catastrophic consequences some mistakes in the field of supply had can be seen, for example, by the fate of French armor where a considerable part of the dreaded Char B battle tanks had to drop out, not because of hits on their hardly penetrated armor, but due to fuel shortages. To that extent, one of the secrets behind the German success also lies in the perfection with which the problem of logistics was solved during Operation Sickle Cut. The logistic after-action report of Panzer Group Kleist contains the following passage: "Between 10 May and the capture of Calais, there was not a single supply crisis that could not be resolved with the resources of the Group von Kleist, without in any way interfering with command functions."[11]

Zeitzler was by no means considered a Panzer expert. Nevertheless, he created precisely the prerequisites for the subsequent success of Sickle Cut. The decisive aspect, above all, was that he was thinking in operational terms also in the field of logistics. Here was his basic idea: Logistical independence had to go hand-in-hand with the Panzer Group's operational independence. This meant that the Panzer Group must not be placed logistically under any field army; it would have to carry with it all the important supply items it needed to carry out the operation. The conclusion to be drawn from that enabled Zeitzler to figure out a highly simple formula, the *Rucksack-Prinzip* (backpack principle): "To use an analogy relating to railroad operations, you might say: The unit must no longer hand its supplies over to the next-higher duty station for transportation; instead, it must have its supplies with itself as a *backpack* or *hand baggage*."[12]

This principle was implemented by means of the following forward-looking measures:

> In addition to its organic supply elements, the Panzer Group was given three truck transport battalions with a total cargo capacity of forty-eight hundred tons.
>
> All 41,140 vehicles used were loaded to the limit of their cargo capacity with ammunition, rations, and above all fuel.

So-called march movement tank depots were spaced along the planned march movement routes from the assembly areas all the way to the border.

Abundantly stocked supply depots were set up near the border so that the units could draw on them during the operation's first phase.

The required ration, fuel, and ammunition convoys were ready for the advance supply base, planned in Luxembourg, before the start of the offensive.

Success during the initial phase was already preprogrammed on the basis of this list of forward-looking measures. In the following, we want to cover each logistical aspect during the ongoing operation.

Ammunition: This was a revolutionary concept of war when compared to World War I. The movement factor and no longer the firepower factor turned out to be decisive. To that extent, the actual ammunition consumption fell far short of prior calculations. The most glaring example of this was the breakthrough at Sedan where the required quantity amounted to only a fraction of the figure calculated earlier in a war game.[13] Thus, there was never any real serious ammunition shortage. The only exception was the bitter fighting for Stonne (south of Sedan), where the 10th Panzer Division and the Infanterieregiment Großdeutschland (Infantry Regiment Großdeutschland) had to beat off what probably was the most dangerous French counterattack. This is where an antitank ammunition shortage developed. Ju 52 transport aircraft turned up in this critical situation and dropped ammunition containers by parachutes.[14]

Fuel: The campaign in the west developed into mobile warfare that far-ranging encirclement maneuvers decided. This kind of operations command was possible only because fuel supply for the mechanized and motorized shock units worked smoothly. Retired Graf von Kielmansegg, who was the supply officer in charge of logistics for the 1st Panzer Division, looking back described the fuel supply movements during the advance to the Meuse River as "one of the toughest tasks" that he ever had to accomplish during the war.[15]

The main problem was a conflict between tactical and logistical requirements. Zeitzler demanded that all vehicles must pass not only the border of Luxembourg but also the Belgian border fully loaded with fuel. But, at the same time, the requirement of the operations officer of the 1st Panzer Division, Major i.G. [Walther] Wenck, was strictly to adhere to the time frame on the march movement table. There was to be no stopping on the move.

Kielmansegg used an improvised system of gasoline can delivery to resolve that conflict. The fuel quantities needed for all the marching groups were calculated precisely and were then stockpiled in gas cans at the planned tactical rest halts along the hundred-kilometer march to the border. In addition, numerous trucks carrying gas cans were inserted into the spearhead of the march movement group. At suitable points, gas cans were simply handed to the crews as their vehicles slowly drove past. Thus, the next stop could be used for refueling—the empty gas cans were simply thrown out on the roadside at designated points. There they were picked up and refilled in the next fuel dump. In that way, it was possible to meet both requirements at the same time: all vehicles drove through the Ardennes fully gassed up with fuel, and it was not necessary to interrupt the march movement to refuel.

During the rapid advance from the Meuse River to the Channel coast, it did become necessary in some cases to airlift fuel forward. The biggest airlift was to the Belval airfield near Charleville after the widening of the bridgeheads beyond the Meuse. On just one day, four hundred tons of fuel were air-delivered here.[16]

Repair: Repair was the only serious problem connected with logistics.[17] The 41,140 vehicles of Panzer Group Kleist had to cover a distance of at least six hundred kilometers all the way to the Channel coast. The actual mileage clocked was much longer because the Panzers were constantly being shifted back and forth. It so happened that by the end of the operation some Panzer formations had breakdowns of up to 50 percent. The astonishingly short time the vehicles spent undergoing repairs offset the astonishingly large number of temporarily broken-down vehicles. Of course, it was a big help that important spare parts were flown in. For example, just a few days after the fall of Dunkirk, the army was again able to start off on the second major operation of the campaign in the west, Case Red, with combat-ready formations.

Summarizing, one can say that while there are a series of publications on the Wehrmacht's logistical problems during the Russian campaign or the African campaign, there are hardly any such investigations on the campaign in the west. That seems to be all the more astonishing because there are a wealth of files handed down to us on that score. Logistics can become a topic only when there are breakdowns; that was not an issue during the campaign in the west. That there were no problems, however, was also due to the astonishingly short duration of the campaign, which actually had been planned as a long war. Suddenly, it was over, and the troops were facing a gigantic mountain of unused supply goods. During the 1941 campaign in the east, the situation was the exact reverse.

Planning the Offensive—A Preprogrammed Chaos

The moment von Manstein had been transferred, von Rundstedt suddenly developed considerable doubts as to the feasibility of the Sickle Cut idea. Those doubts were further reinforced by the warnings from his own field army commanders and his new chief of staff, Sodenstern, about a senseless "sacrifice" of the Panzer force. So, he decided on a two-way solution that ran completely counter to the basic operational idea to put all the money on the Panzer force. Halder actually had made provisions for allowing the Panzer divisions and the motorized divisions of a first echelon to rush on ahead into the attack, something that would have required a rather generous allocation of roads.

Instead, Army Group A wanted to proceed on *two tracks.* The infantry divisions were to attack parallel to the Panzer divisions to achieve the crossing of the Meuse

River, which the Panzer divisions were not believed capable of achieving.[18] The road net in the Ardennes, however, was not sufficient for a simultaneous advance. This ambivalent decision created a traffic chaos and—even without enemy action—would already have caused the Sickle Cut plan to fail in the Ardennes. Headquarters, Army Group A, it so happened, had made two grave operational-level planning mistakes.

Allocation of March Movement Roads

Panzer Group Kleist had 39,373 wheeled vehicles, 1,222 battle tanks, and 545 other tracked vehicles, a total of 41,140 motor vehicles. Including all of the subordinate formations, that added up to a theoretical march movement length of 1,540 kilometers. Lined up on a single road, the march movement column would have stretched from the border of Luxembourg straight across the entire Reich all the way to Königsberg in East Prussia.[19] To that extent, it seems difficult to understand why headquarters, Army Group A, gave that gigantic armada of vehicles only four march movement roads for the advance through the Ardennes. During the first phase, this meant that the Panzer Group had to make up a marching column of almost four hundred kilometers on four different roads—this in the face of a tremendous threat from the enemy's air force. Von Kleist protested against that several times, but he did not get his way even with his minimum requirement to give the Panzer Group at least a fifth road. The official explanation—that there were hardly any Panzer roads in this sector of the Ardennes—seems rather threadbare. The *Military Geography Overview of Belgium and Adjacent Territories,* published by the army general staff, said: "Compared to the number of inhabitants, the road net of the Ardennes region is well developed, the numerous country roads and dirt roads are in very good condition throughout."[20]

In reality, the commanders in chief of the infantry armies were intent on jealously guarding their ownership of roads. The much-cited "eye of the needle" of the Ardennes sprang not so much from the numerous ravines and passes that had to be negotiated but rather from the fact that Army Group A had squeezed this gigantic mass of vehicles belonging to Panzer Group Kleist into a hoselike combat sector. The second planning mistake had an even more fateful effect.

Employment by Echelons Rather Than by Wings

After a quick push through the Ardennes, the Panzer Group was to gain "the west bank of the Meuse River in a surprise attack."[21] Parallel to each other, the Panzer Corps Guderian was to head for Sedan and Panzer Corps Reinhardt was to head to Monthermé, twenty-five kilometers to the north. In light of this arrangement, the deployment of forces already appeared to be preprogrammed. Von Kleist, therefore, planned employment by wings, with the two Panzer corps *next* to each other.

Southern Wing: Panzer Corps Guderian was to push to Sedan on the two left-hand roads.

Northern Wing: Panzer Corps Reinhardt was to attack toward Monthermé on the two right-hand roads.

Motorized Corps Wietersheim was to follow behind the two Panzer corps as the second echelon.

Coordinating with the field armies, in whose deployment area the Panzer Group was located, Army Group A ordered employment by echelons, in other words, the individual corps would be echeloned *behind* each other:

Panzer Corps Guderian (XIX Corps) was to be the 1st engagement (= 1st echelon) and push toward Sedan on all four march routes.

Panzer Corps Reinhardt (XXXXI Corps) was to follow as the second echelon at an interval of 180 kilometers. The right wheel to Monthermé was planned only during the last phase of the advance through the Ardennes in order to reach the assembly area for the Meuse River crossing.

Motorized Corps Wietersheim (XIV Corps) [General der Infanterie Gustav Anton von Wietersheim] was earmarked as the third echelon. It followed at an interval of about 330 kilometers from the lead elements.

This decision caused misunderstanding in Panzer Corps Reinhardt. In the end, both Panzer corps were to cross the Meuse River simultaneously, down to the minute, on the fourth day of the offensive to make use of the Luftwaffe raid into the Sedan-Monthermé area. But how could this be done if Panzer Corps Reinhardt was to advance during the first phase of the approach march not next to but rather behind the Panzer Corps Guderian?

Army Group A, however, refused to allow both Panzer corps to attack side-by-side by wings. The reason was that both would already have to be positioned next to each other in the deployment area. Their past assembly areas had been located behind each other before the order was issued to organize the Kleist Group. Headquarters of Twelfth and Sixteenth Armies, however, did not want any further change in this space arrangement within their deployment area.[22]

The two arguments that they advanced did not sound exactly convincing. First of all, they were afraid that the camouflage measures would thus be endangered. In reality, however, the constant changes in deployment directives again and again led to transfers, especially of the Panzer divisions, although that would not have been a problem. Even more threadbare, however, appears the justification that regrouping an entire Panzer corps in the deployment area would be very awkward and laborious as well as time-consuming. And so it happened that this unavoidable regrouping was not performed calmly far away from the enemy in the rear areas. Instead, a wheeling movement to the right, laterally with respect to the enemy, was to be made in the middle of the attack in the Ardennes woods, so that the former second echelon, Panzer Corps Reinhardt, would be placed parallel and next to Panzer Corps Guderian. That was the only way there could be a simultaneous attack across the Meuse River. That decision proved to be a serious mistake. It meant that traffic chaos was already preprogrammed even without any action on the part of the enemy.

The commanders in chief of the Twelfth and Sixteenth Armies, [Generaloberst Wilhelm] List and [General der Infanterie Ernst] Busch, refused to make any further concessions to Panzer Group Kleist, which they felt to be something like a thorn in the flesh. In their opinion, this isolated Panzer attack was doomed to fail anyway. If the Panzers had gotten stuck along the Meuse River, then the infantry divisions would come to the rescue and force the Meuse River crossing. Only then would the Panzer divisions be able to jump off for their thrust deep into the enemy's rear area. However, headquarters, Army Group A, refused to change the existing deployment plan in favor of Panzer Group Kleist.

The Advance through the Ardennes: A Near Catastrophe

The Problem of Time

The marching columns of Panzer Group Kleist were to cover about 170 kilometers on winding roads from the German border all the way to the Meuse River: 50 kilometers through Luxembourg territory, 100 kilometers through Belgium, and 10 to 20 kilometers from the French border to the Meuse River. In so doing, they had to punch through the following barrier lines:

1. the Luxembourg border barriers
2. the first Belgian fortification line immediately behind the border at Martelange
3. the second Belgian fortification line between Libramont-Neufchâteau-Rulles
4. the valley of the Semois River at Bouillon
5. the French border fortifications made up of pillboxes camouflaged as residential homes (*ligne des maisons fortes* [line of blockhouses])
6. that was to be followed by the most difficult task, the crossing of the seventy-meter-wide Meuse River at Sedan, with the pillboxes of the extended Maginot Line behind it

Luxembourg, of course, was not defended militarily. However, the government had ordered a large number of barriers to be erected along the border, and removing them was quite time-consuming for the German engineers. The Belgian Ardennes were screened by a special unit, the Ardennes Light Infantry. In addition, the French army ordered numerous cavalry units to advance into the Ardennes on 10 May to engage the German attackers in a delaying action. The real problem of that blitz operation was

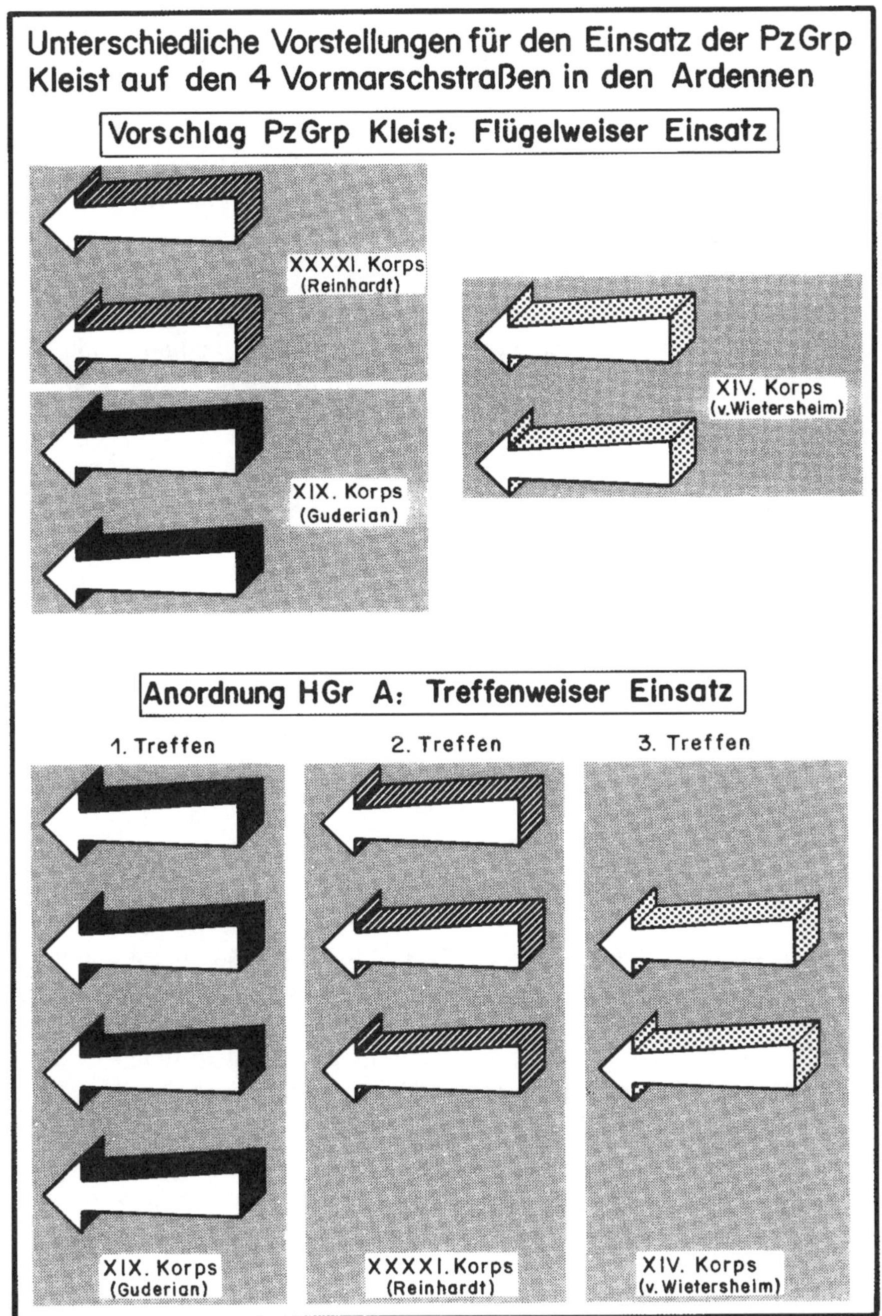

Differing Ideas for the Employment of Panzer Group Kleist on the Four Roads of Advance in the Ardennes

that all these assignments, including the Meuse River crossing, had to be accomplished within four days. Otherwise, the French might be able to move reserves up to the river in time. Graf von Kielmansegg made the following comment on that point in retrospect:

> In planning a major attack operation, an offensive in other words, such as perhaps later on Operation 'Barbarossa,' then, in the course of the general advance of the operation, one need not be accurate down to the last minute. But this was the case here and we all realized that. If we were not across the Meuse River in the evening of 13 May, then the whole thing would fail because the French would now realize that the main effort was here, at Sedan, and not in the north, at Eben Emael, where it was to be simulated. But then the enemy would still have been able to react in time by means of an operational-level move.[23]

With his sixth sense for posterlike slogans, Guderian had ordered the following to be drummed into his soldiers: "In three days to the Meuse, on the fourth day across the Meuse!"[24] During this impetuous advance, the German formations were pressed for time. This meant that in reality they were not the hunters but rather the hunted.

The Traffic Problem

Reinhardt had run through a map exercise on 24 April that only too clearly revealed the design flaw in the deployment plan.[25] Panzer Corps Reinhardt was to pass Panzer Corps Guderian, which was marching ahead in the first echelon, on the right so that it would reach the Meuse River together with Panzer Corps Guderian. However, this lateral movement made it necessary temporarily to switch into the northern neighbor's combat sector. That, in turn, meant that the infantry corps advancing to the right next to Guderian would have to be stopped on reaching the Belgian-Luxembourg border so that Panzer Corps Reinhardt would then be able to veer out to the right through the corridor that would then be developing. What was to be done if the first echelon became jammed? Reinhardt believed that such a complicated maneuver constituted an irresponsible and unjustifiable risk, especially in an absolutely rough sector of the Ardennes. Just four days before the start of the offensive, he was confronted with an additional disaster message. Due to a renewed change in the past deployment plan, the corps that he commanded was now to be given only two march routes. That meant that, looking at the second echelon, only the 6th Panzer Division and the 2d Motorized Infantry Division were to advance on both of the northern march routes, whereas the 8th Panzer Division was shuttled back into the third echelon.

As Reinhardt put it, the march planning done by Army Group A "collapsed quickly, like a house of cards" on the very first day.[26] The moment the leading marching groups of the second echelon had lined up on 10 May, they ran smack into the tail end of the first echelon that was already ten hours late. Around noon, Guderian's three

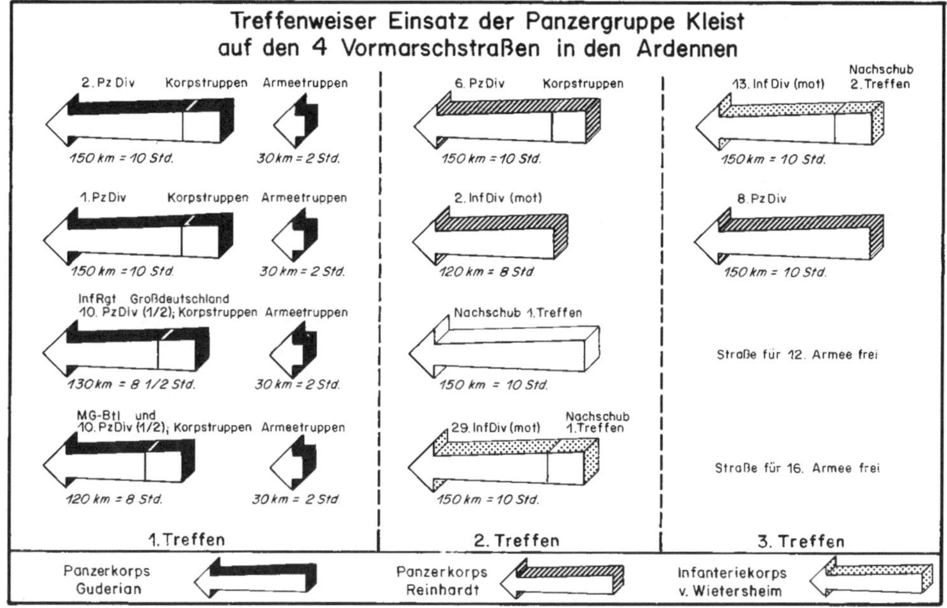

Piecemeal Employment of Panzer Group Kleist on the Four Roads of Advance in the Ardennes

Panzer divisions were already fighting on Belgian territory, but the main body of Panzer Corps Reinhardt was still east of the Rhine, and the Motorized Corps Wietersheim had not even left its assembly area around Marburg and Gießen.[27] Von Kleist, therefore, felt that the success of the operation was already at risk the way it was set up. He ordered the 2d Panzer Division to clear the northern march route on the next day so that Panzer Corps Reinhardt would be able to advance on the right, next to Panzer Corps Guderian. Now came real trouble because this gigantic rally of vehicles had been squeezed together on such a few roads. On top of it all, an erroneous report from the Luftwaffe about a presumed threat to the southern flank from French tank forces created confusion. Guderian felt that he should redirect the 10th Panzer Division; as a result the carefully prepared march movement plan also fell apart on the two southern roads.[28]

The vehicle convoys of the first echelon were caught in a miles-long traffic jam in the Ardennes on 11 May. Apart from the fighting against Belgian and French units, they had to remove barriers or go around them, and improvised bridges had to be built in place of the destroyed river crossings. Again and again, the narrow gorges were blocked by tremendous demolition craters with diameters of 15 to 20 meters and depths of 6 to 8 meters; getting across them was a time-consuming task for the engineers. In other words, on that day, only the 1st Panzer Division was able to stick to its schedule and advance in the evening all the way to Bouillon near the French border. The spearhead of Reinhardt's Panzer units, however, was still on German soil, caught in a traffic jam just before the Luxembourg border.

On the next day, 12 May, there was from time to time a complete breakdown of march movement traffic on the right wing. A hopeless mess developed because vehicle convoys of the infantry divisions again and again forced their way out of the right-hand neighbor's combat sector into the wider roads that were set aside for the Panzer divisions. The infantry units acted like rivals of the Panzer units and did not want them to have all the glory. That resulted in jumbled confusion on the Ardennes trails that turned out to be worse than the disaster scenario that Reinhardt had painted earlier in his war games as a kind of devil's advocate. Instead of immediately being able to start the race to the Meuse River with Guderian's Panzers, his units were senselessly caught in a traffic jam for two days on German soil. The first vehicle of Reinhardt's 6th Panzer Division crossed the Luxembourg boundary only on the third day, at 0600 on 12 May.

Exactly what Reinhardt had feared now happened when this division wanted to wheel to the right in the Ardennes to position itself next to Guderian's 2d Panzer Division. The VI Corps (Infantry), advancing to his right contrary to agreement, did not stop at the Belgian border to clear the corridor he demanded for the complicated wheeling maneuver of the Panzer Corps. Instead, just like the III Corps (Infantry), it used the Panzer roads to push its own divisions forward. When Reinhardt's Panzer units on their highways wanted to push off the vehicles of the infantry divisions that had penetrated here quite arbitrarily to pass them by, the chaos was complete. Here is what the war diary of the 6th Panzer Division says: "The Division was torn apart during the advance by elements of the 2d Panzer Division, as well as the 16th, 23d, 24th and 32d Infantry divisions that slipped in between. In the afternoon and evening, there was no longer any clear picture as to where the march movement groups and their individual formations were located. It was also impossible to get a clear picture by radio because radio communications were poor due to the great distances and radio interference."[29]

Now a general staff officer had to try to untangle the mess from his aircraft. Two columns were next to each other in a traffic jam in segments of the march routes; there was no way of getting through because the vehicles were often bumper to bumper. Reinhardt, the commanding general of that corps, had to hop on a motorcycle to get up front. In this general confusion, it was not only the view of the German units that was lost, but also the distinction between friend and foe. For example, the 6th Panzer Division was warned by its right-wing neighbor about an enemy tank attack from the flank. Immediately, all available guns of the 1st Flak Battalion were ordered into position at Willerzie. Before the firefight began, it was found that those had been armored scout cars of a German reconnaissance battalion.[30]

In the meantime, the operational mistakes made in the decisions of Army Group A had caused the hitherto biggest known traffic jam in Europe. On 12 May the convoys

Traffic jam in the Ardennes on 12 May. *Bundesarchiv Koblenz [Federal Archives]*

were jammed up on the northern (right-hand) advance route up to 250 kilometers from the Meuse River, across French, Belgian, Luxembourg, and German territory, all the way back to the Rhine. March movement traffic flowed only in the center where the 1st Panzer Division formed the spearhead. Here again, there was fear of a raid by the enemy air force. A German officer reported: "Again and again, I cast a worried look up at the bright-blue sky; my Division now presents an ideal attack target because it is not deployed and it is forced to move slowly forward on a single road. But we could not spot a single French reconnaissance arcraft."[31]

During the first few days of the offensive, the air forces of the Allies were presented with the unique opportunity on a silver platter to smash a major portion of the German Panzer force in the Ardennes. But, as if by a miracle, the German Panzers were not bothered. Just why the French and British aircraft remained away is something that will bc looked into later.

The near catastrophe in the Ardennes certainly had consequences as far as the German Panzer force was concerned. The Panzer generals noticed that their primary opponent, paradoxically enough, was not the Belgian and French delaying forces but rather the anti-Panzer way in which Army Group A and the infantry armies were being commanded. Their mistaken decisions could have turned the Ardennes into the "graveyard of the German Panzer Force."[32] In this way, confidence in the competence of the higher command was destroyed in the Ardennes. This again meant that the thrust to the Channel coast turned into a "free-wheeling operation" conducted phase by phase. Increasingly, the Panzer generals ignored the instructions from their superiors, whom they considered to be reactionary, and instead were oriented by the operational guiding idea of the Sickle Cut. In that way, in spite of his exile, Manstein still was invisibly in control.

Finally, we come to the question of why—in spite of a completely erroneous operational deployment plan—the so-called 1940 Ardennes Offensive grew into one of the biggest successes in modern military history. It was due to the flexibility of the middle- and lower-echelon leadership that, out of all this chaos, the Meuse River crossing nevertheless came off successfully both at Sedan and Monthermé on 13 May. In the following section, the advance through the Ardennes will be described from the perspective of the division that attacked in the very focal point of events.

The Impact of Operational-Level Mistakes at the Tactical Level: The Example of the 1st Panzer Division

Among all the German army's 157 divisions, the 1st Panzer Division was considered to be number one due to its modern equipment. It had been assigned the best section for its advance so that it would be able to reach Sedan in time to attack "at the point of main effort of the main effort itself." This division was particularly hard-pressed by the time factor. More than all other divisions, it had to meet Guderian's challenge: "I demand that you go sleepless for at least three nights if that should be necessary."[33]

Graf von Kielmansegg reports that this was not an empty figure of speech. At that time in his capacity as a general staff officer in charge of the 1st Panzer Division's supplies, his job was to bring along twenty thousand tablets of Pervitin. This doping preparation—to put it in modern language—was to be administered to the drivers during their grinding nighttime march movements through the Ardennes to keep them awake longer.[34] Mental doping was much more effective. All soldiers, down to the very last assistant gunner, knew what was at stake. Above all, it had been drilled into them over and over again that every minute counted in the race to the Meuse River.

The Raid against Martelange

Somebody blew a pea-whistle just once at 0535 on 10 May along the border in Wallendorf and a squad of German soldiers rushed across the Sauer Bridge to disarm the Luxembourg border gendarmes. That set the machinery of war in motion for the 1st Panzer Division. The clock began to tick, and it would dictate all future actions. The important thing was to lose as little time as possible while getting through the border barriers. During the preparations for the offensive, German engineers had built models of the concrete barrier on the bridge across the Sauer River to practice the blasting operation and to dose the individual demolition charges in such a way that only the barrier but not the bridge would be destroyed. This was also a problem with the less stable Our River bridge, and it is why a wooden ramp was built to make it possible to bridge the barrier itself. The construction of an additional three bridges was also begun. All the necessary material had been well camouflaged beforehand in Wallendorf so that these bridges were ready after about two hours.[35]

Immediately after the start of the attack, an advance detachment consisting of one motorcycle company plus three armored reconnaissance cars crossed the Our River via a ford. Just three hours later, it had passed through Luxembourg and was approaching Martelange on the Belgian border. As the first armored reconnaissance car approached the destroyed bridge over the Sauer River, it drew fire. About five minutes later, Oberstleutnant [Hermann] Balck, the commander of Schützenregiment 1 (1st Rifle Regiment), arrived at the scene of action. It is astonishing that a staff officer in his position could be found so far forward, but the decision he made once he arrived seems more surprising. Balck ordered the motorcycle company that was under fire in Martelange immediately to attack across the river from the move and frontally to drive the enemy off the hill they were holding above Martelange.

In this attack, a number of factors had to be considered. It was to be a pure infantry assault, with no support by heavy weapons, such as Panzers, artillery, or the Luftwaffe. The three armored reconnaissance cars, with their 2-cm cannon, could not provide any essential fire support either because they were held in check by one Belgian T-13 tank with its dangerous 4.7-cm cannon. That left only a couple of machine guns that went into position along the slope. The attacking force—an infantry company of

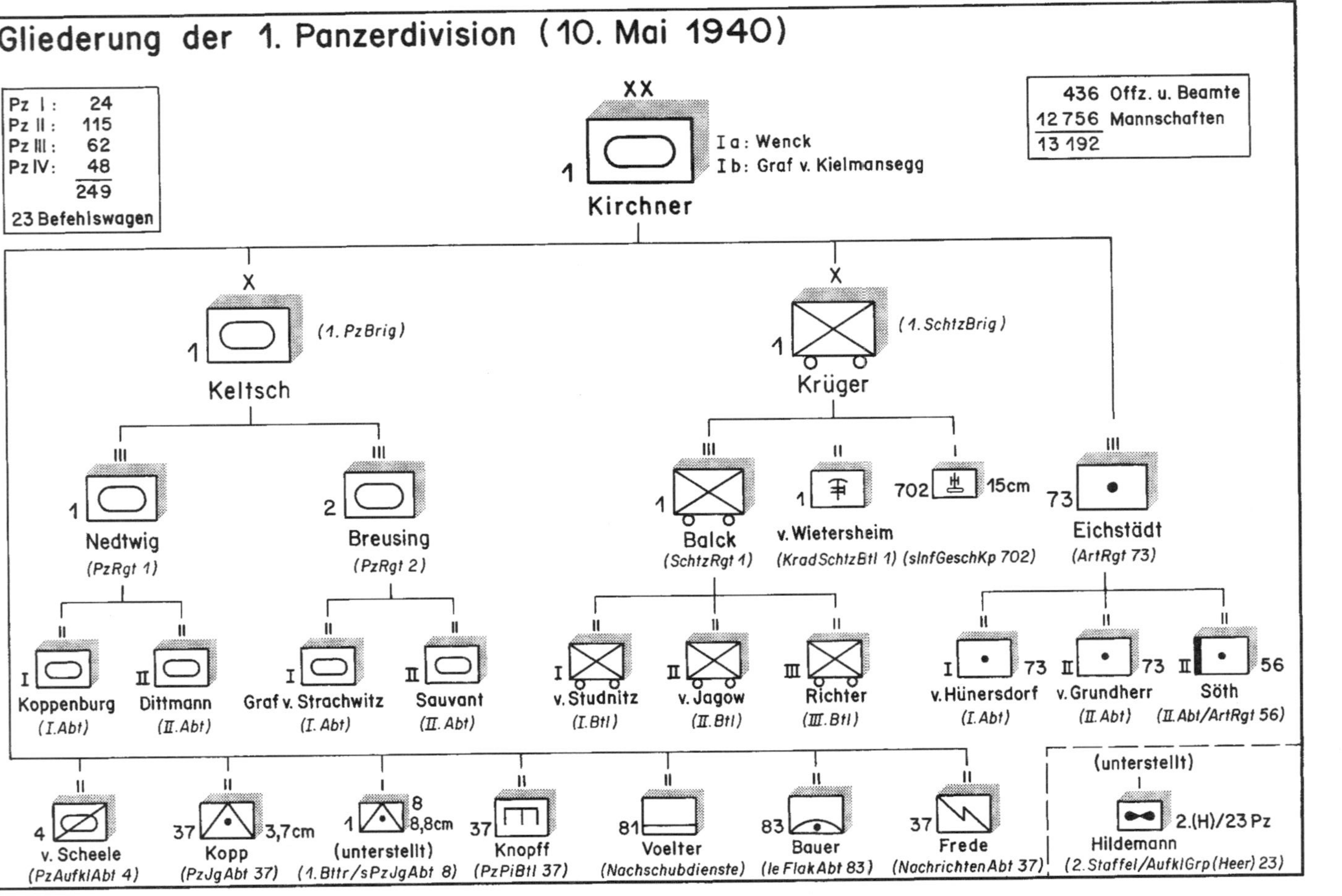

Organization of 1st Panzer Division, 10 May 1940

about a hundred men—was numerically about as strong as the defending force, which was the 4th Company, 2d Battalion, 1st Ardennes Light Infantry Regiment. This unit had ensconced itself in the pillboxes and field fortifications and was protected by minefields and obstacles. The action was to be carried out from the move without any preparation. That meant wading through the Sauer River, pushing through Martelange, and then mounting a frontal attack, uphill, across two hundred meters of open terrain against the positions of an enemy who was entrenched on a hill above the city.

This "suicide mission" turned into a resounding success. When the Germans suddenly stormed up the slope, the Belgians were so surprised by this kind of "crazy" behavior that quite a few of them took flight. Soon thereafter, the company of Ardennes Light Infantry began to retreat.[36] This first fight was to set an example for the course of the entire campaign. The recipe for the attacker's success was simply this: speed and surprise. To that extent, actually, all of Operation Sickle Cut was a raid of operational dimensions, with entire Panzer divisions being used like assault detachments.

Unexpected Resistance at Bodange

From Martelange, the Germans pushed farther to the west, through the valley of the Sauer River that tapers like a funnel. The hill of Bodange rises at the valley's end, something like a cork plugging a bottleneck. The Sauer River and the Basseille, which joins it here, both flow around the locality that at that time consisted of about a dozen farmsteads. Thus, Bodange resembled "a castle, surrounded by both water courses which formed something like a moat."[37] Only one company of Ardennes Light Infantry defended the village, but it was very cleverly employed.

The 1st Panzer Division basically had two possibilities for taking Bodange. It would have had to wait into the evening hours if it had selected a deliberate attack after preparation with Panzers and artillery. This was because the engineers were able to finish the bridge at Martelange only around 1730. On the other hand, air support could be called in only in an emergency for overriding operational reasons. After all, German aircraft were not initially to be employed in the Ardennes but in northern Belgium and Holland to simulate the point of main effort of the offensive there. So, under enormous pressure of time to do that which in this campaign was done again and again with astonishing success, a hasty attack was made with insufficient forces but exploiting the element of surprise. It was believed that things would go as easily as they had gone earlier in Martelange.

The men of the reinforced Kradschützen-Bataillon 1 (1st Motorcycle Battalion) advanced on foot through the valley of the Sauer River into the defile of Bodange. Shortly before, at Wisembach, they ran into a combat patrol screen that withdrew immediately. That gave the enemy enough warning, and the element of surprise was lost. As the Germans tried to approach Bodange around 1250, the Belgians suddenly opened fire from their elevated positions so that the attackers had to withdraw with casualties.

During the course of the afternoon, the Ardennes Light Infantry unit was then squeezed in Bodange from all sides. But all attacks failed; it appeared impossible to take Bodange only with infantry. But then it was possible to bring up a few heavy weapons across a little bridge that was discovered near Martelange. However, neither the 3.7-cm antitank guns nor the light infantry guns (7.5 cm) were able to accomplish anything against the thick walls of the Ardennes houses. The four field howitzers that in the meantime had opened fire from Warnach were also only inadequate artillery support. The turning point came when four 8.8-cm guns were used, and they were able to knock out the most important resistance nests in a short time. Now, the 3d Battalion, 1st Rifle Regiment, assaulted Bodange and, after bitter house-to-house fighting, took the place around 1900. The Ardennes Light Infantry had thus managed to stop the advance of the 1st Panzer Division for six hours.

That was certainly not the end of the trouble at Bodange. Around 1930 an engineer company began to build a military bridge directly south of the demolished bridge over the Sauer River. Because the access ran across a swampy meadow, it was also necessary to build a corduroy road, a job for which several prisoners were used. But the Belgian lieutenant Autphenne, who had been in command of the 3d Platoon in Bodange, protested with striking emphasis against the way his men were being employed in this fashion. That made the Germans suspicious, and after some further questioning, they found out that a minefield was in that meadow.

As Autphenne later explained, surprisingly, the German engineer vehicles had driven to the river across that meadow without triggering any detonations. The explanation was that the mines had been laid in the autumn of 1939 and had in the meantime become useless or had simply sunk into the soft soil. Fortunately, until that moment, only lightweight vehicles had driven over the mined meadow. Graf von Kielmansegg compared this episode to a "ride across Lake Constance," where—as the story has it—a rider was supposed to have ridden across the thin ice of the frozen lake.[38] This led to another delay because the engineers had, first of all, to remove the mines before they could continue with their bridge-building job. The first vehicle rolled across the bridge only at 2115.[39]

Later the Germans kept wondering why the Ardennes Light Infantry had so heroically defended the little village of Bodange, of all places, whereas otherwise they only fought a delaying action and would frequently withdraw after the first exchange of fire. They learned the answer to the mystery only after the end of the war. The defense was an unwanted side effect of an airborne landing operation that took place simultaneously in the area to the rear of Bodange.

The Niwi Airborne Landing Operation and the Friction Problem

Everything in war is very simple, but the simplest thing is difficult. The difficulties accumulate and end by producing a kind of friction that is inconceivable unless one has experienced war. . . . Friction is the only concept that more or less corresponds to the factors that distinguish real war from war on paper.[40]

Clausewitz, *Vom Kriege* (On War)

The timetable for the first day of the attack had always been considered rather skeptically. Consideration was given to employing airborne troops in the enemy's rear areas to open up the Belgian border fortifications from behind. However, all paratroop units and almost all Ju 52 transport aircraft had already been earmarked for employment with Army Group B during the first day of the attack in the north. Then Göring got the extraordinary idea of using Fi 156 liaison aircraft for this purpose. This light aircraft, the famous Fieseler Stork, required only an extremely short takeoff run (85 meters) and an even shorter landing run (27 meters), so that any large meadow could be used as a landing strip. The problem was that a Fieseler Stork could only carry two men in addition to the pilot, but four hundred men had been planned for this commando mission. This meant that one hundred Fieseler Storks would have to be used to transport the earmarked units in two waves with a round trip of two hours. This involved two companies of the 3d Battalion, Großdeutschland Infantry Regiment, reinforced by assault engineers. How could such a big body of aircraft fly over the enemy's positions without drawing fire? The Niwi Airborne Mission, which called for an outstanding aircraft to be used in a completely alien role, thus was nothing but an adventurous-looking improvisation, accepting incalculable risks. It absolutely symbolized that system of expedients that the military command in this particular campaign used to bridge the gap between bold objectives and inadequate resources.

The code name Niwi certainly did not mean *Nicht wissen* (not knowing), as many soldiers trained for this strictly secret mission had come to believe. Instead, it was made up of the initial letters of the two Belgian localities where the landing was to take place, *Ni*ves and *Wi*try.[41]

The Northern Group (11th Company under Hauptmann Krüger) was to land at Nives to support the advance of the 2d Panzer Division. The Southern Group (10th Company) was personally led by Oberstleutnant [Eugen] Garski, the battalion commander. It was to be put down at Witry in order to advance toward Bodange in the attack sector of the 1st Panzer Division.

The mission for the airborne landing operation read as follows:

1. Cut signal communications and message links on the Neufchâteau-Bastogne and Neufchâteau-Martelange roads;
2. prevent the approach of reserves from the Neufchâteau area; and
3. facilitate the capture of pillboxes and the advance as such by exerting pressure against the line of pillboxes along the border from the rear.[42]

The Fieseler Storks took off from their airfields near Bitburg around 0520 on 10 May. Punctually, at 0535, they flew across the border north of Wallendorf. They had to cross

Luxembourg in a low-level flight at an altitude of 15 to 30 meters, which made orientation more difficult. Nevertheless, they passed the Belgian border at Martelange according to plan at around 0550. Exactly at 0600, the aircraft of Garski landed at Witry on the selected landing strip a few hundred meters north of Traimont. As he climbed out of the aircraft, Garski found to his surprise that only five aircraft had arrived.

Just ten minutes earlier, a grotesque sequence of "frictions" had taken place precisely at the critical point, the crossing of the enemy positions along the Belgian border. The Northern Group under Krüger suddenly drew small-arms fire in the area of Martelange, whereupon the pilot of the lead aircraft tried to evade. He lost his way and continued to fly in the wrong direction.

Faithful to the saying it never rains but it pours, the northern group's navigation error also had negative repercussions on the southern group. While flying through a fog bank, the latter had suddenly lost contact between the first five aircraft and the following fifty-one aircraft. Suddenly, however, the latter again spotted a group of Fieseler Storks, right in front. Assuming that this was their own group, they simply followed it. Immediately thereafter, both formations landed at Léglise, about 15 kilometers south of the designated landing site of the Northern Group and about 9 kilome-

Motorcycle infantrymen "mounted." *Bundesarchiv Koblenz [Federal Archives]*

Crash landing of Fieseler Stork (Fi 156) during Operation Niwi on 10 May. *Helmuth Spaeter (Großdeutschland Archives)*

ters south of the Southern Group's landing ground. Some aircraft cracked up during the landing and caught fire. In addition, the groups were completely jumbled up. Krüger had his hands full rounding up his widely scattered soldiers. In the meantime, he ordered several vehicles to be confiscated so that in a motley convoy they could push on northward to the designated action area. At the exit of the village of Léglise, however, he ran into a Belgian patrol, plus some T-15 armored cars. The Germans immediately had to dismount from their vehicles. Krüger and his men then made their way on foot to the north and reached Witry shortly after 1300, where Garski had long been in action with the remainder of the Southern Group.

As he landed around 0600, Garski had initially been able to round up only nine men. Nevertheless, he immediately blocked the Witry-Neufchâteau road "like a highwayman." At last, the second wave arrived according to plan at 0800, so that he was able to beat off a Belgian counterthrust from the Witry area. Early in the afternoon, after a protracted odyssey, Krüger turned up with the men of the first wave that had landed at Léglise by mistake. With its support, Garski continued the advance into the rear of the Belgian border fortifications at Bodange. At 1730 his lead elements ran into the leading elements of the 1st Panzer Division at Fauvillers. This meant that the mission had been accomplished.

In the meantime, the following had been happening to the northern group: The second wave under Leutnant Obermeier landed at Nives at 0805. In spite of an intensive search, it was impossible to find a single man from the first wave. Krüger, who was to direct the actions of the northern group as company commander, was also missing. Nevertheless, Obermeier decided to block the Neufchâteau-Bastogne connecting road even though he only had two weak infantry platoons. On that day, he managed to beat off several attacks launched from the north by the Belgian Ardennes Light Infantry and from a southerly direction by strong reconnaissance elements of the French 5th Light Cavalry Division. In the evening hours, there was a massive French tank attack with infantry support that forced the Germans to retreat. The French, however, fell for a trick. They stopped in front of a dummy barrier and did not continue; instead they withdrew again as darkness fell. On the next morning, the lead elements of the German 2d Panzer Division pushed through the village. In that way, Obermeier had also accomplished his mission, although he was inadvertently confronted with such an important command assignment.

The bottom line was that in spite of all frictions it was nevertheless possible to turn Operation Niwi into a success, although it actually seemed doomed to failure from the very beginning. Without suspecting it, however, Garski precisely in that way created a new, much more fateful friction that turned the purpose of his mission—to speed up the breakthrough of the Belgian border fortifications—into the exact opposite. This can be traced back to a concatenation of odd coincidences. The Ardennes Light Infantry actually did not have any defense mission but only a delaying mission. Accordingly, the 5th Company deployed at Bodange was merely supposed to trigger the demolition barriers, to resist briefly, and then immediately to disengage from the enemy. None of his superiors had demanded that Major [Maurice] Bricart sacrifice himself and his company and defend the defile of Bodange as if he were to imitate Leonidas who, in the year 480 B.C., had blocked the pass of the Thermopylae with his Spartans. Instead, the 1st Ardennes Light Infantry Regiment in Neufchâteau received a division order at 1420 immediately to withdraw the units deployed along the border. That order was to be passed on to the 2d Battalion in Fauvillers and, from there, to the 5th Company in Bodange. If everything had taken its course normally, then Bricart and his men would have left their positions even before 1500 and the Germans would have been spared the trouble of a time-consuming firefight.[43]

That retreat order never reached Bricart. The blame for that goes to Garski, who resolutely accomplished his mission, although in the beginning he only had nine men after the landing at Traimont near Witry. As he emphasized in his after-action report, he immediately ordered the "cutting of the telephone lines and the blocking of the road."[44] He stopped several cars and ordered the capture of two Belgian motorcycle messengers. The stretch between Fauvillers and Neufchâteau had thus been blocked. To be sure, the regiment sent an additional corresponding radio message concerning the withdrawal to Major Agon, the commanding officer of the 2d Battalion, but it could not be decoded correctly in Fauvillers. Without wishing to diminish the bravery of the Belgian Ardennes Light Infantry, the heroic deed at Bodange was actually the result of a communications breakdown. This is precisely why from the German viewpoint the Niwi Airborne Operation must be assessed as a failure with a "boomerang effect." It harmed Panzer Corps Guderian much more than it helped it.

Clausewitz devoted a separate chapter to the subject of "friction in wartime." To illustrate it, one could hardly find a better practical example than Operation Niwi and the attendant fight for Bodange.

Breaking through the French Delaying Line at Neufchâteau

The motto of the first day of the attack actually was "racing to Neufchâteau." In their first onrush, the Germans wanted to punch through not only the Belgian border fortifications at Martelange and Bodange but also the second Belgian fortification line at Neufchâteau. This meant beating the French 5th Light Cavalry Division, which was hurrying over from the Sedan area, to the punch before the latter could set itself up for defense in the positions prepared by the Belgians. But the cavalry division, commanded by General Chanoine, had prepared for that mission for many months. It was alerted at 0640 on 10 May, and the initial reconnaissance units reached Neufchâteau at 0930 from whence they hurried toward the Luxembourg border. Chanoine moved his formations into position along the planned 03 Delaying Line and grouped them around the two so-called corner posts at Libramont and Neufchâteau.

The race to Neufchâteau, on the other hand, had begun as a fatal false start for the 1st Panzer Division. The problem sprang not so much from enemy resistance as from the fact that the traffic routes had been destroyed systematically in the Belgian border region. For example, most vehicles of the division usually had to elbow their way through on a single road and again and again had to drive around demolition craters or barriers.[45] Sometimes they made no headway at all for hour after hour because the engineers had to build a new bridge instead of repairing the old destroyed one.

The attack of Neufchâteau had been scheduled for the evening of 10 May, but it took until 0930 on 11 May before at least the Panzerregiment 2 (2d Panzer Regiment) was ready to attack. Generalleutnant [Rudolf] Kirchner, the division commander, refrained from employing his division in a compact formation for reasons of time. The formations advanced on a single road, lined up behind each other like a pearl necklace, so he decided to send them into action by echelons, one after the other. The thrust was not aimed directly at Neufchâteau, but an attempt was made to skirt the city to the south. The main line of resistance was broken through at Cousteumont at 1030. The continued advance must be described as completely unconventional. The 2d Panzer Regiment did not wheel to the north toward Neufchâteau, but, disregarding the threat to its exposed flanks, pushed straight away deep into enemy territory.

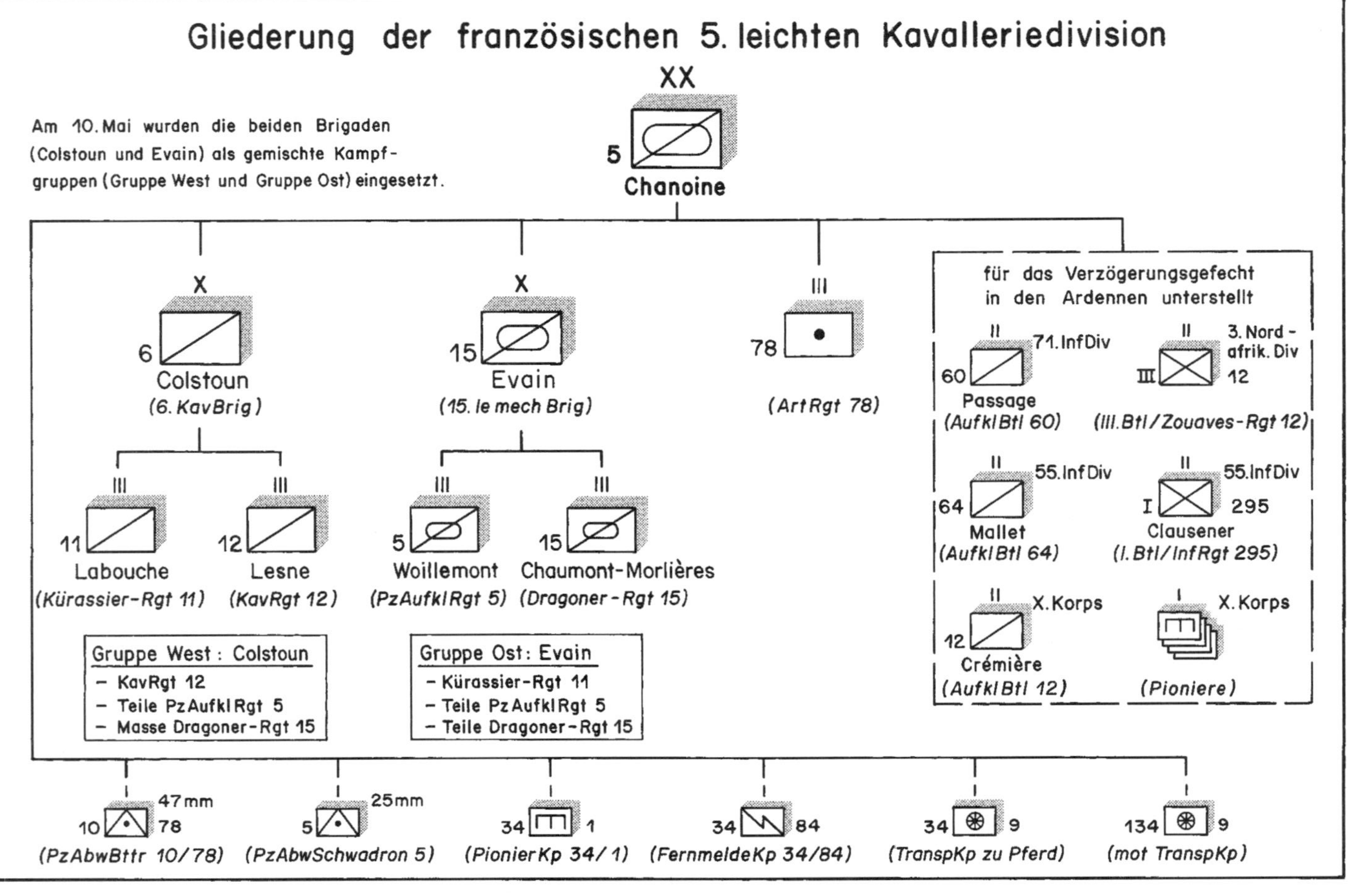
Gliederung der französischen 5. leichten Kavalleriedivision
XX
5
Chanoine
Am 10. Mai wurden die beiden Brigaden (Colstoun und Evain) als gemischte Kampfgruppen (Gruppe West und Gruppe Ost) eingesetzt.
X
6
Colstoun
(6. KavBrig)
X
15
Evain
(15. le mech Brig)
III
78
(ArtRgt 78)
für das Verzögerungsgefecht in den Ardennen unterstellt
II
60
71. InfDiv
Passage
(AufklBtl 60)
II
III
3. Nord-afrik. Div
12
(III. Btl/Zouaves-Rgt 12)
II
64
55. InfDiv
Mallet
(AufklBtl 64)
II
I
55. InfDiv
295
Clausener
(I. Btl/InfRgt 295)
II
12
X. Korps
Crémière
(AufklBtl 12)
I
X. Korps
(Pioniere)
III
11
Labouche
(Kürassier-Rgt 11)
III
12
Lesne
(KavRgt 12)
III
5
Woillemont
(PzAufklRgt 5)
III
15
Chaumont-Morlières
(Dragoner-Rgt 15)
Gruppe West : Colstoun
– KavRgt 12
– Teile PzAufklRgt 5
– Masse Dragoner-Rgt 15
Gruppe Ost: Evain
– Kürassier-Rgt 11
– Teile PzAufklRgt 5
– Teile Dragoner-Rgt 15
10
47 mm
78
(PzAbwBttr 10/78)
5
25 mm
(PzAbwSchwadron 5)
34
1
(PionierKp 34/1)
34
84
(FernmeldeKp 34/84)
34
9
(TranspKp zu Pferd)
134
9
(mot TranspKp)

Organization of French 5th Light Cavalry Division

On 10 May, fate seemed to have been against the 1st Panzer Division, but on this day it had good luck again and again. The advance led through a gap between two loosely connected French delaying formations: the reinforced 11th Cuirassier (Dragoon) Regiment, in the area around Neufchâteau, and the reinforced 60th Reconnaissance Battalion, positioned to the south thereof. That push directly hit the nerve center of the French defense, the village of Petitvoir, just four kilometers to the west of Neufchâteau. This was the location not only of the command post [CP] of the 11th Cuirassier (Dragoon) Regiment but also that of Colonel Evain, who led the east group (mixed 15th Light Mechanized Brigade).[46] In this area, the French had also deployed the 2d Battalion, 78th Artillery Regiment, with the 4th Battery in an open firing position along the southern outskirts of the town.

The attacking German Panzers rolled over the battery at around 1230. Screened by a small forest, they had approached from the southeast and, in a wild ride, burst upon the completely surprised gunners. At the same time, German Panzer IVs went into position on the heights of Warmifontaine and fired on the French who were at the bottom of the valley. Panic spread in Petitvoir. A number of soldiers fled, and riderless horses, galloping through the town, completed the chaos. Looking at it objectively, the Panzer guns caused minor material damage, but the effect on enemy morale was completely out of proportion.

As a matter of fact, in the end even the German officers did not know what to do next because their Panzers, which had penetrated Petitvoir, were not supposed to be used for house-to-house fighting. Kirchner had ordered the 2d Panzer Regiment to mount a probing attack without infantry support at around 0930 while all other formations were still far to the rear. The French managed after all to hold the town. Abandoning Petitvoir would have cut them off from their most important road of retreat to the west, which is why they fought with the courage of desperation.

In the meantime, the Germans had managed to pull the 1st Panzer Regiment forward also, although at the beginning of the attack it was still far behind, stopped at the bridge in Bodange. It now followed through the same breach that the 2d Panzer Regiment had struck and also advanced upon Petitvoir. But now something happened that surprised the French to no end: The 1st Panzer Regiment, newly appearing on the battlefield, did not come to the aid of the bogged down 2d Panzer Regiment, but, instead, pushed past it farther to the west.

Around 1500 it veered slightly to the north and took the highway junction of Biourge. That meant that the French delaying forces had been outmaneuvered. Suddenly, they found that they were cut off from their main line of retreat to Bertrix. The German Panzers were far in their rear, just four kilometers from this city that was protected only by weak elements. Now came one of those dam-bursting collapses of the entire defense organization. The French soldiers, who until then had fought bravely, began to stream to the rear in disorder to seek safety. That had far-reaching consequences because the 2d Panzer Regiment was now able to take the town of Petitvoir. In the meantime, at around 1415, the 3d Battalion, 1st Rifle Regiment, had also driven through that same breach at Cousteumont and immediately wheeled to the north to attack Neufchâteau. While the soldiers of that battalion just the day before had to fight bitterly for many hours over Bodange, which numbered only a dozen houses, Neufchâteau, one of the biggest cities in the Ardennes, fell into their hands like a ripe fruit. The city was taken without major resistance at around 1530.[47]

The breakthrough at Neufchâteau is a classical example of the German Stoßtrupp tactics developed in World War I. This infiltration procedure that the Panzer force took over was intended, after the breakthrough, to push deep into the enemy rear areas via the line of least resistance in order, by means of the resultant panic, to cause a front to collapse indirectly. The 1st Panzer Division, which the day before had been held up for more than eight hours at Bodange, on 11 May during almost the same span of time rushed through almost all of Belgium all the way to Bouillon, just before the French border. During this blitz attack, the French 5th Light Cavalry Division was caught in a maelstrom of precipitous events that were felt to be an *une mêlée digne de l'Apocalypse* (apocalyptic chaos), above all at Petitvoir.[48]

The Panzer Thrust at Bouillon

In planning the offensive, deliberations were concentrated on Bouillon, which was considered a main obstacle to a rapid advance to Sedan. The city's houses were grouped around the ravine of the Semois River, which flowed in a tight bend here to the north. On this peninsula-like spiral turn rises a tall rock massif, topped by the castle of the Crusader knight Gottfried von Bouillon. In the afternoon of 11 May, it was possible to break through the enemy's delaying lines in a first rush. Now the formations of the French 5th Light Cavalry Division rushed pell-mell behind the Semois River. Oberst [Johannes] Nedtwig, the commander of the 1st Panzer Regiment, therefore decided immediately to push on to Bouillon and ordered the 1st Panzer Battalion to mount a probing attack against the two Semois bridges there.

The German Panzers attacked at top speed and punched smack into the middle between the enemy columns that were flooding to the rear in confusion. At 1830 the 3d Company, which happened to be in the lead, rode right into Bouillon when the town was shaken by a tremendous detonation. The company commander, Hauptmann [Matthias] Graf von der Schulenburg, immediately ordered an advance to the northern bridge but only managed to see its just demolished remnants. At the same time, he discovered that the southern bridge was still intact and ordered fire to be placed upon it right away to prevent the approach of the demolition teams.

Events now happened in rapid succession. While the Panzers of the 3d Company went into position along the banks of the Semois River and opened fire, the 4th Company, following behind it, immediately rushed to the southern bridge. When the first

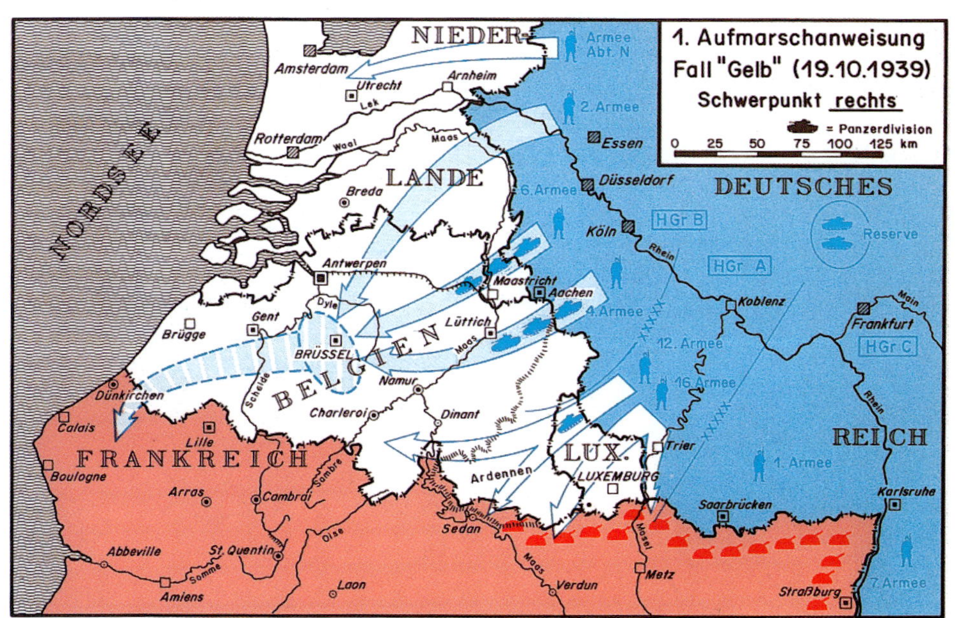

1st Deployment Directive, Case Yellow, 19 October 1939

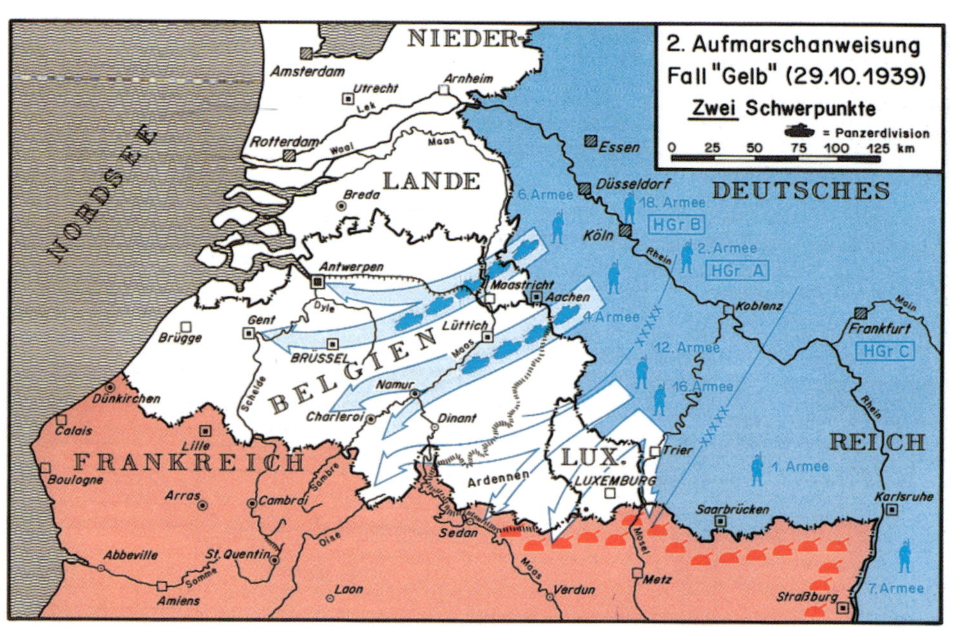

2d Deployment Directive, Case Yellow, 29 October 1939

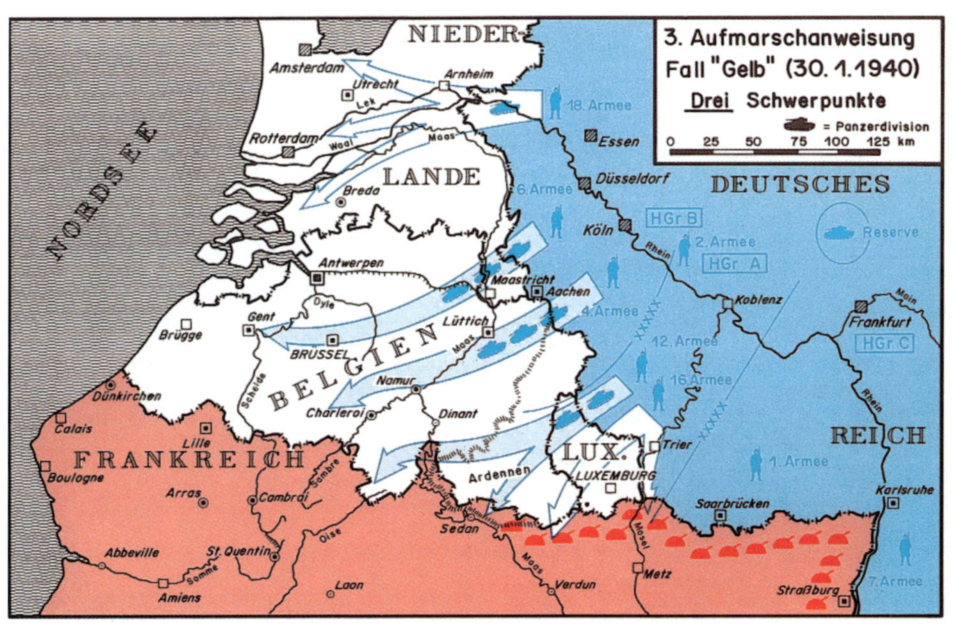

3d Deployment Directive, Case Yellow, 30 January 1940

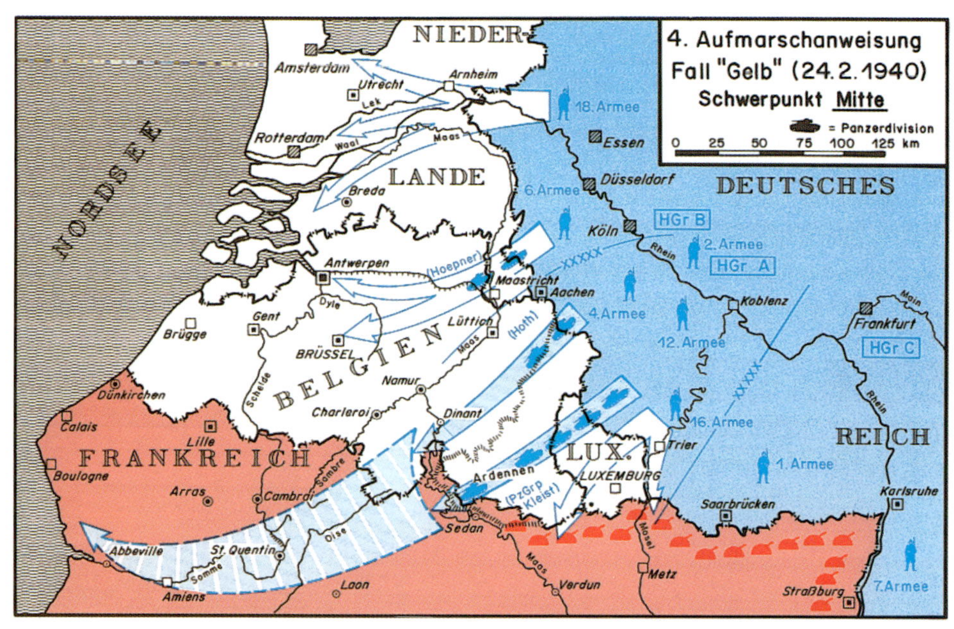

4th Deployment Directive, Case Yellow, 24 February 1940

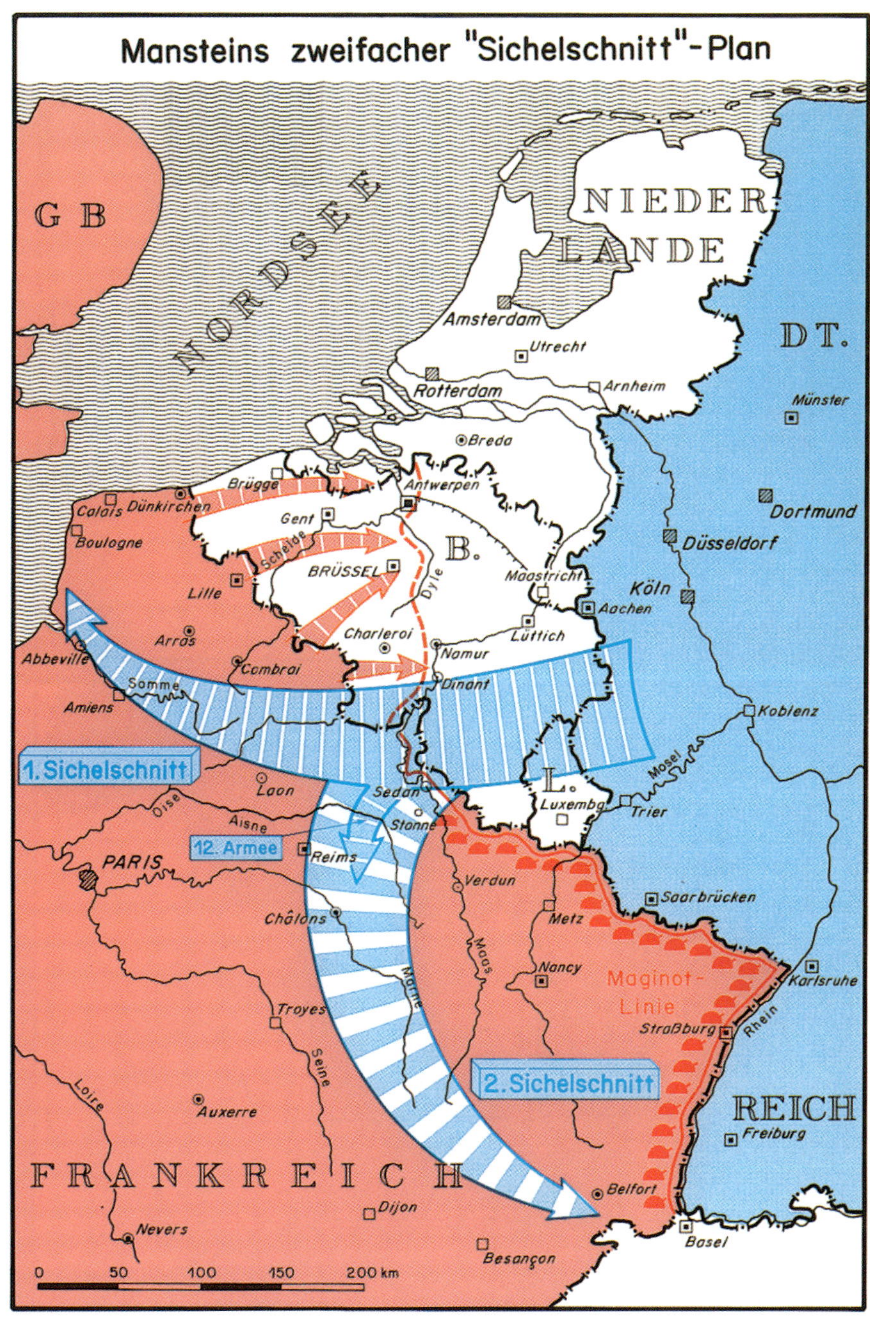

Manstein's Double Sickle Cut Plan

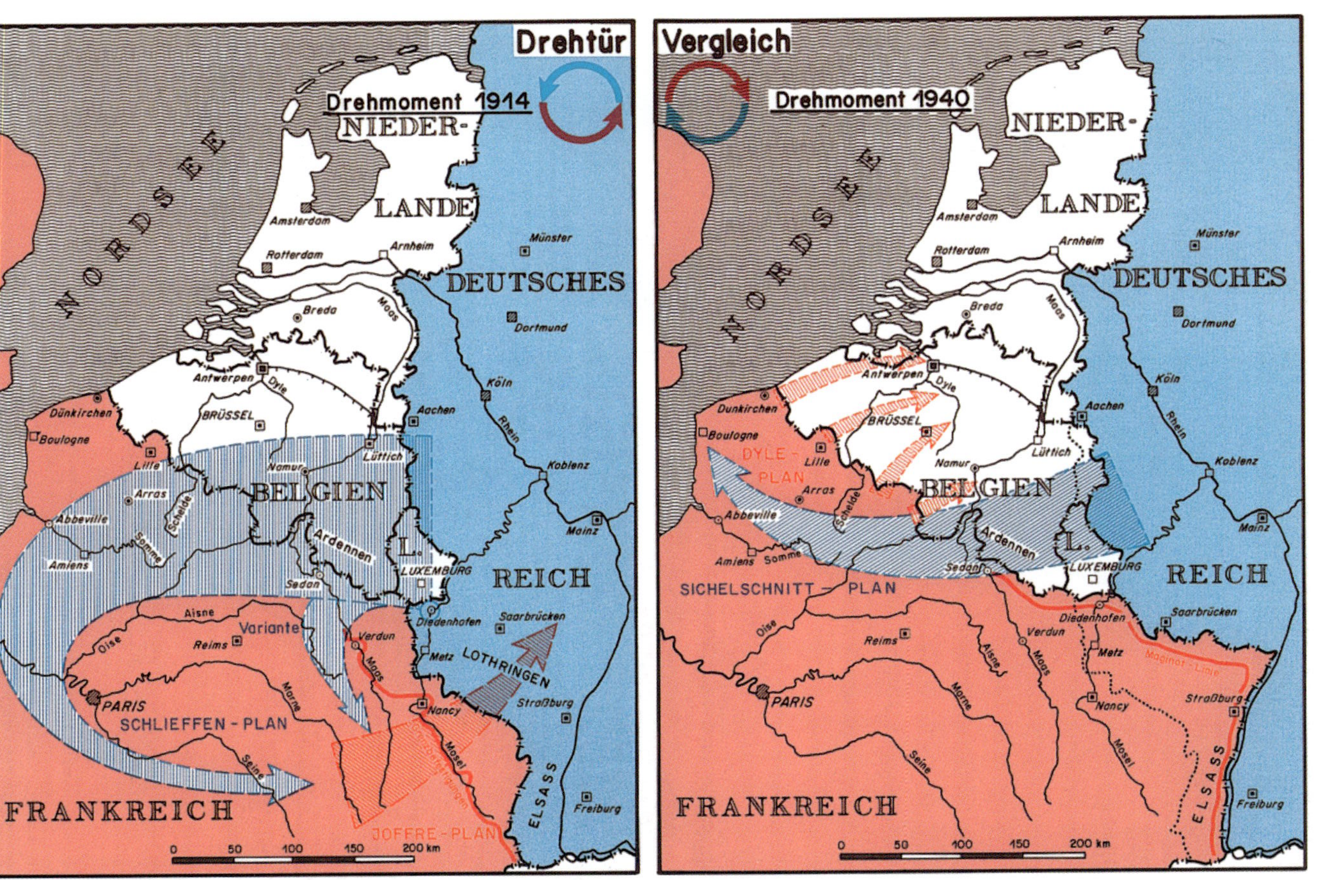

Revolving-Door Comparison: *left*, 1914 pivot; *right*, 1940 pivot

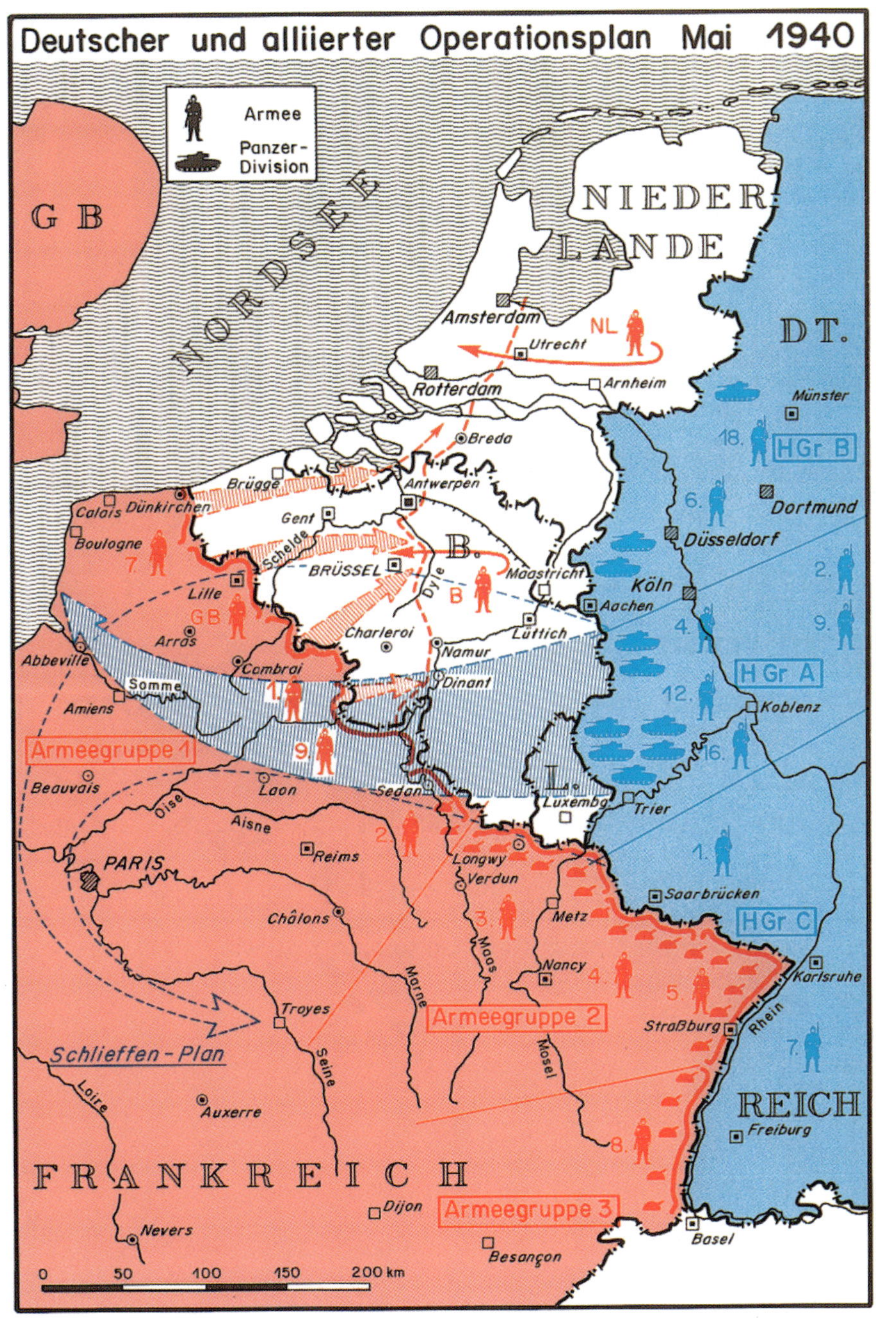

German and Allied Operations Plans, May 1940

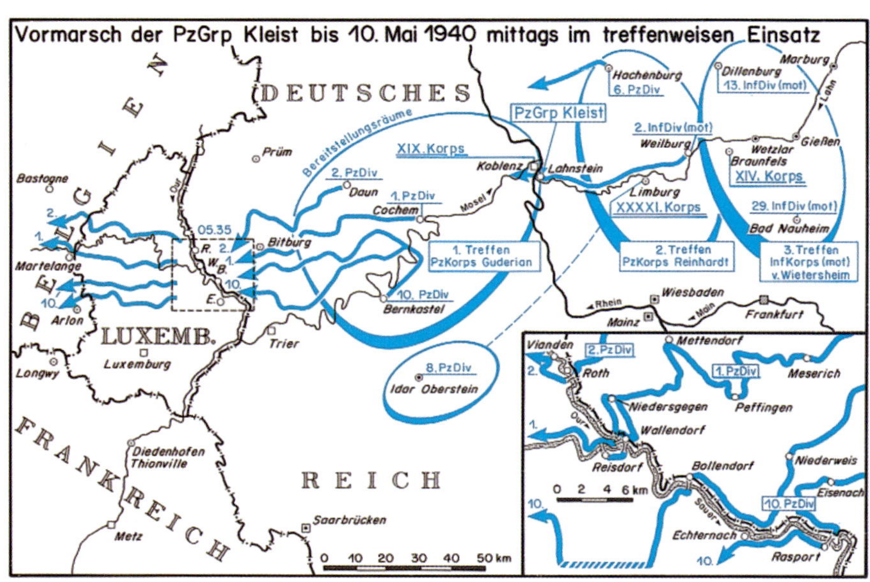

Advance of Panzer Group Kleist up to Noon, 10 May 1940, employment by echelons

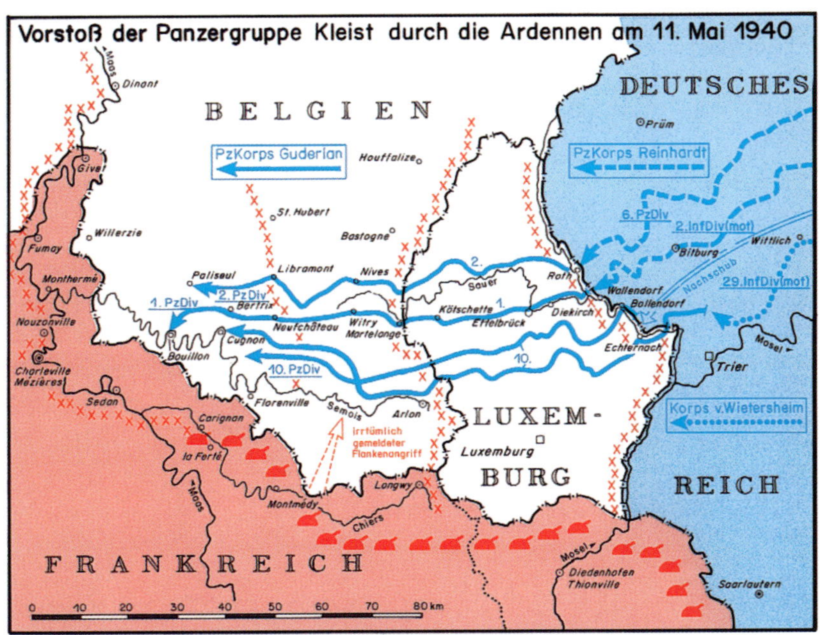

Advance by Panzer Group Kleist through the Ardennes, 11 May 1940

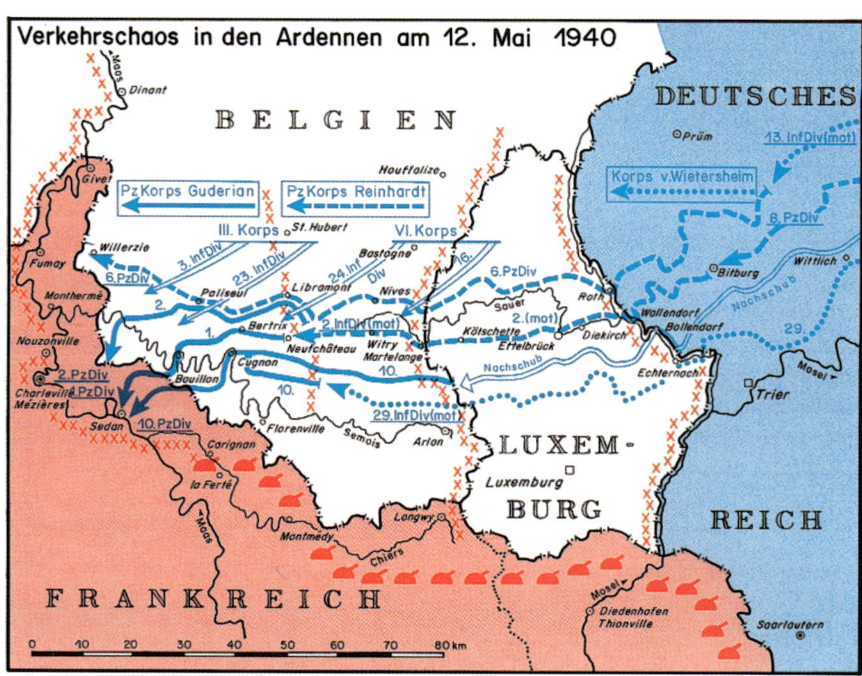

Traffic Jam in the Ardennes, 12 May 1940

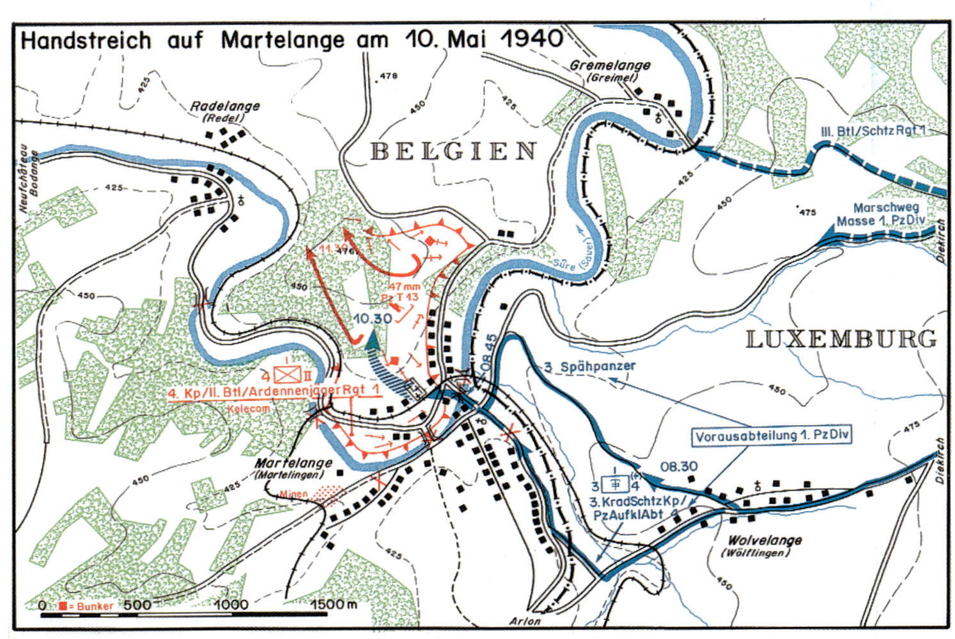

Surprise Coup Against Martelange, 10 May 1940

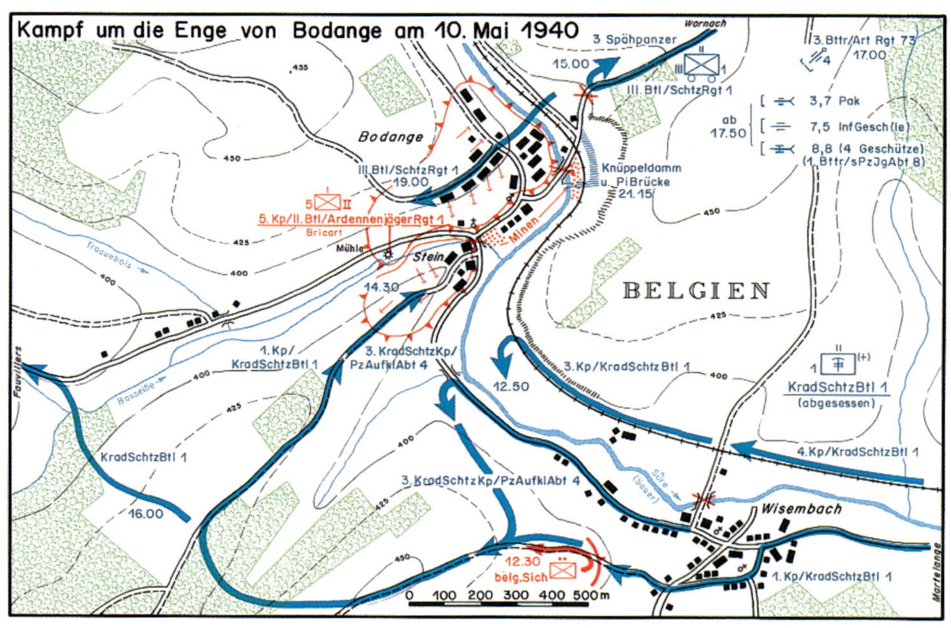

Fight for the Bodange Defile, 10 May 1940

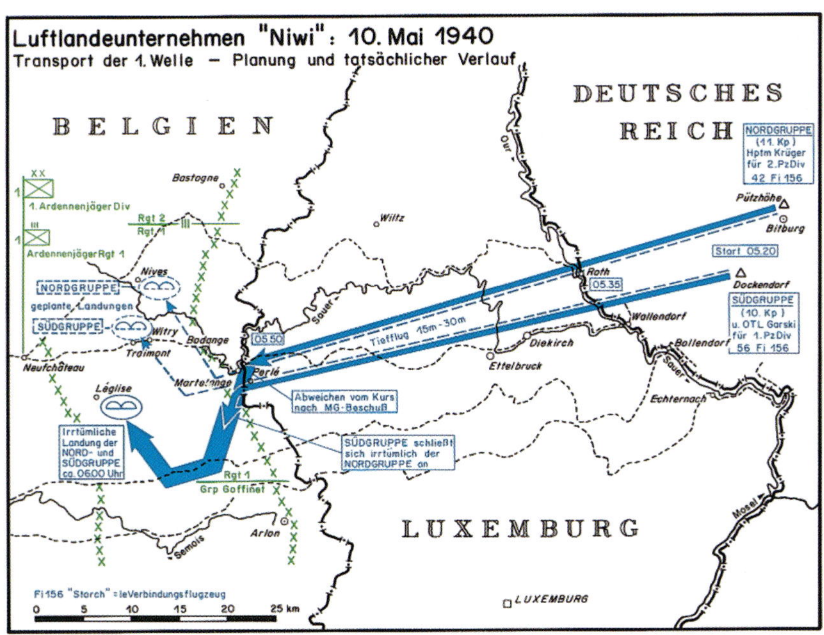

Niwi Airborne Landing Operation, 10 May 1940: Transport of 1st Wave—Planning and Actual Course of Operation

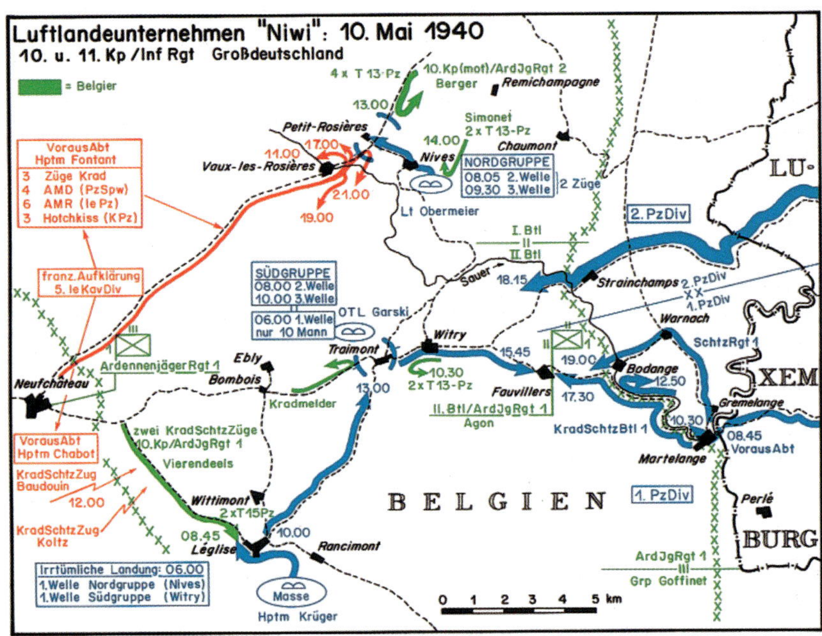

Niwi Airborne Landing Operation, 10 May 1940: 10th and 11th Companies/Infantry Regiment Großdeutschland

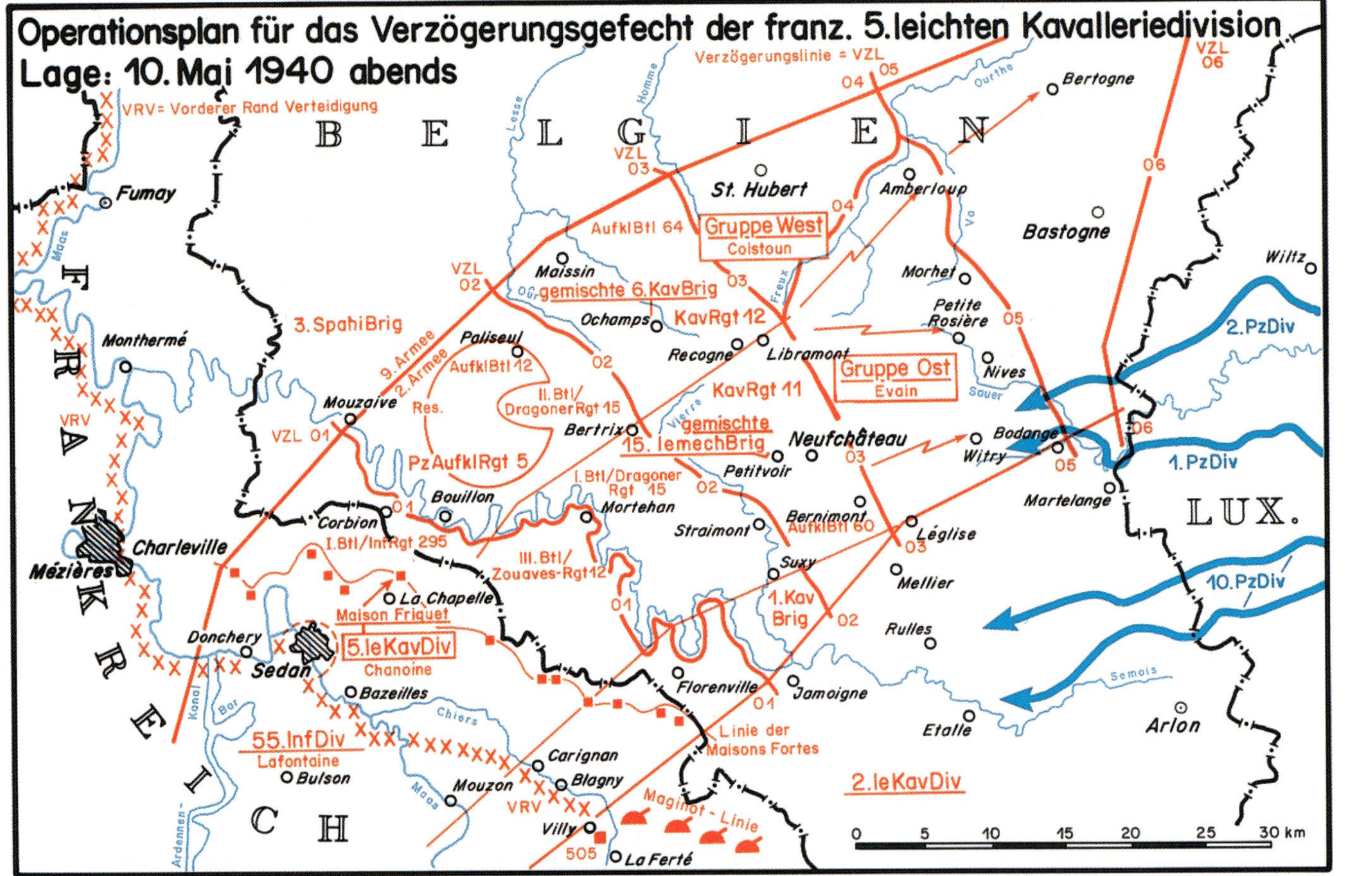

Operations Plan for the Delaying Action of the French 5th Light Cavalry Division; situation as of evening, 10 May 1940

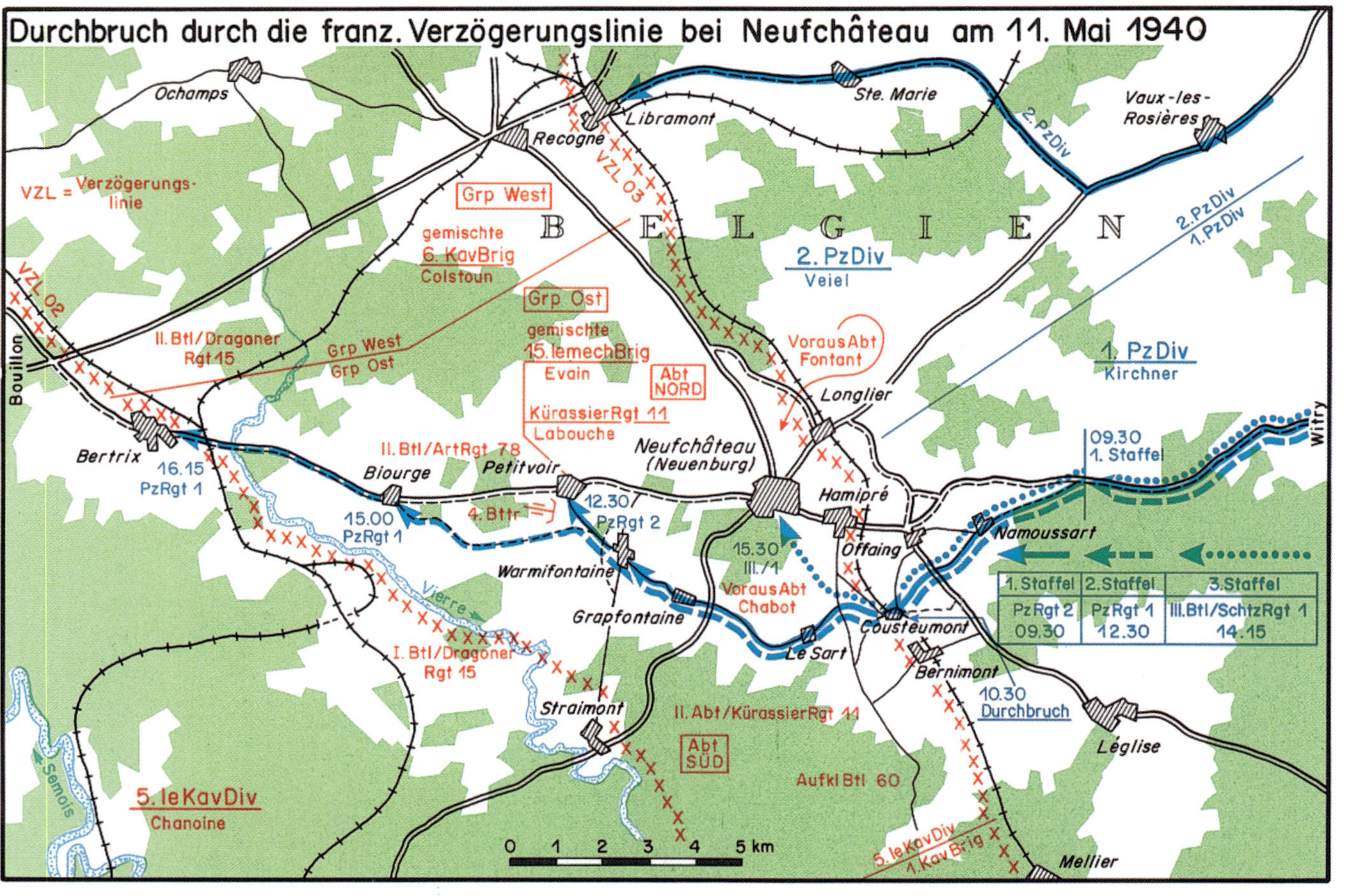

Breaking through the French Delaying-Action Line at Neufchâteau, 11 May 1940

Panzer, manned by Oberleutnant [Ernst] Philipp, the company commander, was just a few yards away, the bridge blew up with a tremendous roar directly in front of him. Immediately thereafter, his Panzer received an antitank gun hit, killing the gunner and putting the vehicle out of action. After both Panzer companies had moved into position between the houses along the Semois River, they were able to neutralize the enemy on the other bank with cannon and machine-gun fire. Under this fire, it was possible, around 1915, for the 2d Company, under the command of Hauptmann [Friedrich Freiherr] von Kreß [von Kressenstein], to cross the Semois River at a ford about three hundred meters downstream from the blasted northern bridge. The raid thus seemed to have succeeded.

The moment the Panzers were on the other bank, however, Bouillon was bombed by about twenty German dive-bombers. All attempts to attract attention by firing white flares were in vain. Immediately thereafter, there was heavy French artillery fire. For the first time, guns positioned on French soil on the southern side of the Meuse participated in this barrage. They were the 15.5-cm long-barrel cannons of the 2d (Heavy) Battery, 4th Battalion, 110th Artillery Regiment, that had moved into position sixteen kilometers farther south next to the Sedan railroad station in the Torcy

Panzer I of 1st Panzer Regiment crossing the ford over the Semois River in Bouillon. In the background, the military bridge built on 12 May. *Bundesarchiv Koblenz [Federal Archives]*

The 1st Battalion, 73d Artillery Regiment, fording the Semois next to the narrow bridge at Mouzaive. *Christa Gampe*

section of the city. Thereupon, the Panzers of the 3d and 4th companies were withdrawn to the area northeast of Bouillon except for the security screens along the Semois River. The 2d Company, however, was on the opposite bank in a narrow loop of the Semois River, as if caught in a trap. There was no infantry support in those narrow little streets. At 0015, on orders from battalion, the Panzers drove through this same ford again to return to the northern bank.

The impetuous German attack did not fail to impress the French defenders. They overestimated the danger and made a critical mistake. At 2130 they voluntarily evacuated Bouillon, the last natural obstacle before Sedan. This withdrawal took place unnoticed by the Germans during a simultaneous artillery barrage. During the night, Bouillon was like a ghost town. On the next morning, the 1st Panzer Division for the first time in this campaign carried out a textbook-style attack, but that action was wasted because Bouillon was clear of enemy forces.[49]

The raid against Bouillon on 11 May thus was an isolated probing attack by a Panzer battalion. Nedtwig had decided to do that because the infantry was still far behind. He deliberately accepted this tactical mistake because he was guided by the higher operational idea of the Sickle Cut that resulted in the requirement of "speed at any price." It was certainly no empty phrase when Guderian maintained that "every minute counts." If the point of the German Panzers had penetrated Bouillon just a few minutes earlier, then perhaps one of the two bridges might have been seized undamaged. That would have opened up entirely new prospects because the bridges across the Meuse River at Sedan were only thirteen kilometers away as the crow flies. So Bouillon had to be taken on the next day by means of a methodical attack. It took until 1900 before the engineers had built a military bridge over the Semois River right next to the blasted northern bridge.

The Raid on Mouzaive

The Wietersheim Group (reinforced 1st Motorcycle Battalion) attacked on the division's right wing in the western Semois sector. The right-hand neighbor, the 2d Panzer Division, was still strung out to the rear. This is why the French delaying forces were still positioned far to the north of the Semois River in this sector of the front. By disregarding regulations and penetrating the combat sector of the neighboring unit, it might be possible to seize a bridge over the Semois River in the rear of the enemy delaying forces. Major [Wend] von Wietersheim therefore determined to mount a raid against Mouzaive (about two kilometers to the west of the division boundary) and assigned the 3d Company to act as assault detachment.[50] The latter penetrated all the way to the bridge by midnight while a withdrawing French cavalry patrol was just crossing it. It was possible immediately to seize the bridge.

As a result of this action, the Germans beat the cavalry troop of Captain Maitre of the 2d Moroccan Spahi Regiment to the punch by just a few minutes as it was moving into the previously reconnoitered positions in the town of Mouzaive. The German assault detachment was already on the south bank and was able to beat off all attempts by the Spahis to attack across the Semois River. The bridge remained in German hands. The command of the 1st Panzer Division covered von Wietersheim's rather independent action. Around 0100, it informed the Panzer Corps Guderian and requested "use of the crossing of the right-hand combat group" at Mouzaive. That was approved because the 2d Panzer Division was still hanging far back.

The few soldiers who participated in this nighttime assault team mission never suspected what a tremendous operational significance their effort was to have. After all, this was a rather modest, narrow bridge. By pure accident, however, those men had bumped precisely into the critical point in the French defenses. It so happened that at Mouzaive ran the boundary line between the Second Army, whose left wing was formed by the 5th Light Cavalry Division, and the Ninth Army, which had employed the 3d Spahi Brigade on the extreme right wing. The latter was therefore responsible for the town of Mouzaive and for the bridge. Because the 3d Spahi Brigade retreated to the Semois later than the 5th Light Cavalry Division, a gap developed for a short time into which the German assault detachment punched. This chain of unfortunate circumstances, again, led to an overreaction by the commander of the 3d Spahi Brigade who, without any contact with his superiors, hastily ordered a retreat. When Second Army was informed about the withdrawal of the left-wing neighbor, a crisis mood was triggered because the left-wing of the 5th Light Cavalry Division was now hanging in thin air. In the end, the only thing left to do was to withdraw that division also.[51]

A German rifle company's rather undramatic thrust toward Mouzaive had triggered a chain reaction. In the end, the French front along the Semois collapsed without any further action by the 1st Panzer Division. The French were still trapped in the linear thinking of World War I. Entire sectors frequently collapsed the moment their lines were breached in just one place. The cause was the fear of the exposed flank, the trauma of which Guderian had successfully been able to rid his officers. Visiting the picturesque valley of the Semois today and passing the little bridge at Mouzaive, one can hardly imagine the dramatic nature of the events of the time and their consequences. The French Ardennes front along the Semois received a tiny crack, precisely at this spot, which spread in erosive fashion so that the dam broke in the end.

The Drive from the Semois to the Meuse

The 1st Panzer Division's continued attack toward Sedan was to be pushed by two battle groups positioned next to each other.[52] The Keltsch Group (mixed 1st Panzer Brigade) was to advance in the right-hand sector via Mouzaive and the Krüger Group (mixed 1st Infantry Brigade) was to advance in the left-hand sector via Bouillon. In the course of the morning, the French 5th Light Cavalry Division, with the remaining elements that were still on Belgian territory, withdrew behind the border to the line of blockhouses. These border pillboxes had been camouflaged as residential homes and were able to block all important lines of communication leading to the Meuse.

The advance party of the Keltsch Group ran into the St. Menges blockhouse around 1000. This pillbox, camouflaged as a forest home, was located three kilometers to the north of St. Menges next to the branch leading to Sugny where a gigantic demolition crater had blocked the fork in the road. The men manning the pillbox and the delaying forces that had withdrawn to that point offered only brief resistance due to the large number of attacking German Panzers. St. Menges was taken around 1430. In that way, the Panzer Corps Guderian had taken fifty-seven hours, not even two and a half days, to push to the Meuse. The first soldiers of the Keltsch Group pushed via Floing into the part of Sedan located on the northern bank of the Meuse around 1815.

The Krüger Group fared entirely differently. Just one and a half kilometers northeast of Fleigneux, it ran into the La Hatrelle pillbox. Only five hundred meters from the southern edge of the Ardennes forest, here it experienced a highly unwelcome surprise. The advance guard of the 3d Battalion, 1st Rifle Regiment, ran into a surprise firefight around 1500. Finally, a Panzer company was moved up front, but its company commander, Oberleutnant [Georg] von Schlieffen, refused needlessly to endanger his Panzers.[53] The pillbox was so well camouflaged along a defile that was secured by mines that it could be engaged only by Panzers advancing individually. The latter would have had to go into position completely exposed along the forward slope and would thus have gotten within the range of the French antitank gun that had opened fire from the pillbox's tiny gun port. Now the infantry again and again tried to attack the pillbox from various directions but failed during the approach. Finally, one Panzer managed to get around the pillbox, driving down a steep slope between the trunks of the dense Ardennes trees. Then it had a technical breakdown and came to a stop.

The pillbox really had the attackers in despair. They had already been trying in vain for three and a half hours to take the French position. At last, a Panzer was able to knock out the French antitank gun with a direct hit on the gun port. But it still took thirty minutes before an assault team seized the pillbox by storm against strong resistance. The men manning the pillbox had managed to hold up the advance guard of the Krüger battle group for four hours. The group reached Fleigneux at the edge of the Ardennes only around 1900.

Summarizing, the fight for the La Hatrelle blockhouse, which had not been mentioned in past reports, contains some parallels to the resistance of the Belgian Ardennes Light Infantry at Bodange. Obviously, in this case likewise, the retreat order did not

Panzer III of the 1st Panzer Regiment advancing from Bouillon to Sedan. *Bundesarchiv Koblenz [Federal Archives]*

St. Menges blockhouse. This border pillbox was to block the access road leading to Sedan out of the Ardennes via St. Menges by means of a demolition crater. *Christa Gampe*

reach the cut-off defenders because when the pillbox was taken by storm around 1900, the last elements of the 5th Light Cavalry Division were just crossing the bridges over the Meuse immediately before they were blown. The example of these brave Belgian and French soldiers shows that it would certainly have been possible to prevent a rapid German thrust through the Ardennes. In spite of the favorable terrain, the French delaying forces refrained from holding key positions as long as possible and, therefore, were never in a position to stop the German attackers for any length of time.

The 1st Panzer Division achieved what had seemed to be impossible in pushing through the Ardennes all the way to the Meuse in just three days. The secret of its success lay in uninterrupted attack. The advance detachment that pushed the attack as the division's spearhead was constantly relieved. The physical and psychological stress was particularly severe for the Panzer crews. This is why the Panzer formations transported relief crews on trucks. The French cavalry formations employed in the Ardennes got no rest, neither during the day nor at night. They were caught up in the confusion of the modern war of movement, and their methodically planned delaying actions frequently degenerated into wild flight.

The thrust through the Ardennes repeatedly has been cited as a classical example of the tactics to be employed in a blitzkrieg. Interestingly enough, however, the German success was not based on any firm system. Von Kielmansegg in this connection speaks of an "ad hoc improvisation."[54] The unusual aspect of this event, he feels, is that there was no concept, there had been no "instructions for use," that could have served as guidance. The important thing was not to translate an as yet undeveloped blitzkrieg strategy into operational-tactical terms. Instead, the task was to accomplish an extraordinary mission. The latter went like this: "In three days to the Meuse. . . ." All the many extraordinary methods that were resorted to here resulted from this requirement due to the situation. The experiences were analyzed in general staff terms only later and were then turned into an abstract system that propaganda journalism referred to as *blitzkrieg.*

The Ardennes Offensive from the Allied Perspective

It [the Ardennes Forest] is impenetrable.[55]

French Minister of War Marshal Pétain
in a statement to the Senate Army Committee on 7 March 1934.

The French-Belgian Misunderstanding

It appears incorrect to describe the Ardennes as the Achilles' heel of the Allied front line because it actually was not a part thereof. The Maginot Line that extended from the Swiss border to shortly before Sedan formed the right wing of the defensive force. From here on, the fortifications extended along the left bank of the Meuse. The Ardennes were located in front of this defense line and were thus outside the line of fortifications. General [René F. C.] van Overstraeten, the military adviser to the Belgian king, had from the very beginning assumed that defending the Ardennes would be difficult and would be beyond the reach of the Belgian army.

During World War I it proved effective not to spread the troops out thinly along the border but rather to concentrate on defending a "redoubt" in the northwest along the Channel coast. But the Ardennes formed a far forward-positioned balcony at the opposite end of the country and, furthermore, were located beyond the Meuse. Thus, to secure them, the Belgians employed only one army corps, "K" Group (named after its commander, Lieutenant General Keyaerts). It consisted of the 1st Ardennes Light Infantry Division, the 1st Cavalry Division, and some reinforcements, above all engineer units. The primary mission was to trigger numerous prepared barriers. Then the Belgian delaying forces were to withdraw as quickly as possible behind the Meuse to the north, between Liège and Namur, to reinforce the defense units stationed there.

So the Belgian army, whose generals very much concentrated on the lessons learned during World War I, fell victim to the Schlieffen plan after the fact. Their operations plan completely accommodated Manstein's Sickle Cut. A dangerous suction developed, as in a whirlpool, because all units rushed into the Flanders trap, whereas a vacuum arose, of all places, in the Ardennes, where the German encirclement forces were easiest to stop. That this could come to pass was also due to the insufficient coordination with the army of the French neighbor. General [André] Doumenc, the French general staff chief, later complained about the "almost complete absence of cooperation between the general staffs of France and Belgium."[56] The French supreme commander Gamelin also said of the Belgian Ardennes Light Infantry: "they evaporated without fighting."[57]

Looking at it today, this latter comment especially seems highly exaggerated. The problem, instead, sprang from a *grave malentendu franco-belge* (very grave French-Belgian misunderstanding).[58] Incredible as it might sound, both sides obviously relied on the neighbor's army supposedly being responsible for defending the Ardennes. An episode that took place in Bouillon, on 10 May, the day of the German invasion, illustrates just how much this displacement process in response to the military threat hit some elements of the Belgian population. General [Charles] Huntziger, the commander in chief of the French Second Army, established contact with the mayor of that city and asked him politely whether he could make one of the many hotels available to him as a military hospital. The mayor answered astonished: "*Mon général,* Bouillon is a spa; our hotels are reserved for tourists!"[59] Just one day later, German Panzers rode through Bouillon and, on the day thereafter, Guderian ordered his corps CP to be set up in the Panorama Hotel, high above the Semois.

Unofficially, both neighboring states had cooperated militarily. For reasons of camouflage, such talks were held only at a higher level and between the intelligence services. In a jointly conducted delaying action that involved the transfer of barriers from one side to the other, this cooperation should have taken place on the lowest echelon. So it happened that the Belgian and French armies in the Ardennes on the one hand did not fight against each other but on the other hand they did not fight side by side either. Instead, two uncoordinated operations plans were carried out here independently of each other. Just how little the operations were coordinated is indicated by the fact that the French conducted their delaying action mostly in an east-west direction, whereas the Belgians withdrew in a lateral movement with respect to the French, heading north toward Namur and Huy. French cavalry formations even found the way forward blocked by demolitions and barriers put up by the Ardennes Light Infantry.

The key terrain in the middle of the Ardennes to some extent became a resistance-free zone because the Belgians had already moved out, whereas the French had not yet moved in. The German commanders did not miss such opportunities and immediately pushed into the gaps. To that extent, many barriers also had a symbolic value because they were not defended. This is emphasized again and again with incredulous astonishment in after-action reports. The engineer units of the Panzer divisions were able to remove a considerable part of the obstacles completely undisturbed. The enormous problems that the Ardennes Light Infantry, considered to be an elite unit, could have created for the German attackers is proved by the fight for Bodange where the 1st Panzer Division was held up for a total of eight hours. This bitter fight was only the result of a communications breakdown and actually ran counter to the operational intentions of the Belgian army.

The French army thus faced a fatal situation because Luxembourg had confined itself to purely passive resistance in that it merely erected barriers along the border with Germany. This meant that the center sector of the French front, manned by only a few weak divisions, was screened by an almost 150-kilometer wide and about 100-kilometer deep area in front of it that, looking at it militarily, was a vacuum. In case of a German attack, French delaying forces were to push into that zone as if racing against the penetrating enemy forces. But the French delaying forces consisted of only five cavalry divisions, three cavalry brigades, as well as some reconnaissance and engineer formations of the divisions that were employed west of the Meuse. Against this area the full might and impetuosity of the German attack were concentrated. The French cavalry units that were a mixture of lightly armored vehicles and mounted units were doomed. In spite of all their bravery, they were just about swept away.

The Myth of the Impenetrable Ardennes

Following World War I, the military thinking of the French general officer corps had been narrowed down in an increasingly dogmatic fashion. Two of the most fatal doctrines related to the Ardennes-Sedan front sector. They were *Les Ardennes sont imperméables aux chars!* (The Ardennes are impenetrable for tanks!) and *La Meuse est infranchissable* (The Meuse cannot be crossed).[60]

This idea was also promoted by the fact that an authority, such as Marshal [Henri Philippe] Pétain, the victor of Verdun, had described the Ardennes as "impenetrable."[61] By the same token, the French supreme commander, Gamelin, described the Meuse as "Europe's best tank obstacle."[62] The geographic twin obstacles of the Ardennes-Meuse appeared to be a strategic barrier that one could go around but not get through. The Sedan area, thus, would obviously be overshadowed by events. This is why the improvement of the fortifications there was neglected in favor of other sectors of the front and only second-rate troops were assigned there. Besides, the French command believed that it would have enough time to bring up reinforcements even if the Germans mounted a big offensive through the Ardennes.

The French general officer corps, of course, did make the mistake of transferring their own time frames, which were handed down from World War I, to the tempo of the German blitz attack. They were convinced that, even in case of a massive thrust (*attaque brusquée*), it would take about another two weeks before the Germans could try to cross the Meuse River.[63]

The French high command figured on at least five but probably nine days for an enemy thrust through the Ardennes. In reality, however, the first German Panzers were at the Meuse River after just two and a half days. The time frame calculation for the preparation of the Meuse crossing turned out to be even more erroneous. This is precisely where the French generals proved that they were still concentrating on the ideas handed down from the last war that had been fashioned by artillery. They figured that the attackers would need about another seven days (!) to move up the artillery pieces, to stockpile ammunition, and so on. To their surprise, however, the German formations, just one day later, launched an attack across the Meuse from the move.

In spite of all of the criticism of the backward thinking of the French generals, one must not forget that most representatives of the higher-ranking German general officer corps did not differ too much from them on that score. Halder originally believed that crossing the Meuse would be possible on the ninth day of the offensive, at the earliest.

During the years between the two wars, there had been many warnings that questioned the myth of the "impenetrability of the Ardennes." British military theoretician Liddell Hart had traveled through this region in 1928 and was astonished at the rather illusionary belief of the French army to the effect that "the terrain would defend itself."[64] In 1933 the British Ministry of War organized larger tank formations. At that time, Liddell Hart—considered to be a tank expert—was asked for advice as to how they could be best employed in a future war. He suggested that they should mount a counterattack through the Ardennes in case of a German invasion of France. The response he got from official sources to his recommendation was that the Ardennes are "impassable for tanks."[65]

Investigations had been conducted in the French army likewise during the 1930s regarding the actual value of the Ardennes as an obstacle. For example, Colonel Bourguignon arrived at the conclusion that a surprise thrust with tanks through the Ardennes would be very possible.[66] Most alarming of all was the result of a map exercise directed in May–June 1938 by General [André] Prételat, the then commander in chief of the French Second Army.[67] This plan described a scenario that resembled Panzer Corps Guderian's attack in May 1940. To the astonishment of his superiors, Prételat arrived at the conclusion that the Germans would be in a position to reach the Meuse in sixty hours and to cross it within one day.[68] In point of fact, Prételat was off by only three hours: the first German Panzers were at the Meuse River loop, north of Sedan, at St. Menges, after fifty-seven hours. When Gamelin learned about the alarming result of this plan exercise, he accused Prételat of pessimism (*jouer le pire*).[69] Thus, the only conclusion reached by the French army high command was the requirement to keep the result of this map exercise secret so that the troops would not be worried.

How Allied Intelligence Assessed the Ardennes

Intelligence Findings Prior to the Start of the Offensive. The German thrust through the Ardennes and the breakthrough at Sedan constitute one of the most successful operational surprises in modern military history. French authors even speak of *une surprise stratégique totale* (a total strategic surprise).[70] Naturally, the German intelligence service left no stone unturned to divert the Allies from the Ardennes and to dangle a rehash of the Schlieffen plan before them, with the point of main effort in the north. However, one extraordinarily important source of information was, of all places, at the very center of German counterintelligence—that was Oberst [Hans] Oster, a passionate opponent of Hitler. He betrayed numerous items of secret information, including the repeatedly postponed attack deadlines, to the Dutch military attaché, Colonel [Jacobus Gijsbertus] Sas.

The Allied intelligence services had pulled off a strategic coup whose significance cannot be estimated highly enough, that is, the piercing of the code processing of the German Enigma deciphering machine. The Poles used a similar machine based on the same patent and in the summer of 1939 sent one copy both to Great Britain and France. The mathematician [Marian] Rejewski, who worked for the Polish intelligence service, very nearly broke the secrecy of the German coding (encryption) system. He was at the decisive breakthrough when the German invasion began in September 1939. After the Polish campaign, the French managed to decipher the German machine coding system for important radio traffic with the help of some Polish specialists who had emigrated.[71] In January 1940 the British were able to break the Enigma code and decipher numerous German radio messages. There was a five-day interruption when the Germans, in the course of their operation Weserübung, which was directed against Denmark and Norway, changed their system; but then it was possible to again decipher numerous army radio messages that pointed to the impending offensive in the west.

At the start of the campaign in the west, the Germans introduced a new encrypting key system. That meant that the electronic oracle of the Allies was silent during an extremely significant phase of the war. Already on 20 and 22 May respectively, radio codes for important radio traffic of the army were deciphered.[72] The German leadership, however, believed that it was impossible for anybody to break its encoding system and used it unsuspectingly to the very end of the war. In that way, the British were precisely informed on almost all the plans being hatched by the Germans. They disclosed the secret of the ULTRA decoding operation only in 1974; this had been one of the strategically most significant successes in World War II.

The French Deuxième Bureau (Army Intelligence Section) did not manage meaningfully to analyze German deployment plans, but there were many indications of the enemy's intention to mount an attack through the Ardennes.[73] As Colonel [Paul] Paillole, the chief of the German Branch, reported as early as 22 March, German agents displayed strikingly unusual interest in these wooded mountains off the beaten path. Besides, they intensively reconnoitered the roads that led from Sedan in the direction of Abbeville to the mouth of the Somme River, and, above all, they studied the carrying capacity of the bridges.[74] The intelligence services of other countries, such as those of Belgium and Switzerland, arrived at similar conclusions as to the probable center of gravity of the German attack. On 1 May, the French military attaché in Bern reported: "The German Army will attack between 8 and 10 May along the entire front, including the Maginot Line. Point of main effort: Sedan."[75]

The French army high command, however, especially Generals Gamelin and Georges, interpreted this as merely a diversionary maneuver and stuck to their preconceived notion that the German main effort would be aimed against northern Belgium.

Misjudging the German Main Effort during the Early Phase of the Offensive. The problem of the Panzer divisions that had been assembled for Sickle Cut was not so much to punch through the rather weakly defended Ardennes as to avoid enemy reconnaissance as long as possible to preserve the element of surprise. How was this to be done since, after all, 41,140 Panzers and wheeled vehicles were bunched together in the Panzer Group Kleist? It seems all the more astonishing how long it took before the Allies spotted the German attack's point of main effort and the French army command drew the proper conclusions from that.

On the first day of the offensive Allied intelligence did not as yet have any suspicions, although the Germans had concentrated tremendous masses of Panzers in Luxembourg and along the eastern edge of the Belgian Ardennes. Thus, the last sentence in the Second Army's summary enemy situation report for 10 May read: "There were no indications of any armored vehicles along the Army Front."[76] During the following night and on the morning of 11 May, however, the pilots of reconnaissance aircraft observed numerous Panzer and motorized columns. On the basis of these messages, the commander in chief of the French air forces in the northern operations zone, General [François] d'Astier de la Vigerie, suspected an enemy secondary thrust toward Givet in the Ardennes. The main effort of the attack was still believed to be definitely in northern Belgium.[77] In the afternoon, French cavalry formations found themselves exposed to such heavy German Panzer attacks that, in some cases, they had to withdraw in flight behind the Semois. Still, there was no suspicion anywhere that this might be the point of main effort of the German attack. The final daily report of Second Army even mentions a *normal* course of delaying operations.[78]

Even more serious seems the mistaken estimate made by Ninth Army whose intelligence section was sometimes referred to as Guderian's "involuntary ally."[79] During the night between 11 and 12 May, the pilot of a reconnaissance aircraft reported numerous, many kilometers-long vehicle convoys that were being driven through the Ardennes with their headlights blacked-out—his report was met with complete skepticism. Thereupon, another aircraft was sent in that direction on the morning of 12 May. Soon, it returned, its wings perforated like a sieve and with a leaking fuel tank due to a German hit. This time, again, the pilot excitedly reported about endless vehicle convoys and furthermore indicated a frighteningly large number of Panzers. Now, the chief of the [Ninth] Army's intelligence section was informed personally. But he refused to believe such an absurd message.[80]

Similar information was received, hard and fast, throughout that day. Reconnaissance aircraft delivered impressive photos, for example, showing German Panzers that were just driving through the ford of the Semois along the northern edge of Bouillon.[81] The thing that worried d'Astier de la Vigerie most of all were the messages from his pilots that the German columns pushing to the Meuse were carrying numerous pontoons for building bridges.[82] During the course of the afternoon, the first German formations reached the river. Nevertheless, the situation continued to be assessed in a definitely positive fashion in the situation reports of the Second and Ninth Armies.[83] Here, however, it must be kept in mind that the French cavalry formations always got to see only the spearhead of the German Panzer divisions that mostly attacked along a single road. The air space was also sealed off almost hermetically. "Like hawks" the German fighters pounced on every Allied reconnaissance aircraft that dared fly anywhere near the Ardennes. So, deep-penetrating air reconnaissance was possible almost only in darkness.

The view that spread before French pilots during the night between 12 and 13 May resembled a procession of lights strung out straight across the Ardennes. In view of the difficult road, some vehicles forgot to black out their headlights. However, the French army command was unimpressed by these presumed "messages of attacking Tartars" and focused its full attention on northern Belgium, as before.

On the morning of 13 May, traffic had broken down along vast sections on the advance routes of the Panzer Group Kleist. Convoys were jammed up for more than 250 kilometers from the Meuse almost back to the Rhine on the northern march route. That was the most threatening moment of the entire Sickle Cut operation. To be sure, German fighters were permanently circling over the Ardennes, and the main body of I Flak Corps had been employed to protect Panzer Group Kleist. Still, a massive raid by Allied bombers could have had devastating consequences. To the astonishment of German soldiers, however, hardly any French or British aircraft showed up that day in the cloudless sky. The Allied air forces instead went into action in northern Belgium where the Luftwaffe was also committed. At noon, however, the Luftwaffe had suddenly vanished and concentrated almost all its forces against the Sedan sector.

A preliminary decision already materialized on 13 May. Although all three Panzer Groups of Army Group A managed to cross the Meuse, Gamelin's headquarters obviously was inadequately informed about that. The final situation report for 13 May, instead, ended with the following sentence: "It is not yet possible to determine the zone in which the enemy will make his main attack." Under that, General [Louis] Koeltz, the chief of the Operations Section, put the following hand-written notation: "Impression [is] very good."[84]

The situation estimate of the French high command, however, appears mysterious even today. It can best be explained if one replicates the four phases of this tragedy of illusions:

First Phase: Apparent Confirmation. The situation reports that Gamelin received on his desk during the first few hours of the campaign seemed almost compellingly to indicate that the Germans this time again would attack with their main effort in northern Belgium. In reality, the reports were much too pretty to be true. Instead, the Germans tried to play their role in Gamelin's script as perfectly as possible. Actually, this was done so perfectly that the French should have become suspicious. So, Colonel [Paul de] Villelume expressed the suspicion that as they marched into Belgium the Allies might run into a trap—after all, there was no explaining why in the course of this forward movement they were not being attacked by the Luftwaffe. Gamelin merely replied that the latter was probably employed some place else.[85]

Second Phase: First Doubts. There were more and more messages about German Panzer columns in the Ardennes that did not fit into this prefabricated picture. They were ignored or dismissed with ironic comments. So, reports to the effect that a reconnaissance aircraft had seen endless chains of lights of vehicles there in the darkness were labeled as "night-time illusions."[86]

Third Phase: Self-Deception. Gradually these reports were so numerous that they added up to certain knowledge. Still, instead of looking reality squarely in the face, the Allies termed the Panzer thrust to the Ardennes a tricky diversionary maneuver that one naturally should not fall for. When there were many indications that the Germans had indeed put their main effort in that place, this did not trigger a crisis mood. Instead, it was believed that this was a positive aspect because the German attack would certainly get bogged down along the Meuse.[87]

Fourth Phase: Admission of Disaster. After Gamelin had consistently disregarded the operational realities and accepted only information he liked, the moment of truth arrived at last. But now it was too late. The German Panzer divisions had long since crossed the Meuse and were now rushing to the Channel coast to close the trap. Gamelin's mistake was not so much in his rather unilateral fixation on the Dyle-Breda plan but rather in his sticking to it undeterred to the bitter end. If he had in time admitted his colossal error, then it would still have been possible—abandoning the entire northern operations area—to withdraw the armies threatened with encirclement behind the Somme River. Hitler could hardly comprehend when it was reported to him on the morning of 14 May, just one day after the Meuse crossing at Sedan, that numerous Allied columns were still rushing northward into the Belgian trap.[88]

France's collapse occurred with the force of an ancient drama. Astonishingly enough, its course even formally resembled a classical Athenian tragedy. For the Greeks, the act of *até,* fateful blindness, always preceded the act of the *catastrophe.*

5

The Decisive Battle

The Breakthrough of Panzer Corps Guderian at Sedan

In *The Second World War* Winston Churchill writes as follows about the events of 15 May 1940: "I was woken up with the news that M. Reynaud [French prime minister] was on the telephone at my bedside. He spoke in English, and evidently under stress. 'We have been defeated.' As I did not immediately respond he said again, 'We are beaten; we have lost the battle.' I said, 'Surely it can't have happened so soon?' But he replied, 'The front is broken near Sedan; they are pouring through in great numbers with tanks and armored cars.' "[1]

Graf von Kielmansegg entitled his 1941 essay "Scharnier Sedan" (The Hinge at Sedan). Sedan formed the hinge between the fixed right wing of the French army along the Maginot Line and the mobile left wing that was to swing up into Belgium in case of a military clash. If this hinge could be smashed, then the swing wing would hang in thin air and the enemy's forces would be cut into two parts.[2]

The French Army's Six Fatal Mistakes at Sedan

Neglecting the Sedan Sector

Under the X Corps, which formed the left wing of the Second Army, the Sedan Sector represented the weakest point in the French front. The French general officer corps considered it completely unlikely that the Germans would place their main attack effort at Sedan of all places. For example, on 7 May—three days before the start of the offensive—Huntziger, the commander in chief of Second Army, said: "I do not believe that the Germans will ever consider attacking in the region of Sedan."[3]

General [Pierre-Paul-Charles] Grandsard, the commanding general of X Corps, believed that the main effort would be in the eastern Mouzon Sector, where he ordered a crash program to improve the defenses along the Chiers River. On the other hand, the Sedan Sector that extended behind the Meuse River appeared to be protected by its terrain, which favored the defenders.[4] Only one Category B Division was earmarked for this sector: General [Pierre] Lafontaine's 55th Infantry Division. This terrain assessment actually appeared to be compellingly logical: The Maginot Line ended twenty kilometers to the east of Sedan at La Ferté, where Fort No. 505 constituted the western corner post of this gigantic fortification system. That was the beginning of the extended Maginot Line, which had not been improved anywhere near as much and ran behind the Meuse River starting at the bend of the river near Sedan. In the Mouzon Sector between La Ferté and Sedan, however, was located the so-called Stenay gap that was not protected by any major natural obstacles. This is why all responsible French generals emphatically advocated strengthening this sector along the Chiers River and, rather fatefully, neglected the Sedan area.

German reconnaissance did not fail to note this weak spot. Nevertheless, in the spring of 1940, von Rundstedt and his field army commanders once again had strong doubts as to whether it was correct to follow Guderian's proposal and to put the main effort of the German breakthrough at the old fortress city of Sedan. The somewhat steeply sloped heights of Marfée rose on the other bank of the Meuse. These slopes were studded with one mighty bunker next to the other—at any rate, that was what the latest aerial photos indicated. Thereupon, once more a photo interpretation specialist was summoned—Major Stiotta, a former Austrian army engineer officer who had been integrated into the German army. His analysis produced a surprising result. The monstrous fortifications that the generals and their advisers thought they had spotted were, in reality, construction sites of bunkers that were shells, not even anywhere near half-finished.[5] With that, Stiotta provided Guderian with the decisive counterargument.

Only a single Frenchman guessed the actual main point of effort of the German attack. Oddly enough, he was not a regular officer, but rather a politician, the Deputy [Pierre] Taittinger.[6] In his capacity as a member of the Parliamentary Army Committee, he visited all sectors of the Ardennes front in March 1940. He was quite shocked about the inadequate defensive preparations in the Sedan Sector. He made the following statement in his report, which he forwarded on 21 March to the then war minister, [Edouard] Daladier, and to the army supreme commander, Gamelin: "In this region, we are entirely too much taken with the idea that the Ardennes woods and the Meuse River will shield Sedan and we assign entirely too much significance to these natural obstacles. The defenses in this sector are rudimentary, not to say embryonic."[7]

Taittinger said that he "trembled" at the thought that a German attack might be aimed at this point. His ominous warning reached its climax in the sentence that became famous later, and afterward earned him the rank of a "prophet" in France: "Il semble qu'il y ait des terres de malheurs pour nos armes" (This place spells misfortune for our troops).[8]

The picture of horror painted by Taittinger, in which Sedan appears as a place of disaster, certainly did not spring from the superstition that there was a curse on the French army on that piece of land. Instead, the deputy was in a position to draw conclusions from the facts of military history and military geography, whereas the gener-

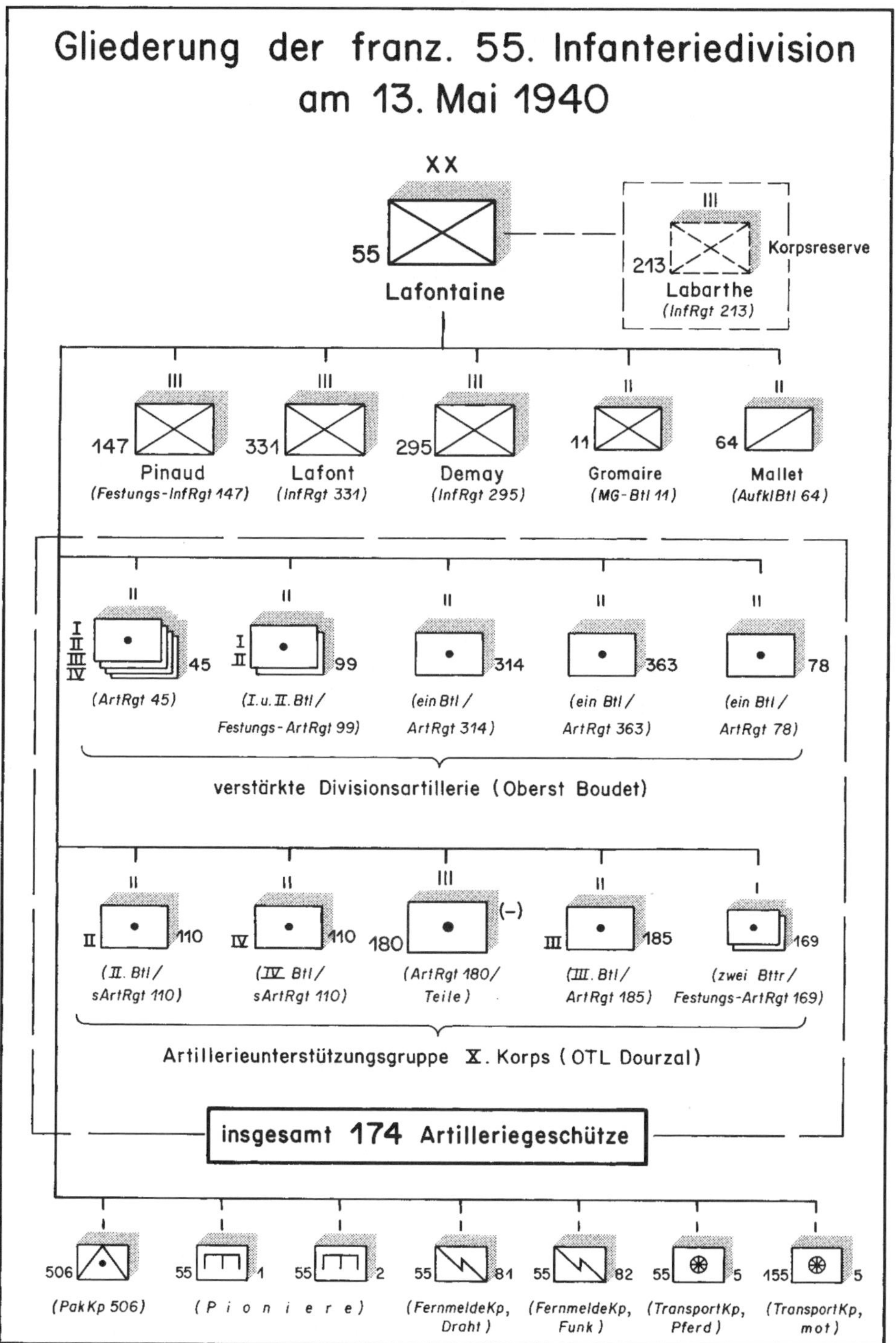

Organization of the French 55th Infantry Division, 13 May 1940

als responsible for this sector were only interested in how many cubic meters of concrete were to be used for what type of bunker. Down through history, Sedan had always been a gateway for invaders who crossed the Meuse at that place.[9] It was here that the Germans in 1870 were able to win their most important victory over France. Why should they not once again select this legendary place for a clash with the French army? Huntziger reacted full of sarcasm in his comment on the Taittinger Report. He challenged the military competence of the parliamentary deputy and declared categorically: "I believe that there are no urgent measures to take for the reinforcement of the Sedan Sector."[10]

The construction of new fortifications was neglected on the basis of this situation estimate. Actually, Huntziger was considered a convinced "advocate of concrete."[11] On the basis of his initiatives, from mobilization in September 1939 to May 1940 the number of bunkers was increased from 2.5 to 5 per kilometer in the western sectors. During that time, the Second Army built a total of fifty-two thousand cubic meters of concrete fortifications.[12] The least effort, however, was made in the Sedan Sector. Before the start of the war, only 42 bunkers of the Barbeyrac type had been built here, along with an artillery casemate erected at the Bellevue crossroads (five hundred meters south of the castle of the same name).

Altogether, 61 additional bunkers were built by 10 May.[13] In addition, there were numerous other bunkers that were just about completed. Official statistics consider only the completion of concrete pouring. Many bunkers lacked the steel gun port shutters that could be used to close the gun ports; some did not even have a door. A report prepared by an officer of the 2d Panzer Division that crossed the Meuse River in the Donchery Sector indicated just what some defensive facilities really looked like: "The road runs along the river. . . . There is a bunker about every 100 meters. Some of these bunkers are still under construction. The wooden shell is still there and the construction pit has not yet been filled up again. Those French really are astonishing! They have been tinkering on their line of fortifications for almost 20 years now; they organized fortress units that are considered to be elite, that wear a special uniform and have a special badge that reads: 'No One Shall Pass.' And now they have not even finished their bunkers along the Meuse River, more than half a year after the start of the war!"[14]

The Gaulier Gap

The original French maps show the planned fortifications that appear to be arranged according to a highly refined system.[15] The bunkers are so placed in the terrain that overlapping fire from various defensive works could guard every sector along the Meuse. One is therefore all the more astonished to find not a single bunker at the most endangered point, at the northern tip of the bend of the Meuse River where the main effort of the breakthrough was later located![16] Here was a yawning 1.5-kilometer-wide gap (measuring almost 2 kilometers along the bend of the river) between Bunker 305 at Glaire and Bunker 211 next to the Pont Neuf [New Bridge], the northernmost bridge of Sedan. Thus, the Germans were able to cross the Meuse River relatively undisturbed at this important place. Between the Glaire and Torcy strongpoints, a wide-open meadowland extending along the south bank was just about ideal for placing mine barriers. But not even that had been done.

From a purely military terrain assessment, such a failure seems incomprehensible because if an attacker coming from the north wants to push out of the Ardennes to the Meuse River, then, at almost a straight line, he has available the St. Menges-Floing-Gaulier axis. In most sectors, such as at Donchery, wide-open terrain has to be crossed to get to the river; but here it is possible to approach the Meuse River shielded by the mentioned villages. Besides, the vast workshops of the Espérance Textile Plant in Gaulier extend directly along the banks of the Meuse River. The Germans were able to use them as an engineer depot to store the numerous rubber boats and assault boats for the river crossing and also the material for the construction of the military bridge. This bridge, over which most of the Panzers rolled, was to assume an operational significance as no other bridge in the campaign in the west. Actually, the French should have learned a lesson from the last war. After all, it was on 26 August 1914 that the attacking German Fourth Army built its first bridge across the Meuse River at almost exactly the same spot.[17]

Absence of Mines

The weakness of the Sedan Sector was not so much due to a shortage of bunkers (this kind of criticism only bears witness to that fateful Maginot mentality) but rather to a shortage of mines. During World War II, the use of mines proved to be the most effective means for stopping enemy tank operations before they got started. In July 1943 the German Panzer divisions trying to break through the Soviet front at Kursk first of all got stuck in kilometer-wide mine belts.[18] At El Alamein, Rommel also had ordered about 500,000 mines to be planted along a front of seventy kilometers.[19] In the spring of 1940 the French Second Army had to watch almost the same frontline width, but it had only 16,000 mines. Of that number, 7,000 each were earmarked for the delaying action of the cavalry divisions in the Ardennes as well as for use in the line of the blockhouses along the border. That left only 2,000 mines for the actual defense line along the Meuse River.[20] Of those, the 55th Infantry Division got only 422.[21]

Looking at it more closely, however, that was actually 422 mines too many because when Guderian's eight hundred battle tanks started out on their final breakthrough on 14 May, almost no mines had been planted in the ground. French officers had concentrated so much on building bunkers that they paid hardly any attention to the mines. At first, only some of them had been laid. Before the German attack, however, the French removed the few mine barriers that did exist in the Sedan Sector. Most of the mines were shipped to a depot near Vrigne-aux-Bois (north of the Meuse

River) where they had to be greased again due to soil moisture. That is where they were discovered in 1941.[22]

Construction Troops Instead of Fighting Troops

The French army's decisive mistake was not that it built too few bunkers but rather that it built too many. Because of all this labor duty involved in building defensive positions, the army had hardly any time for combat training. That is precisely what should have been the most urgent task of the 55th Infantry Division, which, rather unusually, was positioned in the foremost front line, although it was merely in Category B.[23] The division consisted mainly of reservists, most of whom were over the age of thirty and whose active duty time as a rule was far in the past. What little combat training they had was only sufficient to bring out the frightening shortcomings rather than correct them. There also appears to have been no special demand for individual initiative in that area. So, 1st Lieutenant Delas of the 1st Battalion, 147th Fortress Infantry Regiment, was punished with fifteen days of arrest during the winter because he had dared to order firing practice with a 25-mm antitank gun in a quarry.[24]

Lafontaine was of the opinion that building fortifications could best compensate for his division's obvious weaknesses. The quality of bunkers was considered to be more important than the training of personnel. In that way, it was impossible to correct the shortcomings, although eight months were available for proper combat training from mobilization up to the start of the German offensive. Because the men had hardly been trained for combat, many of them at the critical moment lacked the will to fight. All the greater was the shock when on 13 May they were attacked by soldiers who had been given perfect training and who displayed an almost fear-inspiring resoluteness. Many French defenders did not dare offer resistance but instead simply fled. They had been taught very carefully how to build defensive positions, but they had not been taught much about how to defend them.

General der Panzertruppe [Hermann] Balck, at that time an Oberstleutnant in command of the 1st Rifle Regiment that was employed at the main effort near Gaulier, described exactly what preparations on the opposing side were like: "Training was intensively geared toward the future mission. Up to the breakthrough at Sedan, everything was practiced down to the last detail in map exercises and every situation was run through in similar terrain also with live firing and air support. The Mosel [Moselle] River had to stand in for the Meuse River and I did not let up until every last man in my regiment knew how to handle rubber boats like an engineer. I let the exercises run their course, completely and freely, to get everybody accustomed to independent action. This was the best preparation for an offensive that I ever saw."[25] The attack was correspondingly successful. As several German officers emphasized, the Meuse River crossing went as perfectly as if it were a demonstration in the training camp.[26]

The Principle of Rotation

Basically, the defensive organization of the 55th Infantry Division appeared to be uniform and clearly structured:

> The Sedan Sector comprised three subsectors, each for one regiment.
>
> The subsectors were subdivided into (mostly) three *Quartiers* (quarters), each for one battalion.
>
> The Quartiers were (mostly) subdivided into three *Centres de résistance* (CRs, centers of resistance) (position areas), each for one company.
>
> The Centres de résistance consisted of (mostly) four *Points d'appui* (strongpoints), each for one platoon.

However, the many months of duty in this sector had produced the paradoxical effect that the initially rather orderly mosaic of the formations turned into a confused puzzle. The cause of this crazy-quilting was the principle of rotation: The individual companies were repeatedly taken out of the line for construction work, work in agriculture, or training sessions. After this, they were mostly employed not in their former sector but rather in that of the unit that relieved them. That meant that they no longer returned to "their" positions, which they themselves had built and with whose surrounding area they had become familiar.

Out of the nine companies that were employed in the Frénois subsector, where the main effort of the German attack was later placed, most had been in their new positions only a few days as of 13 May. The situation was even worse in the Villers-sur-Bar subsector opposite Donchery. The 213th Infantry Regiment, which was stationed here originally, was taken out of the line on 7 May and was replaced by the 331st Infantry Regiment. In the meantime, the units of the 55th Infantry Division had been so reshuffled that a kind of crazy-quilt pattern resulted. In many cases, the original cohesion had also been lost within the units. The 6th Company, 2d Battalion, 295th Infantry Regiment, stationed in Torcy (the section of Sedan that is located on the south bank of the Meuse River) was a particularly stark example. It was made up of soldiers from four different companies, which, again, had been drawn from three different battalions belonging to three different regiments![27]

Even more serious than the organizational problems were the psychological effects of this crazy-quilting principle upon the internal structure of the major and minor units. The 147th Fortress Infantry Regiment that was to occupy the bunkers along the Meuse River represented the backbone of the 55th Infantry Division. Its soldiers were recruited mostly from reservists from the area around Sedan and quite a few of them had known each other for a long time. Captain Carribou, commanding officer of the 2d Battalion, therefore, described the internal cohesion after mobilization as *cohésion totale* (total cohesion) and judged the regiment rather enthusiastically: "The 147th has a 'soul': It is ready!"[28]

His later reports no longer mention this spirit of unity.[29] Carribou had to accept the fact that his battalion's units were torn apart again and again. When the Germans attacked, he had three companies under his command, which came from three different regiments. Here, the 6th Company, 2d Battalion, 331st Infantry Regiment, was a special problem. It was stationed in the Prés de Queues center of resistance in the rear area of the Torcy quarter, which he commanded. Carribou hardly knew it, and he was never to get to know it in combat either. When he had to withdraw his forward-engaged units all the way to the halt line in the Marfée woods due to the pressure of the German attack, the 6th Company, which was stationed there, had disappeared without a trace.

Scarcely any other battle in World War II has been described as frequently as Guderian's breakthrough at Sedan. These reports are confined mostly to the course of military events. The sociological aspect offers a supplementary perspective here. After all, two military formations with utterly different group cohesion collided with each other in this battle. Guderian's elite formations of enormously strong compactness punched into the amorphous mass of the 55th Infantry Division, whose group cohesion had been destabilized by constant changes. The structures of the primary groups that had grown in the division were constantly torn apart. Instead, ever-new secondary groups were formed, and they were artificially maintained only by the formal structures of the military hierarchy.

This fateful principle of rotation was developed in the French army during World War I, which was fought as battles of matériel. The human factor had become one of anonymous, optional, interchangeable quantities. The rotation system undoubtedly proved itself at Verdun. The German soldier often had to hold out in the foremost front lines for many weeks; the French soldiers on the other hand were taken out of the front line after just a few days of combat and were replaced by fresh troops. The Germans had learned completely different lessons from World War I than did the French, and thus they refrained from tearing apart "units that had grown together." Even on the eastern front they later refrained from replenishing units that had already been heavily decimated by assigning new personnel. Instead, the units were left in the front lines until they had fallen below a minimum in terms of combat strength. Only then were these formations taken out of the front line and reconstituted in the rear areas. In that way, it was possible to integrate the new soldiers before their unit was sent back into action.[30]

Inserting the 71st Infantry Division into the Front Line

Due to the constant reshuffling, the disintegration of the 55th Infantry Division in the meantime had reached worrisome proportions. Now, however, immediately before the start of the German attack, a measure was initiated that made the confusion complete. On 10 May, Grandsard ordered the 71st Infantry Division—which had been held in reserve until then—to be inserted in the front line, smack in the middle between the two divisions of the corps that were committed forward. Everything was very simple in theory: The 55th Infantry Division had to evacuate the right-wing Angecourt subsector, and the neighboring 3d North African Infantry Division was to evacuate the Amblimont subsector on the left-wing to make room for the units of the 71st Infantry Division.

Where was Lafontaine now to put the 295th Infantry Regiment that until then had been employed in the right-hand subsector? He decided on a procedure that is reminiscent of the formal training of a company. His three regiments that initially had moved into position next to each other in three subsectors were to close up to the left so tightly that they would find room in the remaining two subsectors. The right-hand boundary now was no longer at Petit Remilly but rather at Pont-Maugis. That shortened the division's frontline sector from 20 kilometers to 14 kilometers along the Meuse River, or from 14 to 8.5 kilometers as the crow flies. In theory, this was bound to lead to a tremendous concentration of fighting strength, and indeed the density of machine guns in purely statistical terms rose from thirty-two to forty-two per kilometer. As regards the cohesion of the formations, there was reason to fear chaos. However, the restructuring of the 55th Infantry Division, ordered for the night between 13 and 14 May, mostly did not occur because the Germans had in the meantime launched their attack. These measures had been partly begun, so both of the divisions were caught in the middle of the relief operation "on the wrong foot."[31]

German Preparations for the Crossing of the Meuse River

Controversy between Kleist and Guderian on 12 May

The day before the decisive attack across the Meuse River was definitely turbulent for Guderian. In the afternoon, he wanted to plan further operations in Bouillon's Panorama Hotel, where the corps command post had been set up, when British bombers suddenly raided the city. An engineer convoy, heavily laden with explosives, was hit on a street leading past the hotel. A tremendous detonation shook the hotel. A hunting trophy, a gigantic wild boar's head, fell off the wall and missed Guderian's head by "a hair's breadth."[32] An irony of history is that the already beaten Belgian Ardennes Light Infantry had a boar's head in their coat of arms. And so, the animal in their coat of arms almost avenged them by falling on the German general's head.

The subsequent conference at von Kleist's command post turned out to be even more exciting for Guderian. Some military historians quite erroneously described his mood as pessimistic and even depressed. It was even assumed that he was in a kind of shock as a result of the aftereffects of that "hunting accident" in Bouillon.[33] A rather paradoxical situation arose: Guderian, called *schneller Heinz* (Swift Heinz), requested that the attack across the Meuse River be moved up by one day. On the other hand, von Kleist—whose main problem was to put the brakes on the impetuously forward-storming Guderian—insisted on the previously set attack deadline.[34] Guderian certainly understood that there were problems connected with reaching the Meuse River at the right time with all elements, but that hardly was enough reason to drop the idea of the attack from the move, which he had repeatedly demanded. The real reason for his demand actually was to be seen in a kind of spiteful reaction. Von Kleist was in the process of tearing the very heart out of Guderian's operations plan at the very last moment.

Employing the Luftwaffe

The main problem with the Meuse River crossing sprang from inadequate artillery support, primarily because several batteries had become stuck in the Ardennes. Now, everything depended on the employment of the Luftwaffe. But that was precisely the point where the most serious differences of opinion existed between Guderian and his superior. Von Kleist had agreed with General der Flieger [Hugo] Sperrle, the commanding general of Luftflotte 3 (Third Air Fleet), on the conventional method of a brief, concentrated mass bombing raid. After preparatory raids in the afternoon, the bombers and dive-bombers were to wipe out the French forces in the Meuse River loop of Sedan in a single concentrated blow lasting twenty minutes. This mass raid was planned immediately before the infantry's scheduled crossing of the Meuse River at 1600.

In cooperation with Generalleutnant [Bruno] Loerzer, the commanding general of II.Fliegerkorps [II Air Corps], Guderian had developed a novel procedure, the so-called rolling raid, especially for the attack on Sedan.[35] According to that system, only a few Luftwaffe formations were to attack at any one time; but the plan was to repeat these raids throughout the entire day. That would yield the following advantages:

> Enemy artillery could be permanently neutralized.
>
> The effect of the continuous bombing raids on the morale of the defenders would have devastating consequences.
>
> A mass bombing raid, "like a rolling artillery barrage," makes it possible to cover target areas only in a rough fashion; on the other hand, when only a few aircraft at a time attack in a "rolling raid," it would be possible systematically to hit special targets, for example, bunkers.[36]

In close cooperation with the Luftwaffe, Guderian ordered the drafting of a precise fire plan with a detailed target map, which showed target groups and individual targets in minute detail.[37] On the day before the attack, the map was supplemented with target reports from ground reconnaissance. The fire from direct-fire weapons, the artillery, and the Luftwaffe was coordinated in space and time in a kind of perfection that had never been attempted before. Now, von Kleist's decision made the carefully drafted plan useless.[38] In the afternoon of 13 May, Guderian went to Hill 266, south of Givonne, to observe the action of the Luftwaffe. His astonishment was "indescribable" because the dive-bombers attacked precisely according to the method he had worked out with Loerzer. When Guderian in the evening thanked Loerzer by phone for the effective Luftwaffe support, the latter said rather slyly: "The order from Luftflotte 3, that turned everything upside-down, came, well, let us say: Too late. It would only have caused confusion among the air groups; that is why I did not pass it on at all.[39]

Selection of the Point of Main Effort

General Guderian absolutely wanted to mount his main effort at Sedan, while von Kleist wanted it thirteen kilometers farther to the west, at Flize. Guderian insisted that the point of main effort be placed west of the Ardennes Canal. Von Kleist thought that the crossing of the Meuse River would have to be set up in the direction of the operational-level main thrust, in other words, farther to the west, toward Rethel. Advancing via Sedan, on the other hand, signified a detour. By putting the main effort west of the Ardennes Canal, a double river crossing could be avoided: first to the south, across the Meuse River, and then to the west, across the Ardennes Canal. Moreover, von Kleist reasoned an attack directly to the west of the Ardennes Canal would hit precisely the dividing line between the French Second and Ninth Armies.

Guderian argued that the terrain to the west of Sedan offered hardly any covered approaches to the Meuse but instead was wide open and easily observed by the enemy. The attacking troops would also move fully into the effective range of flanking fire from the fortress artillery at Charleville and Mézières. Widening the combat sector to the west would dilute the principle of concentration. In addition, the crossing of the Meuse River at Sedan had been planned for many months in map exercises over and over again, and the firing plan for this mission had been coordinated with the Luftwaffe. Shifting the main effort on short notice would thus invalidate everything.

Above all, however, Guderian pointed out that regrouping his divisions that were right in front of Sedan would mean postponing the attack date by one day. That is precisely what von Kleist did not want to accept, so he simply had to go along.[40] Kleist was right in operational terms, whereas Guderian was correct in tactical terms. But when it comes to a river crossing, it is first of all the tactical factors that count because what good is the best operational-level idea if you do not get across the river! Nevertheless, Guderian's action must be considered a provocation. In a conference on 13 April, von Kleist was impressed by Guderian's arguments and dropped his pet idea of mounting an attack on both sides of Flize but declared unmistakably that the main effort would have to be located west of the Ardennes Canal.[41] He reaffirmed his directive once more in a letter to Guderian on 18 April.[42] But the latter ordered his Panzer Corps, quite arbitrarily and on his own, to swing south in the Ardennes, heading for Sedan, and thus confronted his superior with a fait accompli.

Depth of Bridgehead

Von Kleist believed that forming a bridgehead with a depth of six to eight kilometers would be enough. Guderian, on the other hand, demanded a depth of almost twenty kilometers, including the heights around Stonne. Just exactly what he was thinking in that connection will be pointed out in conjunction with the heavy fighting for this massif of heights. It is interesting to note that Guderian, in this respect likewise, ignored his superior's instructions and ordered his units immediately to push south. This time again his success proved him right.

Guderian's Operations Plan and Its Implementation

For Guderian, 13 May 1940 was thc "moment of truth." Now, it was his to prove that his bold theories were no utopia. If the tremendous significance the breakthrough at Sedan had for him is kept in mind, then it is indeed astonishing that his attack order covered merely three pages. There are two reasons for that. First, according to the German system of *Auftragstaktik* (mission tactics), it was customary to name only the attack objective, whereas the manner of implementation was left to the officer ordered to carry out the attack. Second, the attack on Sedan had already been run through repeatedly in map exercises.[43]

The following episode seems worth mentioning in this connection. On 1 May a map exercise of the 1st Panzer Division was held in Cochem. When the operations officer of 1st Panzer Division, Major i.G. [Walther] Wenck, later carefully filed away the Sedan attack order, which he had drafted and even ordered twenty-five copies to be run off, the division commander, Kirchner, laughed out loud and told him: "Wenck, don't bother; things are not going to happen that way anyway." Events happened hard and fast during the last phase of the advance to Sedan. Wenck suddenly learned early on the morning of 13 May that the attack was to be mounted on that very day, specifically at 1600. His astonishment was even greater when he found that Guderian wanted to use—almost unchanged—the very attack order he had prepared during a war game conducted by the corps in Koblenz on 21 March. That attack order was also the basis of the previous map exercise of the 1st Panzer Division in Cochem. Now Wenck was able triumphantly to show the twenty-five copies of the previously drafted division order, and all he had to do was change the exact time from 1000 to 1600.[44] There are very few operations in modern military history that came off as perfectly as Panzer Corps Guderian's crossing of the Meuse River at Sedan, in spite of the unusual difficulties, due above all to the pressure of time. Then Oberleutnant and ordnance officer in the 1st Panzer Division, Freytag von Loringhoven (later a Generalleutnant in the Bundeswehr), recalls: "Assembly, attack, crossing, and breakthrough actually came off like clockwork."[45]

One thing that is striking to note in Guderian's operations plan is the rigorous practical implementation of his pet idea, the *Schwerpunktprinzip* (concentration principle)

[*Klotzen, nicht kleckern!* or Hit with the fist, don't feel with the fingers!]. The Panzer Corps he commanded consisted of almost sixty thousand men and twenty-two thousand vehicles. During the crossing of the Meuse River at Sedan, he squeezed his three Panzer divisions into a combat sector barely ten kilometers wide between the Ardennes Canal and Pont-Maugis. The actual breakthrough spot between Donchery and Wadelincourt was about five kilometers wide. Here he once again formed a main effort within the main effort in favor of the 1st Panzer Division. He had employed it in the middle, in the segment of the Meuse River at Gaulier, which was particularly favorable for the attack, and assumed that at least it would manage the river crossing. In that way it would be in a position, by wheeling to the left and to the right, to enable the two flanking divisions also to make the Meuse River crossing. The attacks by the 2d and 10th Panzer Divisions were each supported only by two artillery battalions, while the fire of eight artillery battalions, including all of the heavy batteries, was to be concentrated on the only three-kilometer-wide combat sector of the 1st Panzer Division.[46] The Luftwaffe also concentrated its raids on this segment in the Meuse River loop south of Gaulier.

Guderian's biggest problem was completely inadequate artillery support. His Corps had only 141 tubes whereas the French 55th Infantry Division opposite him had concentrated 174 artillery pieces on 13 May.[47] The other artillery units of French X Corps also had to be considered because most of them could be employed against Panzer Corps Guderian's attack.[48] Fire from the artillery units of the French XXXXI Corps on the right flank, mainly from the fortress artillery at Charleville and Mézières, also turned out to be dangerous. The attacker's artillery inferiority to the defender was thus about 1:3! But that number still looks much too advantageous for Guderian's artillery units. Some batteries did not arrive from the Ardennes until much later and had no effect.[49] So it was that the 2d Panzer Division had the most difficult mission of attacking practically without artillery support during the first phase. Even 1st Panzer Division waited in vain for the announced massive employment of the artillery pieces concentrated here: "This announced barrage at first did not materialize at all and was finally expressed around 1600 by a few individual rounds!"[50]

General von Kleist later explained: "my artillery only had 50 rounds per battery [in other words, about 12 rounds per tube] because the ammunition convoys were held up by the traffic jams on the roads in the Ardennes."[51] In this situation, as far as Guderian was concerned, everything depended on the Luftwaffe, the "vertical artillery" of the blitzkrieg.

The Meuse River Crossing on 13 May

Apocalypse over Sedan: The Luftwaffe's Rolling Raid

The gunners stopped shooting and hit the dirt; the infantrymen dove into the trenches and remained there motionless; they were deafened by the

> *crashing of bombs and screeching of the dive-bomber sirens. . . . Just 5 hours of this nightmare sufficed to shatter their nerves; they were no longer able to react to the approaching infantry.*[52]
>
> General [Edmond] Ruby on the effect of the German air raid

The Luftwaffe's mass bombing raid at Sedan on 13 May was the mightiest event of the campaign in the west and also one of the biggest tactical surprises of the war. According to the British and French reports, the psychological shock effect even exceeded the effect of the first poison gas and tank attacks during World War I.[53] Never again would the Luftwaffe carry out anywhere near such a massive attack against such a narrow frontline sector.

As von Kleist emphasized in the order for the Meuse River crossing on 13 May, "almost all German air combat formations were to be employed here."[54] Although this promise was not completely fulfilled, nevertheless, the strongest concentration of aircraft units that had ever been seen until then hit the Sedan Sector.[55]

The Third Air Fleet was employed primarily; II Air Corps under Loerzer was reinforced with formations from I Air Corps and the fighters of Jagdfliegerführer 3 [3d Fighter Command]. At the same time, V.Fliegerkorps (V Air Corps) sealed off the attack in depth. In the afternoon, VIII.Fliegerkorps (VIII Air Corps), which until then had been employed under Luftflotte 2 (Second Air Fleet), also joined the attack. This was the so-called Nahkampf-Fliegerkorps (Close Support Air Corps) under Generalmajor Freiherr [Baron] [Wolfram] von Richthofen that had specialized in close ground support for the army. The 77th Sturzkampfgeschwader (Stukageschwader) (Dive-bomber Group) played a special role; its Commodore, Oberst [Günter] Schwartzkopff (posthumously Generalmajor),[56] had been called the "Father of the Stuka." A total of about 1,500 aircraft supported Panzer Group Kleist:

600 bombers (He 111, Do 17, Ju 88)
250 dive-bombers (Ju 87)
500 fighters (Me 109)
120 destroyers (Me 110)[57]

Only fragments of the Luftwaffe files have been preserved, so it is no longer possible to estimate how many aircraft sorties were flown altogether for direct or indirect support. After all, many of those aircraft went out on several successive sorties on 13 May. Only a smaller air contingent was employed in the Monthermé-Charleville-Mézières Sector to support Panzer Corps Reinhardt. Most of the aircraft were concentrated on the Meuse River loop at Sedan to implement the attack method of the rolling raid that Guderian and Loerzer had developed.[58] A total of 310 bombers, 200 dive-bombers, and 300 fighters and destroyers were available for this mission.[59] There were 1,215 bomber and dive-bomber sorties flown in the four-kilometer-wide main effort sector inside and south of the Meuse River loop at Sedan alone.[60] During the last ninety minutes prior to the Meuse River crossing, 750 bombers and dive-bombers supported Panzer Group Kleist.[61] The Luftwaffe had drafted the following timetable for 13 May:

> Phase 1, 0800–1200: At first, formations of the Third Air Fleet flew nuisance sorties against the French positions along the Meuse River between Flize and Mouzon, with the main effort near Sedan.
>
> Phase 2, 1200–1540: The first dive-bomber formations of VIII Air Corps showed up punctually around noon. The attack procedure was now changed. That meant the systematic bombing of certain target groups.
>
> Phase 3, 1540–1600: The Luftwaffe delivered a massive raid directed mainly against the Meuse River loop at Sedan during the phase immediately prior to the river crossing.
>
> Phase 4, 1600–1730: Luftwaffe sorties were shifted into the depth of the enemy territory while the first infantry wave was crossing the Meuse River. The combined dive-bomber formations flew according to a precisely determined plan, raiding the rear area positions and the artillery.
>
> Phase 5, 1730 to onset of darkness: To finish up, the bridgehead that had now been formed was sealed off in rear areas by engaging approaching enemy reserves.

It was primarily the mass bombing raid shortly before 1600 that presented an infernal spectacle, as was emphasized in the after-action reports. Attacks deep into the French defense system were continued for another one and a half hours, although with reduced intensity. That made it possible to keep neutralizing the artillery of the 55th Infantry Division. The psychological effect of this sheer ceaseless rolling raid, as figured by Guderian, was decisive. Whenever the Stuka pilots came racing at the enemy positions in their dives, they turned on a horribly screeching siren, the Jericho trumpet. In addition, attached to the bomb fins were so-called organ pipes, which produced a shrill whistling sound. Even the German soldiers on the north bank were profoundly impressed. With a mixture of fascination and horror, they contemplated this spectacle, which made the deep and round valley of Sedan resemble an amphitheater of smoke and flames:

> What we now got to see during the next 20 minutes is one of the most tremendous impressions of this war. Squadron after squadron approaches at high altitude, deploys into a line formation and then the first aircraft came diving down perpendicularly, followed by the second, the third, and so on, ten, twelve aircraft pouncing simultaneously like predatory birds on their quarry, releasing their bomb load right over the target. . . . The explosion is immense each time and the noise is deafening. Everything is blurred. . . . The enemy is hit here by an enormous annihilation strike and still, more squadrons keep coming on, climbing to high altitudes in order then to dive steeply down with the same objective, that is, to bust the Sedan invasion gateway wide open. We stand there and watch events as if transfixed.[62]

The German infantrymen felt considerably more queasy directly along the Meuse River bank: "All hell seems to have broken loose. . . . A sulfurous, yellowish-gray wall rises on the other bank; it keeps growing. The enormous air pressure causes glass panes to rattle and crack. . . . The ground is shaken; houses sway. What must it look like on the other side, among the French?"[63]

The soldiers of the 55th Infantry Division were utterly unprepared for this inferno that now broke over their heads. 1st Lieutenant Michard described his horror:

> Explosions keep crashing all over the place. All you can feel is the nightmare noise of the bombs whose whistling becomes louder and louder the closer they get. You have the feeling that they are zeroed in precisely on you; you wait with tense muscles. The explosion comes like relief. But then there is another one, then there are two more and ten more. . . . The whistling sounds are superposed and crisscrossed like a fabric without gaps; the explosions blend in a ceaseless thunder. When the intensity of that sound abates for a moment, you can hear yourself gasping for air.

The Stuka (Ju 87 dive-bomber), along with the Panzer, became the symbol of the blitzkrieg. *Bundesarchiv Koblenz [Federal Archives]*

> So, here we are, motionless, silent, crouched, hunched over, mouth open so that your eardrums will not burst. The bunker trembles. . . . Bombs of all caliber are being dropped. The small ones come down in packets. The big ones do not whistle. As they hit, the noise deceptively sounds like an approaching train. Twice I had acoustic hallucinations . . . that make me think that I own a railroad station; a train comes thundering in. . . . The crashing sound of the explosion shakes me out of my stupor and brutally returns me to reality. Now the dive-bombers join the other bombers. The noise from the siren of the diving aircraft drills into your ear and tears at your nerves. You feel as if you want to scream and roar.[64]

Interestingly enough, the German officers, who observed this terrible spectacle from a safe distance, learned only several years after the war what the essence of the effect of the Luftwaffe raid had really been. Due to the initiative of a lecturer on military history at the French War College, in 1957 a meeting of officers of the former 1st Panzer Division and French veterans who had fought there in May 1940 took place on the former battlefield of Sedan. Graf von Kielmansegg was astonished because the actual destruction caused by the Luftwaffe—measured against the tremendous effort—was minimal. Hardly a single bunker suffered a direct hit that destroyed it, and only fifty-six men were listed as casualties. But the indirect effect was all the more enormous. The command of the 55th Infantry Division was paralyzed because all of the telecommunications cables that were frequently laid out in the open had been cut. Much more serious was the psychological paralysis of individual soldiers whose nerves often were unable to withstand the sustained bombardment of the rolling raids.[65]

The Breakthrough of the 1st Panzer Division

The warnings of the higher-ranking generals that a Panzer division was not at all suitable for making a river crossing were not unjustified. The 1st Panzer Division, for example, had only a single rifle regiment. Guderian had beefed up his most important division that was to form the battering ram for the breakthrough with infantry as best he could. For the Meuse River crossing on 13 May, it was given, among other things, the elite regiment Großdeutschland and the Sturmpionier-Bataillon 43 (43d Assault Engineer Battalion).

Attack of Infantry Regiment Großdeutschland on Hill 247. The river was to be crossed along the northern edge of Sedan at the Pont Neuf bridge. Surprisingly enough, however, all of the bunkers along the Meuse River had remained intact in spite of the Luftwaffe's massive bombing raids. All attempts to cross the river with the help of assault boats and rubber boats failed before they even got started. Now, fire was placed on Bunker 211 that commanded the crossing point; but not even the 7.5-cm short-barrel cannons of the assault gun battery of the Infantry Regiment Großdeutschland were able to accomplish anything against this solid reinforced-concrete structure. Valuable time was lost before it was finally possible to move a self-propelled 8.8-cm gun into position. That gun, of course, immediately achieved a penetrating effect. Now an attempt was again made to cross the Meuse River in assault boats. This time, again, the crossing attempt failed; Leutnant [Alexander] Graf von Medem and two engineers were killed in action. It took a long search before it was possible to figure out where the shots had come from. A bunker had been built into the embankment on the opposite bank in such a clever fashion that the machine gun only had a flanking effect and was thus not recognizable upon frontal observation. The 2d Battalion, which was employed forward, was able to start the crossing only after this bunker had been knocked out.

The 7th Company, under the command of Oberleutnant [Eberhard] Wackernagel,[66] was the first to get across and immediately took the field fortifications of the Pont Ncuf and Cimctièrc strongpoints by storm. Then it pushed forward along the western edge of Sedan and to the south until fire from the bunkers on the opposite height stopped it at the Donchery-Sedan road. The 6th Company, under the command of Oberleutnant [René l'Homme] von Courbière, arrived shortly thereafter. After a brief conference between the two company commanders, the 7th Company remained in its current position to provide fire cover, while the 6th Company was to mount an ad hoc surprise attack on the bunkers. The after-action report described what happened next: "The 6th [Company] quickly made its decision; after all, there was only one decision even though only half the company was available and even though it had no heavy weapons. The decision was: attack! A quick scouting mission showed that a big six-port pillbox [Bunker 104], 200 meters south of the road along the edge of an orchard, offered good approach possibilities while another one—somewhat smaller [Bunker 7 bis]—was 250 meters behind and half-right."[67]

By way of a diversionary maneuver, the main body of the company now mounted a frontal attack against the Bunker 104, but machine-gun fire forced them to seek cover. In the meantime, wheeling out to the left and exploiting the cover offered by several bomb craters, a sergeant and two enlisted men crept up to the bunker. After reaching the dead angle, the sergeant threw a hand grenade through one gun port. The occupants immediately rushed out into the open and surrendered.

Then they stormed Bunker 7 bis, which was directly behind the other one. In the meantime, however, the first casualties were suffered. An enemy antitank gun was firing on the left flank, and, at first, it was impossible to determine its exact position. Finally, it was realized that the rounds had been fired from a barn that stood on a suspicious gray foundation. A dark gun port was spotted in the foundation of what turned out to be Bunker 7 ter, which was also seized quickly. In that way around 1900 the second line of resistance was penetrated, although the soldiers had drifted too far to the right into the combat sector of the 1st Rifle Regiment.

After the 7th and 8th companies had been moved up, the 2d Battalion attacked Hill 247. The Centre de résistance La Prayelle was grouped around that hill with a number

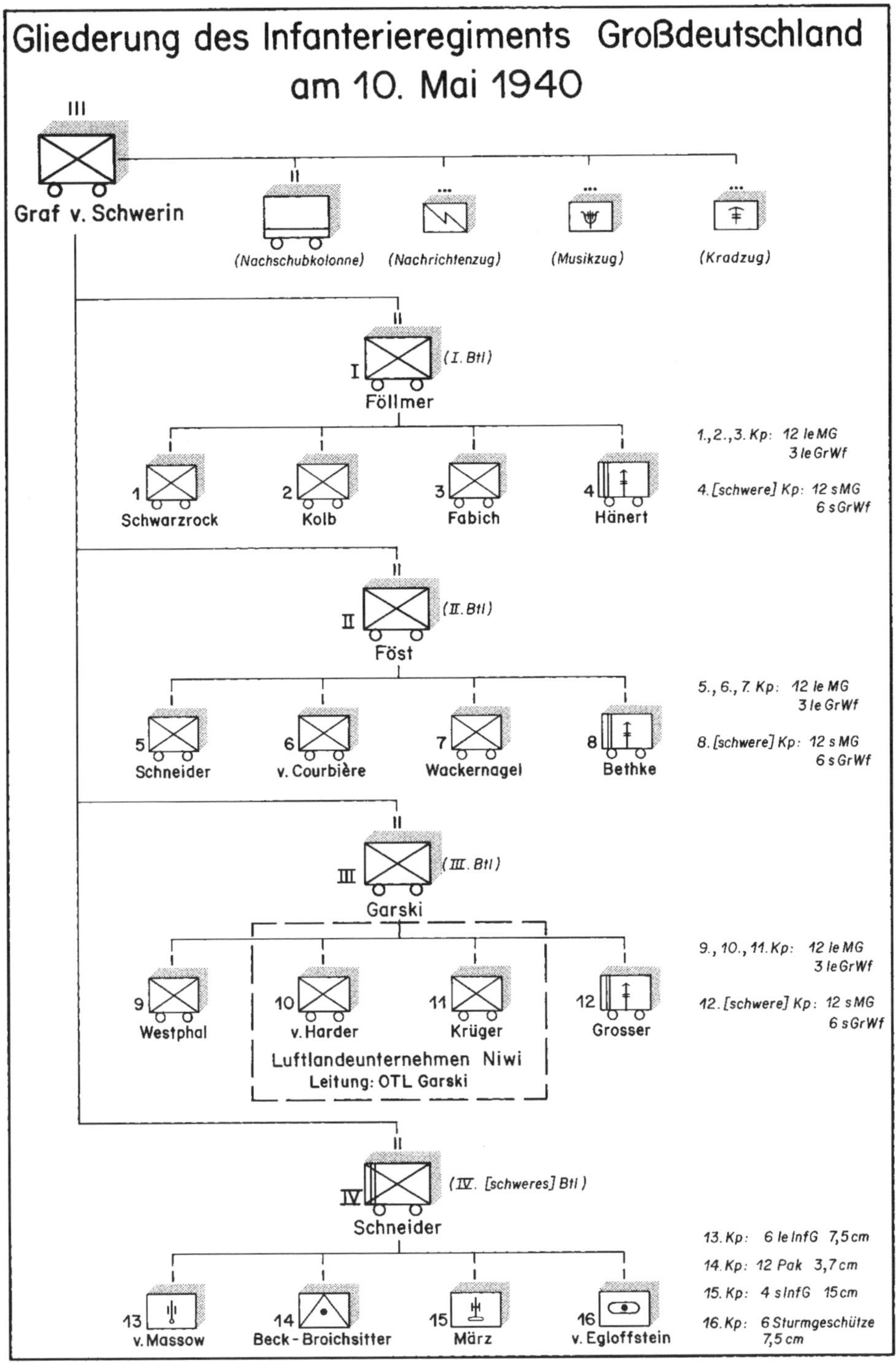

Organization of Infantry Regiment Großdeutschland, 10 May 1940

of bunkers and field fortifications. The hill was taken by storm in hand-to-hand fighting at around 2000. Penetration into the Bois de la Marfée [woods] was impossible because of the completely exposed terrain located in front of the woods. Besides, the 1st and 3d battalions were still hung up far to the rear. They had been involved in time-consuming house-to-house fighting in Torcy, the section of the city of Sedan on the southern bank.[68]

The attack mounted by the 6th Company of the Großdeutschland was an action straight from the move. In spite of enemy fire that forced the men repeatedly to seek cover, the 2d Battalion had just two hours to cover the last ten kilometers to the Meuse River to arrive at the crossing point on time at 1600. During this forced march, the men had to lug the mortars, machine guns, and especially the ammunition. The river crossing commenced as soon as they reached the Meuse.

Thc attack was mounted in a pure infantry fashion, without any heavy weapons' support.[69] The 6th Company's Stoßtrupp mission was a completely isolated action without any contact with neighboring units. The companies put across first did not wait for the following elements but staged a probing attack, regardless of their exposed flanks. The leader of this assault team had neither contact with his superiors nor was he able to refer to any precise orders. The only guidance was the mission assigned to his battalion: "The 2d Battalion will cross the Meuse River as the lead battalion of the Infantry Regiment Großdeutschland; it will break through the Maginot Line and will seize Hill 247."[70]

This was a typical example of the German system of Auftragstaktik where only the attack's objective was specified. The company commander did not follow any prescribed route but took the line of least resistance, sometimes even penetrating into the combat sector of the neighboring regiment because that is where he spotted the decisive gap.

1st Rifle Regiment Takes Hill 301. The 1st Rifle Regiment had a considerably easier mission than the Großdeutschland and crossed the Meuse River in the previously described Gaulier Gap. Many officers took the lead and crossed the river in the very first boats with their men. Guderian, the commanding general of that corps, rode to the opposite bank with the first assault boat of the second wave. Waiting for him there he found Balck, the commander of the 1st Rifle Regiment, who said: "Joy riding in canoes on the Meuse is forbidden." He was referring to Guderian's ironic statement during a map exercise shortly before when he told some young and rather nonchalant officers that crossing the Meuse River under enemy fire could hardly be compared to a "canoe trip."[71] After that, the infantry pushed south to take the intermediate objective, the important crossroads south of Castle Bellevue. France's fate had been decided here once before when Napoleon III capitulated to Prussia's King Wilhelm I in that castle on 2 September 1870. The decisive breakthrough of the so-called extended Maginot Line took place in the immediate vicinity on 13 May. After the château strongpoint around the most important Bunker 103 had been taken, the Sedan-Donchery road was cut at the Bellevue intersection and the center of resistance Frénois penetrated.[72]

However, the fragmentary after-action reports fail to mention that this success was mainly due to a special unit that was only temporarily placed under 1st Panzer Division. This was an assault team commanded by Oberleutnant [Günther] Korthals and consisting of two platoons of the 3d Company, 43d Assault Engineer Battalion.[73] Assault engineers were specialists in attacking bunkers. They had practiced these attacks again and again, using shaped charges and flamethrowers. Airborne assault engineers had carried out the commando mission against the Belgian fort Eben Emael in that same way.

The advance turned into a nightmare for Korthals's company. At 1600 on 13 May, when it was actually supposed to cross the Meuse River with one of the first waves, its vehicles were still stuck in a traffic jam along the southern edge of the Ardennes. Because the company had been more or less torn apart, Oberleutnant Guthy, the company commander, ordered the platoons to fight their way individually through to the Meuse, heading for Gaulier. Korthals arrived there at 1715 with the 3d Platoon and was immediately ferried across. He was in a very tough situation because he was unable to reach any of his superiors, neither his company commander nor the commander of the 1st Rifle Regiment. Thereupon, he also took under his command the 1st Platoon, which had just crossed, and decided to attack all by himself.

The 1st Rifle Regiment's advance had bogged down near the Bellevue intersection on the Sedan-Donchery road. This is why Korthals bypassed the intersection to the west, thus getting into the combat sector of the 2d Panzer Division. He was quickly able to knock out two bunkers along the embankment above the Meuse River after the bunker's occupants had first been blinded by smoke candles.[74] Korthals crossed the road to Donchery at 1830[75] to attack the artillery casemate—the most important defense facility in the Sedan Sector—that was located directly southwest of the intersection. That bunker had assumed almost outstanding significance because it alone was in a position to control the segment of the Meuse River around Donchery and prevent a crossing of or even an approach to the river in the flat terrain that offered no cover. The burning wrecks of some Panzers could be seen on the bank. They belonged to the 2d Panzer Division that was attacking here and had tried to haul rubber boats to the river.

In the meantime, however, the casemate was temporarily neutralized after a Panzer had hit a gun port. In spite of the casualties suffered in the process, the remaining bunker occupants continued to fight. The bunker's commander, Lieutenant Nonat, had his men continue firing with the second gun, although he was now constantly being hit by German Panzers. When the assault engineers threatened to circle around the casemate, the French artillery men left the bunker system, which was difficult to defend because of big gun ports. The occupants of Bunker C, located above the slope and capable of controlling the intersection, acted the same way. Fire from Panzer cannons had earlier made the bunker ripe for assault.

The artillery casemate south of Castle Bellevue commanded the Meuse River bend at Donchery with its 7.5-cm guns. *General a.D. [Lieutenant General, Ret.] Johann Adolf Count von Kielmansegg*

The assault team was thus the first to break through the line of Meuse River bunkers. Korthals now decided to wheel to the west and to take the other bunkers from behind to enable the men of the 2d Panzer Division to make their crossing. These men had tried several times in vain to cross the Meuse River. The two platoons pushed ahead along the road to Donchery that ran above the Meuse River. In the process, they took a number of fortifications, for example, the huge Bunker 102.[76] Then the assault engineers penetrated into the suburb of Donchery that was located along the southern bank of the Meuse River. As darkness fell, the partly abandoned bunkers along the hill located to the south thereof were taken. In the meantime, 2d Panzer Division had also managed to exploit the resulting gap and to get its first elements across the Meuse River.

The independently pushed attack of the two assault engineer platoons also created the prerequisite for the fast breakthrough of the 1st Rifle Regiment, 1st Panzer Division. The flanking effect of the strongpoints to the west of the Bellevue intersection had now been eliminated, which allowed the center of resistance Frénois position to be seized by about 2010. But now the infantrymen seemed to be exhausted because they had been on the attack almost without interruption for days on end. Balck, an uncommonly energetic officer who advanced to the rank of commander in chief of an army group during the war, commanded this regiment. He insisted on seizing Hill 301 (La Boulette), located south of Frénois, on that same evening, come what may. This rather sober-minded regular was not inspired by the romantic-nostalgic memory that this hill in 1870 was Moltke's command post. Instead, he was guided by his own experiences from World War I, the attack on Mt. Kemmel in Flanders. At that time, the assaulting formations were given a break—even though success was almost within reach—because they seemed completely exhausted. In that situation, a senior officer should have been way up front to get the men to rush forward once again and win a final victory. During the night, however, the enemy was able to build up new defenses on the hill with the help of reserves that had been quickly moved up. The hill was taken the next day, but with heavy casualties.

Balck remembered that situation when he said: "Something that is easy today can cost us rivers of blood tomorrow." He described Hill 301 as "the hill of the day" and ordered that the attack be continued even as darkness began to fall. Way up front, Balck advanced together with the 2d Battalion that at the first try took the enemy strongpoint at the top of the hill by storm.[77] Then he ordered the following radio message to be sent to Division: "1st Rifle Regiment took commanding heights [301] just north of Cheveuges at 2240. Last enemy bunker in our hands. Complete breakthrough. Elements, 1st Rifle Regiment, sent toward Chéhéry and heights to the east thereof."[78]

While the fighting for Hill 301 was still going on, reconnaissance units had pushed south through the woods to the east. They reached the northern edge of Chéhéry (five kilometers north of Chémery) around midnight. Within eight hours the 1st Rifle Regiment had thus crossed the Meuse River and had punched eight kilometers deep through three lines of fortifications.

The Meuse River Crossing of 10th Panzer Division and the Role of the Rubarth Assault Team

The 10th Panzer Division, commanded by Generalmajor [Ferdinand] Schaal, was to cross the Meuse River in the sector to the left of the 1st Panzer Division. Two groups were formed for this purpose. Acting as the right attack group, the reinforced 86th Rifle Regiment was to advance from the southern edge of Sedan and from Balan toward the village of Wadelincourt located on the opposite bank. The left attacking group, the reinforced 69th Rifle Regiment, was to cross the Meuse River at Pont-Maugis, coming from Bazeilles.[79]

This mission seemed almost impossible for several reasons:

1. *Lack of Fire Support:* Guderian had employed almost all the reinforcement units available to him with the 1st Panzer Division that was attacking at the point of

main effort. That also applied to the artillery. The 10th Panzer Division even had to detach its heavy batteries to support the neighboring unit and now only had twenty-four light field howitzers (105-mm) with an inadequate ammunition issue. The air raids had also been concentrated primarily on targets in the combat sector of the 1st Panzer Division. This meant that the enemy positions in the Pont-Maugis-Wadelincourt Sector had remained mostly untouched. But above all, it was the flanking fire of the 71st Infantry Division from the Remilly area and from the heavy batteries of X Corps that began to take effect. Their forward observers had an excellent view of the terrain from the commanding heights on the other bank of the Meuse River. The left attacking group mainly felt the crushing fire superiority of the French. A devastating barrage hit the village of Bazeilles just as engineer equipment was to be unloaded from the vehicles, destroying eighty-one out of ninety-six rubber boats. That meant that the attack of the 69th Regiment had failed before it had even begun. The left attack group was then withdrawn from its combat sector and kept in readiness as a reserve behind the 86th Rifle Regiment.[80]

2. *Timetable:* The 1st Panzer Division had the best approach routes and almost all of its elements reached the Meuse River on time. This was impossible for the 10th Panzer Division in spite of its big rush. Just twenty minutes before the attack was to begin, the commander of the 86th Rifle Regiment sent the bad news that the Meuse River crossing had to be postponed because the engineers had still not arrived with their rubber boats. That triggered a vehement reaction from Oberst [Wolfgang] Fischer, the commander of the 10th Rifle Brigade. He demanded that the attack be launched punctually, no matter what, to exploit the psychological effect deriving from the dive-bomber raids. Thus, he ordered everybody "to line up immediately and, if necessary, to swim across the Meuse River."[81] He himself assumed his position at the head of the right attack group. But the rubber boats did arrive after all at the last moment. Still, valuable time passed until the boats were inflated and given to the individual units. Meanwhile, the French defenders had long recovered from their shock and opened fire.

3. *Terrain:* The 1st Panzer Division was able to approach the city of Sedan as well as Gaulier under good cover. On the other hand, there was only a narrow strip of built-up terrain in the sector of the 10th Panzer Division, and that strip extended down to the river along the southern edge of Sedan. This meant that most of the assault teams had to cross wide-open, completely exposed terrain over a stretch of six hundred to eight hundred meters, as if on a silver platter, to get to the river in the first place. The way led through the flat, partly swampy meadows of the Meuse River.[82] In addition to their own gear and weapons on their shoulders, the infantrymen also had to drag rubber boats filled with hand grenades and engineer equipment (such as wire cutters, multiple and satchel charges, etc.). Again and again, French artillery shells hit among them while they drew cannon and machine-gun fire from the heights rising on the other side of the Meuse River. The enemy had

entrenched himself on both sides of Wadelincourt in a defense line reinforced by bunkers.

The confusion became even worse when some French shells exploded and spread a rather strange whitish smoke. The gas alarm was sounded immediately and the sweating and wheezing soldiers now had to continue dragging the heavy rubber boats on to the Meuse River while wearing their gas masks. Then it was discovered to everybody's relief that this was a false alarm. As was found out much later, the presumed gas clouds had come from World War I ammunition that had been stored too long.[83] At first, it was impossible to move even a single rubber boat to the Meuse River. As it says in the regiment's war diary, either "the rubber boats . . . were shot to pieces or their crews got stuck in the swamp."[84] In the end, however, individual squads managed to get to the river. Now, they faced by far the most dangerous moment of this suicide mission, that is, crossing the seventy-meter-wide Meuse River under enemy machine-gun fire.

The attempt to cross the Meuse River failed all along the line in the sector of the 10th Panzer Division. There was one exception, namely, the assault team of Assault Engineer Feldwebel [Sergeant] [Walter] Rubarth. He was a platoon leader in the 2d Company, Panzerpionier-Bataillon 49 (49th Panzer Engineer Battalion), which had been placed under 1st Battalion, 86th Rifle Regiment, for this particular attack. Together with five assault engineers and six infantrymen, he was to cross the Meuse River south of the destroyed railroad station bridge and to seize the bunkers on the opposite bank. His after-action report illustrates how this mission was carried out:[85]

> The pneumatic boats were put on the water and I reached the opposite bank of the Meuse River with my men and an infantry squad. . . . I reached the opposite bank near a strong earth bunker and knocked the crew out together with Gefriter (Private First Class) Podzus. Enemy artillery now placed heavy fire on our crossing point. I cut through a wire obstacle and, ahead of the infantry that was supposed to screen our right flank, we got across a trip wire. We attacked the next bunker from the rear. I attached a charge. At the next moment, a part of the rear bunker wall is bashed in by the force of the detonation. We exploited that opportunity and engaged the occupants with hand grenades. They showed the white flag after a short fire fight. Loud cheering from our comrades reached us from the other bank. Inspired, we pounced on two other timber and earth bunkers that we had spotted about 100 meters in front of us, half-left. . . . With daredevil boldness, Gefreiter Bräutigam attacks the left-hand bunker all by himself and captures the occupants by his skillful action. I seized the second bunker together with Unteroffizier (Corporal) Theophel and Gefreiters Podzus and Monk. This means that the first line of bunkers, directly behind the Meuse River, had been breached over a width of about 300 meters. We continued to advance and reached the road running behind the railroad embankment. Here we drew

> such heavy fire that we had to seek cover temporarily. Only now did I find out that I was all alone on the other bank, together with one sergeant and four enlisted men plus the infantry squad that screened our right flank.[86]

In spite of heavy enemy fire, Rubarth made his way back to the crossing point to pick up reinforcements. In the end, four assault engineers of his platoon managed to row to the other bank. This reinforcement could not in any way make up for the casualties that had been suffered in the meantime. The assault team now penetrated from the railroad embankment into the second line of resistance and took two concrete bunkers (Nos. 8 and 9) north of Wadelincourt.

Quite by accident, Rubarth had hit the spot where the line of bunkers along the Meuse River met the second line of resistance that intersected the Meuse River loop between Wadelincourt and Bellevue. In mopping up the second line of resistance from the flank, without knowing it he penetrated into the combat sector of the 1st Panzer Division and opened up the way to the south for the 1st and 3d battalions of the Großdeutschland that had been involved in bitter house-to-house fighting in Torcy, the southern section of the city of Sedan. Rubarth pushed on through the trenches of the field works here all the way to Bunker 8 ter whose occupants surrendered without

Carrying a rubber boat. *Bundesarchiv Koblenz [Federal Archives]*

Feldwebel Walter Rubarth, assault team leader on 13 May 1940 (shown wearing the Knight's Cross of the Iron Cross). *Bundesarchiv Koblenz [Federal Archives]*

resistance around 1900.[87] However, heavy machine-gun fire from the bunkers of the center of resistance La Prayelle on Hill 247 prevented the attack from continuing, and so the remaining little group prepared for defense in a trench system.

At first, Rubarth could not guess what unexpected consequences were to spring from the action of his tiny group. The assault team he led was the only one that managed to reach the opposite bank of the Meuse River. He had seized a total of seven bunkers and had opened the decisive breach. This individual action turned the attack of the 10th Panzer Division, which seemed to have failed, into a success. Above all one must be astonished that a sergeant led this action. Isolated on the other bank, he by no means acted passively; he did not sit and wait for an officer to give him an order. Instead, he seized the initiative along the lines of Auftragstaktik and acted independently. Rubarth was decorated with the Knight's Cross of the Iron Cross for his achievement and was commissioned with the rank of Leutnant (2d lieutenant). [Rubarth was killed in action in Russia on 26 October 1941.]

The following elements of the 10th Panzer Division used the breach struck by Rubarth's push. The next one to succeed was Leutnant [Heinrich] Hanbauer, who crossed the Meuse River at that same point. With his assault team, he knocked out Bunker 220[88] at the railroad crossing and took the heavily fortified locality of Wadelincourt.[89] In the meantime, the main body of the 1st Battalion, 86th Rifle Regiment, had been ferried across the Meuse River and around 2100 stormed Hill 246 located farther south. German cannon fire had already knocked out most of the bunkers of the Etadan strongpoint located there.[90] Thus, the hill, that was the main attack objective, was taken in a short time.

Initial Failure of the 2d Panzer Division

The 2d Panzer Division[91] had been given the most difficult assignment for the Meuse River crossing. It had advanced through the Ardennes on the notorious northern march route where a 250-kilometer-long traffic jam had formed. Consequently, the division arrived at the Meuse River rather late, at a time when the other two divisions had already launched the attack. For the last two to three kilometers, the division's approach to the Meuse River ran across open terrain without any cover. In the process, the left attack group drew fire from two sides because it had to attack into the bend of the Meuse River at Donchery. It had to advance parallel to the Meuse River that flowed south here and received heavy flanking fire mainly from the park at Castle Bellevue (Bunker 103).

The heights south of the Meuse River rise steeply and tower over the northern bank by about 150 meters. Although the terrain almost defended itself, this sector had been developed into a defensive bulwark with particularly strong fortifications. Some Panzers that tried to drag rubber boats to the banks of the Meuse River were hit and set on fire. The artillery casemate at the Bellevue intersection proved to be most effective. It had been built into the Meuse River loop in a highly refined manner and all vehicles that approached the Meuse River north of Donchery across open terrain drew direct fire from the 75-mm guns.

Artillery observers had an excellent view over the Meuse River from their bunkers in the Donchery terrain sector. They concentrated the fire of the 55th Infantry Division's

174 artillery pieces on the 2d Panzer Division that was attacking here. The batteries of the French 102d Infantry Division that fired from the right flank were also dangerous, as was the heavy fortress artillery from the Charleville-Mézières area. Virtually without any artillery support worth mentioning, the combat elements of the 2d Panzer Division had to approach the Meuse River during the attack's first phase across terrain that offered no cover whatsoever. Like the 10th Panzer Division, the 2d Panzer Division had to turn its heavy batteries over to the 1st Panzer Division and now only had twenty-four light field howitzers. They did not arrive on the battlefield until around 1700 and had only a few shells because the ammunition vehicles were stuck somewhere in the Ardennes.[92]

For these reasons, the officers of the 2d Panzer Division believed that it was impossible to mount the attack that same day. A passage from a report by Oberst [Hans] Koelitz, who at that time (with the rank of Oberstleutnant) commanded the 2d Rifle Regiment, noted: "A dispatch rider tried to get up front with his motorcycle and brought me the 'Division Order for the Crossing of the Meuse River at 1600 on 13 May.'—On 13 May?—What?—Blast! That is today, that is in 2 hours! And we are still sitting in this damned forest (in the Ardennes)!"[93]

The attack across the Meuse River did not commence until around 1730. In the meantime, Panzers and 8.8-cm *Flak* [antiaircraft artillery] guns fired at the bunkers on the opposite bank. All attempts on the part of the infantry to get across the Meuse River failed. Most of the time it was not even possible to move the rubber boats anywhere near the banks. In the right attacking group west of Donchery, a lieutenant and some volunteers swam across the Meuse River. However, they were unable to accomplish anything against the bunkers and had to swim back again. Meanwhile, the neighbor on the left, the 1st Panzer Division, had successfully crossed the river and had pushed all the way to the Meuse River bend at Castle Bellevue. As described earlier, Korthals and his two assault engineer platoons, quite on his own decision, wheeled to the west and attacked the bunkers along the Meuse River from behind. In that way he enabled the left attack group of the 2d Panzer Division to cross the river east of Donchery. A small detail finally reached the other bank in a rubber boat for the first time at around 2000. The crossing point was still under such heavy enemy fire that the regular ferrying of troops across the river was not possible until around 2220 in pitch darkness.[94]

The considerable problems of the 2d Panzer Division at Donchery confirmed Guderian's argument when he had refused to attack with the main body of his corps across the open terrain west of Sedan. His decision to put the main attack effort not to the west of the Ardennes Canal but right at Sedan conflicted with the instructions he had received from his superiors. Even the command of Panzer Group Kleist could not help but state—after the fact—that Guderian's independent action had indeed been correct.[95]

The Myth of the Panzer Breakthrough at Sedan

Guderian had demanded again and again that he be allowed to attack with his Panzer divisions in the lead so that after the infantry had crossed the Meuse River he could immediately thrust deep into enemy territory with the Panzer formations that were ready and standing by. During the night between 13 and 14 May, however, the infantry was already far beyond the Meuse River and had formed a bridgehead. But where were the Panzers? In the meantime, their crews had moved into a standby area along the southern edge of the Ardennes to spend a restful night there and recover from the ordeals of the past days.

The engineers cannot be blamed for the fact that the Panzers still had not crossed the Meuse River. The men of the 505th Engineer Battalion, supported by elements of the 37th Panzer Engineer Battalion, worked with feverish haste on the construction of the pontoon bridge in Gaulier.[96] The first sixteen-ton ferry was already finished at 1910, so that individual antitank guns and light infantry guns could be gradually transported to the other bank. There were no Panzers anywhere that could have been put across.[97] Shortly before midnight, the pontoon ferries that had been built already were hitched together to form a bridge. In that way, the first vehicle was able to cross the famous military bridge of Gaulier at 0010. Astonishingly enough, however, it took until 0720 before the spearhead of the 1st Panzer Brigade rolled across the bridge.[98] To that extent, there was a "Panzer gap" of seven hours or, figuring from the launching of the first ferry, there was a gap of twelve hours. There are three primary explanations for this time gap.

1. Guderian separated the infantry and the Panzers to send them into action, in succession, by echelons.[99] By temporarily holding back the Panzers, he wanted to preserve the element of surprise and then have them punch deep into enemy territory to create a shock effect.[100] But that turned out to have been a mistake. According to von Mellenthin's *Panzerschlachten* (Panzer Battles), Balck criticized Guderian after the fact: "If the 1st Rifle Brigade, during the Meuse River crossing, had had Panzers under its command for immediate use, then things would have been considerably simpler at that time. It should . . . have been possible here to put individual Panzers across the river rather early with the help of improvised ferries. In that case, it would not have been necessary—as actually happened—to order the troops to advance without Panzer support during the night of 13–14 May. If the French counterattack had gotten moving somewhat faster, then the situation of the 1st Rifle Brigade could indeed have become very critical."[101] The breakthrough at Sedan, however, was an experiment for which there were no models. Guderian immediately drew the proper conclusions from that and, thereafter, only employed *Kampfgruppen* (mixed battle groups).

2. Although the 1st Panzer Brigade got the order to advance to the Meuse River bridge from the Corbion standby area, which was about ten kilometers away, at 0120, it took until 0720 before that move was accomplished. Other convoys clogged

all roads leading out of the standby area to Gaulier. In addition, the French artillery fired very accurately, so that burning vehicle wrecks blocked several intersections.

3. The most important reason for this miscalculation resided in the fact that even Guderian, who believed that speed was the attacker's most dangerous weapon, was simply overtaken by the onrush of events: Astonishingly enough the infantry broke through upon its first try. Because far too few rubber boats were available, only a few companies reached the opposite bank of the Meuse River in the beginning. Those companies, however, did not cling to the opposite bank and did not wait for reinforcements. Instead, they immediately mounted a probing attack. In so doing, seeking the line of least resistance, they infiltrated the enemy field works as quickly as possible to punch deep into the enemy positions. The most astonishing phenomenon of the famous breakthrough at Sedan was that it was essentially achieved by just three assault teams, which attacked practically all by themselves: Korthals with two assault engineer platoons, von Courbière with (initially) two platoons of infantry and one squad of assault engineers, and Rubarth with eleven men.

The successful breakthrough of these three assault teams caused the entire French defense system to collapse prematurely. At that time, however, the great mass of Guderian's infantry was still on the northern bank of the Meuse River whereas the Panzer crews were still doing first-echelon maintenance on their vehicles in the standby area in the Ardennes. As the infantry advanced farther into the depths of the enemy positions, some units pushed into a virtual vacuum, which appeared to be so mysterious that a number of German officers feared they were being drawn into a trap. Only after the war did some of them get a vague idea as to the kind of psychodrama that had taken place on the French side during that night.

The Panic of Bulson

Lafontaine's division command post was located eight kilometers south of Sedan in a bunker system in the Fond Dagot woods near Bulson.[102] Probably the oddest incident of the campaign in the west occurred here on 13 May when a mass psychosis erupted into a catastrophe with stunning speed.[103] Shortly after 1900 (1800, French time), 1st Lieutenant Rossignol left the division command post but immediately returned with the bad news that the area was crawling with fleeing soldiers. General [Edmond] Ruby described this episode as follows: "Suddenly, a wave of fleeing infantrymen and artillerymen came rushing at us on the road from Bulson. They hurried along, on vehicles or on foot, many of them without weapons but still carrying their packs, and shouted: 'The Panzers are in Bulson!' Some kept firing their rifles all around like crazy. . . . This was obviously a case of mass hysteria. All of these men maintained that they had seen Panzers at Chaumont and Bulson. Worse than that, officers of all ranks claimed to have gotten retreat orders but were unable to say from whom they had gotten those orders."[104]

Paradoxically enough, there was not a single German soldier—not to mention a single Panzer—in the area at that time. In retracing the chain reaction to the triggering moment, the epicenter of the panic can be placed on Plateau la Renardière, between Bois de la Marfée and Chaumont north of Bulson.[105] After all, this was where the first reports originated about those *chars fantômes* (phantom Panzers) that caused so much confusion. Probably it was Captain Fouques of the 169th Artillery Regiment who triggered this mass panic without intending to. His two batteries, B-7 and B-8, were in position in a wooded depression northeast of Chaumont. Suddenly, a few hundred meters farther north, on Plateau la Renardière, he reported the explosions of shells. He passed this information on via the field telephone and added the assumption that these might be hits of Panzer shells. Soon thereafter, the message spread like wildfire, but in an altered form. The shell hits suddenly became the muzzle flashes from the guns of German Panzers that were allegedly advancing from Plateau la Renardière via Chaumont toward Bulson. Now the wildest rumors and shouting about German Panzers (*chars allemands*) were all over the place: "Les chars sont à Bulson!" . . . "Les chars sont là, les chars nous suivent!" . . . "les boches arrivent, on se replie, vite" . . . "tout le monde se replie!" . . . "sauve qui peut!" (The tanks are at Bulson!—The tanks are there, the

Gen. Pierre Lafontaine's command post (55th Infantry Division), the scene of the Panic of Bulson (Photo taken in 1990). *Author's private collection*

tanks are following us!—The boches [Germans] are coming; we are withdrawing; hurry up.—Everybody is withdrawing!—It's everybody for himself!)

Quickly, the road from Bulson to Maisoncelle was clogged with fleeing soldiers and became the road of panic. This route led smack between the two bunker systems of the division's command post in the Fond Dagot woods. Lafontaine thereupon ordered several trucks to be parked across the road and, together with the officers of his staff, tried to stop the avalanche of fleeing soldiers. Temporarily he threateningly pulled out his pistol, but then he talked to his soldiers in an effort to calm them down. All was in vain. It was possible to stop the southward pushing troops briefly, but soon they had vanished again into the darkness. In the rear areas, officers tried several times to block the way, but in the end even they were swept away by the flood of fleeing soldiers. Some soldiers got all the way to Reims, which was one hundred kilometers away. The military police were also powerless in view of the masses of deserters. Within just a few hours, the 55th Infantry Division had dissolved in the whirlpool of panic, with the exception of just a few elements.

Astonishingly enough, it was the artillery where the first phenomenon of breakup had occurred, whereas the infantry was still fighting up front. The officers allowed themselves to be infected by the general hysteria. Colonel Poncelet, who commanded the heavy artillery of X Corps, urged on by his battalion commanders, finally gave the premature retreat order. When he realized that the report about the attacking Panzers was in error, it was too late. Entire battalions had abandoned their guns and were in flight. As a result of his order, not only the defensive organization of the 55th Infantry Division but also large elements of the neighboring 71st Infantry Division collapsed like a broken dam. The wave of panic now spread there also. The fatal consequences of his order so shocked Poncelet that he committed suicide a few days later.

Lafontaine had made the decisive mistake. Much too early (around 2000) he allowed himself to be persuaded to shift his division command post from the Fond Dagot woods to Chémery, which was four kilometers to the southwest. By so doing, he gave a fateful signal to his units that were in the process of dissolution. In this nightmarelike night, the division command post, which was in the process of evacuating Fond Dagot woods, met with another misfortune of catastrophic consequences. When firing was suddenly heard (coming from panicky soldiers) and a message was making the rounds that the Germans were attacking the bunker, the officers completely lost their heads. Then, the signal communications men hectically burned not only the coding materials but also smashed the telephone exchange. Thus, the division headquarters had decapitated itself in terms of its command capabilities. Now the breakup of the 55th Infantry Division could no longer be stopped.

Subsequently, several commissions were appointed to determine the cause of that unimaginable mass psychosis. Soldiers of all ranks maintained that they had seen attacking Panzers with their own eyes. But they had not fallen victim to German Panzers; they had fallen victim to their own nerves. The spearhead of the 1st Panzer

Brigade crossed the military bridge at Gaulier only on the next morning, around 0720, in other words, twelve hours later.[106] The investigation reports, therefore, assessed this mass panic as *un phénomène d'hallucination collective* (a phenomenon of collective hallucination).

Some historians also suspect that the French soldiers had run away from their own tanks, which they might have confused with German Panzers in the darkness. But even this assumption can be ruled out. At the particular time, there was not a single French tank anywhere in this sector.[107] It was also claimed that the shaky soldiers might possibly have mistaken French *chenillettes*—lightly armored tracked vehicles—for German battle Panzers. During that night, several chenillettes were indeed being driven around on the battlefield to pull antitank guns. This explanation, however, makes no sense in terms of the logic of the time sequence. The order to move these chenillettes around was not the cause but rather the consequence of the Panzer panic. They were sent forward, together with the antitank guns, only after "attacking German Panzers" had been reported there—although those Panzers did not turn up anywhere. When the Panzer panic erupted, there was neither a battle tank nor a chenillette in the area involved, the Plateau la Renardière.[108] And so, one of the oddest Panzer victories of World War II occurred at Sedan. Of course, it did happen over and over again that Panzers forced the enemy to flee without even firing one round—merely by showing up. But in this particular place, they caused the enemy's flight without having appeared at all.

The Advance from the Bridgehead on 14 May

We are facing a new Sedan, much worse than the one in 1870.[109]

General [Gaston-Henri] Billotte,
Commander in Chief, French 1st Army Group,
after the breakthrough by the Panzer Corps Guderian

The Air Battle over Sedan

The Luftwaffe's sustained bombing raids had already prepared the breakthrough in a decisive manner on 13 May. On the following day, German fighters and flak guns played an even more decisive role when they had to protect the military bridges against massive Allied air raids. At first, only the military bridge of the 1st Panzer Division at Gaulier was available to move heavy weapons and Panzers across the Meuse River.[110] Guderian, therefore, decided also to have the Panzer brigade of the 2d Panzer Division roll across the Gaulier bridge. On 14 May, almost six hundred Panzers passed through this eye of the needle. This meant that the success of the operation, conducted under enormous time pressure, depended mostly on that one bridge. It assumed an operational-level significance like no other bridge during World War II. To that extent, it also symbolizes the risky go-for-broke gamble that Hitler's adventurous war policy had forced his generals to adopt. The bridge had been completed with the last yard of available pontoon equipment, and for the time being, no additional reserve equipment was available. Thus, the destruction of the bridge as a result of an air raid or even serious damage to it was bound to have grave consequences.

The tremendous significance of this bridge was not lost on the headquarters of the French and British air forces. At first, the Allied military operations staffs tried to play down the Meuse River crossing at Sedan. Now, they went to the other extreme and put themselves into a disaster mode. General Billotte, commander in chief of 1st Army Group, appealed to d'Astier de la Vigerie, the commander in chief of the air force in the northern operations zone, with the famous words: "*La victorie ou la défaite passent par ces ponts*" (Victory or defeat will depend on these bridges).[111]

At the same time, other bad news became known; for example, from the Houx area where Rommel's 7th Panzer Division was able to cross the Meuse River. Nevertheless, General [Marcel] Têtu, the commander of the Tactical Air Forces, demanded: "Concentrate everything on Sedan. Priority between Sedan and Houx is at 1,000,000 to 1."[112]

Along with the following dramatic appeals to the pilots, there was also a revival of the memories of the "Calvary" (*mission de sacrifice*) of the French cavalry during the Battle of Sedan in 1870. The following statement was made during a mission conference of the 1st Air Force Division: "This operation is a revival of the extremely boldly conducted attack of the Margueritte [Cavalry] Division on 1 September 1870, but this time in the air."[113] At that time, the French cavalry had mounted a desperate attack in an attempt to break through the encirclement ring set up by Moltke's divisions. They rode frontally into the fire of massed German artillery. To memorialize this event, a huge cavalry monument was erected on the hill to the east of Floing from which this heroic attack was launched. The military bridge that was built across the Meuse River at Gaulier on 13 May 1940 was only one and a half kilometers to the southwest of that monument at the foot of the Floing Hill. Ironically German flak batteries were mainly concentrated on the former Cavalry Hill once again to foil a desperate French attack, but this time from the air.

The Allied air force generals were firmly determined to destroy the bridges in the Sedan area—cost what it may. They threw everything they had into the furnace of Sedan (*la fournaise de Sedan*). Now it turned out that they were not in a position to form an operational main effort as quickly as the Luftwaffe. They were able to muster only 152 bombers and 250 fighters. On 10 May, the French Air Force theoretically had 932 bombers (excluding the aircraft in North Africa), of which 242 were operational and ready at the front (see French Combat Aircraft Strength table in chapter 2, page 45). When the decisive air battle erupted on 14 May, the French air force was able to send out only 43 bombers. On the other hand, the Royal Air Force was able to come out with 109 bombers (73 Fairey Battles and 36 Blenheims). To protect the Allied bombers, the French air force, mostly, flew 250 fighter missions.

Guderian from the very first realized that the narrow military bridges at Sedan constituted the Achilles heel of the entire operation. In keeping with his motto *Klotzen, nicht kleckern!* (Hit with the fist, don't feel with the fingers!), he now put a hitherto unheard of concentration of antiaircraft protection in the Sedan area, primarily around the Gaulier bridge:[114]

The 102d Flak Regiment with three heavy battalions (I./18; I./36; II./38) and the 91st Light Battalion[115]
The 83d Light Flak Battalion of the 1st Panzer Division
The 92d Light Flak Battalion of the 2d Panzer Division
The 71st Light Flak Battalion of the 10th Panzer Division

This total of 303 Flak guns[116] could put up such a heavy fire curtain that hardly any aircraft got anywhere near the Gaulier bridge. This is why the Allied pilots who survived that attack kept talking about the "hell along the Meuse." German fighters intercepted many bombers on route. The Allies flew 250 fighter sorties to protect the bombers; the Luftwaffe flew 814 fighter sorties.[117]

The Allied air raids began in the wee hours of the morning around 0530 and were repeated throughout the day until midnight. The problem was that this effort was scattered in the form of twenty-seven individual raids. This is why the Germans most of the time had to contend only with small groups of ten to twenty aircraft, so that the Flak batteries were able to concentrate on individual aircraft. Even the only massive strike, delivered by the Royal Air Force between 1600 and 1700, ended in a fiasco. Out of the seventy-one attacking [Fairey] Battle and Blenheim bombers, forty were shot down during that raid alone. The following comment can be found in the history of the Royal Air Force on that score: "In no comparable operation had the Royal Air Force ever been forced to accept a higher loss rate."[118]

On 14 May, events in the Sedan area took place, phase by phase, not so much on the ground, but rather mostly in the air. An officer, who from time to time was near the Gaulier bridge, reported: "Again and again, the Potez and Morane aircraft attacked their targets with tremendous dash in daredevil low-level flight. It takes dash and daring to dive down so deep into the hell put up by our Flak. But the French know, as we do too, what it means if the bridge were to be destroyed. They failed. . . . Again and again, an enemy aircraft dives out of the sky, trailed by a long black plume of smoke that, after the impact of the following explosion, hovers perpendicularly for a while in the hot air. . . . During the short time I spent at the bridge—hardly an hour—11 enemy airplanes were knocked down."[119]

The most critical moment occurred when a pilot—his aircraft already hit and burning like a kamikaze—dove down at the Gaulier military bridge. The bombs missed the bridge, and so did the aircraft, which exploded as it hit the ground. The pilot had parachuted from the aircraft at the last moment and floated at a height of five meters over a German Panzer that just happened to be driving across the bridge. Not far away, he plunged into the Meuse River, never to be seen again.

The losses suffered by the Allies over Sedan on 14 May were very severe. Out of 109 British bombers, 47 were shot down, and out of 43 French bombers, 5 were shot down. During the 250 Allied fighter sorties, the French lost 30 and the British lost 20 aircraft. Another 65 aircraft were heavily damaged. This meant that on one single day the Allies lost 167 aircraft attacking a single target.[120] The tremendously important bridge at Gaulier could not be hit. The French spoke of a "black day" (*jour noir*),[121] whereas Churchill described the British losses as "cruel."[122]

The day had been nerve-racking also for the German generals. A single bomb hit on the Gaulier bridge would have sufficed to jeopardize the success of the operation where "every minute counted." On 14 May, Guderian kept driving to Gaulier over and over again and, to make a statement, positioned himself on the bridge to set an

The pontoon bridge of the 1st Panzer Division at Sedan—the eye of the needle of Operation Sickle Cut—was the main attack target of Allied bombers on 14 May. On the northern bank, the Esperance textile factory at Gaulier. *Bundesarchiv Koblenz [Federal Archives]*

French Amiot bomber, downed near Sedan on 14 May. *Christa Gampe*

example for his soldiers. After all, on that day there was no more dangerous place in all of France than this bridge. Around noon, even von Rundstedt, the commander in chief of Army Group A, showed up. Guderian made his report to him in the middle of the bridge. Precisely at that moment, enemy aircraft attacked the bridge so that both generals had to seek cover. Then Rundstedt asked: "Is it always like this here?" As Guderian noted in his *Memoirs,* he was able to answer this question "with a clear conscience that it was."[123]

The bottom line is that the air battle on 14 May over Sedan was a success for the Wehrmacht in two ways: (1) For the Luftwaffe, that day was a turning point because it had succeeded in winning air superiority. Above all, the backbone of the Allied bomber fleets had been broken. Their generals no longer dared employ their aircraft in such massive raids. To that extent, the first and only air battle of this campaign was fought over Sedan. (2) On that day, Guderian was able to get the main body of his corps (60,000 men, as well as 22,000 vehicles, including 850 Panzers) across the Meuse River. This meant the breakthrough had attained an operational-level dimension.

Counterattack by the Reserve of X Corps: A Drama of Delays

The first clash between German Panzers and French tanks took place at around 0900 on 14 May on Hill 322 southwest of Bulson, just a few hundred meters away from

Lafontaine's former command post. The French X Corps had run through that situation about three weeks earlier during a map exercise precisely on that same terrain. At that time, the Corps Reserve was to be used in case of German breakthrough at Sedan. At first, it was to occupy a rear defense position (objective 1) between Chéhéry, Bulson, and the edge of the woods south of Haraucourt. Then, using the Bulson springboard, a counterattack was to drive the penetrating enemy all the way back to the edge of the Bois de la Marfée (objective 2) and finally to the banks of the Meuse River (objective 3).

Huntziger, the commander in chief of the Second Army, also participated in the terrain conference. In his final remarks, he stated confidently: "This is one place where they will not get through!"[124] His optimism was by no means unjustified because the terrain definitely seemed to favor the defense.

The race to Bulson commenced at 1600 on 13 May when German infantry crossed the Meuse River. At that moment, Grandsard, the commanding general of X Corps, ordered his reserves to move into the rear defense position at Bulson in accordance with the map exercise. Now everything would take place "according to the script." The 213th Infantry Regiment, reinforced by the 7th Tank Battalion, was to advance along the left-wing axis of attack; the 205th Infantry Regiment, reinforced by the 4th Tank Battalion, was to advance on the right-wing axis of attack. We will first of all look at the left-wing axis of attack because the formations employed in the right-wing sector arrived late.

Grandsard had established the following time table: Within two hours, the 213th Infantry Regiment would be able to move from its standby area southwest of Chémery to the position five kilometers away between Chéhéry and Bulson. For the 7th Tank Battalion, in a standby area 20 kilometers south of le Chesne, he figured a time requirement of 1 hour and 50 minutes.[125]

Then something happened that should never have happened: A total of seventeen hours (fifteen hours after receiving the movement order for the tanks) elapsed from the time the order was issued until the lead French tanks approached Bulson Ridge! To their surprise, there they found German Panzers that had beaten them by just a few minutes.

The Approach March of the Reserves

Around 1600 (1500, French time) on 13 May, Grandsard issued orders to the individual Corps Reserve units to advance into the starting position at Bulson. This order, obviously delivered by a motorcycle messenger, reached the 213th Infantry Regiment at around 1730. At 1830, Lieutenant Colonel [Pierre] Labarthe, the regimental commander, issued his orders and designated 2000 as the departure time. In the meantime, however, the panic occurred in the 55th Infantry Division in position to the north and threatened to spread to the 213th Regiment. The departure was delayed and a wave of fleeing soldiers met the advancing units.

The order to move out reached the 7th Tank Battalion at around 1800. Because it was feared that the enemy Luftwaffe might come over, the French tanks started off only as darkness fell, around 2130. Now, however, the roads were clogged with soldiers and vehicles that were streaming back in flight. Sometimes, the French tank battalion had to make its way forward at the pace of the infantry, with many forced interruptions.

General Lafontaine's Fatal Hesitation

Around 2000 Grandsard ordered Lafontaine by phone to take over command of the counterattack. For this purpose, he gave him the two infantry regiments and two tank battalions of the Corps Reserve. But at that time, Lafontaine had his hands full trying to control the incipient breakup of his division. Moreover, he shifted his command post to Chémery around 2030. Roughly around 2200, he learned from Lieutenant Colonel Cachou, the deputy chief of staff of X Corps, that the advance of the 213th Infantry Regiment to Bulson had not made any headway and that Labarthe therefore decided to stop halfway along and move into a defensive position between Chémery and Maisoncelle.[126] Lafontaine accepted this arbitrary action in a completely passive manner and did nothing to push the counterattack energetically. Instead, he asked Cachou, who was just on his way back, to have corps give him detailed orders.

Lafontaine did not go into action until around 0100 on 14 May. Even then, he did not drive up to the front to make sure at last that the designated starting position was actually taken up. Instead, he went in the opposite direction to the corps command post in La Berlière. This is incomprehensible for two reasons. Personal contact was absolutely unnecessary because there were signal communications links to the corps command post. Moreover, the time left to mount a successful counterattack was running out. Every wasted minute meant a gain for the Germans whose military bridge had been finished since midnight.

Around 0220 Colonel Chaligne, who ran the division command post during Lafontaine's absence, phoned La Berlière. His commanding officer still had not arrived there. Instead, he reached Grandsard who read him the written order for the commitment of the Corps Reserve that had just been drafted. Grandsard gave him full powers to mount the counterattack independently, if his division commander should not turn up in time.

Lafontaine arrived in La Berlière shortly after 0230. Grandsard had just left his command post to go on a longer drive. Unfortunately, Lafontaine also missed the General's deputy chief of staff, Cachou, who had just started out to Chémery to meet him in an effort personally to give him the written order for the counterattack.

Lafontaine arrived in Chémery again around 0400. Although time was relentlessly working against him, he had wasted three hours on a senseless round trip. Meanwhile, the engine noise of the vehicles, which the Germans kept feeding into the bridgehead grew to ever more threatening proportions.

Orders for the counterattack were issued in the division command post shortly after 0400. Several officers had been waiting there impatiently for precise instructions. Lafontaine still hesitated to begin the attack because Cachou had still not arrived with the written orders. The paradoxical thing here was that the division headquarters knew the content of the order quite precisely. About 11/2 hours earlier, Grandsard had personally read that order to Chaligne over the phone. Besides, Lafontaine had just returned from the corps command post where he could have gotten the information. He absolutely wanted to have a written order in his hands. During that night, however, everything seemed to go against him because Cachou, who had started out ahead of him from La Berlière to go to Chémery, still kept everybody waiting.

At last, Cachou arrived at 0445 after a protracted wild-goose chase along roads clogged with fleeing soldiers. The long-awaited corps order that he brought consisted of only a few sentences. Accordingly, the counterattack was to be mounted in the following phases:

Objective 1: Bois la Minière-Bulson-Gros Bois
Objective 2: Reserve defense line (northern edge of Bois de la Marfée)
Objective 3: Main line of resistance (banks of the Meuse River)[127]

After the order had been read out loud, the assembled officers found it difficult to conceal their astonishment. Labarthe called out spontaneously: "But that is the order for the map exercise."[128] That counterattack had been practiced several times during the winter in the course of several map exercises, and, as mentioned before, had again been rehearsed just three weeks earlier during a tactical appreciation of the terrain in the Bulson area. The corps attack order, however, essentially represented what at that time could be considered the school solution. The mission, already forwarded to Lafontaine by Grandsard around 2000, likewise meant nothing but moving into the starting position at Bulson that had been reconnoitered on the terrain at the time (objective 1). Shortly after 0500, Lafontaine at last issued the attack order. This meant that during the night when France's fate was decided he allowed nine hours to pass before he at last acted on the order issued to him to by corps.

After the war, Lafontaine was exposed to severe criticism. His former superior, Grandsard, was particularly relentless and tough on him.[129] It was not only the individual mistakes of the luckless division commander but also the military system to which he was tied that failed at Sedan. During that battle, there was a confrontation between two completely different command systems. According to the method of command tactics customary in the French army, each individual phase was planned in advance in detail and could be carried out only after an express order had been issued. The system of Auftragstaktik looked entirely different. The German officers had been trained in critical situations to act independently—even without specific orders—in terms of the higher-level mission. To get to the point regarding Lafontaine's problem: He did have a *mission,* and he had had it since 2000, but what he wanted was an *order.* That is the only way one can explain his persistent hesitation. This is why, in his despair, he also left the command post and went looking for his superior to at last obtain the formal order without which he did not believe he was authorized to take action.

General Lafontaine's Attack Order

The counterattack was to jump off at 0730. At first only the left (western) attack group—the 213th Infantry Regiment and the 7th Tank Battalion—was available[130] and had to advance alone. The right (eastern) attack group (205th Infantry Regiment and 4th Tank Battalion) was still hanging back and was to follow as quickly as possible in the direction of Raucourt.

Lafontaine ordered the three battalions of the 213th Infantry Regiment to advance, side-by-side, in the left sector: On the left, the 2d Battalion moved along the Bar River on the road to Connage. On the right, the other two battalions advanced across the Plateau of Bulson.

One of the three companies from the 7th Tank Battalion reinforced each infantry battalion. As for artillery, in the beginning only the 1st Battalion, 87th Artillery Regiment, was available with twelve artillery pieces. When Labarthe left the division command post, he said: "*C'est une mission de sacrifice qu'on demande à mon régiment*" (That is a suicide mission for my regiment).[131] The regimental commander's statement did not display excessive confidence in victory.[132]

The Counterattack's Chances

As Grandsard analyzed later, the situation during the night between 13 and 14 May "by no means looked as unfavorable as one might have thought."[133] All was not yet lost. A swift and resolute counterattack could have thrown the Germans back again to the Meuse River, especially since there were some factors in favor of the French.

The entire 55th Infantry Division had not fallen apart in the whirlpool of panic. This mass hysteria had appeared primarily among the rear-echelon elements, especially the artillery, not so much among the infantry. Some strongpoints were able to hold out on the right wing, along the heights of Noyers-Pont-Maugis. In the meantime, a new line of resistance adjoining the strongpoints had been formed south of the Bois de la Marfée. It extended via Chaumont and Ferme St. Quentin all the way to the woods east of Chéhéry at Hill 298. The remaining soldiers were recruited from the rubble of six different battalions and, together, added up to barely two battalions. The decisive thing was that this line of resistance, reinforced by three antitank platoons, extended north of the Bulson Ridge. In that way, the Corps Reserve units were able to reach objective 1 under the protection of that resistance line. The situation was also relatively stable on the left (in the west). Here, elements of the 331st Regiment, flanking the German breakthrough, were still holding strongpoints in the Villers-sur-Bar Sector. Besides, 5th Light Cavalry Division, earlier employed for a delaying action in the Ardennes, had gone into position on the west bank of the Ardennes Canal.

On the German side, the situation during the night of 13–14 May was assessed in absolutely critical terms. Only the 1st Rifle Regiment had managed a deep penetration. This narrow corridor, however, appeared extremely vulnerable, especially from the flanks. Advancing on jammed roads, the 1st Panzer Brigade still took until 0720 to arrive at the Gaulier bridge. Lafontaine did not manage to push into this gap. Actually, he had a total of fifteen hours and twenty minutes between the time the German infantry crossed the Meuse River and the time the Panzer brigade crossed it. A rapid counterthrust by the two infantry regiments and two tank battalions with almost ninety battle tanks that were ready and available for that purpose would inevitably have plunged the Germans into a crisis.

During that night, the German infantry had reached a dead end as far as physical strength was concerned. Guderian's utopian-sounding requirement had been: "In three days to the Meuse, on the fourth day across the Meuse!" As a result, most soldiers got hardly any sleep at all between 9 and 14 May. Balck was able, in the evening of 13 May, to once again drive his exhausted infantry formations forward for an assault on Hill 301 and mobilize the very last ounce of strength. All the more complete was the subsequent personnel collapse. Many of the men simply collapsed during the next break and fell into a leaden sleep. Lafontaine, who had fresh reserves, allowed this chance to slip through his fingers.

The formations of the French X Corps by no means fought alone. Second Army had planned an operational counterattack by several divisions with strong tank forces for the afternoon of 14 May. In addition, support by all available Allied bomber units had been announced for that day.

In that situation, the most important thing would have been to exploit the momentary weakness of the Germans and as quickly as possible to attack the as yet hardly secured bridgehead. If Lafontaine had at least managed to hold the key terrain of Bulson, he would have created an excellent prerequisite for the counterattack of General [Jean-Adolphe-Louis-Robert] Flavigny's tank formations that were moving up from the south.

The Tank Battle of Bulson and Connage

At Bulson around 0845 on 14 May, took place not only the first clash of German Panzers and French tanks south of Sedan but, simultaneously, the collision of two differing concepts of war. This fight virtually symbolizes that revolution in warfare that Guderian's ideas had caused on the German side.

After Lafontaine had issued the attack order around 0500 in Chémery, the units that were standing by along the Chémery-Maisoncelle starting line began moving at around 0730. The tanks did not stage a probing attack in time to occupy the key terrain of Bulson ahead of the approaching Germans. Rather, they moved slowly forward, in step with the infantry. That again was not an individual mistake on the part of Lafontaine. Instead, he acted quite methodically according to the guidelines spelled out in French service regulations, which required tanks to adjust to the tempo of the infantry. Around 0815, both the left-hand column and the middle column ran into German combat reconnaissance that was quickly driven back. However, because the units were advancing next to each other along a line, it was always the slowest unit that determined the speed of movements. The others repeatedly had to wait until the column that was advancing over difficult terrain had caught up. Only about two kilometers had been covered by 0845, in other words, after seventy-five minutes. Then, suddenly, just one kilometer to the north of the two columns attacking on the right, German Panzers showed up on the Bulson Ridge. The French had lost the race for the key terrain around Bulson.

The 2d Battalion fared in a similar way. Supported by a tank company and an antitank platoon, it was attacking along the Bar River and the Ardennes Canal. It advanced along the Chémery-Sedan road and reached the northern edge of the Naumont woods around 0900. Then the French tanks ran into a German antitank gun blocking position at the intersection to the east of Connage. That meant that the counterattack of the unit employed on the left had also been stopped after not even three kilometers.

At this point, a description of the events simultaneously developing on the German side will clarify the most important difference between the two armies, that is, the speed with which combat action took place. The speed of the so-called command process—the time that passed between the realization of a new situation, the response from the military leadership, and actual operations on the battlefield—played an essential role.

The advance of the two rifle regiments of the 1st Panzer Division had come to a halt during the night of 13–14 May on account of complete exhaustion. Reconnaissance patrols carefully probed their way forward only at dawn. On the right (western) wing, the 1st Rifle Regiment had advanced in the Bar Valley all the way to Chéhéry (five kilometers north of Chémery) but had hardly any antitank weapons. The left half of the combat sector was just about bare! That is where the evening before, the Großdeutschland had tried in vain to penetrate into the Bois de la Marfée. To avoid time-consuming close combat, the division commander decided on the next morning to skirt around these woods to the west. Starting at 0645, the Großdeutschland Regiment was shifted to the right into the combat sector of the 1st Rifle Regiment and was just crossing the top of the La Boulette pass west of Hill 301. After that it was to return to its own sector to advance toward Bulson from the southern edge of the Bois de la Marfée woods. That meant that the division at that particular moment was caught "on the wrong foot." If the French had mounted a resolute tank attack from Bulson, they could have thrust almost unhindered to the north toward the military bridge through the uncovered combat sector of the Großdeutschland.

In this situation, it was a good thing that Kirchner, the division commander, was leading his division from way up front, where he had an armored command vehicle with excellent radios. Since the early morning hours, he had been standing on Hill 301, the place from which Moltke had directed his troops in 1870. From that spot, he not only had an accurate overall view of the terrain, but he was also able to check which elements were moving up on the road via the La Boulette pass. Shortly after 0700, aerial reconnaissance had reported French tank concentrations south of Chémery. Thereupon he personally sent out an advance detachment that was to push through the Bar Valley heading to Chémery. The detachment consisted of two anti-tank platoons from the Infantry Regiment Großdeutschland under the command of Oberleutnant [Helmut] Beck-Broichsitter, plus two armored scout cars.

At 0750 a Henschel reconnaissance aircraft from the division's aviation squadron reported that French tanks with infantry support were in the process of attacking northward along two axes: the one from Chémery through the Bar Valley and the other across the Plateau of Bulson, heading toward the Bois de la Marfée. This bit of news triggered a crisis mood at the division's command post. At that moment, only a single German Panzer unit—the 4th Company, 1st Battalion, 2d Panzer Regiment—had crossed the Meuse River and its point had just reached the La Boulette pass. Kirchner ordered the company commander, Oberleutnant Krajewski, to attack immediately via Bulson to tie down the reported enemy force as far south as possible. The Panzers began to move out shortly after 0800. In addition, air support was requested to smash the French tanks that were approaching from Chémery.

At this point, it must be remembered that around 1600 on 13 May—after the start of the German attack—Grandsard had ordered his reserves to move into the starting position for the counterattack at Bulson. Then, at 2000, Lafontaine gave orders to carry out the counterattack, but the units did not get moving until 0730 on 14 May.

In the meantime, fifteen and a half hours had gone by, or eleven and a half hours since Lafontaine had gotten his orders. Lafontaine's opponent on the German side, Kirchner, leading from far up front, took just ten minutes to launch a counteraction.

The attack tempo of the particular armored units on the German and French sides differed as much as did the speed of the command process. The distance up to the ridge south of Bulson was nine kilometers for the German Panzer company, whereas it was only three kilometers for the French tank unit. The German Panzers started out shortly after 0800 and reached the ridge against resistance from enemy forces that had come to a halt around 0845. The French had started the race with a half hour head start at around 0730 and arrived late nevertheless.

The cause of this is to be found in two basically different operational doctrines. In the French army, the tank was considered as a supporting weapon of the infantry and had to move along with the attack tempo of the infantry. On the other hand, in the German Panzer divisions as designed by Guderian, the Panzer was the main weapon and all other arms had to adjust to its speed.

In this situation, time played such an overriding role that Kirchner simply ignored two of the most important action principles: (1) the Panzers mounted a probing attack without waiting for the accompanying infantry;(2) the Panzer force was not employed in a compact fashion, instead, the companies were sent forward individually, one after the other.

Guderian, who had immediately hurried forward after the report of the French counterattack, now had to eat his own words. Actually, he had demanded that the Panzers be employed only in compact formations (*Klotzen, nicht kleckern!* Hit with the fist, don't feel with the fingers!). Now he confirmed the division commander's decision to send the Panzers forward in *kleckerweise* (penny packets), in other words, company by company, the moment they had crossed the military bridge. In that situation, once again "every minute counted," and thus there was no waiting until a complete Panzer battalion or even a regiment had crossed the Meuse River. Krajewski attacked into the unknown with his Panzer company. He had pushed to Bulson, disregarding the enemy forces that were still in place, and the French evacuated Bulson the moment the Panzers appeared. In his report, he describes the decisive scene on Hill 322 as it took place around 0845: "Cautiously, we drove through Bulson, which had been evacuated by the enemy, and slowly, riding single file, we approached the Hill [322] southwest of town. Heavy fire commenced the moment the first Panzers reached the hill. Our two lead Panzers took several direct antitank gun hits and burned."[134]

Krajewski was just able to get a radio message off to regiment before his Panzer was also hit and he had to bail out. The Bulson corridor tapered in funnel fashion south of the ridge and that is where the German Panzers ran head-on into the two French tank companies. Shielded by the edges of the woods on the left and right, two French infantry battalions, with antitank gun support, also advanced and caught the German company that had rushed on ahead in a pincer movement. The main resistance came from the Fond Dagot woods that closed this bottleneck like a cork. The strongpoint that the evening before had still housed the command post of the 55th Infantry Division had been fortified with bunkers and trench systems. Remnants of this division had entrenched themselves here and were fighting with noteworthy stubbornness. The two antitank platoons in position there had hit two German Panzers and set them on fire at the start of the fight, while they disabled a third one so that it just stood there.

The German Panzers had reached the ridge between elevations 322 and 320 just a few minutes ahead of the French tanks. Under cover and from reverse slope positions, they were now able to engage the enemy tanks that were approaching from the south across the plateau. Their most important advantage was that in contrast to the French all Panzers were equipped with radios so that their actions could be coordinated. A nasty surprise, on the other hand, was that the German Panzer guns could penetrate the French FCM tanks only in certain spots.[135] The enemy artillery turned out to be the most dangerous foe. Some guns of the artillery battalion that had gone into position north of Maisoncelle had been moved forward and fired point-blank at the German Panzers.

Labarthe had referred to the mission assigned to his regiment as a "sacrifice" (*mission de sacrifice*). In reality, however, the thrust by the hopelessly inferior German Panzer company turned into a suicide mission. It was wiped out in a short time so that in the end only a single battle-worthy Panzer was left. The latter switched back and forth, shielded by the ridge, and simulated the presence of several Panzers. Just thirty minutes after the start of this meeting engagement, Oberleutnant [Friedrich] von Grolman's 2d Panzer Company, turned up at the scene of the action after crossing the military bridge at Gaulier and taking off at top speed. It managed to stop the French attack. When another Panzer company arrived after some time, the Germans counterattacked. Only the involvement of the advance units of the Großdeutschland changed the outcome. Infantry in close-quarters fighting knocked out the French antitank guns entrenched mainly in the Fond Dagot woods.

At the same time, the French left attack group was stopped just four kilometers to the west. As described earlier, Kirchner had personally given Beck-Broichsitter the mission of advancing toward Chémery with his two available antitank platoons. When he was still about three kilometers away from that village, he spotted thirteen French tanks slowly approaching from there with infantry support. Thereupon, he established an antitank blocking position with his six guns at the intersection east of Connage. The enemy was brought to a halt around 0900, but the inadequate penetrating power of the German 3.7-cm antitank guns was now revealed in a frightening manner. The after-action report says, with unmistakable irony: "The certainty with which the gunners serve their weapons is admirable. Most of the time, they hit with the very first few rounds. Then they change the aiming point on the enemy tank until they have found a spot where our shell can penetrate."[136]

Nevertheless, the enemy battle tanks were stopped for the moment; but then the threat of being outflanked arose. Some tanks penetrated into Connage and pushed past it to the west, while at the same time French infantry advanced on the left flank from the southeast. In the meantime, however, two companies of the 43d Assault Engineer Battalion had arrived and immediately attacked the French infantry battalion. The fortunes of war changed at 0945. Suddenly, German Panzers of the 8th Company, 2d Battalion, 2d Panzer Regiment, showed up under the command of Oberleutnant [Karl Wilhelm] von Kleist and beat back the French battle tanks. The assault engineers in the meantime pushed the French infantry through the Naumont woods all the way back to Chémery, which they penetrated around 1100.

As for the twin actions at Bulson and Connage, which later was upgraded to a tank battle by both sides, only the four German Panzer companies sent forward individually participated in the decisive phase. After the French troops had been stopped and finally beaten back, the main body of the 1st Panzer Brigade was still north of the Meuse River, facing the bridge at Gaulier. At 1045 Lafontaine issued the final retreat order. Only at that point did more and more reinforcements organized by the German division commander arrive. Antitank guns, assault guns, and heavy infantry guns of the Großdeutschland moved onto the Plateau of Bulson. The dreaded self-propelled 8.8-cm gun advanced toward Chémery in the Bar Valley. In the meantime, Guderian had intervened personally and had seen to it that at long last only battle tanks were allowed to cross the bridge at Gaulier.[137]

Around noon, only ten French tanks were left out of the forty; and by the afternoon, the French tank battalion had been almost wiped out. The 213th Infantry Regiment also suffered devastating casualties. Labarthe was wounded and wound up in German captivity. Ruby later wrote about the tragic outcome of this action: "The debacle of the 213th [Regiment] is complete."[138]

The shattered French infantry regiment showed astonishingly high fighting spirit, as did the French tank battalion. This is true above all if, by way of comparison, one looks at the behavior displayed the day before by the 55th Infantry Division.[139] It would also be improper to try to criticize the sluggish tempo of this counterattack too harshly because the right attack group was even slower. The 205th Infantry Regiment had been ready in the standby area at La Besace whose northern edge was only about three kilometers away from the subsequent starting line, the Maisoncelle-Raucourt road. The French 4th Tank Battalion was positioned to the southeast thereof, near Beaumont, and had to cover a distance of about 12 kilometers up to that line. On the evening of 13 May, both units were caught in the panic that the troops of the 55th and 71st Divisions had triggered as they fled south.

During the early morning hours of 14 May, Lafontaine sent Chaligne into the right-wing combat sector to inquire as to the whereabouts of the units under his command. The colonel finally found them north of Bois de Raucourt at 0715. That meant that the main body of the 205th Regiment, since starting out on 13 May at around 2100, had advanced only up to a line about one kilometer (!) to the north of the standby area. There, the infantry units, as well as the subsequently arriving tank battalion, had assumed a screened halting position. Chaligne now ordered these units to advance approximately two kilometers to the starting line, the road between Maisoncelle and Raucourt, and to attack to the east, past Bulson.

However, as during the evening before, the advance turned into a debacle. When the soldiers in the lead column at last got going around 0900, they became involved in a fire fight with a scattered French unit, which they mistakenly believed to be German paratroopers. The starting line was reached only at 1045, after almost two hours. But now it was too late; Lafontaine had just broken off the counterattack. A further thrust by the right-wing attack group would have made no sense, and so he also ordered the 205th Regiment and the 4th Tank Battalion to fall back to the south.

That was not the end of the drama. Lieutenant Colonel Montvignier-Monnet, the commander of this infantry regiment, now wanted to establish contact with a higher command authority in the rear areas as quickly as possible to get a new mission order. On the way there, he ran into a roadblock by the French military police who at first mistook him for a German agent and finally arrested him as a presumed deserter. Ironically this officer had been highly decorated for extraordinary bravery during World War I and had been made a member of the Legion of Honor. During the last twenty-four hours, his main problem was to keep his panicky soldiers from just running away. Now, he, of all people, was arrested in Verdun on the absurd suspicion of desertion.[140] Thus, the regiment had become leaderless in a highly critical situation. The orderly withdrawal turned into a wild flight and, in the end, elements of the regiment simply fell apart in the whirlpool of retreating formations. The 213th Regiment's counterattack ended in tragedy, but the action of the 205th Regiment just about turned into a farce.[141]

The rejoicing of the 1st Panzer Division at this victory was also subdued. A commanders' conference began at 1200 in the square in front of the church in Chémery, which had just been captured. At that same moment, German dive-bombers attacked the village and hit the vehicles parked on the square. The commander of the 43d Assault Engineer Battalion and three officers of the 2d Panzer Regiment were killed, and the commander of the 1st Panzer Brigade and a number of other officers and enlisted men were seriously wounded. At 1000 Guderian had gotten on the radio and repeatedly asked that the previously requested dive-bomber raid be scrubbed or that it be shifted to the south.[142] Obviously, however, he was too late to stop the Luftwaffe in the midst of its attack. The Panzers had attacked with such speed that they were even too fast for the Luftwaffe.

Guderian's Unauthorized Thrust to the West

As earlier emphasized, the operations plan of the army high command was only a half-hearted and inconsistent implementation of Manstein's bold Sickle Cut idea. The decisive breach point was at Sedan. Manstein and Guderian had assumed that after crossing the Meuse River the Panzer formations would immediately have to push to the Channel coast, disregarding their exposed flanks, or otherwise lose the race against the Allies. All of the higher-ranking generals from the army high command and all the way down to Army Group A and von Kleist had discarded precisely this requirement as being too risky. After crossing the Meuse River at Sedan, the Panzers were at first to be held back in the bridgehead until the following infantry divisions had secured it. Only then was the thrust deep into enemy territory to be ventured.[143] So, Halder noted unmistakably: "An immediate operational-level effect deriving from the Panzer units that are first across the Meuse River is not expected. . . . Only after infantry formations with adequate strength have taken up the required movement space west of the Meuse and have a firm grip on it, can one consider combining the still usable Panzer units with an operational objective."[144]

Hitler was also afraid of the threat from the exposed flanks and had put his own personal reservation on any "further measures after forcing the Meuse River crossing."[145] Guderian, on the other hand, was in favor of the *ununterbrochenen Angriffs* (uninterrupted attack). He believed that it was senseless to try to break through the Meuse River line without immediately pushing deep into enemy territory, thus to encircle the enemy. Waiting in the bridgehead for the infantry divisions that were approaching from the Ardennes would have given the enemy many days to build up a new line of resistance. Then that astonishing breakthrough came off successfully on 13 May. On the next day at 1230, Guderian received the message that a unit of the 1st Panzer Division had seized the bridge at Malmy, one kilometer to the west of Chémery, undamaged and was in the process of pushing farther West.[146] The little bridge over the Ardennes Canal at Malmy thus became the pivotal point of the Sickle Cut movement. Immediately thereafter, Guderian hurried to the command post of the 1st Panzer Division in Chémery where one of the most significant decisions of the campaign was made. The conflicting goals shaped up as follows: (1) Should he obey the tactical necessity and, first of all, secure the unstable bridgehead against the anticipated French counterattack from the south? (2) Or should he exploit the enemy's confusion and, going along with the operational idea of the Sickle Cut, should he immediately push west with the main body of the Panzer units?

Guderian found himself facing a very grave responsibility. His forces were not sufficient for a "both-and solution." Still, if he wanted to exploit this favorable moment, he had to make a decision immediately. At that point, Wenck, the operations officer of the 1st Panzer Division, gave him the decisive key word by reminding him of his favorite saying: *Klotzen, nicht kleckern!* (Hit with the fist, don't feel with the fingers!). "That really answered my question," Guderian wrote in his *Memoirs.* At 1400, he ordered the 1st and 2d Panzer Divisions, with all of their units, to wheel westward from the move and to attack "toward Rethel" (forty kilometers away as the crow flies).[147]

This meant that on 14 and 15 May the bridgehead was to be protected mostly only by the 10th Panzer Division and the Infantry Regiment Großdeutschland! Only then could the Motorized Infantry Corps Wietersheim, coming from the Ardennes, have any effect. Guderian believed that he could accept this risk because he figured on the methodical slowness of the French command system. Developments were to prove him right. He managed to punch through the chains of hills located west of Chémery before the approaching enemy reserves were able to entrench themselves in this terrain, which favored the defenders. Even a slight delay of the attack would have created a new situation favoring the enemy. As Guderian explained later, "the essence" of the success at Sedan was not to be found in the "breakthrough action" as such but rather in the immediate exploitation of the breakthrough by the thrust of the Panzer Force deep into enemy territory.[148]

Sedan 1940—Turning Point in Military History

We have gone to war with a 1918 army against a German Army of 1939. It is sheer madness.[149]

General [Maxime] Weygand,
the newly appointed supreme commander,
in a conversation with the French
prime minister Reynaud on 25 May 1940

In most battles, armies equipped with similar weapons and using similar methods fight each other. The nature of war changes—as does military technology—in an evolutionary fashion and only rarely in a revolutionary fashion by major mutational leaps. Now and then, however, it happens that one army intends to start the next war with the tried and proven system of the last war, whereas the other army faces it with completely new and modern methods. One of the best-known examples is Napoleon's victory over the Prussian army in the Battle of Jena. On that score Clausewitz wrote: "When in 1806 the Prussian generals . . . , plunged into the open jaws of disaster by using Frederick the Great's oblique order of battle, it was not just a case of a style that had outlived its usefulness but the most extreme poverty of the imagination to which routine has ever led."[150]

To this very day, the Arc de Triomphe in Paris bears witness to that victory in which the spirit of progress smiled upon France's flags. In July 1939 there was a glittering military parade at that monument on the occasion of the 150th anniversary of the French Revolution. Just a year later, it turned out that France's military leaders had simply slept through a revolution that meanwhile had taken place in their very own trade. So, in May 1940 Sedan became the French Jena. On this historical battlefield two armies collided, and, as the tank fight at Bulson demonstrated, one was moving in the slow-motion tempo of World War I while the other one forged ahead in the time-lapse photography tempo of the blitzkrieg.

The German attack, especially the breakout of the Panzers from the bridgehead, was so fast that there were hardly any major combat actions. Moreover, many French soldiers were in such severe shock as a result of the flood of events that they either fled in panic or allowed themselves to be taken prisoner almost without resistance. That also explains the astonishingly low casualty rate in this battle. The assault team of two assault engineer platoons under Korthals achieved the most important individual success. At the Bellevue intersection, this team created the prerequisites for the breakthrough of the 1st and 2d Panzer Divisions. As Korthals emphasized in complete astonishment in his after-action report, he took eleven concrete bunkers and mopped up numerous field works during this assault team mission *without a single dead or wounded.* The French appeared to be paralyzed. The British major [Philip] Gribble, a liaison officer to the French army, wrote in his diary about the breakthrough at Sedan: "Recently I walked through the fortifications along this front and estimated that well-organized and resolute resistance would cost the Germans half a million casualties, if they actually managed to achieve their breakthrough. But what happened? The Germans marched through 8-kilometer deep fortifications with a loss of perhaps 500 men."[151]

This estimate would appear to be quite close to reality. During the Sedan breakthrough battle on 13 and 14 May, Panzer Corps Guderian suffered about 120 dead and 400 wounded.[152] This low casualty rate is bound to cause astonishment when compared to the casualty figures of the big breakthrough battles of World War I, all of which failed. For example, in 1916, the British lost 60,000 out of 140,000 attacking soldiers on the very first day of the Battle of the Somme. Overall, the Allies lost 660,000 men and the Germans lost 500,000 men during that battle. It achieved no breakthrough and no decision, just as in the case of the slaughter of Verdun, also in 1916, where the Germans lost 330,000 men and the French 362,000 men. In May 1940, on the other hand, the Germans at Sedan achieved within five days after the start of the campaign what they had attempted in vain for four years during World War I: the decisive, operational-level breakthrough.

The key scene took place at 1400 on 14 May in Chémery when Guderian, without proper authorization, ordered his Panzers to charge westward. In so doing, he not only violated the clear orders given him by his superiors plus Hitler's instructions but he also went against "all rules of the art of warfare." With this decision, he also triggered an avalanche effect because he swept the other Panzer divisions along with him. Those other Panzer divisions formed an operational wedge that headed for the Channel coast completely isolated. In the process, there was no flank protection from the infantry divisions. This is why the thrust finally took on the shape of a narrow sickle; hence the term "sickle cut," later coined by Winston Churchill. It was highly significant that Guderian's initiative had wrested the controls from the hands of the general officer corps on the operational echelon. The operation increasingly took on a dynamism of its own and developed the way Manstein had figured it would. In the end, the Panzer divisions simply took off and ran away from the following infantry armies so that the umbilical cord to the infantry, marching behind in clouds of dust, was ripped off. This, indeed, was the initial independent operational employment of the Panzer force.

Sedan in 1870 represented a high point in operational command skill because here Moltke had successfully fought that famous encirclement battle that became the "Cannae of the nineteenth century." Of all places, here in May 1940 there was a rebirth of that very same trend of thought that had been stifled in the firestorm of World War I. The pendulum of military technology had swung back from the fire factor to the movement factor. The British general [J. F. C.] Fuller, who can be considered the trailblazer for Guderian's ideas, later referred to Operation Sickle Cut as the "second Battle of Sedan."[153] He drew a parallel between Moltke's envelopment operation and Manstein's even bolder envelopment idea. In 1870 the meeting point of the two pincer armies was at Illy, nine kilometers from Moltke's command post; in 1940, the operation was a gigantic, almost four-hundred-kilometer-long envelopment movement that extended in "sickle fashion" from the border of Luxembourg all the way to the Channel coast. In 1870 a French army of 120,000 men was encircled in Sedan; in 1940, about 1.7 million Allied soldiers walked into the Sickle Cut trap.[154]

Today, military historians agree that France's defeat was sealed after the breakthrough at Sedan. One could already tell on 14 May that the Allied troops had been outmaneuvered because of their false deployment and had thus lost the campaign. "In the 1939–1940 Campaign, 14 May was the real turning point. It was indeed on that day that the Battle for France was decided."[155] Even more significant is the turning point this battle represents in modern military history. The image of the modern operational war of movement abruptly replaced the image of position warfare dating back to 1918. It is just this concept that is behind the rather evocative catchword blitzkrieg.

6

The Collapse of the Meuse Front

The exploitation of success is the key to victory.[1]

Guderian's comment on the occasion of the operations staff officer training course in 1940

Seal the Gap and Counterattack: French Operational Countermoves after the Breakthrough at Sedan

The French command fatally underestimated the threat that grew from the initially tiny bridgehead at Sedan. The only information on that development that the headquarters in Vincennes received on 13 May was a message that came in at 2125 from General Georges, the commander in chief of the northeast front. In his message he merely mentioned that there had been "*un pépin assez sérieux*" (a rather serious pin prick) at Sedan.[2] The British historian [Alistair] Horne commented that that "was the understatement of the century."[3] At noon on 14 May, the French supreme commander, Gamelin, still referred to the breakthrough at Sedan as "merely a local interlude."[4] He did not grasp the full measure of the disaster until 15 May.[5] The rather sluggish flow of information that came out of the obsolete French telecommunications system caused this mistaken situation estimate.

Nevertheless, the French army had sufficient opportunities for responding. Several divisions standing by behind the front had already been moved forward at the start of the German offensive on 10 May. Some elite divisions from the operational central reserve were even dispatched to the Sedan area when there were indications of a push through the Ardennes. After the breakthrough the operational concept that emerged was that in the west the Ninth Army was to seal off the enemy who had broken through with a refused right wing. Second Army was to mount a counterattack from the south with strong armored units. From a southwesterly direction the newly formed Sixth Army was inserted between Second and Ninth armies.

The divisions that were on standby would have been more than enough to stop the isolated German Panzer units, which not even Chief of the General Staff Halder credited with any "directly operational effect."[6] But it was the speed of the units that counted in this campaign not their numerical strength. Their availability in the right place and at the right time was the decisive factor.

Second Army Attempts an Operational Counterattack

Huntziger, commander in chief of the Second Army, very nonchalantly countenanced a German attack in view of his own considerable reserves. He was not really worried either when a message arrived during the afternoon of 13 May that the Luftwaffe had hit the French units around Sedan with devastating bombing raids. All he said was: "Well, they have to have their baptism of fire sooner or later."[7] Shortly after 1800, he was informed that forty German infantrymen had crossed the Meuse River at Wadelincourt. His laconic reply was: "There will be just that number of prisoners."[8] Not even the bad news about the catastrophic collapse of the 55th Infantry Division made him nervous. He knew that the counterattack by the reserve of the X Corps was bound to be launched any moment and expected that the situation would be stabilized as a result. This was not supposed to be just an initial probing attack, for immediately to the rear he had concentrated a mighty force with which to mount the counterstrike.

The subsequent action appears highly interesting inasmuch as this was the only French attempt at launching an operational counterattack throughout the entire western campaign. Normally, French countermoves were mostly uncoordinated and were mounted, at best, in a division context. In this case, however, two reinforced army corps were to be combined to launch a single overall operation against the bridgehead at Sedan. If Guderian had guessed the threat building up to the south behind the massif of Stonne, he would hardly have accepted the risk of breaking out of the bridgehead prematurely. The 10th Panzer Division that had been left behind to cover the bridgehead now faced the following overwhelming enemy strength.

(1) Flavigny Group (XXI Corps)
- 3d Armored Division
- 3d Motorized Infantry Division
- 5th Light Cavalry Division
- 1st Cavalry Brigade

(2) Roucaud Group
- 2d Light Cavalry Division
- 1st Colonial Infantry Division
- 3d Tank Battalion

(3) Remnants of X Corps
- 12th and 64th Reconnaissance Battalions
- elements of the 71st Infantry Division, the 205th Infantry Regiment, the 4th Tank Battalion

The Second Army was able to assemble about three hundred tanks for this counterattack,[9] and numerous armored reconnaissance vehicles in the cavalry units also joined them. With its 138 battle tanks,[10] half of them Hotchkiss and Char B1 models, the 3d Armored Division alone would have sufficed to overrun the few outfits Guderian had left behind to protect the bridgehead. The most powerful German combat vehicle, the Panzer IV, had 30-mm thick armor, while the Hotchkiss tank had 45-mm of armor and the Char B even had 60-mm. The latter was thus just about invulnerable when engaging German tank and antitank guns. Its twin armament of 47-mm and 75-mm guns definitely made it superior to all German models. In an open field engagement—tank versus Panzer—Guderian's 10th Panzer Division would not have had a chance against those giants. On 14 May, it only had about 30 Panzer IV models, and two-thirds of its combat vehicles were the lightweight Panzer I and II models that were unsuitable for engaging even light French tank types on account of their weak armament. The attempted French counterattack at Sedan is the best answer to the question of why the French failed to exploit the superiority of their tank arm in operational terms in this campaign.

Flavigny, commanding general of XXI Corps, was ordered to carry out the counterattack. For this purpose, the Roucaud Group[11] and elements of X Corps[12] were formally subordinated to him on 14 May. Huntziger had demanded that his army reserve mount its attack immediately following the attack by the reserve of X Corps so that any developing local success could be exploited immediately. The axes of attack of Bulson-Sedan as well as the intermediate objectives that had been ordered for 3d Armored Division and the 3d Motorized Infantry Division were extensively identical to those of the corps reserve. This meant that two counterattacks, echeloned in succession, were to be mounted in the same terrain: The first one on the *tactical* echelon and the second one on the *operational* echelon.

The counterthrust by X Corps reserve under Lafontaine moved in a strikingly slow fashion compared to the tempo of the German attack. The employment of the 3d Armored Division demonstrated even more clearly that French armor planned to attack with 1918 speed as if time had come to a standstill since then. One seemingly secondary technical feature that turned out to be particularly significant with regard to the employment of tanks during this campaign was the volume of the fuel tank. This is precisely what symbolized the differing tank philosophy of the two armies. The German Panzer Force was intended for operational missions. Accordingly, German Panzers had comparatively large fuel tanks that gave them operational combat range and enabled them to accomplish deep penetrations. The French tanks, on the other hand, had a tactical mission to accomplish in close cooperation with the infantry. The daily movement distance covered during the infantry advances of World War governed their fuel tank volume and their range. The 32-ton French Char B was extremely heavy for tank designs at that time. Its disadvantage was not only its lack of speed but also that, when operating in difficult terrain, it could be employed for only about two hours before it had to be refueled.[13]

First Attempt at a Counterattack on 14 May. Initially, the 3d Armored Division was in a standby area near Reims. At 1600 on 12 May, General [Antoine] Brocard, the division commander, was given the mission of moving up to the front and initially of occupying a standby area near Le Chesne (a sixty-kilometer movement). It took until 0600 on 14 May for the last elements to reach the new assembly area. A dramatic conference took place that morning at 0500 at the XXI Corps command post. In view of the rather surprising German penetration, Flavigny's superiors had been urging him to move with extreme haste. He told Brocard that the 3d Armored Division had to attack that same morning. Brocard thought that he had not heard the date right and requested that the attack be postponed by one day. He mentioned the following time requirements to justify his request:

refueling his tanks: 5–6 hours

marching to the starting position along the northern edge of the Bois du Mont-Dieu (a movement covering between fourteen and eighteen kilometers): 2–3 hours

refueling once more for the attack against Sedan, which was fifteen kilometers away: 2–3 hours

Flavigny, a tank expert, was rather annoyed by this time frame requirement, which in his opinion was excessive. He demanded that the jump-off line for the attack be taken up on that same day by 1200, but finally moved the time up to 1400. Now, the French army's inadequate communications system revealed itself for what it was. Brocard's order reached his headquarters only between 0800 and 0900. It took him from 1100 to 1300 to pass the order on to all units. The first French tanks did not start to move toward the Bois du Mont-Dieu until 1300. The Flavigny Group was finally ready to launch its attack at 1730. In the meantime, the Roucaud Group had also moved into its starting position to the east of Stonne.

This brings us to one of the decisive moments of the campaign in the west. If there was ever a chance to stop the German Panzers, that chance came in the afternoon of 14 May. The irony of history was that the attack would have been mounted at the best possible moment precisely because of the constant delays. To secure the bridgehead, the Germans no longer had the 1st and 2d Panzer Divisions available, while the 10th Panzer Division had not yet arrived. The French could thus have pushed into a gap. The 1st Panzer Division had, in the meantime, made a ninety-degree flanking movement to the west at Chémery and presented its unprotected flank to any attack that would have come from the south. A thrust into the soft underbelly would have hit the supply columns head-on, specifically at the moment when the Panzer units, which had pushed to the west, had run out of supplies. In the afternoon, the 1st Panzer Brigade reported that it had "no ammunition and no fuel."[14] On the other hand, the 10th Panzer Division at that time was still held up far to the rear engaging the bitterly resisting remnants of the French 71st Infantry Division and had not yet even reached its designated phase line east of Bulson. This meant that at that particular time the Germans essentially only had the Infantry Regiment Großdeutschland to defend the bridgehead against an attack from the south. The Germans would not have had the slightest chance of coping with an attack by Flavigny's and Roucaud's divisions.

The fighting spirit of these elite divisions was praised as "most magnificent" and "splendid" in the combat reports on 14 May.[15] The French soldiers, especially the tank crews, were eagerly heading into their first engagement; they were spurred on by their officers. The commander of a tank battalion shouted to his men: "Forward men! We'll whip them! Long live France!"[16] But the attack order did not come. Now came the wearying wait. At last, a new order arrived during the evening hours. It had an almost paralyzing effect: The attack had been called off.

What had happened? On his way to the front, Flavigny over and over again heard tales of disaster as the panic-stricken soldiers streamed back, reporting hundreds and even thousands of attacking German Panzers. When he wanted to give the attack order on the afternoon of 14 May, some officers from the smashed 213th Infantry Regiment arrived and, horror-stricken, reported about the recently failed counterattack of the corps reserve. In addition, Flavigny was completely shaken up by the constant breakdowns and delays as his tank units tried to take up positions on the starting line. Thus, he canceled the attack at the very last moment. After the war he cited the rather astonishing justification for that decision of his: "I wished to avoid disaster."[17] In the rather thinly held Sedan bridgehead, the German soldiers would have had every reason to thank him for that.

Flavigny then committed an even more critical error. He decided to switch to the defense and ordered his formations, which really were supposed to attack from south to north, dispersed to the east and west. In so doing, he distributed his tanks on a line of twenty kilometers on both sides of the Ardennes Canal between Omont and La Besace. So-called *bouchons* (corks), composed of one heavy tank and two light ones, clogged all roads and passes. Thus, all French tank formations were broken up and scattered. Flavigny, the commanding general responsible for the counterattack, in this way managed to dissolve the French 3d Armored Division as a major unit capable of carrying out a military operation. This led to the complete dilution of an attack operation that, in the words of Huntziger, was to have been carried out "*avec la plus brutale énergie sans aucun souci des pertes*" (with the most brutal energy and in utter disregard of casualties).[18]

The failure of the counterattack had been preprogrammed in the way Huntziger worded his attack order. In his Ordre général d'opérations No 24 (General Operations Order No. 24), dated 14 May at 0000, Huntziger had ordered troops (1) to take up the second prepared reserve position between La Cassine and Mont-des-Cygnes [southeast of Stonne] and to seal off the enemy penetration frontally; (2) after the enemy had been successfully blocked, to mount the counterattack as quickly as possible toward Maisoncelle, Bulson, and Sedan[19] That was a contradiction in terms because the defensive and offensive parts of the mission to "seal the gap and counterattack" (*colmater et contre-attaquer*) were mutually exclusive. Defending meant spreading the units out in a linear pattern along a front line. Attacking, on the other hand, meant concentrating all forces at one point in the form of a narrow and deep deployment pattern.

To this extent, it is psychologically entirely understandable that Flavigny—in view of the constant flow of bad news—initially concentrated on the defensive portion of the order, even though he was not at all attacked directly and thus was unable to seal off any enemy thrust. He also had the units of X Corps in front of him. The roots of the problem were much deeper. Many Frenchmen later considered the cause of the defeat in 1940 to be the word *colmater* (to seal off) or, rather, the wrong line of thinking concealed behind that order. Huntziger's order was completely in consonance with the principles of command dating back to World War I.

At that time, the reaction to the German penetration attempts was (1) seal off the penetration frontally (*colmater*); (2) wipe out the attacker with artillery fire; (3) clear the terrain of enemy. This concept, which was aimed at restoring the linear cohesion of the front, appeared outdated in an era of a modern mobile warfare. In similar crisis situations, the Germans reacted not with any frontal blocking action but instead with a counterattack against the flank using their Panzers. Paradoxically, Flavigny's attack quite by accident would have thrust into the exposed flank of Guderian's Panzer Corps, if his rather respectable armored fighting force had moved just a few more kilometers to the north.

The Second Attempt at a Counterattack on 15 May. In the evening, when Georges, the commander in chief of the northeast front, learned of the Second Army's so-called successful defense, he furiously told Huntziger: "The 3d Armored Division was put at your disposal to counterattack toward Sedan."[20]

The commander in chief of Second Army, on the other hand, allowed the night to pass without taking any action whatsoever. After all, he was busy moving his headquarters from Senuc to Verdun, which is about fifty kilometers farther to the rear. On the next morning, however, the right moment had passed because the front line along the Meuse River collapsed over a width of more than one hundred kilometers on 15 May, primarily on account of the disaster at Sedan. In the meantime, the 1st and 2d Panzer Divisions had continued their thrust to the west and were out of range. Moreover, the 10th Panzer Division was now fully available. Nevertheless, a resolute attack would inevitably have led to a crisis in the German operational command setup.

Georges once again urged Huntziger to make haste during a telephone conversation at 0715 on 15 May. That is when Huntziger at last went into action. At 0800 he gave Flavigny the *mission impérative* (express order) to mount a counterattack with his tank formations. That directive did not reach Flavigny until 0830. He summoned the commanding generals of the 3d Armored Division and the 3d Motorized Infantry Division to his command post at 1000 (note the time delay) and ordered them to continue the counterattack together with the neighboring divisions. He set a deadline of 1400. Now it turned out that it had been much easier to spread the French tanks out than to concentrate them again for a renewed attack. In some cases, the commanders simply did not know where their vehicles were. That was particularly noticeable when the widely scattered French tank units were to be refueled. In addition, most of the radios had failed because there had been no time in recent days to recharge the storage batteries.

The same drama of constant delays as the day before now began all over again. Flavigny ordered the attack to be postponed from 1400 to 1600 and then to 1830. But there was no end to the problems. Besides, it was impossible to maintain a constant hold on the key terrain around Stonne, which in the meantime the Germans had attacked several times. In the end, Flavigny, completely shaken up, canceled his attack order at 1815.

The 1st and 2d companies of the 49th Tank Battalion, however, had not been informed in time that the order had been canceled. Attacking all by themselves with their Char B tanks, they advanced from the northern edge of the Bois du Mont-Dieu toward Chémery without any artillery and infantry support. After only two kilometers they ran into a blocking position of German antitank guns between Artaise and Neuville. Now, the Germans were able to concentrate their defensive fire on these few tanks that had been pushed too far ahead. Although the Char B tanks had been hit several times, the Germans managed to put only two of them out of action. When the two French company commanders realized that they had attacked all by themselves, they ordered a retreat. Their German opponents ran into no end of surprises. First of all, they found to their amazement that their projectiles, with which they literally covered the French Char B tanks, bounced off the French armor almost without any effect. Then they could not figure out why these colossuses that threatened to overrun them suddenly turned around and drove away. This isolated thrust showed what the Germans would have run into if a French tank attack had indeed been mounted on a broad front. What Manstein and Guderian feared most was a French countermove immediately after the breakthrough at Sedan. The counteroffensive, which in the Flavigny's words was to be pushed "*avec le plus grand esprit de sacrifice*" (with the utmost spirit of sacrifice),[21] consisted merely of the mistaken thrust by two French tank companies that had not been informed in time that the attack order had been countermanded.[22]

General Flavigny, the Real Loser of the Battle of Sedan. The only attempt at a French counterattack on the operational echelon had failed before it had begun. As the British author Len Deighton put it, the French army "had been defeated by its own commanders" at Sedan.[23] Now Flavigny and Huntziger tried to put the blame on Brocard, the commander of the 3d Armored Division, and relieved him of command. On 14 May he had refused the order given to him by his corps commanding general to attack immediately, pointing out that he had not yet completed his supply operations. Thereupon, Flavigny conjured up the image of the "suicide mission" (*mission de sacrifice*), which was used so frequently during that campaign. Brocard merely replied rather dryly: "Suicide mission or no suicide mission—the tanks cannot move without gas."[24]

Oddly enough, Flavigny had decided against leading the attack himself. Instead, he placed the 3d Armored Division under the commander of the 3d Motorized Infantry Division, General Bertin-Boussu. That leads to the question as to what Flavigny was intending to command when he had placed one division under the other? Above all, it is astonishing that he put the tanks under the infantry instead of the other way around! Besides, this was not to be any shocklike tank thrust in the style of commanders such as Rommel or Guderian but rather an "infantry attack supported by tanks" according to the 1918 system. In this extraordinary situation, Flavigny acted rigidly according to the conventional method that had been taught at the École Militaire since World War I and that Lafontaine had also applied as the corps reserve advanced slowly toward Bulson. Further cause for astonishment is that it was Flavigny, of all people, who made such a fatal mistake. After all, he was considered to be a tank expert and in some way he was believed to be "the Guderian of the French army."[25] No other general in the French army had anywhere near as much experience in handling armor as he had. Not only had he commanded all sizes of armored units but he was also instrumental in the development of the SOMUA S-35, the world's best tank at that time. Thus, he seemed to be just about predestined for the mission he now faced.

At no time during this campaign was the contrast between German and French command theory more striking than at Sedan. To get right down to brass tacks: The French were able to respond to the operational challenge from German Panzers only in a tactical sense. While the Wehrmacht concentrated several Panzer divisions for a single operation, the French always threw battalion by battalion, division by division, into battle one after the other. Only at Sedan was it possible to combine several divisions, including strong armored forces, into one operational counterattack. Although Flavigny in the end felt responsible for only two of these divisions, he was not in a position correctly to coordinate the attack of these two major units. More than enough men and tanks were available, but the French army had neither the command principles nor the proper regulations, neither well-trained staffs nor suitable radio sets to carry out such an operational counterattack. Above all, there was no intellectual infrastructure for operational thinking because nothing like that had ever been run through in war games.

The crucial, decisive moment during the campaign in the west came late in the afternoon on 14 May when Flavigny's units had just moved into their starting positions for the attack. This was a unique, never-to-recur opportunity "to turn defeat into victory," as German Panzer General [Hermann] Hoth put it later.[26] Flavigny, however, missed his rendezvous with history.

This just about cries out for a comparison to the Battle of Waterloo where, for a brief moment, the fate of France was in the hands of Marshal Grouchy. But he hesitated too long before he dared to deviate from Napoleon's by then outdated order and came to his aid. Thus, the Prussians under Blücher arrived on the battlefield before Grouchy's troops and wrested victory from Napoleon's hands. In a similar manner,

Flavigny at Sedan shied away from the magnitude of his responsibility. Concerning the role of Marshal Grouchy, Stefan Zweig wrote in his book *Sternstunden der Menschheit* (The Tide of Fortune): "Fate smiles on the mighty and the violent," men such as Caesar, Alexander, and Napoleon. Then he continued: "But sometimes, very rarely in all ages, and in a rather odd twist of fate, it falls for just any nonentity. Sometimes—and these are astonishing moments in world history—fate settles on a trivial being for just one twitching minute. Always, such individuals are more scared than happy by the onrush of responsibility that embroils them in a heroic world game, and almost always they allow the fate that has been flung at them to slip out of their trembling hands."[27]

Stonne: The Verdun of 1940

> *Stonne! That word has become a concept for us. The name of this mountain village was written in blood in our regimental history.*[28]
>
> From a battle report of the Infantry Regiment Großdeutschland

The bitterest fighting during the campaign in the west erupted over the village of Stonne that changed hands 17 times between 15 and 17 May. Its geographic location tells us why, of all places, there was such furious fighting over this little village that numbered only a dozen farmsteads. The heavily wooded Mont-Dieu (God's Mountain) rises steep and threatening just fifteen kilometers south of Sedan. This massif blocks the terrain to the south like a natural fortress. The village of Stonne stands exposed along the northeast edge, the highest and steepest point of this ridge. Right at the eastern edge of this settlement rises the conical Pain de Sucre, which the Germans called Zuckerhut (Sugarloaf), the best observation point far and wide, whose military significance had been recognized by the ancient Romans. Before the start of the campaign, the French had fortified the northern edge of this massif with pillboxes and barriers and had developed it into a blocking position. At the same time, they were able to exploit the terrain as a point of departure for an attack to the north. The struggle for this ridge at times took on the character of positional warfare of World War I. The French compared the "hell of Stonne"[29] over and over again to the "hell of Verdun."[30] A German officer later said: "There are three battles that I can never forget: Stonne, Stalingrad, and Monte Cassino."[31] The fighting for Stonne was of great operational significance inasmuch as the Germans tried at this point to nip the French counterattack in the bud—a counterattack that was very dangerous to them. To that extent, it seems by no means an exaggeration to say that the Battle of Sedan was actually decided at Stonne.

The first fight for Stonne had already taken place in the evening of 12 May at the command post of the Panzer Group von Kleist. During this dramatic staff conference, there was a dispute over the expansion of the planned bridgehead at Sedan. Von Kleist believed that a depth of six to eight kilometers along the line Noyers-Pont-Maugis-Chéhéry was sufficient. But Guderian demanded the formation of an operational bridgehead with a depth of almost twenty kilometers, including the northern edge of the massif of Stonne. He argued that the bridgehead ordered by von Kleist was much too small for his Panzer Corps of about twenty-two thousand vehicles and that the improvised bridges across the Meuse should really be beyond the range of French artillery. Moreover, the massif of Stonne would have to be seized before it could be used as a point of departure for an enemy counterattack.[32]

More than anything else, it was the last argument that was decisive, and it definitely goes back to Manstein's operations draft. Manstein had demanded that following the crossing of the Meuse at Sedan the left flank not be sealed off passively but that a part of the breakthrough forces immediately push south, smack into the middle of the enemy's anticipated deployment area, before the enemy's attack could get going. With this idea, which amounted to aggressive defense, Manstein had earned strong approval from Guderian who put all his cards on movement to begin with. Halder, on the other hand, did not go along with this unconventional idea of Manstein. Kleist also outright rejected any such daring thought, and, anticipating possible extracurricular activities on the part of Guderian, he had ordered a "definite prohibition."[33] Von Rundstedt, commander in chief of Army Group A, visited Guderian on the Sedan battlefield early in the morning on 14 May. At that time, Guderian immediately wanted to use this opportunity to bring about a ruling on the situation. Thereupon, in a telephone call to Guderian's command post at 1145, Rundstedt had his staff make it absolutely clear that von Kleist's directive continued to be binding.[34] The following rather succinct sentence concerning the further course of this controversy can be found in the files of the von Kleist Group: "XIX Corps [Panzerkorps Guderian], however, stuck to its decision to push toward Stonne."[35]

This was an almost incredible case of military disobedience! But 14 May was the day when Guderian, encouraged by the unexpectedly rapid breakthrough, discarded all rules and commandments and imprinted his very own stamp on the operation, "contrary to express instructions."[36] Success, however, proved him right, and so we find the following comment on the thrust toward Stonne in the operational analysis of the Panzer Group Kleist that was written after the campaign: "The unauthorized measures taken by the commanding general of XIX Corps, General of Panzertruppe Guderian, resulted in a great success for the von Kleist Group, and thus for the entire course of operations, and averted a big threat."[37]

On 14 May Guderian broke out of the bridgehead in two directions at once: with 1st and 2d Panzer Divisions to the west, heading for the Channel coast, and with the 10th Panzer Division, mounting an aggressive defense toward the south. On the morning of 14 May, he had already refrained from stopping at the prescribed Noyers-Pont-Maugis-Chéhéry line and had pushed on to Bulson and Chémery, right into the middle of the French X Corps' counterattack. In that way he triggered a chain reaction because the repulsed French units now were streaming in wild flight to the south, into the Bois du Mont-Dieu where Flavigny was just marshalling his forces for the big counterblow. The frightening messages that now spread so heavily impressed Flavigny that he switched to the defensive instead of attacking.

The Stonne massif constituted an ideal springboard for an attack to the north. When Flavigny wanted to attack on the next day, 15 May, his units could not jump off because the enemy had in the meantime already gotten a stronghold on the springboard. The 10th Panzer Division had thrust into the middle of the French assembly area. Actually, it had the mission of screening the southern part of the bridgehead between the Meuse and the Ardennes Canal. However, being a Panzer Division, it did not have enough infantry for this mission, although the Infantry Regiment Großdeutschland supported it. If the enemy counterattack had really gotten rolling with the Char B tanks that were employed at the point of main effort like a battering ram, then the division would not have had any suitable antitank weapons to stop the French. Because the 10th Panzer Division was too weak for defensive action, Guderian decided to have it attack! It was better suited for that sort of fight because of its Panzers. The enemy had to be engaged at the very moment he was weakest—as he was in the process of lining up for the attack in the assembly area. The important thing was to tie his forces down at Stonne for one or two days until the divisions coming out of the Ardennes could take over the job of protecting the bridgehead.

Possession of Stonne was of overriding significance against the background of the fighting that was now erupting. The battle reached its climax in that village. It began at the crack of dawn on 15 May when the Großdeutschland, supported by the 2d Battalion, 8th Panzer Regiment, staged a probing attack. Just a single road led up the steep slope via two tight hairpin curves. The German Panzers were able to attack only in column formation and lost seven Panzers in the attempt to penetrate the village. The infantry did not finish clearing Stonne out until 0800. Now it turned into a slugging match. Stonne changed hands four times by 1045. Each time, the French tanks penetrated into the village and forced the German defenders, who were powerless against those French tanks, to retreat. The French attacks, however, were poorly coordinated with the infantry. The French tanks had to withdraw again and again, and the Germans would immediately reoccupy the village.

In some combat actions, there are situations where victory or defeat hangs in the balance for a brief moment and where the outcome is decided by individual actions at the very lowest tactical echelon. Such a crucial scene took place on that day in Stonne at around 1100. The French were preparing for a new attack and concentrated the following units: the 3d Company, 49th Tank Battalion, with Char B tanks; the 1st Company, 45th Tank Battalion, with Hotchkiss tanks; the main body of the 2d Company, 4th Tank Battalion, with FCM tanks[38]; the 1st Battalion, 67th Infantry Regiment; and the 1st Company, 51st Infantry Regiment. The French infantry was slow in getting ready, so the Char B tanks at first mounted a probing attack all by themselves. At that time, Stonne was held only by the 1st Battalion of the Großdeutschland, supported by nine out of twelve of the regiment's antitank guns.

Suddenly the widespread, frightening cry of "tank" circulated. At that moment, Oberfeldwebel [Hans] Hindelang rode into the village, "quite by his own decision," with his three antitank guns that had been held in reserve until then. He was barely able to get into position at the southwestern exit of Stonne near the water tower when the Char B tanks came at him. The following scene took place according to the after-action report: "Hindelang is being attacked by three 32-ton enemy tanks. Every round fired bounces off the enemy tanks. The tracer then gets lost somewhere. The tanks crunch on through the orchards. One tank knocked out the right-hand gun at a range of 100 meters. Then it empties its machine gun at the rubble pile. The gun commander, Corporal Kramer, is wounded, and his gunner is hard-hit; the others are dead. Kramer, though himself wounded, under machine-gun fire, crawls over to the gunner and, in a tremendous effort, drags him behind a house."[39]

This situation produced the first signs of panic in the elite Großdeutschland Regiment. The soldiers felt that they were powerless against these monster tanks. Most of all, they were terrified by the thought of being crushed by the tracks of these steel giants. Some infantrymen now simply took off, but the crews of the antitank guns continued to hold their positions, although the situation became increasingly hopeless. Hindelang's antitank platoon had only two of its three guns left:

> The fire from the three heavy enemy tanks threatened to wipe out the platoon. . . . At one point, one of the giants stood sideways. The left gun commander, Acting Corporal Giesemann, spotted a small ribbed surface in the middle of the enemy tank's right side, apparently a kind of radiator. It was no bigger than an ammunition chest. He aimed at it. A jet of flames shot out of the tank. . . . Now the two guns fired only at those little squares in the side of the 32-ton enemy tanks. The left gun was knocked out shortly thereafter by a direct hit. Now, Hindelang withdrew the surviving gun into the village. The three 32-ton enemy tanks had been finished off.[40]

At that moment, things began to turn around. The crews of the Char B tanks had felt completely safe against the German antitank projectiles. But now the three enemy tanks—Hautvillers, Gaillac, and Chinon—were burning brightly along the southern edge of Stonne. Suddenly, the crews of the other French tanks panicked and drove away to the south.

Around noon, the French managed to take the village again after their hitherto most massive assault. But that was just a brief episode. Hindelang's unexpected successful defense had broken the spell, and the myth of the invulnerability of the Char B tanks had been destroyed.[41] The Germans did not abandon Stonne as lost and prepared a new attack. In the afternoon, the French tanks had to be withdrawn again because Flavigny was regrouping his units for the ordered counterattack against Sedan. The 10th Panzer Division immediately exploited this break and dispatched the 1st Battalion, 69th Infantry Regiment, to support the Großdeutschland Regiment so that the Germans were able to take the village around 1730 for the fourth time within about nine hours.

The fact that Stonne—the springboard for the thrust at Sedan—had been lost again produced considerable operational consequences on the French side. Flavigny decided to cancel the attack that had been scheduled for 1830 and instead ordered that Stonne be attacked the next morning. That meant that the chance for a successful operational counterattack was gone once and for all because on the next day it was too late. Guderian had figured things out correctly. His opponent was still completely mired in World War I thinking and was mesmerized by the taboo of the exposed flank and the dogma of the linear front line. It seemed that it was more important for Flavigny first of all to restore the linear cohesion of the front and to recapture Stonne, the "thorn in the side." Only then was the methodically planned assault to be launched. In that context, he was even able to refer back to the wording of the order he got from his army commander: "After you have sealed off the enemy, you must counterattack."[42]

Huntziger, later to be minister of war of the Vichy government, turned out to be quite flexible. He managed to reinterpret the disaster of the failed assault attempt at Stonne as "successful defense."[43] He even trotted out the old battle slogan of Verdun *ils ne passeront pas!* (they [the Germans] shall not pass!). In that way, these historical events were just about turned upside down because after all the French were the attackers during the decisive phase on 14 and 15 May and they had missed an opportunity that would never come back. The fighting for Stonne, in which the Germans later mounted an attack on a broad front, continued for many days. In operational terms, the decision had already been made on the afternoon of 15 May when Flavigny canceled his attack order. From then on, the fighting there was only of subordinate tactical significance.

During the night of 16–17 May, the VI Corps replaced the 10th Panzer Division, which now followed Guderian's attack units that had already penetrated far to the west. The Großdeutschland had recorded the loss of 570 men[44] and was given a short break. The Panzerjägerkompanie 14 (14th Panzer Antitank Company), which again and again was in the very thick of the fighting, suffered the heaviest losses. They numbered 13 dead and 65 wounded, along with half of its 12 guns destroyed.[45] In the meantime, Stonne looked something like a tank cemetery with the wrecks of 33 French and about two dozen German Panzers among the rubble of the houses and along the outskirts of the village. But the fighting continued undiminished, with the Germans now employing mainly the 16th and 24th Infantry Divisions. The village changed possession for the seventeenth and last time on 17 May at 1745. After renewed, desperate French thrusts had been beaten off on 18 May, the Germans attacked, pushing farther south. It took them until 25 May before they had once and for all seized the plateau of Stonne. The longest and severest fighting in the campaign ended on that day.[46]

The Fighting for Stonne

Only two episodes will be picked out from among the confusing number of combat actions that took place after the decisive events of 15 May. In spite of the initial apparent success, these episodes clearly demonstrate one of the most important factors in the French defeat. The main body of two French tank battalions, supported by one infantry battalion, attacked the tiny village of Stonne around 0700 on 16 May after a forty-five-minute barrage from two artillery regiments. In the end, it was one single tank that took the village practically all by itself. Captain Billotte, commanding officer of the 1st Company, 41st Battalion, in his Char B Eure, broke through the German positions and pushed into Stonne. A German Panzer company from the 8th Panzer Regiment that had moved into positions on both sides of the village street now opened fire from all barrels. But the Char B drove smack through the column, shooting up all 13 German Panzers with its 4.7-cm and 7.5-cm guns and also wiping out two antitank guns. The Char B itself received 140 hits, but not a single one of the German projectiles penetrated its armor.[47]

Char B Riquewihr of the 49th Tank Battalion spread even greater terror on the next day. Its commander, Lieutenant Doumecq, on that day was dubbed *le boucher de*

Char B Gaillac (3d Company, 49th Tank Battalion) was put out of action on 15 May along the southern edge of Stonne by an antitank gun of Oberfeldwebel Hindelang (14th Company, Infantry Regiment Großdeutschland). *Helmuth Spaeter (Großdeutschland Archives)*

Knocked-out Panzer IVs of the 8th Panzer Regiment at the eastern edge of Stonne. They were presumably shot to pieces by Char B Eure of the French captain Billotte (1st Company, 41st Tank Battalion). *Bundesarchiv Koblenz [Federal Archives]*

Stonne (the butcher of Stonne) by his comrades. Around 1700 he attacked in the direction of Stonne. Some eight hundred meters to the northwest of the village, he ran into a column of German infantrymen who were seeking cover in a section of ditch along the way.[48] When those infantrymen rather light-heartedly opened fire with their small arms, he simply rolled over the entire column.[49] Then, firing wildly all around, he pushed into the village that was being held by men of the 64th Rifle Regiment. Those men panicked and fled from the village as they spotted the fire-spitting monster with its still-bloody tracks.

At this point the question arises: How could the inferior German Panzer force in just a few days simply overrun the French armored force, which had considerably more and better tanks and whose tankers in some cases fought with noticeable resolution? The most important answer has already been given with the example of Flavigny—the French did not know how to combine their tanks into a coherent action on the operational echelon. As demonstrated at Stonne, moreover, they could not do that even at the tactical echelon in the context of combined arms combat. Spectacular though the highly praised actions of Captain Billotte, Lieutenant Doumecq, and many others may have been, these were usually individual exploits that were nothing but piecework, as it were, and whose success in most instances could not be exploited.

The example of the feared French Char B tank demonstrated precisely the shortcomings of the French tank arm. To begin with, few tanks had radios. The quality of those radios was so poor that they frequently failed, especially in the case of protracted combat operations. In that way, the tank commanders were hardly in a position to coordinate their own operations not to mention joint actions with the infantry. On the other hand, almost all German Panzers were equipped with modern radios. Huge formations attacked as if governed by a single will. Whenever radio contact failed now and then, the principle of Auftragstaktik (mission-type tactics) took over. In that respect, what happened at Stonne was practically a tragedy. There were hardly any other major French units that fought with such self-sacrifice as the men of the French 3d Motorized Infantry Division and the 3d Armored Division. In the end, however, all this bravery was in vain because the French army was operating on the basis of an obsolete command system that had been handed down from World War I.

	Stonne in German Hands	**Stonne in French Hands**
(1) 15 May	0800	
(2)		0900
(3)	0930	
(4)		1030
(5)	1045	
(6)		1200
(7)	1730	
(8) 16 May		0730
(9)	1700	
(10) night 16–17 May	Stonne unoccupied	
(11) 17 May	0900	
(12)		1100
(13)	1430	
(14)		1500
(15)	1630	
(16)		1700
(17)	1745[50]	

The Operational Effects of the Thrust to Stonne

Guderian's breakthrough at Sedan caused the utmost confusion among the French command. From that point, the Germans could push on in three different directions: to the west, to the Channel coast; straight ahead, toward Paris; and to the east, into the rear of the Maginot line.

For a brief but decisive moment, the French general staff was paralyzed. According to Alistair Horne's analogy, the French general staff was like a hunting dog whose instincts were blocked because it faced three different hares that were at the same distance from it.[51] Guderian's additional thrust toward Stonne had embroiled the French general staff in this decision-making dilemma. The trauma of August 1914 still held the French in thrall. At that time, the German Fourth Army had also crossed the Meuse in the Sedan area and had pushed from there southeastward toward Verdun to envelop the French fortification line from the rear. It was possibly this association that misled the otherwise cool and calm Huntziger into making a fatal snap decision. Mistaking the direction of the German attack, he believed that the Maginot Line was in danger and ordered the entire left wing of his army to swing southward on the way to Inor on the Meuse. The pivotal point here was Fort No. 505 at La Ferté. That meant that all the many fortifications in the Mouzon sector, in whose favor the Sedan sector had been neglected, now fell into enemy hands without a fight. More than 130 pillboxes had to be abandoned. Without any action on the part of the Germans, the breakthrough point at Sedan that had formed only a six-kilometer-wide bottleneck now opened like a breach in a dam to a width of almost thirty kilometers.

Even worse was the fact that the French, quite mistakenly, believed that Guderian's aggressive defense at Stonne constituted the main effort of an operational thrust to the south. Instead of mounting a counterattack, they used the best divisions from their operational reserve to block this presumed major offensive while neglecting the western part of the bridgehead where the breakout had actually taken place. This meant that they once again fell for a deception maneuver. At the start of Operation Sickle Cut, the Germans feigned the point of main effort of the attack on the right wing but broke through in the center, while at Sedan, on the other hand, Guderian simulated a thrust in the center but broke through to the right toward the west. This once again bears Manstein's signature because he had from the very beginning called for that same simultaneous thrust to the south, using elements of the breakthrough forces. The French command, first and foremost Huntziger, later was subjected to severe criticism because it was completely taken in by the bluff. But it must be kept in mind here that the German generals also did not know what to do with the brilliant chess move that Manstein had suggested. It was solely due to Guderian's disobedience that the chess move was successfully made.

French Ninth and Sixth Armies Attempt Blocking Action in the West

The boundary between the French Second and Ninth Armies lay just west of where the Ardennes Canal runs into the Meuse. This is why von Kleist wanted to place his point of main effort there, along the line where the two armies met and not seven kilometers to the east thereof at Sedan. In that way, it would also have been possible to avoid a double river crossing, first to the south bank of the Meuse and then to the west bank of the Ardennes Canal. As his superior later had to admit, Guderian was right in rejecting the idea because the chances of getting across the Meuse to begin with were incomparably better at Sedan. Now it so happened that several French units had moved into position to the west of the Ardennes Canal or that they were in their approach march.[52]

Second Army: In the northern sector (at the place where the canal runs into the Meuse), the extreme left wing of the 55th Infantry Division still held its position along the western edge of the Ardennes Canal. Besides, the 5th Light Cavalry Division, which had already faced the Panzer Corps Guderian in the Ardennes, was ordered to set up defenses along the west bank during the night between 13–14 May. The 1st Cavalry Brigade was placed under its command for this purpose.

Ninth Army: The right wing was swung back to the south. This meant that several new units were additionally put into line along the Ardennes Canal and that the 5th Light Cavalry Division, which belonged to the neighboring Second Army, was at last able to concentrate on the southern sector. Until that moment, the 102d Division had formed the right wing of Ninth Army. Elements of that division were to reinforce the strong points set up for the purpose of defending the bridges across the canal in the northern sector of the Ardennes Canal. The 53d Infantry Division was put into line to support those units. The previously mentioned 3d Spahi Brigade, which had returned from the Ardennes, was ordered to the south thereof to form the link with the 5th Light Cavalry Division and thus with the Second Army. In addition, the newly formed Sixth Army was to be inserted between the Ninth and Second Armies.

It now became obvious how eminently important Guderian's decision had been immediately to break out of the bridgehead to the west. The French hardly had any time left to regroup their units. On the morning of 14 May at around 0730, an assault team from the 1st Panzer Division had already swiftly seized the Ardennes Canal Bridge at Omicourt and formed a small bridgehead. Even more important was the advance around 1200 by two Panzers that seized the important canal bridge at Malmy near Chémery with infantry support. In addition, the 2d Panzer Division took the bridge of Pont à Bar at the place where the Ardennes Canal closed in to the Meuse, and its Panzers began crossing the bridge at 1430. That division pushed another five kilometers to the west by evening, all the way to Flize as well as on to Sapogne, while the 1st Panzer Division was able to push almost ten kilometers to Singly as well as to Vendresse. This meant that it had penetrated deeply into the heavily wooded chain of hills that formed a natural barrier to the west of the Ardennes Canal.

Even this success was due not only to the ability of the Germans but also to the incomprehensible mistakes of the enemy. In that campaign, which was so marked by failures and breakdowns, the insertion of the 53d Infantry Division into the front line represented "a record achievement in the art of scattering troops all over the terrain."[53] This division's tragedy was that without any action by the Germans it was checkmated by an absurd sequence of contradictory orders from its own command. During the night of 13–14 May, the 53d Infantry Division received the following orders and counterorders:

> On the evening of 13 May, General Etcheberrigaray was ordered to march north in order to move into position along the Meuse on the right wing of Ninth Army.
>
> Around 2200, General [André-Georg] Corap, the commander in chief of the Ninth Army, instead ordered [Etcheberrigaray] to march east to man a defense line along the Ardennes Canal.
>
> At midnight, a new order arrived, directing the division again back to the north, along the Meuse.
>
> But that directive was countermanded that same night; now General Etcheberrigaray and his division were again to march eastward to the Ardennes Canal.[54]

This jumbled mess of orders shows what confusion prevailed among the French command in the meantime. The next morning no one knew where the widely scattered formations were as they wandered around the area. The division was now so busy rounding up its scattered units that it hardly had any chance to participate in the fighting. However, it was precisely this major unit that was to play the most important role in containing the German thrust to the west. When Etcheberrigaray finally managed to get his division together again, Guderian's troops were well along the way to the Channel coast. This principle of "order, counterorder, disorder" created constant confusion during those days.[55]

The collapse of the French army cannot be blamed on the soldiers but rather on its command. Whenever those men were correctly employed, they displayed astonishing examples of bravery, such as on 15 May at La Horgne, 20 kilometers southwest of Sedan. The 3d Spahi Brigade had gone into position here. Earlier, this brigade had played a fateful role at the Mouzaive Bridge in the Ardennes during the night 11–12 May when its premature pullout had caused the collapse of the delaying-action line along the Semois. Now it was preparing a mean surprise for the 1st Panzer Division on its seemingly relentless push to the west because it stopped the northern battle group for eight hours. Apart from Stonne, this was probably the bitterest fighting in the campaign. Balck later wrote about the fighting in which the 1st Rifle Regiment was involved at La Horgne: "I fought against all foes in both wars and I was always in the thick of it. Rarely did anyone fight as outstandingly as the 3d Spahi Brigade. Its commander, Colonel Maré,[56] was captured after having been wounded. . . . Out of the brigade's 27 officers, 12 were killed in action, 7 were wounded, along with 610 Spahi dead or wounded. The brigade had ceased to exist. It had sacrificed itself for France. I gave orders that the few prisoners we took be given especially good treatment."[57]

On that day, the 1st Rifle Regiment recorded by far the heaviest losses during the campaign. In some respects, this fighting represented a parallel to the fight for Bodange on 10 May in the Ardennes. For reasons of time, the Germans could not afford the luxury of mounting a methodical attack with adequate fire support. The effect of the Panzers was also restricted in this heavily wooded and mountainous terrain. The decision thus came as a result of close-quarter infantry combat. That same evening, it was important to take Bouvellemont, at which time Balck had to go into action personally because his men were completely exhausted.

> We are right in front of Bouvellemont, a wide and broad plain extends to the village from whose edge we are drawing fire from numerous MG [machine guns] and Pak [antitank guns]. The Studnitz Battalion is deployed in a long line along the edge of the plain. The men are completely exhausted. Rations have run out. There is nothing to drink in this oppressive heat. Ammunition is short. But losses . . . kept piling up considerably . . . I called the officers together: We cannot go on; we need one night's sleep; tomorrow we can go on. I cut them short: Gentlemen, we are attacking or we are simply giving victory away. This was the kind of situation in which you can give orders until you are blue in the face—the men simply will not follow you. I turned around and said, if you do not want to go on, I will take the village myself; and so I marched off toward Bouvellemont, across thc open field, 50 meters, 100 meters, then they all got up and followed me. Men and officers, who just a few seconds earlier were at the end of their tether, passed me by. Nobody was thinking of seeking cover. Everybody rushed on ahead. Our fixed bayonets glistened in the setting sun. There was no stopping us. From everywhere came the sound of wild cheering as a thin line of completely exhausted riflemen pushed into the village. Bouvellemont was ours.[58]

At 0900 on 14 May, Georges, the commander in chief of the French northeast front, had already given orders to move up the Sixth Army and to insert it in the front line between the Ninth and Second armies. But General [Robert-Auguste] Touchon, who was suddenly cast in the role of "France's savior," was a general without troops. He had a staff and a few motley units. From the operational reserve, he was given two elite divisions: the 2d Armored Division and the 14th Infantry Division, which was commanded by General [Jean] de Lattre de Tassigny, later a Marshal. These units were joined by the 36th Infantry Division and other formations that were made up in an improvised fashion. He also got the XXXXI Corps, which until then had formed the right wing of Ninth Army.

Now, however, the French army's main problem in this campaign cropped up once again. Unable to combine major units quickly enough into one operational countermove, it instead proceeded at the same tempo with which it had launched counteroffensives during World War I. A sufficient number of major units could not be moved into position to prevent the German thrust to the west. Of course, the 14th Infantry Division's courageous fight in the Bouvellemont-Chagny area was praised again and again, but essentially it was only the 152d Regiment that could be moved forward in time. Thus, Touchon finally confined himself to sealing off the southern German flank along the Aisne. On the morning of 16 May, Guderian had once and for all punched through the chain of hills to the west of the Ardennes Canal. Between him and the Channel coast there were now almost no Allied troops that could block his way. The campaign had been decided. Everything happened so quickly that the French, with a few exceptions, had not even noticed anything. On the morning of 16 May, Guderian's Panzers kept pushing relentlessly west. At the same time, the French were able to read the following report in the latest edition of *L'Epoque:* "The enemy has not succeeded in breaking through our battle front and emerging from the Sedan-Mézières region. He has thrown wave upon wave, division on division, into the furnace. Our plains, our fields, our roads are filled with his corpses. . . . We must say this and say it again and cry it to the four winds of France's sky: 'He wanted to break through, as he wanted to at Verdun, but he did not get through!' "[59]

Panzer Corps Reinhardt Breaks Through at Monthermé—A Victory over His Own Command

> *When facing an enemy who has fast and mobile reserves, an effective breakthrough or a timely envelopment is possible only if the attack is ceaselessly pushed with the utmost speed and force deep into the enemy's deployment.*[60]
>
> Generalmajor [Werner] Kempf, Commander,
> 6th Panzer Division, on 25 January 1940

Crossing the Meuse

General [Hans] Reinhardt entitled his essay on the fighting at Monthermé rather characteristically "*Im Schatten Guderians*" (In Guderian's Shadow). The Panzer Corps that he commanded at that time was at a disadvantage in every respect when compared to Panzer Corps Guderian that was attacking to the south of his unit. When List, the commander in chief of Twelfth Army, briefed him on his new mission, he told him: "Where you are to attack I would best like to use mountain troops. I put in a mountain division to the right, next to your corps."[61]

In the area around Monthermé, the Meuse meanders through the Ardennes in a canyonlike gorge that greatly resembles the valley of the Rhine near Lorelei Rock. The bizarre rock formations, which attract so many tourists, created a nightmare here for Reinhardt. Along the northern bank of the Meuse, opposite Monthermé, rises a 200-meter high cliff, called Enveloppe, which several rockfalls interrupt. From here, the Germans had to try to get to the river. In the process, they were completely under the observation of the enemy who was superior in artillery. Here is what Reinhardt wrote on that score: "The terrain really scares you. The only road leading to Monthermé snakes down . . . into the deeply cut Meuse valley. . . . The riflemen are having trouble climbing down the steep slopes leading to the Meuse River while manhandling their heavy weapons. The rubber boats have to be taken down to the Meuse in the armored personnel carriers because it was impossible to carry them down."[62]

Support from the Luftwaffe, which was considerably less than at Sedan, was a big disappointment. As noted sarcastically in the journal of the 6th Panzer Division, it was "rather ineffective when it came to hitting the enemy facing the division. But it did a real good job in hitting our own units."[63] Some pilots lost their way over the heavily wooded terrain through which the Meuse River meanders and hit German units by mistake. It was mainly the rather scant artillery that was decimated. In addition to two guns, it lost thirty men, including fourteen killed.[64]

The most drastic consequences sprang from Army Group A's disastrous deployment planning. Panzer Corps Reinhardt and Guderian were to cross the Meuse River simultaneously and next to each other, down to the minute, after prior Luftwaffe bombing raids precisely at 1600 on 13 May. As a result of the previously mentioned planning mistakes, the Panzer Corps Reinhardt had been stuck in a chaotic traffic jam in the Ardennes. Thus, the 8th Panzer Division did not reach the Meuse until 16 May. The mission of the 2d Motorized Infantry Division, which was also a part of Panzer

The village of Stonne, perched high on a hill (south of Sedan), changed possession seventeen times between 15 and 17 May. View from Pain de Sucre. (Photo taken in 1990.) *Author's private collection*

The destroyed bridge over the Meuse River at Monthermé. On 13 May the 3d Battalion, 4th Rifle Regiment, 6th Panzer Division pushed its attack down from the two-hundred-meter-high cliff. Enveloppe in the background. *Bundesarchiv Koblenz [Federal Archives]*

Corps Reinhardt, was supposed to have been to cross the Meuse at Nouzonville (seven kilometers south of Monthermé). When it arrived there one day late on 14 May, the 3d Infantry Division of the neighboring III Corps was already at the designated crossing point.

While Reinhardt's major units were caught in the traffic jam, the 3d Infantry Division coming from the north had pushed forward and was now given the mission of being the first to cross the Meuse River. In that way, the sequence established in the movement plan was turned upside down. At the designated moment of 1600 on 13 May, the 3d Battalion, 4th Rifle Regiment, 6th Panzer Division, supported by one Panzer battalion and one artillery battalion, was the only infantry battalion of Reinhardt's three divisions in position along the Meuse. Still, they managed to cross the Meuse River and to take Monthermé that same evening and form a bridgehead.

That did not mean that anything had been decided—far from it. Monthermé stands on the northern end of a narrow spit, with the Meuse River flowing around it, and was thus easily isolated. The 2d Battalion, 42d Colonial Infantry Regiment, defended that peninsula.[65] It was part of the 102d Fortress Infantry Division, a regular division, whose personnel were superbly trained and fought extremely tenaciously in contrast to the 55th Infantry Division deployed to its south near Sedan. On 14 May, the Germans could not break out of this peninsula. The French had established a blocking position at the southern end and had reinforced the positions, which were partly dug into the rocks, with concrete pillboxes and armored cupolas.

Panzer Group Kleist Threatened with Breakup

From the very beginning, von Kleist had demanded operational independence for his Panzer Group, which was to be placed immediately under Army Group A. On the other hand, the commanders in chief of the field armies in whose combat sectors the Panzer Group was to attack demanded that it be placed under their command. Thereupon, von Rundstedt decided on a disastrous compromise. If the Panzer Group Kleist managed to cross the Meuse on its first attempt, then it would retain its operational independence. Otherwise, it would be taken out and placed under one of the following field armies as an operational reserve. On 14 May, the Panzer Corps Guderian achieved a brilliant success and Reinhardt's 6th Panzer Division was just about to break through.

Nevertheless, the command of Army Group A took the difficulties reported at Monthermé as an occasion for prematurely terminating the experiment of an operationally independent employment of the Panzer Force—an experiment that had always been eyed with suspicion. On 14 May, Army Group ordered that effective at 1200 on 15 May Panzer Group Kleist would be placed under Twelfth Army. That arrangement led to the most serious crisis of Panzer Group Kleist during the campaign in the west. Its war diary on 14 May noted: "Everything depends on whether we are now able to get across the Meuse, where we are temporarily stopped, on our own strength so that we may thus retain operational freedom of action. Otherwise there would be reason to fear that the fast-moving formations would now be employed, sticking very closely to the infantry corps with a correspondingly shorter-range objective. That would practically have signified the end of the von Kleist Group as an independent operational formation."[66]

Twelfth Army's very first orders confirmed von Kleist's worst fears. At 0400 on 15 May that army's command issued an order that Panzer Corps Reinhardt was to be taken out of the front line and assigned to the operational reserve. Only the 6th Panzer Division was to be left in the front line, although it was to be placed under III Corps. The latter's divisions were now to accomplish the mission that the 6th Panzer Division, very deficient in infantry, apparently could not.

Even the otherwise loyal von Kleist now became rebellious. He ignored his superiors' directives and ordered that all major units continue the attack. Reinhardt now urged the 6th Panzer Division on to achieve a breakthrough at all costs. This elite unit needed no further motivation. When the men of the 6th Panzer Division learned that an ordinary infantry division was to replace them, they once again returned to the attack with maximum effort. In this attack a pontoon bridge that had been built across the Meuse River under cover of darkness around 0100 on 15 May helped the division. The attack on the blocking position, which closed the peninsula off to the south, commenced at 0500. The forest terrain, which was heavily broken up by rocks, rather restricted the effect of the Panzers that had been moved up. Once again, close-quarter infantry combat with the assault engineers attacking the pillboxes with flamethrowers and explosive charges achieved the objective. The blocking position and another reserve position had been penetrated in depth by 0930.

Retreating Forward: The Push from Monthermé to Montcornet

The command of Army Group A first of all intended the infantry divisions of Twelfth Army to "gain an adequate and secure bridgehead along the Meuse" and therefore had placed the Panzer divisions under that army. Only then was the operation to be continued "with strong forces."[67] The 3d Infantry Division of III Corps could not get across the Meuse at Nouzonville, so Reinhardt was directed to order elements of the 6th Panzer Division, which had just broken through, to pivot to the south to open up the crossing point for the neighboring division "from the rear." Reinhardt, however, went along with Manstein's operational concepts and rejected that idea. He was most concerned with thrusting as deeply as possible into the enemy's positions.

The unauthorized action of Generalmajor [Werner] Kempf, the commander of 6th Panzer Division, rather abruptly terminated this operational controversy. On 15 May, he pulled off one of the most spectacular coups of the campaign and confronted all his superiors with a fait accompli. He did not wait for the units of his Panzer division to cross the Meuse River in full strength. Instead, he used immediately available elements to put together an ad hoc unit, the so-called Pursuit Detachment von Esebeck.[68] That unit was to exploit the breakthrough's success and to push into the enemy rear areas as deeply as possible. The unit was made up as follows:

65th Panzer Battalion
6th Motorcycle Rifle Battalion
2d Company, 57th Panzer Engineer Battalion
2d and 6th Batteries, 76th Artillery Regiment
1st Company, 41st Antitank Battalion
a reconnaissance school detachment
one antiaircraft artillery battery

The vehicles earmarked for this unit were given preference in crossing the river over the pontoon bridge. By 1500, the Pursuit Detachment was complete and pushed west with lightning speed. By around 2000, attacking relentlessly, it had reached Montcornet, which was fifty-five kilometers away as the crow flies. Indescribable scenes took place on the way there. Again and again, the Germans simply rolled all over the French columns. In most cases, there were not even any noteworthy combat actions. Rather, the French, who did not expect any enemy formations that far to the rear, acted as if paralyzed. On several occasions the dust-covered German vehicle columns were confused with French or British columns and were greeted with friendly waves before the French realized their terrible mistake. More than two thousand enemy soldiers were taken prisoner, although the Germans had hardly any time as they rushed on ahead.

The French command's operational planning collapsed like a house of cards within just a few hours after the push to Montcornet. It had become useless for the Sixth Army to form a new defense line to the west of the Ardennes Canal to block Panzer Corps Guderian because the Panzers of another German division were now far to the rear of that line. On the next day, Kempf and Guderian met in the marketplace at Montcornet and congratulated each other on their success. Two bridgeheads had been merged into one and the entire French defense in the central sector of the Meuse had collapsed.[69]

The fact that the German army command, just like the high command of the Luftwaffe, concentrated its interest completely on Sedan also yielded an advantage. By breaking through immediately, Guderian attracted all attention to himself. As a result, the French army command simply overlooked the threat coming at it from Monthermé. When the 6th Panzer Division also broke through on 15 May, its Panzers were able to push into a vacuum.

From the viewpoint of von Kleist, the most important result of the push to Montcornet was that Kempf had saved the establishment of the Panzer Group. Because of this unexpected success, the command of Army Group A reversed a portion of its rather restrictive orders. That meant, above all, that the Panzer Corps Reinhardt again came under the command of the Panzer Group Kleist. Of course, the Panzer Group continued to be subordinated to Twelfth Army, but that had no further effect for the time being. Instead, Panzer Group Kleist was now again given permission to attack far ahead of the Twelfth Army's infantry divisions.

Panzer Corps Hoth Breaks Through at Dinant

You are too fast, much too fast for us. That's all there is to it![70]

Remark of a French general captured at
St. Valery in conversation with Rommel

Panzer Corps Hoth had been placed under Fourth Army and, charging ahead of it, attacked to the west. Its mission was to screen the right flank of the Panzer Group Kleist, especially if the Allied formations encircled along the Channel coast should try to break out to the south. That corps had the 5th and 7th Panzer Divisions and was commanded by Hoth, one of best-known Panzer generals of World War II. During the campaign, however, one of his division commanders, Rommel, attracted the attention of the international public by a series of sensational actions. The 7th Panzer Division, which he commanded, again and again turned up so surprisingly behind enemy lines that the French called it *la division fantôme* (the ghost division).[71] By the same token, Rommel's name finally became synonymous with the German blitzkrieg.

Paradoxically, it was Rommel, of all people, who prior to World War II as an infantry officer with a reactionary way of thinking vehemently rejected the ideas of a man such as Guderian. But then, during the Polish campaign, he saw the light when, as commandant of Führer Headquarters, he watched the new Panzer force in action. Quite in keeping with his passionate and uncompromising character, he immediately became a Panzer devotee. On 12 February 1940 he was able to get command of the newly organized 7th Panzer Division for himself—a decision that was generally tied in with Hitler's predilection for this general.

As a Panzer leader in the campaign in the west, Rommel won breathtaking victories, ironically because he knew so little about Panzer operational principles. The old rules, as spelled out in regulations, no longer applied because the entire nature of war had been so revolutionized. Instead, Rommel acted intuitively to the particular situation he faced. He had a sure sixth sense for development of emerging situations and reacted quickly and resolutely. To that extent, he acted much like he did as an assault team (Stoßtrupp) leader in World War I. In October 1917 he led a successful commando raid near Tolmein in eastern Alps, capturing fourteen hundred Italian soldiers and seizing eighty-one artillery pieces. Storming the summit of Monte Matajur was his most spectacular success. Thereupon, he was promoted to the rank of captain and decorated with the highly coveted German order Pour le Mérite. During the campaign in the west, Rommel acted, so to speak, as assault team leader in a general's uniform. He led his Panzers like an infantry assault detachment and employed the same infiltration tactics he had when he was an Oberleutnant during World War I. This unorthodox way of employing the Panzer force became the nightmare of his methodical French counterparts. At the same time, Rommel's successes constitute impressive evidence of the thesis that German Panzer tactics were in the end crystallized from the assault team tactics of World War I.

Probing Attack against the Meuse River Bridges on 12 May

Panzer Corps Hoth pushed through the Ardennes parallel to Panzer Group Kleist about thirty-five kilometers to the north. The sector of the Meuse River they had to cross was located in Belgian territory. This meant that the [Allied] intervention forces of the French Ninth Army employed here would have to advance to the northeast as part of the Dyle maneuver from the national boundary for about another 90 kilometers to occupy the positions that had been reconnoitered on the west bank. In this "race to the Meuse," Hoth saw an opportunity for getting across the river by exploiting the element of surprise before the enemy could set up strong defensive positions there.

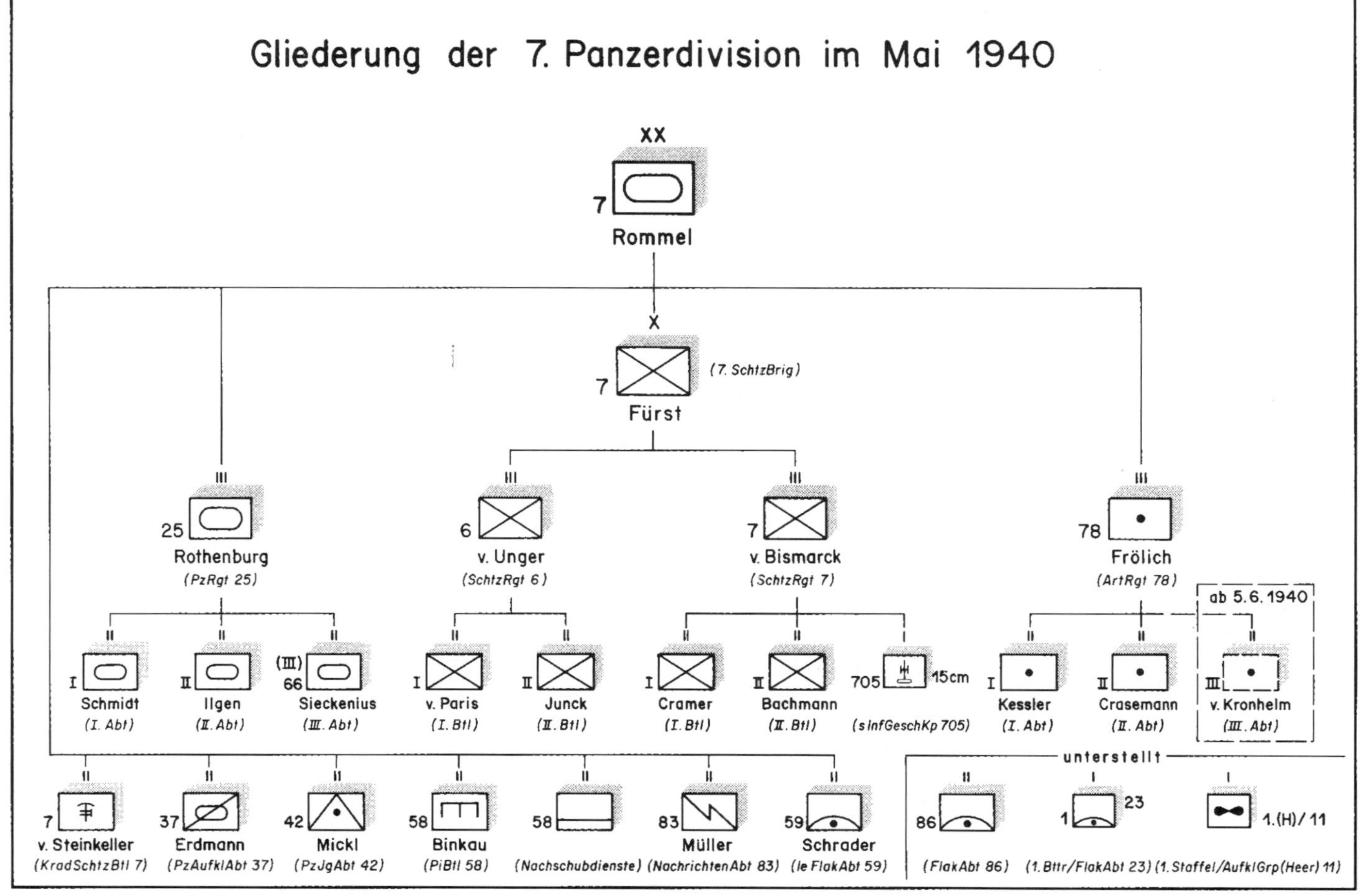
Gliederung der 7. Panzerdivision im Mai 1940
XX
7
Rommel
X
7
Fürst
(7. SchtzBrig)
25
Rothenburg
(PzRgt 25)
6
v. Unger
(SchtzRgt 6)
7
v. Bismarck
(SchtzRgt 7)
78
Frölich
(ArtRgt 78)
ab 5.6.1940
Schmidt
(I. Abt)
Ilgen
(II. Abt)
(III) 66
Sieckenius
(III. Abt)
v. Paris
(I. Btl)
Junck
(II. Btl)
Cramer
(I. Btl)
Bachmann
(II. Btl)
705
15cm
(sInfGeschKp 705)
Kessler
(I. Abt)
Crasemann
(II. Abt)
v. Kronhelm
(III. Abt)
unterstellt
7
v. Steinkeller
(KradSchtzBtl 7)
37
Erdmann
(PzAufklAbt 37)
42
Mickl
(PzJgAbt 42)
58
Binkau
(PiBtl 58)
58
(Nachschubdienste)
83
Müller
(NachrichtenAbt 83)
59
Schrader
(le FlakAbt 59)
86
(FlakAbt 86)
1
23
(1. Bttr/FlakAbt 23)
1.(H)/11
(1. Staffel/AufklGrp(Heer) 11)

Organization of 7th Panzer Division, May 1940

To get to that point, his two Panzer divisions had to cover a distance of about 115 kilometers. In the process, they had to overcome not only the numerous barriers put up by the Belgian Ardennes Light Infantry, but also the resistance of the French delaying forces that had rushed ahead across the Meuse River. In this sector of the Ardennes, formations of the 1st and 4th Light Cavalry Divisions blocked them. Rommel's 7th Panzer Division attacked so energetically that it finally charged far ahead of the 5th Panzer Division. Thereupon, Hoth decided in the morning of 12 May also to put the Werner Advance Detachment (under Oberst Paul Hermann Werner, commander, 31st Panzer Regiment), which belonged to the 5th Panzer Division, under Rommel's command.

The 7th Panzer Division's attempt to quickly get across the Meuse River by surprise failed. To be sure, a Panzer company sent on ahead as an advance guard crossed the Meuse River at Dinant at 1645, but the bridges there had just been blown. The fighting in the northern sector was even more dramatic. Werner received a message from close-support air reconnaissance in the afternoon that the bridge at Yvoir (seven kilometers north of Dinant) was still intact. He immediately ordered Leutnant [Heinz] Zobel's armored assault team of two armored scout cars and one Panzer platoon to head to the bridge at top speed.

Belgian engineers under the command of 1st Lieutenant de Wispelaere had prepared the bridge for demolition while a platoon of Ardennes Light Infantry and elements of a French infantry battalion screened the bridge. In the course of 12 May, formations of the 4th Light Cavalry Division, returning from the delaying action in the Ardennes, withdrew across the bridge. Although the last soldiers had already passed the bridge, de Wispelaere delayed the demolition because civilian refugees were still approaching. At that point, it was believed that the Germans were still very far away. Suddenly, at around 1725, there was a cry of alarm *Ils sont là!* (They are here!). At that moment, one could see the first German vehicles driving from Yvoir along the road paralleling the east bank of the Meuse River. The two German armored scout cars charged toward the bridge while the following three Panzers opened fire. De Wispelaere immediately pushed the electrical ignition, but there was no explosion. Obviously, a shell fragment had damaged the ignition system that had been checked a few minutes earlier.

In the meantime, the first German scout car drove onto the bridge but was stopped by a hit from a Belgian antitank gun. Immediately, a soldier carrying wire cutters jumped out of the armored car hatch to cut the ignition wire that he had spotted, but he was laid low by fire from the machine guns. However, more German soldiers were already approaching under covering fire from the Panzers. Wispelaere now left his shelter and worked the manual ignition device. Trying to get back to his bunker, he was hit by a burst from a German machine gun and fell to the ground, mortally wounded. At the same time, the explosive charge went off. After the gigantic smoke cloud had drifted away, only the remnants of the pillars could be seen. The bridge and the armored scout car on it had sunk into the water.[72]

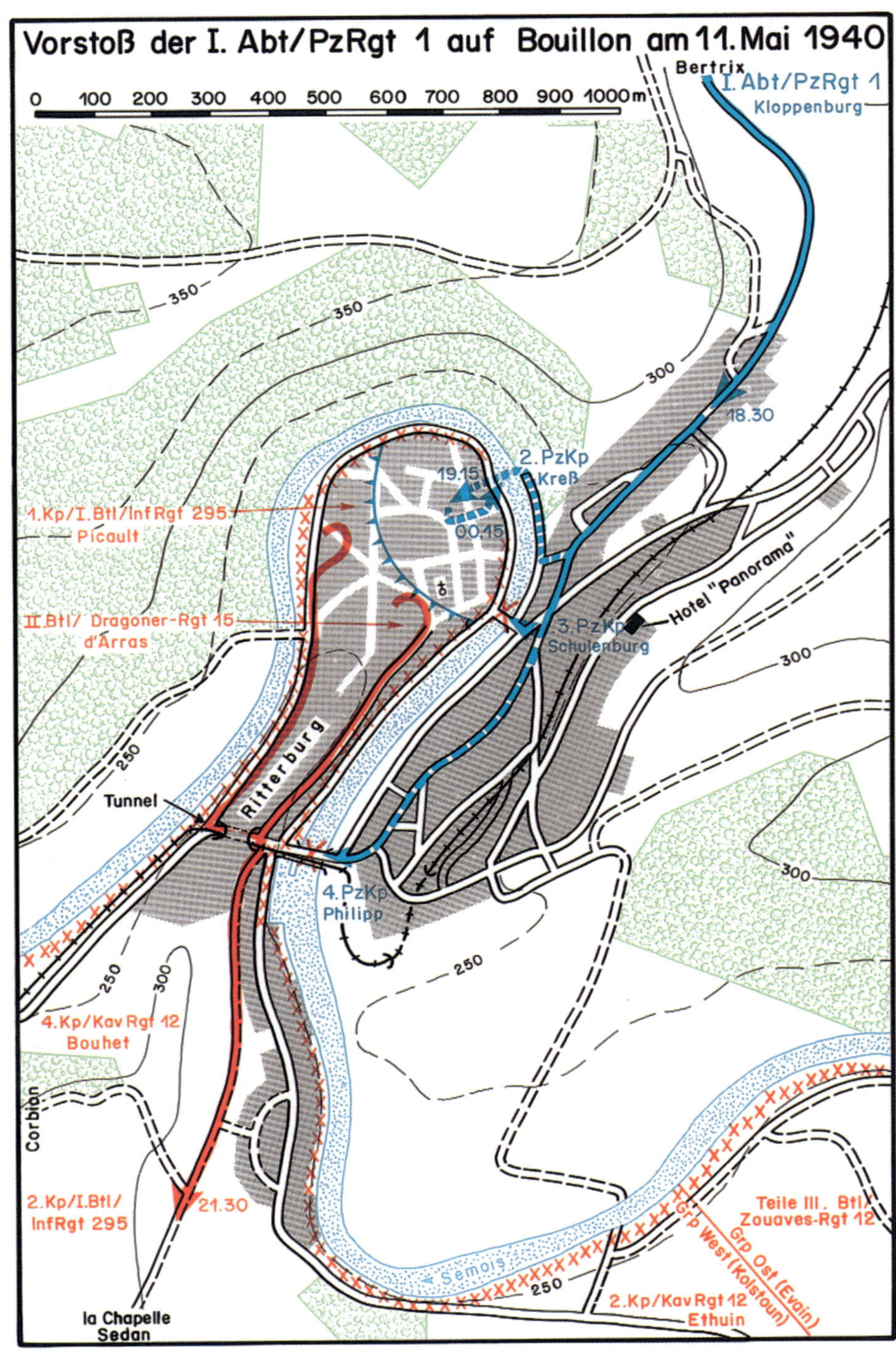

Advance Attack of 1st Battalion, 1st Panzer Regiment to Bouillon, 11 May 1940

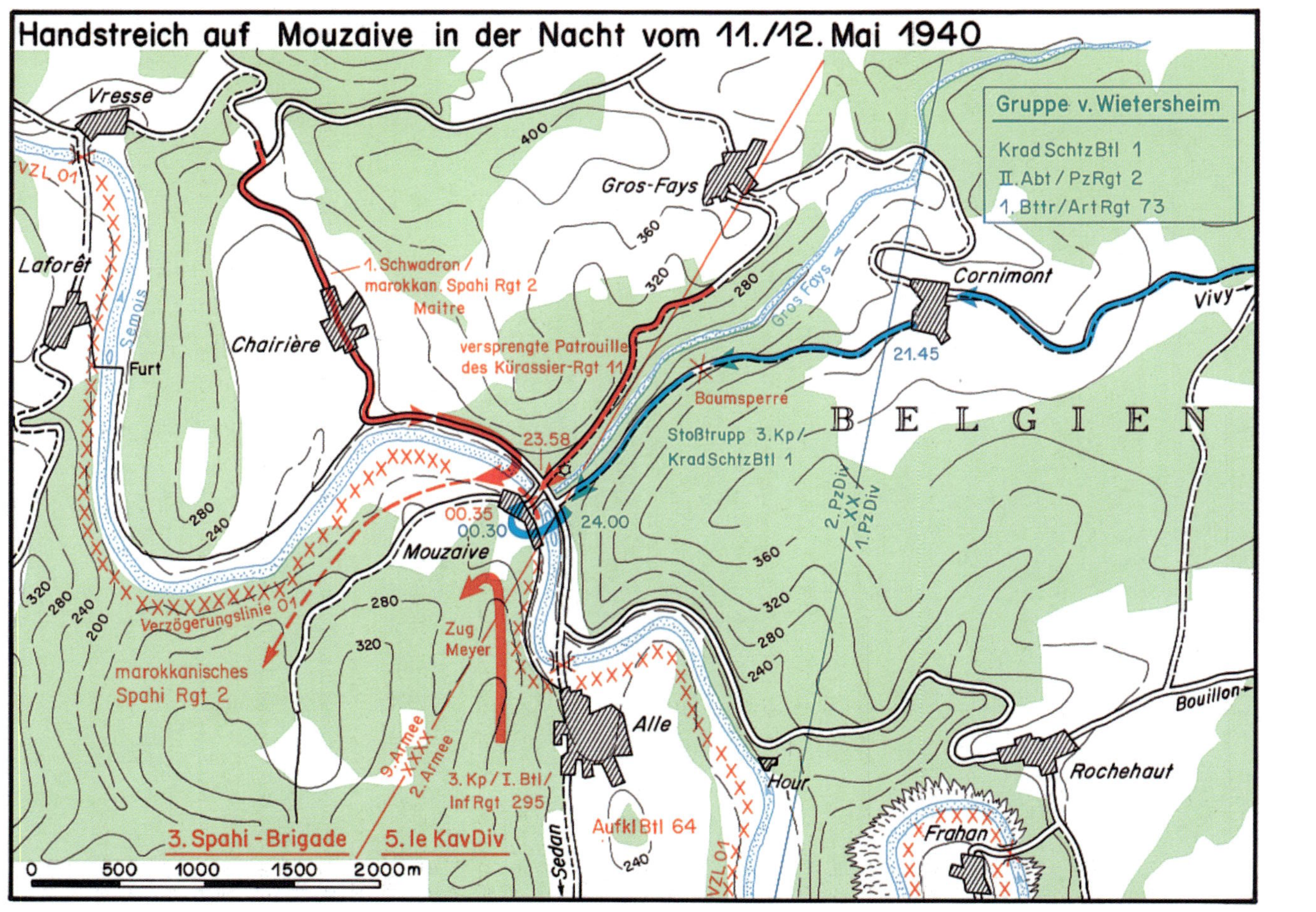

Surprise Attack at Mouzaive during the Night of 11–12 May 1940

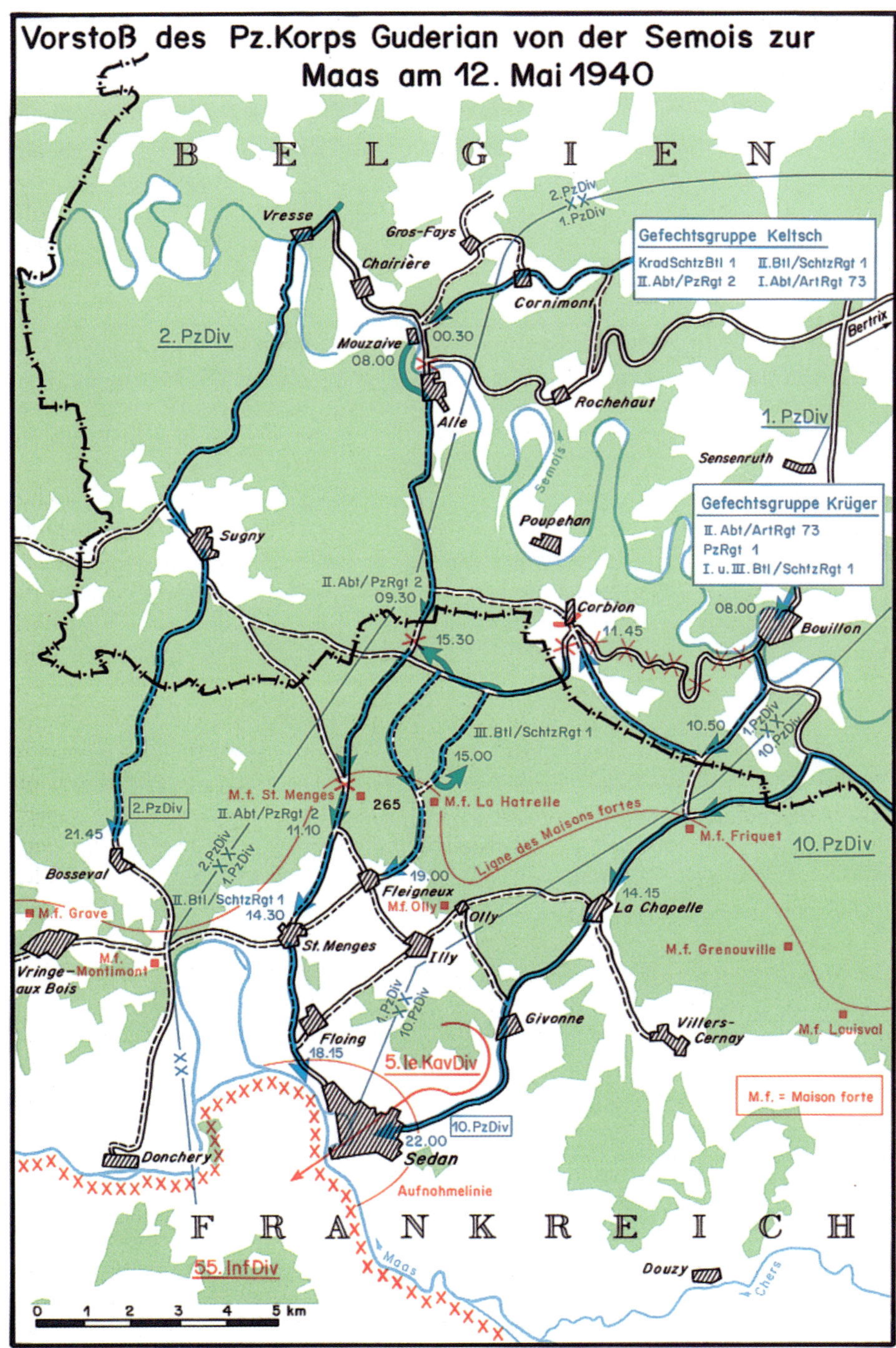

Advance of Panzer Corps Guderian from the Semois to the Meuse, 12 May 1940

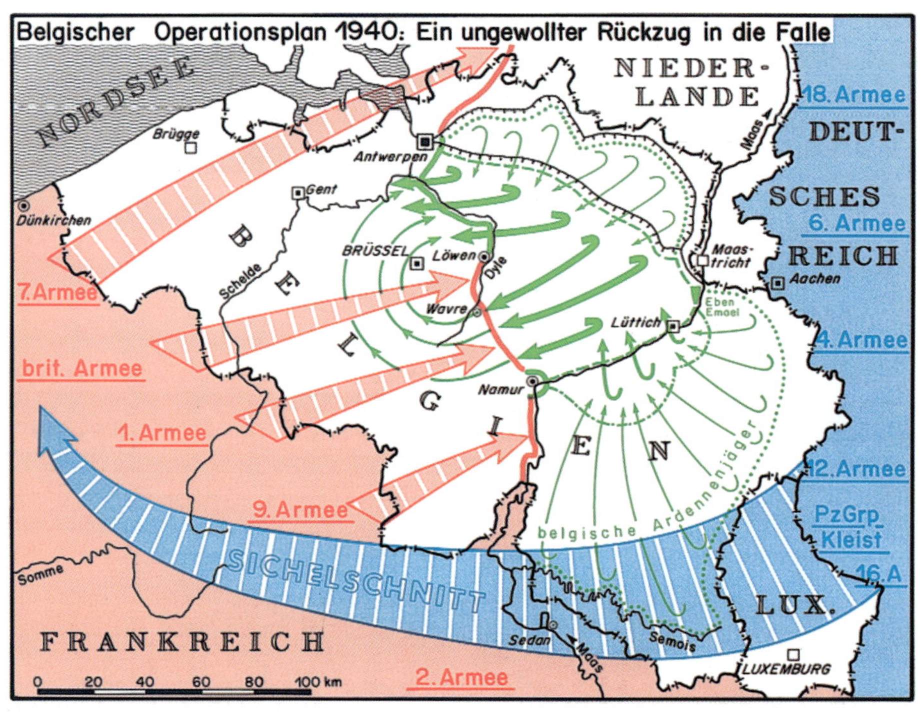

The 1940 Belgian Operations Plan: An Unwanted Retreat into the Trap

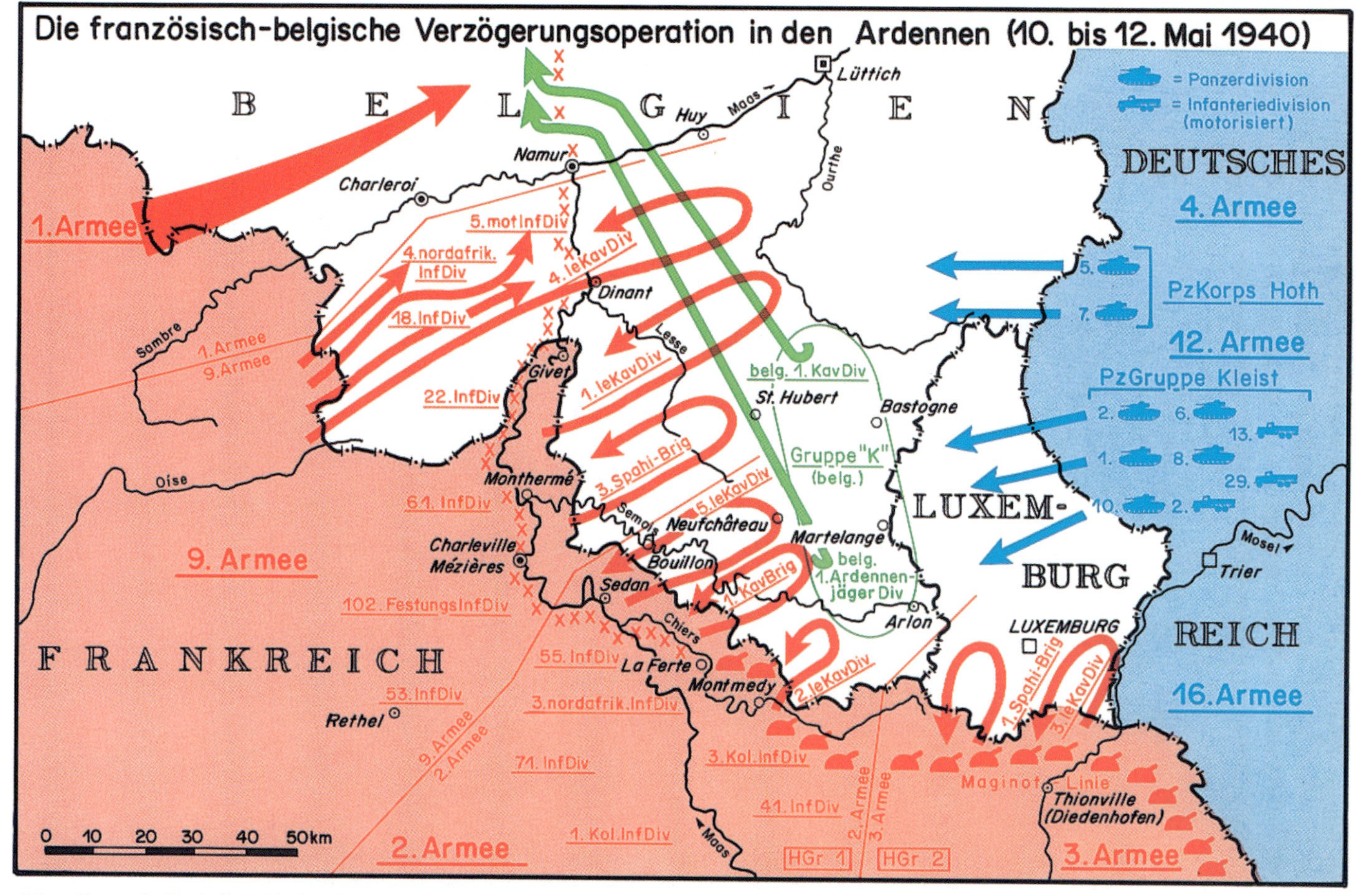

The French-Belgian Delaying Operation in the Ardennes, 10–12 May 1940

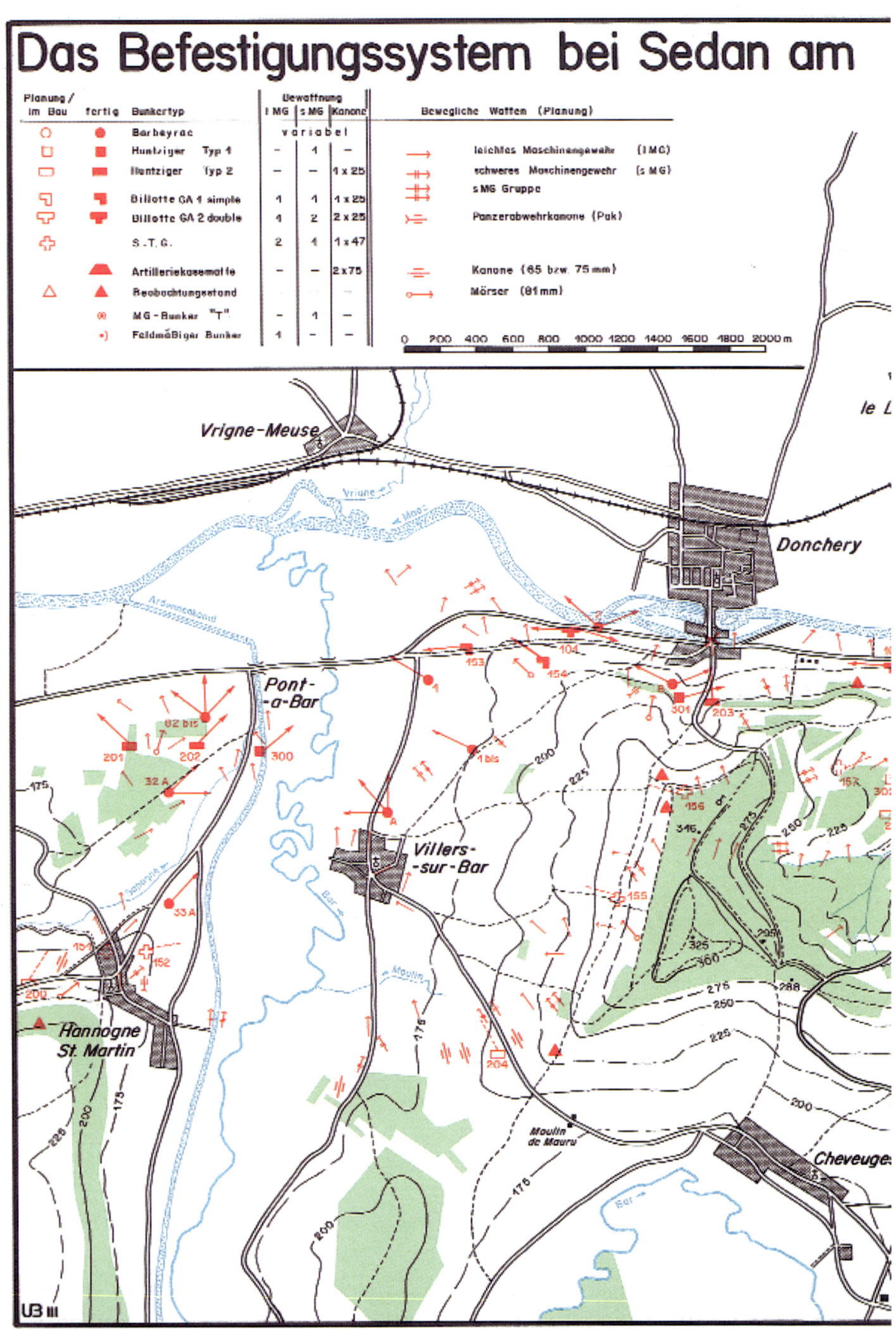
Das Befestigungssystem bei Sedan am
Planung / im Bau
fertig
Bunkertyp
Bewaffnung
I MG
s MG
Kanone
Barbeyrac
variabel
Huntziger Typ 1
Huntziger Typ 2
Billotte GA 1 simple
Billotte GA 2 double
S.T.G.
Artilleriekasematte
Beobachtungsstand
MG-Bunker "T"
Feldmäßiger Bunker
Bewegliche Waffen (Planung)
leichtes Maschinengewehr (l MG)
schweres Maschinengewehr (s MG)
s MG Gruppe
Panzerabwehrkanone (Pak)
Kanone (65 bzw. 75 mm)
Mörser (81 mm)
0 200 400 600 800 1000 1200 1400 1600 1800 2000 m
Vrigne-Meuse
Donchery
Pont-a-Bar
Villers-sur-Bar
Hannogne St. Martin
Moulin de Mauru
Cheveuges
Ardennenkanal
Bar
Moulin

The Fortification System at Sedan, 13 May 1940

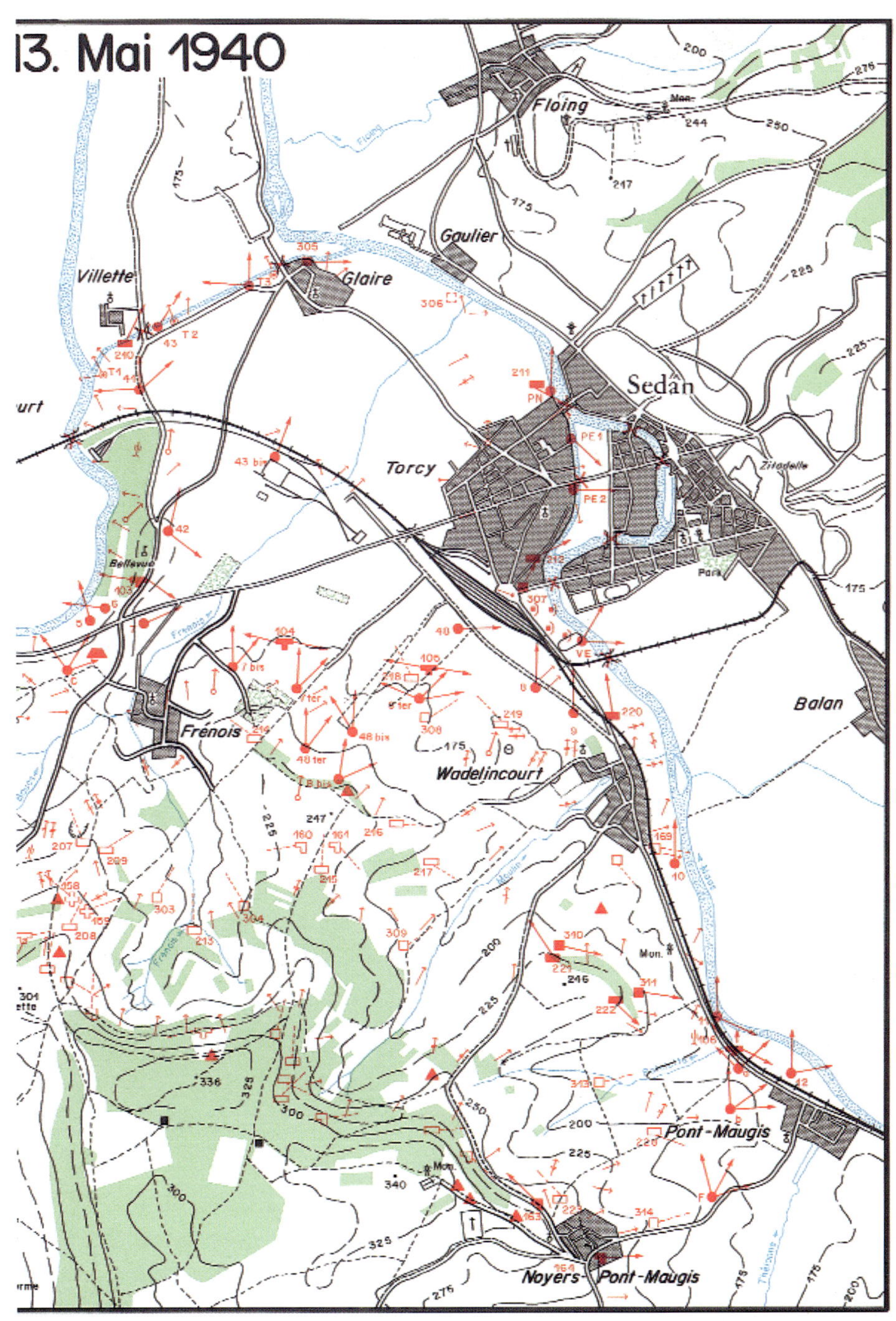

13. Mai 1940
Floing
Gaulier
Glaire
Villette
Sedan
Torcy
Zitadelle
Bellevue
Frénois
Balan
Wadelincourt
Pont-Maugis
Noyers-Pont-Maugis

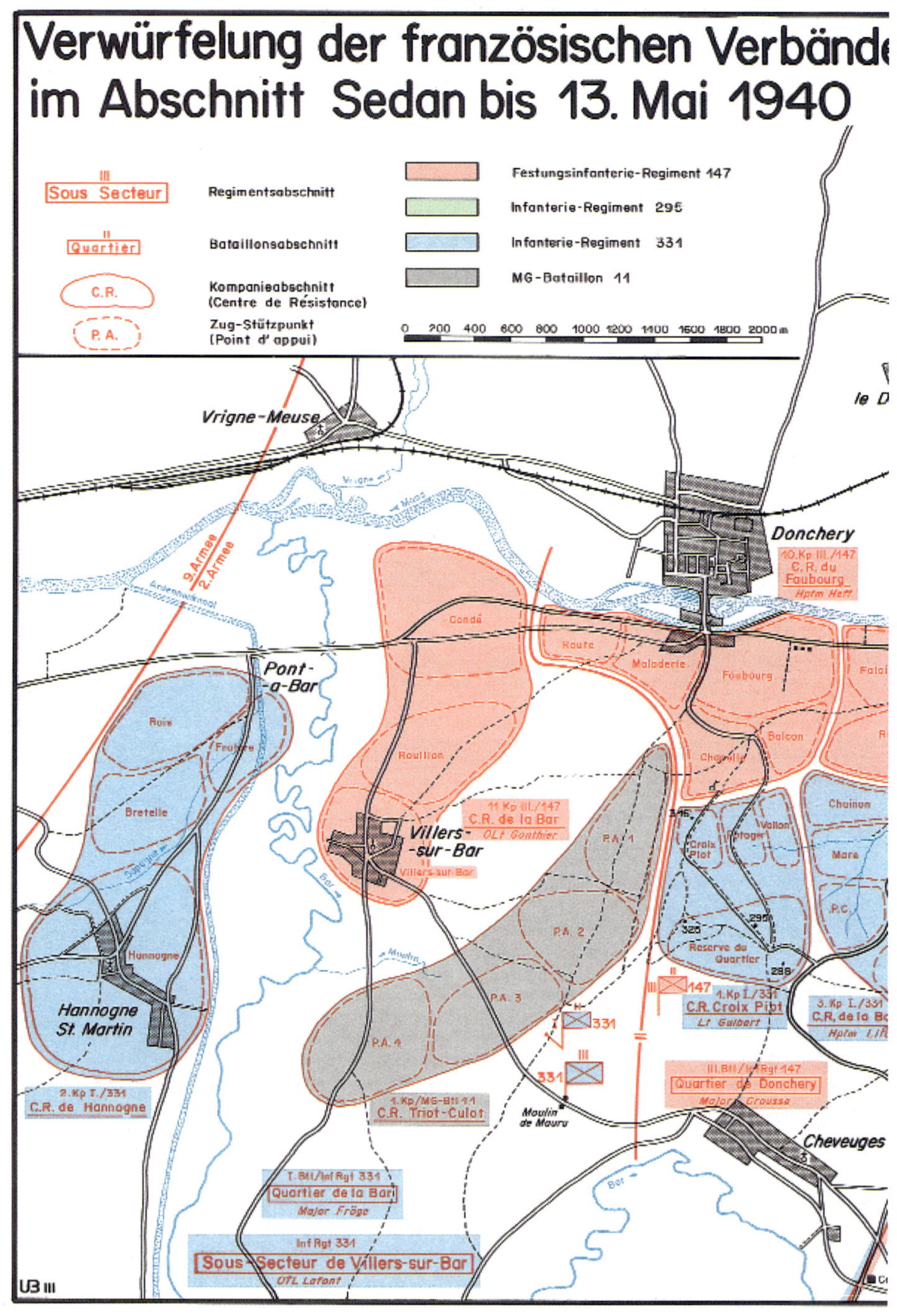

Crazy-Quilting Deployment of French Units in the Sedan Sector until May 1940

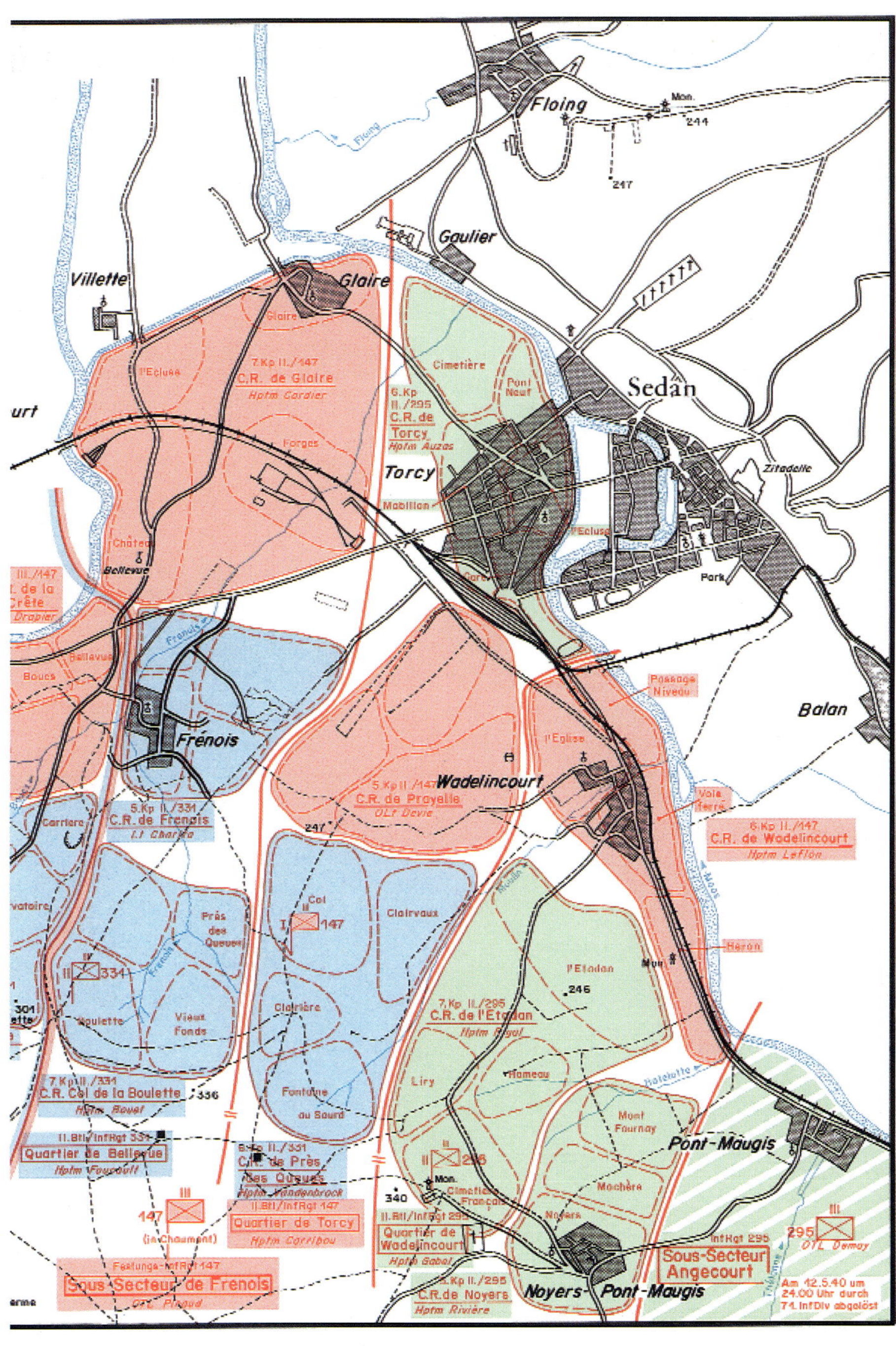
Floing
Mon.
244
247
Gaulier
Villette
Glaire
Sedan
7.Kp II./147
C.R. de Glaire
Hptm Cordier
6.Kp
II./295
C.R. de
Torcy
Hptm Auzas
Cimetière
Pont
Neuf
Torcy
Zitadelle
Forges
Château
Bellevue
Mobilion
l'Ecluse
Gare
Park
III./147
de la
Crête
Drapier
Boucs
Frénois
Passage
Niveau
Balan
l'Eglise
Wadelincourt
5.Kp II./147
C.R. de Prayelle
OLt Devie
5.Kp II./331
C.R. de Frenois
Lt Charlia
Carrière
247
Voie
ferrée
6.Kp II./147
C.R. de Wadelincourt
Hptm Leflon
Col
147
331
Clairvaux
Prés
des
Queues
Héron
l'Etadan
246
Clairière
Vieux
Fonds
7.Kp II./295
C.R. de l'Etadan
Hptm Rigal
Liry
Hameau
Fontaine
au Sourd
336
7.Kp II./331
C.R. Col de la Boulette
Hptm Rouel
Mont
Fournay
Pont-Maugis
II.Btl/InfRgt 331
Quartier de Bellevue
Hptm Foucault
6.Kp II./331
C.R. de Prés
des Queues
Hptm Vandenbrock
295
Mon.
340
Machère
Noyers
II.Btl/InfRgt 147
Quartier de Torcy
Hptm Carribou
II.Btl/InfRgt 295
Quartier de
Wadelincourt
Hptm Gabal
147
(in Chaumont)
InfRgt 295
Sous-Secteur
Angecourt
295
OTL Demay
Festungs-InfRgt 147
Sous-Secteur de Frenois
OTL Pinaud
5.Kp II./295
C.R.de Noyers
Hptm Rivière
Noyers-Pont-Maugis
Am 12.5.40 um
24.00 Uhr durch
71.InfDiv abgelöst

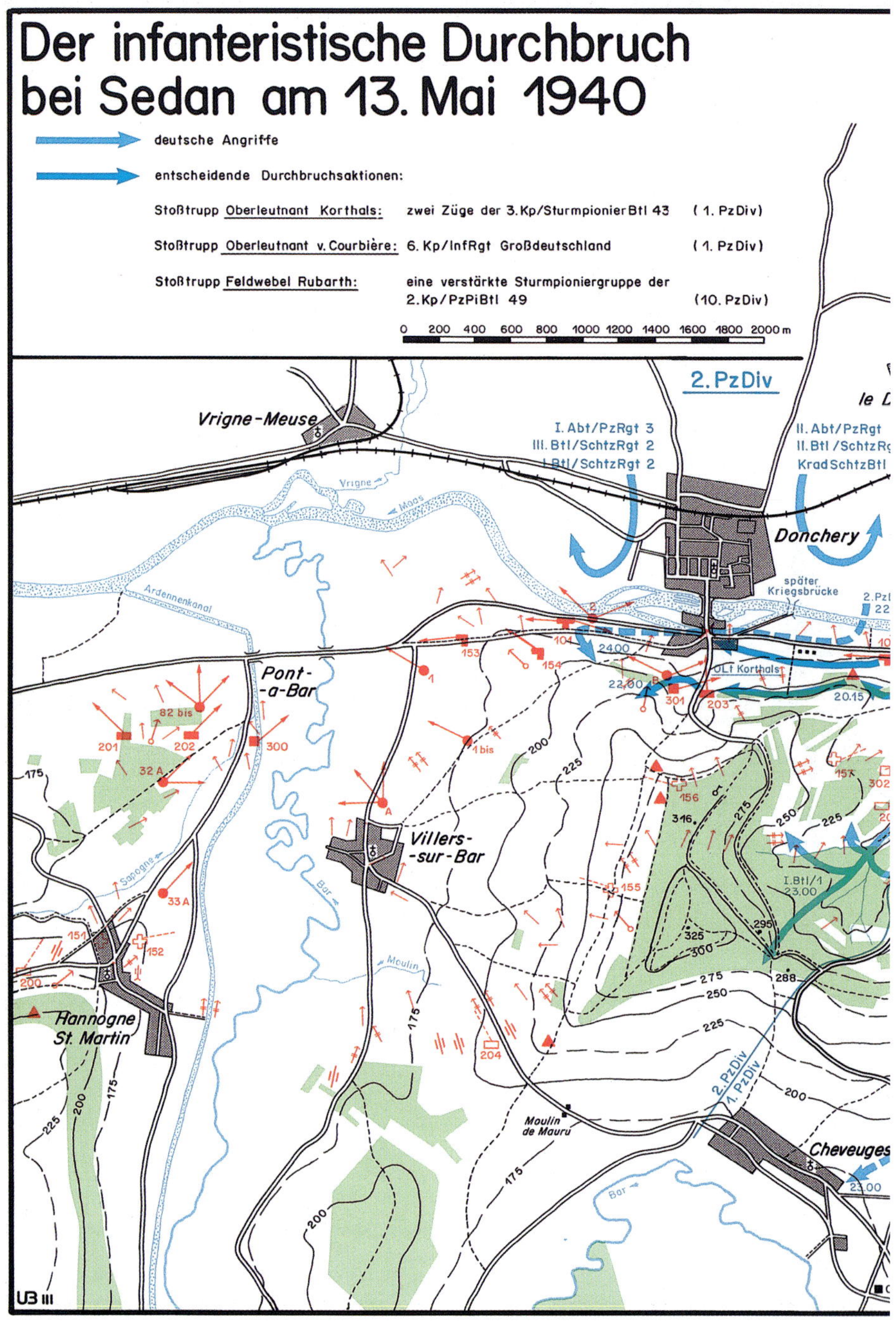

Der infanteristische Durchbruch bei Sedan am 13. Mai 1940
deutsche Angriffe
entscheidende Durchbruchsaktionen:
Stoßtrupp Oberleutnant Korthals: zwei Züge der 3. Kp/Sturmpionier Btl 43 (1. PzDiv)
Stoßtrupp Oberleutnant v. Courbière: 6. Kp/InfRgt Großdeutschland (1. PzDiv)
Stoßtrupp Feldwebel Rubarth: eine verstärkte Sturmpioniergruppe der 2. Kp/PzPiBtl 49 (10. PzDiv)
0 200 400 600 800 1000 1200 1400 1600 1800 2000 m
2. PzDiv
Vrigne-Meuse
I. Abt/PzRgt 3
III. Btl/SchtzRgt 2
I. Btl/SchtzRgt 2
II. Abt/PzRgt
II. Btl/SchtzR
KradSchtzBtl
Vrigne
Maas
Donchery
später Kriegsbrücke
Ardennenkanal
Pont-a-Bar
Villers-sur-Bar
Hannogne St. Martin
OLt Korthals
I. Btl/1 23.00
2. PzDiv
1. PzDiv
Moulin de Mauru
Cheveuges
Sapogne
Bar
Moulin
UB III

The Infantry Breakthrough at Sedan, 13 May 1940

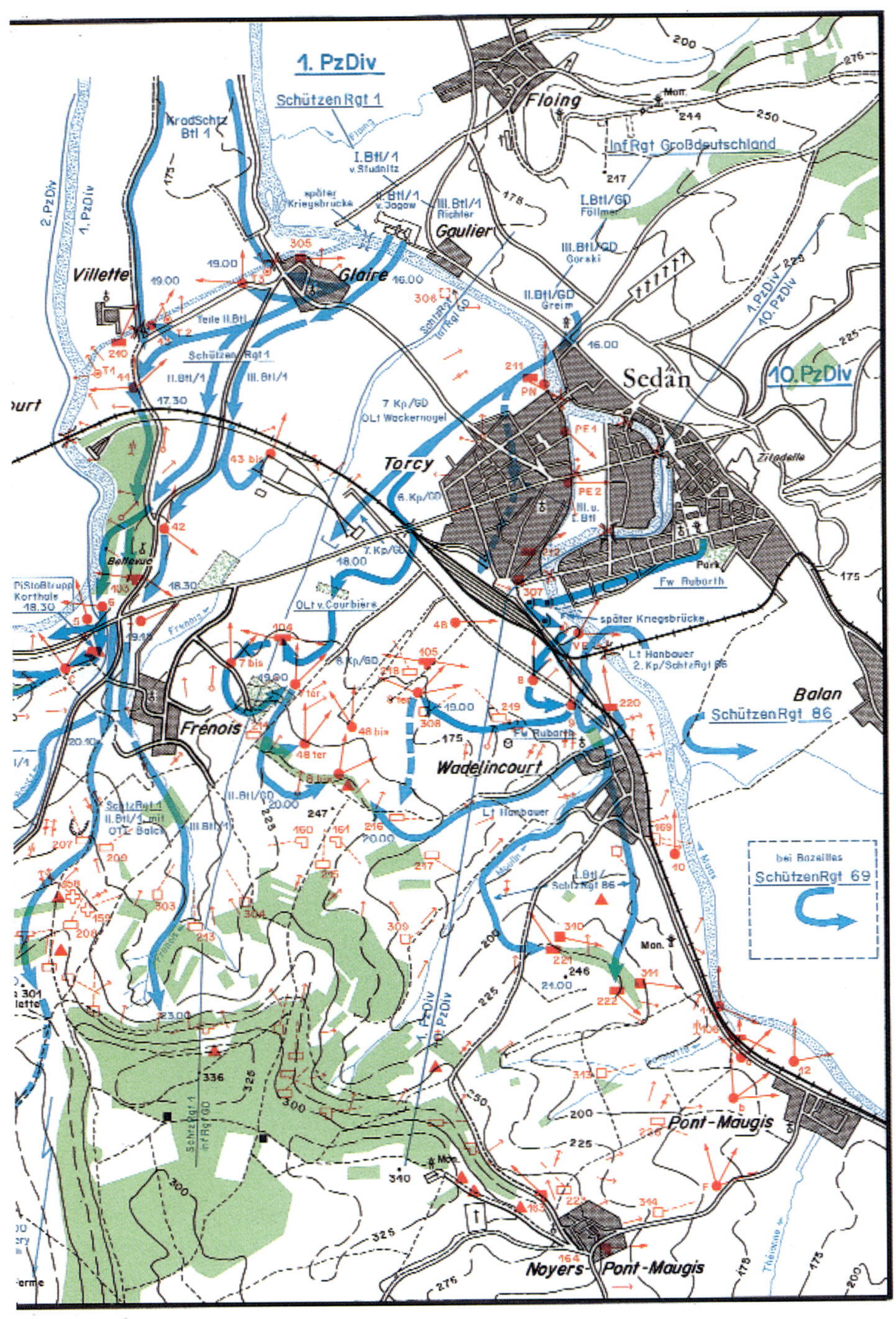

1. PzDiv
Schützen Rgt 1
KradSchtz Btl 1
I. Btl/1 v. Studnitz
II. Btl/1 v. Jagow
III. Btl/1 Richter
später Kriegsbrücke
Floing
Inf Rgt Großdeutschland
I. Btl/GD Föllmer
III. Btl/GD Garski
II. Btl/GD Greim
Gaulier
Glaire
Villette
Sedan
10. PzDiv
1. PzDiv
10. PzDiv
2. PzDiv
1. PzDiv
Zitadelle
Torcy
7 Kp/GD OLt Wackernagel
6. Kp/GD
7. Kp/GD
OLt v. Courbière
Bellevue
PiStoßtrupp Korthals 18.30
Fw Rubarth
später Kriegsbrücke
Lt Hanbauer 2. Kp/SchtzRgt 86
Balan
SchützenRgt 86
Frénois
Wadelincourt
Fw Rubarth
Lt Hanbauer
SchtzRgt 1 II. Btl/1 mit OTL Balck
III. Btl/1
II. Btl/GD
I. Btl/SchtzRgt 86
bei Bazeilles
SchützenRgt 69
SchtzRgt 1 Inf Rgt GD
1. PzDiv
10. PzDiv
Pont-Maugis
Noyers-Pont-Maugis

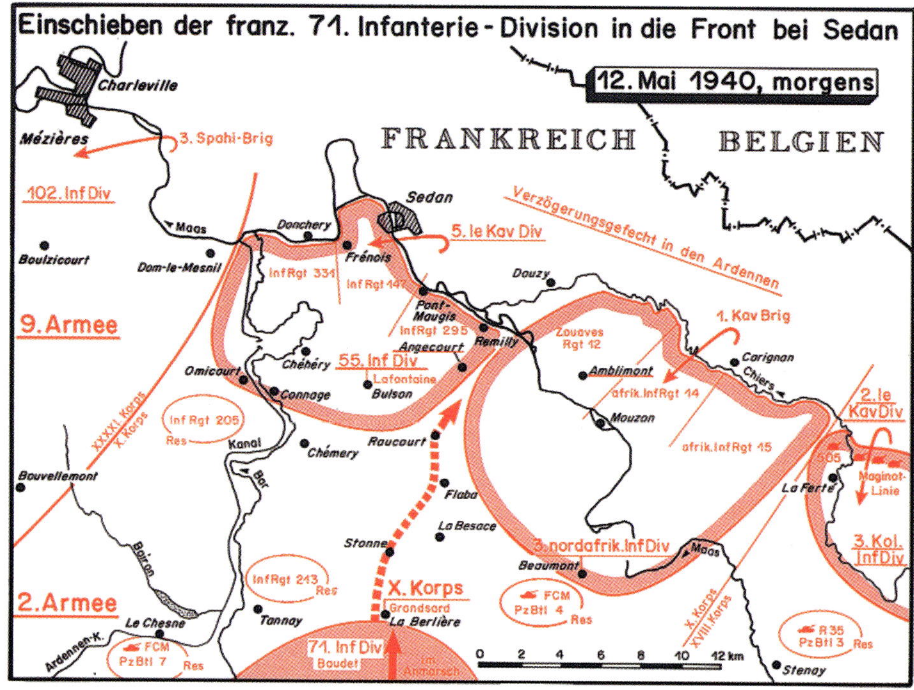

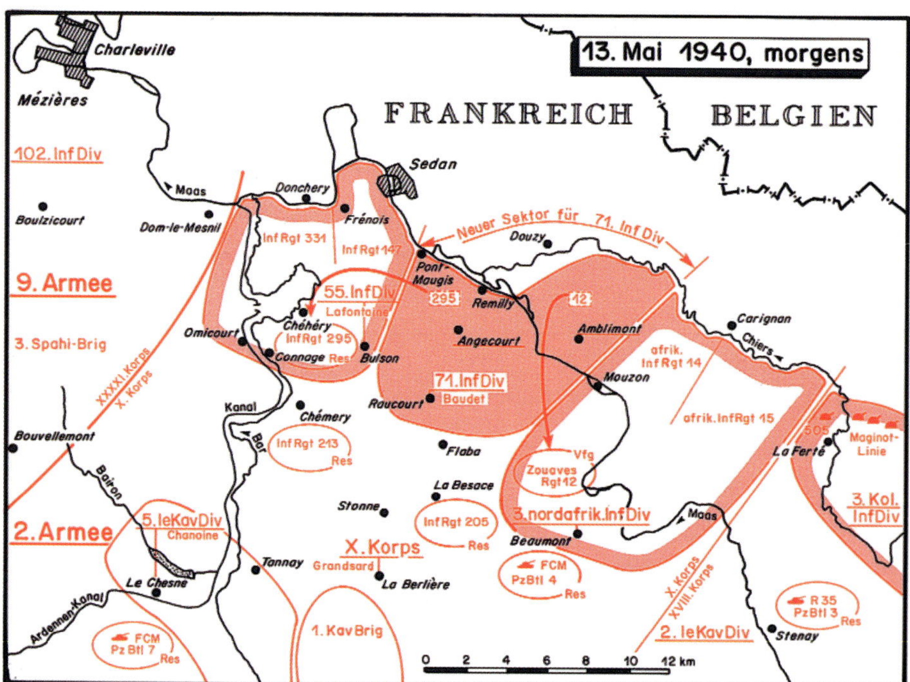

Insertion of the French 71st Infantry Division into the Front Line of Sedan

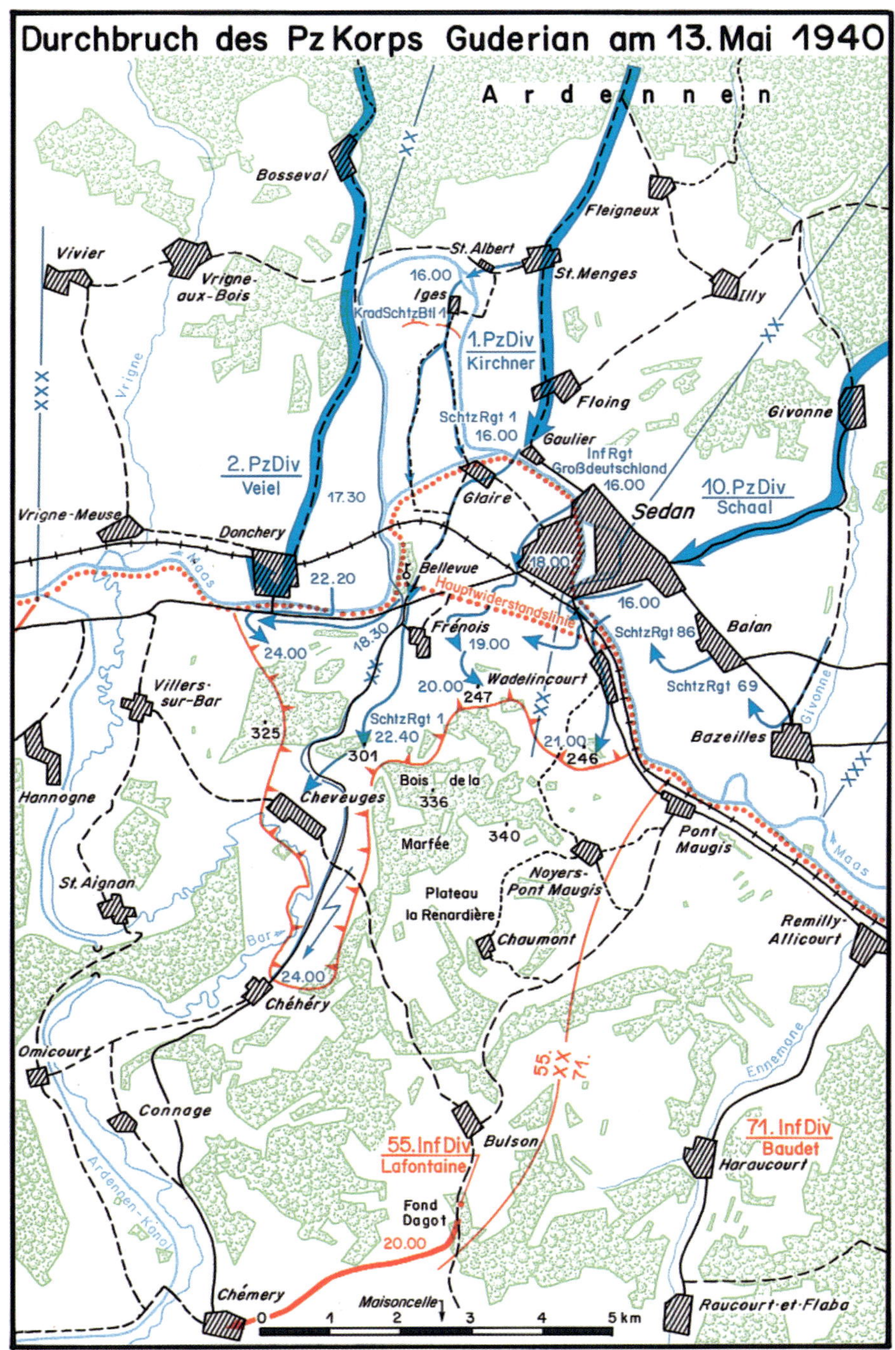

Breakthrough of Panzer Corps Guderian, 13 May 1940

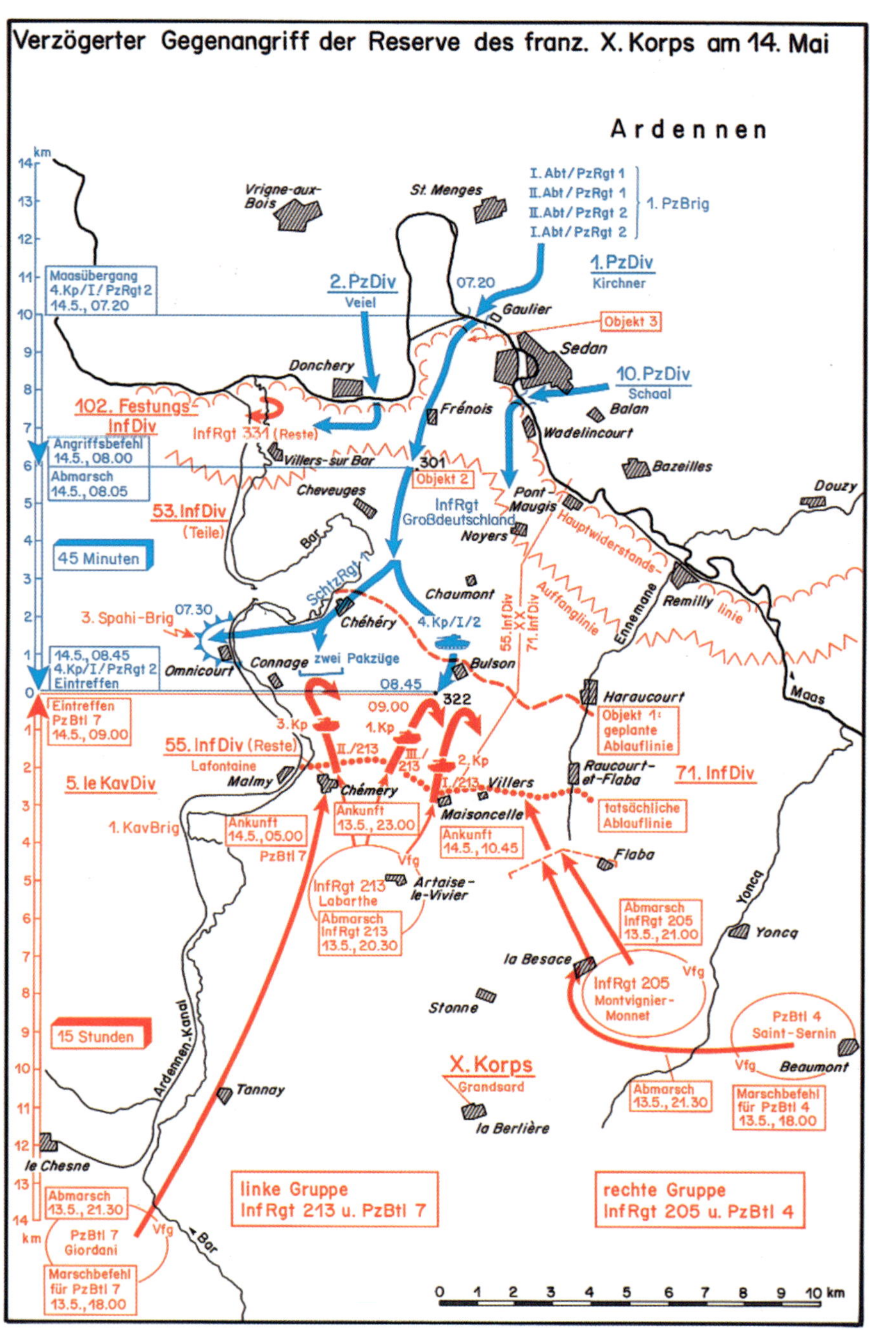
Verzögerter Gegenangriff der Reserve des franz. X. Korps am 14. Mai
Ardennen
I. Abt/PzRgt 1
II. Abt/PzRgt 1
II. Abt/PzRgt 2
I. Abt/PzRgt 2
1. PzBrig
1. PzDiv
Kirchner
2. PzDiv
Veiel
10. PzDiv
Schaal
Maasübergang
4.Kp/I/PzRgt 2
14.5., 07.20
Angriffsbefehl
14.5., 08.00
Abmarsch
14.5., 08.05
45 Minuten
14.5., 08.45
4.Kp/I/PzRgt 2
Eintreffen
Eintreffen
PzBtl 7
14.5., 09.00
15 Stunden
Vrigne-aux-Bois
St. Menges
Gaulier
Sedan
Objekt 3
Donchery
Frénois
Balan
Wadelincourt
Bazeilles
Douzy
102. Festungs-InfDiv
InfRgt 331 (Reste)
Villers-sur Bar
301
Objekt 2
Cheveuges
Pont-Maugis
53. InfDiv
(Teile)
InfRgt Großdeutschland
Noyers
Bar
Hauptwiderstands-linie
Auffanglinie
Remilly
Ennemane
SchtzRgt 1
Chaumont
3. Spahi-Brig
07.30
Chéhéry
4.Kp/I/2
55. InfDiv
X X
71. InfDiv
Omnicourt
Connage
zwei Pakzüge
Bulson
08.45
322
Haraucourt
Maas
Objekt 1:
geplante
Ablauflinie
3. Kp
09.00
1. Kp
II./213
III./213
2. Kp
I./213
55. InfDiv (Reste)
Lafontaine
Malmy
Chémery
Villers
Raucourt-et-Flaba
71. InfDiv
5. le KavDiv
Maisoncelle
tatsächliche
Ablauflinie
1. KavBrig
Ankunft
14.5., 05.00
Ankunft
13.5., 23.00
Ankunft
14.5., 10.45
PzBtl 7
Vfg
Flaba
InfRgt 213
Labarthe
Artaise-le-Vivier
Abmarsch
InfRgt 213
13.5., 20.30
Abmarsch
InfRgt 205
13.5., 21.00
Yoncq
la Besace
InfRgt 205
Montvignier-Monnet
Stonne
PzBtl 4
Saint-Sernin
Beaumont
Ardennen-Kanal
X. Korps
Grandsard
Abmarsch
13.5., 21.30
Marschbefehl
für PzBtl 4
13.5., 18.00
Tannay
la Berlière
le Chesne
Abmarsch
13.5., 21.30
PzBtl 7
Giordani
Marschbefehl
für PzBtl 7
13.5., 18.00
linke Gruppe
InfRgt 213 u. PzBtl 7
rechte Gruppe
InfRgt 205 u. PzBtl 4
0 1 2 3 4 5 6 7 8 9 10 km

Delayed Counterattack by Reserves of French X Corps, 14 May 1940

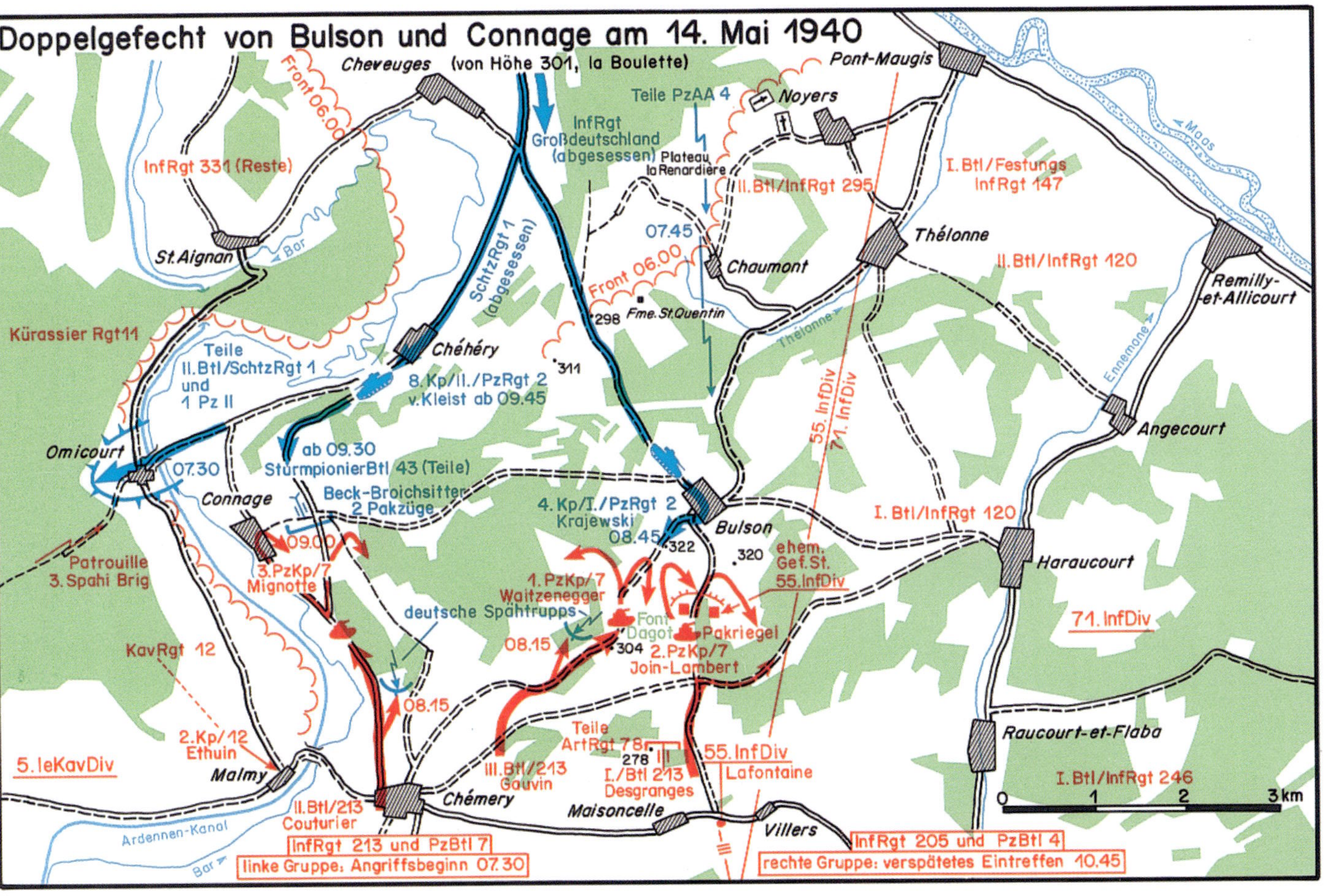

Doppelgefecht von Bulson und Connage am 14. Mai 1940
(von Höhe 301, la Boulette)
Cheveuges
Pont-Maugis
Noyers
Teile PzAA 4
InfRgt
Großdeutschland
(abgesessen)
Plateau
la Renardière
Front 06.00
InfRgt 331 (Reste)
II. Btl/InfRgt 295
I. Btl/Festungs
InfRgt 147
Maas
Thélonne
St. Aignan
Bar
07.45
Chaumont
II. Btl/InfRgt 120
Remilly-
-et-Allicourt
Front 06.00
298
Fme. St. Quentin
SchtzRgt 1
(abgesessen)
Kürassier Rgt 11
Teile
II. Btl/SchtzRgt 1
und
1 Pz II
Chéhéry
311
8. Kp/II./PzRgt 2
v. Kleist ab 09.45
Ennemone
55. InfDiv
71. InfDiv
Angecourt
Omicourt
07.30
ab 09.30
SturmpionierBtl 43 (Teile)
Connage
Beck-Broichsitter
2 Pakzüge
4. Kp/I./PzRgt 2
Krajewski
08.45
322
Bulson
I. Btl/InfRgt 120
320
ehem.
Gef. St.
55. InfDiv
Haraucourt
09.00
Patrouille
3. Spahi Brig
3. PzKp/7
Mignotte
1. PzKp/7
Waitzenegger
deutsche Spähtrupps
Font
Dagot
Pakriegel
71. InfDiv
KavRgt 12
08.15
304
2. PzKp/7
Join-Lambert
08.15
Teile
ArtRgt 78
278
55. InfDiv
Lafontaine
Raucourt-et-Flaba
2. Kp/12
Ethuin
5. leKavDiv
Malmy
III. Btl/213
Gauvin
I./Btl 213
Desgranges
I. Btl/InfRgt 246
0
1
2
3 km
II. Btl/213
Couturier
Chémery
Maisoncelle
Villers
Ardennen-Kanal
Bar
InfRgt 213 und PzBtl 7
linke Gruppe: Angriffsbeginn 07.30
InfRgt 205 und PzBtl 4
rechte Gruppe: verspätetes Eintreffen 10.45

Twin Action at Bulson and Connage, 14 May 1940

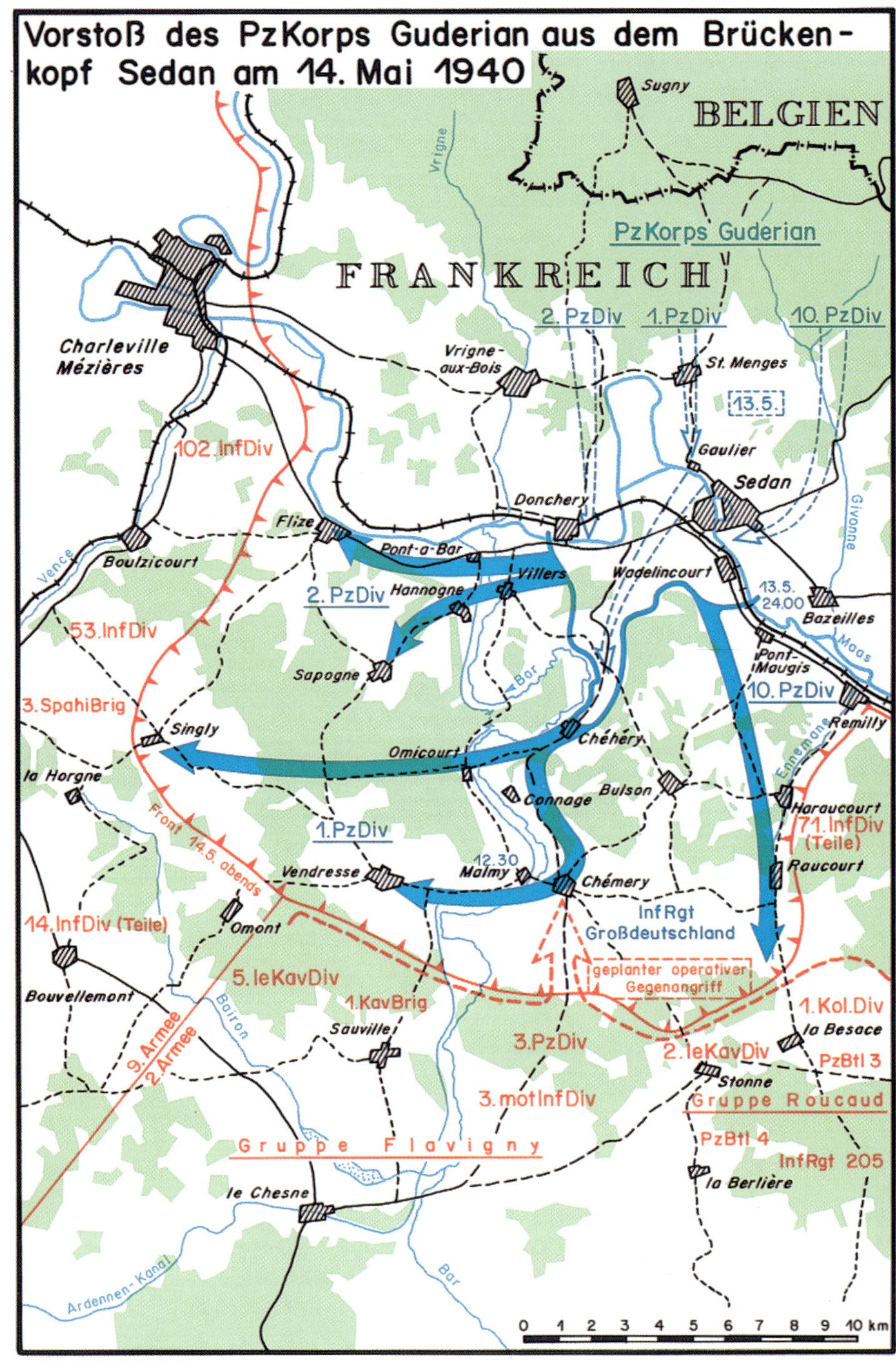

Advance by Panzer Corps Guderian from the Sedan Bridgehead, 14 May 1940

The men of the Werner Advance Detachment had better luck three kilometers south of the dynamited bridge at Yvoir. At this point in the Meuse River, a weir and a lock system connect an island at Houx to both banks. In spite of considerable concern, the Belgians and French had refrained from blasting Lock 5 because they were afraid that the water level would drop too much. That lock was precisely at the boundary between the French II and XI Corps, and, moreover—as will be described later—nobody really felt competent to take action for just one short but fatal moment.

After the failure of the coup at Yvoir, Werner had sent out several reconnaissance patrols of motorcycle riflemen who were to look for crossing sites along the Meuse River. One of these patrols rode by Evrehailles and passed through Houx. When the motorcycle riflemen spotted the Meuse River island, they were astonished because the weir leading across to the island was neither destroyed nor blocked. The scouting patrol waited until darkness had fallen, and then a few volunteers gingerly tiptoed their way on the slippery weir across to the island. They stopped there for a short time in the shelter of the trees and then sneaked to the other bank via a lock catwalk. Shortly before 2300, they were the first men from Army Group A to reach the west bank of the Meuse River. When they tried to push farther west, they were stopped by French fire. In the meantime, Werner had sent reinforcements. At first, they consisted of only a few motorcycle riflemen who were able to form an infantry bridgehead on the opposite bank.

As happened earlier at Sedan, a whole series of grave mistakes committed by the opposite side helped the Germans. Oddly enough, German soldiers previously crossed the Meuse River at the Island of Houx in August 1914.[73] This is precisely where the critical weak point was in May 1940. The fatal breakdown in the northern sector of the Meuse River at Dinant occurred because the mistakes the French made in their calculation of the time element once again tripped them up. They figured that the Germans, even if they mounted an energetic attack, would take 10 to 14 days before they could cross the river. Thus, they believed they would have enough time to take up their previously reconnoitered positions along the Meuse River, which the Belgians had prepared in some places. The 5th Motorized Infantry Division of the II Corps was positioned north of the Island of Houx. It had already arrived in full strength, ready to take up defensive positions on 12 May. Directly south of the 5th, the 18th Infantry Division of XI Corps was to go into position, but had few vehicles. By the evening of 12 May, only five of its nine infantry battalions had marched to the Meuse River whereas, according to the schedule drawn up long before, the other formations together with the heavy artillery were to arrive in full strength only by the evening of 14 May.

This meant that during the "race to the Meuse" the two German Panzer divisions took considerably less time to cover the 115 kilometers of their attack through the Ardennes than did the French 18th Infantry Division for its undisturbed 80-kilometer march. Units of the 1st Light Cavalry Division that had just returned from the Ardennes were inserted in the line but that only served to increase the confusion. Most importantly, however, the command of the 18th Infantry Division overlooked the fact

In the evening of 12 May reconnaissance patrols of the 5th Panzer Division were the first German soldiers to cross the middle course of the Meuse River over the unguarded lock on the Island of Houx. View to the south. *Brussels Military Archives*

that there was a small hole on the extreme left wing along the boundary between two army corps. When the neighboring 5th Motorized Infantry Division reported this, the 2d Battalion, 39th Infantry Regiment, was dispatched from the army reserve and placed under the command of the 18th Infantry Division. Although [French Ninth] Army had ordered that the first defense line be manned directly along the riverbank, the battalion commander deviated from that and initially posted his men only on the rock plateau behind. That meant that during the night of 12–13 May, this was the sector in which the Germans got to the west bank across the lock catwalk that was not being watched. When the men of the 6th Company positioned there noticed the German infiltration shortly before midnight, they opened fire. Otherwise, they behaved passively and did not mount a counterattack to wipe out the weak German bridgehead.

The spectacular crossing of the weir at Houx is mentioned in almost all accounts of the campaign. Erroneously, however, it is almost always assumed that those were men of the 7th Motorcycle Rifle Battalion of the 7th Panzer Division. Rommel was not entirely uninvolved in the creation of this tale. He by no means denied the reports

An armored scout car of the 7th Panzer Division being ferried across the river on a pontoon ferry south of the Island of Houx. *Bundesarchiv Koblenz [Federal Archives]*

according to which men of his division were the first to have reached the west bank of the Meuse River. In reality, those motorcycle riflemen were members of the 5th Division, specifically, the 3d Company, 8th Reconnaissance Battalion, and also some men from the 1st Battalion, 13th Rifle Regiment. The Werner Advance Detachment had been placed under Rommel formally on 12 May but reverted to the 5th Panzer Division after the latter part of his units had closed up along the Meuse River. Moreover, the Meuse Island at Houx was still in the combat sector of 5th Panzer Division.[74]

Crossing the Meuse River on 13 May

Three rifle battalions of the 5th Panzer Division (I/14th; II/14th; I/13th) crossed the weir at Houx in single file starting at 0530 on the morning of 13 May. The Panzer company did give them covering fire, but it did not adequately neutralize the machine guns that repeatedly opened flanking fire from the rocks. Moreover, French artillery fire was concentrated on the crossing site. Commenting on this situation, the after-action report noted: "The dead are floating in the water. The wounded desperately cling to the lock gates. They call for help but nobody can help them."[75]

The crossing proceeded briskly only after the last resistance in the rocks had been knocked out. On that day, the infantry pushed about four kilometers to the west, all the way to Haut-le-Wastia. A bitter firefight broke out on 13 and 14 May for this village that was perched high up and that the Germans referred to as "the mountain fortress." Here the disadvantage was that the 5th Panzer Division's infantry at first had to attack without heavy weapons, whereas the French occasionally also employed tanks.

The 7th Panzer Division had a considerably tougher time in getting across the Meuse River. It was not as lucky as the 5th Panzer Division in whose sector the now famous weir was located. That its operations were nevertheless more successful than those of the neighboring division was mainly due to the person of the commander. It is certainly correct to say that Rommel was a master of self-aggrandizement and that a veritable cult grew up around him later. Nevertheless, it must be noted quite objectively that during this particular phase of the campaign there was probably no other commander who gave his division such decisive impetus as did Rommel. He had designated two sites for crossing the Meuse River: the first one immediately south to the Island of Houx for the 6th Rifle Regiment and the 7th Motorcycle Rifle Battalion; and the other one in Leffe on the northern edge of Dinant for the reinforced 7th Rifle Regiment.

The main effort was with the crossing detachment to the south, near Dinant (commander, Oberst [Georg] von Bismarck). Under the protection of the morning mist a part of the first wave was indeed successful in getting across the river at around 0430. Then those soldiers just clung to the other bank and did not dare leave their covered positions due to enemy fire. From then on, it seemed almost impossible to row rubber boats to the west bank across the Meuse River, which is about a hundred meters wide there. The French had put their machine guns in position in the houses opposite and opened fire from the bunkers that had been built into the rocks high above the river. The superior enemy artillery was particularly dangerous as the French forward observers had a wide-open view of the German crossing site from the ruins of the castle at Bouvignes. The 7th Panzer Division, on the other hand, only had two light artillery battalions. Support from the Luftwaffe was also minimal because almost all bombers and dive-bombers were concentrated near Sedan on that day.

On 13 May, crisis followed crisis in the sector of the 7th Panzer Division so that Rommel was constantly shuttling back and forth between the two crossing sites. His forte, however, was always to lead from way up front. He sent Panzer units forward and personally directed them into their positions; he coordinated fire support and somehow managed to round up more rubber boats. Nevertheless, as Rommel himself reports, the mission seemed to be failing: "The crossing had now come to a complete standstill, with the officers badly shaken by the casualties their men had suffered."[76]

A renewed crossing attempt was ventured only after he had ordered additional Panzers and even individual artillery pieces to move forward to fire on the enemy bunkers. To inspire his demoralized soldiers, Rommel again slipped into his role as World War I assault detachment leader: "I now took over personal command of 2nd Battalion of 7th Rifle Regiment and for some time directed operations myself. . . . I crossed the Meuse in one of the first boats and at once joined the company which had been across since early morning."[77]

In the afternoon, Rommel mostly stayed with the northern crossing group. Although French artillery was still placing unobserved fire on the crossing site, he ordered the engineers to build a ferry at this early point in time. For this purpose, he, the division commander himself, jumped into the water up to his hips and for a while pitched in personally. When the ferry was ready, he was the first to cross over in his command Panzer. Two bridgeheads had been formed by the evening: a larger one in the north by the 6th Rifle Regiment together with the 5th Panzer Division, and a smaller one at Dinant. On account of the superb traffic connections, Rommel believed that the main effort was here with the 7th Rifle Regiment. During the night, therefore, he ordered construction to be started on a military bridge between Leffe and Bouvgnes on the northern edge of Dinant. Moreover, the engineers had ferried about thirty Panzers across by 0800 the next morning.

Advance Out of Bridgeheads on 14 May

For the following day Panzer Corps Hoth had given orders to merge the two bridgeheads and to extend them so far to the west that the crossing sites were no longer under enemy artillery fire. Rommel did not wait until he had gotten enough men and material across the river, but during the night he ordered elements of the 7th Rifle Regiment under von Bismarck to mount a probing attack against Onhaye. Actually, everything should have gone according to plan because the division had run through the attack from Dinant against Onhaye, which was five kilometers away (as the crow flies), in the course of a map exercise in Bad Godesberg shortly before the start of the campaign. However, so-called friction points were unavoidable due to Rommel's excessively rapid operations. At 0800, he received an alarming message that triggered a crisis mood that escalated all the way to the echelon of army headquarters: "*Bismarck bei Onhaye eingeschlossen*" (Bismarck encircled in Onhaye).[78]

Radio contact was lost immediately thereafter, and all attempts to reach von Bismarck were in vain. Rommel immediately ordered the Panzers that had in the meantime been ferried across to push on toward Onhaye. Hoth had no more reserves. This is why Generaloberst [Hans-Günther] von Kluge, commander in chief of Fourth Army, decided to dispatch elements of II Corps to assist in resolving the "Onhaye crisis." All at once, however, the situation returned to normal when contact was reestablished with von Bismarck's headquarters. This artificial crisis turned out to have been a case of "misspeak" on the radio. The original text of the radio message was: "*Bismarck bei Onhaye eingetroffen*" (Bismarck arrived in Onhaye), but *eingetroffen* (arrived) became *eingeschlossen* (encircled) when somebody simply "misheard."

Onhaye was to have a fateful significance for Rommel also in other ways because this is where his life was in serious danger. The way he told the story, he was riding in a Panzer III right behind the spearhead of the Panzer column heading toward the edge of the woods. Suddenly, several French antitank guns opened fire, along with two 7.5-cm batteries:

> Shells landed around us and my tank received two hits one after the other, the first one on the upper edge of the turret and the second in the periscope. . . . The driver promptly opened the throttle and drove straight into the nearest bushes. He had only gone a few yards, however, when the tank slid down a steep slope on the western edge of the wood and finally stopped, canted over on its side, in such a position that the enemy, whose guns were in position about 500 meters away on the edge of the next wood, could not fail to see it. I had been wounded in the right cheek by a small splinter from the shell which had landed in the periscope. It was not serious though it bled a great deal.[79]

Rommel barely managed to bail out of the Panzer and get away from enemy fire. Onhaye was taken after a stiff firefight against units of the French 1st Light Cavalry Division. Subsequently, the 7th Panzer Division pushed on all the way to Morville, twelve kilometers west of the Meuse. This meant that the second French line of resistance had been pierced. The military bridge at Dinant was finished by 2000 so that the now available vehicles could be used to exploit the breakthrough completely for a thrust into the depth of enemy positions.

On that day the 5th Panzer Division at last took the hotly contested Haut-le-Wastia and pushed on to Sommière. This meant that French resistance had also collapsed in this sector. Even more interesting than the course of combat operations in this phase appears to be the feud between the two rival division commanders. When it turned out that the bridge building material coming from the Ardennes would initially suffice only to build a single military bridge, Rommel, after some tough bargaining with Hoth, managed to get all the equipment put under his command. The commanding general of the 5th Panzer Division, Generalmajor [Max] von Hartlieb [Walsporn], protested, but without success, and now also had to ask for permission to have his division's heavy Panzers routed across the military bridge after the neighboring division.

In a rather arbitrary and unauthorized fashion, Rommel immediately exploited the opportunity to put those heavy Panzers under his command to push his own division's attack. He was not at all impressed by the furious protests from the 5th Panzer Division, but instead he complained about the alleged passive attitude of the neighboring division that was always caught somewhere back. Thus, he told Hoth that the 7th Panzer Division could "not be expected to fight the war all by itself all the time."[80] Hoth was not fond of Rommel's egocentric style, but the latter was always able to fall back on the operational logic that the few Panzers ferried across the Meuse River were not enough for simultaneous breakthroughs at two points.

Though Rommel's ruthless action can be criticized, one must keep in mind that he managed the crossing of the Meuse River faster than did Guderian at Sedan, although he had to attack almost without any support from the Luftwaffe. Besides, he was confronted with more difficult terrain conditions due to the rocks that rose like a wall along the west bank of the Meuse River. The particular irony of this comparison is that Panzer expert Guderian made a mistake when he waited to put his Panzers across until the military bridge had been built. The "infantry-type" Rommel, on the other hand, decided to put some of his Panzers across via ferries from the very first moment and thus broke out from the bridgehead even before the bridge had been finished.

The Attempted Counterattack of the II and XI Corps

In his diary, Rommel emphasized several times that the success at Dinant hung in the balance for quite some time, above all because the weak infantry elements in both bridgeheads initially had to attack without Panzers and heavy weapons. The French, on the other hand, had enough mobile forces in this sector and those forces, supported by battle tanks and armored scout cars, could have mounted a powerful counterattack. For example, elements of the 4th Light Cavalry Division supported the 5th Motorized Infantry Division and formations of the 1st Light Cavalry Division assisted the 18th Infantry Division. In addition, the French 6th Tank Battalion was available. As at Sedan, however, the slow speed of the French command system again took effect here. An initial exchange of fire with the German soldiers who had penetrated to the west bank of the Meuse River occurred on the Island of Houx shortly before 2400 (German time) on 12 May. It took until 0500 on 13 May before General [Julien-Francois-René] Martin learned that an infiltration had taken place on the left boundary of XI Corps, which was under his command. Corap, commander in chief, Ninth Army, received some vague information from the Houx-Dinant area only around noon. At 1330 the French high command in Vincennes for the first time took note of the fact that German forces had crossed the Meuse River. Georges, the commander in chief of the northeast front, merely reported, however, that "a battalion had gotten into trouble" near Houx.[81]

What were the French counteractions at that time? The sector opposite the Island of Houx, where the first German infiltration had taken place, belonged to the 18th Infantry Division. On the morning of 13 May, that Division's command setup was in a mess. According to Doumenc [chief of the French general staff], contact with 66th Regiment had been broken; "contact had been lost with the 77th and could not be restored with 125th. The radios did not work and there were no motorcycles."[82] Above all the 2d Battalion, 39th Infantry Regiment—which was placed under division on 12 May and inserted into the front line at the boundary between the two army corps—was completely isolated. However, on that critical day, the headquarters, 18th Infantry

Division, made no serious attempt to push the Germans back. Mainly the cavalry formations that meanwhile had been inserted between the division's units merely made local counterthrusts, including the employment of a few armored scout cars.

Martin, commanding general, XI Corps, was initially informed only about the midnight episode at the Island of Houx. When he visited the command post of the 18th Infantry Division around noon, he found out that the Germans had been attacking across the Meuse River since 0430 and had formed two bridgeheads. He now ordered Colonel Dugenet, the commander of the 39th Infantry Regiment, which was in reserve, to mount a counterattack against the northern bridgehead. He was to be supported by 3d Company, 6th Tank Battalion, as well as several armored scout cars from the 1st Light Cavalry Division. He was also promised fire support from four artillery battalions. But the designated attack jump-off time of 2000 could not be met and was postponed to 2100 (French time: 2000) at Dugenet's request. A quarter of an hour before, the colonel phoned again and reported that the infantry was still not ready. Thereupon, the Renault 35 tanks and the armored scout cars at first had to attack all by themselves. They pushed through the northern bridgehead, past Grange, into the vicinity of the Meuse River. But as darkness fell and the infantry had still not arrived, they withdrew. That was the end of the XI Corps' countermeasures on 13 May.

Just as ineffective were the II Corps' efforts, although the 5th Motorized Infantry Division positioned north of the breakthrough point was an elite formation. General Boucher had known since 0200 that German infantrymen had pushed to the western bank of the Meuse River on his division's right wing. But he did not react until 0730. Then he sent elements of his reconnaissance battalion to the right-wing neighbor to restore contact with the 18th Infantry Division, which had been broken off in the meantime. Only now did he learn that the Germans had also expanded their bridgehead into his division's combat sector. Thereupon, Boucher, around 1100, ordered the 2d Battalion, 129th Infantry Regiment, to stage a counterattack. The push was to be made at 1400 but had to be postponed to 1500. During its approach march, the battalion was caught in a German dive-bomber raid and beaten back.

Now, pushed by his superiors, Boucher decided to launch a massive counterattack. For this mission, he picked the 2d Battalion, 129th Infantry Regiment, from his division, plus the reconnaissance battalion. They were to be supported by elements of the 4th Light Cavalry Division, specifically, by the 1st Squadron, 14th Dragoon Regiment, plus one company of Hotchkiss tanks from the 4th Armored Reconnaissance Regiment. The attack was to be mounted from several directions against Haut-le-Wastia and initially was scheduled for 2015. Because the approach of the infantry was delayed, it was postponed to 2100 and finally 2200 (French time: 2100). But now, the commanding officers of the supporting artillery raised objections because darkness was beginning to fall. Thereupon, the attack was postponed to the next morning.

That was all the two army corps did by way of counteractions on the crucial day of 13 May: the temporary thrust by one tank company in the sector of XI Corps and an attack by II Corps postponed to the next day. When Corap, the commander in chief, Ninth Army, found out about that, he sarcastically spoke about a "comedy."[83] On the next day, 14 May, the forces assembled by II Corps mounted a courageous attack against Haut-le-Wastia and temporarily recaptured it. But now it was too late because the Germans had ferried enough Panzers across the Meuse River during the night. While there was still bitter fighting for Haut-le-Wastia, Rommel achieved the decisive operational breakthrough in the south at Onhaye.[84]

The Tank Battle at Flavion

Because the countermeasures at the corps' level were not initiated in time and thus were ineffective, there had to be a response at the army level. By way of reserves, Ninth Army in this sector had the 4th North African Infantry Division and the newly subordinated 1st Armored Division in addition to some minor formations. On 13 May, when the Panzer Corps Hoth was crossing the Meuse River at Dinant and Houx, the French 1st Armored Division was in a standby area near Charleroi, not even 40 kilometers away. There, it was to be held in readiness as reserve of the First Army, which had advanced all the way to the Dyle Line for employment against "the Gembloux Gap."

The French supreme command still believed that the German main effort was in northern Belgium and thought that the attack on the Meuse River line was a diversionary maneuver. Only shortly before midnight, in other words twenty-four hours after the first German soldiers had crossed the Meuse River, did the French 1st Armored Division receive a preliminary order that it was to mount a counterattack toward Dinant under the Ninth Army. The division had spent the entire morning of 14 May in its standby area without doing anything. Due to a communications breakdown, it got the actual execution order only around 1400. Around 1600, in other words, two hours later, the division's first elements finally got going. They took about five hours to cover a distance of thirty-five kilometers before they reached the area north of Flavion at around 2100 (French time: 2000). The roads were jammed with fleeing soldiers and civilians, and some units got lost and had to be "corralled." Just how explosive the situation estimate was is revealed by the words of Corap, the commander in chief of the Ninth Army. In a phone conversation he implored General Bruneau, the commander of the French 1st Armored Division: "You must counterattack this evening with all that you have. That's a formal order."[85]

In the meantime, Rommel's 25th Panzer Regiment had arrived near Morville, just five kilometers away from Bruneau, and moved into a standby area for the night. Oddly enough, neither of the two sides guessed who their dangerous neighbors were during the night. If Bruneau, as had been planned, had continued his advance toward Dinant, then his tanks would have rolled over the 7th Panzer Division's Panzer regiment that was not ready for a fight. In the meantime, however, the Char B battle tanks had run out of gas because they had only a small fuel tank. A mistake was made during march planning when the fuel vehicles were placed at the end of the convoy. When they were urgently needed up front, nobody knew where they had gotten stuck. All the division could do was to break off its attack and move into a standby area near Flavion to spend a quiet night.

A tragedy struck the French 1st Armored Division on 15 May. German dive-bombers had in the meantime smashed several fuel convoys, and the remaining vehicles did not arrive until 0900. Now another elementary difference emerged between the two armies: under Guderian's influence the German Panzer force's logistics were geared toward "high-speed warfare." Thus, the introduction of gas cans solved the fuel supply problem. All vehicles were able to transport them and, if necessary, they could be hand-carried for a short distance out in the field. The trucks of the fuel groups quickly unloaded the full gas cans at the individual distribution points and then made the same round-trip once more to pick up the gas cans that had been emptied. Time losses were thus minimized if the organization was well set up. However, on the French side special fuel trucks whose cross-country capability was very restricted handled refueling for the tanks. Because these tank trucks had to refuel each individual tank in succession, like mobile gas stations, it always took a very long time, even when the vehicles were favorably positioned. When on the morning of 15 May the French 1st Armored Division wanted to refuel in the standby area, Rommel's Panzers attacked it.

At this point, we must dispel another legend. Numerous reports assert that Rommel's 7th Panzer Division wiped out the French 1st Armored Division on that day. In the morning, Rommel and his Panzer regiment did push into the French standby area, catching the 28th Tank Battalion (Char B) and the 25th Tank Battalion (Hotchkiss 39) in the act of refueling. But when the first Panzers of the 5th Panzer Division arrived to the north of his position late in the morning, he left the further engagement of the French tanks to the neighboring division. With the 25th Panzer Regiment, he himself carried out a breathtaking maneuver by circling around the southern flank of the French armored division and pushing far to the west. So, it must be noted that the "tank battle of Flavion," which lasted into the evening hours, was decided not by Rommel but by Werner, the commander of the 31st Panzer Regiment, 5th Panzer Division. In contrast to the 7th Panzer Division, the 5th Panzer Division had two Panzer regiments,[86] but the 15th Panzer Regiment, which was stuck farther back, at that moment was still east of the Meuse River. The military bridge of the 5th Panzer Division was not completed until the afternoon, which is why the lead elements of that regiment arrived only after the battle had already been decided.

According to the French version, the 1st Armored Division faced the overwhelming force of two German Panzer divisions at Flavion. In reality, however, the Panzers of Werner were in a situation of dramatic inferiority after Rommel's Panzers had left the battlefield in a completely surprising manner after a short episode during the morning. The 31st Panzer Regiment had two Panzer battalions, whereas Bruneau's 1st Armored Division had four. The difference becomes even more striking if one looks at the precise number of models suitable for tank action. On the French side, there were around 90 Hotchkiss 39s, 65 of the feared Char Bs, and at least 12 Renault 35 tanks of the 6th Independent Tank Battalion.[87] This meant that the French had just about 170 battle tanks, of which some had already been destroyed during the prior action against Rommel's Panzers. Werner, on the other hand, had a total of 30 Panzer IIIs and IVs. The remaining 90 German battle tanks were the lightweight Panzer I and II models and could not be used to engage enemy battle tanks because of their inadequate armament. Here again, the first clash with the Char B battle tanks was a shock to the German Panzer soldiers. The commander of a Panzer III reported in his after-action report: "We were really shook up as we saw our tracer rounds bounce off the French tanks like just so many marbles!"[88]

In view of this force ratio, the question arises of how it was possible for the French 1st Armored Division to be smashed in just a few hours. One of the factors had to do with radio equipment. There was hardly any other combat action during the campaign where commanding units with the help of radios played such an overwhelming role as they did at Flavion. All German Panzers had modern radio equipment whereas the few French radios had mostly broken down because of their weak batteries. This resulted in a rather strange situation in which the French tanks mostly fought in a disconcerted pattern

Char B Gard (2d Company, 37th Tank Battalion) was put out of action near Flavion on 15 May. In the foreground, the graves of two French soldiers who were killed in action. *Bundesarchiv Koblenz [Federal Archives]*

Wreck of Char B Poitou, knocked out on 15 May near Deneé (Flavion); in the foreground, the turret that was blown off after an artillery hit. The tank commander, Captain Lehoux, and his crew were killed. The 3d Company, 37th Tank Battalion, which he commanded, was wiped out at Deneé. *Bundesarchiv Koblenz [Federal Archives]*

against a German Panzer regiment that had a single leader. Werner was in a position to direct his units by radio. Cooperation within platoons and companies also worked outstandingly well. Again and again, German Panzers as part of the "wolf pack tactic" surrounded small groups of French battle tanks that were then fired upon from all sides. Whenever the Germans had to tackle a Char B, they concentrated on smashing its tracks. The Panzer I and Panzer II, which were unsuitable for tank action, were held back at a respectful distance, but Werner repeatedly used them for simulated attacks on the flanks.

Another reason for the French defeat was that they fought only with tanks whereas the Germans fought a "combined arms combat." Bruneau had positioned his artillery so far back that it was hardly able to go into action during the battle. On the other hand, the 5th Panzer Division had moved some of its batteries so far forward that they could engage enemy tanks pointblank. Werner in some cases also had his tanks withdraw to coax the French battle tanks right in front of the barrels of German artillery and flak pieces whose projectiles could pierce even the armor of a Char B.[89] Finally, the Luftwaffe dive-bombers also went into action and pounced on the enemy tanks. The biggest tragedy of the French 1st Armored Division was that a number of Char B battle tanks had simply run out of gas. Now these gigantic monsters stood on the battlefield like beached battleships. Several of them were set on fire by their own crews.

Bruneau finally gave the order to retreat. In the evening, out of the 170 battle tanks of his reinforced division, he had only about 36 left, and they disengaged toward the French border. The next morning, their number had dwindled to 16. The French tank crews had fought with extraordinary bravery but with hopelessly inferior methods. On top of everything else, Rommel had pushed deep into the enemy deployment during the Flavion tank fight and had cut the supply lines of the French tank formations in their rear. The resulting panic caused several units simply to turn tail. Rommel's Panzers reached the Philippeville-Cerfontaine area before the still intact units of the Ninth Army were able to withdraw there. This meant that the enemy had crossed the new defense line, which the French army high command had planned, before French troops could occupy those positions.[90]

On 15 May the French Meuse River front collapsed completely. Three isolated thrusts sufficed to do the job: in the north, Rommel's 7th Panzer Division; in the center, Kempf's 6th Panzer Division; and in the south, the Panzer Corps Guderian. Although the three breaches were rather narrow in the beginning, they finally caused the dam to break. On that day, the French front between La Ferté south of Sedan and Namur was ripped open for a width of far more than 100 kilometers.

Panzer Corps Hoepner Attacks the Dyle Line: A Diversionary Maneuver on the Operational Level

The first tank battle of World War II, and the biggest one during the Campaign in the West, originated from this first tank-vs.-tank fight over the next 48 hours.[91]

Heinrich Bücheler about the tank battle of Hannut on 12 May

While Army Group A advanced through the Ardennes, Army Group B attacked north of the line Liège-Namur. The Eighteenth Army after five days had already punched through the rear resistance lines of the Dutch army. The official capitulation occurred on 15 May. To the south, the Sixth Army attacked through the Maastricht bulge and overcame the strong Belgian border fortifications at Liège. Now the road ahead was clear for the thrust of the Panzer Corps Hoepner (XVI Motorized Corps) [General der Kavallerie Erich Hoepner]. It was to attack at the exact spot where the French army command mistakenly expected the German main effort, that is to say, in the Gembloux Gap northwest of the bend of the Meuse River near Namur.

Using the previously mentioned comparison of British military historian Liddell Hart, the Panzer Corps Hoepner represented the cape of the bullfighter, which, like a "red cloth," was to entice the Allies to charge into the Flanders trap like an enraged bull. Now the Panzer divisions of Army Group A were able to thrust into the unprotected flank like the sword of the bullfighter. The spectacular German airborne landing operations in northern Belgium and Holland brought about the same indirect effect, for example, the missions against Eben Emael, the Albert Canal bridges, the airfields near the Hague, and the bridges of Rotterdam.[92] The Allied field army headquarters now indeed looked in the wrong direction, to the north, as if transfixed.

Immediately after the start of the German attack, Gamelin had launched the long-planned Dyle maneuver. Because the Luftwaffe did not disturb the advance to the Dyle Line—quite deliberately, of course—everything seemed to be running smoothly at first. The Allied field armies were employed as follows for this wheeling maneuver by the left wing:

> Over to the far left in the north along the Channel coast, the French Seventh Army was to push toward Breda via Antwerp and establish contact with the Dutch army.
>
> The British Expeditionary Force had the mission of advancing past Brussels, all the way to the Dyle River, and occupying the sector between Wavre and Louvain.
>
> The French First Army was to go into position next-door between Wavre and the Meuse River bend at Namur.
>
> Farther to the south, the French Ninth Army had to wheel its left wing forward up to the Belgian section of the Meuse River between Namur and Givet.

Inside the Dyle Line, which was also reinforced by the Belgian army, the First Army's sector was the critical spot. This is the location of the so-called Gembloux Gap (*la trouée de Gembloux*), which was not protected by any natural obstacles. This is why six elite divisions, reinforced by several independent tank battalions, had been concentrated here in the only thirty-three-kilometer-wide sector. In front of this sector, eight kilometers east of Perwez, extended a tank obstacle (*le barrage de Cointet*) that the Belgian army had constructed. This was a kilometers-long heavy iron grill made up of T-beams that were positioned on rollers. The obstacle, which was 2.5 meters high and 3 meters deep, was additionally reinforced by concrete blocks and barbed wire and was secured by mines.

In case of a German attack through Flanders, the plan was to move additional formations, including the 1st and 2d Armored Divisions, northward also and occupy an assembly position behind First Army to form a counterweight to the German attack's main effort that was expected here. The most important forward-looking measure, however, was that the Prioux Cavalry Corps was sent ahead, thirty kilometers beyond this line, toward Liège, to cover the move into the Gembloux Gap. This huge formation, comparable to a German Panzer corps, was to occupy a reserve line between Tirlemont (Tienen), Hannut, and Huy, and, in the course of a delaying action, hold up the attackers at least to the fifth day of the campaign, until the infantry divisions to the rear had adequately improved their positions.

The Tank Battle of Hannut

Hoepner's Panzers and Prioux's tanks collided frontally near Hannut on 12 May. First of all, the important thing is to track down the assertion, frequently found in the literature on the subject, that 415 French tanks had faced an overwhelming force of 623 German Panzers at Hannut. At first sight, the strength ratio seems to be correct. General [René-Jacques-Adolphe] Prioux had the 2d and 3d Light Mechanized Divisions, with a total of 239 Hotchkiss and 176 SOMUA tanks.[93] Hoepner's Panzer Corps again had the 3d and 4th Panzer Divisions, with 280 and 343 Panzers, respectively. However, it must be kept in mind here that the 623 German Panzers include 498 Panzer Models I and II. Oddly enough, the literature on this battle only rarely mentions the fact that the French Cavalry Corps also employed numerous armored reconnaissance vehicles. The Renault AMR-ZT-63 proved at least equal to or even superior to the German Panzer Is and IIs in terms of armament. That applies all the more to the 90 Panhard 178 armored scout vehicles whose modern 25-mm cannon was able to penetrate even the German Panzer IV. Counting only the models that could be used for Panzer-against-tank action and disregarding the armored reconnaissance vehicles, there were 239 Hotchkiss and 176 SOMUA against merely 73 Panzer IIIs and 52 Panzer IVs on the German side.

This quantitative superiority (415 against 125) appears even greater if the qualitative superiority of the French battle tanks is considered. It is characteristic of the backwardness of German Panzer development at the time that the armor of the "heavy" Panzer IV was only 30-mm compared to the 45-mm of the French "light" Hotchkiss 39 tanks and the 55-mm of the "medium-heavy" SOMUA.[94] Many experts described the SOMUA as the most modern and best battle tank that was employed in this theater of war at that time. The crews of the German Panzer III were in for a nasty surprise as they discovered that the projectiles from their 3.7-cm gun bounced off the enemy armor without any effect. Thus, we are left with only the 52 Panzer IV whose cannon could do something against the SOMUA, but only at close range. Another advantage enjoyed by the French was that they were employed in a delaying pattern and were again and again able to fight in villages and in the terrain from covered positions. Just how desolate the situation looked for the crews of the German light Panzers is indicated by the desperate action of the commander of a Panzer I in Jauche on 13 May. "Armed" with a hammer, he jumped on the Hotchkiss tank of 1st Lieutenant Le Bel, obviously intending to smash the periscopes of that tank. In the process, however, he fell off the moving French tank, which ran over him.[95]

When the fight began, French armor was still fighting according to the rigid tactics of World War I. The German Panzers were being commanded in a mobile manner and were constantly being shifted back and forth. French tanks were employed in much too static and too linear a fashion. This battle revealed also the advantages of superior German radio equipment. The German commanders were always able to unexpectedly shift the point of main effort. On the other hand, few French tanks had a working radio. Therefore, several times officers had to dismount and run from tank to tank to issue orders. In the process, they were taken by surprise by a German attack while they were outside their tanks. The first clash of the two armored forces revealed yet another difference between the German and French models—the way the armored turrets were designed. The French tanks had one-man turrets. That meant that the tank commander, who should actually be the tactical leader, had, at the same time, to be the gunner and assistant gunner. In contrast, the German Panzer commanders were able to concentrate fully on their command task. A critique prepared by the 35th Panzer Regiment characterized French tank employment at Hannut as "leaderless, aimless, poorly led, tactically inferior."[96]

The Germans were at an advantage especially in combined arms combat. Hannut was not only the scene of the first and, at the same time, biggest tank battle of the campaign; it also turned into a tremendous tank-air battle, in which the Wehrmacht demonstrated what nowadays is called the air-land battle.[97] The VIII Air Corps under Freiherr [Baron] von Richthofen, which specialized in direct, close army ground support in its capacity as the Close Support Air Corps, participated massively in the ground fighting. It was above all the German dive-bombers that cleared the way for the German Panzers and disabled a number of French tanks. The VIII Air Corps switched its operations area only at noon on 13 May and took off for its rolling raid at Sedan. During the next several days, the Second Air Fleet also supported the advance with its other combat units.

The Battle at Hannut developed as follows. On 10 May the Panzer Corps Hoepner had advanced from the Aachen area through the Maastricht bulge and had begun to cross the Meuse River. On 11 May very close to the captured Belgian Fort Eben Emael, it crossed the Albert Canal on one of the bridges that airborne troops had swiftly seized. For a time the corps was allowed to use only a single bridge, and this is why only the 4th Panzer Division, which was committed forward, was available. On 12 May German Panzers ran into the French forward defensive position at Hannut. Now began that memorable tank battle during which, on the very first day, French armor—contrary to German reports—definitely emerged victorious. A few German Panzer commanders tried entirely too boldly to tackle the French tanks during this first clash. Individual duels, especially with SOMUA tanks, revealed the superiority of the French models in a shocking manner. That the defenders nevertheless were hard hit and shaken up was primarily due to the Luftwaffe.

On the next day, the French fell victim to their ineffective tactics, that is, their preference for contiguous lines. They had lined up their formations almost like a string of pearls on the line between Tirlemont (Tienen) and Huy, a distance of thirty-five kilometers. In that way, the delaying action lacked any and all depth, and, above all, there was no adequate reserve available for a counterthrust. Hoepner, however, on 13 May, the second day of the tank battle, concentrated his two Panzer divisions on a narrow sector opposite the French 3d Light Mechanized Division and at last achieved a breakthrough here. The tanks of the 2d Mechanized Division, however, were "passed by on the left" and to some extent stood almost inactive in the field.

It would be unjustified to blame only Prioux for this kind of rigid combat leadership. He had protested vehemently but in vain against this way of employing his tanks. The bottom line of the 12–13 May tank battle is that the 2d Light Mechanized Division lost almost no tanks and the 3d Light Mechanized Division lost a total of 75 Hotchkiss and 30 SOMUA tanks. On the other hand, the approximately 160 German Panzers that had been disabled can be claimed mainly by this one French division. However, due to the linear deployment of the French, a breakthrough in one single spot sufficed and their entire Cavalry Corps had to abandon the field of battle.

Breaking Through Gembloux

The retreat of the French once again displayed the basic difference in the armor tactics employed by these two armies. When the Prioux Cavalry Corps fell back to the west, this was not done by way of a delaying action, as would have been in keeping with German employment principles. It would have been possible to force the enemy again and again to run into numerous obstacles and to hit his advanced elements in the flank. The French armor was unable to carry out this kind of active delaying maneuver, first and foremost on account of its miserable radio equipment. Instead, the French fell back mostly in one swift move. When the German Panzer commanders noticed that, they started the pursuit on 13 May and, caught by the suction effect of the withdrawal movement, in some cases pushed directly into the middle of the French units that were flooding to rear. That created a difficult situation for the French artillery that was to screen this withdrawal because in some cases it could no longer distinguish between friend and foe since both were so closely intermingled. Hoepner recognized this big opportunity and on 14 May ordered the German Panzer spearheads that had raced far ahead to continue the attack relentlessly: "The important thing is to penetrate into the Dyle position simultaneously with the beaten enemy."[98]

The Perwez tank obstacle (*le barrage de Cointet*) turned out to be rather ineffective because it had big gaps. The attempt to punch through the well-developed Dyle position during the attack from the move failed on 14 May. Hoepner, an extremely courageous man, who later on paid with his life for his resistance to Hitler, proved that he was determined to achieve an immediate breakthrough. He wanted to prevent the enemy from getting reinforcements and therefore attacked the next day only with the two Panzer divisions, without waiting for the arrival of the infantry divisions that were under his command. That meant that the Panzer units to some extent had to attack the antitank gun blocking position frontally, even though the position had not yet been put out of action by the infantry. This thrust seemed doomed to failure in spite of air support. For example, the 4th Panzer Division sent out the following report around 1600: "5th Panzer Brigade has heavy losses. . . . Continuing attack against this enemy, in well-developed defensive positions, today no longer looks promising since it was impossible to neutralize his strong artillery (10–12 batteries). There are

The kilometers-long Belgian tank obstacle called Barrage de Cointet near Perwez was not able to delay the advance of Panzer Corps Hoepner for any length of time. *Bundesarchiv Koblenz [Federal Archives]*

serious doubts as to whether the troops can resume the attack on 16 May under the same combat conditions."[99]

The situation report submitted by the commander of the 5th Panzer Brigade was particularly impressive because he arrived at the division command post with a face wound. He had run into an ambush far up front and got out of it only because he played dead for three hours in a shell crater. He commented that he had not experienced that kind of artillery "even during the World War." Resuming the attack on the next day, he indicated, "would be suicide."[100] Hoepner now believed that the attack had failed solely because the Panzer divisions did not have enough infantry. He wanted to avoid senseless casualties and therefore immediately sent out the following radio message: "Suspend attack. Continue tomorrow morning from line reached, employing 35th Infantry Division and 20th Infantry Division (Motorized)."[101]

That order obviously did not reach all elements of the 3d Panzer Division, which attacked farther to the north near Ernage. Suddenly, there was a completely surprising message that the 3d Rifle Regiment had punched through not only the main line of resistance but also through the rear defense line around 2045. This meant that what corps

A Panzer company of Panzer Corps Hoepner forming up for the attack against the Dyle position at Gembloux. *Bundesarchiv Koblenz [Federal Archives]*

headquarters had no longer considered possible on that day, the breakthrough of the Gembloux position, had indeed been achieved. Here again, the impractical employment of French armor had facilitated Hoepner's success. After its withdrawal behind the Gembloux position, the French First Army employed the Prioux Cavalry Corps no longer in a compact fashion but rather distributed the individual tank battalions behind the infantry divisions. This tactical breakup of a major operational formation seems all the more incomprehensible as the First Army employed here had four independent tank battalions anyway. When Panzer Corps Hoepner achieved its surprisingly swift breakthrough, the French were no longer in a position to respond to it on the operational level.

In conclusion, it must be noted that there are different interpretations among military historians as to who actually won the tank battle at Hannut: Hoepner or Prioux? There is a two-part answer to that.

(1) Looking at it *tactically,* Prioux achieved complete success. His mission had only been to offer temporary resistance and to give the First Army time to get settled in the Gembloux position by the fifth combat day (in other words, 14 May). His

mission was more than accomplished because the Germans could mount a massive attack against this line only on 15 May. Moreover, the French tanks were able to inflict considerable losses on the Germans. The Germans had to accept tremendous losses not only at Hannut but also at Gembloux. For example, the 4th Panzer Division had only 137 fighting vehicles on the morning of 16 May, including just four Panzer IVs. The statistics compiled on the same day reported 20 to 25 percent of the Panzers as not being operational in the area of the 3d Panzer Division, while the 4th Panzer Division indicated that as many as 45 to 50 percent of its Panzers were not combat ready. Of course, some of the disabled fighting vehicles were quickly repaired. Nevertheless, the attack strength of this Panzer Corps was initially greatly weakened.

(2) Looking at it *operationally,* however, one can say that the mere fact that the Battle of Hannut took place at all can be described as a big success on the part of Hoepner. The corps which he commanded after all—to put it somewhat strongly—was supposed to be the bait to coax the enemy into a direction that would be ineffective in operational terms. Among all the major French formations on the northern wing, the Prioux Cavalry Corps had given the German command its biggest headache. In terms of organization and equipment, it would have been outstandingly suited for slicing up Sickle Cut from the north. After the counterattacks at Sedan had failed on 14 May, French Supreme Commander Gamelin during the following night seriously considered ordering the Prioux Cavalry Corps—as his last trump card—to punch into the right flank of the German Panzer divisions that had rushed forward. In the meantime, Hoepner's Panzers, in conjunction with the Luftwaffe, had so decimated the formations of his opponent Prioux that there was no possibility of employing the Cavalry Corps in that way for the moment. This meant that Panzer Corps Hoepner had accomplished its first mission. Now it did not have to create a diversion from Sickle Cut but instead was itself to participate in this Panzer thrust. For this purpose, it was placed under the command of the Army Group A on 18 May.[102]

French Divisions Pinned Down in the Maginot Line

The vanquished contributes to a victory just as much as the victor.[103]

Field Marshal Graf von Schlieffen

The missions of Army Group B and Army Group C were basically identical. They were to create a diversion away from the actual main effort in the center, in the sector of the Army Group A, and coax the strongest possible enemy forces away from the center toward the wings. Von Leeb, the commander in chief of Army Group C, thought that it would be incomparably more difficult to simulate the kind of strength that was not there. Most of his formations had rather inferior equipment and were more suitable for defense than for taking the mighty Maginot Line, opposite which they were positioned. Above all, this army group did not have a single Panzer formation. Its mission, therefore, was to attract the enemy's attention to this area through deception measures, to tie down as many enemy divisions as possible.

Numerous elite formations that were to be moved to the central sector of the western front after the Polish campaign, were first routed to the south, either to First Army in the Saarbrücken area or to Seventh Army along the Upper Rhine. After these troops had moved into their final standby areas, an attempt was made to suggest the presence of Panzer Troops by using misleading tactical symbols, stories in the press about maneuver damage, and so on. This resulted in a rather strange masquerade, as part of which several officers had to put on the uniforms of the Panzer Troops and to make a big show in public. Finally, Army Group C got some limited-service Panzers that were now permanently run back and forth near the border.

Seventh Army was assigned the most important deception measure. With only four divisions, it was to cover the far-flung sector between Karlsruhe and the Swiss border. It was to simulate preparations for an offensive against Switzerland to envelop the Maginot Line from the south. Nowhere else along the front did the Germans employ such a repertoire of ruses of war. There were some very ostentatious train switching movements at the marshaling yards in Freiburg im Breisgau, where General der Artillerie [Friedrich] Dollmann, the army commander in chief, had his headquarters. Most of the time, however, these movements were carried out only in darkness so that the enemy's agents would not notice that this was always the same military train. In that way it would also be very difficult to determine whether Panzers and big artillery pieces were really hidden under the canvas covers, as one might assume by the general outline. Hush-hush "headquarters" were set up in ostentatious mansions and spa hotels, although, in reality, only the very military-looking guards out front were genuine.

In the end, the southern portion of the Black Forest looked like a huge army camp because there were permanent German troop movements in the side valleys that were open toward Switzerland—all in keeping with precise instructions in the script for this show. These troop movements were so managed that they could be observed from the south and the Swiss guards conscientiously took down all observations on paper. The clanking noises of moving Panzers and the engine noises from vehicle convoys were heard over and over again near the border during the long winter nights. In reality, however, this noise was manufactured from loudspeakers and was played from tape. The German Counter-Intelligence Service, under Canaris, also participated in these deception measures with a specifically target-oriented disinformation drive according to which an attack through Switzerland was allegedly planned.[104]

In reality, however, the German general staff never seriously considered an offensive through Swiss territory to outflank the Maginot Line to the south. Obviously, the German general staff had too much respect for the reputed Swiss bravery. According to the later Generalmajor Liß, at that time chief of the Foreign Armies West Section of Army Intelligence, this option was looked into within the army high command but was soon dropped.[105] There was indeed a harvest from these deception measures. Thus, it happened that at the start of the campaign in the west thirty-six French divisions were concentrated in the area of the heavily fortified Maginot Line facing only nineteen divisions of Army Group C on the German side.

Immediately after the start of the German offensive, however, the French high command should have realized that there was no danger threatening on the right wing. Now the important thing would have been to employ many of the divisions, stationed needlessly behind the Maginot Line, as part of a countermove heading north. The real clincher came only at that particular point in time when Propaganda Minister Goebbels set the scene. The German troops had just broken through the front at Sedan when in a radio address he stated that "within twice 24 hours, there will no longer be any neutral states in Europe."[106] The way things looked at the moment that could only have meant an attack against Switzerland. Now the Wehrmacht Intelligence Service (Abwehr) launched a furious deception operation, employing numerous diplomats in various countries for the purpose of spreading rumors. The French and British were made so nervous that they began to prepare for the evacuations of their embassies in Bern. On 15 May, Colonel Gauché of the French Intelligence told the Swiss military attaché in confidence: "We know from an absolutely reliable source that the German attack against Switzerland scheduled for 16 or 17 May, in the morning, is firm."[107] The French leadership fell victim to a mirage: the German attack against Switzerland never took place.

The German general staff believed that the biggest threat was located along the northern wing of the Maginot Line, which extended to within just a few kilometers of Sedan. The Achilles heel of Sickle Cut was that the French could take many uncommitted formations out of this sector and employ them for a counterattack into the left flank of the Panzer Corps Guderian while shielded by the mighty fortification line. As mentioned earlier, von Bock, had remarked rather sarcastically to Halder: "You will be creeping by 10 miles from the Maginot Line with the flank of your breakthrough and hope that the French will watch inertly!"[108]

But the enemy did indeed stand by and do nothing. This can be traced to the following operational chess move: The German Sixteenth Army initially only had the mission of providing a defensive screen for the left breakthrough flank of Panzer Corps Guderian. Its VII Corps, however, was to make a maximum effort and attack the left flank of the Maginot Line at La Ferté in order to tie down strong enemy formations here. The 71st Infantry Division was to attack Fort No. 505 that constituted the western corner post of that fortification line. The fight for La Ferté finally was played up as much as if the Battle of Verdun had to be fought a second time at this spot. So, Georges, the commander in chief of the Allied northeast front, already on the afternoon of 15 May had personally phoned the commanding general of XVIII Corps and appealed to him with these words: "You must hold at all costs the Inor-Malandry shoulder [at La Ferté]. The whole issue of the war may depend on it."[109]

The Germans had concentrated around 250 artillery pieces on this narrow frontline sector. Not even the heavy mortars (230-mm) could do any damage to the fort. Once again, the employment of assault engineers achieved the decision. On 18 May, an assault detachment led by Oberleutnant [Alfred] Germer advanced all the way to Block II of the fortification. He attached a 40-kg demolition charge to the slewing ring of its retractable armored turret. No major damage was inflicted on the steel armored cupola, but the force of the detonation was so great that the cupola was flung upward and then came to rest obliquely jammed on the slewing ring. Germer then threw smaller demolition charges and smoke candles into the resultant opening, triggering a chain reaction. Now occurred one of the most dramatic events of this campaign, that is, the "*tragédie souterraine*" (underground tragedy) of La Ferté.

The explosives that Germer had thrown inside caused a fire in the armored turret that spread immediately and, due to the heat generated, gradually caused the shells stored there to explode. The blast waves from the detonations ripped the steel doors open and made way for the fire. Thereupon, the occupants fled to the lower floors down to a connecting gallery that was 35 meters below ground and led to Block I of the fort, 250 meters away. In the end, Germer's assault team also put out of action that fortification, with its steel gun turrets and observation cupola.[110]

A fire also broke out inside, so that the occupants there had to flee to the connecting gallery. Now the disaster was complete. The situation of the trapped men resembled a disaster in a coal mine, where the fire from the higher galleries not only blocks the exit for the mine workers but also deprives them of oxygen. The air became increasingly worse so that the soldiers had to put on their gas masks. Again and again, blast waves blew through the galleries as more ammunition was ignited, knocking the trapped men to the ground. Finally, the electric lights also failed.

But there was continuous contact with the outside world via a field telephone. The French commander, 1st Lieutenant Bourguignon, requested permission to surrender the fort that the Germans had already put out of action because poisonous powder gases kept spreading more and more inside the system of galleries and tunnels. Because the explosions let up, there was still a chance of climbing up to one of the blocks and getting out into the open from there. His superiors required him to hold out—an order that a French historian later on described as a "monstrous absurdity."[111] The last contact with the trapped fort occupants took place at 0539 on 19 May. The French sergeant Sailly reported in a weak voice, interrupted by coughing: "I cannot stand it anymore. . . . The 1st lieutenant is next to me. . . . We will try to climb up again."[112] Several days later, after the smoke and the poison gases released during the explosions had evaporated, German soldiers climbed down into the underground tunnel system. There they found the corpses of the 107 men of the fort garrison who had died as a result of carbon monoxide poisoning.[113]

In their theatrical plays and novels, the French existentialists again and again gave full rein to their imagination in order to conjure up hopeless situations. But reality by far outdid them in the light of this drama that took place thirty-five meters below ground. Perhaps the real tragedy of 1st Lieutenant Bourguignon and his men was that holding on to Armored Fort No. 505 for such a length of time had not only become meaningless but,

Armored Fort No. 505 at La Ferté was taken by storm; it was the scene of an underground tragedy. *Bundesarchiv Koblenz [Federal Archives]*

in an operational sense, was even counterproductive. After all, the VII Corps attack against La Ferté was primarily a deception maneuver to divert attention from the real point of main effort at nearby Sedan. When the Germans launched their attack on the fort on 16 May, a crack in the front line, amounting to far more than a hundred kilometers, already gaped north of La Ferté—the entire Meuse River line had collapsed.

Widening the breach by three or four kilometers to the south was bound to seem insignificant. The issue in this fight for Fort No. 505 that was fought so bitterly by both sides was something entirely different, that is, the myth of the "impregnability of the Maginot Line." No French general could afford to give up even a small piece of it.

The irony of destiny, however, was that this myth fatally tripped up the French. After the breakthrough at Sedan, the situation was so desperate that the only chance was to strip the Maginot Line, which "almost defended itself," of all personnel and to use the bulk of the formations not tied down here to attack the southern flank of the German breakthrough. Instead of shifting the troops, the French generals even dispatched reinforcements from the Sedan sector of all places to protect the Maginot Line. And so, the Char B tanks of the 41st Tank Battalion, 3d Armored Division, were

The armored cupola of Fort No. 505, blasted into an oblique position by Oberleutnant Alfred Germer using a 40-kg charge. *Bundesarchiv Koblenz [Federal Archives]*

taken out of the bitter fighting around Stonne and sent to mount a counterattack against La Ferté. The attempt to relieve the encircled Fort No. 505 failed.

This incomprehensible behavior cries out for a comparison to the situation in August 1914. The French supreme commander Joffre had concentrated his troops precisely on the wrong wing, that is to say, on France's eastern border. Now the Germans who were attacking according to the Schlieffen plan had outflanked his left wing and threatened to hit him in the rear. In that situation, he did the only correct thing: He stripped the right wing that was protected anyway by strong border fortifications, such as the Maginot Line in 1940, and dispatched as many troops as possible by rail to the opposite wing. In doing so, he was even inclined, if necessary, to sacrifice the prestige target of Verdun and ordered artillery pieces to be withdrawn from there. In that way, he was successful in hitting the Germans by surprise in the flank and stopping them along the Marne River. For his successors, however, the Maginot Line had almost become an end in itself. To that extent, during the crucial phase, the nineteen moderately armed divisions of Army Group C were successful in checkmating the thirty-six French divisions that were protected by the Maginot Line.

7

The Push to the Channel Coast and the Problem of the Exposed Flank

The breakthrough wedge is developing in a positively classic manner.[1]

General Halder in his diary, 16 May 1940

Hitler's Halt Order at Montcornet and the No-Show French Counterattack

Operation Sickle Cut is considered to be a perfectly planned and executed blitzkrieg campaign that "went like clockwork."[2] In reality, however, the map exercises were merely confined to the advance through the Ardennes and the hasty Meuse River crossing from the move that was considered "hardly possible." The further course of operations seemed to be problematical and decision was postponed for the time being. Then suddenly came the "miracle of Sedan." Now the Panzers were on the other side of the Meuse River, but there were no specific ideas as to how things were going to go from there. That turned up already during the previously mentioned conference on 15 March in the Reich Chancellery where Guderian's plan for a breakthrough at Sedan was received with skepticism and irony. Only Hitler had put the question to him: "And then what are you going to do?" In his *Memoirs* Guderian commented: "He was the first person who had thought to ask me this vital question."[3] Above all, he noted: "I never received any further order as to what I was to do once the bridgehead over the Meuse was captured. All my decisions, until I reached the Atlantic seaboard at Abbéville, were taken by me and me alone. The Supreme Command's influence on my actions was merely restrictive throughout."[4]

Guderian immediately seized the initiative and pushed deep into the enemy's territory with his Panzers the moment they had crossed the Meuse River. The blitzkrieg that now emerged in outline revolutionized the operational nature of war that had prevailed until then. It signified a major switch from *linear* to *nonlinear* combat operations. To that extent, there were two simultaneous disputes during the advance to the Channel coast: one of them took place on the battlefield; the other one occurred among the German general officer corps. The traditionalists showed that they were still trapped in the linear way of thinking. Their instinctive fear of gaps and exposed flanks came from a time when there were as yet no Panzers. The advance of the completely isolated Panzer divisions through the enemy's rear areas was a dizzying proposition to them. On top of that came the breathtaking tempo of that attack. This is why they repeatedly demanded the slowing of the advance of the Panzers so that the infantry divisions assigned to provide flank protection could close up.

For the progressives, on the other hand, first and foremost Guderian, things could not go fast enough. The latter had said that "any hesitation means strengthening the enemy."[5] Here is his watchword: "So long as you yourself stay in motion, so long will you also keep the enemy in motion and prevent him from getting a strong foothold."[6] He was not afraid of exposed flanks but rather believed that confusing the enemy was the best flank protection. During the preceding years, Guderian had to do an intensive job of persuasion among his Panzer soldiers to help them get rid of their deep-seated fear of a threat to their flanks. So he stated at one time: "Exposed flanks are the nicest thing there is for Panzer units; the longer they are, the better."[7]

Guderian's Temporary Relief on 17 May

The dispute within the German general officer corps culminated in the controversy between Guderian and Kleist who belonged to the old school of operational thinking. At 2230 on 13 May, the day of the Meuse River crossing, Guderian ordered an attack for the next day with the main effort "along the Aisne toward Rethel."[8] That directive probably sprang from a touch of euphoria; after all, Rethel was fifty kilometers away as the crow flies. On the following day, however, the general bug of confidence in victory infected the rather cautious von Kleist. And so, at 1830, agreeing with Guderian, he ordered that the troops were to push all the way to Rethel by 15 May. Then Kleist began to worry again about his left flank. He canceled his order and instead, at 2200, specified that the attack be pushed only to the line Montigny-Bouvellemont. However, that line was only four kilometers from the line that had been reached on 14 May. Guderian reacted impulsively; he pressured his superior and accused him of "giving victory away" as a result of his order. His superior finally gave in and ordered the movement to be continued again all the way to Rethel.[9] The same procedure was repeated on the next day, 15 May, because Kleist wanted to stop the Panzers once again. Here is how Guderian described this incident in his *Memoirs:* "I neither would nor could agree to these orders, which involved the sacrifice of the element of surprise we had gained and of the whole initial success that we had achieved."[10]

In his energetic fashion, he once again got release for the movement for twenty-four hours, whereupon he ordered his soldiers "relentlessly onward."[11] The next day, 16 May, brought an overwhelming success. In the morning came the final breakthrough of the chain of hills to the west of the Ardennes Canal, where the French had made a last attempt to seal off the Sedan bridgehead. From there on, the Panzer formations pushed to the west almost unhindered. In the meantime, the so-called operational command echelon had lost control of the operations. The Panzer force instead led itself. As previously mentioned, the episode that took place on that day in the market square of Montcornet is characteristic of this. Guderian and Kempf met, although the latter's 6th Panzer Division was actually under Panzer Corps Reinhardt. Both generals congratulated each other on their success; then they began to untangle their tangled-up columns and distributed among themselves the advance routes for the continued attack. That actually should have been von Kleist's job. The first reconnaissance units reached the Oise River on that same evening. The following story indicates what a euphoric mood the German soldiers were in at that time: "During the next several days, our Panzer wedge pushed from Sedan in the direction toward the Channel coast. The strategists had given that operation the name 'Sickle Cut.' . . . Of course, we knew nothing about the strategic intentions but we were euphoric. . . . We sat in our vehicles, dust-covered, dead-tired, but all wound up."[12]

This euphoria was quite in keeping with the actual military situation because the enemy's resistance had been broken. Winston Churchill writes on that in his wartime memoirs, *The Second World War:* "The German tanks—the dreaded 'chars allemands'—ranged freely through the open country . . . without the slightest opposition, their officers looking out of the open cupolas and waving jauntily to the inhabitants. Eye-witnesses spoke of crowds of French prisoners marching along with them, many still carrying their rifles, which were from time to time collected and broken under the tanks. I was shocked by the utter failure to grapple with the German armour . . . and by the swift collapse of all French resistance once the fighting front had been pierced."[13] There was nothing that could have stopped the German Panzers—except their own leadership.

Early in the morning on 17 May, Guderian received the order from Panzer Group Kleist to stop the attack immediately. He himself was directed to report to the airfield at Montcornet by 0700. Von Kleist arrived there punctually by plane. He was so furious that he forgot to greet Guderian and instead accused him of disregarding his halt order and having continued the attack arbitrarily and without authorization. According to Guderian's version, the dispute culminated in the following scene: "When the first storm was passed, and he had stopped to draw a breath, I asked that I might be relieved of my command. General von Kleist was momentarily taken aback, but then he nodded and ordered me to hand over my command to the most senior general of my corps. And that was the end of our conversation."[14] Thereupon, Generalleutnant [Rudolf] Veiel, the commander of the 2d Panzer Division, was given command of the corps, and Generalmajor [Heinrich] von Prittwitz [und Gaffron] took over his job.

The odd thing about the "command crisis at Montcornet" was that Guderian—who had consistently ignored the instructions he got from his superior—was unjustly accused on this occasion. The crisis had sprung from the development of a paradoxical situation. At around 0045 on 17 May, Guderian received an order from Panzer Group

Kleist that had been sent out at 1630 on 16 May. It prohibited the crossing of the Vervins-Montcornet-Dizy-le-Gros line on 17 May. Only "strong advance detachments" were to be sent up front to seize the bridges across the Oise River.[15] However, Panzer Corps Guderian had already pushed far beyond the "halt line"—that became known only after the fact—for a distance of thirty kilometers on the day before. Guderian thus quickly realized that the ordnance officer, who was to bring this order, could no longer reach him in time. He therefore believed the order to be outdated and radioed to Panzer Group Kleist that he would continue to attack.

The "Montcornet command crisis" caused tremendous excitement all the way to the highest command authorities. In the afternoon, List, the commander in chief of Twelfth Army, to whom the Panzer Group had been subordinated since 15 May, turned up at Guderian's headquarters. List did everything he could to calm things down and, by direction of von Rundstedt, restored Guderian to his command. At the same time, he managed a conciliatory compromise with the approval of Army Group A. He allowed Guderian to push "strong reconnaissance forces" forward on the condition that Guderian would not move his corps command post forward.

Guderian took this golden opportunity. He immediately attacked again with his Panzers, but he, of course, now no longer issued his orders directly by radio but initially routed them via field telephones to the corps command post that had been left behind as a kind of telephone exchange. The command post was connected with his advanced command echelon by a four-kilometer-long field cable. Thus, Guderian had no need to send radio messages any longer and could not be located by the monitoring service of the next-higher command authorities.

Hitler's Flank Panic

> *Until 18 May 1940, in other words, in its decisive initial phase after the breakthrough along the Meuse River, "Operation Sickle Cut" . . . continued to be a movement that was not permitted by Hitler and with regard to which generals risked their necks.*[16]
>
> Wolfgang Paul, *Brennpunkte. Geschichte der 6. Panzerdivision* (Focal Point: The History of the 6th Panzer Division)

In the opinion of Panzer expert von Mellenthin, only two decisive mistakes were made in the campaign in the west: the halt order of Montcornet and the halt order of Dunkirk.[17] One may even argue that the "miracle of Dunkirk" would hardly have been possible without the brakes having been put on the German attack between 16 and 18 May.[18] The French front was about to collapse when the delay in the German advance brought an unexpected breathing spell. On 16 May, most units of the Ninth Army had to be considered as having been smashed. General [Henri] Giraud replaced Corap, the commander in chief of that army, on 15 May. Even the latter was not able to reorganize the remnants of that army. Instead, the French continued their retreat, which finally turned into flight. It appears almost symptomatic that Giraud was captured a few days later by a field kitchen detachment of the 11th Panzer Regiment that was just in the process of moving into a shed in which the general had been hiding. On 16 May, there was an approximately hundred-kilometer-wide gap in the front line. The German Panzers, however, were not allowed to push into that gap and so the French high command managed once again to stabilize the front line along the Oise and Sambre rivers. That leads to the question as to who is responsible for this fatal halt order.

Von Kleist cannot be considered in this connection. As Guderian found out only later, von Kleist followed orders from higher-ups, but did so only reluctantly. As Zeitzler, his chief of staff at that time, described it later, von Kleist had to stop the attack "with a heavy heart."[19] At this point, one must put into perspective the stereotype of the "reactionary Cavalry Officer Kleist," above all because his only function was believed to be to "constantly put the brakes" on Guderian. In reality, he held a midway position between the traditionalists and the progressives and appeared to be a conservative counterpole only in contrast to the impetuous innovator Guderian. Until 17 May he covered up for the actions of his subordinate who more and more frequently overstepped the bounds to the point of disobedience. For example, after the breakthrough at Sedan, Kleist sent cosmetic situation reports to army group because Guderian would certainly have been stopped immediately if the higher-ranking superiors had gotten an unadorned picture of the situation.

List, the commander in chief of Twelfth Army, only acted as a "relay station" in passing on the halt order, which he had gotten from Army Group A. Rundstedt's headquarters, of course, can be considered one of the "inhibiting factors." The war diary of Army Group A contains the following entry on 15 May (at 2330): "For the first time, one must consider that it might become necessary to temporarily stop the motorized units along the Oise River. In particular, the O.B. [commander in chief] (Rundstedt) emphasized that the enemy must under no circumstances achieve even any only local success along the Aisne River or, later on, in the area around Laon. That would be more harmful to the operation as a whole than would be the case if we temporarily 'slowed' the tempo of our motorized units."[20]

On the morning of 16 May, von Rundstedt decided temporarily to stop the Panzer formations to enable the following infantry divisions "to close up." The Beaumont-Montcornet Line was to be crossed only by advance detachments. On that same day, he directed that crossing the Sambre-Oise Line would be made contingent upon his approval. Nevertheless, he cannot be considered to be the only person responsible for the Montcornet halt order. As Halder emphasized, it was much more Hitler who stopped the Panzers beyond that point "by personal order" on 17 and 18 May.[21] To do that, the dictator interfered in the course of operations by means of verbal instructions and furthermore issued Directive No. 12.[22] Kleist, Manstein, Blumentritt, and Heusinger also emphasized that Hitler bears the responsibility for this senseless interruption of the operation.[23] Guderian also expresses his astonishment and his disappointment over the fact that "Hitler himself"—who after all had approved the bold idea behind this attack operation—"would order our advance to be stopped at once."[24] Guderian was not the only one who was unable to catch the meaning of that instruction. This became particularly clear in a telephone conversation whose content Heusinger—later the inspector general of the German Bundeswehr (Federal Armed Forces)—managed to preserve. At that time, in his capacity as deputy chief for operations of the Operations Section, army general staff, he had to forward Hitler's halt order to headquarters, Army Group A. Here is its explosive content: "The Führer has ordered: 'The bulk of the Panzer formations will not cross the line Le Cateau-Laon to the West.' "

Heusinger's man at the other end of the line was von Tresckow, who later stood out in the resistance against Hitler. Tresckow reacted furiously: "But that is sheer madness. We have got the whole thing rolling now. We have to get to the Coast as quickly as possible. And we are supposed to stop now? Did somebody change the operations plan? And why?"[25]

Hitler provided the justification for this step on 17 May in the headquarters of von Rundstedt in Bastogne. The war diary of Army Group A contains the following entry on that point: "The Führer . . . underscores the special significance of the southern flank not only to the operations of the Army as a whole but also in political and psychological terms. Under no circumstances must there be, at this particular moment, anywhere, any setback that would give a fatal boost not only to the military but also above all to the political leadership of our enemy. At this particular moment, the decision is not to be found so much in a rapid thrust to the Channel Coast but rather . . . in as quickly as possible establishing absolutely reliable defense readiness along the Aisne, in the area around Laon, and later on, along the Somme."[26]

It was not just at Dunkirk but earlier already at Montcornet that the politician Hitler—something entirely new in German military history—massively interfered in the course of a military operation. To that extent, 17 May 1940 marks a break. The German general staff, which at that time was highly regarded all over the world, constituted an intellectual elite whose decisions were guided by sober professionalism. Now an element of incalculability and even irrationality had infiltrated this institution. The problem was not so much Hitler's deficient military knowledge but rather the dependence on his extreme mood swings. The Führer again and again swung back and forth between extreme overestimation of the possibilities and exaggerated disaster moods.[27] The strange thing was that his nervousness grew more and more during Operation Sickle Cut, the more clearly success began to emerge. Hitler, who allegedly was the only one who was convinced of the operation's success, could hardly grasp the facts when he learned of the final breakthrough at Sedan and stammered about a "miracle."[28] Horrified, he looked at the situation map as the German Panzers, without any units along their flanks, pushed forward in the form of a narrow sickle. On 17 May

Halder wrote on that point in his own personal war diary: "An unpleasant day. The Fuehrer is terribly nervous. Frightened by his own success, he is afraid to take any chances and so he would rather pull the reins on us. Puts forward the excuse that it is all because of his concern for the left flank!"[29] On 18 May, likewise, Halder reports about a "highly unpleasant dispute" at Führer Headquarters: "The Fuehrer unaccountably keeps worrying about the south flank. He rages and screams that we are on the best way to ruin the whole campaign and that we are leading up to a defeat."[30]

Thus, the Panzer formations were forced mostly "to mark time" for about two days. The advance was secretly continued during that phase in some sectors just the same due to the unauthorized actions of individual commanders who accepted a high risk. Rommel's thrust at Avesnes, which represents a noteworthy example of military disobedience, will be covered in detail later on. As later at Dunkirk, Halder already tried to circumvent the halt order at Montcornet. He thought he could interpret this instruction as applying only to the rear area supply services but not to the Panzer spearheads.[31] At least, the order was loosened up to the effect that La Cateau and St. Quentin, which were on the other side of the designated holding line, were allowed to be taken "with strong advance detachments." But when Hitler figured out Halder's intentions, he responded with a fit of rage and ordered army headquarters "in the severest manner" immediately to take the "necessary measures" to cover the south flank.[32] Only at 1800 on 18 May, after another situation briefing, did the army chief of staff secure the "permission to start for the next day."[33]

The threat from the south, which seemed to hypnotize Hitler, in reality did not exist at all. Halder said later: "The Army was at all times most accurately informed by Luftwaffe reconnaissance. I was able to command as if during a map exercise."[34] Liß, at that time chief of the Foreign Armies West Section of Army Intelligence, also reported that it was already realized on 15 May that there was no threat whatsoever of counteroffensive against the southern flank: "On the German side, we got the impression that the French command was completely paralyzed. Five days had gone by and we were still not able to detect anything pointing to a major counteroperation."[35] In this connection, he emphasized: "It is certain that the French command, on 15 May, at all echelons, dropped the idea of mounting a counterattack against the southern flank of the breakthrough."[36]

Hitler's military advisers, who based their evaluations on precise and clear situation reports of the Army Intelligence Service's Foreign Armies West, tried in vain to talk him out of his instinctive fright. The dictator was mesmerized by the mad delusion of a repeat of the "miracle on the Marne," which, in September 1914, led to the failure of the Schlieffen plan. At that time, the German right-wing army had approached all the way to Paris across the Marne River. Spotting the Eiffel Tower in the distance, the German troops thought that victory was within their grasp when they were hit in the exposed flank by a French surprise attack. This trauma obviously depressed Hitler when, on 18 May, while the Panzers were still stopped, he wrote to Mussolini: "The 1914

Miracle on the Marne will not be repeated!"[37] No matter how logical, there was no argument that could rid him of his flank fright. As Manstein noted rather ironically, he constantly had the specter of a threatening setback before his eyes.[38]

During this phase, there was a complete mood swing in two men who were as opposite as Hitler and Halder. It was, of all people, Hitler who, being a gambler by nature, accepted almost criminal risks in his foreign policy adventures but was suddenly scared stiff by his own courage and found himself at the brink of a nervous breakdown. Halder, on the other hand, suddenly exuded self-confidence and belief in victory. As he confided to his diary on 16 May, "Our breakthrough wedge is developing in a positively classical manner."[39] The entries on 17 May contain the following rather noteworthy sentence: "A great decision must be taken now!"[40]

In this situation, Halder fell back to that bold idea that he had rejected at the time in connection with Manstein's operations draft. To prevent the formation of a solid Allied defensive front along the Somme and Aisne rivers, strong elements of Army Group A were no longer to march to the coast but were to wheel southwest via Compiègne. Reinforced by the Fourth Army as well as some Panzer divisions, Army Group B was given the job of encircling and smashing the enemy forces that were already breaking up along the Channel coast. Now Halder became "more Mansteinish" than his rival. While the latter wanted to defeat the Allies in two separate major operations [Case Yellow and Case Red] he now sought success "in one fell swoop"—as did Schlieffen once upon a time.[41] Hitler was aghast at this breathtakingly bold idea and rejected it gruffly.[42] That meant that Manstein's idea of an "offensive solution for covering the south flank"[43] had been filed away, and so the French high command managed to build up a new defensive front along the Somme and Aisne.

In a subsequent presentation, Liß also addressed the question as to whether it would have been possible, simultaneously with the push to the Somme River mouth, "also to smash the French forces that were being assembled along the Aisne River by means of a second push to the south." He arrived at a positive result: "In retrospect, one might regret that this operation did not materialize. From what we know today about the enemy situation at that time, it would probably have been successful and would then have shortened the entire campaign by several weeks."[44]

The Montcornet halt order, when Hitler in panic pulled the emergency brake, represents the dictator's first interference in Operation Sickle Cut. The rejection of Halder's intended southwest wheel by elements of Army Group A was the second intervention. Here, again, Hitler took the wheels of action, so to speak, away from the chief of the general staff who was responsible for the execution of the operation. His order to build up a defense front along the southern front, specifically, using divisions that until then had been earmarked for the immediate thrust to the Channel coast, was the third interference. Originally, Halder had planned to push west with the Fourth and Twelfth Armies and to use the Second Army, following behind, to screen the southern flank. In the meantime, Hitler had so slipped into the flank psychosis that he stopped the Twelfth Army in the midst of its attack movement and ordered it to be employed for static defense along the Aisne River. And so the Second Army had to be inserted in the gap between the Fourth and Twelfth Armies.[45] That delayed the advance even further. The threat from the left flank, however, proved to have been a phantom. The actual situation of the Allies shows how irrational Hitler's fear of a serious enemy threat was.

Why the French Counterattack Did Not Come

Right now, it looks like the biggest military catastrophe in history.[46]

General [William] Ironside, the British
Chief of the [Imperial] General Staff, commenting on the
situation of the Allies as of 17 May 1940

The French army had already lost the campaign on 14 May, but its leaders did not yet know that. The sudden awakening during the following days was all the more horrible. Georges, the commander in chief of the northeast front, seems to have been the only one who had a premonition of catastrophe. He suffered a nervous breakdown when, early in the morning on 14 May, he was informed of the breakthrough at Sedan. General [André] Beaufre was a witness to this oppressive scene: "The atmosphere was that of a family in which there had just been a death. Georges . . . terribly pale. 'Our front has been broken at Sedan! There has been a collapse. . . .' He flung himself into a chair and burst into tears. . . . He was the first man I had seen weep during this campaign. Alas, there were to be others. It made a terrible impression on me. . . . Doumenc [the chief of the general staff], taken aback by this greeting, reacted immediately. 'General, this is war and in war things like this are bound to happen!' "[47]

Georges, who had gotten hardly any sleep since the start of the German blitz offensive, quickly recovered from this sudden faint feeling. But all the measures he initiated to check the German thrust proved in vain. In the evening, the French prime minister Reynaud sent the following telegram to Winston Churchill in London: "The situation is really very serious. The German Army has pierced our fortified lines south of Sedan. . . . Between Sedan and Paris there are no more fortifications comparable to those."[48]

Churchill, on the other hand, thought that the French prime minister's reaction was exaggerated. He did not wish to grasp the seriousness of the situation even when Reynaud awakened him with a phone call the next morning at 0730 on 15 May. The French prime minister excitedly reported not only about German Panzers that were streaming through the breach at Sedan but also added: "We are defeated; we have lost the battle."[49] Churchill tried to calm him down: "All experience shows that the offensive will come to an end after a while. I remember the 21st of March 1918. After five or six days, they have to halt for supplies, and the opportunity for counterattack is presented."[50] The French prime minister stuck to his pessimistic situation estimate whereupon Churchill promised immediately to visit him in Paris.

On that same evening, the French supreme commander Gamelin had to make full disclosure and admit the unavoidable defeat. If the American ambassador in Paris, William Bullitt, had not accidentally been an eyewitness to this historical moment, then posterity would never have learned of that fateful dialog. Thus, President Roosevelt was informed about France's inevitable military disaster that same evening.

Bullitt was in the office of French war minister Daladier at 2030 on 15 May when a telephone call from Gamelin was put through. While the latter reported on the latest situation at the front, Daladier sat there "totally incredulous and stupefied." Suddenly he shouted: "No! What you tell me is not possible! You must be wrong! It's impossible!" Gamelin had reported that a German Panzer column had broken through and was approaching Rethel and Laon (130 kilometers northeast of Paris). Thereupon, Daladier screamed into the phone: "Then you must counterattack at once, like 1918!" But Gamelin retorted: "With what? I don't have the reserves." As Bullitt reports, Daladier now slumped while his facial features became petrified. Unbelieving, he asked: "Then the French Army is finished?" Gamelin replied: "It's finished."[51]

From the British angle, probably the most dramatic scene of the campaign took place not on the battlefield but in the French Foreign Ministry at the Quai d'Orsay in Paris. There, Winston Churchill, who had hurried over from London on the morning of 16 May, met Reynaud and Daladier. The French supreme commander Gamelin stood next to a big situation map where the front line had been drawn with black ink. The front line revealed "a small but sinister bulge at Sedan." At first, Gamelin delivered a situation briefing with his usual rhetorical brilliance. After he finished, Churchill wanted to know where the strategic reserve was. He repeated this question in his own inimitable French: "*Où est la masse de manoeuvre?*" (Where is the strategic reserve?)[52]

Gamelin's reply was shattering; it consisted of one single word: "*Aucune*" (None)—it was no more. There was a long silence in the room. From the window, one could see smoke clouds rising from the inner courtyard of the Foreign Ministry. Venerable old officials came with pushcarts full of files that were to be burned. Obviously, the evacuation of Paris was already under way. Winston Churchill later wrote: "I was dumbfounded. What were we to think of the great French Army and its highest chiefs? It had never occurred to me that any commanders having to defend five hundred miles [804 kilometers] of engaged front would have left themselves unprovided with a mass of manoeuvre. . . . I admit this was one of the greatest surprises I have had in my life."[53]

As noted earlier, Seventh Army originally had been kept as operational reserve in the area around Reims. Then, on orders from Gamelin, it had been shifted to extreme left wing, where it was to advance toward Holland as part of the Dyle-Breda maneuver. At that time, Georges had vehemently protested against this measure because he now no longer had any major cohesive reserve. Precisely what he had warned against had now happened. The Germans attacked with their point of main effort from an entirely different direction, but he no longer had any operational possibility of immediately reacting to that. For Supreme Commander Gamelin this was tantamount to an operational declaration of bankruptcy just a few days after the start of the campaign. As Colonel Minart wrote, "the wind of panic" blew through Gamelin's headquarters in the Château de Vincennes in the evening of 16 May. The supreme commander himself was running around, looking sad. Nobody dared to approach him. Everybody knew that the battle was lost.[54]

At this point we come to the question as to why the French, in view of the incipient catastrophe, did not fall back on their far superior armored force of 3,254 battle tanks. Here again, we can see the differing employment principles. The Germans had combined their fighting vehicles in major, operational formations and used them at the point of main effort. The bulk of the French tanks, however, was scattered along the entire front line, in tiny formations, "like small change."[55] The numerous independent tank battalions, however, could only inflict tactical pinpricks. The only outfits that were suitable for operational countermeasures were the Prioux Cavalry Corps and the four armored divisions that had very recently been organized only as a reaction to the German Panzer successes during the Polish campaign. The employment of French armor in this campaign turned into a cascade of tragedies. For example, the Prioux Cavalry Corps achieved a tactical success in the north but brought about the exact opposite in operational terms because it was employed in the wrong place. The French 1st Armored Division, as stated earlier, was wiped out near Flavion when a number of Char B battle tanks simply ran out of gas. The French 3d Armored Division, again, had a unique opportunity at Sedan to stop the Panzer Corps Guderian with a flank attack. However, Flavigny canceled his attack order at the last moment. That left only the 2d and 4th Armored Divisions, whose actions will be described shortly.

The Breakup of 2d Armored Division in the Whirlpool of Mobile Warfare. Among all of the French armored formations, the 2d Armored Division suffered the saddest fate.[56] The other armored divisions were wiped out only after strong resistance and after inflicting considerable losses on the enemy, but the French 2d Armored Division perished without having fought a single coherent combat action. The blame for this can be found in the hectic sequence of contradictory orders issued by the French command that was confused by the German attack tempo. Between 11 and 15 May, General Bruché received five different operations orders:

(1) Assemble as a reserve for the intervention forces advancing into Belgium.
(2) Support the First Army.
(3) Counterattack toward Dinant as part of Ninth Army.
(4) Move into a standby area at Signy-l'Abbaye.
(5) Defend the Oise-Sambre Canal Sector as part of Sixth Army.[57]

The result was that the French 2d Armored Division was unable to accomplish any of these missions and simply broke up in chaos. The fateful aspect here was that the tracked vehicles had to be transported on railroad flatcars, whereas the wheeled vehicles advanced separately on roads. That meant that cohesion was lost. Bruché no longer had any picture of where his troops were wandering around. On the morning of 16 May, the division was to report its location to Georges's headquarters, but, at that time, it could locate only seven out of the twelve tank companies. Those seven companies were scattered in an oval area with a width of eighty kilometers and a depth of sixty kilometers.[58] Moreover, higher headquarters did not know how far the German Panzer spearheads had already pushed. Thus, during their march to the designated assembly area at Signy-l'Abbaye some of Bruché's units bumped into Reinhardt's Panzers "to be cut up."

On 15 May, during its push from Monthermé to Montcornet the 6th Panzer Division had already rolled over several French supply convoys. On 16 May, Reinhardt managed to move his 8th Panzer Division up also. Now, this newly formed Panzer wedge thrust its way right through the middle of the scattered elements of Bruché's division, which was thus torn apart into two halves along the Liart-Montcornet Line. As if things could get any worse, most of the supply elements with the fuel trucks and the repair units were in the south, whereas the French tanks were cut off from them farther north. A number of Char B battle tanks were standing on the railroad flatcars, almost without gas, in the unloading stations, when they were surprised by Reinhardt's Panzers. A later report prepared by the Parliamentary Investigating Commission said: "As of 16 May, there is no longer any 2d Armored Division; there are only scattered units whose commanders are trying as best they can to maintain order and to carry out all kinds of amended orders, to avoid air raids and German Panzer spearheads, while command agencies of all kinds, trying to get through to them, only add to the confusion."[59]

De Gaulle's 4th Armored Division Counterattacks at Montcornet. At the start of the campaign, the French Army, strictly speaking, only had three armored divisions because the 4th Armored Division was still being organized. To that extent it seems paradoxical that, of all of these divisions, this one was able to cause the Germans the most trouble. Its commander, however, was none other than Col. [Charles] de Gaulle, later president of France. He had advocated ideas similar to Guderian's for many years and had demanded the creation of an operational armored force.[60] What he wrote in 1934 about the future role of tanks seems almost clairvoyant: "They will clear the way for tremendous victories. . . . Their swift thrusts, aimed deep into enemy territory, will cause the enemy's collapse, the way the fall of a pillar sometimes can bring a cathedral to the point of collapse."[61] The conservatively oriented general officer corps had rejected those ideas. When he was given his command on 11 May 1940, Georges therefore told him: "There, de Gaulle! For you who have for so long held the ideas which the enemy is putting into practice, here is the chance to act."[62]

Now, when it was too late, when the German Panzers had created chaos along and behind the front, de Gaulle was at last to be allowed to implement his ideas to bring about a turning point. In his *Memoirs,* he describes how hopeless the situation had become:

> Miserable processions of refugees crowded along all the roads coming from the north. I saw, also, a good many soldiers who had lost their weapons. They belonged to the troops routed by the Panzers during the preceding days. Caught up, as they fled, by the enemy's mechanized detachments, they had been ordered to throw away their arms and make off to the south so as not to clutter up the roads. "We haven't time," they had been told, "to take you prisoners!" . . . Then, at the sight of those bewildered people and of those soldiers in rout, at the tale, too, of that contemptuous piece of insolence of the enemy's, I felt myself borne up by a limitless fury. Ah! It's too stupid! The war is beginning as badly as it could.[63]

Although the French 4th Armored Division had not been completely organized, it was immediately thrown into the battle. Its first mission was to screen the buildup of a new defense line in the Laon area along the Aisne River. De Gaulle decided to attack. He wanted to thrust into the flank of the German Panzer formations that were advancing to the north thereof and interrupt their rear communications lines by taking the Montcornet highway intersection. On the morning of 17 May, he did have three and a half tank battalions but very few supporting forces; infantry had not as yet arrived. Still, he did not want to lose any time and immediately attacked with his tanks. He was lucky. His thrust was aimed precisely at the crucial point, that is, the area around Montcornet, where the Panzer Corps Guderian had its headquarters, along with the rear area services of the 1st Panzer Division. Moreover, the Germans did not expect such a bold flank attack because, in view of the otherwise customary French tank employment tactics, he was bound to appear utterly atypical.

The attack began rather promisingly because only isolated security units protected the southern flank of the German breakthrough corridor. The French tank columns ran into some vehicle convoys that they managed to shoot up with their cannon. As they finally approached Montcornet, the situation seemed to become very critical for the Germans. The first officer who noticed this was Graf von Kielmansegg, the supply officer of the 1st Panzer Division: "Leaving Montcornet and continuing along the main highway—the Division's only route of advance—I saw several Germans running back toward me. They were engineers who said that there were French tanks coming after them! I did not want to believe that because the direction in which they pointed was the direction of our own front line."[64]

Von Kielmansegg recognized the danger, ordered the engineers immediately to put up a mine barrier, and improvised a defensive position with randomly collected troops. He was lucky to find some antitank and flak guns. He managed to move supply convoys to safety, immediately to the south, from the village of Lislet, before French tanks overran the village. Finally, Kielmansegg was able to throw into the fight some German Panzers that had just come back from the repair depot. The French attack was stopped in the end. Dive-bombers of the VIII Air Corps showed up in the afternoon and pounced on de Gaulle's formations. In turn, he was now threatened in his flank. In the meantime, 10th Panzer Division had been taken out of the fighting at Stonne and had been moved up into the area of Montcornet. "We were lost children thirty kilometers in advance of the Aisne River," de Gaulle later described this situation.[65] Thus, all he could do was to retreat.[66]

Interestingly enough, the two main actors at that time happened to meet some years after the war. At that time, de Gaulle was the president of France and resided in Élysée-Palace in Paris where he had invited General Graf von Kielmansegg, who meanwhile had become commander in chief of NATO Forces in Central Europe. The latter assured him during their conversation that, in the entire campaign, the French tank thrust at Montcornet was the only French counterattack that "was completely correct in terms of time, place, and direction."[67]

De Gaulle attacked again just two days after his thrust toward Montcornet, specifically against Crécy-sur-Serre, which was located about thirty kilometers farther to the west. Once again it was mainly due to the Luftwaffe that this threat to the German left flank was quickly sealed off. The French 4th Armored Division, on the other hand, once again had to fight without support from French aircraft. Later, de Gaulle was reproached for having informed the French Air Force neither about the time nor the direction of his attack. That appears symptomatic inasmuch as, in his theoretical writings, he mentioned close coordination between armor and air only in passing.[68] This is one of the main differences that distinguishes him from Guderian in whose concepts Panzers and aircraft are a pair of twins. Looking at it from the purely technical aspect, however, close cooperation with the French air force would hardly have been possible anyway because the French armed forces—in contrast to the Wehrmacht—had neither suitable liaison staffs nor suitable radios. And so, de Gaulle's flank attacks had no lasting effect.

Rommel's Unauthorized Push at Avesnes

Your raid cost me a sleepless night.[69]

Hitler's admonition to Rommel after the latter's "private offensive" at Avesnes

Rommel's night attack at Avesnes is probably the most spectacular individual operation during the campaign. This operation earned the 7th Panzer Division, which was led by Rommel, the French nickname "*la division fantôme*" (the ghost division).[70] The

Montcornet halt order had stopped not only Panzer Group Kleist but also Panzer Corps Hoth, which was under Fourth Army. While it was possible to stop Guderian along the northern flank of the breakthrough wedge, Rommel completely broke out of the straitjacket of the orders he got. As noted earlier, when the tank battle of Flavion was still in progress, he had pushed west on 15 May and approached the Belgian-French border on 16 May. Behind it was the so-called extended Maginot Line, which was not nearly as well developed as the real Maginot Line that ended at La Ferté. At 0750 on 16 May, headquarters, Fourth Army, received an order that very clearly forbade breaking through this fortification line: "The directive from Army Group, that the lead elements are for the time being not to cross the French fortifications southeast of Maubeuge and providing enough of a security screen in the north, assumes increased significance."[71]

The night before von Sodenstern, the chief of staff of Army Group A, had already ruled a swift move against the fortification line as impractical. Instead, the Panzers were to be spared for "subsequent missions."[72] The chief of staff of Fourth Army also commented along these lines. If the extended Maginot Line should turn out to be heavily occupied, then he wanted to allow Panzer Corps Hoth "to rest and freshen up." Instead, the V Corps with the 87th and 62d Infantry Divisions would achieve the breakthrough.[73] Only then was the Panzer Corps to be employed for the thrust deep into enemy territory. This once again brought up the same question as during the map exercises for the breakthrough at Sedan: Should the Panzers be up front or should the infantry lead? When von Brauchitsch, the commander in chief of the army, arrived at headquarters, Fourth Army, on the afternoon of 16 May, he likewise spoke in favor of giving the Panzers a break soon. He wanted to keep them "on a shorter leash."[74] Moreover, he rejected the idea of pushing the advance to the west and instead demanded that the northern flank be screened. Finally, he was afraid that the Allied intervention troops that advanced into Belgium might launch a counterattack into the right flank of the Fourth Army.

The files show contradictory data as to how the orders were issued at Fourth Army in the afternoon and evening of 16 May. The report by Hauptmann i.G. [Hans] Meier-Welcker appears most reliable here.[75] In his capacity as administrative officer of Fourth Army, he accompanied his commander in chief, von Kluge, on a trip to the front on 16 May and prepared a report on it.[76] According to that report, at 1225 Kluge ordered 7th Panzer Division to advance toward the French border and to scout the fortification line behind it. But he emphasized: "No breakthrough!"[77] This directive was also in keeping with the army order for 16 May: "We will mount a swift surprise attack against the French border fortifications only if the weakness of the garrison promises a sure success. There will be no push to the west beyond those lines, into the enemy rear areas, without approval from Army."[78]

With no indications whatsoever of an enemy counterattack reported from the northern flank, von Kluge decided around 1445 to deviate partly from the orders received from army group and to attempt a limited push to the west by the Panzers. Thereupon, Hoth immediately radioed the order to 7th Panzer Division to punch through the French fortifications and to attack in the direction of Avesnes.[79] This directive was at first only a preliminary order. The written corps order that restricted the type of advance in terms of time and place arrived late at the command post of 7th Panzer Division. That was to have considerable consequences because, at that moment, Rommel and his Panzers had already disappeared.

The French border was crossed around 1800 at Clairfayts. Soon thereafter, Rommel saw the sharp contours of the extended Maginot Line with its concrete bunkers, armored cupolas, minefields, and barbed wire entanglements. Any other general probably would have hesitated and mounted the attack on the next day under more favorable conditions. After all, support from heavy artillery, additional infantry, and Luftwaffe dive-bombers had been promised. That would have meant forgoing the element of surprise. Rommel could not resist the temptation, contrary to instructions from his superiors, to attempt a sudden surprise attack. After all, when he was an assault team leader during World War I, he again and again achieved astonishing successes as a result of surprise raids. But what he wanted to attempt now was something entirely novel in military history: a massive Panzer night attack against a well-fortified position, without preparation, and straight from the move. The surprise was complete. Rommel's advance detachment punched smack into the first lines of the enemy around 1830 before the latter was able to react. Then, of course, the French defenders of the 84th Regiment, 101st Fortress Infantry Division, offered considerable resistance.[80] A German Panzer commander reported encountering the French fortified positions: "It [the bunker] spits fire. Two vehicles are knocked out; and also from the right an anti-tank gun fires and hits the Command tank of the heavy company. The radio operator has a leg shot off, commander unhurt. I am close by with my tank, but take cover. Enemy artillery fires heavily on us with medium calibre guns. How are we going to get through the bunker line? Big question. In front of us is a thick wire entanglement, behind it a broad and deep panzer ditch, and in the middle of the road anti-tank obstacles have been built. . . . Meanwhile it is night."[81]

In the meantime, however, the Panzers had already penetrated so far into the enemy's field works that they were able to neutralize some dangerous bunkers by firing on the gun ports. Artillery fire neutralized the rear portions of the fortified zone. The men of the motorcycle rifle battalion attacked antitank gun positions and machine-gun nests under cover of falling darkness. The engineers once again accomplished the primary mission during the actual breakthrough phase. They put concrete pillboxes out of action with satchel charges and flamethrowers and blasted gaps in the barrier belts. Finally, they destroyed the roadblock west of Clairfayts that consisted of big, interconnected steel hedgehogs. The Panzers punched through this breach deep into the fortification zone, firing to both sides as they raced along. They were followed by the motorcycle riflemen on their motorcycles and by the reconnaissance battalion.

Around 2300, they punched through a second fortification line at Solre-le-Château.[82] By the light of the moon, the German soldiers now saw wide-open terrain before them. Rommel describes his feelings about this tremendous breakout in his diary: "The way to the West was now wide open. . . . We were through the Maginot Line! It was hardly conceivable. Twenty-two years before, we had stood for four and a half long years before this self-same enemy and had won victory after victory but yet finally lost the war. And now we had broken through the renowned Maginot Line and were driving deep into enemy territory. It was not just a beautiful dream. It was reality."[83]

Immediately thereafter, Rommel and his Panzers ran frontally into French artillery position that opened fire on them. He quickly made one of his typical decisions—he started on his escape forward and ordered his Panzers to race at the French guns at top speed, firing "from all barrels" while bouncing along. He was actually successful. Later, he commented on this: "The method that I have ordered, of driving into the enemy with all guns firing . . . has worked magnificently. It costs us a lot of ammunition, but it saves tanks and lives. The enemy have not found any answer to this method yet. When we come up on them like this, their nerves fail."[84]

Now he acted intuitively, like the former assault detachment leader he was, employing the same principle as Guderian. A successful breakthrough would be in vain if it were not immediately exploited by a thrust deep into enemy territory. He decided to continue to push on the road to Avesnes, in spite of the darkness. Happenstance would have it that the French 5th Motorized Infantry Division had set up a nighttime bivouac along this road. Its vehicles were parked to the left and right along the road, lined up neatly. In between, elements of the 18th Infantry Division and the French 1st Armored Division were spending the night. Suddenly, the German Panzers raced right through the vehicles that were lined up like targets in a shooting gallery, firing "broadsides from all barrels" on Rommel's command. They spread panic and terror, as indicated in the following report: "Hundreds upon hundreds of French soldiers and civilians are shaken out of their sleep by the Panzer regiment that thundered at top speed along the roads; their faces distorted with fear, they lay in the gutters and roadside ditches, to the right and left of the route of advance. The fire from the Panzer regiment reaches far into the area off to the side of the streets and causes boundless confusion during this night."[85]

Never again in this campaign were there such apocalyptic scenes as during the night of 16–17 May on the road from Solre-le-Château to Avesnes. The German Panzers literally crunched over the 5th Motorized Infantry Division while it was asleep. Even German soldiers, whose units a few hours later drove on this road during daylight were thunderstruck: "I have never seen anything like the scenes along Rommel's route of advance. His tanks had run into a French division coming down the same road, and they had just kept advancing right on past it. For the next five or six miles, there were hundreds of trucks and tanks, some driven into the ditches, others burned out, many still carrying dead or injured. More and more Frenchmen came out of the fields and woods with abject fear written on their faces and their hands in the air. From up front came the short, sharp crack of the guns of our tanks, which Rommel was personally directing—standing upright in his ACV [armored command vehicle] with two staff officers, his cap pushed back, urging everybody ahead."[86]

Around midnight, the Panzers rode into Avesnes. With his lead units, Rommel raced through it and did not stop until he got to the hills to the west of the town. In the meantime, contact within his column had broken off, so he waited for quite some time to enable the following units to close up. At last, one could hear the clanking of the approaching Panzers and the outfit continued its advance. In reality, however, those were French tanks, that is, the last sixteen tanks that were still left of the French 1st Armored Division that was decimated at Flavion. They also included some Char B tanks. They drew the Panzer battalion that had gotten stuck in Avesnes into a long-drawn-out firefight with many losses. Rommel had to stop his advance and send reinforcements. Under cover of darkness, Leutnant [Karl] Hanke,[87] riding in a Panzer IV, thrust into the rear of the French and smashed the tracks of some Char B tanks. The nighttime firefight in the streets of Avesnes was decided around 0400 and the last three tanks of the French 1st Armored Division began their retreat.

Bunker No. 2/152a (west of Clairfayts) was taken in the evening of 16 May during the breakthrough of Rommel's 7th Panzer Division as it punched through the extended Maginot Line. *Bundesarchiv Koblenz [Federal Archives]*

An artillery battalion of the 7th Panzer Division driving through Avesnes on 17 May. Knocked-out Hotchkiss 39 tanks of the 25th Tank Battalion, French 1st Armored Division, can be seen on both sides of the street. *Bundesarchiv Koblenz [Federal Archives]*

Now Rommel decided to make the most of his opportunities. He smashed right through the rows of confused enemy all the way to Landrecies, which was eighteen kilometers away, to seize the important bridge over the Sambre River there. Once again, his advance detachment ran into French elements that acted as if paralyzed by the surprising approach of the Panzers. A former Panzer commander reports that Rommel simply drove up to them and told them to throw their weapons away. The reaction was almost always the same: "Many willingly follow this command, others are surprised, but nowhere is there any sign of resistance. Several times his [Rommel's] tank men were questioned, somewhat hopefully: 'Anglais?' "[88]

Around 0600 the Sambre River bridge in Landrecies was taken in a swift assault. Rommel kept chasing forward as if possessed and allowed his Panzers to stop only as the point of the advance detachment reached the hilly terrain east of Le Cateau around 0630. In the meantime, not only ammunition but also fuel began to run out. Only now it began to dawn on Rommel into what a fatal situation he had maneuvered himself. He noticed that in his attack in the end only two Panzer battalions and a few motorcycle rifle platoons had followed him. The third Panzer battalion and the main body of the reconnaissance battalion had gotten stuck under way. The worst surprise was still in store for Rommel. In his impetuous advance, he failed to notice that he had conducted the entire push—almost fifty kilometers as the crow flies—with the advance detachment only! The main body of his division, including the two rifle regiments, was still in front of the extended Maginot Line on Belgian territory and in the meantime had settled down for the night!

There was big excitement at the division command post that had been left behind at Froid-Chapelle. Rommel's operations officer, Major i.G. Heidkämper, was now the only man in charge there and was unable to answer the nervous inquiries that were coming from corps who wanted to know where his commander and his Panzers had disappeared to. A written corps order arrived at 2230, giving permission for the continuation of the attack across the border fortifications only for the morning of 17 May: "7th Panzer Division will cross the line reached in the evening of 16 May at 0800 and, as its first attack objective, will seize Avesnes and will then stand by for further advance in the direction toward Landrecies."[89]

Radio contact with Rommel's command echelon had been lost rather mysteriously. Because almost all radio messages from 7th Panzer Division during that night are preserved in the records, one can clear up some things that simply don't rhyme.[90] It is thus striking to note that Rommel simply could not be reached, of all times, during the phases when he did not want to be stopped by his superiors under any circumstances. Radio contact had been lost for several hours and was not restored until 0340 on 17 May. This seems paradoxical inasmuch as Rommel, at the time of his last contact, had pushed fifteen kilometers farther to the west. Looking at it from the purely technical viewpoint, that could hardly have improved the radio contact situation. Rommel did not check in again on the radio until the fight for Avesnes was mostly decided and until he had created a fait accompli. It is also odd that there was in the meantime "good contact" with the command echelon of the motorcycle rifle battalion that was also a part of the advance detachment.[91] The radio equipment of Rommel's command echelon, however, was definitely better. At 0420 Heidkämper received an urgent order from corps at the division command post: "Do not advance beyond Avesnes."[92]

At that point in time, Rommel's command echelon was roughly in the same place where it had accepted the radio message at 0340. Now contact had been lost again in some strange fashion. The Operations Staff of the Panzer Corps also radioed several times "Stop immediately."[93] But it was all in vain. Rommel simply could not be reached. As a result of this unauthorized push, however, contact with the division command post was finally lost completely. Heidkämper, who was the only one left behind, stuck strictly to the corps order and allowed the division to move up toward Avesnes only around 0800. Now, a traffic jam in front of the French fortifications caused further delays, which are explained by a report from the 6th Rifle Regiment:

> On reaching the Maginot Line, we saw the following picture: A lane ran through the line of pillboxes with their dense barrier belt. The pillboxes on both sides of

> the route of advance had been knocked out by the Panzers; but we found that the pillboxes farther south were completely untouched. A lane had been blasted or cut through the thick and deep wire entanglement, just about the width of a road, and our battalion now pushed through that opening. We thought we would at any moment get a sudden and devastating barrage from the bunkers. Nothing of the sort! Not a round was fired! We could not believe that we were supposed to be sending an entire division through such a narrow lane. To some extent, we believed that the French were trying to coax us into a trap here and that they would close the little loophole behind us.[94]

In the meantime Rommel had gotten so far away that no radio contact was possible anyway. He was rather miffed that the division was still hanging back because, by mistake, he thought it was somewhere behind the advance detachment on the way to Landrecies. This is why he decided around 0700 to hand command of the advance detachment to Oberst [Karl] Rothenburg, the commanding officer of the 25th Panzer Regiment. He himself wanted to double back on the road to Avesnes again to get the division to move up. On his ride, his command vehicle, an eight-wheeled armored scout car, was escorted only by one Panzer III, which, however, had mechanical trouble on the way and was left behind.

Now began probably Rommel's craziest adventure during the campaign. His little advance detachment was far to the west, completely isolated, like an island, in the vast ocean of the enemy rear areas. In the meantime, using the roads over which the German Panzers had rolled during their advance, French elements were again marching toward Rommel on their retreat to the west. It seems difficult to believe that the General did not turn around but instead continued undeterred on his way east. Obviously, he had in the meantime lost any sense of danger. He charged through the baffled Frenchmen, ordered fire to be opened several times, and skirted dangerous spots from which he was getting fire. Whenever he ran into a superior enemy unit, he charged it and directed the particular commander—in his command tone that brooked no contradiction—to surrender along with his men. In that way, he managed every time to take the French by surprise, as shown by the following example: "Just one kilometer to the east of Marbays (Marbaix), a French civilian car, coming from the left, crossed the road just ahead of us. We called out to him and he stopped. An officer got out. Behind him came a whole convoy of trucks and machine gunners who had set their machine guns up so they could fire at aircraft. We took the convoy over and told them to start out for Avesnes. Leutnant Hanke had climbed on the lead truck. I myself drove next to the convoy. He indicated to the French by sign language that they were to lay their weapons down and that the war was over for them."[95]

Oddly enough, Rommel used that trick successfully over and over again. A British author commented on the risk he was taking: "It would have taken only one trigger-happy Frenchman to end Rommel's career there and then. He made no attempt to conceal his rank or his person: his natty army uniform, his high peaked cap, his medals and loud voice marked him out above his tank commanders. But he continued to lead this charmed existence, as countless episodes revealed."[96] At last, Rommel arrived in Avesnes trailed by a convoy of forty French trucks. There he ran into the lead elements of his division's formations that were gradually closing up. Now everybody was greatly relieved—even the higher headquarters, all the way to the Wehrmacht high command. The message that Rommel and his Panzers had disappeared without trace caused great excitement. And so, the 7th Panzer Division had become a "ghost division" not only for the French general staff but also for the German general staff.

However, it was impossible to court-martial such a successful general, so Rommel instead got the Knight's Cross. The consequences of his nighttime push seemed breathtaking. After the extended Maginot Line, he had also punched through the Sambre-Oise Line behind it. In the process, the Sambre River bridge at Landrecies fell into German hands even before the withdrawing French troops were able to set up defensive positions behind the river. II Corps, which had been heavily mauled in the prior fighting in Belgium, simply dissolved in panic. The French 1st Armored Division was also wiped out once and for all. In addition, Rommel's Panzers rode over some units of the 8th Infantry Division, the 4th Light Cavalry Division, the 1st Light Mechanized Division, the 1st North African Infantry Division, and the 9th Motorized Infantry Division. On 17 May, about ten thousand French soldiers were taken prisoner in this sector. About thirty-five hundred of them fell into the hands of 7th Panzer Division although, in the course of its impetuous advance, it had hardly any time for such things.[97] The division's losses for 16 and 17 May only amounted to forty killed in action and seventy-five wounded.[98]

Rommel's push seems to be significant also as part of the development toward the modern operational war of movement. In this particular campaign, it represents the extreme example of the transition from linear to nonlinear combat command. After all, the advance detachment had pushed on, like a moving island, drifting through the enemy's rear areas, over dozens of kilometers, without flank protection, and even without contact to division in the rear. The psychological shock element had become the most effective weapon.

The British Counterattack at Arras: A Tactical Failure with Unsuspected Operational Consequences

A critical moment in the drive came just as my forces had reached the Channel. It was caused by a British counterstroke southward from Arras toward Cambrai, on 21 May. For a short time it was feared that our armoured divisions would be cut off before the infantry divisions could come up to support them.[99]

Field Marshal von Rundstedt, in retrospect

Reaching the Channel Coast

On 17 May, Halder decided to restructure the German attack formations. Accordingly, if at all possible, all "fast units" (Panzer divisions and motorized infantry divisions) were to be combined under the command of Fourth Army.[100] After Hitler had approved its move, that army had the mission of pushing west as quickly as possible to cut off the Allied intervention troops that were returning from Belgium even before they reached the Somme River and to encircle them along the Channel coast. According to Halder's comparison, in the process Army Group B was to be the anvil in the north while Army Group A, with its Panzer divisions, was to be the hammer that would come swinging up from south.[101] In the meantime, of course, Army Group B was running the risk of driving the enemy—contrary to operational intentions—entirely too quickly in front of it, while the advance of Army Group A was being slowed down by Hitler's halt order. Von Bock, therefore, was given the mission of taking Panzer Corps Hoepner (XVI Corps) and the XXXIX Motorized Corps (Generalleutnant [Rudolf] Schmidt) out and transferring them to Army Group A. These reinforcements were to be placed under the command of Hoth whose Panzer Corps (XV Corps) was now expanded to form the so-called Panzer Group Hoth.[102]

After speaking to Hitler several times, Halder managed to get approval for resumption of the push to the Channel coast on 19 May. Now there was no holding the Panzer formations any more: "We have the feeling that a noble race horse might have that is being held back on a short rein by its rider out of cool calculation and that now suddenly, the bit in its mouth and its head straight forward, can gallop to the finish line and win the race."[103]

The advance led through the ill-fated terrain of the battlefields of World War I, where the Germans and the Allies had faced each other in trench warfare for year after year. On that same day, the 1st Panzer Division was able to take Amiens and form a small bridgehead south of the Somme River. The 2d Panzer Division was even more successful—on that day, it advanced ninety kilometers. Near Albert, it surprised a British artillery unit that was conducting a terrain exercise without live ammunition, using only practice cartridges. The operational objective designated by von Manstein, Abbeville at the mouth of the Somme River, was reached at 2030. At 0200 that same night, moreover, the 3d Battalion, 2d Rifle Regiment, penetrated right to the Channel coast west of Noyelles. This meant that the decisive phase of Operation Sickle Cut had been completed successfully.

The German Panzers had driven a wedge through the Allied front and had encircled the entire northern wing, including the main body of the elite divisions, along the Channel coast. This gigantic pocket, 200 kilometers long and up to 140 kilometers wide, now contained not only the Belgian army, but also the 1st Army Group with the British Expeditionary Force, French First and Seventh Armies, as well as scattered elements of Ninth Army. The Allied divisions almost throughout were facing east and north from which directions they were attacked frontally by German Army Group B. Now, Fourth Army, supported by all the "mobile units," was to thrust the pocket's rear from the south—the Panzer Group Kleist along the Channel coast via Dunkirk and Panzer Group Hoth to the east thereof, in the Arras area.

7th Panzer Division Beats Off British Flank Attack

After his impetuous advance via Avesnes all the way to Le Cateau, Rommel had first of all been stopped by his superiors. After he was given the go-ahead again, he pushed via Cambrai into the area south of Arras. For 21 May, 7th Panzer Division was given the mission of performing a wheeling movement to the west around Arras, heading north, and seizing the crossings over the Scarpe River at Acq. This clockwise semicircular movement represented a considerable risk because, throughout the entire long, drawn-out wheeling maneuver, the right flank was open toward the city. To the right of Rommel's attack formations, actually, the 5th Panzer Division was to attack to relieve the pressure on the flank of 7th Panzer Division. As it turned out in the end, its advance was delayed so that it was unable to accomplish its mission.

On a high in view of all his successes, Rommel threw caution to the winds. He decided to have his 25th Panzer Regiment stage a probing attack toward the Scarpe River bridges at Acq that were more than ten kilometers away. The two rifle regiments were to follow later. The fact that the division's main body was at first left behind without a single Panzer further increased the risk. While Lady Luck had astonishingly favored Rommel until then, his division now ran into bad trouble in the form of one of the most dangerous attacks that a German division ever had to beat off during the entire campaign in the west. Accident had it that the British tank attack, mounted without any prior reconnaissance exactly at the worst moment and in the worst spot, punched full-force into the unprotected flank of the German infantry columns.

At first, Rommel had been followed by his charging Panzers. But when the infantry did not come up, he drove back, and around 1600 experienced an attack by about 40 British tanks against 2d Battalion, 7th Rifle Regiment. He then hurried up to Hill 111, one kilometer northwest of Wailly, where several artillery pieces had gone into position. At first, the situation did not look too dramatic. As the division commander noted with satisfaction, his gunners were "calmly hurling round after round into them in complete disregard of the return fire."[104] Several British Mark I tanks were knocked out. A British captain climbed out of a heavily damaged tank and, quite stunned, wobbled toward the Germans, his hands raised in surrender. Suddenly, the crews serving the antitank guns acted irritated. Between the British tanks there were also some cumbersome giants that relentlessly drove toward the German positions. The German gunners fired from all barrels but it was no good: All shells bounced off without causing any effect. These were Mark II (Matilda) infantry tanks whose 80-mm armor was the thickest among all models employed during the campaign.[105] An after-action report reads as follows: "Our own antitank guns do not have a sufficient effect even at close range against the heavy tanks of the English. *The enemy simply breaks through the defensive fronts they form; the British tanks shoot the German antitank guns to pieces or crunch over them and the crews are mostly killed in action.*"[106]

With the help of a nearby artillery battery, it was possible with a major effort to stop the attack shortly before Hill 111. The threat to the 7th Rifle Regiment, which was spearheading the attack, seemed eliminated for the moment. Now individual British tanks pushed past to the north and south. The left (southern flank) of 7th Panzer Division was to be screened by the motorized SS-Totenkopf [Death's Head] Division, that however did not as yet have any combat experience. Rommel watched as British tanks rolled into a position of the neighboring division. Some soldiers panicked there and simply fled.

As early as thirty minutes before the attack on the 7th Rifle Regiment, another British tank formation attacked the 6th Rifle Regiment, which was advancing parallel to it, farther north at Agny. It bumped frontally into a British tank column that was approaching from Dainville. Some vehicles were shot to pieces. Soon thereafter, there were several more attacks by British tanks and infantry from the north. They hit the long, drawn-out vehicle convoys of the 6th Rifle Regiment on its unprotected right flank. Division headquarters received the following radio message: "Strong enemy tank attack from Arras. Help, Help."[107] The Panzerjägerabteilung 42 (42d Antitank Battalion) hastily put up a blocking position between Agny and Beaurains. British tanks simply rolled over it. After they had punched through the 6th Rifle Regiment, the vehicle convoys of the 7th Rifle Regiment, advancing to the south between Mercatel and Ficheux, met the same fate to some extent. A few British tanks then relentlessly pushed farther south where they caused confusion among the ranks of the SS-Totenkopf Division and threatened its command echelon.

The principle of leading from up front proved itself in view of this situation because German commanders practiced that principle in contrast to the Allied commanders. Nobody did it to such extremes—and often quite exaggerated—as Rommel. His favorite saying was that no admiral ever won a sea battle from the coast.[108] This leadership principle had a twin effect at Arras: psychologically and in terms of command technique.

First of all, Rommel's actions served as a model. He was in the thick of the fighting, amid his own men. Although in some cases there were nightmarelike scenes when enemy tanks rolled over German antitank gun positions, there was no panic. In contrast to the SS-Totenkopf Division, there were no bugout movements worth mentioning. Because the division commander personally exposed himself to this danger, his men could only do likewise. And so, enemy tanks broke through the German lines but the latter held. That made it possible to beat back the British infantry that was trying to follow the British tanks. The situation into which Rommel moved was by no means without danger. As the British tanks opened fire on the German gun positions, among which the general was running back and forth, his orderly officer, Oberleutnant Most, who was right next to him, suddenly fell, mortally wounded. Just a few days earlier, Hauptmann Schraepler, his ordnance officer, had been wounded right by his side. Each time, the round could have hit him also.

Rommel's command behavior also had an advantageous effect in other respects. While the Allied commanders were mostly miles away from the focal point of events, he was able quickly to grasp the situation and react instantly since he was way up front. There were four measures that brought about a turning point:[109]

1. At first, he organized a forward containment line made up of antitank guns and light flak pieces. That, of course, did not stop the Matilda battle tanks but did stop some of the lighter tanks.
2. As indicated by several of Rommel's radio messages to his division headquarters, he ordered a second containment line made up artillery pieces and flak guns to be formed deep to the rear.[110] When the British, in the open terrain between Mercatel and Tilloy, ran frontally into these positions, they lost two dozen tanks in just a few minutes. The 8.8-cm flak guns played a particularly important role in beating this thrust off.
3. Shortly after 1800, about two hours after the request from 7th Panzer Division, the first aircraft of I and VIII Air Corps arrived. At that moment, the British attack had already been beaten off. Now the German aircraft pounced on the retreating tanks. There were three hundred dive-bomber attacks by 2030.[111]
4. In the meantime, Rommel had also ordered the 25th Panzer Regiment, which had rushed far ahead to the north, to come back. It was to cut the route of retreat of the withdrawing British formations. South of Duisans, however, it bumped into a column of French tanks that—as will be described later—were to screen the right flank of the British. The German Panzers were able to prevail only after bitter fighting with heavy losses. Then the important thing was to break through a British antitank gun blocking position between Duisans and Warlus. The so-called tank battle of Arras had been decided long before the German Panzers in darkness arrived at the battlefield that the British tanks had already left.

The fighting of 21 May inflicted by far the most painful losses in the campaign on 7th Panzer Division. They were just as heavy as those during the first four days of combat, including the Meuse River crossing, taken together. The figures added up to 89 killed in action, 116 wounded, and 173 missing. Among the latter, however, 90 soon thereafter found their way back to their units.[112]

The Counterattack at Arras from the Allied Viewpoint

Looking at the planning and execution of the Allied counterattack, we are struck by the inability of the British and French operations staffs to react quickly enough to the German Panzer thrust. Here, they would have had one more chance to turn things around. The farther the German Panzers pushed to the Channel coast, the longer were their exposed flanks. The breathtaking aspect of this nonlinear operations management was that there was an isolated Panzer wedge, pushing its way to the west, behind which almost a vacuum had been formed in individual sectors. The few motorized infantry divisions were not enough by far to secure the entire territory seized by the Panzers, while the infantry divisions marching on foot in some cases were still several days' march away. Thus, only a forty-kilometer-wide corridor had developed in the Arras sector—the flanks of that corridor just about cried out for a pincer attack. Winston Churchill had sent Gamelin a corresponding dispatch already on 19 May, very figuratively comparing the onrushing German Panzer formations to the head of a tortoise: "The tortoise has protruded its head very far from its shell. Some days must elapse before their main body can reach our lines of communication. It would appear that powerful blows struck from north and south of this drawn-out pocket could yield surprising results."[113]

Now, the dangerous turnabout—which Clausewitz calls the "encirclement of the encircler"[114]—could very easily materialize. If the Allies had exploited the weak moment of the attacker at the right time, then it would have been possible to make a "Dunkirk" for the Germans—in the reverse direction. The Panzers would then be cut off from their supplies, and they would be encircled along the Channel coast. But Halder accepted this risk readily because he knew how weak his opponents were. He did not think that the headquarters of the Allies were capable of combining several major formations quickly enough into an operational counteraction. Actually, there were two such attempts, one from the French side and another one from the British. Just what results they produced will be taken up below.

The Weygand Plan. Gamelin had left the execution of operations mostly to Georges, the commander in chief of the northeast front. On 19 May, however, he interfered for "his first and last" time in the battle.[115] In Directive No. 12 he observed that a big gap had developed behind the leading German echelon into which one would have to push with "particularly mobile forces." In that way, one could get into the rear of the German Panzer divisions and prevent the encirclement of the 1st Army Group along the northern wing. But his directive bore the character of a vaguely worded memorandum rather than that of a bold operations plan. The only really specific admonition consisted of the now famous sentence: "Everything depends on the next few hours."[116]

However, several days passed until an operations plan materialized somehow. On the same day, 19 May, the luckless Gamelin was relieved of command and was replaced by the seventy-four-year-old General [Maxime] Weygand, who had been recalled to active duty. During World War I, Weygand was considered to be the right-hand man of Marshal Foch who, in the spring of 1918, was able to stop the dangerous German large-scale offensive in the Amiens area. In addition, in 1920, as adviser to Polish marshal Pilsudski, he participated in the "miracle on the Vistula," when the offensive of the Red Army was brought to a halt before Warsaw. Weygand seemed to have the kind of charisma that was expected of the "savior of France."

As it turned out, he was even more than his predecessor captive to the comfortable tempo of command processes as they took place during World War I. His first measure was to cancel his predecessor's directive for the execution of an immediate counteroffensive. He wanted to get a picture of the situation for himself. In this connection, following his World War I role model, Foch, he considered it indispensable, first of all, to visit the front line and to have a personal talk with the most important field army commanders. That was bound to be almost anachronistic in view of the tempo of the German blitzkrieg. Gamelin's appeal that every moment counts had been absolutely correct. With every passing hour, the German Panzer formations pushed farther and farther west. On 20 May, they reached their major operational objective, Abbeville at the mouth of the Somme River.

But, on that day, Weygand wasted considerable time paying courtesy visits to political dignitaries in Paris, including newly appointed Interior Minister Mandel.[117] On the morning of 21 May, he flew into the pocket of Flanders to drop in on General Billotte, the commander in chief of the Allied 1st Army Group that was encircled there. Organizational breakdowns and the constant need to evade German aircraft resulted in the fact that he arrived there only around 1500. After a conversation with French and Belgian commanders as well as the Belgian King in Ypres, he took off again around 1730 and, after a time-consuming trip by air, sea, and rail, did not return to Paris again until around 1500 on 22 May.[118] In between, the Germans had plenty of opportunity to move sufficient divisions into the corridor and had pushed farther along the Channel coast to cut the encircled Allied army off from the ports. The push at Arras, beaten off by Rommel's 7th Panzer Division, which will be described in greater detail from the British viewpoint, had in the meantime been discontinued without result.

Only now, on 22 May, did the newly appointed French supreme commander issue his Operations Order No. 1, which became known as the Weygand plan. Churchill, who participated in the pertinent session of the Allied War Council in Paris, commented as follows on this in *The Second World War:* "It will be seen that Weygand's new plan did not differ except in emphasis from the canceled Instruction No. 12 of General Gamelin."[119] This meant that, since Gamelin's relief on 19 May, three days had been wasted—a loss of time in dealing with the Germans that could never be made up! Weygand's operations plan was simplicity personified. A pincer attack was to be mounted against the Arras "corridor": from the north, by 1st Army Group, encircled along the coast, under Billotte; from the south, by the newly formed 3d Army

Group under General [Antoine-Marie-Benoît] Besson, which was behind the Somme River.

The situation just about cried out for punching through the corridor as quickly as possible with as many troops as possible to avert what General Ironside said might be the "greatest military catastrophe in history."[120] In that way, it would be possible not only to break open the encirclement ring around the encircled 1st Army Group but also to encircle the German Panzer divisions along the coast. The threatened defeat might even be turned into victory.

While Joffre in 1914 managed the "miracle on the Marne," Weygand could not repeat this miracle on the Somme. Actually, one should have expected the formations of the 1st Army Group, encircled in the Flanders pocket, to break through south to the Somme as quickly as possible. However, when Weygand discussed his plan on 22 May during the meeting of the Allied War Council in Vincennes, he said: "There can be no talk of expecting the bulk of the French-English-Belgian forces, that are still in the north . . . simply to withdraw south and somehow link up with the main body of the French armies."[121] Even more depressing was the result in 3d Army Group that, symmetrically, was to carry out a pincer attack from the south. It remained motionless in its position behind the Somme River and confined itself to moving against the German bridgeheads on the south bank.

The last possible chance for a counteroffensive would have been on 23 May. On that same evening, however, General [Lord John] Gort, the commander in chief of the British Expeditionary Force, decided to retreat to the Channel coast and allowed the British troops near Arras to fall back to the north. Although in the next day he still declared that he was ready with the two requested divisions to participate in an Allied counteroffensive, he no longer believed that the French army would be able for its part to supply the necessary troops on schedule. The endeavors of the French command had suffered a bitter setback anyway because Billotte, the commander in chief of the 1st Army Group, was killed in a traffic accident on the evening of 21 May while returning from Ypres where Weygand had revealed his operations plan for the first time. Now the only man who was thoroughly familiar with the ideas of the French supreme commander was dead. Nonetheless, the French supreme commander took his time and General [Georges-Marie-Jean] Blanchard was not officially appointed Billotte's successor until three days later so that for some time there was almost a leaderless state in the Flanders pocket. Weygand actually wanted to launch the counteroffensive on 23 May, but then postponed it to 24 May and finally to 26 May or 27 May before finally canceling it altogether. This meant that the last chance to avert the catastrophe had been missed.[122]

The British Initiative of a Counterattack at Arras. The vain attempt at an Allied counteroffensive also cast a characteristic light on the deficient cooperation between the French, British, and Belgian armies. The French supreme commander, who commanded all Allied formations on the northeast front, made no energetic effort to execute a counterattack in time. This is why Ironside, the British chief of the imperial general staff, developed his own initiative.

It seems worth noting that the Gamelin plan, the Weygand plan, and the Ironside plan were basically almost identical. The only thing missing was tight leadership by a supreme commander to translate this joint operational idea into action at the right time. On 20 May, Ironside visited both Gort, the commander in chief of the British Expeditionary Force, and his French superior, Billotte, the commander in chief of the 1st Army Group. They agreed on the following operations plan for an attack against the German corridor: On the next day, two British infantry divisions, reinforced by one tank brigade, were to push south from Arras. At the same time, the attack of the French V Corps, with two divisions, was planned to the east thereof, in the area of Cambrai. It was expected that the Cavalry Corps of Prioux would provide support with its particularly great striking force. Prioux, this daredevil tank specialist, would have been just the right man for executing the counterattack. The tanks of his 2d and 3d

Left to right: General Ironside, General Georges, Winston Churchill, General Gamelin, General Gort. They were gathered to award the Grand Cross of the Legion of Honor to the two British generals just a few weeks before the beginning of the campaign in the west. *E.C.P.A. Fort d'Ivry*

Hitler and Generalfeldmarschall Göring meet during the campaign in the west; on the right, Generalleutnant Bodenschatz. *Bundesarchiv Koblenz [Federal Archives]*

Light Mechanized Divisions had already created enormous problems for the Germans at Hannut and Gembloux.

In the meantime, he had also again been given the 1st Light Mechanized Division, which had been temporarily placed under Seventh Army, so that the Cavalry Corps was again complete. This major formation seemed almost predestined for this important mission. In the meantime, however, Prioux had to stand by and watch as a considerable number of his tanks were distributed by companies to the individual infantry divisions. Now it was impossible to round these tanks up quickly enough for a coherent operation. Only after a draconian order from army group in which the responsible commanders where threatened with court-martial did they begin hesitantly to send the tanks back again.

Ironside informed Weygand by phone about his intention and complained about the lack of cooperation on the part of Billotte. He had met the latter in his headquarters at Lens (north of Arras), together with Blanchard, the commander in chief of First Army. Both French generals seemed completely discouraged and undecided, as Ironside confided to his diary: "No plan, no thought of any plan, just ready to be slaughtered."[123] Ironside, a giant of a man, lost his self-control, as he later admitted, and grabbed Billotte by a button on his tunic.[124] He finally managed to get him to approve a joint offensive. Actually Billotte or at least Blanchard personally should have directed this kind of decisive inter-Allied operation. They delegated this job to General [René-Félix] Altmayer, the commanding general of V Corps. The latter, however, was in a state of deepest depression when he got the order to launch the attack. Major Vautrin, the liaison officer of the French First Army with the British Expeditionary Force, recorded this scene: "General Altmayer, who made an exhausted and beaten impression, sat on my cot and wept quietly. He said we have to see things the way they are, that his troops were finished, that he was ready to take upon himself the consequences of his refusal to carry out the order and that he would take up his position at the head of a battalion and fall in battle. But he would not continue to sacrifice his army corps, which had already lost half its personnel strength."[125]

To make things even worse, there was also a linguistic misunderstanding. Ironside wanted under all circumstances to attack "on 21 May." But Blanchard, in his directive to Altmayer, wrote that the attack was to begin "from the 21st on" (*à partir du 21*). Thereupon, Altmayer reported that his Corps would not be ready until 22 May. As Colonel Lyet writes, "The entire drama of the failure of the French-British operation sprang from these words."[126] Thereupon, the British had to attack mostly alone on 21 May.

There was no end to the chain of misunderstandings. Accident would have it that General [Harold E.] Franklyn, who was charged with the higher-level planning of the British offensive, originally had a different although apparently similar mission. The direction of the attack was even identical. Accordingly, there was likewise to be a push south from Arras. This was only an attack with a limited objective to relieve the important garrison at Arras and to cut the German lines of communication. Oddly enough, he was not sufficiently informed of the fact that this rather tactical objective had, in the meantime, assumed operational significance due to Ironside's new plan. Franklyn did not even find out that, parallel to this, there was also to be a French attack. Thus, he did not throw all his troops onto the scales but employed most of the formations of the 5th and 50th Infantry divisions under his command in a purely defensive role to reinforce the troops already in position at Arras or he held them back as reserve. In the end, there were only two reinforced infantry battalions left for the so very important attack.

In the meantime, the two British tank battalions that had been moved up for this purpose had dwindled considerably due to mechanical failures. They only had 88 battle tanks: 58 Mark I infantry tanks, 16 Mark II infantry tanks (Matilda), and 14 light tanks. On the other hand, the 3d Light Mechanized Division from the Prioux Cavalry Corps was subordinated for the attack. Its SOMUA tanks could have been used as battering rams for the breakthrough. But this division was only employed to protect the right flank.

General Giffard Martel, who had been charged with the execution of the attack on the tactical echelon, organized his formations in two columns: on the right, 7th Battalion,

Royal Tank Regiment, and 8th Battalion, Durham Light Infantry Regiment; on the left, 4th Battalion, Royal Tank Regiment, and 6th Battalion, Durham Light Infantry Regiment. Each column was supported by one artillery battalion, one heavy antitank battery, one antitank platoon, and scouting units.[127] The impetus of the British attack has been overdramatized in German reports. Ronald Lewin wrote: "Myth and act now part company. The British attack . . . so often applauded, is actually a model of how not to launch a combined infantry/armoured assault."[128]

The problem of frequency allocation showed just how badly the attack was organized. Radio contact worked neither between the tank units nor to the infantry. The thrust by the right-wing column was launched in a particularly confused fashion. Next, 7th Battalion, Royal Tank Regiment, lost its way and attacked along the wrong road, severing contact with the infantry. At first, it drifted west, getting itself into a brief firefight with French tanks at Duisans before the mistake was noticed. Additional confusion was caused by a sudden exchange of fire with the rear guard of Rommel's Panzer regiment that had already pushed past them, far to the north. Thereupon, the 7th Battalion, Royal Tank Regiment, moved too far to the east and, north of Dainville, ran into the formations of the left-wing attack column. Now, the British tank battalion, like a bouncing billiard ball, swung too far back to the west instead of attacking in a southern direction, as had been intended. In the process, British tanks from time to time executed a lateral movement with respect to the German artillery pieces that had gone into position at Wailly. The attack against this village, where Rommel was personally in command, failed. Only a few isolated British battle tanks continued the attack, circling around Wailly to the left and right.

The left-wing column's push began more promisingly. The 4th Battalion, Royal Tank Regiment, at Achicourt south of Arras, smashed a marching formation of the 6th Rifle Regiment and broke through a German antitank gun blocking position. But, in the end, it ran frontally into the positions of the German artillery pieces and flak guns between Mercatel and Tilloy. A British officer describes the outcome of this tragedy as follows: "I went forward through the tanks of 'A' and 'B' Company and thought it very off that they were neither moving nor shooting. Then I noticed that there was something odder about them: their guns were pointing at all angles; a number of them had their turret hatches open and some of the crews were half in and half out of the tanks, lying wounded and dead. . . . In that valley, the best of our crews were left behind."[129] Individual tanks, nevertheless, managed to push through farther south, all the way to the formations of the SS-Totenkopf Division where they were stopped after severe fighting. When the dive-bombers showed up in the sky, the British were already retreating.

The push by a tank column of the French 3d Light Mechanized Division was also rather confused. The French were to screen the British right flank but were inadequately informed as to the exact timing and direction of the attack mounted by their Allies. As noted earlier, there was already a fatal collision at the start of the attack. The

French SOMUA tanks successfully broke through a hastily built-up antitank position. Only then was it realized that those were British troops. Nevertheless, the French tanks later on did provide valuable support for the British formations. In the evening, the latter were in danger of having their retreat cut off by the 25th Panzer Regiment, which Rommel had ordered back. The German Panzers became involved in a bitter fight with about 60 French tanks south of Duisans. The Germans managed to break through after suffering rather heavy losses, but in the meantime the British troops were able to withdraw to the north.[130]

The counterthrust at Arras ended in a disaster—only twenty-eight out of a total of eighty-eight British tanks returned from the battlefield. In the evening, the formations that got away were exactly in the same place where they had begun their action in the afternoon. Actually, the attackers were extremely lucky because, at first, they only had to deal with German infantry and not with Panzers. The British soldiers fought extraordinarily bravely and the British tank crews, inspired by their initial successes, attacked in daredevil style. That is above all true of Major King and Sergeant Doyle who were the only ones of their unit to push past Wailly toward Mercatel in their tanks. Their

This Matilda II tank of the 7th Battalion, Royal Tank Regiment, was put out of action on 21 May, along the northern outskirts of Wailly near Arras. *Bundesarchiv Koblenz [Federal Archives]*

two Matilda tanks—the "queens of the battlefield"[131]—rolled over anything and everything in their way. Two German antitank gun companies, opening fire from all barrels, could not stop them. They were finally halted at Mercatel by fire from 8.8-cm flak guns.

Here again, we cannot help but note the parallel to the employment of the French Char B and SOMUA tanks. All these spectacular actions, written up in numerous after-action reports, were merely individual successes that could not be exploited tactically. The combined arms combat that the Germans had drilled so perfectly was practically not to be found in this British attack because contact between the individual arms was inadequate. Due to radio equipment problems, coordination of combat actions did not work even among the tanks. Thus, the officers were forced partly to dismount from their tanks or, in the midst of enemy fire, to open their hatches and lead by means of hand signals. That took the lives of Lt. Col. H. M. Heyland as well as his aide during the right-wing column's attack against Wailly. The only command system that still seemed possible was "attacking by instinct."[132] And so, the British tanks charged on ahead at random, as impetuous as they were uncoordinated. The isolated British tank commitment at Arras was the exact opposite of what Guderian had been teaching. Laconically, Liddell Hart cites three reasons for the failure: "little infantry support, less artillery support, and no air support."[133]

The French push to Cambrai on the next day, 22 May, ended in an even bigger failure. Altmayer was actually supposed to attack with V Army Corps, reinforced by the tank units of the Prioux Cavalry Corps. The actual force commitment was reduced to one infantry regiment and two smaller tank battalions. Nevertheless, the attackers had a big opportunity because they just about punched into a vacuum. The German Panzer divisions had already left Cambrai behind, but the infantry divisions marching on foot behind them had not reached the place. They were not scheduled to arrive in the city, which was held only by small screening detachments, until sometime during the day. The attack was smashed almost solely by the Luftwaffe, and the French formations that had already reached the outskirts of Cambrai had to withdraw to the north again.[134]

Halder had accepted a risk in allowing the Panzer Divisions to push on ahead to the Channel coast, far in front of the infantry divisions. On 23 May, he wrote in his diary that "it will take days yet" until the strong infantry forces can reach the area around Arras.[135] But, in spite of their superiority, the Allies were no longer in a position to assemble their formations to mount an operational counterattack. More than 1 million men, including most of the Allied elite divisions, were encircled in the Flanders pocket. All those forces managed to accomplish was just two tactical pinpricks at Arras and Cambrai.

Operational-Level Effects of the Arras Counterattack

The failed British push at Arras achieved an astonishing effect after the fact. The operational and strategic consequences were way out of proportion to the tactical cause. The explanation of this phenomenon can once again be found in exaggerated flank fright. The overreaction of the German command clearly shows how far removed the thinking of most higher-ranking generals still was from the concepts of a blitzkrieg, in other words, an operational war of movement. Von Kleist suddenly thought he could see a "serious threat" to the operation.[136] He had Oberstleutnant i.G. [Heinz] von Gyldenfeldt, the liaison officer to the army high command, inform Halder that he felt he "cannot tackle his task as long as the crisis at Arras remains unresolved."[137] Von Kluge ordered the movement of the Panzers to be stopped, which meant that he was fully in agreement with von Rundstedt, the commander in chief of Army Group A. On 22 May, by which time the British counterthrust had long been beaten off, the latter decided "*first of all* to straighten out the situation at Arras and *then* only to push toward Calais—Boulogne with the Kleist Group."[138]

The biggest panic erupted, of all places, in the Wehrmacht high command where Hitler at last thought he found confirmation for his fears that Halder had discounted again and again. At 0130, during the night leading up to 22 May, the Führer ordered his chief military aide, Schmundt, to phone headquarters, Army Group A, to get information on the Arras crisis. He even sent Keitel, the chief of staff of the Wehrmacht high command, there. The latter arrived at 0900 and once again personally delivered Hitler's directive that had already been sent by phone. Accordingly, "all possibly available fast units" were to be employed on both sides of Arras and to the west thereof, while the infantry divisions were to be employed to the east thereof.

The so-called crisis of Arras was homemade and had an effect only among the higher-level staffs. It seems paradoxical that there was no crisis mood to be detected at all among the Panzer divisions that should have felt threatened. Rommel kept attacking quite unconcernedly and, on the next day, pushed into the area north of Arras. On 23 May the 5th Panzer Division, which he had sent forward, took the Lorette Heights that had been so bitterly fought for during World War I. There, Werner's men were able to read the famous inscription: "Who holds Lorette Heights holds France."[139] On the same day, Halder made the following entry in his diary: "Notre-Dame-de-Lorette! The fate of France is in our hands!"[140]

The chief of the general staff made a correct estimate of the consequences deriving from the failed British attack. Like Guderian, he felt that the threat was now no longer represented by a possible flank attack executed by the Allies but rather by the fact that the Allies might withdraw to the Channel coast too fast. Now began the last phase of the operation, the race to the Channel ports. To that extent, 22 May is a significant date for the fate of the British army. Guderian had aimed his three Panzer Divisions at the three Channel ports: 1st Panzer Division at Calais, 2d Panzer Division at Boulogne, 10th Panzer Division at Dunkirk.

At that point in time, the main body of the British and French divisions was still stuck in the country's interior about a hundred kilometers from salvation along the Channel coast. Now, however, the German Panzers threatened to push to the Channel ports along the coast behind the back of the British and French. The British command immediately recognized the danger and tried to transfer troops from England to Calais and Boulogne in order, from there, to block the way of the Germans to Dunkirk. It was hoped that this port could be held open for an evacuation. The embarkation of the contingents that were to come to the aid of the trapped Allies was delayed so much that this race became a matter of hours. British military historian Kenneth Macksey arrived at the following result: "But it would be the morning of the 22nd before Boulogne received its main garrison and so it follows that, if Guderian or Reinhardt had been sent there immediately on the 21st at the same rate as they travelled on the 20th, they would have found the port virtually undefended. Likewise they could have had Calais for the asking since that port's garrison was not properly in position until the 22nd."[141]

The most important role was assigned to the 10th Panzer Division. At that time, it would have been possible, without any problems, to push through to Dunkirk, which was hardly defended. But, after the first halt order at Montcornet, the Panzers were now stopped once again at Arras. Without this intervention, however, the famous halt order of Dunkirk on 24 May would not have had any consequences because that port would already have been in German hands.

After the arrival of the first reports about the British counterthrust, the advance of the Panzers toward the Channel ports was interrupted for about twenty-four hours on 21 May. But just as significant was the fact that, subsequent thereto, the Germans were allowed to attack only with half their strength. Of all units, it was the 10th Panzer Division that was supposed to push on through to Dunkirk, which was now held back uselessly as a reserve for Panzer Group Kleist—a decision that Guderian accepted "with a heavy heart."[142] He was furthermore forced to leave strong units along the Somme River to screen the southern flank although, in the meantime, more and more fresh troops—who actually were supposed to take over this task—were being moved up. Quite contrary to operational logic, those troops were used to secure the Arras sector, although the British had begun to retreat after their failed attack. The Arras halt order was met with noncomprehension above all in Panzer Corps Reinhardt. On 21 May, it was only fifty kilometers from Dunkirk and, among all of the German army corps, it could have reached that port fastest. Absurdly enough, Reinhardt was now ordered to wheel a portion of his Panzer formations in the wrong direction, that is to say, east, to stop the enemy who allegedly had broken through at Arras.

After twenty-four hours had been wasted, as Guderian saw it, he was allowed on 22 May to continue the attack with the rest of his Corps. Now the big opportunity of quickly seizing the Channel ports was gone. It took the 2d Panzer Division three days at last, after bitter house-to-house fighting, to capture Boulogne on 25 May. The infantry had to storm the medieval city walls using ladders. It took even longer until Calais was at last taken on May 26. Here is what Churchill wrote on that point:

"Calais was the crux. Many other causes might have prevented the deliverance of Dunkirk, but it is certain that the three days gained by the defense of Calais enabled the Gravelines waterline to be held, and that without this, . . . all would have been cut off and lost."[143]

Now we come to the question as to how the failed British attack at Arras could in the end have brought all this about. Rommel must indirectly shoulder a part of the responsibility here. First of all, we must establish that he indeed was the victor of Arras. In a style completely atypical for Allied generals, Rommel had led his division from far up front, where all the firing was going on. To that extent, his courage and calmness in coping with extreme danger must be emphasized. Reacting with lightning speed, he managed to convert a disaster that threatened his formations into a victory. But there is another side to the coin, and it is also rooted in Rommel's extreme personality. His excessive ambition led him astray to the extent that he magnified the danger to make his achievement look even better than it already was. So he sent exaggerated disaster dispatches to his superiors and reported about "hundreds of enemy tanks" that would attack him.[144] In the so-called Rommel-Album that was presented to Hitler after the campaign in the west, there is a real horror painting consisting of red arrows that are supposed to represent the attacking British tank formations. There is mention of a total of five enemy divisions.[145]

During this critical phase of the operation, Hitler and some of the higher-ranking generals waited daily for the operational counterattack by the Allies, which was considered to be unavoidable. Since that attack was delayed, their nerves were just about at the breaking point. At last came the long-expected news that put an end to this state of tension. According to the figures initially reported by Rommel, there seemed to have been a counterattack on an operational-level order of magnitude, something that triggered an overreaction among his superiors. Of course, these statistics were immediately denied and the situation turned out to be "defused."[146] It was, however, too late because Hitler and some of his advisers had already lost their nerve. The war diary of Panzer Corps Reinhardt, which attacked in the left-wing neighboring sector, reveals what the situation actually looked like: "By the way, today is marked by exaggerated and partly false news and reports. And so, there is talk of a breakthrough by an enemy tank formation with about 50 tanks that is reported to be advancing toward Doullens [from Arras]. This bit of news turns out to be completely false. All other messages about the . . . counterattack are also exaggerated."[147]

The situation reports from the right-wing neighboring sector reveal an even greater contrast. The Intelligence Section of the Hoth Group on that same evening reported that the enemy is "demoralized" and "in a process of complete disintegration; moreover, there is supposed to be a confusing mess resembling headlong flight."[148] The messages that reached headquarters, Fourth Army, on the morning of 22 May made the incident at Arras appear in an entirely different light. For example, Schmidt, the commanding general of XXXIX Corps, under whose command Rommel now was, described the “enemy attack as being executed rather lamely.”[149] Von Kluge failed in his attempts to persuade headquarters, Army Group A, to allow a general continuation of the attack. Von Rundstedt simply could not be persuaded that there was no considerable threat to the flanks and insisted on stopping Panzer Group Kleist.[150] So, paradoxically, the failed British counterattack on 21 May not only led to the Arras halt order but also had an indirect effect at Dunkirk.

8

The "Miracle of Dunkirk"

We shall have lost practically all our trained soldiers by the next few days—unless a miracle appears to help us.[1]

British Chief of the Imperial General Staff,
Gen. Sir Edmund Ironside, 25 May 1940

Background of the Halt Order

On 24 May the Germans had pushed to within fifteen kilometers of Dunkirk, the only remaining Channel port of the Allies. The lead elements had already crossed the Aa Canal, the last natural obstacle. No enemy troops worth mentioning were positioned between the German Panzers and Dunkirk. It was just a matter of a few hours and the last gap would have been closed and about 1 million British, French, and Belgian soldiers would have been sitting in the trap. In most cases, those men were still a hundred kilometers away from Dunkirk, fighting against the divisions of Army Group B, and they had no opportunity to respond to the deadly threat that emerged in their rear. Then one of the strangest episodes in the military history of the twentieth century took place—the "miracle of Dunkirk." With incredulous astonishment, Allied soldiers discovered that the German Panzers had suddenly come to a halt, as if stopped by magic.

Contrary to widespread opinion, Hitler did not originate the halt order. On 24 May, the dictator was no longer able to stop the Panzers because, at that moment, they had already been stopped. Instead, he intervened only at the climax of a command crisis within the general officer corps. The immediate cause for the halt order was in that controversy that constitutes the essence of this episode, that is, the conflict between the traditionalists and the progressives. On the day before, there had been considerable differences of opinion among the general officer corps regarding the further employment of the Panzer force. This split can be illustrated with the help of the following layered model:

The Panzer generals (on the divisional and corps echelon) wanted to attack as quickly as possible.

> The commanders in chief at the army and army group echelon (Kluge and Rundstedt) pleaded for briefly stopping the Panzers to allow [other units] to close up.
>
> The army high command came out in favor of a rapid advance.
>
> Hitler, and with him the Wehrmacht high command, was inclined toward putting the brakes on the Panzer formations.

The cause of this controversy was once again the flank psychosis. Von Rundstedt later said to von Bock: "I was worried that Kleist's weak forces would be overrun by the fleeing English!"[2] His chief of staff, von Sodenstern, also believed that it "was not a good thing" to "assess the situation too optimistically."[3] On 25 May, when the encircled Allied divisions were already flooding back toward Dunkirk, headquarters, Army Group A, was afraid that it might itself be encircled: "One cannot rule out the possibility that the enemy is conducting his movements according to a uniform plan with the intention of breaking through the Fourth Army and its subordinate mobile troops by attacking from north *and* from south in order thus to restore contact between his separated army elements."[4]

This crisis psychosis appears, so to speak, to be endogenous because the crisis can be traced not so much to an external threat from the enemy, but rather to the thinking of some high-ranking military leaders who, facing an incomprehensible victory, at the last moment lost their nerve. At that time, there was no reason to fear any serious counteroffensive from the north or south. Von Bock, whose Army Group B was driving the already beaten and dissolving Allied divisions frontally from the north, had a considerably more realistic situation estimate. Full of sarcasm, he wrote in his diary of the flank fright of headquarters Army Group A: "I had no worries of this sort whatsoever; if they were ever at all justified, they have become completely invalid ever since the Eighteenth and Sixth Armies got the English by the throat, making them happy just to escape with their lives."[5]

Halder, who among all generals had the best overview, both on 23 and 24 May noted that the situation was developing "in an entirely satisfactory manner."[6] He stated several times that there was no reason to expect any serious counterattack, from any direction, and emphasized: "no threat south of the Somme."[7] In saying that, he referred to the accurate situation reports from the Army Intelligence Service, Foreign Armies West. Still, Hitler and some of his generals were so fixated on preventing a repetition of the "miracle of the Marne" that they conjured up the "miracle of Dunkirk."

The 23 May Close-Up Order

If we track the development of the halt order back to its point of origin, we find that von Kleist was the man who, without wanting to do so, got the ball rolling. His message, which he sent out on the morning of 23 May, triggered dramatic consequences. Orders from army group had forced Kleist to disperse his units for various assignments, for example, providing flank protection toward the south. Thus, he was no longer in a position "to line up for the decisive attack." This is why he declared, rather annoyed: "Following the losses suffered during the past 14 days of fighting, particularly in terms of tanks, which amount to more that 50 percent, the Group is no longer strong enough to mount an attack to the east, against *strong* enemy forces. If the enemy attacks in major strength, then I would like to note for the record that the Panzer Divisions are little suited for defense."[8]

Halder made fun of Kleist because Kleist felt "that he [could not] tackle his task," and he downplayed the risks in view of the "magnitude of his task." He would not even allow Panzer losses, which, as will be shown, were by no means as bad as indicated, to serve as an excuse.[9] But this message had an effect on von Kluge. At that particular moment, he was overloaded by the situation anyway because, in addition to his army's infantry divisions, he also had to command a total of ten Panzer Divisions and six motorized divisions of the Wehrmacht. The latter had been combined as *Schnelle Truppen* (mobile forces) on the left wing of his army, between the Channel coast and Arras, while the infantry divisions on foot were advancing on the right wing between Arras and Valenciennes. At 1640, Kluge had a talk with Rundstedt in which he used the fatal term *aufschließen* (close up) for the first time. He suggested that the fast left wing be stopped in order to let the following formations "close up." Von Rundstedt agreed fully and issued the following order: "In other words, the right wing and the Center are to be pushed forward, the rest are to close up, infantry divisions [are to be] advanced."[10] Thereupon, headquarters, Fourth Army, at 2000, issued a "close-up order" for 24 May. Accordingly, only II and VIII Corps (two purebred infantry corps) were allowed to continue the attack east of Arras. On the other hand, Panzer Groups Kleist and Hoth were to interrupt their advance for one day "to make all preparations for continuing the attack on 25 May."[11]

At this point, it must be emphasized that the Panzers were already stopped by the close-up order issued by Kluge and Rundstedt, dated 23 May—in other words, long before the famous halt order of 24 May. Both of these cases of interference in the course of operations have been confused in many descriptions of events during the campaign in the west.[12] When the close-up order reached the troops during the night of 23–24 May, it was greeted with noncomprehension and protests. Reinhardt believed that interrupting the attack was wrong. He wanted to exploit the moment because his Panzer formations were momentarily facing only weak "quickly moved-up enemy forces."[13] And so he emphasized that any stopping "could only help the enemy." In saying this, he referred to the reconnaissance findings that the enemy was moving up fresh formations "to strengthen his defenses and, under their protection, to move the bulk of his troops to the ports for embarkation."[14] Panzer Corps Guderian's war diary also notes rather critically that the new order would "practically discard the attack concept such as it has been used until now."[15] "Now it appears essential . . . to push toward Dunkirk, the last major port, whose fall would make the encirclement complete.

But that attack has for the moment been shelved."[16] The divisions in the very front line should have felt threatened if any did. Instead, they were understandably disappointed, as indicated in the war diary of the 6th Panzer Division: "In contrast to combat operations in the past, the tempo of the advance, dictated by operational considerations, has become slower than the tactical conditions would have permitted. The Division could have attacked out of the bridgehead it had been able to win with full force at dawn on 24 May against an inferior enemy to the east."[17]

Rundstedt's Temporary Disempowerment

The close-up order issued by headquarters, Army Group A, contradicted the basic idea of Sickle Cut and triggered vehement counteractions. During the night of 23–24 May, the controversy within the general officer corps was escalated further due to the interference of the army high command. Brauchitsch and Halder felt that the conservative headquarters, Army Group A, was a fifth wheel. Disagreements had become increasingly hardened during the course of the operation, which was important inasmuch as Army Group A played an outstanding role in the practical implementation of Sickle Cut. Army Group B had originally started the campaign with twenty-nine divisions, but in the meantime had shrunk to twenty-one. On the other hand, the number of divisions in Army Group A had risen to seventy-one, including all mobile forces. However, Rundstedt and his chief of staff, von Sodenstern, were typical representatives of the old school and did not stand out as protagonists of the modern operational war of movement. Several entries in Halder's diary revealed how tense relations with the army high command were. An entry, dated 23 May, is characteristic in this respect: "The developments of the past few days show that AGp.A is indeed experiencing considerable difficulties in managing this unwieldy mass of seventy-one divisions. I have a good idea its staff has not been energetic and active enough."[18]

Von Brauchitsch, the commander in chief of the army, had essentially left the execution of the operation to his chief of staff, Halder. But now he rigorously intervened in events. Around midnight, Army Group A received a telephone order from the army high command that the Fourth Army would no longer be under Army Group A but rather under Army Group B as of 2000 on 24 May.[19] That meant that Rundstedt, who had been in command of all German Panzer divisions, would now have not a single Panzer. Instead, he was to concern himself with flank protection along the Somme River. Brauchitsch officially justified Rundstedt's "disempowerment" on the basis of his desire "to unify direction of operations under AGp.B for the last phase of the encircling battle" and to combine the participating armies under a single command.[20] Halder also basically favored the idea of relieving Rundstedt's overloaded headquarters of the responsibility for the Panzer divisions. Doing this immediately prior to the completion of the operation, however, seemed to him to be a rather unhappily chosen time. He was afraid of difficulties in terms of technical command procedure because Army Group B did not have any well-established communications to the Panzer troops.

The Halt Order

On the next day, 24 May, Hitler visited Rundstedt's headquarters in Charleville in the morning to discuss the further employment of the Panzer force with him. To his astonishment, he learned that Rundstedt was to turn over the Fourth Army, with all its Panzer divisions and motorized divisions, to Army Group B, and was to be responsible no longer for Dunkirk but only for the Somme sector. This radical measure, however, had been ordered without Hitler's approval and even without his knowledge. He immediately declared the orders from the army high command to be null and void. At the same time, he "fully and entirely"[21] agreed with Rundstedt's pessimistic situation estimate because it is "entirely identical to his thoughts."[22] The famous halt order of Dunkirk was issued by headquarters, Army Group A, at 1245: "On orders of the Führer, the attack to the east of Arras is to be continued with VIII Corps and, to the northwest, II Corps in cooperation with the left wing of Army Group B. On the other hand, the general line Lens-Bethune-Aire-St. Omer-Gravelines (Canal line) will *not* be crossed northwest of Arras. On the western wing, instead, the important thing is to get all mobile units to close up and to force the enemy to run into the mentioned favorable defense line."[23]

Later, Rundstedt tried to put all the blame on Hitler, as if the latter had forced the halt order on him.[24] Blumentritt also spread this myth, which Liddell Hart above all propagated in the historiography.[25] In reality, the halt order merely signified the confirmation and continuation of the close-up order that Rundstedt had already issued the day before and that originally was supposed to have applied only to 24 May. In this connection Hitler merely issued Directive No. 13, which states: "The next object of our operations is to annihilate the French, English, and Belgian forces which are surrounded in Artois and Flanders, by a concentric attack by our northern flank and by the swift seizure of the Channel coast in this area."[26]

Hitler likewise pleaded for at least a temporary halt by the Panzers. But, as regards individual measures, above all the duration of the stop, he expressly gave Rundstedt freedom of action, as the Führer's army aide, Engel, noted full of "surprise."[27] Jodl, the chief of the Wehrmacht operations staff in the Wehrmacht high command, wrote the following in his diary on 25 May: "Führer . . . leaves decision to Army Group A."[28] The war diary of Army Group A provides the final certainty on this point when it states that Hitler "expressly left the manner of handling the fighting by the Fourth Army" to von Rundstedt.[29]

The Reactions of the Generals to the Halt Order

During World War II hardly any other directive within the German army was so passionately protested as the halt order of Dunkirk. Hitler's chief military aide, Schmundt, reportedly commented on the reaction of some corps commanders: "They resembled a pack of hunting dogs that are halted at a dead stop, directly in front of the game, and that see their quarry escape."[30] Liß described the mood the halt order triggered in Halder: "I learned of this . . . completely incomprehensible measure only in the evening, when General Halder, contrary to his customary habit, turned up almost one hour late for the evening briefing. He was livid with anger, such as I have never seen him before nor ever saw him thereafter."[31] The explanation for this can be found in Halder's personal war diary: "The battle plan I had drafted called for AGp. B, by heavy frontal attacks, merely to hold the enemy, who is making a planned withdrawal, while AGp. A, dealing with an enemy already whipped, cuts into his rear and delivers the decisive blow. This was to be accomplished by our armor. . . . This is a complete reversal of the elements of the plan. I wanted to make AGp. A the hammer and AGp. B the anvil in this operation. Now B will be the hammer and A the anvil. As AGp. B is confronted with a consolidated front, progress will be slow and casualties high."[32]

That nobody at the army high command understood the "what and wherefore" is indicated by the words of the then Oberstleutnant Heusinger: "What is this nonsensical order to stop the Panzer formations south of Dunkirk supposed to mean? Do we want to build golden bridges for the English whose entire expeditionary army is being squeezed in around Dunkirk? Do we want to give the English an opportunity to evacuate their troops? That is sheer nonsense."[33] Protests were also expressed among the generals of the Luftwaffe, such as Richthofen and General der Flieger [Alfred] Kesselring. They believed that Göring's promises were unrealistic. As will be described later, he wanted to have the Luftwaffe alone wipe out the Dunkirk pocket. Von Bock was likewise unable to grasp why his Army Group B, with its infantry divisions, was to push toward Dunkirk, which was seventy-five kilometers away, while the Panzer Divisions of Army Group A were standing around in the enemy's rear, facing the port city, and doing nothing: "I then said that I considered the capture of Dunkirk absolutely necessary; otherwise, the English might transport what they wanted out of Dunkirk under our noses."[34] Von Kluge, who on 23 May had still advocated having the formations close up (with a twenty-four-hour limit), also joined Kleist in urgently pleading for a continuation of the attack. In a phone conversation on the evening of 25 May, he reproached Sodenstern: "If I had been given my way today, the Panzers would have been positioned on the heights around Cassel."[35]

It had been his intention to push from there through the corridor of Kemmel, the narrowest point of the pocket, heading for Courtrai in the east to link hands with Army Group B that was attacking from there to the west. This inland-facing pocket would have meant that the French and British divisions—most of which were still south of the Lys River in the area around Lille—would have been cut off from their retreat to Dunkirk that was still fifty kilometers away. But now, the German Panzer divisions were lined up neatly side by side from the coast at Gravelines all the way to Arras as if during a parade. They had to watch helplessly as the Allied units marched unhindered right past them, day-after-day, heading for Dunkirk.

The otherwise loquacious Guderian, as he himself put it, was "speechless" when he learned of the halt order.[36] Nobody could give him a plausible reason for this measure. Later on he wrote "the Supreme Command intervened in the operations in progress, with results that were to have a most disastrous influence on the whole future course of the war."[37] Strictly speaking, for many formations, this was not a halt order but rather a retreat order because they had to evacuate their bridgeheads east of the Aa Canal, where Allied units now went into position. This instruction seemed so absurd that of all people Sepp Dietrich, the commander of the Leibstandarte Adolf Hitler [SS Bodyguard Regiment, Adolf Hitler], repudiated it, although it was said that Hitler himself had issued the order. The SS-Obergruppenführer [SS Lieutenant General] crossed the Aa Canal with his men and occupied [the hill] Mont Watten that was located on the other bank. Guderian was rather astonished at this expression of disloyalty on the part of Hitler's most loyal troops, but tolerated this unauthorized action.[38]

Brauchitsch and Halder Attempt to Amend the Halt Order

The Dunkirk halt order was generally considered to be so absurd that it really could not have constituted a problem to persuade Hitler to change his mind with a view to the disastrous consequences. Von Brauchitsch was summoned to him late in the afternoon of 24 May and thus had an opportunity to convince him of the irrationality of this measure. However, the "very unpleasant interview"[39] developed in an entirely different fashion. The Führer did not talk about the stopped Panzers at all but immediately forced Brauchitsch onto the defensive. He reproached him vehemently for his unauthorized actions against Rundstedt, which he believed to be a "crisis of confidence."[40] He denied the commander in chief of the army the right on his own to direct the employment of the field armies and made every future alteration in the command structure dependent on his own personal decision.

Brauchitsch had been appointed commander in chief of the army precisely because Hitler considered him to be the most obedient among all of the candidates. He could not tolerate any strong personalities in his immediate vicinity. That was to be his undoing because there was nobody who dared to alert the military amateur Hitler forcefully enough as to Rundstedt's mistaken situation estimate. Von Brauchitsch, of course, had an overwhelming body of arguments on his side, but he now turned out to be so intimidated that he had no persuasiveness whatsoever. Once again, the sensitive and highly cultivated aristocrat's nerves failed as he faced Hitler, the man of violence, in his undisguised fury. As he tried to argue, he got the feeling as "if somebody was strangling him."[41] Rumbling and roiling Hitler, on the other hand, feasted on the general's weakness and let him feel his dependence. Thus failed the attempt to persuade the dictator to revoke the halt order. Depressed and humiliated, Brauchitsch returned to Halder at around 2000.

While the commander in chief of the army was obviously resigned to his fate, his chief of staff figured a way out. Together with the chief of the operations section, Oberst i.G. [Hans] von Greiffenberg, he developed an idea as to how one could get around the halt order. Thus, he sent the following radio message to Army Groups A and B: "Expanding on the directives in the 24 May 1940, Army High Command order . . . the go-ahead is hereby given for the continuation of the attack up to the line Dunkirk-Cassel-Estaires-Armentières-Ypres-Ostende."[42] The decisive words were "the go-ahead is given" while the term "is ordered" was intentionally avoided. Moreover, the partial amendment of the hitherto ordered holding line did not signify a general lifting of the halt order. Halder had some ulterior motives in doing this. Headquarters, Army Group A, would forward this vaguely drafted directive, through normal command channels, to the "Panzer generals" whose powerful drive could hardly be slowed down anyway in this situation. Everything else seemed to be a question of Auftragstaktik. Army Group B understood this little hint very clearly. In it they saw for the Fourth Army positioned south of the pocket "the opportunity of moving closer to Dunkirk in order to stop the ship traffic that was increasing there."[43]

But now something happened that, in the words of Hans-Adolf Jacobsen, was "probably unique in modern German military history."[44] Von Rundstedt refused to pass on this directive from army high command. The procedure seems so incredible that we want to quote the pertinent entry in the war diary of Army Group A: "At 0045, received a new telephone directive from army high command, allowing the Von Kleist Group to also cross the Canal line by way of continuation of the attack, on 25 May. It is not forwarded to Fourth Army. The O.B. [Rundstedt]—to whom the Führer expressly left the manner of handling the operations of Fourth Army—considers it urgently necessary to let the motorized groups close up, if they are supposed to advance at all."[45]

The first hour of 25 May, which had just broken, thus became an hour of destiny in the campaign in the west. Rundstedt had the chance of producing an entirely different result with Operation Sickle Cut—with catastrophic consequences above all for the British. But he stubbornly refused to correct his past situation estimate. After the war, his former Anglo-Saxon opponents expressed much respect for the subsequent Field Marshal von Rundstedt. Gen. Dwight D. Eisenhower paid tribute to him as "the ablest of the German generals" and Field Marshal B. L. Montgomery stated: "Rundstedt is the best German general I have come up against."[46] As for Operation Sickle Cut, one must state that it was essentially Rundstedt who deprived it of real success by constantly slowing it down. Since his chief of staff, Manstein, whose Sickle Cut idea he had initially supported, had been transferred away, he finally turned into an opponent of Manstein's basic ideas because he did not want to bear the risk of an isolated Panzer thrust without flank connection with the infantry divisions.[47]

On the morning of 25 May, urged on by Halder, Brauchitsch once again reported to Hitler and, once more, requested that the Panzers be allowed to push toward Dunkirk. But, once again, he was turned down. Jodl wrote the following rather succinctly:

"Führer is against the idea, leaves decision to Army Group A. The latter for the moment rejects idea because Panzers are to recuperate and refit so as to be ready for missions in the south."[48] An entry in the personal war diary of Halder, who had met his superior immediately after the latter's return, reveals that Brauchitsch's backbone had now been broken.[49] Until then, no general in that war had been forced to submit to this kind of humiliating treatment. During the most important phase of the operation, the commander in chief of the army was no longer master of his decisions. Instead, he depended on the good graces of one of his army group commanders who, on top of everything else, repudiated him brusquely.

Halt Order Lifted on 26 May

Rather soon, it turned out that stopping the Panzer divisions had been a grotesque and fatal mistake. The infantry divisions, which were now entirely on their own, had trouble making headway. However, the Luftwaffe also proved that it was completely overloaded and overtaxed. Precisely at that moment, the German pilots ran into a fresh, rested opponent, that is, the British home defense fighters. Despite calls for help from the French government, Churchill had kept most of the British fighter squadrons back on the island instead of sending them to the continent. The clash with a completely new British fighter, the Spitfire, signified a particularly bad surprise. For the first time, the pilots of the Messerschmitt 109 had to cope with an aircraft that was equivalent and in some respects even superior. Dunkirk, so to speak, was right at the front door of the British fighter formations—all they had to do was fly over the fifty-kilometer-wide Strait of Dover, and they were thus able to take off several times a day. Overall, the British fighter squadrons flew 2,739 sorties during the evacuation operation, which was called Dynamo.[50] For the German fighters, on the other hand, Dunkirk was at the "outermost limit of their effective range," and they could stay over the operations area only "a very short" time."[51] So the Germans for the first time in this campaign lost air superiority and, moreover, suffered painful losses.[52]

The order for Operation Dunkirk had come so quickly and so unexpectedly for the Luftwaffe that it was not in a position to prepare a "new air deployment."[53] It had just begun to build up the corresponding ground organization in Belgium. Most bomber formations, therefore, had to take off from Germany. This meant that, for example, squadrons stationed in Bavaria, would first have to fly across Reich territory, then be refueled during a stopover, before flying straight across France all the way to the northwestern tip of that country. The Luftwaffe was not able to concentrate fully at Dunkirk because it was employed at the same time for army ground support. Besides, at that time, important targets along the Somme River and in the French hinterland had to be bombed in preparation for the second phase of the campaign in the west (Case Red).

However, one factor had an even more devastating effect on the Luftwaffe—the weather had become a "decisive ally of the British Admiralty."[54] During the first two weeks of the campaign, the German pilots had gotten the benefit of so-called Hermann Göring weather. But now, rain clouds covered the hitherto bright blue sky. From time-to-time, the cloud cover was as low as one hundred meters, which is why the bomber and fighter sorties had to be aborted again and again. During the nine-day British evacuation operation, the Luftwaffe was available only for the first seven days. On account of the unfavorable weather conditions, however, it was able to go into action with the stronger units only on two and a half days.[55] Von Richthofen had from the very beginning vehemently protested against this unilateral commitment of the Luftwaffe. In the war diary of VIII Air Corps, which he commanded, the Dunkirk chapter ends with the following sentence: "A victory over England was simply given away."[56]

The Luftwaffe was unable to prevent, and the Panzer Force was not allowed to prevent, the Allied troops from being evacuated. After the halt order took effect, the English, according to Loßberg, "almost within visual observation of the Panzers, marched off to the coast undisturbed and embarked."[57] Halder commented rather sarcastically: "Our Panzer and motorized forces have stopped as if paralyzed on the high ground between Béthune and Saint Omer in compliance with top-level orders, and must not attack. In this way, cleaning out the pocket may take weeks."[58]

Rundstedt grumbled about the army high command that had wanted to take away his Panzers. Contrary to any and all operational logic, he stuck to the halt order far too long—as a matter of principle. His corps commanders, likewise, were in the beginning unable to get him to stop being so stubborn. Not until the morning of 26 May, when it was by far too late, did Rundstedt gradually begin to get nervous. He "apparently could not stand it any longer"[59] and drove to the front to see Kleist and Hoth, both of whom very forcefully urged that they be given the go-ahead. Now the only thing left for him to do was to inform Hitler as to the latest developments of the situation whereupon the latter, in keeping with Rundstedt's proposal, lifted the halt order at 1330.[60] The formations in the meantime had stood down, were in the midst of reorganization, or were busy doing repair work. Once again, valuable time slipped by before the order at last had reached the very last unit and before the Panzer divisions again assumed attack formation. The offensive was not resumed until 0800 on 27 May. This meant that most of the Panzer divisions had been forced to mark time in front of Dunkirk for a total of three days and eight hours.

However, the situation had basically changed unfavorably for the Germans between 24 and 27 May. Several enemy divisions had gone into position in front of Dunkirk, where just days before only a couple of British companies had formed a thin screen. No sooner had the German attack begun on 27 May than it bogged down. In addition, numerous Allied troops were able to withdraw to safety at the coast from the interior of the country. For example, four British and several French divisions came streaming out of the pocket around Lille. It would have been easy for the Germans to close the narrow corridor at Kemmel, but their attack formations, including Rommel's 7th Panzer Division, were being held in place on orders from higher up. When this pocket within a pocket capitulated on 1 June, there were only thirty-five thousand French soldiers in the trap.

The British had also had sufficient time to assemble an evacuation fleet, a measure that would have been meaningless if the German Panzers had been allowed to continue their push to Dunkirk on 24 May. The weather had also changed. That restricted not only the employment of the Luftwaffe, but, with the soil softened by rainfall, the Panzers also had a more difficult time advancing.

Liß subsequently said, "We had missed the great moment."[61]

Operation Dynamo: The Evacuation of the Allies

Both the British and the French began considering an evacuation for the first time on 19 May.[62] By 26 May, it was possible to embark 27,936 soldiers from Dunkirk, Boulogne, and Calais.[63] Now, however, only the port of Dunkirk was left, and even that city might fall into German hands within a short time. In utmost haste, the British assembled an evacuation fleet, which, reinforced by French and Belgian units, grew to a total of 861 ships.[64] This quickly improvised mosquito fleet consisted of 1 cruiser as well as 56 destroyers and torpedo boats, plus a motley gathering of minesweepers, yachts, fishing boats, barges from the Thames River, excursion steamers, and so on.

Operation Dynamo commenced at 1857 on 26 May, but the British Admiralty did not entertain any great expectations. It was believed that at most two days would be available, and it was hoped that up to 45,000 men could be rescued during that time.[65] Even more pessimistic was the prognosis of Ironside who figured on a maximum of 30,000 men.[66] But the evacuation operation started even more sluggishly than had been feared. By 28 May, only 9,965 men were embarked. In the meantime, however, the Allied troops—not bothered in any way by the Germans in three days—were able to build up a deeply echeloned defensive position around Dunkirk that turned out to be very stable. Moreover, Operation Dynamo was now running full speed. In that way, 47,310 men were evacuated on 29 May and as many as 68,014 on 31 May.[67]

Now things happened, one after the other, to make the "miracle of Dunkirk" come true. The weather also played an important role. Normally, the seas are rough in the Channel. Rarely do the waters remain calm for several days in a row. During the nine days of Operation Dynamo, however, the surface of the sea was smooth as a millpond. According to Walter Lord, all the old salts reported that they had never seen the Channel as quiet.[68] That meant that the soldiers could be embarked not only in the harbor but also from the open beach. Just one day after the end of the evacuation, the wind turned suddenly and the surf smashed huge breakers upon the empty beaches. Another advantage was that the mostly low cloud cover protected the Allied troops against Luftwaffe attacks during the evacuation. Only at 0940, on 4 June, did the Germans manage to capture the harbor of Dunkirk after bitter fighting.[69]

During Operation Dynamo, from 26 May to 4 June, the Allies were able to transport 338,682 men to England.[70] Together with the 27,936 soldiers evacuated earlier from various Channel ports, plus approximately 4,000 British who were rescued in French ports, this makes a total of about 370,000 men. Of that number, about 247,000 were British and 123,000 were French. Nevertheless, 80,000 French soldiers were left behind in the area around Dunkirk and thus wound up in captivity.[71] Just a few days earlier, 35,000 Frenchmen had capitulated in the "witches' cauldron of Lille."[72] The Belgian forces that had also wound up in the trap capitulated officially on 28 May. About 500,000 men had to lay down their weapons.[73] It is no longer possible to determine just how many of thc morc than 1 million Allied soldiers who had been trapped in the Flanders pocket since 20 May died during the bitter fighting or during the evacuation.

Scenes of despair took place on 4 June in the harbor of Dunkirk and along the beaches where tens of thousands of French soldiers were waiting for evacuation but the rescue ships were no longer able to approach due to German fire. That morning Lieutenant Cameron once more took his motor torpedo boat into the smoke-covered harbor but returned without having accomplished anything. He saw an apocalyptic picture: "For nine days the port had been a bedlam of exploding bombs and shells, the thunder of artillery, the hammering of anti-aircraft guns, the crash of falling masonry; now suddenly it was a graveyard—the wrecks of sunken ships . . . abandoned guns . . . empty ruins . . . silent masses of French troops waiting hopelessly on the pierheads and the eastern mole. . . . 'The whole scene,' he later recalled, 'was filled with a sense of finality and death; the curtain was ringing down on a great tragedy.' "[74]

Of the 861 Allied ships employed, 272, including 13 destroyers, were sunk.[75] In addition, during those nine days, the Royal Air Force lost 177 aircraft.[76] The German soldiers, who were advancing toward Dunkirk, encountered chaos. The British Expeditionary Force had left almost all its equipment behind. That included about 63,000 vehicles, 20,000 motorcycles, 475 tanks and armored vehicles, 2,400 artillery pieces, as well as vast quantities of handguns, ammunition, and gear.[77] Thus, von Bock wrote in his war diary: "The scene on the roads used by the English retreat was indescribable. Huge quantities of motor vehicles, guns, combat vehicles, and army equipment were crammed into a very small area and driven together. . . . There lies the materiel of an army whose completeness of equipment we poor wretches can only gaze at with envy."[78]

Nevertheless, many German officers, who now at the end of Operation Sickle Cut stood along the Channel coast as victors, had rather mixed feelings. They did not really know whether they should be triumphant or whether they should be mad as hell: Dunkirk had been taken but the English were gone!

The beach at Dunkirk. *Bundesarchiv Koblenz [Federal Archives]*

Digression: Did the Dunkirk Halt Order Decide World War II?

> *Had the BEF had been wiped out in northern France, it is difficult to see how Britain could have continued to fight; and with Britain out of the battle, it is even more difficult to see what combination of circumstances could have aligned America and Stalin's Russia to challenge Hitler.*[79]
>
> Alistair Horne, *To Lose a Battle*

As noted earlier, World War II actually seemed lost to the German Reich in strategic terms before it had even begun in operational terms. Then the incomprehensible happened. The breakthrough at Sedan had outmaneuvered the French army. At Dunkirk now beckoned the chance to inflict a decisive defeat on Great Britain, an island power that until then had been considered invincible because it was unreachable. It had been possible to encircle in Flanders the British Expeditionary Force, a small but excellently trained elite force of regular soldiers. This force was almost identical to the regular, standing army because Great Britain did not have universal military service in peacetime. In another way, Dunkirk looked like a double catastrophe. Great Britain was not only about to lose almost all its trained soldiers, but also, as a consequence of that, it would hardly have had any active duty personnel who could have trained new recruits.[80] Most irreplaceable, however, would have been the commissioned officer losses because who would then have provided the tactical and operational leadership of the newly organized units? Almost all higher-ranking British officers, who later on fought against Rommel in North Africa or who in June 1944 directed the invasion in Normandy, including Montgomery and Alexander, were encircled in Dunkirk at that time. Looking back, Field Marshal [Lord Alan] Brooke—who, in May 1940, had been trapped along with II Corps, which he commanded—later wrote: "Had the B.E.F. not returned to this country it is hard to see how the Army could have recovered from the blow."[81] The future field marshal and British chief of the imperial general staff was also talking here about the psychological shock that would have been a severe damper on the readiness of the British to continue the war. But now, the population was aroused once again because the "spirit of Dunkirk" brought a change in mood.[82]

To be sure, later Winston Churchill maintained that his government would have continued the war under any circumstances, even if the expeditionary force had not been rescued. He indicated that he was prepared to continue the fight from the colonies, even if "this island or a large part of it were subjugated and starving."[83] The question, of course, is just how many days that government could have remained in office in case of a complete disaster at Dunkirk. Hitler, whose irrational Anglophilia we will go into in detail later on, emphasized again and again that he wanted a settlement with England and that he would offer his opponent an honorable peace. The captured expeditionary force would have been an extremely valuable ace in the hole for him.[84] The United States would also have been less ready, after such a complete British defeat, to invest vast amounts of money in the long drawn-out development of a new British army. The threat of an invasion of the British Isles now left without any active duty personnel would have increased the readiness to end the war.

To that extent, most Anglo-Saxon authors assume that without the "miracle of Dunkirk" the Churchill government would have been ousted, something that would have meant Great Britain's dropping out of the war. At the same time, they visualize a horrendous scenario for that case: Germany, whose armed forces at the time of the campaign in the west were just being built up, could have engaged in a gigantic wartime armament drive without being bothered by the Royal Navy and Royal Air Force. Hitler would not have had to take troops away for the Balkans (for example, Crete) or for North Africa, but could have concentrated all his armies on the Soviet Union.[85] Norman Gelb writes:

> For the Soviet Union, the consequences would have been grim indeed. The Battle of Britain . . . would not have taken place. During that historic battle, which commenced six weeks after the conclusion of Operation Dynamo, the Luftwaffe lost 1,882 aircraft as well as great numbers of its most experienced pilots and bomber crews. Had they not been lost, Hitler would have had an air force more than half again as large as the one at his disposal when his blitzkrieg against the Soviet Union was launched the following June.
>
> In addition, he would have been able to dispatch up to forty more divisions against Russia, ones he would not have needed to deploy on his Atlantic Wall, elsewhere in Western Europe, or in combat against the British in Western Egypt and Libya. Even without those additional divisions and aircraft, the German army took some three million Soviet prisoners of war during the first four months of its invasion of Russia. . . . Moscow might have fallen. Leningrad too.[86]

Naturally, one must not overestimate the Dunkirk legend, which British historians are busily cultivating. It only too clearly conceals the intention of crediting Great Britain with the decisive role in the Allied victory during World War II. Whether Hitler's Wehrmacht, without the "miracle of Dunkirk"—as some authors suggest—could have overrun the Soviet armies in a blitzkrieg is something that must remain pure speculation. There is, however, one fact that must be kept in mind and that is that the halt order of Dunkirk was one of the most serious mistakes of World War II.

Hitler's Alleged Motives for the Halt Order

Men in high position who make a fatal mistake rarely tell the truth about it afterwards, and Hitler was not one of the most truth-loving of great men. It is more likely that his evidence would confuse the trail.[87]

Liddell Hart on the background of the halt order

First Thesis: The Swampy Terrain

Hitler later maintained that the "unfavorable terrain around Dunkirk" caused him to spare the Panzers.[88] A comment by Keitel is also cited to support this thesis: "He maintained that he knows the terrain of Dunkirk only too well because, during World War I, he [Keitel] was a general staff officer of the German Marine Infantry Corps in Flanders. The soil is supposed to be swampy and the Panzers would only get stuck in it."[89] Some historians even want to claim Panzer expert Guderian as a star witness for the so-called swamp theory.[90] Looking at the rain-softened reclaimed polder land, he supposedly said, "An attack in the reclaimed Polder land with Panzers is believed to be wrong. This would mean needlessly sacrificing our best soldiers."[91]

However, the protagonists of this argument overlooked the fact that Guderian came up with this situation estimate not on the fatal 24 May but only on the afternoon of 28 May. In the meantime, soil conditions turned out to be entirely different because the heavy rainfall, setting in after 24 May, had softened up the reclaimed polder land. At the time of the halt order, on the other hand, Guderian was firmly determined to charge ahead to Dunkirk with his Panzers—right through the (at that time still dry) reclaimed polder land.[92] He also notes clearly in his memoirs: "The reason he [Hitler] subsequently gave for holding back my corps—that the ground in Flanders with its many ditches and canals was not suited to tanks—was a poor one."[93]

Halder later criticized this threadbare argument even more forcefully: "The reason he gave at the time was the unsuitability of tanks for use in waterlogged country. In flat contradiction to this were his actions in 1941, during the Russian Campaign, when in spite of all warning to the contrary he personally ordered tanks of the very same type into waterlogged marshlands, first around the Ilmensee [Lake Ilmen], later at Schlusselburg, and finally at Tikhvin."[94]

Second Thesis: Sparing the Panzer Force

On 24 May, Hitler emphasized that "it is necessary, to begin with, to husband the Panzer forces for the coming operations."[95] To document the allegedly critical Panzer situation, the literature mostly quotes the message from von Kleist, according to which "more than 50 percent" of his Panzers were out of commission.[96] But the files of Panzer Group Kleist contained no indications as to a Panzer crisis. Kleist himself later on spoke of an "exaggeration."[97] In reality, he wanted to protest against having to fritter away his forces to the four winds in this decisive phase and, moreover, quite superfluously, to set aside a reserve for Fourth Army.[98] Hence, the reference was made to the annoyed Kleist and the allegedly alarming "Panzer situation."[99] It is interesting to note that the units themselves viewed the readiness level of the fighting vehicles quite calmly. The records of 1st Panzer Division note that the "Panzer situation" by no means could have constituted "a valid excuse for the 24 May 'Halt Order.' "[100]

Halder at that time likewise did not want to go along with the pessimistic situation estimate regarding the operational readiness of the Panzers. He pointed out that "the crisis will be over within 48 hours."[101] After all, most Panzers were out of commission only for a short time.[102] The time the Panzers spent at the repair facilities mostly amounted to only a few hours.[103] That there could be no talk of a serious crisis in the Panzer force is also indicated by the fact that the Panzers, just a few days later, immediately after the fall of Dunkirk, were able to start off for the second big offensive of the campaign, Case Red.

Third Thesis: Fear of Allied Flank Attack

On 1 June in Brussels, talking to several generals from Army Group B, Hitler tried to justify the order to stop the Panzers: "I was anxious lest the enemy launch an offensive from the Somme and wipe out the Fourth Army's weak Panzer force, perhaps even going so far as Dunkirk."[104] Hitler's fear of an Allied counteroffensive at that time was completely irrelevant. The enemy situation reports appeared much too unambiguous for that. Perhaps there were reasons for keeping several Panzer divisions in reserve to be able to react to any and all eventualities, but a single Panzer regiment would have been enough to push to Dunkirk on 24 May. However, the halt order pinned down all available Panzer divisions and motorized divisions on the spot. In other words, this was a decision based on *principle.* Accordingly, Hitler must have had reasons other than the fear of a counteroffensive from the already beaten French army that acted as if paralyzed.

Fourth Thesis: Change in Concerns Relating to the Second Act of the Campaign

Jodl, one of Hitler's closest collaborators, justified the order to halt the Panzers on 24 May because "the war is won; all we have to do is finish it."[105] But precisely because the campaign was already considered to have been won and the second part (Fall Rot) was considered only to be an epilogue, there were no grounds to stop the Panzers so abruptly, as if one had to pull the emergency brake. Rundstedt also subsequently commented: "You bring *one* operation *to a conclusion* before you can think of *the next one!*"[106]

There is, thus, little to support the thesis that the German Panzer generals on 24 May were hardly any longer interested in the Flanders pocket but supposedly were already concentrating on the second part of the campaign. Here again one must consider the date of the particular entries in the war diaries so as not to reverse the sequence of cause and effect. It is striking to note that it was above all Guderian who suddenly displayed an almost provocative lack of interest in the attack on Dunkirk. It was only on 28 May that this attitude emerged as a reaction to the 24 May halt order.

Fifth Thesis: Lack of Information on the Number of Encircled Units

Another attempt to provide an explanation is the argument that the German command did not guess what a large number of Allied units had gotten into the trap or it would hardly have allowed such booty to escape. Halder's war diary is often cited as evidence of the fact that the German general officer corps allegedly had no idea as to what was in the pocket. On 29 May, Halder noted that he was really eagerly looking forward to finding out "how much of the enemy is still caught in this pocket, 45 km in length and 30 km in width."[107] This sentence has repeatedly been misinterpreted to mean that Halder had not the faintest idea as to how many Allied divisions were encircled. The critical word in this sentence (neglected in some translations) is "*noch*" (still). It contains a certain bitterness and irony. After all, the army chief of staff had to stand by powerlessly while the Allies started the evacuation of their troops and the spoils of the victory began to shrivel hour after hour. In reality, Halder was very thoroughly informed on the strength of the encircled Allied units, specifically by his outstanding Intelligence Service.[108] In the Dunkirk pocket, the latter identified 22 Belgian, 12 British, and 29 French divisions, quite a few of which were already heavily decimated. As Liß noted later on, not without a certain measure of professional pride, his section at that time was wrong by only one single French division (29 instead of the actual 28).[109] To that extent, the assumption that Hitler fatally underestimated the number of encircled major units is totally in error. In a letter to Mussolini, dated 25 May, he even maintained that 72 Allied divisions were encircled there—10 divisions more than were actually there.[110]

Sixth Thesis: Continental Thinking

At first sight, it seems entirely plausible to assume that Hitler and his generals—trapped in continental thinking—never really seriously figured on the possibility of such a vast evacuation operation by sea and were taken completely by surprise as it developed.[111] But the German command was by no means as unsuspecting as some historians maintain. On 21 May the Intelligence Service very carefully recorded "heavy occupation of the ports of Dunkirk and Boulogne" and the "departure of a larger number of transport vessels." This is why it pointed to the possibility that "English units might also be evacuated from there."[112] On 26 May, when Operation Dynamo was launched, it also reported "that the evacuation of the British Expeditionary Corps has begun."[113] An intercepted radio message of the British War Ministry to the garrison at Calais played an important role.[114] In this connection, Liß established later on: "The Intelligence Service thus . . . very early pointed to the probability of embarkation . . .—for the first time on 21 May, two days after Lord Gort had suggested the idea of embarkation in London and five days before 'Operation Dynamo' was set in motion in London."[115]

It is certainly correct that Hitler, the Austrian who grew up at the foot of the Alps, had little familiarity with maritime issues. Nevertheless, he, too, saw the danger that the British might be able to evacuate a considerable portion of their troops across the Channel. This emerges clearly from his Directive No. 13 that he drafted on 24 May. In it, he unmistakably demanded that the Luftwaffe have the mission "to prevent the escape of English forces across the Channel."[116]

Seventh Thesis: Using the Luftwaffe Alone

While most of the reasons cited for the halt order lose very much of their plausibility upon closer examination, the following argument deserves more consideration. Hitler believed Göring's big-mouthed promise that the Luftwaffe could wipe out the Dunkirk cauldron all by itself. Obviously, this idea came to the commander in chief of the Luftwaffe very spontaneously. On the afternoon of 23 May, he attended a conference with members of his operations staff, when the news of the impending formation of the Flanders pocket suddenly arrived: "Göring reacted in a flash. His heavy hand thumped down on the table: 'This is a special job for the Luftwaffe! I must speak to the Führer at once. Get a line through by phone!' "[117]

In the subsequent phone conversation, he predicted to Hitler a "gigantic victory of the Luftwaffe,"[118] maintaining that the Luftwaffe could give the English the "coup de grace" all by itself. The army would then only have to "occupy the territory."[119] But the feasibility of Göring's boastful announcement was in doubt from the very beginning. Some of Hitler's advisers from the Wehrmacht operations staff even reacted furiously. For example, Jodl commented on the notoriously glory-hunting Göring: "He is shooting his mouth off again."[120]

Protests within the Luftwaffe general officer corps were even stronger. Von Richthofen, the commanding general of VIII Air Corps, never left a stone unturned in his effort to get missions for his close air support corps. But when he heard of this strange mission, he was against it. After all, this was a typical mission for the army, which could best be accomplished by "a sudden surprise attack on Dunkirk."[121] He said, rather annoyed: "We flyboys are supposed to do everything."[122] In addition, the Luftwaffe did not have enough bombs for hitting naval targets.[123] In vain, Richthofen turned to his friend [Hans] Jeschonnek, the chief of staff of the Luftwaffe, to get him to cancel this mission order. The commanding general of Second Air Fleet, Kesselring, also protested. According to his information, "These operations exhausted our men and material, and reduced our strength to 30–50 per cent."[124] He therefore severely criticized Göring: "The C.-in-C. Luftwaffe must have been sufficiently aware of the effect of almost three weeks of ceaseless operations on my airmen not to order an operation which could hardly be carried out successfully by fresh forces. I expressed this view very clearly to Goering and told him it could not be done even with the support of VIII Air Corps."[125]

During the first phase of the campaign in the west, the German Luftwaffe achieved tremendous successes, but at the same time it also suffered severe losses. Between 10 and 24 May (inclusive), it lost 1,005 aircraft, including 810 that were totally destroyed.[126] In view of that, it is bound to seem just about absurd to think of employing the completely worn-out Luftwaffe to accomplish a mission that is typical of the army—with the excuse of wanting to relieve the burden on the Panzer force. In reality, the Luftwaffe would have needed a breather much more urgently.

Göring's questionable assurance that the Luftwaffe could do "everything by itself" may certainly have influenced Hitler's decision to affirm Rundstedt's halt order. But this statement, made by the commander in chief of the Luftwaffe already on 23 May, initially only played a background role. On the other hand, historiography long ago clarified the fact that Hitler, on 24 May, did not come to Rundstedt with the previously developed firm intention of stopping the Panzers. The triggering event, as will be shown later, took place after his arrival at headquarters of Army Group A.

Eighth Thesis: Intentionally Going Easy on the English

Among the many attempts at explaining the halt order, no other has caused as much irritation as this one. Allegedly, Hitler fully intended to build "golden bridges" for the English to let them escape across the Channel. Looking at it superficially, there would even seem to be some grounds for that. Just a few weeks before his suicide, Hitler recorded the following declaration in his "Political Testament": "I intentionally spared the fleeing British at Dunkirk. If only somebody could have made them realize that recognition of our leadership role on the Continent—which I had just accomplished painlessly but which they rather selfishly resisted—could have brought nothing but advantages for them."[127]

As an English historian emphasized, the dictator had "for the English . . . a maudlin, unrequited affection."[128] Germany had a tradition of Anglophile thinking anyway, and this might possibly be due to the ethnic relationship between the Anglo-Saxons and the Germans. After all, the ancestors of the Anglo-Saxons had moved to England from present-day Lower Saxony back during the fifth century. This preference for everything English, which in the past was rather confined to north Germany, was accentuated in ideological terms during the time of National Socialism, stressing the common Germanic roots. Hitler had only praise for the British Empire and "her mission for the white race."[129] In 1937 he ordered German schools to replace French with English as the first foreign language. Not only in his book *Mein Kampf,* but also later on, as Reich Chancellor, he left no doubt that the English really were his favorite partners for an alliance.[130] The foreign policy goal was "to arrive at an understanding with Britain on the basis of a division of the world."[131] In January 1940 Halder explained Hitler's objective to chief of Wehrmacht intelligence, Admiral Canaris: "The Führer wants to win the war *militarily:* defeating France, then a grand gesture to Britain."[132]

On 20 May, the very day the German Panzers encircled the Allies along the Channel coast, Hitler told Jodl that the English could have "a special peace at any time."[133] Hitler's predilection for the English, who, for their part, considered him to be a mortal enemy, indeed bore some irrational features and several times caused noncomprehension among his foreign policy advisers. For example, Envoy Hewel, Ribbentrop's liaison with Hitler, reported that the Führer, on the evening of the fateful 24 May, confided to him that "he simply could not have allowed himself to wipe out an army of the 'good consanguineous English race.' "[134] On 2 June, Hitler delivered a thirty-minute lecture in Rundstedt's headquarters: Ritter von Leeb, the commanding general of Army Group C, was also invited.[135] To the astonishment of the audience, Hitler sang the praises of the English. Blumentritt reconstructed the comments:

> Hitler was in very good humour . . . and gave us the opinion that the war would be finished in six weeks. After that he wished to conclude a reasonable peace with France, and then the way would be free for an agreement with Britain. . . . He then astonished us by speaking with admiration of the British Empire, of the necessity for its existence, and of the civilization that Britain had brought into the world. . . . He compared the British Empire with the Catholic Church—saying they were both essential elements of stability in the world. He said that all he wanted from Britain was that she should acknowledge Germany's position on the Continent. The return of Germany's lost colonies would be desirable but not essential, and he would even support Britain with troops if she should be involved in any difficulties anywhere. . . . He concluded by saying that his aim was to make peace with Britain on a basis that she would regard as compatible with her honour to accept.[136]

After this speech, von Rundstedt commented "with a sigh of relief": "Well if he wants nothing else, we shall have peace at last."[137] As Rundstedt said later on, Hitler assured him on that day he hoped England "was inclined to make *peace,*" in that he "allowed the escape" of the British Expeditionary Force at Dunkirk.[138] Allegedly, he wanted to spare the British "a shameful defeat."[139] Blumentritt later noted: "If the B.E.F. had been captured at Dunkirk, the British might have felt that their honour had suffered a stain which they must wipe out. By letting it escape Hitler hoped to conciliate them."[140]

Hitler's pertinent comments on 2 June have partly been erroneously back-dated to 24 May, the day of the halt order, when he likewise visited Rundstedt's headquarters. In reality, however, more than a week had gone by and the halt order had turned out to be a fatal error. There can be no doubt that the legend of the English being intentionally spared was put out by Hitler himself. Obviously, he wanted to anticipate certain arguments and embellish his military mistake, after the fact, to make it look like a far-sighted political decision. Instead, however, the dictator was far from granting the British Expeditionary Force a free and easy exit as a noble gesture. He would never have voluntarily let such an invaluable bargaining chip slip through his fingers. His real intentions are indicated only too clearly by the first words in his Directive No. 13 that was drafted on 24 May: "The next object of our operations is to annihilate the French, English, and Belgian forces that are encircled in Artois and Flanders. . . . The task of the Air Force will be to break all enemy resistance on the part of the surrounded forces."[141]

Upon closer contemplation, Hitler's Anglophilia looks more like a love-hate relationship that only too easily flipped over into his so striking desire to annihilate the English. And so, he wanted to cause a mass bloodbath among the English who were waiting for rescue, jammed together tightly on the beaches. When he learned that artillery shells were ineffective in the sand dunes, he suggested that antiaircraft shells with time fuses be used instead.[142] It seems extraordinarily indicative when the political leader of the Third Reich interferes in the lowest tactical echelon and even specifies the kind of ammunition that is to be used. According to a statement by his army aide, he particularly wanted "SS units to participate in the final annihilation" of the encircled English.[143] Hitler's destructive intentions are also disclosed by a remark made by Göring who once again made fun of the army general officer corps: "The army always wants to act the gentleman. They round up the British as prisoners with as little harm to them as possible. The Führer wants them to be taught a lesson they won't easily forget."[144]

There is no need to take a closer look at yet another thesis that would explain the halt order because it runs along the same lines. It so happens that Hitler tried, in talking to Halder, to make stopping the Panzers look plausible by noting that Flanders, which was inhabited by (Germanic) Flemings, was not to be devastated.[145] With this abstruse argument that did not convince Halder in the slightest, the dictator also tried to simulate racial-ideology aspects to divert from his true intentions.

Hitler's Real Motive: Asserting His Leadership Claim against the General Officer Corps

In the course of the many attempts to solve the riddle of Dunkirk, the questions always were only aimed at objective reasons, without going into the purely subjective motives of this egomaniacal dictator. In reality, there was a motive that seemed far more important to him than all tactical, operational, strategic, or political-ideological arguments—his personal authority as military leader. To get straight to the point: At Dunkirk, Hitler wanted to stop not the Panzers but the general officers corps in the army high command. He was simply concerned with a basic principle, the *Führer-Prinzip* (Führer principle). In his view, the Third Reich was a *Führerstaat* (Führer state) in which everything was to be oriented toward his person and that applied especially to the military leadership.

At this point, we must once again recapitulate the events from Hitler's very subjective viewpoint. The attack against the Western powers was very definitely his war. All military advisers at first predicted that the campaign in the west could not be won. He really had to force it on his reluctant generals. But then it turned out how right he apparently had been because this campaign turned into one of the most spectacular victories in the history of warfare. Now it looked as if not he, but his generals, would emerge as the big victors. Above all, Halder, who was mocked before the campaign as timid and anxious, now exuded self-confidence. The army high command was in the process of downgrading Hitler to a mere extra.

As described earlier, the key scene took place at 1130 on 24 May at the headquarters of Army Group A in Charleville. When the dictator arrived there, he found Rundstedt, the man who had his confidence, almost "disempowered." The army high command had ordered this radical measure not only against his will but also without informing him at all. Hitler felt that he had been struck at his most sensitive spot—his prestige. Now his power instinct began to rebel because never before had a general dared to go over his head in this way and leave him high and dry. This was precisely the moment for the explosion. Jodl's diary entry, to the effect that the "Führer" reacted "very unwilling"[146] looks like an understatement in view of Hitler's dreaded choleric eruptions. In his desire for revenge, which on occasion could take on downright irrational features, he decided to set an example. He wanted to restore the so-called pecking order and demonstrate who was the undisputed military leader.

Now he turned the tables and degraded Brauchitsch and Halder to the position of extras by letting Rundstedt determine how much longer the already stopped Panzers were to be held back. The provocation was that he, so to speak, at the very climax of Operation Sickle Cut, sidetracked the army high command and left the decision as to the employment of the Panzer force to a subordinated command echelon. But this tremendous affront was tantamount to a temporary disempowerment of the army high command. Hitler enjoyed his revenge when, immediately thereafter, von Brauchitsch reported to him and requested that the halt order be canceled. He referred him to Rundstedt, so that Brauchitsch, in his capacity as commander in chief of the army, had to go to his subordinate like a supplicant.

On top of all this, one must not forget the suspicious mood with which the Führer had started out to Charleville in the first place. The day before, Göring, the intriguer, who had a particularly good grasp of Hitler's psyche, had already managed to stir him up against the army generals.[147] He even advised that the triumph of Dunkirk not be granted to the conservative army but rather to the National Socialist Luftwaffe that was created under Hitler's regime.[148] Halder later commented on this scene as follows: "Goering warned Hitler against leaving such a success to the Generals, suggesting that if he did they might win a prestige with the German people which would threaten his own position."[149]

For Hitler, the halt order thus was not a military necessity but rather a reflex action on the basis of his power instinct. As star witness for this thesis, one can cite Hitler's army military aide, the subsequent Generalleutnant a.D. Engel. When Meier-Welcker after the war questioned him about the halt order, he revealed that some of Hitler's decisions "had nothing whatsoever to do with objective arguments but were merely intended to let the Commander-in-Chief of the Army know that he [Hitler] was in command and nobody else."[150]

Of all things, it was this example that was set on 24 May 1940 that spoiled the success of Operation Sickle Cut. Thus, there was no complete Cannae, as the Schlieffen school was thinking of. Instead, the escape of the British Expeditionary Force meant that the strategic victory, which von Manstein had wanted, was downgraded to just an ordinary operational victory. And so, the campaign in the west was nothing but one of many "lost victories," to use the title of Manstein's memoirs.

Dunkirk was actually a decisive turning point of the war. That applies not only to the success of the British evacuation operation but also to the power shift within the military leadership of the German Reich. The German general staff was an excellently functioning military brain. This instrument of the art of operational leadership would, in Hitler's hands, have been a dangerous weapon to carry out his own expansion plans. But because he considered himself to be a military genius, he considered the generals, with whom he surrounded himself, in the end to be only a backdrop for his lonely decisions. To that extent, Dunkirk indeed marks a break. When, on 17 June, the armistice request of the French government was received at Hitler's command post, Keitel described the Führer as the "greatest warlord of all times."[151] In that way, the latter once and for all completely fell under the spell of his Caesar mania. A frightening amateur slipped on the far too big warlord's cloak and finally led the victorious army into catastrophe.

9

The End of the Campaign in the West

Case Red—Only an Epilogue

In keeping with Manstein's basic concept, the campaign was subdivided into two major operations. Fall Gelb (Case Yellow) was aimed at encircling the Allied northern wing along the Channel coast. Following that, the Allied southern wing, which extended along the Maginot Line from Sedan to Switzerland, was to be encircled as part of Fall Rot (Case Red).[1] At the same time, strong forces were to push deep into France. After the Dunkirk encirclement battle, however, the campaign was decided and so Case Red was only an epilogue. The French army had practically no chance of turning the tide because the initial superiority of the Allies in manpower had now turned into the exact opposite. General Weygand only had 66 divisions.[2] On the other hand, the Germans could now muster 104 divisions and had an additional 19 divisions in reserve.[3]

On 5 June, one day after the seizure of Dunkirk, Army Group B launched a new offensive to push southwest along the coast. Surprisingly enough, however, the attacks were stopped initially with heavy losses. Von Bock stated rather astonished: "It appears as if we are pinned down!"[4] There were two reasons for this: Manstein had demanded "that an *offensive* solution should be found for securing the southern flank of the thrust toward the lower Somme."[5] As described earlier, during the push to the Channel coast, one of the field armies was to advance, not to the west, but to the south to prevent the enemy from forming a strong defensive front along the Somme and Aisne rivers. However, as Manstein observed regretfully in his memoirs, this big opportunity "had been needlessly sacrificed."[6] In the meantime, the French had erected the so-called Weygand line precisely along the line of the Somme and Aisne rivers as he had predicted, and that line had to be pierced in a frontal attack with heavy losses. Thus, there was a phase-by-phase reversion to the tactics of World War I with the same kind of bloody "chopping through the enemy defensive positions"[7] before it was again possible to switch to an "operational war of movement" after considerable loss of time.

Another reason why the offensive got stuck at first was that the fighting spirit of the French soldiers was now considerably stronger than during the days of May along the

Meuse River, where many were in a kind of shock. They now seemed visibly recovered and offered bitter resistance. Besides, the French had in the meantime changed their defensive tactics. Instead of the old rigid linear operational style, they now echeloned their defense in depth, setting up the checkerboard-like towns and woods as strong points for all-around defense. Characteristically enough, it was Rommel who most quickly adjusted to this new tactic. He simply attacked cross-country and avoided wide highways and outstanding terrain features. After the resistance zone had been pierced, the continued thrust deep into France in certain stretches took on the character of a pursuit race. Here, Rommel's 7th Panzer Division established a special record when, on a single day, 17 June, it covered 240 kilometers "without any contact on the right or on the left."[8] In the meantime, units of the Eighteenth Army had marched into Paris, the undefended capital, on 14 June, something that had a considerable psychological effect on the French.

At first, Army Group A had to reorganize its units. So, Guderian, whose corps on 31 May was expanded into a Panzer Group, had to return his units from the Channel coast to a new deployment area southwest of Sedan. While the main body of Army Group A attacked to the south, Guderian was to wheel southeast toward the Swiss border to circle around the rear of the French Second Army Group that was positioned between Sedan and Switzerland. In that way, he followed the operational line that Manstein had already charted in the autumn of 1939. The then chief of staff of Army Group A had proposed forcing the French during this phase to fight a battle with the fronts reversed in the rear of the Maginot Line.[9] As he emphasizes in his memoirs, he was quite deliberately thinking "after the pattern of the Schlieffen Plan."[10] The Army Group A offensive, launched on 9 June, began so promisingly in spite of bitter French resistance that Halder wrote rather euphorically in his diary on the next day: "A 'Battle of Cannae' is in the making."[11]

Guderian attacked past Châlons-sur-Marne toward Besançon and reached the Swiss border on 17 June. The tempo of this push seemed so breathtaking that in the beginning not even his superiors wanted to believe it. In his *Erinnerungen* (Memoirs) he wrote: "We sent a message to supreme headquarters informing them that we had reached the Swiss border at Pontarlier, to which Hitler signalled back: 'Your signal based on an error. Assume you mean Pontailler-sur-Saône.' My reply, 'No error. Am myself in Pontarlier on Swiss border,' finally satisfied the distrustful *OKW*."[12]

In the meantime, the Seventh Army of Army Group C had crossed the Rhine at Breisach and had punched through the Maginot Line.[13] It attacked through southern Alsace and, on 19 June, established contact with the northward-wheeling elements of Panzer Group Guderian at Belfort. Thus, a gigantic pocket now held the three French field armies that were squeezed together between Nancy and Belfort. This had been Schlieffen's vision in his time.[14] In contrast to Dunkirk, this time there was a complete Cannae, with about five hundred thousand French soldiers caught in the trap of Lorraine. Actually, the campaign in the west had to be considered as ended on 17 June.

On that day, Marshal [Henri Philippe] Pétain, the newly appointed French prime minister, requested an armistice in view of the hopeless situation. Now French resistance let up considerably, and only the defenders of some forts in the Maginot Line still offered bitter resistance. The armistice was signed in the forest of Compiègne on 22 June. Hitler had very deliberately picked the site of the armistice agreement of 11 November 1918. The signing ceremony took place in the same dining car in which German negotiators had then signed.

Italy, which was allied with the German Reich, had stayed out of the war for the time being. Due to the haste with which German successes occurred, however, the Italian government was caught in a kind of "missing the bus" panic and was afraid it would come away empty-handed after Europe's redistribution. With undisguised cynicism, [Benito] Mussolini told Marshal [Pietro] Badoglio that he needed "several thousand dead" to be able "to sit at the negotiating table."[15] Very few out of the total of seventy-three Italian divisions were combat ready.[16] Then, during the last few minutes of the campaign in the west, on 21 June, an Italian army group launched an offensive in the Alps. It ran into bitter French resistance and could make only minimal territorial gains. The Italian-French Armistice was signed in Rome on 24 June. The guns finally fell silent at 0135 on 25 June. That meant the end of the French Third Republic that had been born of the defeat of Sedan (1870). Soon thereafter, Pétain established an authoritarian regime in Vichy that was under the control of the German government.

The Campaign in the West: The Statistics

Case Yellow

Sickle Cut represents probably the mightiest encirclement operation in military history. Cooperation between two army groups resulted in an oversized pocket that encompassed the three Benelux countries as well as northern France from Sedan to the mouth of the Somme River. In the trap were the Dutch army (which capitulated on 15 May),[17] the Belgian army,[18] the British Expeditionary Force, and the northern wing of the French army, including the First Army as well as large elements of Second, Sixth, Seventh, and Ninth Armies.

The number of Allied soldiers who wound up in this pocket was estimated at about 1.7 million. Many of them were able to escape from the trap: not only the 370,000 men evacuated from the Channel ports but an undetermined number of French soldiers who, leaving their heavy equipment behind, escaped to the south through the gap between the advancing German Panzer divisions and the following infantry divisions. Officially, more than 1.2 million men were taken prisoner.[19] The precise number of those killed in action can hardly be determined. By that time, France had lost a total of 400,000 men (including those evacuated).[20] Weygand deplored this situation:

"Three-quarters, if not four-fifths, of our most modern equipment was captured. Our units in the north were the best armed. *They were our spear-head. The best of the French army was captured.*"[21]

The dimensions of this encirclement operation can be gauged only if one compares them to the numbers of prisoners of war captured during other battles of World War II. In the summer of 1941, 665,000 Soviet soldiers were taken prisoner at Kiev in the biggest encirclement battle of the eastern campaign[22] and 110,000 German soldiers wound up in captivity during the Battle of Stalingrad.[23]

The low casualty rate of the attackers in the Case Yellow encirclement operation is astonishing. In May 1940, the German army recorded a total of only about 21,000 dead and missing.[24] By the end of May, a number of the infantry divisions bringing up the rear had not had any enemy contact at all. For example, von Manstein's XXXVIII Corps was inserted into the front line only on 27 May. The ten Panzer divisions and six motorized infantry divisions that had been combined to carry out Sickle Cut had almost solely decided the operation. But, here again, the losses remained within limits. The 1st Panzer Division that was always employed at the point of main effort suffered only 267 killed in action. That amounts to 2.2 percent for a mobilization strength of 13,162 men.[25] These low casualty figures lay in a revolution in the conduct of battle. The German army avoided the tactical slaughter that was so typical of World War I and instead tried to outmaneuver the enemy in an operational manner. To that extent, the Panzer divisions had an exclusively operational mission, that is, to reach the mouth of the Somme River as quickly as possible. The ill-fated Battle on the Somme took place in this blood-soaked landscape in 1916, and, on the very first day, the British lost a total of 60,000 (including 20,000 dead) out of 140,000 men. In this bloodiest battle of World War I, the Allies lost 700,000 men and the Germans lost 500,000 men (killed in action and wounded). Nevertheless, neither side was able to achieve any significant territorial gains, not to mention a breakthrough.

The Bottom Line of the Campaign in the West: Cases Yellow and Red

In May–June of 1940, the German army recorded only about 49,000 killed in action and missing.[26] Those figures came to 120,000 for the French army,[27] 7,500 for the Belgian army,[28] and 3,000 for the Dutch army.[29] The British (army and air force) lost about 5,000 killed in action, and their total losses (including prisoners of war and wounded) were reported to be about 70,000.[30]

In view of the fact that the German Panzer force was still in the developmental stage and, by way of a direct comparison, was inferior to the Allied models, the loss figure of 714 fighting vehicles was certainly within reason. Of these, 428 were the Panzer I and II models whose combat capability was limited.[31] The Luftwaffe suffered considerable losses, with 1,236 aircraft destroyed plus 323 damaged.[32] In contrast, the

French Air Force lost 892[33] and the Royal Air Force lost 1,029 aircraft.[34] A surprise raid during the very first few hours of the campaign had smashed most of the potential of the Belgian and Dutch air forces. Looking at it overall, the campaign in the west appeared to be an unexpectedly easy victory, which led to the rather dangerous assessment that in the future it would be possible everywhere to win easy victories with a minimum of effort.

10

Causes of Victory and Defeat

France's Collapse

Social and Psychological Reasons

> *The young German soldiers were astonished at the . . . weak resistance. After all, they had been told that the French were going to be tough foes. But even more astonished were the veterans of World War I; after all, they had gotten to know the* Poilu *during the battles around Verdun, along the Somme, in the Argonne and elsewhere as a brave fighter. What was wrong with the French of today?*[1]
>
> From the records of the 7th Panzer Regiment

World War I, which France won with the help of its allies, had become a Pyrrhic victory. Among all the warring countries, France paid the highest price in blood: 1.5 million dead and missing. This meant that 27 percent of the male population between the ages of eighteen and twenty-seven had been killed in action on the battlefield.[2] Besides, a trauma, the Verdun complex, was left behind. The exhausted French population had still not recovered from this maximum effort. To that extent, it is no wonder that war weariness and yearning for peace were widespread. It had become fashionable to draw a caricature of allegedly decadent and pacifist French society prior to World War II. In reality, conditions were considerably more complex, although pacifist ideas were certainly influential. Some circles believed that any and all war was senseless, even a war against Hitler. On 10 July 1939, Marcel Déat, in the magazine *L'Œuvre,* published an editorial whose title, "*Mourir pour Dantzig?*" (Why Die for Danzig?), became a thoroughly misunderstood slogan.[3]

Hitler had pursued his rearmament effort camouflaged behind clever peace propaganda.[4] To conceal his intention, he several times received influential pacifists from England and France for personal talks. George Lansbury, the former leader of the British Labour Party, after such a meeting enthusiastically proclaimed in the press and on radio that he was most deeply impressed by Adolf Hitler's love of peace.[5] The veterans associations of the Allies were special target groups. In July 1937 Freiburg im Breisgau was the scene of a peace spectacular that numerous French World War I veterans attended. Immediately thereafter, in August, about one hundred thousand delegates attended a meeting of war victims.[6] In a weepy voice, Hitler reported again and again how much he suffered as just a plain soldier during the war and how he had gone blind after a gas attack. He regained his eyesight only after spending a long time in a military hospital. It was interesting to note that leading National Socialist propagandists at that time in their verbal and written announcements behaved as if they were the heads of organized pacifism in Germany.[7] Neither German rearmament nor the Sudeten Crisis, not even the attack on Poland, completely disillusioned the western Europeans. And so, many Frenchmen found refuge in the dream world of a utopian pacifism.

France's Left found itself torn two ways when Stalin allied himself with his archenemy Hitler. Parts of the Communist Party of France in fact collaborated with the National Socialists. The German soldiers who marched through French towns did not believe what they saw when they read, for example, the following slogans on leaflets and posters: *On ne tire pas contre les Allemands.—Pas un coup de feu! Vive Stalin—Vive Hitler!* (Do not fire on Germans.—Not a single round! Long live Stalin—Long live Hitler!)[8]

The Communist Party had, of course, been outlawed in September 1939 and most of its deputies arrested. But numerous subversive measures provided underground support for Stalin's and Hitler's policies. For example, Communist workers carried out a series of sabotage acts in arms plants. Some of the aircraft delivered by the Farman Works exploded mysteriously in the air shortly after takeoff. At last, the security police caught Roger Ramband, a young French Communist, in the act. He had just tampered with the fuel supply in seventeen aircraft so that the flowing fuel dripped on the red-hot exhaust pipe, which was bound to lead to an explosion. In the Renault Works, armament workers threw screws into the gears of Char B tanks that were ready for delivery, which damaged the gears after a few hours of driving. In another plant, two hundred barrels of the urgently needed 2.5-cm antiaircraft guns—equivalent to the equipment of four divisions—were rendered unusable.[9]

The tremendous force of the German offensive not only caused the front to collapse in May 1940 but also spread chaos behind the front. Now, one of the most successful propaganda coups of World War II took effect—the fear of the Fifth Column, which Goebbels had stirred up. It triggered "a mass hysteria that is unique in modern history."[10] It caused "spy-itis" to spread like an epidemic.[11] The aroused imagination of the fearful French suspected spies and agents everywhere. When a rumor suddenly sprang up that German paratroopers would be causing trouble dressed up as nuns and monks, all similarly dressed persons were suspected of being spies. As a rule, however, the nuns were real nuns and the monks were really members of religious orders.[12]

A secret German radio station, camouflaged as a Communist underground transmitter Radio Humanité, played a particularly disastrous role in rattling the French population.[13] Millions of fleeing French further increased the panic among the civilian population. The French writer [Alfred] Fabre-Luce wrote about this in his diary: "This flight is suicide. . . . Along all roads leading south, the refugees encounter armies marching north to defend the homes left behind by the civilians. They stop the marching troops, they embroil them in their terrible confusion, and infect them with their panic. The avalanche grows from city to city. It rolls all the way to the Pyrenees. This is also something that Hitler had made provision for. . . . Although this mass of people may curse him, it nevertheless works right along with his plan."[14]

After the defeat, a search for the guilty ones began in France. Now came the day of reckoning with the so-called Left, with the socialists and Communists. The French Right, including some generals, accused them of having corroded society with the poison of pacifism. In this way, the strength of the army was undermined in the end. Thus, the alleged decadence of certain population strata became an alibi for the failure of the general officer corps. It was not the many military mistakes but rather society alone that was responsible for the collapse. During the Vichy Regime, the Riom Trials took place in which, not so much the generals (except for Gamelin), but primarily politicians and intellectuals of the defunct Third Republic were accused. Also, of all people, Huntziger, one of the main defendants in the debacle, became minister of war. The historian Marc Bloch came out against this French "stab-in-the-back legend"—in spite of all criticism of pacifism. As a reserve officer, he had witnessed the complete failure of the military command and blamed it for the incomprehensible catastrophe. In his book *The Strange Defeat,* he accused the French general officer corps of being "incapable of thinking in terms of a *new* war."[15] Instead, the generals cocooned themselves against the reality of a modern war in a kind of "reality loss."

Military Causes

Maginot Thinking: Confinement to Passive Defense

Whosoever stays behind his entrenchment is beaten.[16]

Napoleon

One of the commonplaces of historiography is that the Maginot Line was a gigantic investment mistake. But, of all people, Winston Churchill, who in his assessment of French military strategy was not always very lenient, commented: "In the after-light, the policy of the Maginot Line has often been condemned . . . yet it is always a wise precaution in defending a frontier of hundreds of miles to bar off as much as possible by fortifications, and thus economize the use of troops in sedentary roles and 'canalize' potential invasion. Properly used in the French scheme of war, the Maginot Line would have been of immense service to France."[17]

The Maginot Line, with which France wanted to protect itself against *furor teutonicus* (Teutonic fury), offered a series of advantages:

A sudden surprise attack (the prerequisite for a blitzkrieg) had no chance of success.

The Germans found themselves forced to attack on the detour via the territory of three neutral countries whose potential thus enhanced the French potential.

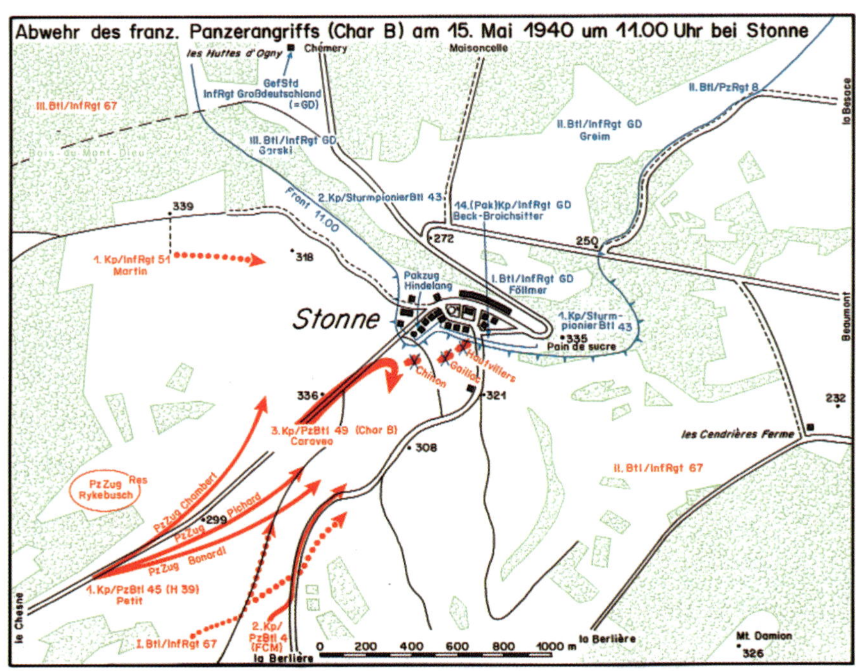

Repulse of French Tank Attack (Char B) at 1100, 15 May 1940, near Stonne

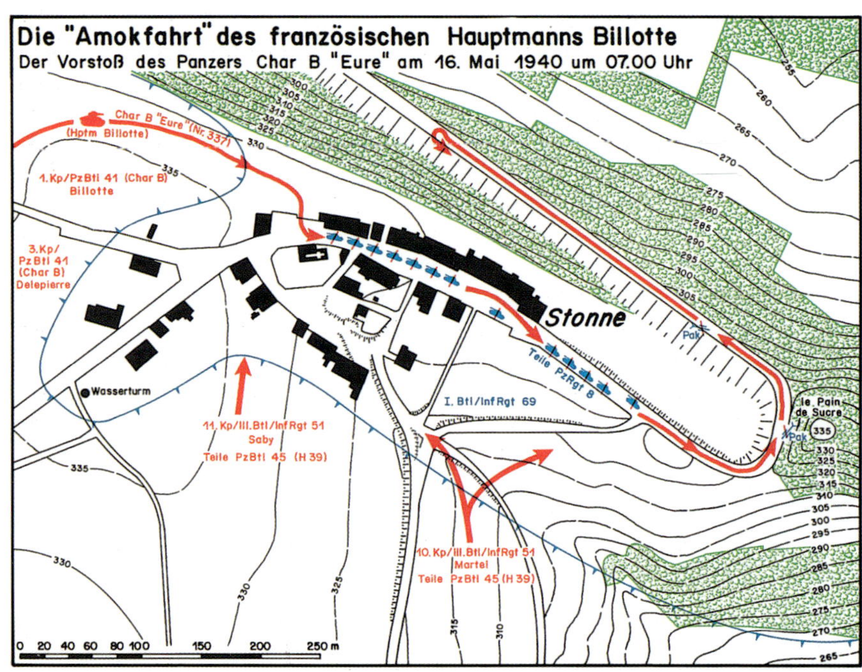

French Captain Billotte's Wild Ride; the Thrust Made by Char B Eure at 0700, 16 May 1940

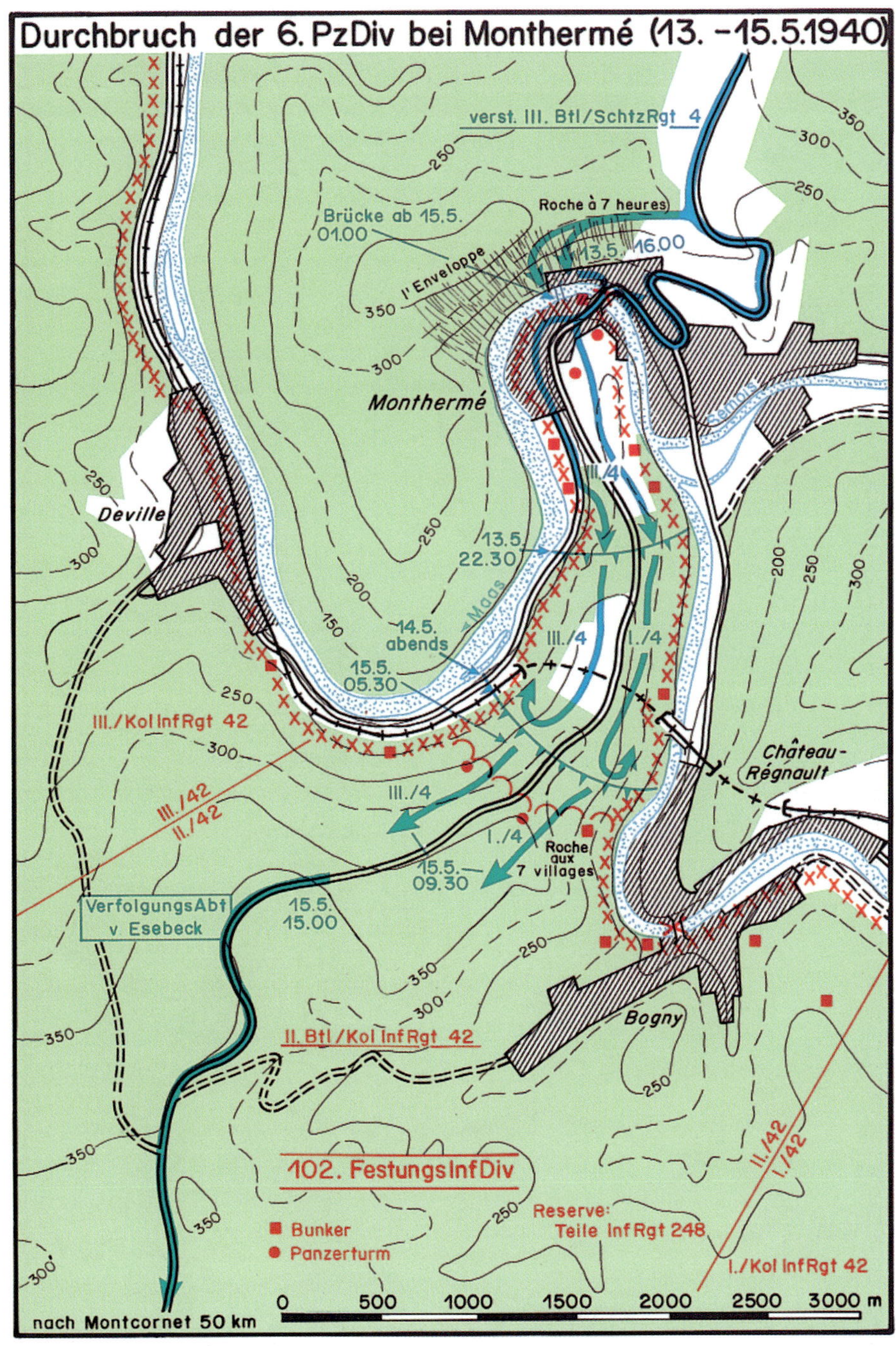

Breakthrough by the 6th Panzer Division at Montherermé, 13–15 May 1940

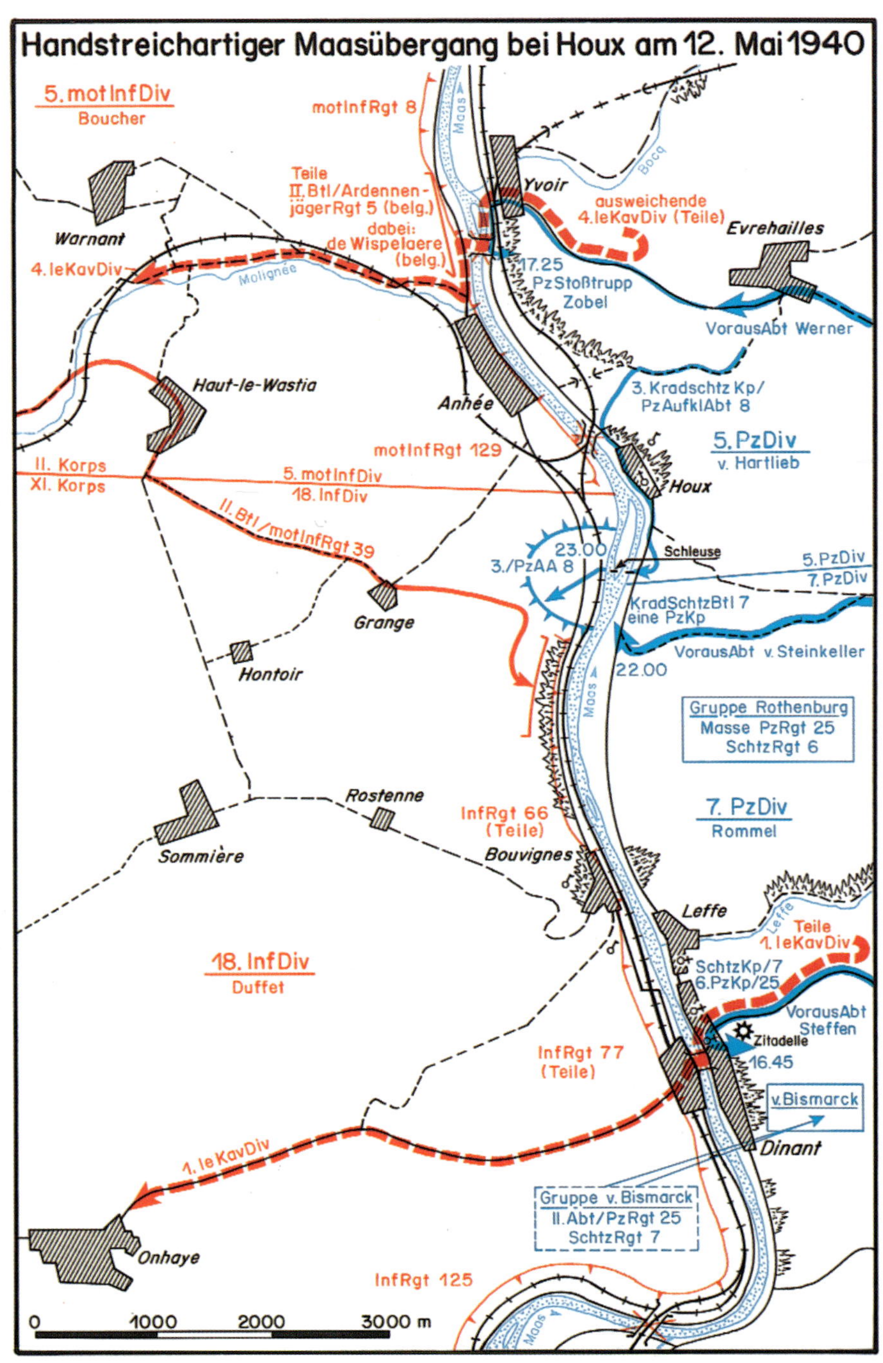

Handstreichartiger Maasübergang bei Houx am 12. Mai 1940
5. mot Inf Div
Boucher
motInfRgt 8
Maas
Teile
II. Btl/Ardennen-jägerRgt 5 (belg.)
dabei: de Wispelaere (belg.)
Yvoir
ausweichende 4.leKavDiv (Teile)
Evrehailles
Bocq
Warnant
4. leKavDiv
Molignée
17.25
PzStoßtrupp Zobel
VorausAbt Werner
Haut-le-Wastia
Anhée
3. Kradschtz Kp/
PzAufklAbt 8
5. PzDiv
v. Hartlieb
motInfRgt 129
Houx
II. Korps
XI. Korps
5. motInfDiv
18. InfDiv
II. Btl/motInfRgt 39
23.00
3./PzAA 8
Schleuse
5. PzDiv
7. PzDiv
KradSchtzBtl 7
eine PzKp
Grange
VorausAbt v. Steinkeller
22.00
Hontoir
Gruppe Rothenburg
Masse PzRgt 25
SchtzRgt 6
Rostenne
InfRgt 66
(Teile)
7. PzDiv
Rommel
Sommière
Bouvignes
Leffe
Teile
1. leKavDiv
18. InfDiv
Duffet
SchtzKp/7
6.PzKp/25
VorausAbt Steffen
Zitadelle
16.45
InfRgt 77
(Teile)
v. Bismarck
Dinant
1. leKavDiv
Gruppe v. Bismarck
II. Abt/PzRgt 25
SchtzRgt 7
Onhaye
InfRgt 125
0
1000
2000
3000 m

The Surprise Crossing of the Meuse River at Houx, 12 May 1940

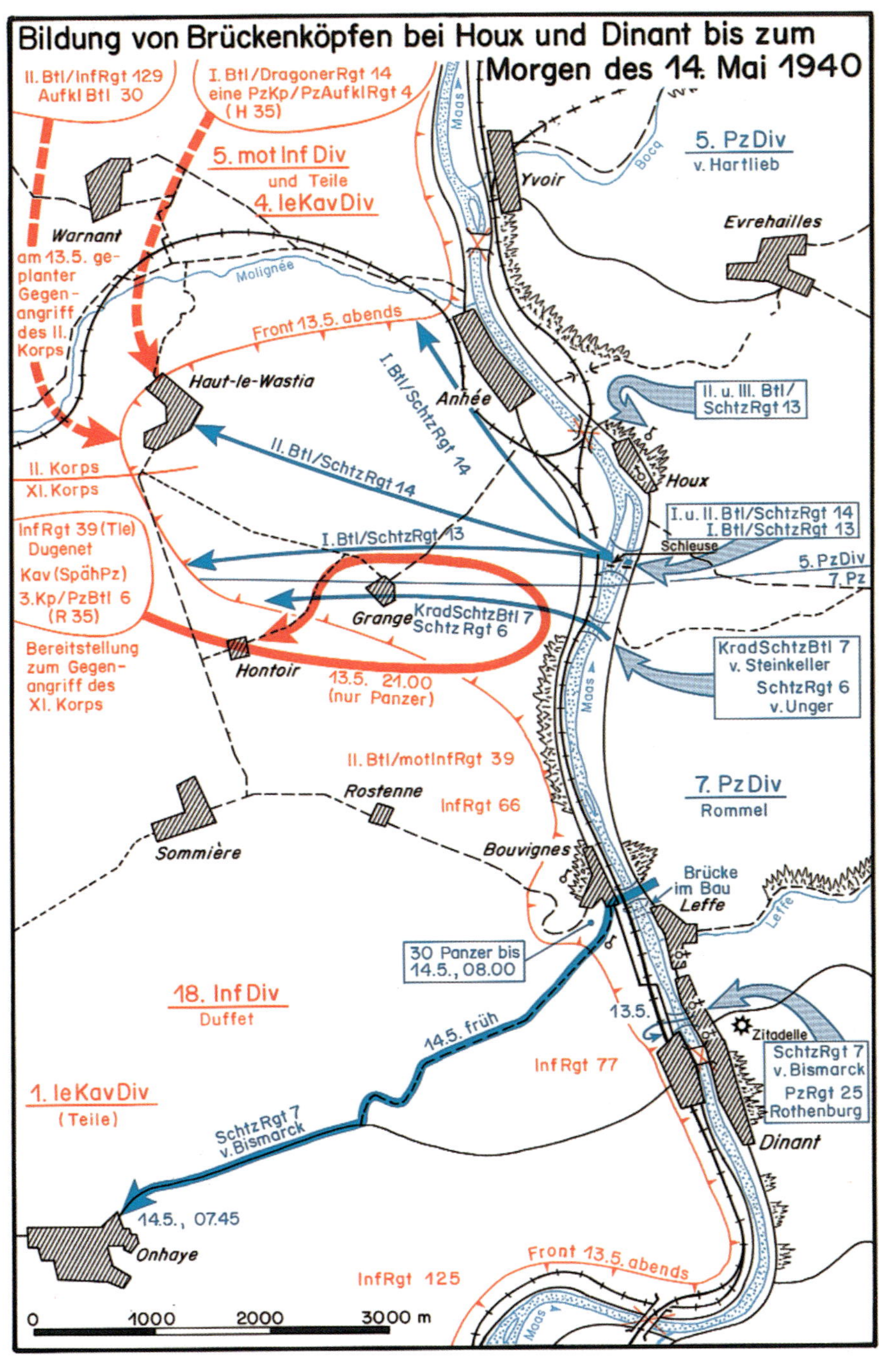

Forming Bridgeheads at Houx and Dinant by the Morning of 14 May 1940

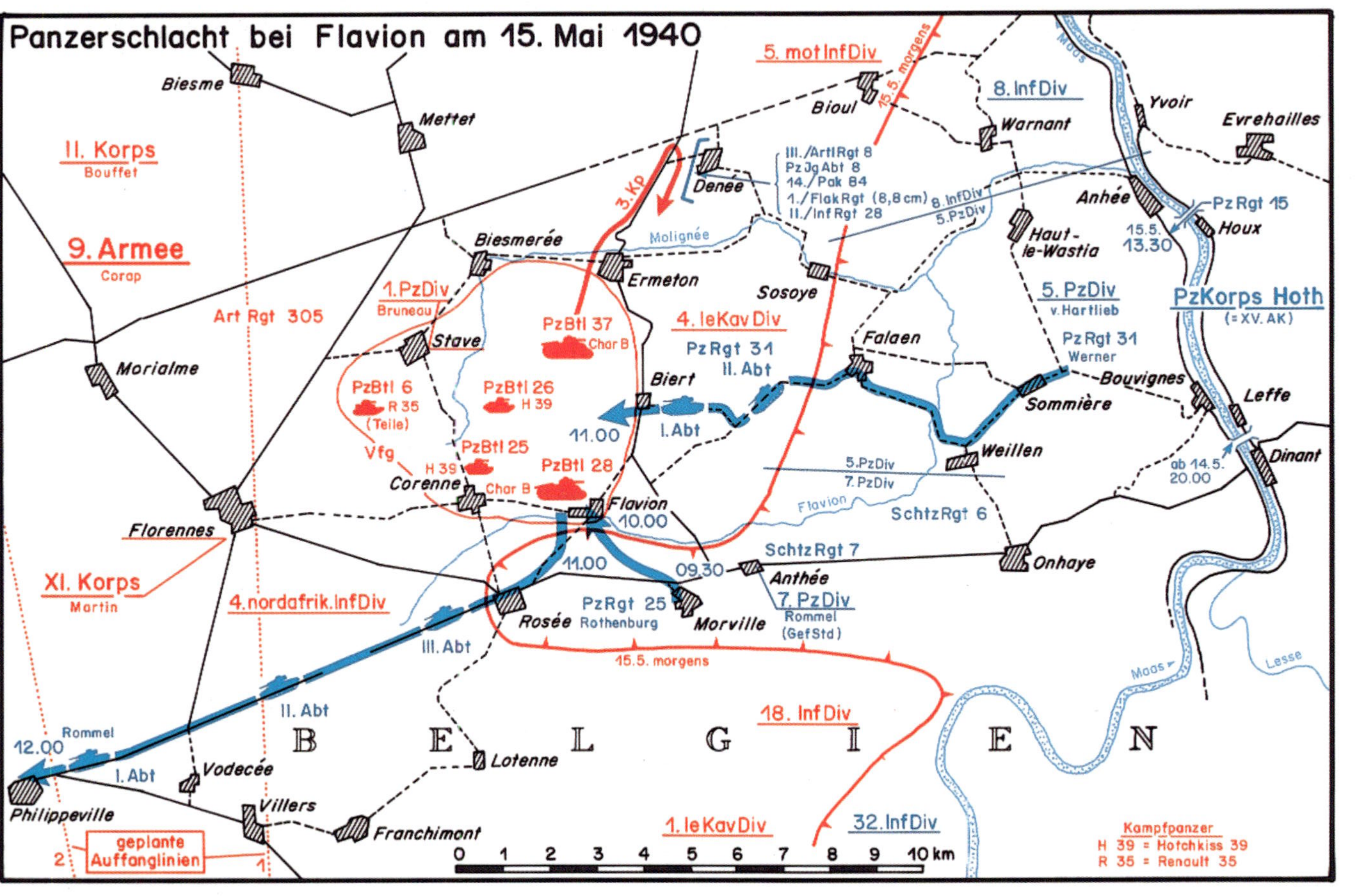

Tank Battle at Flavion, 15 May 1940

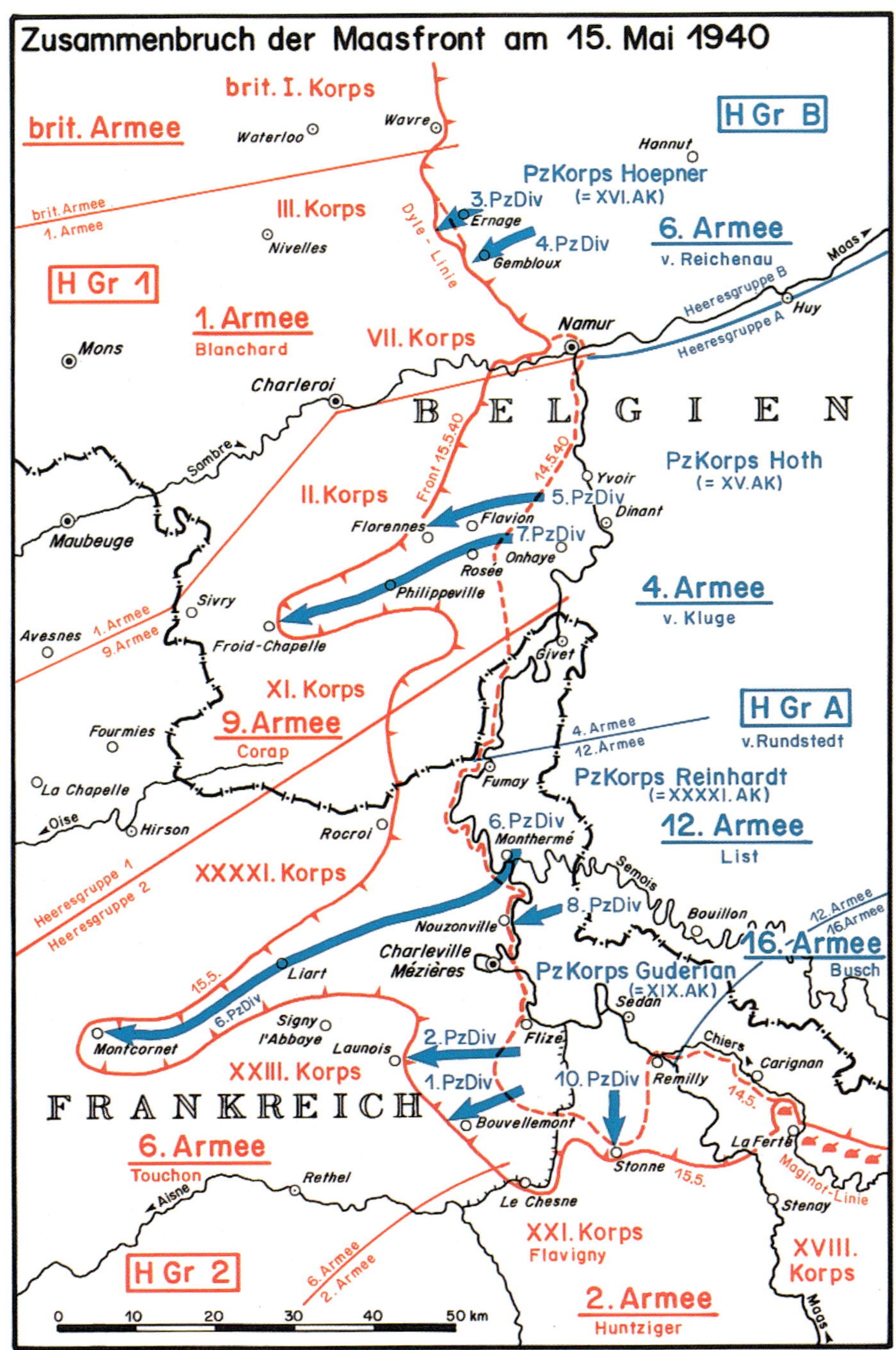

Zusammenbruch der Maasfront am 15. Mai 1940
brit. I. Korps
brit. Armee
Waterloo
Wavre
H Gr B
Hannut
PzKorps Hoepner
(= XVI.AK)
3.PzDiv
Ernage
4.PzDiv
Gembloux
6. Armee
v. Reichenau
Maas
III. Korps
Nivelles
Dyle-Linie
brit. Armee
1. Armee
H Gr 1
1. Armee
Blanchard
VII. Korps
Namur
Heeresgruppe B
Heeresgruppe A
Huy
Mons
Charleroi
BELGIEN
Sambre
Front 15.5.40
14.5.40
PzKorps Hoth
(= XV.AK)
Yvoir
II. Korps
5.PzDiv
Dinant
Florennes
Flavion
7.PzDiv
Onhaye
Rosée
Maubeuge
Philippeville
4. Armee
v. Kluge
Sivry
Avesnes
1. Armee
9. Armee
Froid-Chapelle
Givet
XI. Korps
H Gr A
v. Rundstedt
9. Armee
Corap
4. Armee
12. Armee
Fourmies
PzKorps Reinhardt
(= XXXXI. AK)
Fumay
La Chapelle
6.PzDiv
Monthermé
12. Armee
List
Oise
Hirson
Rocroi
XXXXI. Korps
Semois
8.PzDiv
Bouillon
12. Armee
16. Armee
Heeresgruppe 1
Heeresgruppe 2
Nouzonville
16. Armee
Busch
Charleville
Mézières
PzKorps Guderian
(= XIX.AK)
Liart
15.5.
Sedan
6.PzDiv
Signy l'Abbaye
2.PzDiv
Flize
Chiers
Carignan
Montcornet
Launois
XXIII. Korps
1.PzDiv
10. PzDiv
Remilly
14.5.
FRANKREICH
Bouvellemont
La Ferté
6. Armee
Touchon
Stonne
15.5.
Maginot-Linie
Rethel
Aisne
Le Chesne
Stenay
XXI. Korps
Flavigny
XVIII. Korps
H Gr 2
6. Armee
2. Armee
2. Armee
Huntziger
Maas
0 10 20 30 40 50 km

Collapse of Meuse River Front, 15 May 1940

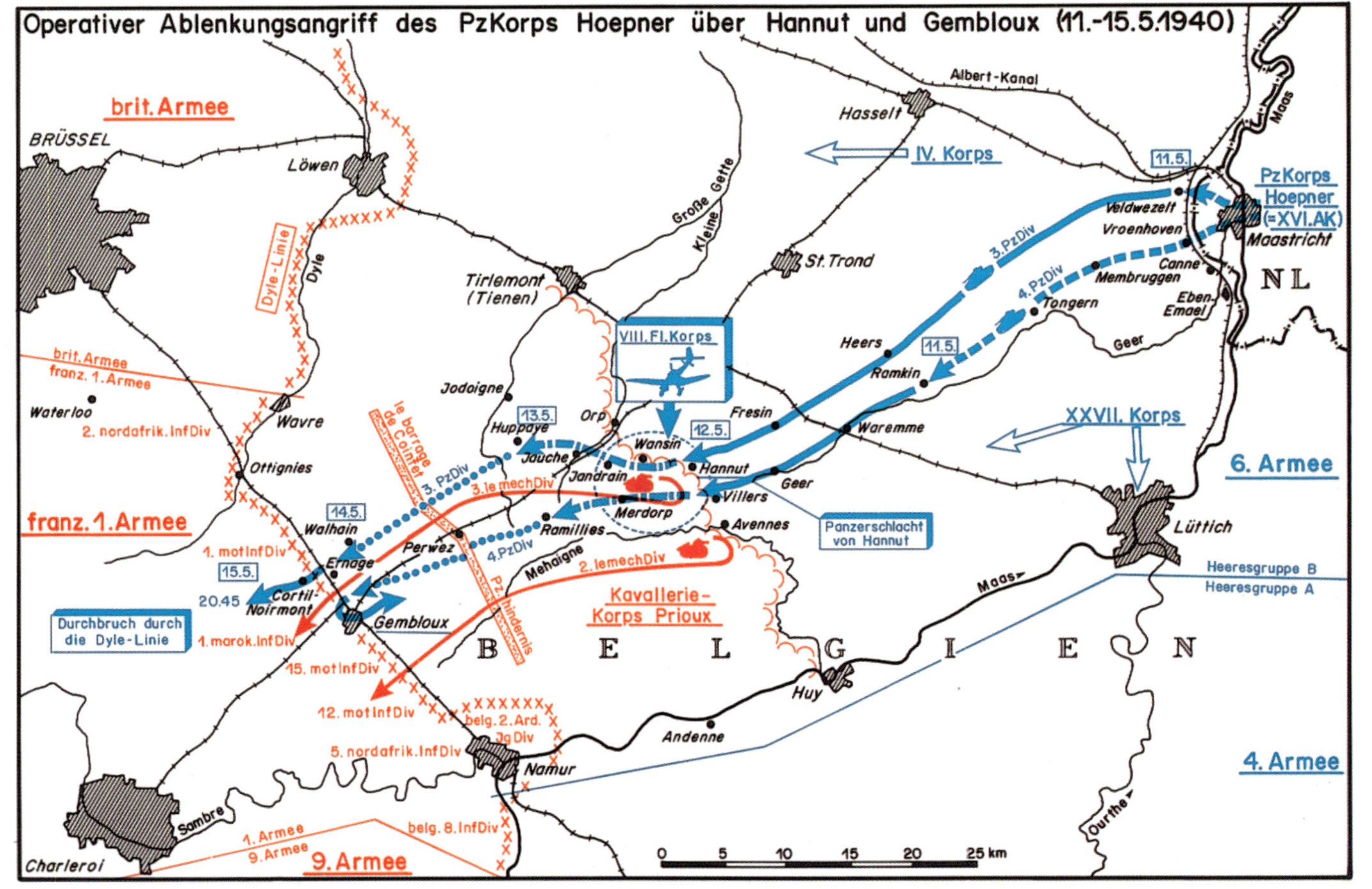

Operation-Level Diversionary Attack by Panzer Corps Hoepner via Hannut and Gembloux, 11–15 May 1940

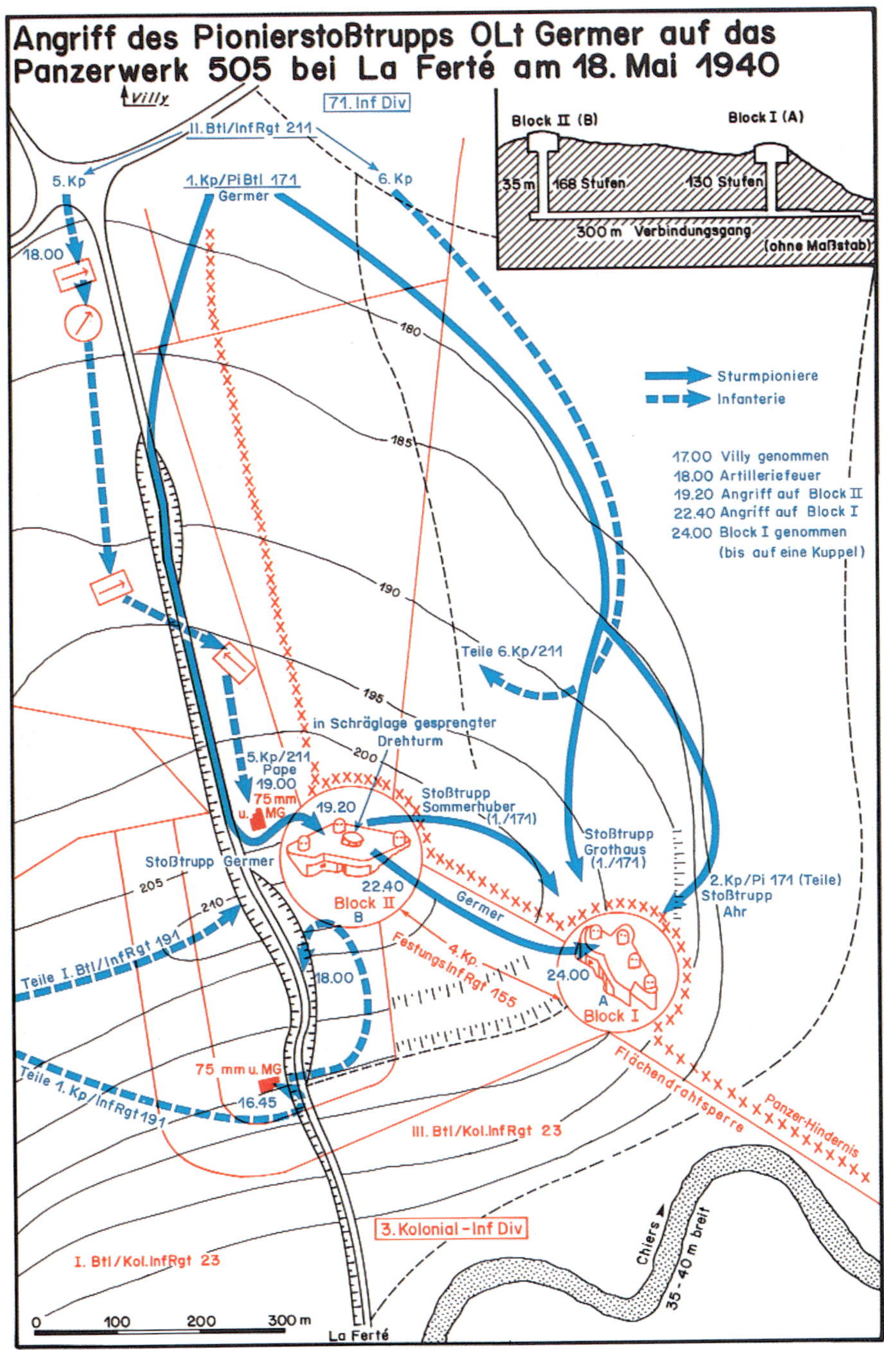

1st Lieutenant Germer's Engineer Assault Team Attack against Fort No. 505 at La Ferté, 18 May 1940

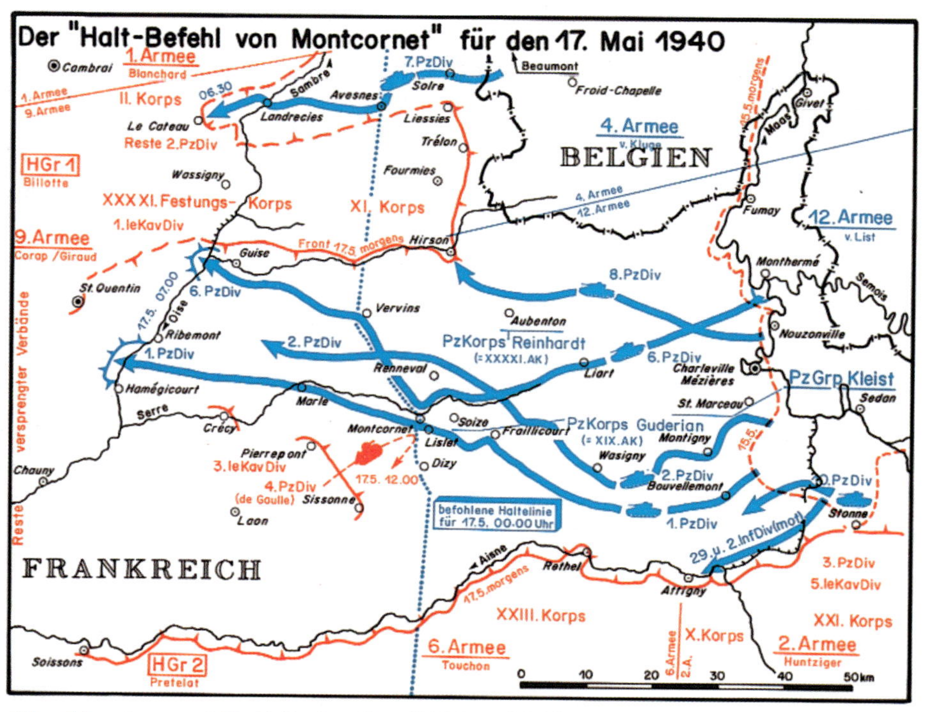

The Montcornet Halt Order for 17 May 1940

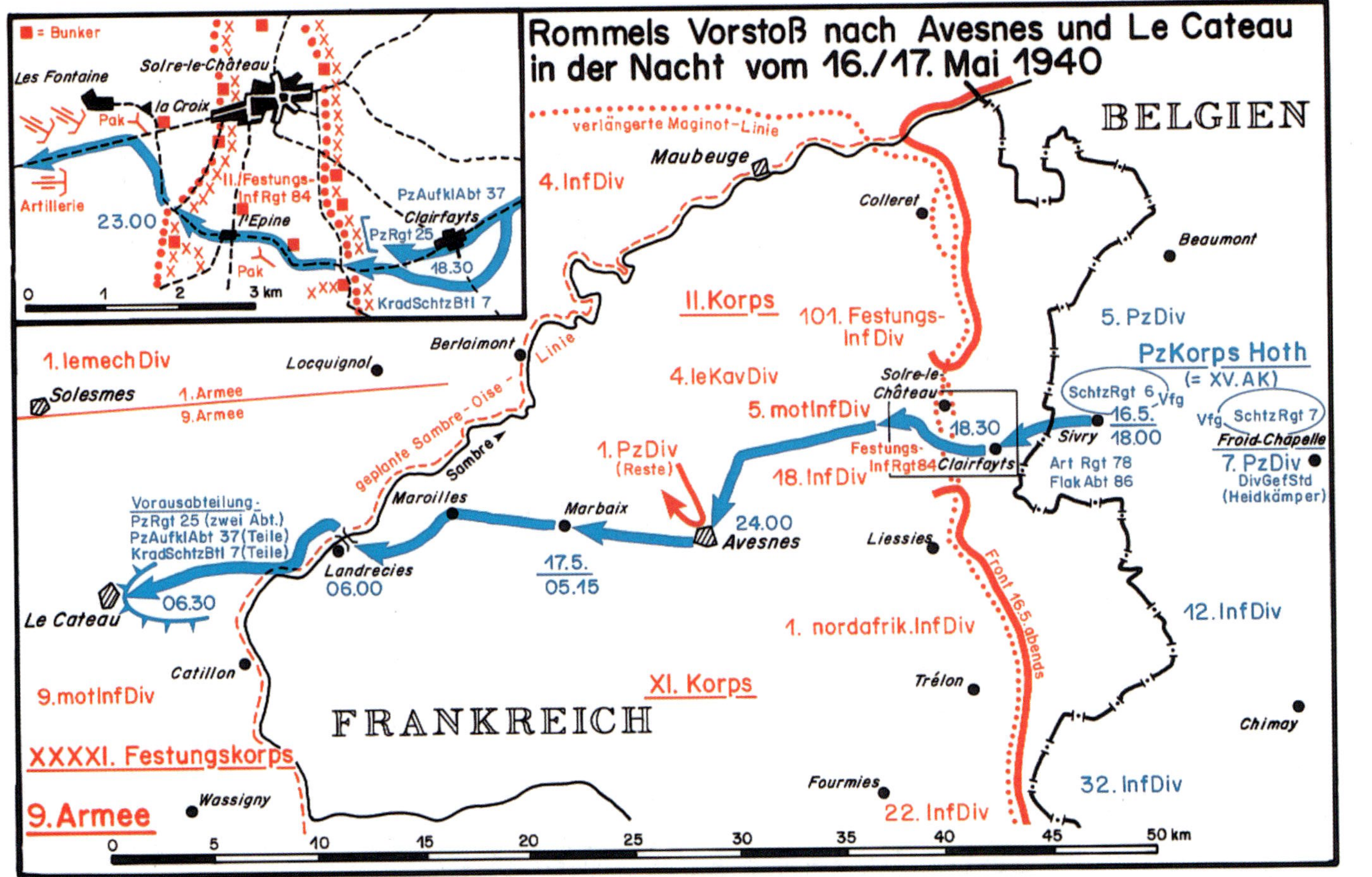

Rommel's Push to Avesnes and Le Cateau during the Night of 16–17 May 1940

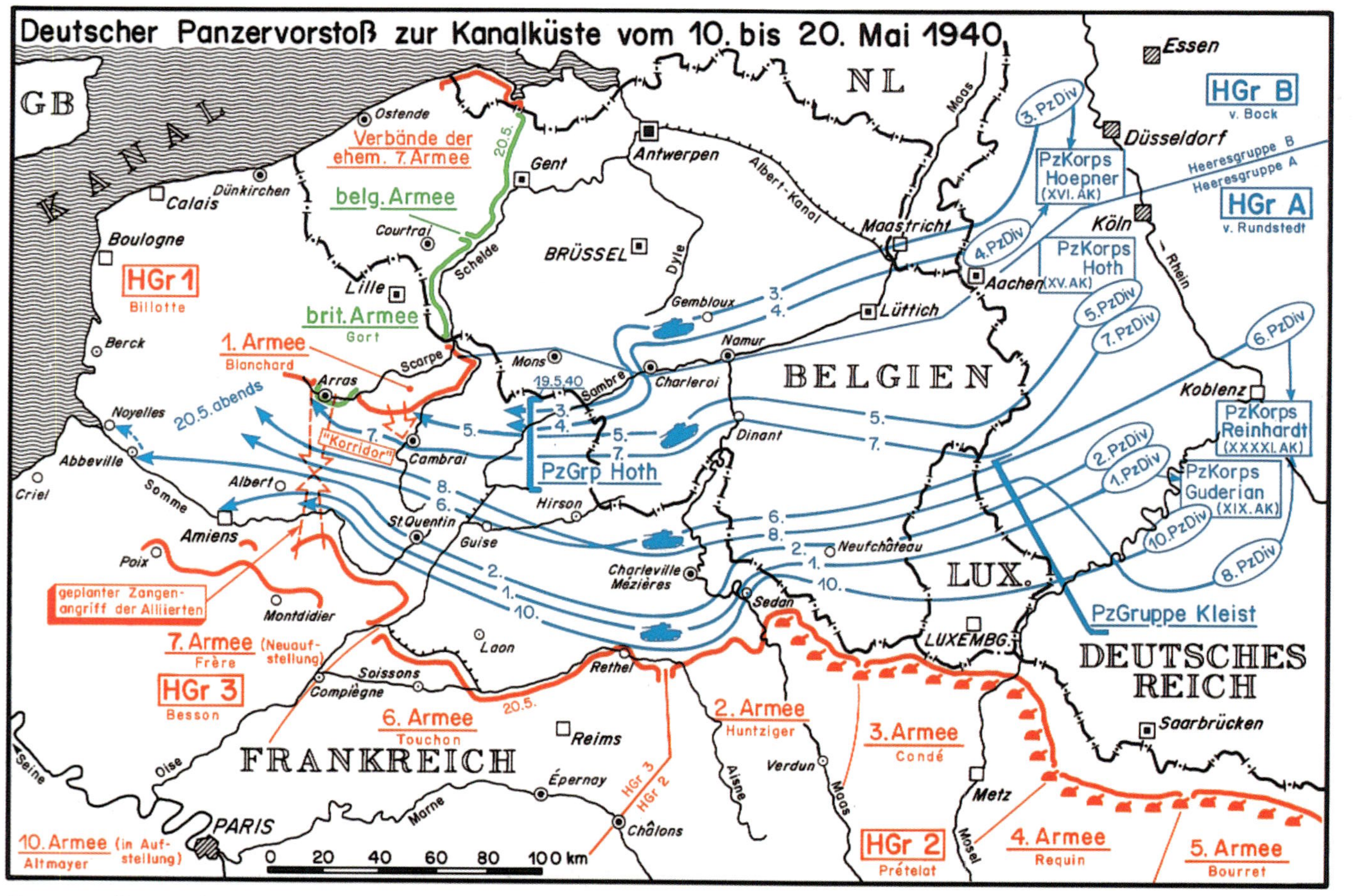

German Panzer Thrust to Channel Coast, 10–20 May 1940

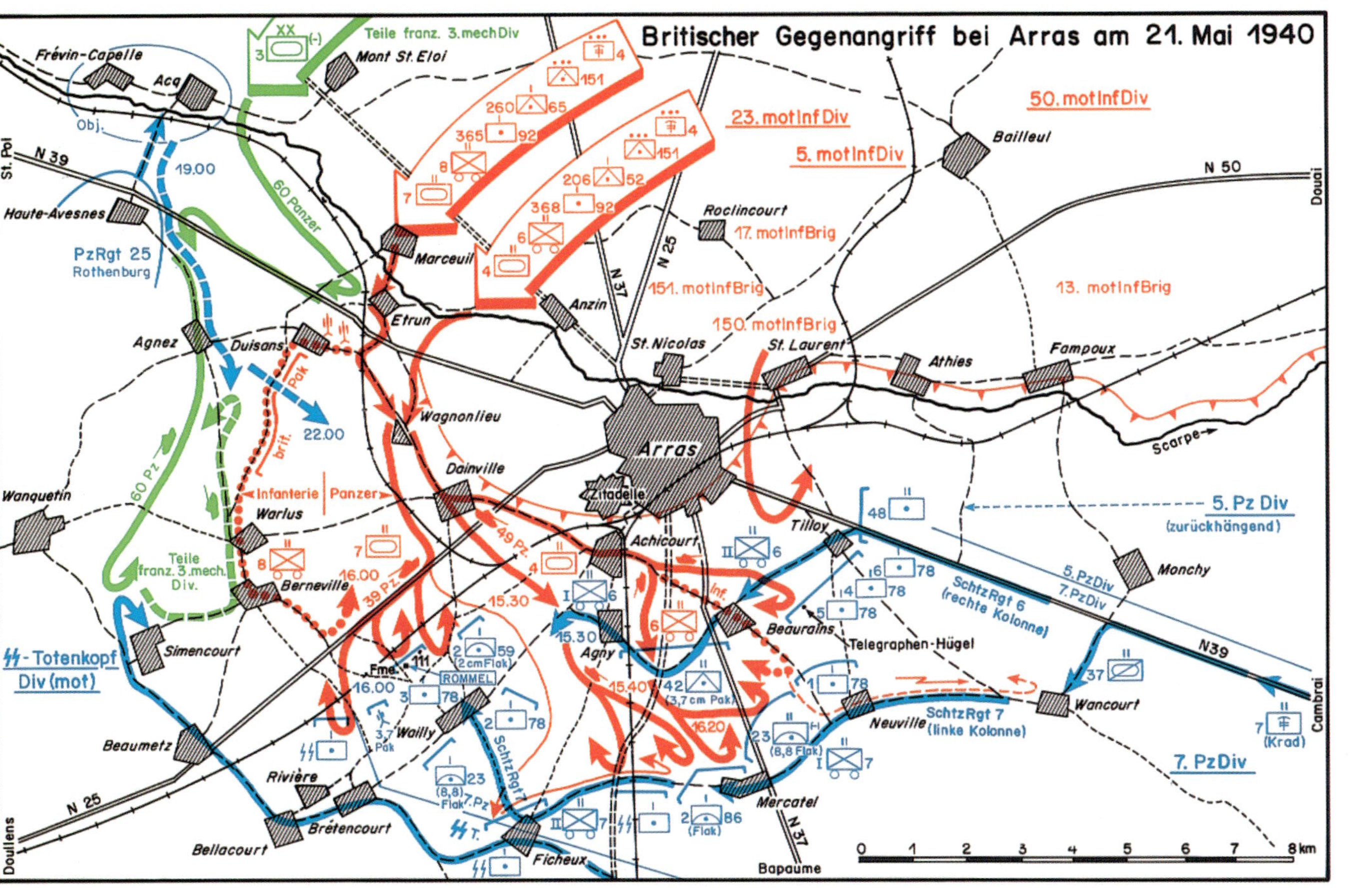

British Counterattack at Arras, 21 May 1940

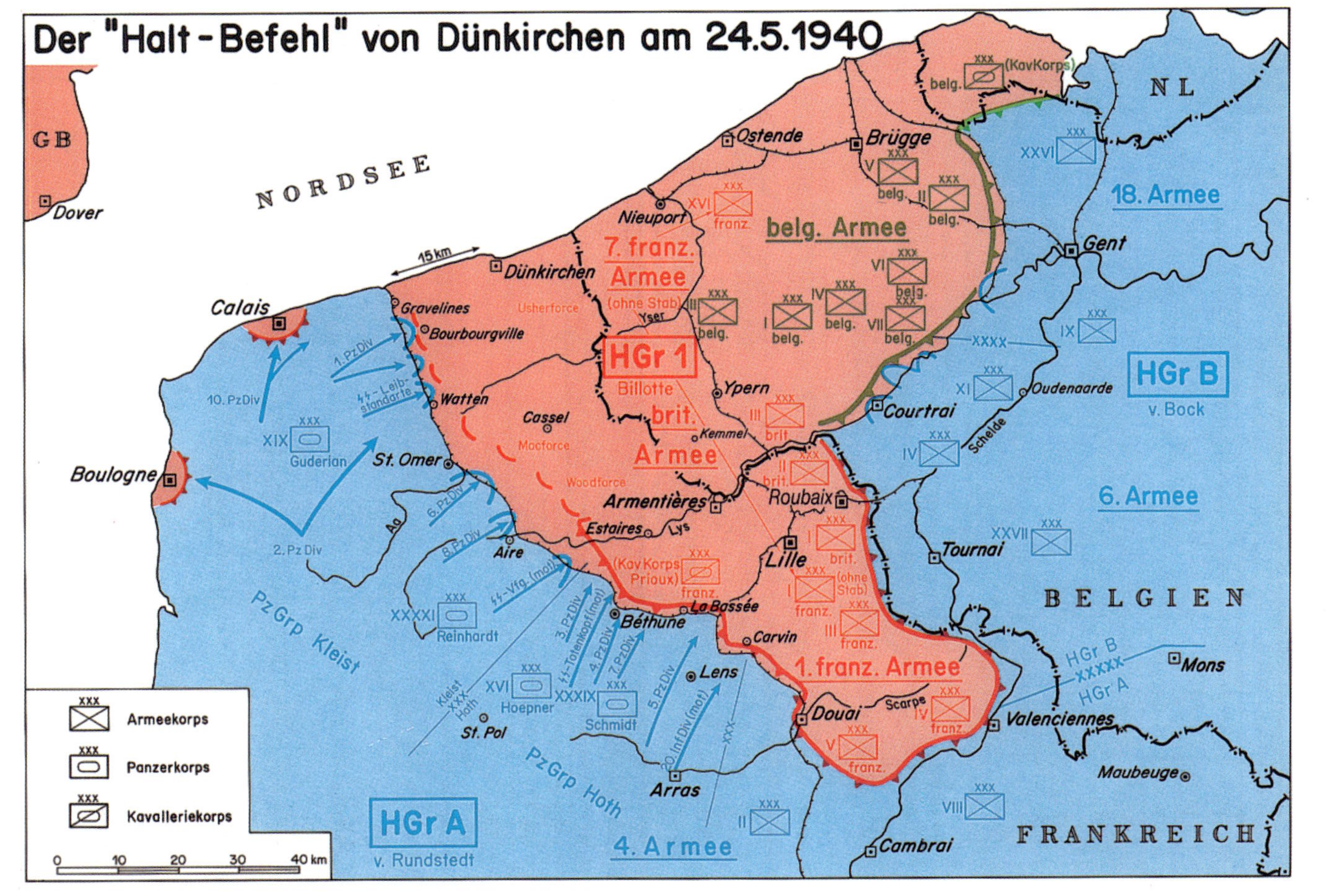

The Dunkirk Halt Order, 24 May 1940

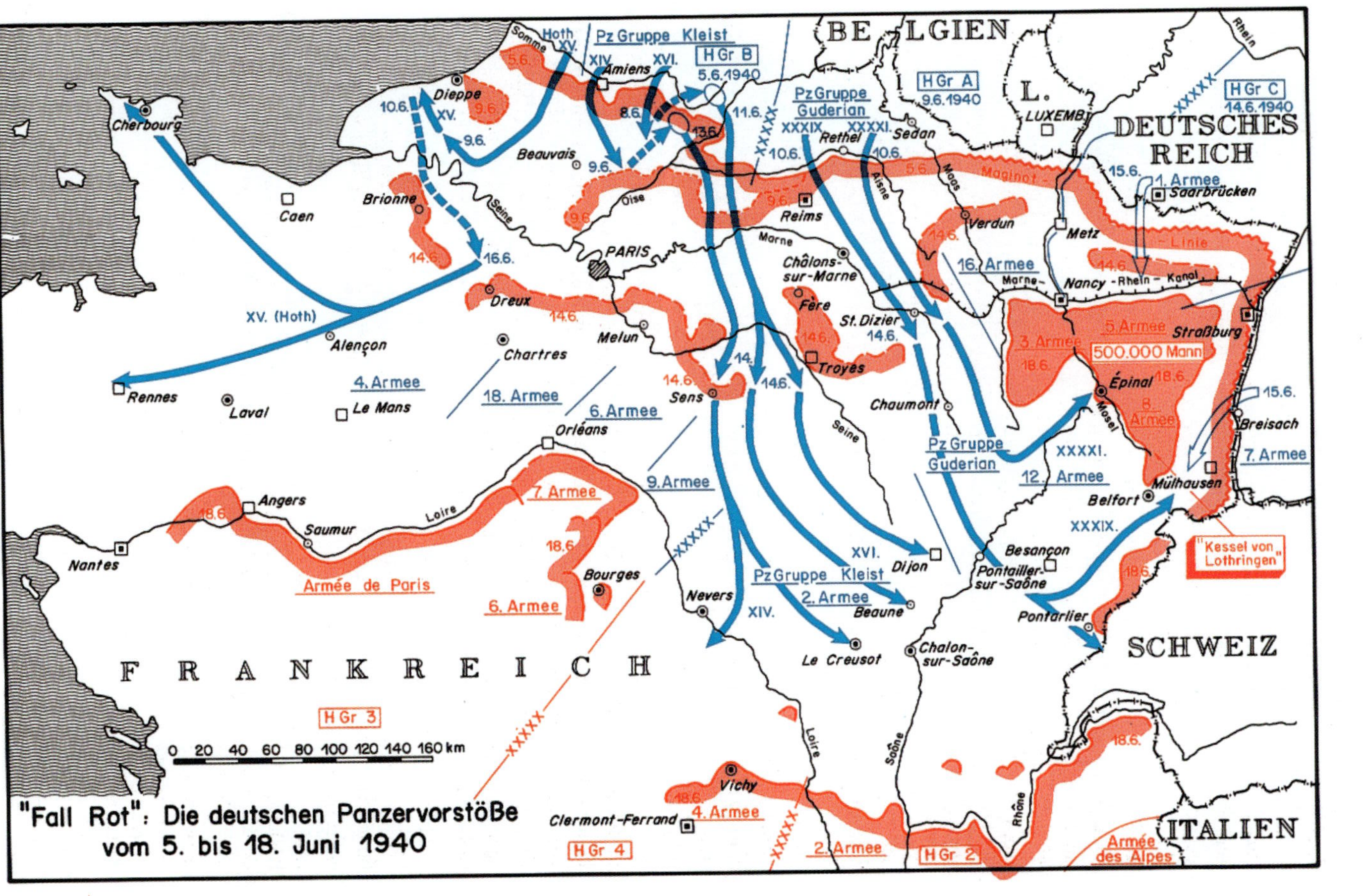

Case Red: German Panzer Thrusts from 5 June to 18 June 1940

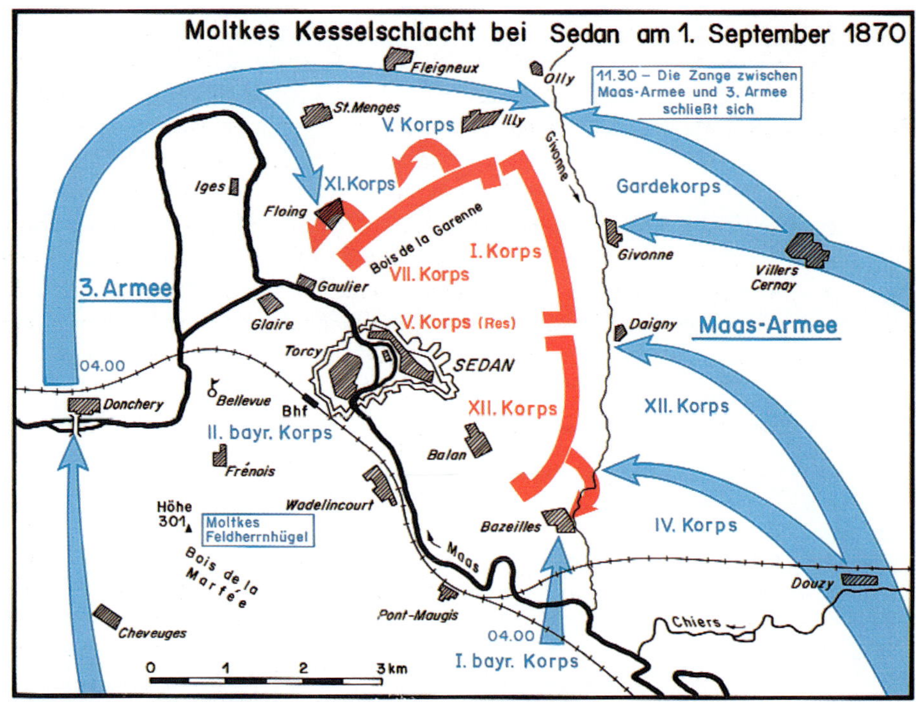

Moltke's Battle of Encirclement at Sedan, 1 September 1870

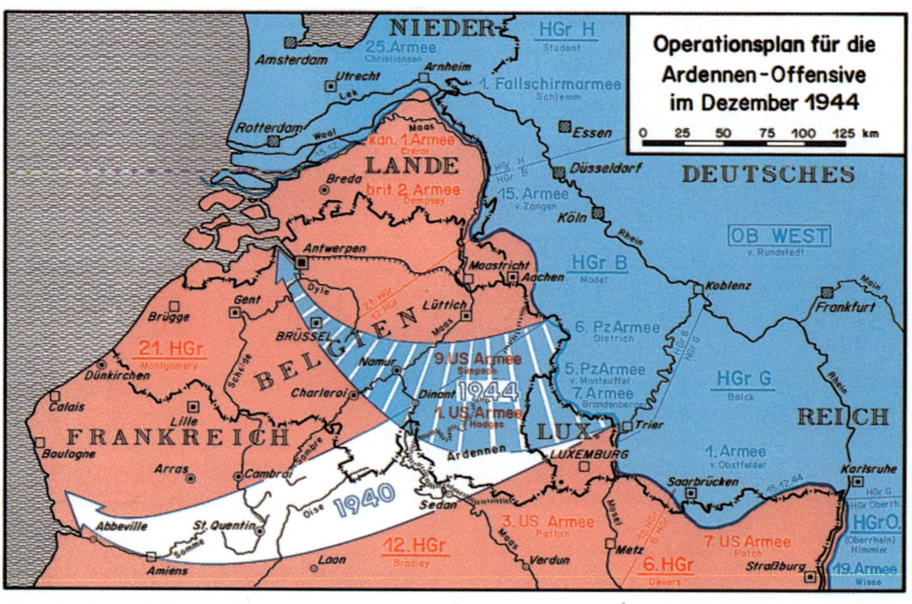

Operations Plan for the Ardennes Offensive, December 1944

The industrial regions along the northeast border, whose loss was so painful during World War I, were protected.

Especially after the severe manpower sacrifices of the past war, it seemed necessary to make up for the numerical inferiority against the Germans. Verdun demonstrated the value of fortifications. A soldier in a well-developed defensive system was the equivalent of seven in position out in the open field.

It is a myth that the Maginot Line was originally designed as an expression of a purely defensive strategy. That line forced France on the defensive just as little as the Westwall (Siegfried Line) forced Germany on the defensive. On the contrary, it was precisely this reinforcement of the border that released troops that could be used for operations elsewhere. To that extent, the Maginot Line certainly accomplished its purpose, but so-called Maginot thinking had a disastrous effect. While the Germans were aiming at a rebirth of an operational war of movement, the French seemed under all circumstances to want to avoid the open battle in the field and decided to hide out behind the Maginot Line. French generals stuck to the doctrine of linear defense as if the important thing were to repeat the trench fighting of World War I. In the process, the idea of the compact front line was solidified into a dogma just like the articles of faith relating to the primacy of the defensive and the superiority of fire over movement.

However, this exclusively defensive tactic and military strategy were in conflict with France's foreign policy. After all, France was considered the hegemonic power of the Continent and viewed itself as playing the role of the policeman of Europe. When Hitler launched his expansion policy and pounced on France's allies, the allegedly strongest army of the world stood inactive behind the Maginot Line. France's military establishment had walled itself in. The bad thing about the Maginot thinking to that extent was represented by passivity, by self-restriction to the defensive, and by forgoing the initiative. That emerged during the fighting in its own country, when the French army could not react to the German breakthrough with an operational counterattack.

Nobody criticized the so-called pure defensive more severely than Clausewitz, although—in contrast to the Schlieffen school—he only asserted that "the defensive form of warfare is intrinsically stronger than the offensive."[18] At the same time, however, he termed it the "negative" form of war, which one must employ only so long as this is necessary due to one's own weakness. Clausewitz stated: "A sudden powerful transition to the offensive—the flashing sword of vengeance—is the greatest moment for the defense. If it is not in the commander's mind from the start, or rather if it is not an integral part of his idea of defense, he will never be persuaded of the superiority of the defensive form. . . . Moreover, it is a crude error to equate attack with the idea of assault alone, and therefore, to conceive of defense as merely misery and confusion."[19] French generals, however, were not striving for an active form of defense. It was mostly the renunciation of armor that could be employed in an operational setting, as demanded by de Gaulle, that proved to be so disastrous. Thus, in the Maginot Line the army did have a mighty shield, but it had no sword.

Urged on by Great Britain, France declared war on the German Reich on 3 September 1939. But then its army stayed behind the Maginot Line. Now began that strange suspended state, the Drôle de guerre, which the British called the "Phony War" or "Twilight War." The Sitzkrieg (Sit-Down War) that preceded the blitzkrieg to some extent turned into a "sit-down strike against war."[20] For eight months, French soldiers—doing nothing, devoid of any recognizable war aim—rested under the illusionary shell of the Maginot Line, while defeatist thinking spread around already before the war sprouted "as if in a hothouse."[21] At the same time, French soldiers were exposed to the barrage of German propaganda. And so, that bizarre half-way state deteriorated into the caricature of a war. While Poland was bleeding to death in September, there were even some fraternization scenes on the German-French front. Posters had been put up on both sides, reading: "If you do not shoot, we will not shoot either!"[22]

At Winterfeld, there were several instances of barter trade between enemy soldiers via an incompletely demolished bridge. At one time, the French transported a slaughtered cow to the other side and then came back with a German radio. On Christmas Eve, friend and foe together put up a Christmas tree on that bridge, illuminated by German and French antiaircraft artillery searchlights. Entrenching work continued undisturbed and bored French soldiers even played soccer right behind the border.[23] During this "funny war" German power plants along the Saar River supplied French border towns with electric power for several months. One fine day, a French soldier got lost along the Lauter River and wandered over to the German side where he was taken prisoner. Immediately thereafter, an officer appeared under a flag of truce and asked that the man be returned. The French officer declared rather indignantly that this kind of capture was against all past custom. Moreover, he pointed out, "his sector is so weakly occupied that he really could not get along without that man."[24] What Otto Abetz, Hitler's expert on France, reported now appeared to be all too typical: "On invitation of some officers I knew I once drove along the Westwall from Karlsruhe all the way to the bend of the Rhine River at Basel and, in front of various positions, I witnessed how German and French soldiers were chatting like buddies across the river. The only shots I heard in this entire stretch of the front line were fired in Breisach. A rather long, skinny straw man with an umbrella had been suspended from a crane in the harbor. Shotguns and machine guns from the Westwall and from the Maginot Line engaged in a shooting match at this unmistakable target."[25]

Hitler had actually managed to put the French to sleep behind the Maginot Line. All the greater was the shock when the Germans suddenly attacked with unexpected force and completely novel methods. Rarely in military history has an army been so carefully equipped and trained for the next war as was the French army at that time. The individual French administrations invested huge sums of money in the defense budget.

But suddenly, the Germans fought a war that was completely different from the war that France's forces had been preparing for.

The Anachronistic Command System of the French Army

The General Staff on 1914 was prepared for the war of 1870, and, in 1940, for the war of 1914.[26]

Guy La Chambre, French Minister of Aviation, 1939–40

Marshall Foch, who had won World War I for France, is credited with a statement that one can consider as already containing the germ of a future defeat: "The next war begins the moment the World War ended."[27]

By building the Maginot Line, the French generals wanted to cast the scenario of Verdun in concrete—in reality, however, they thus blocked the view to any future prospects. They slept through a technological revolution, which, in turn, led to the revolution of warfare. In view of the blitzkrieg of 1940, it turned out that the Maginot Line had become frozen into an anachronism of reinforced concrete. Thus, the French officers were trapped in methodical leadership principles that were no longer valid for the modern operational war of movement. In the words of Marc Bloch, "the German triumph was, essentially, a triumph of intellect—and it is that which makes it so particularly serious."[28] In his analysis, he arrived at the following conclusion: "The ruling idea of the Germans in the conduct of war was speed. We, on the other hand, did our thinking in terms of yesterday or the day before. Worse still: faced by the undisputed evidence of Germany's new tactics, we ignored, or wholly failed to understand, the quickened rhythm of the times. So true is this, that it was as though the two opposed forces belonged, each of them, to an entirely different period in human history."[29]

It was not so much society as a whole or the individual soldier who failed. The root of the trouble instead rested with the military leadership that had fallen victim to a strange intellectual rigidity. The backward thinking of the army certainly was also because the officer corps in the top-level positions was simply too old. Thus, the army was led by an "assortment of Methuselahs."[30] They not only clung to their positions and social privileges but also stuck to the old ideas with which, once upon a time, they were able to win victories on the battlefield. The advancement of talented younger officers with new ideas (such as, for example, de Gaulle) was blocked.[31] After the disaster of Sedan, the "lethargic philosopher" Gamelin was replaced as supreme commander of the armed forces.[32] But, of all people, it was his predecessor Weygand who became his successor. In other words, a seventy-three-year-old man relieved a sixty-eight-year-old man. Soon thereafter, eighty-four-year-old Marshal Pétain, the "hero of Verdun," was summoned to head the government—the challenge of the present was to be countered by the spirit of the past.

This overage leadership also used an obsolete command system. Incredible as it may sound, there was not a single radio at Gamelin's headquarters in the Château de Vincennes near Paris, and an aide complained that they did not even have carrier pigeons.[33] When an officer suggested that at least a teletype station be set up, his tradition-conscious superiors told him that "military orders cannot be compared to horserace results."[34] The underground command center at Vincennes was therefore referred to as "a submarine without periscope."[35] When Gamelin wanted to establish contact with Georges, the commander in chief of the northeast front, he only rarely used the phone. Instead, he got into his staff car and had himself driven to the latter's headquarters or apartment. This approximately sixty-kilometer ride lasted about two hours, round-trip—an unimaginable waste of time! Because the phone network broke down again and again, motorcycle messengers frequently delivered important dispatches. On the roads that were jammed with refugee convoys, those motorcycle messengers often wound up in the ditch and in some cases died in traffic accidents. As Gamelin later admitted to the Parliamentary Investigating Committee, "it generally took 48 hours" before an order reached the "executing unit at the Front."[36]

When headquarters in Vincennes had to be evacuated as the Germans approached, the chaos became even worse. Weygand finally moved headquarters to the out-of-the-way Castle Briare where, however, there was only one telephone. During this phase, when France's fate hung in the balance, the supreme commander regularly was cut off from the outside world every afternoon between 1200 and 1400. The switchboard girl on duty who operated the manual exchange in the nearby little town insisted on her lunch break.[37]

On top of these technical problems came the cumbersome nature of the French battlefield bureaucracy. The headquarters, corresponding to the system of command tactics, were geared to planning all combat operations schematically in advance. That involved drafting interminable orders in a time-consuming fashion in which every little detail was prescribed for the subordinate units. Marc Bloch concluded that "from the beginning to the end of the war, the metronome at headquarters was always set at too slow a beat."[38]

By the time an important order reached the field unit, it was as a rule already outdated. In this campaign, the French actually never managed to seize the initiative. They were hardly ever able to take action, and most of the time their reactions came too late.[39]

The Myth of the National Socialist Blitzkrieg

On 20 May 1940, during a press conference in Berlin, Göring announced that the operations plan for campaign in the west was "the very own personal work of the Führer." His statements culminated in the rather clear-cut sentence to the effect that "Adolf Hitler's genius as a warlord also caused a revolution in warfare in that it breached strategic principles that had been held sacrosanct until now."[40] Propaganda pictured the blitzkrieg as an invention of Hitler, the "greatest warlord of all times." Thus, for example, Wilhelm Weiß, the chief editor of *Völkischer Beobachter* (Peoples' Observer) got himself all worked up: "It was Adolf Hitler, the National Socialist, who demonstrated the ability to master this task and successfully to stride the bold path from static to dynamic warfare. The revolutionary spirit of his Brown Army swept over Europe's battlefields together with his Panzer divisions and bomber wings."[41]

Generalleutnant [Friedrich] von Rabenau, the chief of army archives, arrived at a completely different result in an analysis drafted during the campaign in the west.[42] In his opinion, the secret of German victory did not lie in "getting over conventional strategy,"[43] but rather in the "return of the war of movement."[44] He noted: "This was nothing other than that conventional strategy that always led from Leuthen via Waterloo, Sedan, Tannenberg, all the way to the victorious Campaign in Romania during the World War. It was also the inheritance of the Great General Staff."[45] In this connection, Rabenau emphasized: "The basic trend in the war of movement simultaneously contained the basic old Schlieffen truth, the idea of Cannae, involving envelopment and annihilation by means of encirclement."[46] In that way, of course, von Rabenau violated one of the taboos of National Socialist propaganda.[47] It is, therefore, no wonder that this essay was finally censored. The file contains Keitel's marginal entry: "I am against releasing this!"[48] Jodl's assessment is even more informative: "Relaxing censorship regulations would not be proper for this article. The objections are that the article praises Schlieffen and von Seeckt and that does not appear to be practical at this time in my view."[49]

Konstantin Hierl's article on the campaign in the west reads almost like a direct answer to this question: "It was not along the lines of the 'Schlieffen Plan' or on the grounds of the Cannae doctrine or some other rigid theories, but rather through free artistic creativity that sprang from the inspiration of martial genius that the Führer led the German Wehrmacht to the most glorious victories in their glorious history."[50] During the western campaign, Chief of the General Staff Halder wrote in a letter to his wife: "I have to be extremely cautious because any hint as to any merit earned by the Army High Command is in itself already a crime against the State."[51]

Guderian had already drafted the ideas that led to the rebirth of operational war of movement during the 1920s, completely independent of Hitler's later plans of conquest.[52] Upon closer contemplation, therefore, the slogan about the "National Socialist Panzer Force" turns out to be a propaganda illusion. The Panzer force fascinated Hitler only in purely technical terms because he was unable correctly to assess its future operational significance.[53] As Manstein emphasizes in his memoirs, "The foundations in terms of arms technology had been created before his [Hitler's] accession to office by the Army High Command. One can say that—apart from the assault guns . . . —all new weapons had been developed already before the [Nazi Party's] 'seizure of power.'"[54] By the way, ideas similar to those implemented in Germany had also been developed abroad, for example, by Fuller, Liddell Hart, de Gaulle, and Tukhachevskiy. To that extent, the military phenomenon of the blitzkrieg and the political phenomenon of National Socialism were indifferent toward each other. The apparent agreement sprang from the fact that, quite by accident, there was a revolution in the nature of war in May 1940 that led Hitler's go-for-broke gambling policy—which was already considered to have failed—quite suddenly to a triumphal military success. But there cannot be any talk of a blitzkrieg program that was drawn up by Hitler with supposedly strategic farsightedness. The National Socialist regime did not create the foundations for the buildup of the Panzer force and the development of modern operational war of movement; it only benefited from it. These new methods were used consciously and deliberately only after the campaign in the west, when Guderian's bold theories proved to have been correct.

The assertion that the fighting spirit of the German soldiers can be traced back to the "spirit of National Socialism" is also questionable. Also similarly wide of the mark is the contention that the war-crazed Germans jumped all over the war-weary French. Just how depressed the mood really was in Germany at the start of the war was described, for example, by Karl Wahl, the Nazi Gauleiter [party province governor] of Swabia: "Nothing of all I experienced in 1914 . . . did I observe again on this trip: No enthusiasm, no joy, no rejoicing anywhere. Wherever you went, there was depressing quiet, not to say a deep feeling of despondency. The entire German people seemed to be seized by a paralyzing terror."[55]

Hitler's expert on France, Otto Abetz, expressed the mood in similar terms: "For Germany and France, the war that broke out on 3 September 1939 at any rate was the 'most unpopular war' in their history. Neither in Paris nor in Berlin was there the remotest indication of any chauvinist enthusiasm, such as had accompanied the outbreak of the wars of 1914 and 1870 and such as had also appeared in the wake of the Napoleonic Wars."[56]

To that extent, the same conclusion can be drawn regarding Germany that Marc Bloch had already done for the French side: It was not so much social and ideological factors that decided the outcome of the campaign in the west as it was military factors. The fighting power of the German Wehrmacht was not based on the dynamism of National Socialism but rather primarily on the kind of efficiency that is purely inherent in the military system. This was the result of hundreds of years of development during which the German military establishment had developed extraordinary, perfectly functioning machinery.[57] That kind of organization—which was geared to efficiency and nothing else—could then be used for all kinds of purposes. Its soldiers fought bravely for National Socialist Germany, just as they would have fought for an Imperial or Communist Germany. This mechanism was revealed with particular clarity by Israeli military historian [Martin] van Creveld in his book *Kampfkraft* (Fighting Power) that has already become a classic.[58] In his opinion, it was the "internal organization of [the] Army" that was decisive.[59] He arrived at the following judgment: "The

German Army was a superb fighting organization. In point of morale, élan, unit cohesion, and resilience, it probably had no equal among twentieth-century armies."[60] The German army had displayed similar qualities during earlier wars, for example, during World War I. The fighting power factor was, of course, the prerequisite, but it was not a specific feature of blitzkrieg.

The Secret of the Success of the German Blitzkrieg: The Blend of Traditional Military Principle with Modern Technology

Strategic Constant: The Tradition of the Quick War

The goal of any military leadership is to beat the enemy decisively in the shortest possible time.[61]

Generalmajor [Georg] Thomas, 29 November 1939

According to Clausewitz, there are two contrasting possibilities of winning a war: a victory of annihilation or a victory of exhaustion.[62] Accordingly, the first goal can be attained by a rapidly fought "main battle"[63] (in modern terms: operational battle of decision); the second goal can be attained by a long, drawn-out war of attrition. Clausewitz developed this theory against the background of the wars of Frederick the Great and Napoleon. Both of them repeatedly found themselves facing a superior enemy coalition and attacked immediately to force a swift decision. The historian [Hans] Delbrück later was guided by the same dualist principle as Clausewitz when he differentiated between "strategy of annihilation" and "strategy of exhaustion."[64] In Germany, this developmental trend finally resulted in the "strategy of annihilation" becoming absolute. This strategy was aimed at a swift decision and was expressed in the terms "quick war" as well as "short war." That this theory could become so dominant in Germany is due to the central position of the Reich in the center of Europe, a position that is unfavorable in military-geographic terms. Here, once again, we discover the truth in Napoleon's maxims that a country's policy is dictated by its geography. During the Seven-Years' War, England, on its island, was mostly untouchable while its Prussian ally was exposed to attacks from all quarters—France, Sweden, Russia, and the Habsburg monarchy. Frederick the Great, therefore, tried to fight short wars and seek an immediate decision on the battlefield. He demanded: "Our wars must be short and lively, because it is not good for us to drag the thing out, because a long, drawn-out war inevitably will cause our admirable discipline to fall apart and would depopulate the land and exhaust our resources."[65]

The trauma of the war finally gave rise to the postulate of the preventive strike and the dogma of the battle of annihilation.[66] Moltke's encirclement victory at Sedan became the ideal type of that trend of thought that was expressed in the Schlieffen school. Thus, the phenomenon of blitzkrieg also appears merely as the superlative escalation of the short war.[67]

The Revival of Operational Thinking

Operation is movement.[68]

Graf von Schlieffen

It was Moltke who placed the concept of "operation" on the "hitherto unnamed area between strategy and tactics."[69] In doing so, he started with the following consideration: "All individual successes achieved by the bravery of our troops on the battlefield are useless if they are not guided by a grand idea and if they are not combined toward and aimed at the purpose of the campaign, yes, the entire war."[70]

The reason why the art of operational command was to become the domain of the German general staff can also be found in Germany's unfavorable geostrategic position. The permanent encirclement anxiety, the risk of becoming simultaneously involved in a war against several neighboring countries, led to a very specific kind of military thinking. Thus, German generals in their planning almost always started with the basic assumption that Germany's own forces were inferior to those of the enemy. Skillful leadership had to compensate for this disadvantage.[71] The basic principle of the Schlieffen school therefore was: "From inferiority to victory."[72] The much-cited law of the superiority of numbers applies primarily to the strategic echelon and is noticed mostly in a long war. On the other hand, on the operational echelon where battles are decided, the important thing is to employ the right units in the right place at the right time. As Frederick the Great had already demonstrated, one can get around strategic force ratios operationally by faster maneuvering. To that extent, the blitzkrieg that springs from this trend of thought is nothing but the attempt to turn strategic necessity into an operational virtue.

Actually, in World War I, when the Schlieffen plan failed at the very beginning, this overemphasis on operational thinking seems to have led to absurdity. The battle of matériel no longer required a high level of military command skills because, in the end, victory always went to the side that had the most shells. Even Ludendorff himself was resigned to the solidification of the western front into a positional war. In spite of tremendous sacrifices, success seemed possible only in small steps on the tactical echelon.[73] Deeply disappointed, he said on 5 April 1918: "I never want to hear the word 'operation' again. We will just smash a hole in the front line. The rest will come by itself."[74]

After World War I began the interim period of the Reichswehr, one of the strangest armies in military history. Its officers lived in the past and for the future, but they were unable to identify with the sad present. The soldiers were actually trained for the day when Germany's military establishment would again play a commensurate role in the world. On that point, Manstein wrote: "The most important thing of all was that our little Reichswehr, once rather looked down upon by many people, had revived Germany's great tradition of training and leadership after carrying it through the aftermath of the 1918 defeat. The new German Wehrmacht, as the child of that Reichswehr, had found—and was probably alone in doing so—how to prevent warfare from degenerating into a static war. . . . In the German Wehrmacht it had been found possible, with the help of new means of warfare, to reacquire the true art of leadership in mobile operations."[75]

Limited by the restrictions of the Versailles Treaty, the Reichswehr was numerically much too small to be able to provide complete protection for Germany's borders. Because the Reichswehr was too weak for defense, it necessarily picked attack for its map exercises. A penetrating enemy was to be defeated by mounting an operational counterattack into the flanks. [Hans] von Seeckt, the chief of the army directorate, therefore dropped the idea of a "linear forward defense" and picked the concept of "free operating" in Moltke's tradition. Seeckt bequeathed to his successors not only "a gospel of mobility"[76] but tied it in with the idea of the "elite army." He said: "The mass becomes immobile, it can no longer maneuver, in other words, it cannot win; it can only oppress."[77]

Seeckt started with the assumption that quality would prevail over quantity. In his opinion, large masses of poorly armed and badly trained draftees were nothing but cannon fodder whenever they would run into the elite force of a smaller, but superbly equipped and trained, professional army. He therefore postulated: "I see . . . the future of warfare residing in the use of high-quality and mobile, hence smaller, armies, whose effectiveness is considerably enhanced by the air force."[78]

Supplementing his demand, he called for a kind of militia army consisting of draftees for general national defense. However, the spearhead represented by the elite forces would achieve the decision in a war. Only those forces, operationally assembled, would be in a position to mount a fast and decision-seeking type of warfare. And so, there was a rebirth of operational thinking during the time of the Reichswehr. To be sure, these war games with army corps that existed only on paper appeared somewhat utopian. In that way, during a period of weakness, which was thought to be "army-less—defenseless—honor-less," Seeckt laid one of the most important theoretical foundations for the latter blitzkrieg.[79] This produced an infrastructure of operational thinking that all German generals shared in common. In this way one can also explain why Manstein, although he was not a Panzer expert, could develop the idea for the brilliant Panzer operation called Sickle Cut. Most generals, of course, did believe that this style of "free operating" (such as, for example, during the Polish campaign) could not simply be transposed to the western theater of war. But after Guderian, in his own impetuous way, provided evidence to the contrary, the other generals were also able almost overnight to switch to this type of operational command.[80]

The Schwerpunkt *Principle*

> *An operation without a Schwerpunkt [point of main effort] is like a man without character.*[81]
>
> von Hindenburg

Once upon a time, a French marshal submitted to Napoleon a campaign plan in which the French army was to be positioned in a linear pattern, from one end of the border to other. Napoleon remarked sarcastically: "Are you trying to prevent smuggling?"[82] Another time, he said: "The art of warfare can be boiled down to a single principle: Concentrate a greater mass than the enemy at one single point."[83]

Napoleon's successors seemed to have completely forgotten this principle. They were sworn to uphold the dogma of linear defense along the compact front. This one-dimensional thinking had its most devastating effects in the case of the armored force. Mostly, the French generals distributed the mass of tanks by companies to the infantry units and, in the end, the respectable armored force had been split up and scattered between the Channel coast and the Swiss border. The numerically inferior German Panzers, on the other hand, were assembled in ten Panzer divisions, seven of which were concentrated in the operational Schwerpunkt between Sedan and Dinant. This meant following Guderian's principle: *Klotzen, nicht kleckern!* (Hit with the fist, don't feel with the fingers!). The French tank general Charles Delestraint reduced the differing armor tactics of the two armies to the following common denominator: "We had 3,000 tanks and so did the Germans. We used them in a thousand packs of three, the Germans in three packs of a thousand."[84]

There was a tradition for the use of the principle of concentration in German military thought. If you wished "to bring a war to a swift decision," then you proved your courage in picking the Schwerpunkt. Nobody stressed this principle as heavily as Schlieffen. The important thing each time was to convert the enemy's absolute strategic superiority into one's own relative operational superiority at the decisive point.

The Principle of Encirclement

> *The battle of annihilation can today be fought according to the same plan as Hannibal elaborated in the long forgotten past. The enemy front is not the objective of the principal attack. Against it the mass of troops need not be assembled nor the reserves be deployed; the essential thing is to crush the flanks. . . . The annihilation is completed by an attack against the enemy's rear.*[85]
>
> Schlieffen, *Cannae*

The German general staff's operational style of thinking developed against the background of the nightmare of a two-front war that kept threatening again and again. In this connection, the following objective was pursued, almost as if by tradition: If one enemy could be defeated in the course of an immediate battle of decision, then the other one could subsequently be concentrated on to the maximum extent. In that way, *one* war on two fronts could be divided into *two* successive wars, each on one front. As Schlieffen emphasized, one must not strive for an ordinary victory that enables the enemy to continue the war but for a victory of annihilation that creates a fait accompli. Such a victory must be won above all by the complete encirclement of the enemy army. He thought that he had found the ideal type of this "battle of annihilation" in Hannibal's victory over the Romans at Cannae (216 B.C.). But there was yet another battle that resembled this ideal image: Moltke's victory at Sedan in 1870. Schlieffen enthusiastically wrote about that victory: "At last a battle at Cannae had been fought and the enemy's complete encirclement was achieved."[86]

To be sure, Schlieffen allowed that "apart from Sedan, no complete Cannae" was ever achieved again.[87] In his studies on the history of war, however, he described a series of additional "approximate battles of annihilation." In their cases, he maintained, it had been possible again and again by a single operational maneuver to bring about a final victory of strategic proportions. But Schlieffen and his pupils gazed upon this secret of victory with such fascination that the idea of the encirclement gradually became the operational end in itself. The gigantic encirclement movement of the Schlieffen plan failed in World War I. The fighting along the western front solidified into position warfare. On the other hand, the two-faced image of war on the eastern front appeared in the form of several phases in the nature of a classical war of movement. There were also several encirclement battles, and the victory of Tannenberg was upgraded to a new Cannae. The officers of the Reichswehr and, later on, of the German Wehrmacht, kept practicing—if only on the paper used during map exercises—the procedure of operational encirclement as the *non plus ultra* (very utmost) in the art of military command.

The encirclement idea took on new dimensions in Germany as a result of the invention of aircraft. The encirclement demanded by Schlieffen was not carried out mostly because the fast encirclement forces were too weak in artillery. Now, however, the fire delivered by the Luftwaffe could be used to seal off the encircled enemy's breakout attempts. The Wehrmacht was particularly interested in testing the airborne units, which were organized amid strict secrecy and were referred to as "youngest child of Mars, the God of War."[88] That force had created the possibility for vertical encirclement, which meant that a three-dimensional Cannae was within the realm of the doable.

Removing the Taboo against the Breakthrough

The first few days of the campaign in the west showed that fortifications of the traditional type could no longer stand up to combined air and ground

> *attacks. The Luftwaffe prepared the way for the capture of a fortification system; Panzer and infantry finished the job.*[89]
>
> Cajus Bekker on the breakthrough of the Meuse River Line

Schlieffen believed that frontal attacks were hopeless and rejected the idea of the breakthrough in view of the greatly increased destructive force of modern firearms. This went so far that the regulations drafted under his influence no longer contained the term *Durchbruch* (breakthrough). As far as is known, he never directed a war game or maneuver in which the breakthrough was practiced.[90] Instead, he developed a fixation on the idea of encirclement. In point of fact, neither the Germans nor the Allies ever achieved an operational breakthrough on the western front during World War I. All the more abstruse must Manstein's idea have appeared to the German general officer corps as he proposed breaking through the Meuse River line at Sedan by way of an immediate attack from the move. But the nature of war had changed in the meantime. During World War I, the defense had won out over the attack. Now, the pendulum of the technique of warfare swung back from the factor of fire to the factor of movement. Guderian, therefore, trusted the striking power of the operationally combined Panzer force and Luftwaffe. To that extent, Sickle Cut tied in the method of the *breakthrough,* which was rejected by Schlieffen, with the idea of *encirclement,* which he had propagated. Strictly speaking, this plan can be divided into two suboperations: During the breakthrough phase, the Germans were to punch frontally through the Meuse Line at Sedan; and during the encirclement phase, the German units could be sent through this breach to thrust into the enemy's rear.

The Push Deep into Enemy Territory and Overcoming the Linear Style of Thinking

> *After the breakthrough, it is a matter of decisive importance to push ahead as far as the fuel will permit, regardless of the threat to the flanks, making full use of engines, without rest or breaks, marching day and night. Neutralizing enemy flank attacks is the mission of all following corps.*[91]
>
> Guderian 1941

In planning the encirclement phase, Manstein violated yet another taboo of the Schlieffen school, that is, the taboo of the exposed flank. Schlieffen could visualize an encirclement only in the form of the compact turning movement of one wing. He wanted to have entire armies wheel, the way companies do during close-order drill. According to the Sickle Cut plan, however, a Panzer group was to push through enemy rear areas completely isolated, like a wedge. Revolutionary though this may seem at first, Manstein and Guderian here adopted the tactic of the German assault teams from

World War I and transferred them to a higher, operational echelon. The germ of the blitzkrieg idea can be seen precisely in this tactic, and this is why we will now look more closely at its development.

During World War I, the Allies relied on their quantitative superiority and tried to express it in tremendous battles of matériel. On the other hand, in accordance with the old proverb "Necessity is the mother of invention," the Germans developed a new attack tactic, getting away from the linear style of thinking represented by positional warfare. During the Allied attacks that were systematically planned in advance, the units had to advance uniformly next to each other, and precisely determined lines could be crossed only at a certain time to ensure coordination with the artillery. The German Stoßtrupp leaders, on the other hand, attacked completely independently, without regard to communications and exposed flanks. Later, the British military writer Liddell Hart described this method as an "expanding torrent" (an ever-widening mountain torrent)[92] because the assault teams—like water, which always seeks its lowest level—advanced along the line of least resistance.

While the Allies systematically retained the point of main effort determined before the start of the offensive, the Schwerpunkt (point of main effort) in the attack by assault teams was adapted in a flexible manner to the development of combat operations as such. The employment of reserves was also entirely contrasting: the Allies concentrated reserves at the point of strongest resistance, whereas the Germans concentrated their reserves at the point of weakest resistance. The attackers in the first waves were to go around centers of enemy resistance and leave their elimination to the following troops. This method of uninterrupted attack had the objective of pushing deep into enemy territory as quickly as possible.[93]

The secret of the German assault teams' success, as far as Liddell Hart was concerned, was in the "indirect approach." These assault teams were not concerned with engaging and annihilating enemy troops but, instead, pushed past them deep into enemy rear areas where they threatened the enemy's supply lines, command centers, and lines of retreat. Most significant was the resultant psychological effect of confusion. When a Stoßtrupp managed to punch deep into the rear of the enemy frontline units, panic would frequently break out because the Allied soldiers were fixated on fighting along continuous lines. Thus, entire defense sectors collapsed even though the front had been pierced only at a single, tiny spot.

This Stoßtrupp-Taktik (assault team tactics) was probably tried out for the first time in December 1915 at the Hartmannsweilerkopf in the Vosges Mountains. Similar methods were tried out also in other sectors of the front. The first major attempt on a larger scale took place near Riga in September 1917, where Gen. Oskar von Hutier achieved a sensational success with the help of Stoßtrupp-Taktik. German assault teams achieved the most spectacular success during the famous Ludendorff Offensive in March 1918. This operation can be considered as the predecessor of Sickle Cut because a similar direction of attack was pursued in the original planning. At that time, likewise, the English were to be encircled along the Channel coast by a push to the mouth of the Somme River. For several days before the offensive was barely stopped, it looked as if the Germans would manage after all to pull off the big breakthrough, which they had tried to achieve in vain for so many years.[94] What the Germans lacked was the right number of Panzers to widen the *tactical* breakthrough into an *operational* breakthrough. In this connection, it is interesting to note that Gen. Otto von Below, a few weeks earlier, in January 1918, made the following revolutionary proposal to Ludendorff: "Forget about the offensive and shorten the front lines as much as necessary; build Panzers throughout all of 1918 and, with your Panzer squadrons, break through all the way to the Channel coast in the Spring of 1919."[95]

The German Panzer success of 1940 thus had entirely historical roots. Guderian took over the basic principles of the old Stoßtrupp-Taktik almost down to the last detail and integrated them into the modern Panzer force. The main element of the blitzkrieg had thus been created.

The Traditional Principles of Command

The most important factor in the victory of 1940 was the system of command. In the context of this account, however, only those two command principles in which the Wehrmacht and the Allied armies differed most clearly from each other will be singled out.

Leading through Mission

> *Individual leadership was fostered on a scale unrivaled in any other army, right down to the most junior N.C.O. or infantryman, and in this lay the secret of our success.*[96]
>
> Manstein

American historians, not without irony, commented on the cliché-like characterization of the Germans in Anglo-Saxon war films.[97] The soldiers of the Wehrmacht appear rather stereotyped as robots of war who sullenly carry out orders and always—in the movie—are taken in and outsmarted by their more flexible Anglo-Saxon opponents. In reality, however, the situation was somewhat different. Thus, Rommel was astonished at the rigid "order-based tactics" of his British opponents in North Africa: "The cumbersome, methodical style of command, the schematic issuing of orders, down to the smallest detail that left junior commanders little freedom, and the poor adaptability to the situation that results from the development of the actual fighting—these can be blamed extensively for British failures."[98]

The feature that was typical of the German command system was not the so-called Prussian blind obedience but, on the contrary, the Auftragstaktik that emerged from the Prussian army.[99] The latter left the subordinate commanders a measure of freedom of action not practiced in any other army of the world. In contrast to an order, a mission regulates only *what* is to be done but not *how* the job is to be done. The reforms of Scharnhorst created the foundations of Auftragstaktik, which Gneisenau then developed further. However, the decisive aspect was practical implementation by Moltke who preferred to lead via directives.[100] Stricter regulations were put out during World War I due to the influence of the Schlieffen school. In contrast, Seeckt again more heavily emphasized the decentralization of responsibility.[101]

The rigorous provisions of the Versailles Treaty indirectly increased the trend toward mission tactics. The Reichswehr was allowed to have only four thousand officers, although there would have been ten times as many applicants from the dissolved Imperial Army. Thus, only the very best of the best were taken.[102] Seeckt believed that he could give this tactically outstandingly trained elite the freedom to take independent action. In addition was the fact that the Reichswehr in reality was a *Führerheer* (army of leaders). The hundred thousand soldiers were to be the officers and noncommissioned officers of an army to be organized in the future. Therefore, each of them was trained for one step higher than his particular position—a company commander was trained as battalion commander; a battalion commander, as regimental commander. This also meant that every commander was in a position to act along the lines of the mission of the next-higher unit.

The fact that Seeckt was already thinking of a future war of movement also played a role here. The combat operations of motorized units would take place with such speed that issuing orders necessarily would fall behind. This is why the officers were trained so that they could seize the initiative on their own and push into the gap even without orders. This proved highly effective in the whirlpool of the war of movement where the military commanders found themselves in one unforeseen situation after the other.[103] Never during World War II did leading through mission play such an overwhelming role as in May 1940. The campaign in the west led to a revolution in the operational-tactical nature of war. The old doctrines collapsed. However, there were not as yet any new rules, and so many orders were reduced to absurdity by themselves because they were in line with an outdated way of thinking. This development was a surprise for both sides. The German officers proved to be so superior during the campaign not because they had already applied the rules of a blitzkrieg but because, on the basis of mission tactics, they were in a position to adapt to the new situation of a blitzkrieg considerably faster than the Allies.

Leading from Up Front

> *The times of men such as Seydlitz and Ziethen have come back. We must view today's war from the cavalry viewpoint—we must lead Panzer units like squadrons, we must issue commands from the Panzers as they race along, just as commands were given out earlier from the saddle.*[104]
>
> Rommel

When the German infantry began to cross the Meuse River at Sedan at 1600 on 13 May, the company commanders were frequently in the very first boats. Guderian crossed to the other bank with the first assault boat of the second wave, where Balck, the commander of the 1st Rifle Regiment, was already waiting for him. On the next day, even von Rundstedt, the commander in chief of Army Group A, turned up and inspected the important military bridge at Gaulier, although the latter was constantly being attacked by Allied aircraft. While the German officers led from up front, the French commanders were in their command bunkers, far behind the front. Lieutenant Colonel Pinaud, the commander of the 147th Fortress Infantry Regiment employed in the Meuse River loop of Sedan, had his command post at Chaumont, 7 kilometers south of the Meuse River. The division commander, Lafontaine, was 10.5 kilometers away from the Meuse River loop at Bulson. Grandsard was in his corps command post 21 kilometers away in La Berlière; and the army commander in chief Huntziger led from Senuc, which was about 45 kilometers away.

The French officers were by no means less brave than the Germans, but they followed a completely different doctrine that was still guided by the trench fighting of World War I. At that time it had proved effective to move the command posts far behind the front line—out of range of dangerous artillery fire. There the officers were able calmly to analyze the situation, to make decisions, and to draft orders. The front's negative effects (fear, sweat, filth, blood) were not to influence their thinking.[105] On the other hand, in their underground bunkers, they were cut off from actual events on the battlefield. During the campaign in the west, however, it turned out that the nature of war had in the meantime changed from a static to a dynamic type of combat. Only the military leader who was constantly at the focal point of events would be able to respond quickly enough to surprising situation changes. And so, the German commanders endeavored to lead from up front in order immediately to make use of the favorable moment by a lightning-fast decision. As far as the German Panzer commanders were concerned, command process (situation assessment—planning—issuing orders—monitoring) as a rule occurred on the spot with a direct view of actual events. This was one of the most important causes of the surprising German victory: The cycle of the command process took place on the German side several times faster than among the French and British. At one time, Napoleon defined the striking power of an army as the product of mass and speed.[106] Because the Allies started with the static picture of World War I, their armies, though numerically superior, constituted a cumbersome mass and were outmaneuvered by the German Panzer divisions that were attacking in blitzkrieg tempo.

Führen von vorn (leading from up front) yielded not only tactical but also psychological advantages. It was precisely in critical situations, when panic threatened to break out, that the presence of a higher-ranking superior in the foremost front line was a matter of considerable significance. That emerged, for example, during the British tank attack at Arras. There was probably nobody who practiced the principle of "leading from up front" in a more extreme fashion than Rommel. In that way, he became a nightmare for his staff officers. On the other hand, Rommel had the intuitive talent for anticipating situation changes. Again and again, he turned up completely by surprise at the right time and in the right place and brought about the decisive turning point in the fighting through his intervention.

Combination of Tactics and Technology

> *Technology has advanced with giant strides since the World War and it will force tactics to follow it.*[107]
>
> Guderian in *Bewegliche Truppenkörper* (Mobile Troop Units), 1927

The Allies had the same weapon systems as the Germans, and their tanks were technically even better. The fundamental difference, however, was in the basic principles of employment. On the other hand, German employment principles were long known and had been used already during earlier wars. It was only their combination with modern technology that led to something new, the blitzkrieg. Therefore, the synthesis of individual, rather inconspicuous, elements when considered in isolation resulted in a highly explosive mix. It achieved its spectacular explosion at Sedan in May 1940, and its effect even surprised Guderian. Now Sickle Cut could be pulled off successfully, whereas it had failed in the spring of 1918, mainly due to the lack of a Panzer force. In the following pages the most important of these technical factors will be discussed: radio, the Panzers, and aircraft.

Telecommunications Technology. Characteristically, Guderian, while a junior officer, had several assignments with the Signal Corps. He had already operated a radio station in 1914 during the advance through the Ardennes. He was guided by the idea that the large number of individual Panzers could be turned into a tactical and even operational instrument only if all fighting vehicles were equipped with radios. The commanders were to have special Panzer command vehicles that were equipped with long-range radios. In that way, even the generals commanding the Panzer corps were able to lead their units from up front. Accompanied by a small command echelon, they hurried from focal point to focal point and were in a position to react immediately to every new development. While they forwarded their command decisions within seconds to the appropriate units, it often took hours before their Allied opponents, isolated in their bunkers, learned about the change in the situation in the first place. It is rather interesting to note that the German army had twelve times as many trained radio operators as the French army.[108] An operational war of movement above all is a problem of command technique. And so, the command post of Panzer Group Kleist moved

General der Panzertruppe Guderian in his command Panzer—in the foreground on the left, an Enigma coding machine. *Bundesarchiv Koblenz [Federal Archives]*

thirty-four times during the forty-six days of the campaign in the west. In this connection, the signal communications regiment of the Panzer Group connected 5,000 kilometers of telephone lines on poles, laid 2,500 kilometers of field telecommunications cables, and sent out 3,500 radio messages.[109]

The Total System of the Panzer Force

The engine of the Panzer is its weapon just as much as the cannon.[110]

Guderian

The basic principle of the navy that "the slowest frigate determines the speed of the flotilla" was also considered to be correct by French generals when it came to land warfare. To that extent, the tank was considered merely as a weapons system to accompany the infantry and had to adapt to the latter's speed. Accordingly, the French combat vehicles mostly were designed as heavy, slow infantry tanks whose operating radius would suffice only for a tactical breakthrough but not for an operational encirclement. Guderian went exactly the opposite way.[111] He figured the Panzer as being the fastest element to whose speed all others had to adjust.[112] So he built up a Panzer division around the Panzer, complete with Panzer grenadiers [armored infantry] in armored half-tracks, Panzer reconnaissance units riding in armored scout cars, and artillery pieces on self-propelled mounts. All components of this system, all the way to supplies, had to be mechanized or motorized. Above all, cooperation with the Luftwaffe represented the decisive aspect. Panzer and aircraft were to constitute a "pair of twins" and the dive-bomber was used as the vertical artillery of the blitzkrieg.

That this innovative concept could materialize at all was paradoxically also rooted in the restrictive provisions of the Versailles Treaty. The Germans, who had been able to build only very few tanks during World War I due to the raw material shortage,[113] were now not allowed to have any tanks at all. To that extent, they went exactly the opposite way when compared to the neighboring armies—first they developed Panzer tactics and then the corresponding Panzer equipment.

It is also incorrect to say that Guderian only acted on what Western tank theoreticians, who did not get anywhere in their own countries, figured out for him. Thus, the alleged influence of Liddell Hart is pictured as a legend in more recent research.[114] The writings of de Gaulle, who pursued a different concept, were not published until later.[115] To that extent, only the British general Fuller is left as an important source of impetus. But the latter's theories were very much fixated on the tank, whereas Guderian was thinking in terms of the Panzer force system as a whole and drew more heavily on the supporting arms.[116] The essential feature of the German Panzer philosophy seems to be that it actually goes back to the operational style of thinking of men such as Moltke and Schlieffen.[117] The Panzer force was thus a means toward an end, that is, to accomplish the revival of the classical war of movement and to facilitate a motorized Cannae.

The Luftwaffe as Flying Battlefield Artillery. One of the biggest riddles of the campaign in the west seems to be that the French air force had "vanished" in May 1940. The question "where is our air force?" runs like a thread through numerous accounts. D'Astier de la Vigerie, the commander in chief of the northern zone of air operations at that time, even felt called upon to give his subsequent account the following apologetic title: *Le ciel n'était pas vide 1940* (The Sky Was Not Empty in 1940). Yet the French air force was reproached for its absence at Sedan on 13 May.[118] Almost all the after-action reports of army officers employed here contained phrases such as *absence totale de notre aviation* (total absence of our aviation),[119] *aucun avion français dans l'air* (no French aircraft in the air),[120] *que fait notre aviation?* (what is our aviation doing?).[121] As explained earlier, the French air force had about roughly the same number of aircraft as the Luftwaffe. At the start of the campaign in the west, however, this 1:1 ratio had been converted into a ratio of 1:3 [in favor of the Luftwaffe] in terms of operational readiness and, for actual missions in the air, the ratio turned out to be 1:12.[122] There are primarily two reasons why such a striking disproportion developed.

First-Strike Thinking. The Germans had to avoid a long, drawn-out war of attrition in the air. Hitler said in January 1940, "There must be no Verdun in the air."[123] The concept developed by the Luftwaffe command called for a surprise strike against the enemy's ground organization during the very first few minutes of the campaign to destroy any aircraft, if at all possible, on the ground. This first strike required the use of all reserves and was executed so ruthlessly that the Luftwaffe on the very first day lost 347 aircraft.[124] But losses on the opposing side were also so considerable that the Luftwaffe was able to gain air superiority in a very short time.

On the other hand, the Allies believed that victory in the war would go to the side that, after many long years of struggle and loss, would still be able to throw the most aircraft into the last battle. This is why the Allies did not want to place the entire potential on the scales and initially mobilized only a part of the air force. As already explained in connection with the force balance, most of the Allied aircraft were deep in the hinterland at airfields or in depots but not operational at the front. Vuillemin, commander in chief of the French air force, had ordered the "strategy of economical employment" soon after the start of the war in the autumn of 1939.[125] All the more surprising was the tremendous force of the German attack because the campaign in the west was decided in the first battle. This meant that the race that the Germans had run in one dash had been lost because the Allies wanted to move at the speed of a long-distance run to economize.

Differing Operational Principles: The Luftwaffe as Strategic or Operational-Tactical Instrument? The theories of the Italian general [Giulio] Douhet very heavily influenced the Western powers. Douhet assumed that future wars, like World War I, would rigidify into position warfare and would be fought purely in strategic terms as wars of attrition. He argued in favor of the primacy of air warfare because no operational decision seemed possible any longer in land warfare. He believed that the purpose of the air force was not so much to provide ground support for army operations as to mount independent strategic missions far behind the front lines into the enemy hinterland. Victory in war would go to the side that was able to smash the enemy's economic infrastructure by air raids and that could break the morale of the civilian population.

According to the 1940 French "Operational Regulations for the Bomber Fleet," strategic missions were standard. Direct involvement in the army operations was to take place only if "crisis situations" necessitated such action.[126] Thus, according to French air force historian [Lucien] Robineau, missions to provide direct air support to the ground army were accepted only "reluctantly and in exceptional cases."[127] Whenever a French commander at the front wanted to request air support, his request first of all had to clear several bureaucratic hurdles. The problem sprang from the confusion resulting from overlapping jurisdictions that were so "nontransparent" that "even the commanding generals did not know what was going on."[128]

Another disadvantage of the French air force was that the missions were not centrally controlled. This meant that it was hardly ever possible quickly to form points of main effort. Instead, the aircraft were distributed to the army groups for individual days on a percentage basis and from there, again, they were distributed to the individual field armies on a percentage basis, something like the watering can principle.[129] It is also astonishing that a number of aircraft squadrons, which hardly ever got any mission orders, were held in readiness behind the front. General Massenet de Marancour, the commanding general of the 3d Air District, reported that in Tours alone 200 aircraft stood around, unused, including 150 Bloch 151 fighters. He said: "An entire month passed but no orders came."[130] Even more astonishing is an assertion by the then commander in chief of the northern air operations zone, d'Astier de la Vigerie: "Almost every evening, I had to take the initiative and phone the commanders of an army or army group and inform them that I had a certain number of air units for the next day that did not have any mission orders; I would inquire whether they had any assignments. Their answer was always the same: 'Thank you very much, but we have no requirement.' "[131]

The Luftwaffe command, on the other hand, believed that the Luftwaffe had to be employed mainly for *indirect* (operational) and *direct* (tactical) army ground support.[132] This is why the Luftwaffe had the primary mission of providing massive support for the offensives of the army to force an immediate decision. This one-sided fixation meant that most German aircraft did not have any strategic range. Later on, during the air war against Great Britain and in the campaign in the east, this had a highly disadvantageous effect. But this specialization had an advantageous effect during the campaign in the west because it took place as a blitzkrieg.[133]

A structural comparison of the German and French forces clearly shows that on the French side the army and the air force stood mostly independent next to each other, like two isolated columns. On the German side, on the other hand, a number of overlapping liaison elements had been created, also on the middle and lower echelons, that facilitated direct and rapid establishment of contact without any time-consuming procedures of going through channels.[134] The prerequisite for this was technically high-quality radio equipment—a factor whose absence was noted very painfully among the French armed forces. Besides, the Wehrmacht had drilled close cooperation between the army and the Luftwaffe over and over again, in both theory and practice.[135] Thus, the appropriate staffs were also billeted near each other wherever possible. Just how close the link between the two components of the Wehrmacht was is indicated by the fact that on occasion Zeitzler and Seidemann, the chiefs of staff of Panzer Group Kleist and VIII Air Corps, commanded while standing at the same map table. The Luftwaffe detailed special liaison teams to the army that in some cases accompanied the fighting units all the way up front in eight-wheeled armored scout cars. When everything went smoothly, requirements to the Luftwaffe sometimes took effect on the battlefield within forty-five minutes.[136] So, it is no wonder that during the campaign in the west each German fighter flew about 4 sorties per day whereas a French fighter only got up to 0.9 sorties.[137]

Speed and Surprise

> *It [Guderian's blitzkrieg] was to employ mobility as a psychological weapon: not mobility to kill but to move; not to move to kill but to move to terrify, to bewilder, to perplex, to cause consternation, doubt and confusion in the rear of the enemy, which rumor would magnify until panic became monstrous.*[138]
>
> British Major General [J. F. C.] Fuller in an analysis of the campaign in the west in *The Conduct of War, 1798–1961*

The blitzkrieg of 1940 at first seems like nothing other than the revival of the classical operational war of movement of men such as Moltke and Schlieffen. But that is only half the truth. The tie-in of traditional command principles with modern technology resulted in such a tremendous increase in speed during combat operations that there arose a dialectical turnabout, leading to a new, psychological quality. That is the essence of the revolution in the nature of war. The principle of psychological confusion replaced the old principle of physical annihilation. This, in the final analysis, is also the essence of the "indirect approach" as described by Liddell Hart. If at all possible, the advancing German Panzers avoided all kinds of combat actions. After they had thrust deeply enough into the enemy's rear areas, the enemy front collapsed by itself amid wild chaos. Here we also come to an elementary difference with respect to the annihilation battle postulated by von Schlieffen. According to the classical system, the enemy was to be clutched and squeezed to death as if by a boa constrictor. The effect of the blitzkrieg, however, was not directed against the muscles but rather against the nerves of the enemy so that the latter would be paralyzed—the way the rabbit is by the gaze of the snake.

To that extent, this new type of warfare employed an age-old psychological trick: it generated terror. The onrushing German Panzers spread fear and horror like the horsemen of the Apocalypse. That often applied even to the rather puny Panzer I models that their own crews mocked as "tin cans." As the panic at Bulson demonstrated, Panzers—even when they were just phantoms—were able to cause a front to collapse through a mass psychosis. But it is not true that the German command had anticipated and calculated this effect to such an apocalyptic extent. Even Guderian, who was particularly convinced as to the psychological shock effect of the Panzer and the aircraft, was so surprised during the breakthrough at Sedan that he spoke of a "miracle."[139] There were, however, also weapons systems in which the terror effect was planned from the very beginning, such as, for example, the Stuka [dive-bomber]. The British major general [Lord] Trenchard had already asserted—in view of the bombing raids during World War I—that the effect on morale was in a ratio of 20:1 to the material effect.[140]

The special characteristic of the German dive-bomber was that it did not attack in horizontal flight but plunged vertically at the target. Thus, the attack targets thought that they could see "death on wings" racing toward them. Besides, during each dive, the pilot would turn on a howling siren, the so-called Jericho trumpet. The horrible screeching of that siren became the terror fanfare of the blitzkrieg. Following the model of the assault team missions of World War I, the Panzers mounted shock attacks so that the success was based above all on the element of surprise. To that extent, the mission simply could not be betrayed by a lengthy preparatory artillery barrage. That occurred before the crossing of the Meuse River at Sedan. The Luftwaffe appeared "like a bolt out of the blue." One of the most overwhelming surprise effects of World War II was thus achieved.

Marc Bloch experienced the hopelessly disastrous confusion of French headquarters in response to the tempo of the German blitzkrieg and reported: "From beginning to end of the campaign, the Germans showed the same embarrassing skill in appearing where they ought not to have appeared. They did not, in fact, play the game. . . . The war was a constant succession of surprises."[141]

The French and British wanted to run through combat operations that had been planned systematically in advance—military command had degenerated to battlefield management. Thus, the stereotyped matériel battles of World War I turned war into a mathematical problem where the most important thing was to calculate the ammunition tonnages. There was no room in this rigid pattern for the incalculable. Suddenly, the Allies were attacked by an enemy who deliberately disregarded the rules of war and whose only system seemed to consist of unsystematic, unmethodical action. An American author writes: "On the other hand, the more fluid, the more obscure, the more chaotic the battle became (or could be *made to be*), the more the Allied leaders were subject to bewilderment, panic, and despair. . . . The Germans, on the other hand, accepted chaos as a natural substance of combat. For them, the fog of war and friction were paramount forces with which the methodology of combat should seek to harmonize, not suppress. By developing the methodology of *Auftragstaktik* . . . the Germans inured themselves to the effects of confusion and uncertainty in the tangled frenzy of combat. They accepted chaos as inevitable and lived with it."[142]

11

Summary and Epilogue

Summary

It had always been the maxim of the Prussian-German general staff to fight quick wars to avoid the danger of a long, drawn-out two-front war. The unfavorable central geostrategic position of the German Reich necessitated that. The famous 1940 blitzkrieg, however, had not been planned as a blitzkrieg. An investigation into the preparatory measures prior to the campaign in the west, particularly in the field of armament, clearly shows that the German command was planning a rehash of the many long years of struggle during World War I. To that extent, it was completely surprised by the course of operation. The "miracle of 1940" cannot be traced back to a blitzkrieg strategy that is repeatedly played up largely in historiography. Instead, it is based mostly on the following three factors.

The Changing Nature of War

The campaign in the west marked a turning point in military history. The pendulum of martial technology, which during World War I had favored the defender, now swung in favor of the attacker. Mainly due to the operational employment of the Panzer force and Luftwaffe, there was no positional warfare and the operational war of movement of men such as Moltke and Schlieffen was reborn. Because of new technical developments, the effect of traditional German command principles was enhanced in undreamed of ways. Quite by accident, this led to a revolution in the nature of war that plunged the armies of the Western powers into unholy confusion. They were still trapped in the static style of thinking that was in fashion during World War I and perished in the whirlpool of the war of movement. The German officers seemed to be likewise surprised by this development, but, on the basis of their well-drilled mission tactics and their operational training, they were much quicker when it came to adapting to new situations.

Allied Mistakes

Manstein's Sickle Cut idea led to a success that nobody had thought possible before, that is, to an immediate operational decision. The prerequisite, however, was that the

Allies allowed themselves to be deceived and ran into the trap. So a complete encirclement (Cannae principle) materialized that is so rare in military history. The "strange defeat" of the Western powers was thus also the result of the extremely serious mistakes of their military leaders. Again and again, German successes hung by a thin string, but, again and again, luck favored Hitler's attack formations, which often beat their opponents to the punch only by a matter of hours. After the incomprehensible victory, both Nazi propaganda and Allied reporters—for different reasons—created the myth of the overwhelmingly powerful Wehrmacht. The reality was, however, that the Western powers were definitely superior, as proved by a detailed strength comparison. However, they managed to adjust to the methods of the German war of movement only during the second half of the campaign (Case Red). By then it was too late.

Unauthorized Actions

The spectacular course of Operation Sickle Cut had not been planned in advance. The army high command completely shied away from accepting Manstein's bold Sickle Cut idea and would venture only a half-hearted plan. Besides, the anti-Panzer command of Army Group A wanted to adjust the tempo of the attack to that of the infantry divisions marching on foot, something that would have implied a blitzkrieg in slow motion. But the immediate breakthrough of the Meuse River line at Sedan gave the operation such a dynamism of its own that the Panzer divisions in the end simply took off and left the infantry divisions eating dust. The attack rolled at maximum speed like an avalanche, and the top command occasionally lost control. In this very special situation, numerous officers were increasingly less inhibited when it came to disregarding all orders and regulations, claiming, as they did, their implementation of mission tactics. The key scene of the operation was Guderian's unauthorized breakout from the Sedan bridgehead. Only that brought about, by force, the success of Manstein's far-sighted Sickle Cut idea—quite contrary to the desire of the higher-level command.

The 1940 blitzkrieg, thus, is in no way connected with the blitzkrieg strategy that Hitler is credited with. According to this theory, the major objective of world power or world rule allegedly was to be achieved no longer in a single total endeavor, as in World War I, but stage by stage, on the basis of a phased plan, by fighting short blitzkriegs. However, at the time, Hitler had not planned any war against the Western powers—and certainly not a blitzkrieg. After all, the Wehrmacht was still being built up due to the Versailles Treaty and even its own general staff graded it as "not ready for war." Instead, it was Great Britain and France that declared war on Hitler after the German invasion of Poland. Thus, the dictator—as a result of his failed go-for-broke gambler's policy—had maneuvered the German Reich into a situation from which there was no way out. A war against the Western powers, with their superior strength, looked hardly winnable. Because time, in the long run, worked against Germany, there was really only the chance of starting out on a flight forward, putting all the money on one card, and overrunning the enemy by a surprise attack. But the German command shied away precisely from this kind of venturesome undertaking, mindful of the trauma of the Schlieffen plan that had failed during World War I.

As Clausewitz explained, people act "not reasonably during big crises, since, driven to utter despair, they see no salvation other than risking a daring leap."[1] This "daring leap" across the Meuse River and all the way to the Channel coast was Manstein's Sickle Cut. The Allied generals had not figured on that kind of daredevil action. They faced these breathtaking developments as nonplussed as did Hitler, the hesitator, himself, as the controls were ripped from his hands by an operation that became increasingly independent. By stopping the Panzers before Dunkirk, he allowed himself to be trapped in a mistake that, in the end, undid the desired strategic success. The campaign in the west thus was not a planned campaign of conquest. Instead, it was an operational act of despair to get out of a desperate strategic situation. What is called "blitzkrieg thinking" did not develop until *after* the campaign in the west. It was not the cause but rather the consequence of the victory. Something that, in May 1940, had come off successfully to everyone's surprise, was now to serve the implementation of Hitler's visions of conquest in the form of the secret of success.

Epilogue: The Delusion of the Worldwide Blitzkrieg

"Cannae"—no catchword has become so disastrous for us as this one.[2]

Generaloberst von Seeckt about the failure of the Schlieffen plan

For the Wehrmacht, the campaign in the west was at once triumph and tragedy because the glitter of victory misled Hitler and his generals into a fatal case of hubris. The myth of Sedan played a special role here. This is where the Germans in 1870 and 1940 had been able to win two of their most significant victories, but each time they drew false conclusions from these victories, which had their negative effects in two world wars. For the French army, Verdun led to an overestimation of position warfare; on the German side, the victories at Sedan always resulted in an overestimation of the operational war of movement. After the campaign in the west, those very same generals who earlier had been so skeptical in viewing the new ideas worked themselves into a blitzkrieg euphoria. In contrast to World War I, swift, operational battles of decision now again seemed possible, even against an economically and thus also strategically superior enemy. And so, the blitzkrieg led to a *motorized* rebirth of the Cannae idea. As previously happened under Schlieffen, the generals forgot who really won the Second Punic War: Cannae was only a passing operational success by Hannibal over Rome, the strategically superior sea power. Clausewitz warned against making the fate of a state dependent upon an immediate operational battle of decision and instead gave preference to strategic defense. Thus, he put it rather drastically: "We must add unequivocally, however, that we consider it beneath our dignity to notice the clamor of those whose vague emotions and even vaguer minds impel them to expect everything from attack and movement, and whose idea of war is summed up by a galloping hussar waving his sword."[3]

Just as the Western powers were overestimated before, so now did the German command underestimate the Soviet Union. During World War I, it had not been possible to defeat France and its allies, but Russia was defeated. Now that the Western powers were conquered in just a few weeks, it was believed that the Soviet Union would be easy pickings. Immediately after the campaign in the west, Hitler, drunk with victory, told the chief of the Wehrmacht high command: "Now we have shown them what we can do. Believe me, Keitel, a campaign against Russia would be child's play compared to that."[4]

The successful blitzkrieg against France had not been based on any previously determined doctrine; but, as Halder observed, it was an improvisation born of necessity.[5] A year later, they wanted to try the same trick against the Soviet Union, with the difference, however, that this time a blitzkrieg was really planned and, in strategic respects, the way it was set up. The Germans had figured on a long, drawn-out war against the Western powers, without any time limit set in the beginning. However, they wanted to smash the Soviet Union militarily in a campaign planned for just three months. The mobilization of personnel and matériel was coordinated with this exact final target date.[6] However, it was impossible to reach Moscow before the onset of winter. And so it happened that, in December 1941, a sudden cold spell of minus 36 degrees [centigrade] forced most German soldiers to fight while still wearing their summer uniforms because too little winter clothing had been prepared. Hitler and his generals had actually believed that they could flatten the Red Army, the "giant with feet of clay," in their first onrush—even though the Wehrmacht was already committed on other fronts, on land, on the sea, and in the air. The army high command planned a "super Cannae" to smash the Soviet armies that were deployed along the border in a series of encirclement battles—and they figured that this alone would mean that the campaign had been won. The crucial mistake was that the most important prerequisite for a blitzkrieg in the strategic sense did not exist, that is, a first-strike capacity (at least a temporary one). In spite of the attempt to convert to a campaign with a time limit on it, German armament was not able to keep up and so, in June 1941, thirty-six hundred German Panzers attacked a total of twenty-four thousand Soviet tanks.[7]

Nevertheless, in the beginning everything looked like a gigantic blitzkrieg success. The Red Army was overrun, real and proper; encirclement battle followed encirclement battle: Bialystok, Minsk, Smolensk, Uman', Kiev, Vyaz'ma, Bryansk, just to mention the most important ones. Approximately 4 million Soviet soldiers were taken prisoner during the first months of the campaign from June to December 1941.[8] Operations began so successfully that Halder noted in his war diary as early as the twelfth day [3 July 1941]: "It is thus probably no overstatement to say that the Russian Campaign has been won in the space of two weeks."[9]

The chief of the general staff, who had been so cautious before the campaign in the west, following the initial successes, worked himself into a blitzkrieg mania and charted visions of an intercontinental Cannae. Immediately after the eastern campaign, which was already considered to have been won, he wanted to mount a gigantic encirclement movement, over three continents, with three spearheads, "against the land route between the Nile and the Euphrates"[10]: (1) via Russia through the Caucasus toward Iran, (2) from Bulgaria via Turkey toward Syria and Iraq, (3) from North Africa through Rommel in Libya across Egypt and the Suez Canal to Palestine.

Hitler had lost all sense of reality and was caught up in the vision of a Weltblitzkrieg (worldwide blitzkrieg).[11] After the Soviet Union had been quickly smashed militarily and following the push all the way to the Persian Gulf, he wanted to push deep into Asia. The offensive was to be routed via Afghanistan to India to threaten the "heart of the British Empire." At the same time, the Germans expected a Japanese push against India from the east so that this subcontinent would be caught in a pincer movement from two compass directions.[12]

The blitzkrieg against the Soviet Union had already failed in the winter of 1941 before Moscow. To boil it down to a simple formula, the difference between the campaign in the west and the campaign in the east was that the 1940 campaign in the west was an unplanned but successful blitzkrieg, whereas the 1941 campaign in the east was a planned but unsuccessful blitzkrieg. To be sure, when the Germans again went on the offensive in 1942, they were able to advance all the way to the Volga and into the Caucasus, but the German Wehrmacht was operationally winning themselves to death. Looking at it strategically, it was bound to run out of steam sooner or later. Now the economic superiority of the Soviet Union and its allies began to take effect. This can be shown especially by citing Panzer production statistics. Neglecting all other arms, the German Reich concentrated primarily on the Panzer force. Still, the Germans were able to build only a total of twenty-five thousand battle tanks due to raw material shortages. On the other hand, the three most important Allies—the United States, the Soviet Union and Great Britain—were able to turn out two hundred thousand battle tanks.[13] Thus, World War II, just like World War I, was decided not on the battlefields but in the factories.

At the end of 1944, there was once again a large-scale German offensive operation against the Western powers. But the so-called Ardennes offensive [Battle of the Bulge] was only the last gasp of a German Reich that was already laboring in agony. At this point, the cycle is closed, so to speak; it so happens that Hitler employed the first offensive in the Ardennes in 1940 as the inspiration for the second one in 1944.[14] This time, Sickle Cut was to be directed against the port city of Antwerp and to drive a wedge between the British and American forces. This offensive represented the nadir of the German art of operational command.

The plan was not based on any rational, general staff–style calculations, but was only an irrational act of despair on the part of Hitler. How could anyone plan an offensive with such an ambitious objective as the Port of Antwerp if fuel for some Panzer units was available only for the first sixty kilometers? That fuel was barely enough to reach the enemy fuel dumps after whose seizure the advance was to be continued—freshly gassed up.[15] Such a "blitzkrieg without gasoline" is bound to appear just about absurd in retrospect. By comparison, one may refer to the perfect logistic preparation, especially the precise fuel calculations, for the 1940 offensive. There was also another factor that had been so decisive in 1940, that is, at least temporary air superiority—but it was not present in 1944. How were the German Panzer units to reach Antwerp if they could sneak there only at night and in fog? While so-called Göring weather in May 1940 favored the smooth operation of the Luftwaffe, the encore of this operation in 1944 was dogged by a protracted period of bad weather. The Ardennes offensive of 1944 that sprang from Hitler's delusions did not even have a chance of operational success. It was but a poor copy, yes, even a satire, of the operation in 1940. Once upon a time, Karl Marx, who was also an avid reader of Clausewitz, commented on the questionability of historical analogies: "Hegel noted somewhere that all major events in world history happen, so to speak, twice. He forgot to add that they take place, the first time, as a tragedy, and the next time, as a farce."[16]

An episode that appears symbolic of the entire campaign in the west is recounted in an after-action report of the infantry regiment Großdeutschland. On the morning of 14 May 1940, after the breakthrough at Sedan, a German advance detachment pushed south toward Chémery. As it says in the after-action report, there was a scene as if out of a dream. Southeast of Connage, French cavalry suddenly came charging out of the woods. Machine guns immediately put an end to this mounted attack. Immediately thereafter, in the roadside ditch, next to the discarded baggage of a French officer, a book famous in world literature was found: *Don Quixote* by Miguel Cervantes.[17] Don Quixote was the very symbol of an anachronistic picture of war. It was the end for the knights as they clashed with armies of mercenaries equipped with modern firearms. And so, the uprising of the knights against modern weaponry resembled an act of jousting with windmills. By the same token, many French soldiers, who had fought bravely, played but a tragic role. Nobody stated this more clearly than Weygand who, after the disaster at Sedan, tried to save France, in spite of everything, in his capacity as newly appointed supreme commander. He said, "We have gone to war with a 1918 army against a German Army of 1939. It is sheer madness."[18]

At this point, we come to the following question: Should we not also label the phenomenon of the blitzkrieg as anachronism in some respects? In the industrial age, when two world wars were decided in purely strategic terms—specifically, by the productivity of the factories—Hitler and his generals had become fixated in an entirely too one-sided manner upon the military operational level. To that extent, the blitzkrieg seems both revolutionary and reactionary. Looking at it purely in operational terms, the German generals did use the most modern methods. In strategic respects, on the other hand, they were guided by an anachronistic concept of war. Back during the nineteenth century, the American Civil War demonstrated that the militarily more efficient southern states, in the long run, did not have a chance against the economically superior northern states. Thus, the Panzer operations of the German blitzkrieg were very much like jousting against the windmills of superior industrial potentials.

Table of Equivalent Ranks

U.S. Army	German Army and Luftwaffe	German Waffen-SS
	Officers	
None	Reichsmarschall	None
General of the Army	Generalfeldmarschall	Reichsführer-SS
General	Generaloberst	Oberstgruppenführer
Lieutenant General	General der Infanterie	Obergruppenführer
	Artillerie	
	Flakartillerie	
	Flieger	
	Kavallerie	
	Luftwaffe	
	Panzertruppen	
	Pioniere	
Major General	Generalleutnant	Gruppenführer
Brigadier General	Generalmajor	Brigadeführer
None	None	Oberführer
Colonel	Oberst	Standartenführer
Lieutenant Colonel	Oberstleutnant	Obersturmbannführer
Major	Major	Sturmbannführer
Captain	Hauptmann	Hauptsturmführer
1st Lieutenant	Oberleutnant	Obersturmführer
2d Lieutenant	Leutnant	Untersturmführer
	Enlisted	
Master Sergeant	Stabsfeldwebel	Sturmscharführer
Technical Sergeant	Oberfeldwebel	Hauptscharführer
Staff Sergeant	Feldwebel	Oberscharführer
Sergeant	Unterfeldwebel	Scharführer
Corporal	Unteroffizier	Unterscharführer
Private 1st Class	Gefreiter	Rottenführer
Private	Soldat	SS-Mann

Source: U.S. War Department, *Handbook on German Military Forces,* Technical Manual TM-E 30–451, 15 March 1945, 6–7, 204.

Notes

Abbreviations used in notes and bibliography:

EWKde	*Europäische Wehrkunde* (European Military Science)
MGM	*Militärgeschichtliche Mitteilungen* (Military History News)
MWR	*Militärwissenschaftliche Rundschau* (Military Science Review)
ÖMZ	*Österreichische Militärische Zeitschrift* (Austrian Military Journal)
RBHM	*Revue belge d'Histoire militaire* (Belgian Military History Review)
RHA	*Revue Historique des Armées* (Army Historical Review) (until 1973: *Revue Historique de l'Armée de Terre* [Army Historical Review])
RHDGM	*Revue d'Histoire de la Deuxième Guerre Mondiale* (World War II History Review)
WWR	*Wehrwissenschaftliche Rundschau* (Military Science Review)

Introduction

1. HGr C (Ia), Notiz Besprechung in Versailles am 28.6.1940, Bundesarchiv-Militärarchiv, RH 19 III/141, Anl. 23, Bl. 44 (Army Group C [Operations], Note on Conference in Versailles on 28 June 1940, Federal Military Archives, app. 23, sheet 44), hereafter BA-MA.
2. Quoted from Jaques Benoist-Méchin, *Der Himmel stürzt ein: Frankreichs Tragödie 1940* (The Sky Is Falling: France's Tragedy in 1940) (Düsseldorf: Droste Verlag, 1958), 9.
3. Patrick Turnbull, *Dunkirk: Anatomy of Disaster* (New York: Holmes and Meier Publishers, 1978), 7.
4. *The Ciano Diaries, 1939–1943,* ed. Hugh Gibson (New York, 1946), 201.
5. Golo Mann, *Deutsche Geschichte des 19. und 20. Jahrhunderts* (German History of the 19th and 20th Centuries) (Stuttgart and Hamburg, 1958), 922. English-language version, *The History of Germany since 1789,* trans. Marian Jackson (New York: Frederick A. Praeger, 1968), 470.
6. Basil Henry Liddell Hart, *Geschichte des Zweiten Weltkrieges* (History of the Second World War) (Wiesbaden: FourierVerlag,1970), 102. English-language version, *History of the Second World War* (New York: G. P. Putnam's Sons, 1970), 73.
7. Barrie Pitt, *Angriffswaffe, Einleitung zu:* Macksey, *Deutsche Panzertruppen* ("Attack Weapon," introduction to Kenneth J. Macksey, *German Panzer Forces*) (Vienna and Munich: Moewig, 1985), 10f.
8. "Catastrophic Failure: The French Army and Air Force, May–June 1940," Eliot A. Cohen and John Gooch, *Military Misfortunes. The Anatomy of Failure in War* (New York: Vintage Books, 1991), 197.
9. William L. Langer, *Our Vichy Gamble* (New York: Alfred A. Knopf, 1947), 3; translation from Benoist-Méchin, *Der Himmel stürzt ein,* 5.
10. Gen. d.Inf a.D. Günther Blumentritt, Der Westfeldzug 1940, Bd. 2: Darstellung der Operationen (The Campaign in the West, 1940; vol. 2, Description of Operations),

Studies of the Historical Division, Headquarters, U.S. Army, Europe, Study P–208, 46, BA-MA. On another occasion, Hitler described the first phase of the campaign in the west as "an absolute miracle," Günther Blumentritt, *Von Rundstedt. The Soldier and the Man* (London: Odhams Press, Ltd., 1952), 71, 78.

11. B. H. Liddell Hart, *Jetzt dürfen sie reden. Hitlers Generale berichten* (Now They Can Speak Out. Hitler's Generals Report) (Stuttgart: Stuttgarter Verlag, 1950), 213; English-language versions: first published in England as *The Other Side of the Hill. Germany's Generals. Their Rise and Fall, with their own Account of Military Events, 1939–1945* (London: Cassell, 1948); the American edition was, *The German Generals Talk* (New York: William Morrow, 1948), 134; Blumentritt, *Rundstedt,* 68–74.
12. Heinz Guderian, *Erinnerungen eines Soldaten* (Memoirs of a Soldier) (Stuttgart: Motorbuch Verlag, 1986), 95; English-language version, *Panzer Leader,* trans. Constantine FitzGibbon (Cambridge, Mass.: Da Capo Press, 1996), 106.
13. About Germany's wartime objective in World War I, see also the controversial book by Fritz Fischer, *Griff nach der Weltmacht: Die Kriegspolitik des kaiserlichen Deutschland 1914/18* (The Grasp for World Power: The War Policy of Imperial Germany, 1914–18) (Düsseldorf: Droste Verlag, 1961).

Chapter 1

1. Max Domarus, *Hitler. Reden und Proklamationen 1932–1945* (Hitler: Speeches and Proclamations, 1932–1945) (Würzburg, 1962–63), 1776.
2. Larry H. Addington, *The Blitzkrieg Era and the German General Staff, 1865–1941* (New Brunswick, N.J.: Rutgers University Press, 1971), 234n.53. *Blitzkrieg* was not a translation of the English term "lightning war"; instead, it was exactly the other way around. German emigrants introduced this word into the English language before World War II. See the book by Fritz Sternberg, published in 1938, titled *Germany and a Lightning War* (London: Faber and Faber, 1938). The German version, titled *Die deutsche Kriegsstärke: Wie lange kann Hitler Krieg führen?* (German War Strength: How Long Can Hitler Fight a War?) (Paris: Editions Sebastian Brant, 1939 [1938 copyright]), repeatedly contains the word *blitzkrieg* (e.g., see pp. 8 and 11).
3. Von Schwichow, "Die Ernährungswirtschaft als Wehrproblem" (The Food Economy as a National Defense Problem), *Deutsche Wehr* 39, no. 18 (1935): 257f.
4. Braun, "Der strategische Überfall" (The Strategic Surprise Attack), *Militär-Wochenblatt,* no. 18 (1938): col. 1134.
5. Additional evidence of the use of the word *Blitzkrieg* before World War II can be found, for example, in Stefan T. Possony, *Die Wehrwirtschaft des totalen Krieges* (The War Economy of Total War) (Vienna: Gerold, 1938), 82, or in Wolfgang Foerster, *Generaloberst Ludwig Beck: Sein Kampf gegen den Krieg. Aus nachgelassenen Papieren des Generalstabschefs* (Generaloberst Ludwig Beck: His Fight against the War. From the Posthumous Papers of the Chief of the General Staff) (Munich: Isar Verlag, 1952), 123.
6. Among others, the following examples might be mentioned from the vast *Blitzkrieg* literature published in 1940 or shortly thereafter: Rudolf Vogel, *Grenzerjunge im Blitzkrieg. Eine Erzählung aus dem Polenfeldzug* (Border Youth in the Blitzkrieg. A Tale from the Polish Campaign) (Stuttgart, 1940); Oberstleutnant Köhn, "Die Infanterie im 'Blitzkrieg'" (The Infantry in the "Blitzkrieg"), *Militär-Wochenblatt* 125, no. 5

(1940): 165f.; "Blitzkrieg und Panzerdivisionen" (Blitzkrieg and The Panzer Divisions), *Ostasiatischer Beobachter* (East Asian Observer), 30 November 1940, 11–13; Gaul, "Der Blitzkrieg in Frankreich" (The Blitzkrieg in France), *Militär-Wochenblatt* 125, no. 35 (1941): cols 1513–16; "Blitzkriegmethoden (von Dr. F. K.). Erfolge und Gefahren einer neuen Kriegführung" [Blitzkrieg Methods (by Dr. F. K.). Successes and Dangers of a New Method of Warfare], *Weltwoche,* 4 July 1941; "Deutsche Blitzkriegsstrategen" (German Blitzkrieg Strategists), *Weltwoche,* 4 July 1941; Philip Gribble, "Blitzkrieg" in *Die Auslese* 41, no. 3: 185–90; no. 4, 307–12, first published in the *Saturday Evening Post,* 7 December 1940. In the book by Eugen Hadamovsky titled *Blitzmarsch nach Warschau* (Lightning March to Warsaw) (Munich: Zentralverlag der NSDAP Franz Eher, 1941), the word *Blitz* (lightning) shows up three times on p. 84, with the following variations: *Blitzkrieg* (lightning war), *blitzschnell* (lightning fast), and *Blitzschlag* (lightning strike). The secret situation report of the SS Sicherheitsdienst (Security Service), no. 88, dated 16 May 1940, states that "vast circles of the population" would believe "that there was also a 'Blitzfeldzug' (lightning campaign) in the West"; see *Meldungen aus dem Reich 1938–1945. Die geheimen Lageberichte des Sicherheitdienstes der SS* (Messages from the Reich, 1938–1945. The Secret Situation Reports of the Security Service of the SS), vol. 4, ed. Heinz Boberach (Herrsching: Pawlak, 1984), 1139.

7. H. Mußhoff, "Blitzkriegpsychose" (Blitzkrieg Psychosis), *Ostasiatischer Beobachter* 8, ser. 86, 31 August 1940: 3–7.
8. See also the quotation at the beginning of this chapter, according to which Hitler described the word blitzkrieg as a "stupid word" that he "never" used. In reality, the word *Blitz* (lightning) had always been one of Hitler's favorite metaphors. As shown in Hoßbach's notes, the dictator had already stated during the conference on 5 November 1937 that the sudden attack on Czechoslovakia would have to be mounted "*blitzartig schnell*" (lightning fast) (ADAP [Documents on German Foreign Policy], ser. D., vol. 1, 31). He also had this to say on 27 March 1941: "Politically it is particularly important that the strike against Yugoslavia . . . be carried out '*in einem Blitzunternehmen*' (in a lightning operation)" (Domarus, *Hitler,* 1677). The author's colleague Dr. Reinhard Stumpf alerted him that Hitler, after the German defeat near Moscow, wanted to blame the Italians for this word that suddenly seemed suspect to him. Thus, he said in January 1942: "Blitzkrieg, that word is a pure Italian invention, Italian phraseology, a translation from Italian." (Adolf Hitler, *Monologe im Führer-hauptquartier 1941–1944. Die Aufzeichnungen Heinrich Heims* [Monologues at Führer Headquarters, 1941–1944. The Notes Taken by Heinrich Heims]), ed. Werner Jochmann (Hamburg: Albrecht Knaus, 1980), 17. Possibly, he was referring to a book—not published until 1940—titled *La guerra lampo* (The Lightning War) by Aldo Cabiati. However, there is no reliable evidence as to Hitler's statement.
9. Generalmajor Teiß, "Der Blitzkrieg" (The Blitzkrieg), *Rheinisch Westfälische Zeitung,* 1 October 1942.
10. See also: R. Hargreaves, "Blitzkrieg: Illegitimate Son of Mars," *The Cavalry Journal,* no. 5 (1940): 386–91; S. L. A. Marshall, *Blitzkrieg: Its History, Strategy, Economics, and the Challenge to America* (New York: William Morrow, 1940); Henry J. Reilly, "Blitzkrieg," *Foreign Affairs* 18, no. 2 (1940): 254–65, and "Can 'Blitzkrieg' Be Stopped?" *Illustrated London News,* no. 5282 (1940): 50; Ferdinand Otto Miksche, *Blitzkrieg* (London, 1942).
11. The Swedes spoke about *Blixtkrieg* and *Blixtanfall* [e.g., "Blixtanfallet," (ed.), *1939 års Färsvarsförbund* (Stockholm, 1940); "'Blixtkrig' och försvar mot 'blixtkrig,'" *Kungl.*

Krigsvetenskaps-Akadem. Handlingar och Tidskrift, no. 3 (1942): 56–80; "Blixtkriget och sprängberedskapen," *Tidskrift i fortification* 66, no. 3 (1943): 121–137; Carl August Ehrensvaerd, *Hårt mot hårt. Blixtanfallet och blixtförsvar* (Stockholm: 1943); the Dutch spoke of *Bliksemoorlog* (Henry J. Reilly, "Bliksemoorlog," *De Kern* 10 (1940): 161–64; the Russians mentioned "*molnienosnaya voyna*" ("Diskussiya o 'molnienosnoy voyne'"), *Voenniy Zarubeznik* no. 10 (1940): 13–31; Henry J. Reilly, "Na fone molnienosnoy voyny," *Voenniy Zarubeznik* no. 9 (1940): 36–44; Paul W. Thompson, "Inzenernye voyska v molnienosnoy voyne," *Voenniy Zarubeznik* no. 11–12 (1940): 72–79); the Hungarians talked about *villámháború* (S. Lipcsey-Magyar, "Villámharcászat-zsakhadászat," *Magyar szemle* 11, no. 11 [1941]: 257–67); the Portuguese talked about *guerra relámpago* (A. Botelho, "O commando e a guerra relámpago," *Revista militar* [Lisbon], no. 9 [1942]: 522–33); the French talked about *la guerre éclair;* the British and Americans talked about "lightning war."

12. George Raudzens, "Blitzkrieg Ambiguities: Doubtful Usage of a Famous Word," *War and Society* 7, no. 2 (1989): 77ff.
13. In the terminology used in World War II, the dividing line between "operational" and "strategic" is rather fluid; the latter term continued to be used in a purely military context. The modern definition of "strategic matters" takes into consideration considerably more extra-military components, for example, the areas of economics, diplomacy, ideology, and psychology.
14. "Blitzkriegmethoden" (by Dr. F. K.).
15. Laszlo M. Alfoldi argues against that in his essay "The Hutier Legend," *Parameters* 5, no. 2 (1976): 73. He points out General von Hutier was by no means the sole inventor of "*Stoßtrupp-Taktik*" (assault team tactics). Instead, this was an evolutionary development in which various German officers participated independently of each other.
16. Braun, 1135.
17. See, for example, the book by Dermot Bradley, *Generaloberst Heinz Guderian und die Entstehungsgeschichte des modernen Blitzkrieges* (General Heinz Guderian and the Origin of the Modern Blitzkrieg) (Osnabrück, 1978).
18. B. J. Rolak, "Fathers of the Blitzkrieg," *Military Review* 49, no. 5 (May 1969): 74ff. This connection—which hereafter will play an important role—was also confirmed for the author in a communication from retired Bundeswehr Generalmajor Heinz-Günther Guderian, the son of the World War II Panzer general. See also Hubertus Senff, *Die Entwicklung der Panzerwaffe im deutschen Heer zwischen den beiden Weltkriegen* (The Development of the Panzer Force in the German Army between the World Wars) (Frankfurt, 1969), 28f.
19. Alan S. Milward, "Der Einfluß ökonomischer und nicht-ökonomischer Faktoren auf die Strategie des Blitzkriegs" (The Influence of Economic and Non-Economic Factors on the Strategy of the Blitzkrieg), Friedrich Forstmeier and Hans-Erich Volkmann, eds., *Wirtschaft und Rüstung am Vorabend des Zweiten Weltkrieges* (The Economy and Armaments on the Eve of the Second World War) (Düsseldorf: Droste Verlag, 1975), 189. The same author published a series of additional standard works on so-called Blitzkrieg strategy: *Die deutsche Kriegswirtschaft 1939–1945* (The German War Economy, 1939–1945) (Stuttgart: Deustche Verlags-Anstalt, 1966); *Der Zweiten Weltkrieg. Krieg, Wirtschaft und Gesellschaft 1939–1945* (The Second World War: War, Economy and Society) (Munich: Deutscher Taschenbuch Verlag, 1977); "Hitlers Konzept des Blitzkrieges" (Hitler's Concept of Blitzkrieg), Andreas Hillgruber, ed., *Probleme des Zweiten Weltkrieges* (Problems of the Second World War) (Cologne: Kiepenheuer and Witsch, 1967).

20. Burton H. Klein, *Germany's Economic Preparation for War* (Cambridge, Mass.: Harvard University Press, 1959). For a discussion of this subject, see Bernhard R. Kroener, "Die personellen Ressourcen des Dritten Reiches im Spannungsfeld zwischen Wehrmacht, Bürokratie und Kriegswirtschaft 1939–1942" (The Manpower Resources of the Third Reich in the Context of the Wehrmacht, the Bureaucracy, and the War Economy), Bernard R. Kroener, Rolf-Dieter Müller, and Hans Umbreit, *Organisation und Mobilisierung des deutschen Machtbereichs. Kriegsverwaltung, Wirtschaft und personelle Ressourcen 1939 bis 1941* (Organization and Mobilization of the German Sphere of Power. Wartime Administration, Economy and Personnel Resources 1939 to 1941), vol. 5, pt. 1, *Das Deutsche Reich und der Zweiten Weltkrieg* (The German Reich and the Second World War) (Stuttgart: Deutsche Verlags-Anstalt, 1988), 694.
21. Andreas Hillgruber, *Hitlers Strategie. Politik und Kriegführung 1940–1941* (Hitler's Strategy: Politics and Warfare, 1940–1941) (Munich: Bernard and Graefe, 1982), Postscript to the 2d ed., 717. Among the historians who developed this idea further, we might mention above all Ludolf Herbst in *Der totale Krieg und die Ordnung der Wirtschaft. Die Kriegswirtschaft im Spannungsfeld von Politik, Ideologie und Propaganda 1939–1945* (Total War and the Organization of the Economy: The War Economy in the Context of Politics, Ideology, and Propaganda, 1939–1945) (Stuttgart, 1982), 98ff.
22. Michael Salewski, for example, believes that Hillgruber's "*Stufenplan*" (step-by-step plan) model is too monocausal: "There were indeed more than enough steps but there was not just one staircase but an entire series of staircases with many main and back staircases" ["Knotenpunkt der Weltgeschichte? Die Raison des deutsch-französischen Waffenstillstands von 22. Juni 1940"] (Crucial Junctures in World History. The Rationale behind the German-French Armistice of 22 June 1940), Claude Carlier and Stefan Martens, eds., *La France et l'Allemagne en guerre. Septembre 1939–Novembre 1942* (France and Germany at War, September 1939–November 1942) (Paris: I.H.A.P.-I.H.C.C, 1990), 119. See also Bernd Stegemann, "Hitlers 'Stufenplan' und die Marine" (Hitler's "Step-by-Step Plan" and the Navy), *Historische Studien zu Politik, Verfassung und Gesellschaft* (Historical Studies on Politics, Constitution, and Society) (Frankfurt am Main: Peter Lang, 1976) as well as his "Hitlers Ziele im ersten Kriegsjahr 1939/40. Ein Beitrag zur Quellenkritik" (Hitler's Objectives during the First Year of the War, 1939–1940: A Contribution to Criticism of the Sources), *MGM* 27, no. 1 (1980): 93–105. Hartmut Schustereit advocates the most decisive antithesis to Hillgruber's step-by-step plan in his monograph *Vabanque. Hitlers Angriff auf die Sowjetunion 1941 als Versuch durch den Sieg im Osten den Westen zu bezwingen* (The Go-for-Broke Gamble: Hitler's Attack on the Soviet Union as an Attempt to Defeat the West through Victory in the East) (Bonn and Herford: E. S. Mittler and Sohn, 1988).
23. Karl-Dietrich Erdmann, *Deutschland unter der Herrschaft des Nationalsozialismus 1933–1939* (Germany under the Rule of National Socialism, 1933–1939), Gebhardt, *Handbuch der deutschen Geschichte* (Handbook of German History), vol. 20 (Munich: Deutscher Taschenbuch Verlag, 1980), 34.
24. Reference is frequently made here to the following passage from the *Weisung für die einheitliche Kriegsvorbereitung der Wehrmacht* (Directive for the Uniform Wartime Preparations of the Wehrmacht) of 24 June 1937: The German Armed Forces were to be able "to start a war by a surprise attack in terms of strength and timing" (see also *Der Prozeß gegen die Hauptkriegsverbrecher vor dem internationalen Militärgerichtshof, Nürnberg, 14.11.45–1.10.46* (The Trial of the Major War Criminals before the International Military Tribunal, Nuremberg, 14 November 1945–1 October 1946), vol. 34, 735, hereafter cited as *Prozeß*. In reality, this sentence is taken out of context.

The introductory part of this directive speaks of different purely hypothetical scenarios of a future war and touches on just as many different possibilities for corresponding preparations. In other words, this does not involve a single option in a monodimensional fashion.

25. For blitzkrieg literature in the historiography of the former German Democratic Republic, see Gerhard Förster, *Totaler Krieg und Blitzkrieg* (Total War and Blitzkrieg) (East Berlin, 1967); Paul Heider and Richard Lakowski, "Theorie vom totalen Krieg. Blitzkriegskonzeption und Wehrmacht in Vorbereitung des zweiten Weltkrieges" (The Theory of Total War. The Blitzkrieg Concept and the Wehrmacht in Preparation of the Second World War), *Militärgeschichte* 28, no. 4 (1989): 291–300; Erich Menke, "Militärtheoretische Überlegungen im deutschen Generalstab vor dem zweiten Weltkrieg über den Einsatz von Panzern" (Military Theory Considerations in the General Staff before the Second World War Regarding the Employment of Panzers), *Revue Internationale d'Histoire Militaire,* no. 71 (1989): 151–63; Helmut Otto, "Entstehung und Wesen der Blitzkriegsstrategie des deutschen Imperialismus vor dem ersten Weltkrieg" (Origin and Essence of Blitzkrieg Strategy of German Imperialism before the First World War), *Zeitschrift für Militärgeschichte* 6, no. 4 (1967): 400–14, and "Illusion und Fiasko der Blitzkriegsstrategie gegen Frankreich, 1914" (Illusion and Failure of the Blitzkrieg Strategy against France, 1914), *Militärgeschichte* 28, no. 4 (1989): 301–8. See also the "*Wörterbuch zur Deutschen Militärgeschichte*" (Dictionary of German Military History), vol. 1, 90f., published by the Institute of Military History of the German Democratic Republic.
26. Uwe Bitzel, *Die Konzeption des Blitzkrieges bei der deutschen Wehrmacht* (The German Wehrmacht's Blitzkrieg Concept) (Frankfurt am Main: Peter Lang, 1991), 35, 53, 80f., 405ff. Of course, this rather neatly formulated thesis should be taken with a grain of salt because the author falls back only on literature and does not take any archival records into consideration. For example, Bernhard R. Kroener and Rolf-Dieter Müller, who analyzed the files of the Federal Military Archives, arrived at considerably different results. Published in *Organisation und Mobilisierung des deutschen Machtbereichs. Kriegsverwaltung, Wirtschaft und personelle Ressourcen 1939 bis 1941,* vol. 5, pt. 1 (1988), of the series *Das Deutsche Reich und der Zweiten Weltkrieg,* their descriptions, unfortunately, were not considered by Bitzel although his monograph was published three years later.
27. Bitzel, *Konzeption,* 63, 405.
28. Timothy W. Mason, "Innere Krise and Angriffskrieg 1938/39" (Domestic Crisis and War of Aggression, 1938–39), *Wirtschaft und Rüstung,* 188.
29. Hew Strachan, *European Armies and the Conduct of War* (London: George Allen and Unwin, 1983), 163. More recent literature increasingly rejects the idea of tying in Guderian's armor tactics, already developed during the 1920s, with Hitler's political objectives. Williamson Murray ["The German Army Doctrine, 1918–1939, and the Post–1945 Theory of 'Blitzkrieg,' " Carole Fink, Isabel V. Hull, and MacGregor Knox, eds., *German Nationalism and the European Response, 1890–1945* (London, 1985), 93] stated: "The German Army did not develop armored tactics to meet strategic needs." See also William Carr, "Rüstung, Wirtschaft und Politik an Vorabend des Zweiten Weltkrieges" (Armament, Economy, and Politics on the Eve of the Second World War), Wolfgang Michalka, ed., *Nationalsozialistische Außenpolitik* (National Socialist Foreign Policy) (Darmstadt, 1978), 446f.; Michael Geyer, "German Strategy in the Age of Machine Warfare, 1914–1945," *Makers of Modern Strategy,* ed. Peter Paret (Princeton, N.J.:

Princeton University Press, 1986), 584f.; Winfried Heinemann, "The Development of German Armoured Forces, 1918–40," J.P. Harris and F. H. Toase, eds., *Armoured Warfare* (London: B. T. Batsford Limited, 1990), 57; Matthew Cooper, *The German Army 1933–1945: Its Political and Military Failure* (London: Macdonald and Janes, 1978), 115f., 151, 166, 219; Daniel J. Hughes, "Blitzkrieg," Trevor Dupuy et al., eds., *International Military and Defense Encyclopedia* (Washington D.C., 1993), vol. 1: A-B, 377ff.

30. Georg Thomas, "Operatives und wirtschaftliches Denken" (Operational and Economic Thinking), *Kriegswirtschaftliche Jahresberichte* (War Industry Annual Reports) (Hamburg, 1937), 16.
31. Vortrag Ob.d.M. [Oberbefehlshaber der Kriegsmarine] am 3.2.37, S. 21 (Lecture, commander in chief, Navy, 3 February 1937, 21), BA-MA, RM 8/1491, sheet 75.
32. Ibid.
33. Foerster, *Beck,* 123.
34. Possony, 82.
35. Johann Wolfgang von Goethe, *Faust* (Munich, 1962), 59.

Chapter 2

1. Strachan, *European Armies,* 163.
2. Paul Schmidt, *Statist auf diplomatischer Bühne 1923–45. Erlebnisse des Chefdolmetschers im Auswärtigen Amt mit den Staatsmännern Europas* (An Extra on the Diplomatic Stage, 1923–45: Experiences of the Chief Interpreter in the Foreign Office Dealing with Europe's Statesmen) (Bonn: Athenäum, 1954), 473f.
3. In the summer of 1939, the general officer corps repeatedly alerted Hitler to the fact that the German Army was not ready for war; see Klaus-Jürgen Müller, *Das Heer und Hitler. Armee und nationalsozialistisches Regime 1939–1940* (The Army and Hitler. The Army and the National Socialist Regime, 1939–1940) (Stuttgart: Deutsche Verlags-Anstalt, 1969), 407ff., as well as Wilhelm Deist, "Die Aufrüstung der Wehrmacht" (The Rearmament of the Wehrmacht), Wilhelm Deist, Manfred Messerschmidt, Hans-Erich Volkmann, and Wolfram Wette, *Ursachen und Voraussetzungen der deutschen Kriegspolitik* (Causes and Conditions of German War Policy), vol. 1, *Das Deutsche Reich und der Zweiten Weltkrieg* (Stuttgart: Deutsche Verlags-Anstalt, 1979), 448.
4. Karl Dönitz, *Zehn Jahre und zwanzig Tage* (Ten Years and Twenty Days) (Munich, 1977), 44.
5. Liddell Hart, *Zweiten Weltkrieges,* 19, 32.
6. Bernhard von Loßberg, *Im Wehrmachtführungsstab: Bericht eines Generalstabsoffiziers* (In the Wehrmacht Operations Staff: Report of a General Staff Officer) (Hamburg: Nölke, 1950), 23.
7. Hans-Adolf Jacobsen and Jürgen Rohwer, "Planungen und Operationen der deutschen Kriegsmarine im Zusammenhang mit dem Fall 'Gelb'" (Planning and Operations of the German Navy in Conjunction with Case 'Yellow'), *Marinerundschau* (Navy Review) 57, no 2 (1960): 66.
8. Quoted from Carl-Axel Gemzell, *Raeder, Hitler und Skandinavien. Der Kampf für einen maritimen Operationsplan* (Raeder, Hitler, and Scandinavia: The Fight for a Maritime Operations Plan) (Lund: C. W. K. Glerrup, 1965), 196.
9. According to Horst Rohde, the personnel strength of the Wehrmacht on 1 September 1939 on the Eastern Front was 1.5 million while the Poles had 1.3 million men

("Hitlers erster 'Blitzkrieg' und seine Auswirkungen auf Nordosteuropa") [Hitler's First "Blitzkrieg" and Its Effects on Northeastern Europe], Klaus A. Meier, Horst Rohde, Bernd Stegemann, and Hans Umbreit, *Die Errichtung der Hegemonie auf dem europäischen Kontinent* (The Establishment of Hegemony on the European Continent), vol. 2, *Das Deutsche Reich und der Zweiten Weltkrieg* (Stuttgart: Deutsche Verlags-Anstalt, 1979), 111. After mobilizing all reserves, the Polish ground forces had a total of 3.6 million men; see Karl Ploetz, *Geschichte des Zweiten Weltkrieges* (History of the Second World) (Würzburg: Ploetz Verlag, 1960), prepared by Percy Ernst Schramm and Hans O. H. Stange, 2d, expanded edition, pt. 2, 339.

10. *The Trial of the Major War Criminals before the International Military Tribunal, Nuremberg, 14 November 1945–1 October 1946),* vol. 10 (Nuremberg, 1947), 519; *Prozeß,* vol. 10, 583.
11. See William L. Shirer, *The Rise and Fall of the Third Reich: A History of Nazi Germany* (New York: Simon and Schuster, 1960), 634; *Aufstieg und Fall des Dritten Reiches* (The Rise and Fall of the Third Reich) (Cologne and Berlin: Kiepenheuer and Witsch, 1961), 580, which quotes Halder's testimony before the Nürnberg Military Tribunals on 8–9 September 1948 in "The Ministries Case" (*Trials of War Criminals before the Nuernberg Military Tribunals under Control Council Law No. 10,* vol. 12 [Washington D.C.: 1950], 1086). Generaloberst a.D. Alfred Jodl, then the Chief of the Wehrmacht Operations Staff, expressed the same judgment later, *Prozeß,* vol. 15, 385f.
12. ADAP, ser. D, vol. 7, 170; see also Franz Halder, *Kriegstagebuch* (War Diary), vol. 1, ed. Hans-Adolf Jacobsen (Stuttgart: Kohlhammer, 1962–64), 13, hereafter cited as Halder *KTB;* Adolf Heusinger, *Befehl im Widerstreit. Schicksalsstunden der deutschen Armee 1923–1945* (Conflicting Orders: The Fateful Hours of the German Army, 1923–1945) (Tübingen: Rainer Wunderlich, 1957), 56.
13. See, for example, Gerhard Engel, *Heeresadjutant bei Hitler 1938–1943* (Hitler's Army Aide, 1938–1943), ed. Hildegard von Kotze (Stuttgart: Deutsche Verlags-Anstalt, 1974), 58.
14. Loßberg, *Im Wehrmachtführungsstab,* 37.
15. Ibid.
16. Erich von Manstein, *Lost Victories* (Chicago: Henry Regnery, 1958), 24; *Verlorene Siege* (Lost Victories) (Koblenz: Bernard and Graefe, 1987), 14.
17. Georg Thomas, *Geschichte der deutschen Wehrand- und Rüstungswirtschaft* (1918–1945) (History of the German Defense and Armament Industry [1918–1945]) (Boppard: Boldt, 1966), 11.
18. Loßberg, *Im Wehrmachtführungsstab,* 37.
19. Heusinger, *Befehl,* 60.
20. Ibid. Mussolini likewise could not refrain from taking a swipe at the German Foreign Minister. In a letter to Hitler, he noted that "Ribbentrop's predictions as to England's and France's non-interference did not come true" (ADAP, ser. D, vol. 8, doc. 504, 476); see also Ulrich von Hassell, *Die Hassell-Tagebücher 1938–1944: Aufzeichnungen vom Andern Deutschland* (The Hassell Diaries, 1938–1944: Diary Entries about the Other Germany), ed. Friedrich Freiherr Hiller von Gaetringen (Berlin, 1988), 160.
21. Schustereit, *Vabanque,* 120, and "Heeresrüstung und 'Blitzkriegskonzept.' Fakten zur Materiallage im Herbst 1939" (Army Armament and the 'Blitzkrieg Concept.' Facts Regarding the Matériel Situation in the Autumn of 1939), *Soldat und Technik* (Soldier and Technology) 33 (1990): 126; Ihno Krumpelt, *Das Material und die Kriegführung*

(Matériel and Warfare) (Frankfurt am Main: Mittler and Sohn, 1968), 38. Hillgruber, who otherwise stressed the programmatic aspect of Hitler's actions, also notes that the Supreme Wehrmacht Command did "not entertain any kind of considerations as to an overall strategy in case of a war against the Western Powers" (*Hitlers Strategie,* 40).

22. Loßberg, *Im Wehrmachtführungsstab,* 25.
23. Hillgruber, *Hitlers Strategie,* 40.
24. Loßberg, *Im Wehrmachtführungsstab,* 27.
25. Franz Halder, *Halder War Diary, 1939–1942,* ed. Charles Burdick and Hans-Adolf Jacobsen (Novato, Calif.: Presidio Press, 1988), 67; Halder *KTB,* vol. 1, 93 (29 September 1939).
26. Cooper, *German Army,* 169ff.; Len Deighton, *Blitzkrieg. Von Hitlers Triumphen bis zum Fall von Dünkirchen* (Blitzkrieg: From Hitler's Triumph to the Fall of Dunkirk) (Munich: Heyne, 1983), 225. English-language version, *Blitzkrieg: From the Rise of Hitler to the Fall of Dunkirk* (New York: Alfred A. Knopf, 1980); Strachan, *European Armies,* 164.
27. At that time the division (today the brigade) was the lowest command echelon for "combined arms combat." On the other hand, the operational level as a rule began at army echelon.
28. Akte OKH/GenStdH, "Kampf um ständige Befestigungen, Grafenwöhr, 20.–25.8. 1939" (File, Army High Command/Army General Staff, "Fighting to Seize Permanent Fortifications, Grafenwöhr, 20–25 August 1939"), BA-MA, RH 2/181, 162 (489)ff., 279 (527)ff.; see also RH 2/182 a and b as well as Akte Chef der Schnellen Truppen im OKH, "Bestimmungen für Marschand- und Gefechtsübung motorisierter Verbände 1939" (File, Chief of Mobile Forces, Army High Command, "Regulations for the March Movement and Combat Exercises of Motorized Formations, 1939"), BA-MA, RH 10/1.
29. Guderian, *Erinnerungen,* 64
30. Wilhelm Ritter von Leeb, *Tagebuchaufzeichnungen und Lagebeurteilungen aus zwei Weltkriegen* (Diary Entries and Situation Estimates from Two World Wars), ed. Georg Meyer (Stuttgart: Deutsche Verlags-Anstalt, 1976), 184f.
31. HGr A, 5.3.1940 (Army Group A, 5 March 1940), 7 (BA-MA, RH 19 I/38, sheet 310); see also Kenneth Macksey, *Deutsche Panzertruppen,* 55.
32. This false estimate was particularly serious on the French side; see William L. Shirer, *Der Zusammenbruch Frankreichs. Aufstieg und Fall der Dritten Republik* (The Collapse of France: The Rise and Fall of the Third Republic) (Munich: Droemersche Verlagsanstalt, 1970), 561f., [English-language version, *The Collapse of the Third Republic: An Inquiry into the Fall of France in 1940.* New York: Simon and Schuster, 1969] as well as Gerd Brausch, "Sedan 1940. Deuxième Bureau und strategische Überraschung" (Sedan 1940. French Army Intelligence and the Strategic Surprise), *MGM,* no. 2 (1967): 87.
33. This is indicated in the captured text of a speech by French Prime Minister Reynaud, dated 7 June 1940 (Akte OKH/GenStdH/Fremde Heere West [Files, Army High Command/Army General Staff/Foreign Armies West], BA-MA, RH 2/1556, 12).
34. In this connection, Hans-Adolf Jacobsen refers to the factors of armament and ammunition but arrives at the same result when looking at other factors, for example, motorization. See *Fall Gelb. Der Kampf um den deutschen Operationsplan zur Westoffensive 1940* (Case Yellow: The Fight for the German Operations Plan for the 1940 Offensive in the West) (Wiesbaden: Franz Steiner Verlag, 1957), 20.

35. *Halder War Diary,* 66; Halder *KTB,* vol. 1, 90 (27 September 1939).
36. *Halder War Diary,* 62; Halder *KTB,* vol. 1, 86 (27 September 1939). See also Handakten Halder (Halder's Notes), BA-MA, RH 2/768, sheet 6 (reverse side).
37. Bitzel, *Konzeption,* 70.
38. Deist, "Aufrüstung," 444; Hans Umbreit, "Kampf um die Vormachtstellung in Westeuropa" (The Struggle to Achieve Hegemony in Western Europe), *Die Errichtung der Hegemonie auf dem europäischen Kontinent,* vol. 2, *Das Deutsche Reich und der Zweiten Weltkrieg,* 265ff.; Hans-Erich Volkmann, "Die NS-Wirtschaft in Vorbereitung des Krieges" (The Nazi Economy in Preparation for War), *Ursachen und Voraussetzungen der deutschen Kriegspolitik,* vol. 1, *Das Deutsche Reich und der Zweiten Weltkrieg,* 359ff.
39. *KTB OKW (Kriegstagebuch des Oberkommmandos der Wehrmacht) (Wehrmachtführungsstab)* (War Diary of the Wehrmacht High Command [Wehrmacht Operations Staff]), comp. and ed. Hans-Adolf Jacobsen, vol. 1, *1.8.1940–31.12.1941* (1 August 1940–31 December 1941), pt. 2 (Munich, 1982), 950.
40. Denkschrift, 9.10.1939, S. 13 (Bl. 17), Handakten Jodl (Memorandum, 9 October 1939, 13 [sheet 17], Jodl's Notes), BA-MA, RW 4/35.
41. *Halder War Diary,* 63 (27 September 1939); Halder *KTB,* vol. 1, 87.
42. HGr B, KTB, 16.3.1940 (Army Group B, *KTB,* 16 March 1940) BA-MA, RH 19 II/19, 159.
43. See also Jacobsen, *Fall Gelb,* 141.
44. Denkschrift, 9.10.1939, S. 11 (Bl. 15), Handakten Jodl (Memorandum, 9 October 1939, 13 [sheet 15], Jodl's Notes), BA-MA, RW 4/35.
45. Halder *KTB,* vol. 1, 99.
46. David Irving, *Die Tragödie der deutschen Luftwaffe. Aus den Akten und Erinnerungen von Feldmarschall Milch* (The Tragedy of the Luftwaffe: From the Files and Memoirs of Field Marshal Milch) (Frankfurt am Main: Ullstein, 1970), 139; English-language version, *The Rise and Fall of the Luftwaffe: The Life of Field Marshal Erhard Milch* (Boston: Little, Brown, 1973).
47. Aktenvermerk Thomas, 19.(21.)11.1939 (File entry by Thomas, 19 [21] November 1939), BA-MA, RW 19/1792, 21; Notiz Hünermann, 22.11.1939 (Notation by Hünermann, 22 November 1939), BA-MA, RW 19/261, Anl.23 zum KTB Rüstungswirtschaftliche Abteilung (app. 23, KTB, Armament Industry Department). The memorandum mentioned here dated back to 27 August 1939.
48. Halder *KTB,* vol. 1, 93.
49. Rolf-Dieter Müller, "Die Mobilisierung der Deutschen Wirtschaft für Hitlers Kriegführung" (The Mobilization of the German Economy for Hitler's Warfare), *Organisation und Mobilisierung des Deutschen Machtbereichs,* 406ff., 425f., 466ff.; and "Die Mobilisierung der Wirtschaft für den Krieg—eine Aufgabe der Armee? Wehrmacht und Wirtschaft 1933–1942" (The Mobilization of the Economy for the War—A Task for the Army? The Wehrmacht and the Economy, 1933–1942), Wolfgang Michalka, ed., *Der Zweiten Weltkrieg. Analysen, Grundzüge, Forschungsbilanz* (The Second World War: Analyses, Characteristics, and Research Balance) (Munich: Piper Verlag, 1989), 357f.
50. Jacobsen, *Fall Gelb,* 19.
51. Burkhart Müller-Hillebrand, *Die Blitzfeldzüge 1939–1941* (The Blitz Campaigns, 1939–1941), vol. 2, *Das Heer 1933–1945. Entwicklung des organisatorischen Auf-*

baus (The Army, 1933–1945: The Development of the Organizational Build-up) (Frankfurt am Main: Verlag E. S. Mittler and Sohn, 1956), 41; Müller, "Mobilisierung der deutschen Wirtschaft," 554.

52. Denkschrift, 9.10.1939, S. 12 (Bl. 16), Handakten Jodl (Memorandum, 9 October 1939, 12 [sheet 16], Jodl's Notes), BA-MA, RW 4/35.
53. *Halder War Diary,* 65 (27 September 1939); Halder *KTB,* vol. 1, 90.
54. Jacobsen, *Fall Gelb,* 19, 180ff., 192ff.
55. Ibid., 309.
56. Müller, "Mobilisierung der deutschen Wirtschaft," 554. These figures refer to production statistics from industry but not all Panzers had been delivered to the units as of 10 May. Looking at the production statistics for Panzer III models, they also include the chassis for the Command Panzer III models.
57. Henri Amouroux, "Kollabos, Helden und Verräter. Die Franzosen unter deutscher Besetzung" (Collaborators, Heroes, and Traitors. The French under German Occupation), *Der Spiegel* 44, no. 20 (1990): 151.
58. Kroener, "Personellen Ressourcen," 731, 834, 959.
59. Burkhart Müller-Hillebrand, *Das Heer bis zum Kriegsbeginn.* Bd. 1: *Das Heer 1933–1945. Entwicklung des organisatorischen Aufbaus* (The Army to the Beginning of the War; vol. 1, The Army, 1933–1945: The Development of the Organizational Build-up) (Darmstadt, 1954), 32ff.
60. Ibid., 731.
61. See Jacobsen, *Fall Gelb,* 20.
62. Kroener, "Personellen Ressourcen," 821.
63. *Prozeß,* vol. 37, 552.
64. Milward, "Einfluß," 189; *Der Zweiten Weltkrieg,* 43; "Hitlers Konzept," 24.
65. Kroener, "Personellen Ressourcen"; "Squaring the Circle. Blitzkrieg Strategy and Manpower," in Wilhelm Deist, ed., *The German Military in the Age of Total War* (Leamington Spa: 1985), and "Der Kampf um den 'Sparstoff Mensch.' Forschungskontroversen über die Mobilisierung der deutschen Kriegswirtschaft 1939–1942" (The Struggle for the Scarce Resource Called Manpower. Research Controversies Concerning the Mobilization of the German War Economy, 1939–1942), Wolfgang Michalka, ed., *Der Zweiten Weltkrieg.* See also Müller, "Mobilisierung der deutschen Wirtschaft" and "Mobilisierung der Wirtschaft für den Krieg"; R. J. Overy, "Blitzkriegswirtschaft? Finanzpolitik, Lebensstandard und Arbeitseinsatz in Deutschland 1939–1942" (Blitzkrieg Economy? Finance, Living Standards, and Labor in Germany, 1939–1942), *Vierteljahrshefte für Zeitgeschichte* (Quarterly Journal for Contemporary History) 36 (1988): 432.
66. Vortrag des Generalmajors Thomas am 29.11.1939 vor der Reichstruppe Industrie (Lecture to the Reich Industrial Group, Generalmajor Georg Thomas, 29 November 1939), reprinted in his *Geschichte,* 499.
67. Ibid., 501.
68. Mason, "Innere Krise," 181f.
69. Kroener, "Kampf um den 'Sparstoff Mensch,'" 407, 409.
70. Quoted in Müller, "Mobilisierung der deutschen Wirtschaft," 688.
71. *Hassell-Tagebücher,* 164.
72. *Prozeß,* vol. 37, 552.
73. Ibid., 553.
74. BA-MA, RW 19/1022, 1.

75. Müller, "Mobilisierung der deutschen Wirtschaft," 466, 479.
76. Rüstungsinspektion des Wehrkreises III (Berlin, 3.5.1940) (Armament Inspectorate of Military Area III [Berlin, 3 May 1940]), BA-MA, RH 8/1012, sheet 104.
77. Stab Heereswaffenamt, Rüstungsstand (Headquarters, Army Weapons Bureau, Armament Status), BA-MA, RH 8/1023, sheet 70/261.
78. Kroener, "Personellen Ressourcen," 999, and "Kampf um den 'Sparstoff Mensch,'" 412.
79. Kroener, "Personellen Ressourcen," 695, 999, 1001, 1014; Schustereit, *Vabanque,* 32.
80. Handakten Jodl, Bl. 39 (S.3) (Jodl Notes, sheet 39, p. 3), BA-MA, RW 4/35.
81. BA-MA, RH 19 II/72, sheet 125.
82. General Sir John Hackett in the foreword to Bryan Perrett, *A History of Blitzkrieg* (New York: Stein and Day, 1983), 15.
83. Kroener, "Personellen Ressourcen," 995.
84. Cooper, *German Army,* 159.
85. Adolphe Goutard, *1940. La guerre des occasions perdues* (1940. The War of Lost Opportunities) (Paris: Hachette, 1956), 76.
86. Müller, "Mobilisierung der deutschen Wirtschaft," 460; Michael Salewski, *Die deutsche Seekriegsleitung, 1935–1945* (The German Supreme Naval War Staff, 1935–1945) (Munich: Bernard and Graefe, 1970), vol.1, 169.
87. Jeffrey A. Gunsburg, *Divided and Conquered: The French High Command and the Defeat of the West, 1940* (Westport, Conn.: Greenwood Press, 1979), 103.
88. Halder *KTB,* vol. 1, 180.
89. Müller, "Mobilisierung der deutschen Wirtschaft," 426ff., 436 ff.
90. Halder *KTB,* vol. 1, 180.
91. Müller, "Mobilisierung der deutschen Wirtschaft,"434ff.; Umbreit, "Kampf," 267.
92. Halder *KTB,* vol. 1, 181.
93. Cooper, *German Army,* 163; see also Heinrich Walle, "Krampnitz. Von der Kavallerieschule zur Panzertruppenschule II 1937–1945" (Krampnitz: From Cavalry School to Panzer Force School II, 1937–1945); Bernard R. Kroener, ed., *Potsdam. Staat, Armee, Residenz in der preußisch-deutschen Militärgeschichte* (Potsdam: State, Army, Residence in Prussian-German Military History) (Frankfurt am Main and Berlin: Propyläen Verlag, 1993), 476.
94. Kroener, "Personellen Ressourcen," 826.
95. This comparison was used by Dr. Daniel J. Hughes, then of the Combined Arms Center at Fort Leavenworth, Kansas, during a lecture titled "Preparations of the German Army," Annual Meeting of the American Military Institute, Washington, D.C., 30 March 1990.
96. Theodore Ropp, introduction to Addington, *The Blitzkrieg Era,* xv.
97. Regarding the following statements, please see Kroener, "Personellen Ressourcen," 710ff., 726ff., 819ff., as well as Müller-Hillebrand, *Heer,* vol. 1, 71f., vol. 2, 39f.
98. See Ia der HGr C, Oberst i.G. Müller, an OKH vom 24.9.1939 (Operations Officer, Army Group C, Oberst i.G. Müller, to Army High Command, 24 September 1939), BA-MA, RH 19 III/92.
99. Typical of this is Ernst Jünger's diary from the campaign in the West, *Gärten und Straßen. Aus den Tagebüchern von 1939 und 1940* (Gardens and Streets: From the Diaries of 1939 and 1940) (Berlin: Verlag E. S. Mittler, 1942), that rather looks like a very interesting and illustrative travel log. The regiment to which the author belonged had the first enemy contact worth mentioning just a few days before the end of the

campaign in the West. One could hardly imagine a contrast greater than Jünger's World War I autobiographical account *In Stahlgewittern. Aus dem Tagebuch eines Stoßtruppführers* (The Storm of Steel: From the Diary of an Assault Team Leader) (Berlin: E. S. Mittler and Sohn, 1929).

100. Senff, *Die Entwicklung der Panzerwaffe,* 30.
101. Heinz Guderian, *Panzer Leader,* 32, see also 30; *Erinnerungen,* 26, see also 24.
102. Guderian, *Panzer Leader,* 21; *Erinnerungen,* 15f.
103. Guderian, *Panzer Leader,* 21; *Erinnerungen,* 16.
104. The author was able to talk about this topic several times with General a.D. Johann Adolf Graf von Kielmansegg, the then commander in chief, Allied Forces Central Europe. The latter not only participated actively in the campaign in the West but, later on, was assigned to the Operations Section where he obtained important background information in conversation with officers who were involved in planning the campaign. They also included the then chief of the Operations Section, Heusinger, the subsequent Generalinspekteur (commander) of the Bundeswehr (Federal Armed Forces).
105. Akte HGr C (Files, Army Group C), BA-MA, RH 19 III/141, sheet 44 (see *Einleitung* [Introduction]).
106. Quoted from Ferdinand Otto Miksche, *Atom-Waffen und Streitkräfte* (Atomic Weapons and Armed Forces) (Bonn: Westunion/Offene Worte, 1955), 40.
107. Carl von Clausewitz, *Vom Kriege* (On War), 19th ed. (Bonn: 1980), 373; Carl von Clausewitz, *On War,* ed. and trans. Michael Howard and Peter Paret (New York: Everyman's Library, 1993), 228.
108. Müller, "Mobilisierung der deutschen Wirtschaft," 486ff., 523 ff.
109. The author is indebted to his colleague Prof. Dr. Bernhard R. Kroener for these statistics. They spring from an interpolation of the graphs given in his study "Personellen Ressourcen," 834 and 959.
110. See, for example, Jacobsen, *Fall Gelb,* 258f.; Müller-Hillebrand, *Heer,* vol. 2, 40; Werner Haupt, *Sieg ohne Lorbeer. Der Westfeldzug 1940* (Victory without Laurels: The 1940 Campaign in the West) (Holstein: E. Geerdes, 1965), 356; Trevor N. Dupuy, *Numbers, Prediction, and War: Using History to Evaluate Combat Factors and Predict the Outcome of Battles* (London: 1979), 15; Ulrich Liß, *Westfront 1939/40. Erinnerungen des* Feindbearbiters *im O.K.H.* (Western Front, 1939–40: The Memoirs of the Intelligence Officer in the O.K.H.) (Neckargemünd: Kurt Vowinckel, 1959), 145.
111. Liß, *Westfront,* 25; Amouroux, "Kollabos," 151.
112. Liß, *Westfront,* 145; Ploetz, *Geschichte des Zweiten Weltkrieges,* pt. 2, 386f.
113. Ploetz, *Geschichte des Zweiten Weltkrieges,* pt. 2, 495.
114. Umbreit, "Kampf," 273.
115. Liß, *Westfront,* 145. See also Ploetz, *Geschichte des Zweiten Weltkrieges,* pt. 2, 363, 374; "Ein Überblick über die Operationen des belgischen Heeres im Mai 1940. Dargestellt nach belgischen Quellen" (An Overview of the Operations of the Belgian Army in May 1940. Described According to Belgian Sources), *MWR* 6, no. 3 (1941): 274.
116. Müller-Hillebrand, *Heer,* vol. 2, 44f. (For the tables, see 45); Kroener, "Personellen Ressourcen," 826; Jacobsen, *Fall Gelb,* 258f.
117. See graph on 33. Müller-Hillebrand, *Heer,* vol. 2, 44f; Jacobsen, *Fall Gelb,* 258f.
118. Umbreit, "Kampf," 282; see also Shirer, *Zusammenbruch,* 643; Hellmuth Günther Dahms, *Geschichte des Zweiten Weltkriegs* (History of the Second World War) (Munich and Berlin: F. A. Herbig, 1983), 164; Liß, *Westfront,* 141, 145; Claude Paillat, *La guerre éclair. 10 mai–24 juin 1940* (The Lightning War: 10 May–24 June 1940), vol.

3, *Le désastre de 1940* (The Disaster of 1940) (Paris: Laffont, 1985), 631. On the other hand, Franz Uhle-Wettler in *Höhe- und Wendepunkte Deutscher Militärgeschichte* (High Points and Turning Points of German Military History) [Mainz: Hase and Köhler Verlag, 1984], 256) considers this figure and several other Allied strength figures to be much too low.

119. One British division was stationed in the Maginot Line.
120. For a discussion as to the precise strength of British divisions, see Uhle-Wettler, *Höhe- und Wendepunkte,* 256.
121. These statistics are mentioned throughout the literature on the subject. On the other hand, Hans-Adolf Jacobsen, *Dünkirchen* (Dunkirk) (Neckargemünd: Kurt Vowinckel, 1958), 15, and Cooper, *German Army,* 214, use a figure of 23 Belgian divisions.
122. Umbreit, "Kampf," 282; Haupt, *Sieg ohne Lorbeer,* 357.
123. Deighton, *Blitzkrieg,* 132 (175, 218, German edition).
124. R. H. S. Stolfi, "Equipment for Victory in France in 1940," *History* 55 (1970): 9.
125. Dirk Rottgardt, "Die deutsche Panzertruppe am 10.5.1940" (German Panzer Forces on 10 May 1940), pt. 1, *Zeitschrift für Heerskunde* (Army Affairs Journal) 49, no. 319 (1985): 65. The table does not list 135 armored command vehicles. These tracked vehicles, that were "armed" with radios, were used only as command Panzers and must definitely not be included among the battle tanks. Some actually did have a "cannon," but that was only a wooden mockup. Some authors confuse the number of 2,439 battle tanks available for the Western Offensive in May 1940, with the output figures of the German armament industry. By May 1940, it had turned out 3,360 Panzer Models I to IV. For example, among the total of 1,445 Panzer I models produced, only 523 were on the West Front. This type of Panzer proved mostly useless for combat operations and had been partly taken out of the inventory. A few were converted into special vehicles by industry, using the old chassis. Both models were used as practice vehicles in training. The ratio was similar on the French side. Only 3,254 French tanks were stationed on the Northeast Front on 10 May, whereas French industry had produced 4,688 tanks by then (Stolfi, "Equipment," 10–12).
126. The statistics given by Stolfi in "Equipment" appear particularly reliable. Older reports frequently consider the light German Panzer I and Panzer II models but not the corresponding French models. The French AMR and AMC were equipped partly with machine guns but mostly with 2.5-cm or 3.7-cm guns and were thus superior to the German light tanks. One series of the AMC was even equipped with a 4.7-cm gun. Besides, in May 1940, the French Army also had 1,500 Renault F.T. models that were employed mostly to protect airfields. But there were also 500 to 600 Renault F.T. tanks in a modernized version. Of that number, 315 were stationed on the Northeast Front on 10 May. As regards their armament, which featured a 3.7-cm gun, they were superior to the German Panzer I and Panzer II models.
127. Liß, *Westfront,* 269.
128. The statistics concerning British combat vehicles differ in the literature as regards the count of "light" models as well as the inclusion of the formations that were on standby in England.
129. Steven J. Zaloga, *Blitzkrieg. Armor, Camouflage and Markings, 1939–1940* (Carrolton, Texas: Squadron/Signal Publications, 1980), 9f., 78.
130. See, for example, Christopher F. Foss, *Die Panzer des Zweiten Weltkrieges* (The Panzers of the Second World War) (Friedberg: Podzun-Pallas, 1988), 57; Janusz Piekalkiewicz, *Krieg der Panzer 1939–1945* (The War of the Panzers, 1939–1945) (Gütersloh: Bertelsmann, n.d.), 281.

131. BA-MA, RH 27–1/170, 29.
132. Wolfgang Paul, *Brennpunkte. Die Geschichte der 6. Panzerdivision (1. leichte)* (Focal Points: The History of the 6th Panzer Division (1st Light Division) (Osnabrück, 1984), 73.
133. Gérard Giuliano, *Les combats du Mont-Dieu. Mai 1940* (The Fighting at Mont Dieu. May 1940) (Charleville-Mézières: Éditions Terres Ardennaises, 1990), 51n.15.
134. Geschichte 4.PzDiv (History of the 4th Panzer Division), RH 27–4/199, 55 (sheet 57), BA-MA.
135. Quoted from Shirer, *Collapse,* 616; *Zusammenbruch,* 647.
136. Concerning the following statistics, note above all Die Akten des Generalstabs der Luftwaffe (Generalquartiermeister) (Files, Luftwaffe General Staff [Supply and Administration]): BA-MA, RL 2 III/736, as well as RL 2 III/707. After the war, the Air War History Studies Group, which also included some former generals of the Luftwaffe, prepared various studies in which the strength figures, listed in that file, were estimated as being too high. The difference regarding operational readiness is lower by a total of about 300 aircraft, depending on the counting method. The above-mentioned files in the BA-MA show statistics that also include the "matériel reserves." A calculation according to "unit strength figures" would result in statistics that would be somewhat too low. One cannot determine an absolutely precise total strength figure because most of the Luftwaffe files were burned. See also Wilhelm Speidel, Der Einsatz der operativen Luftwaffe im Westfeldzug 1939/40 (The Employment of the Operational Luftwaffe in the 1939–40 Campaign in the West), pt. 3, 55–59, Study Lw 3/2, BA-MA; Gen. d/Fl. a.D. Joseph Kammhuber, Das Problem der Erringung der Luftherrschaft durch Gegenmaßnahmen der Luftwaffe (The Problem of Winning Air Superiority by Luftwaffe Countermeasures), BA-MA, Study Lw 12, vol. 2 (see also pt. C, Westfeldzug [Campaign in the West], 3–8), as well as the tables in Materialsammlung: Stärken (Ist-Stärken und Einsatzbereitschaft) der Fliegenden Verbände der Luftwaffe 1938–1945 [Collection of Materials: Strength Figures (Actual Strength Figures and Operational Readiness) of Luftwaffe Flying Units, 1938–1945], BA-MA, Lw 106/7. In this file, it is above all the figures based on the air situation map of the Oberbefehlshaber der Luftwaffe (commander in chief, Luftwaffe) that are of interest. The author is indebted for important information to Mr. Ulf Balke who was able to collect additional documents from private owners; see also his study, *Der Luftkrieg in Europa. Die operativen Einsätze des Kampfgeschwaders 2 im Zweiten Weltkrieg* (The Air War in Europe. The Operational Missions of the 2d Bomber Wing during World War II) (Koblenz: Bernard and Graefe, 1989), vol. 1, 400ff., 407.
137. At the start of the campaign in the west, the Wehrmacht, in addition to combat aircraft, also had 656 reconnaissance aircraft (512 operational), 474 transport aircraft (436 operational), and smaller numbers of liaison squadrons, weather reconnaissance squadrons, etc. For this we must also add 235 Navy aircraft (156 operational).
138. The units, employed at that time against Norway, included the following aircraft, in addition to the reconnaissance aircraft: 143 bombers (80 operational), 39 dive-bombers (25 operational), 51 fighters (34 operational), 53 destroyers (28 operational); see also Balke, *Luftkrieg,* vol. 1, 406f.
139. Speidel, Der Einsatz, pt. 3, 58f., BA-MA, Study Lw 3/2.
140. See also the overall study prepared by a team of authors under the direction of Generals Christienne and Lissarrague, *Histoire de l'aviation militaire française* (History of French Military Aviation) (Paris: Limoges, 1980), 373ff. One of the authors, Patrice Buffotot, had prepared an individual study earlier with Jacques Ogier, titled "L'armée

de l'air française dans la campagne de France (10 mai–25 juin 1940)" (The French Air Force in the Campaign in France [10 May–25 June 1940]), *RHA* no. 3 (1975): 88–117. The following table is based primarily on that material.

141. In a new investigation, Faris Kirkland calculated an actual strength of 2,517 fighters and 1,059 bombers that slightly deviates from that figure; see his "French Air Strength in May 1940," *Air Power History* 40, no. 1 (1993): 23.
142. Shirer, *Zusammenbruch,* 647, 746.
143. Deighton, *Blitzkrieg,* 270 (328, German edition); see also Shirer, *Zusammenbruch,* 649.
144. Shirer, *Zusammenbruch,* 649f.
145. Pierre Cot, "En 40 où etaient nos avions?" (Where Were Our Aircraft in 1940?), *Icare* no. 57 (spring–summer 1971): 42.
146. Ibid., 38; that number also includes the models purchased in the United States.
147. Ibid.
148. Shirer, *Zusammenbruch,* 648; Deighton, *Blitzkrieg,* 328 (German edition); Janusz Piekalkiewicz, *Luftkrieg 1939–1945* (The Air War 1939–1945) (Munich: Südwest-Verlag, 1978), 83.
149. Shirer, *Zusammenbruch,* 650.
150. Cot, "En 40," 42.
151. Ibid., 38.
152. Most reliable appear to be the latest calculations by Kirkland, "French Air Strength," 24. See also Gunsburg, *Divided,* 108; Brain Bond, *France and Belgium, 1939–1940* (London, 1975), 171; Shirer, *Zusammenbruch,* 647; Isabelle Sormail, "Le Haut commandement aérien française et la participation de la RAF à la bataille de France: une note du Géneral Vuillemin du 8 juillet 1940" (The French Air Force High Command and the Participation of the RAF in the Battle of France: A Note by General Vuillemin on 8 July 1940), *RHA* no. 168 (1987): 5; Umbreit, "Kampf," 282; Piekalkiewicz, *Luftkrieg,* 67; Turnbull, *Dunkirk,* 66; Patrick Facon, "Chasseurs et bombardiers dans la bataille" (Fighters and Bombers in Battle), in *Historia Spécial* (Historia Special), no. 5 (1990): 36; A. D. Harvey, "The French Armée de l'air in May–June 1940: A Failure of Conception," *Journal of Contemporary History* 25, no. 4 (1990): 450; L. F. Ellis, *The War in France and Flanders* (London: Her Majesty's Stationery Office, 1953), 309.
153. It was Uhle-Wettler in *Höhe- und Wendepunkte* (298f.) who pointed out this discrepancy.
154. Gunsburg, *Divided,* 108; Raymond Danel, "En mai–juin 1940: Ils étaient les plus forts" (In May–June 1940: They Were Stronger), *Icare* no. 54 (summer 1970): 51; Ellis, *The War in France,* 309; Cot gives a figure of 1,850 British aircraft (see "En 40," 41).
155. R. J. Overy, *The Air War, 1939–1945* (London: Europa Publications, 1980), 23.
156. Danel, "En mai–juin 1940," 51, and "La conquête de la Hollande: Opération secondaire?" (The Conquest of Holland: A Secondary Operation?), *Icare* no. 79 (winter 1976–77): 23; Cot, "En 40," 41. This does not include the 43 Dutch Navy aircraft, few of which saw any action.
157. A similar distortion of yardsticks also happened in the case of the antiaircraft guns belonging to the Luftwaffe. Allegedly, a total of 10,000 antiaircraft guns protected the German attack divisions in France. But the statistics given include the antiaircraft guns set up for home defense in the territory of the Reich itself. That mistake obviously is the result of a mistranslation but has since then been passed on by numerous histori-

ans. Harvey pointed that out. According to his calculations ("French Armée de l'Air," 449), the German attacking armies had only 1,696 antiaircraft guns.

158. See also, for example, Sormail, "Haut commandement," 5; Liß, *Westfront,* 145; Umbreit, "Kampf," 282.
159. In his 1993 study, Kirkland employed different counting criteria (e.g., also considering the reconnaissance aircraft) but arrived at a similar result. Accordingly, the Germans had 76.8 percent operational at the front whereas the French only had 25.3 percent of the aircraft ready for operations at the front; see his "French Air Strength," 28.
160. Overy, *Air War,* 23, 28; Kirkland, "The French Air Force in 1940. Was It Defeated by the Luftwaffe or by Politics?" *Air University Review* 36, no. 6 (1985): 103; Cot, "En 40," 41; Gunsburg, *Divided,* 107f.
161. Shirer, *Zusammenbruch,* 650.
162. Overy, *Air War,* 28.
163. Kirkland, "French Air Strength," 26.
164. Kroener, "Personellen Ressourcen," 717.
165. Cot, "En 40," 42, 53; Buffotot and Ogier, "L'armée de l'air," 111.
166. Harvey, "French Armée de l'Air," 455; Kirkland, "French Air Force," 117n.4.
167. Akten des Genst der Luftwaffe (Generalquartiermeister) (Files of the Luftwaffe General Staff [Supply and Administration]), BA-MA, RL 2 III/1173 as well as 1174.
168. Winston S. Churchill, *Their Finest Hour,* vol. 2, *The Second World War* (Boston: Houghton Mifflin, 1949), 49, and *Zweiter Weltkrieg* (The Second World War), vol. 2, bk. 1 (Stuttgart, 1948–49), 68.
169. Golo Mann, *Deutsche Geschichte,* 915f.; *History of Germany,* 466–67.
170. Engel, *Heeresadjutant,* 6 (29 August 1939).
171. Ibid., 68 (18 November 1939).
172. Ibid., 70 (6 December 1939).
173. ADAP, ser. D, vol. 8, 346, 349. Concerning the *Befehlsempfang* (Command Conference) on 23 November, see also Jacobsen, *Fall Gelb,* 59ff.
174. ADAP, ser. D, vol. 8, 350.
175. Nicolaus von Below, *Als Hitlers Adjutant 1937–1945* (Hitler's Military Aide, 1937–1945) (Mainz, 1980), 210.
176. Jacobsen, *Fall Gelb,* 8.
177. Hans Bernd Gisevius, *Bis zum bitteren Ende. Vom Reichstagsbrand bis zum Juli 1944* (To the Bitter End: From the Reichstag Fire to July 1944) (Hamburg, n.d.), 431.
178. Leeb, *Tagebuchaufzeichnungen,* 188.
179. Ibid., 104.
180. Peter Hoffmann, *Widerstand-Staatsstreich-Attentat. Der Kampf der Opposition gegen Hitler* (Resistance-Coup d'etat-Attempt on His Life. The Opposition's Fight against Hitler) (Munich: R. Piper, 1969), 215.
181. Helmuth Groscurth, *Tagebücher eines Abwehroffiziers 1938–1940* (Diaries of an Intelligence Officer, 1938–1940), Helmut Krausnick and Harold C. Deutsch, eds., with Hildegard von Kotze (Stuttgart: Deutsche Verlags-Anstalt, 1970), 218.
182. *Generalfeldmarschall Keitel—Verbrecher oder Offizier? Erinnerungen, Briefe, Dokumente des Chefs OKW* (Field Marshal General Keitel—Criminal or Officer? The Memoirs, Letters, and Documents of the Chief of the OKW), ed. Walter Görlitz (Göttingen, Berlin, and Frankfurt am Main: Musterschmidt, 1961), 223f. English-

language version, *The Memoirs of Field Marshal Keitel,* ed. Walter Görlitz, trans. David Irving (New York: Stein and Day, 1966).

183. *KTB OKW,* vol. 1, pt. 2, 950.
184. *Memoirs of Field Marshal Keitel,* 102; *Keitel,* 225.
185. Halder *KTB,* vol. 1, 98, 120; see also Fedor von Bock, Kriegstagebuch, Bd. 1, Teil 1: Tagebuch-Notizen zum Polenfeldzug, Mai-Juni 1939–3.Oktober 1939 (War Diary, vol. 1, pt. 1: Diary Entries during the Polish Campaign, May–June 1939–3 October 1939), Study P–210, 43–45, BA-MA, hereafter cited as Bock, KTB, with pertinent citation information; Engel, *Heeresadjutant,* 66ff.; *Keitel,* 222ff.; see also Jacobsen, *Fall Gelb,* 46f.; Umbreit, "Kampf," 243f.
186. Heinrich Bücheler, *Carl-Heinrich von Stülpnagel. Soldat, Philosoph, Verschwörer* (Carl-Heinrich von Stülpnagel. Soldier, Philosopher, Conspirator) (Berlin and Frankfurt a.M.: 1989), 164; Harold C. Deutsch, *Verschwörung gegen den Krieg. Der Widerstand in den Jahren 1939–1940* (The Conspiracy against the War. The Resistance in the Years 1939–1940) (Munich: Beck, 1969), 33.
187. Bock, KTB, Bd. 1, Teil 2: Tagebuchnotizen Westen. Vorbereitungzeit, 4.10.1939–9.5.1940 (War Diary, vol. 1, pt. 2: Diary Entries West. Preparatory Period, 4 October 1939–9 May 1940), Study P–210 2f., BA-MA; Halder, *KTB,* vol. 1, 115ff.; Jacobsen, *Fall Gelb,* 25f., 44ff., 48ff.; Müller, *Heer und Hitler,* 507ff.; Gerd R. Ueberschär, "Generaloberst Halder im militärischen Widerstand 1938–1940" (General Halder in the Military Resistance, 1938–1940), *Wehrforschung* (Defense Research), 25ff.; Umbreit, "Kampf," 243f. This meeting is mentioned only briefly in Leeb's diary entries (199), without any exact hints as to his intentions at that time. According to a statement by General von Sodenstern, Leeb was considering retiring when he failed in his attempt to persuade the other two commanders to join ranks and support his ideas (see Leeb, *Tagebuchaufzeichnungen,* 199n.154).
188. Klaus-Jürgen Müller, "Witzleben-Stülpnagel-Speidel—Offiziere im Widerstand" (Witzleben-Stülpnagel-Speidel: Officers in the Resistance), *Nr. 7 Beiträge zum Widerstand* 1933–1945 (No. 7 Contributions to the Resistance, 1933–1945) (Berlin, 1988), 14.
189. See Jacobsen, *Fall Gelb,* 48.
190. Müller, *Heer und Hitler,* 512.
191. Groscurth, *Tagebücher,* 223; cf., Christian Hartmann, *Halder. Generalstabschef Hitlers* (Halder. Hitler's Chief of the General Staff) (Paderborn: Ferdinand Schöningh, 1991), 167.
192. Quoted from Kurt Sendtner, "Die deutsche Militäropposition im ersten Kriegsjahr" (The German Military Opposition in the First Year of the War), *Die Vollmacht des Gewissens.* Bd. 1: *Probleme des militärischen Widerstandes gegen Hitler* (The Power of Conscience. vol. 1: The Problems of the Military Resistance against Hitler) (Frankfurt am Main and Berlin: Alfred Metzner Verlag, 1960), 401.
193. Heidemarie Schall-Riaucour, *Aufstand und Gehorsam. Offizierstum und Generalstab im Umbruch. Leben und Wirken von Generaloberst Franz Halder, Generalstabschef 1938–1942* (Insurrection and Obedience. Commissioned Officers and the General Staff in Revolution. The Life and Work of Generaloberst Franz Halder, Chief of the General Staff, 1938–1942) (Wiesbaden: Limes Verlag, 1972), 329ff.; Gerd R. Ueberschär, *Generaloberst Franz Halder. Generalstabschef, Gegner und Gefangener Hitlers* (Generaloberst Franz Halder. Chief of the General Staff, Opponent and Prisoner of Hitler) (Göttingen: Musterschmidt, 1991), 81ff.

Chapter 3

1. Liddell Hart, *Jetzt dürfen sie reden,* 173; The German Generals Talk, 107.
2. Winston S. Churchill, *His Complete Speeches, 1897–1963,* ed. Robert Rhodes James, vol. 6: *1935–1942* (New York and London: Bowker, 1974), 6226.
3. Jacobsen, *Fall Gelb,* 9.
4. Reprinted in: *Dokumente zur Vorgeschichte des Westfeldzuges* (Documents on the Background of the Campaign in the West), ed. Hans-Adolf Jacobsen (Göttingen, Berlin, Frankfurt am Main: Musterschmidt, 1956), 4–21.
5. H. R. Trevor-Roper, *Blitzkrieg to Defeat: Hitler's War Directives 1939–1945* (New York: Holt, Rinehart and Winston, 1964), 13; *Hitlers Weisungen für die Kriegführung 1939–1945. Dokumente des Oberkommandos der Wehrmacht* (Hitler's Directives for the Conduct of the War, 1939–1954. Documents of the Wehrmacht High Command), ed. Walther Hubatsch, 2d revised edition (Koblenz: Bernard and Graefe, 1983), 32f.
6. Oberbefehlshaber des Heeres, Aufmarschanweisung "Gelb" (19.10.1939), Akte Chef Heeresnachrichtenwesen [Commander in Chief of the Army, "Deployment Directive 'Yellow' " (19 October 1939), Files, Chief of Army Signal Service], BA-MA, RH 6/1.
7. Jacobsen, *Fall Gelb,* 32.
8. *Memoirs of Field Marshal Keitel,* 102; *Keitel,* 226. Hitler described the operations draft of the Army High Command also as the "same old Schlieffen hat"; see Engel, *Heeresadjutan*t, 69; David Irving, *Hitlers Krieg. Die Siege 1939–1942* (Hitler's War. The Victories, 1939–1942) (Munich and Berlin: F. A. Herbig, 1983), 129. English-language version, *Hitler's War* (New York: The Viking Press, 1977).
9. Oberkommando des Heeres/GenStdH/Op.Abt., Aufmarschanweisung "Gelb," Neufassung (29.10.1939), Akte Chef Heeresnachrichtenwesen [Army High Command/Army General Staff/Operations Section, "Deployment Directive 'Yellow,' " New Version (29 October 1939), Files, Chief of Army Signal Service], BA-MA, RH 6/2.
10. Fernschreiben OKH an Heeresgruppen A u. B vom 11.11.1939, Akte Chef Heeresnachrichtenwesen (Teletype message from Army High Command to Army Groups A and B, 11 November 1939, Files of the Chief of Army Signal Service), BA-MA, RH 6/3; see also OKW/WFSt, KTB, Notizen Hptm. Deyle (Wehrmacht High Command/Wehrmacht Operations Staff, War Diary, entries by Captain Deyle), BA-MA, RW 4/41, 4.
11. Umbreit, "Kampf," 247.
12. HGr B, KTB, BA-MA, RH 19 II/19, 11ff.; General der Infanterie a.D. Kurt von Tippelskirch, Die Vorgeschichte, Bd. 1, Teil 2 Der Westfeldzug 1940 (The Early History, vol. 1, pt. 2, The Campaign in the West 1940), Studies by the Historical Division, Headquarters, U. S. Army, Europe, Study P–208, 76ff., BA-MA; see also Jacobsen, *Fall Gelb,* 90, 93ff.
13. Oberbefehlshaber des Heeres vom 30.1.1940, "Neufassung der Aufmarschanweisung 'Gelb' " (Commander in Chief of the Army, 30 January 1940, "New Version of Deployment Directive 'Yellow' "), BA-MA, RH 19 II/21.
14. Halder *KTB,* vol. 1, 161, 166; Tippelskirch, Westfeldzug, vol. 1, pt. 2, Study P–208, 81ff., BA-MA; Jacobsen, *Fall Gelb,* 99ff.
15. Engel, *Heeresadjutant,* 75.
16. That comparison was one of Hitler's favorite expressions; see also, for example, Paul Berben and Bernard Iselin, *Die Deutschen kommen. Mai 1940. Der Überfall auf Westeuropa* (The Germans Are Coming. May 1940. The Surprise Attack on Western Europe) (Hamburg: Christian Wegner, 1969), 326; Irving, *Hitlers Krieg,* 93.

17. Akte der HGr A (Files of Army Group A), BA-MA, RH 19 I/26, 14f., sheet 216f. The memorandum was signed by von Rundstedt, the commander in chief of Army Group A, but was actually written by his Chief of Staff, von Manstein. This basic idea runs through all other memorandums that von Manstein drafted. See above all his lecture note on 19 January 1940. In it, he criticized not only the Army High Command for lacking the will to bring about "the complete decision on the ground," but also he even spoke of the "well-known negative attitude of the O.K.H. with regard to the offensive in the west to begin with" (ibid., sheet 100).
18. Manstein, *Lost Victories,* 109; *Verlorene Siege,* 107.
19. Guderian, *Panzer Leader,* 89; *Erinnerungen,* 79.
20. Six of these seven memorandums are reprinted in Manstein, *Verlorene Siege,* 625ff. They can also be found in Akte der HGr A, BA-MA, RH 19 I/26.
21. Frederich Wilhelm von Mellenthin, *Schach dem Schicksal* (Checkmating Destiny) (Osnabrück, 1989), 79f.
22. Engel, *Heeresadjutant,* 73f.
23. Akte HGr A: Entwurf einer Notiz Mansteins für das KTB, 17.2.1940 (Files, Army Group A: Draft of one of Manstein's notes for the War Diary, 17 February 1940), BA-MA, RH 19 I/41, app. 51 (sheet 174f.); Notiz über Führer-Vortrag (Note on Führer briefing), RH 19 I/26, sheet 121f.; see also Manstein, *Verlorene Siege,* 118ff.
24. Following this conversation, Hitler reportedly commented as follows on Manstein: "Certainly a particularly bright fellow with great operational talent, but I do not trust him" (Heusinger, *Befehl,* 81, 93). Engel, Hitler's Army Aide, reported roughly the same (see his *Heeresadjutant,* 74f.). The dictator considered von Manstein to be a typical representative of that old-line Prussian officer caste that he rejected as being reactionary, although he was dependent on it for the purpose of attaining his wartime objectives. David Irving had the following judgment on this point: "Hitler's respect for General von Manstein's abilities bordered on fear" (Irving, *Hitler's War,* 81; *Hitlers Krieg,* 129). Conversely, Prussian aristocrat Manstein, who had once been a page at the Emperor's court, could not conceal his aversion to Hitler, the vulgar man of violence. Although he had a critical attitude toward National Socialism, he did place his operational skills in the service of the unloved dictator. His tremendous ambition would appear to have been the most important motive for this.
25. Engel, *Heeresadjutant,* 75; "Jodl Diary," in *Prozeß,* vol. 28, 405.
26. "Jodl Diary" in *Prozeß,* vol. 28, 402.
27. For the map exercises on 27 December, in January, and on 7 and 14 February, see also Tippelskirch, Westfeldzug, vol. 1, pt. 2, Study P–208, 64ff., BA-MA; Ulrich Liß, "Die deutsche Westoffensive 1940 vom Blickpunkt des Ic" (The German Offensive in the West from the Viewpoint of the Intelligence Officer), *WWR* 8, no. 4 (1958): 212; Akten der HGr A, BA-MA, RH 19 I/25; RH 19 I/35; Akten der 12. Armee, BA-MA, RH 20–12/11; RH 20–12/20; Manstein, *Verlorene Siege,* 117; Guderian, *Erinnerungen,* 80f.; Halder, *KTB,* vol. 1, 185f.
28. Oberbefehlshaber des Heeres/GenStdH/Op.Abt., Akten HGr A (Commander in Chief of the Army/Army General Staff/Operations Section, Files, Army Group A), BA-MA, RH 19 I/38, sheets 286ff.
29. Joachim Engelmann, *Manstein. Stratege und Truppenführer. Ein Lebensbericht in Bildern* (Manstein: Strategist and Troop Leader. A Report on His Life in Pictures) (Friedberg: Podzun-Pallas Verlag, 1981) 43ff., 55ff.

30. A controversy had arisen already during the Polish campaign because Manstein, who was inclined toward taking action on his own, simply wanted to ignore Halder's instructions. See Schall-Riaucour, *Aufstand und Gehorsam,* 150.
31. Perrett, *Blitzkrieg,* 83; and his *Knights of the Black Cross: Hitler's Panzerwaffe and its Leaders* (New York: St. Martins Press, 1986), 48; Addington, *The Blitzkrieg Era,* 54; Kenneth Macksey, *Guderian: Der Panzergeneral* (Guderian: The Panzer General) (Düsseldorf and Vienna: Econ Verlag, 1976), 105.
32. Alistair Horne, *To Lose a Battle: France 1940* (Boston: Little, Brown, 1969), 144, and the German edition, *Über die Maas, über Schelde und Rhein. Frankreichs Niederlage 1940* (Across the Meuse, the Scheldt, and the Rhine. France's Defeat in 1940) (Vienna, Munich, and Zurich: Molden Verlag, 1969), 132.
33. Franz Halder, *Hitler als Feldherr* (Hitler as Warlord) (Munich: Münchener Dom-Verlag, 1949), 28f. English-language version, *Hitler as War Lord* (London: Putnam, 1949).
34. See Jacobsen, *Fall Gelb,* 273f. n. 14.
35. Actually, Halder made history twice with respect to the campaign in the west: The first time as German army chief of staff and the second time as a key leader of a group of high-ranking German officers who, by direction of the Historical Division of the U.S. Army [European Command], were writing so-called studies about military experiences during World War II. It was indeed significant that the authors to some extent were able to refer to the initially not yet generally accessible German military files, most of which were in American custody. Halder distinguished himself in that project by strictly observing scientific criteria and by virtue of his incorruptible objectivity. But he was unable to conceal his old rivalry with Manstein only when it came to describing the Sickle Cut. That tendency is also revealed in some individual supporting studies that back up Study P–208 (Campaign in the West), whose authors were not always able to get out from under his overpowering intellectual influence.
36. See especially Günther Blumentritt, Westfeldzug, Kritik (Campaign in the West, Critique), sketch on p. 31 (BA-MA Study for P–208, vol. 2, sec. E), BA-MA. Halder greatly exaggerated his role as creator of the Sickle Cut plan in the work titled *Hitler als Feldherr* (Munich: Münchener Dom-Verlag, 1949) (28f.), which was published in English in 1949 (*Hitler as War Lord,* London: Putnam). In his monograph *Fall Gelb* (75 and 150), Jacobsen also made use of the differentiation between Manstein's alleged "sickle movement" and Halder's "sickle cut." This is one of the less serious points of critique that can be found in Hans-Adolf Jacobsen's monograph *Fall Gelb.* It is rightfully considered a classic example of modern military historiography, although it was published in 1957 when far from all files were available.
37. This thesis, which Jacobsen also mentioned, was questioned particularly emphatically by Generaloberst a.D. Hermann Hoth. The controversy thus triggered was argued out in the magazine *EWKde* in 1958. See Hermann Hoth, "Buchbesprechung zu: Jacobsen, *Fall Gelb*" (Book Review of Jacobsen, *Case Yellow*), *EWKde* 7, no. 2 (1958): 118f.; his "Mansteins Operationsplan für den Westfeldzug 1940 und die Aufmarschanweisung des O.K.H. vom 27.2.1940" (Manstein's Operations Plan for the 1940 Campaign in the West and the Deployment Directive of the OKH of 27 February 1940), *EWKde* 7, no. 3 (1958): 127–30; and his "Zu 'Mansteins Operationsplan für den Westfeldzug 1940 und die Aufmarschanweisung des O.K.H. vom 27.2.1940'" (On 'Manstein's Operations Plan for the 1940 Campaign in the West and the Deploy-

ment Directive of the OKH of 27 February 1940'), *EWKde* 7, no. 8 (1958): 459. See also Jacobsen's response: "Zur Entstehung des Sichelschnittplanes vom 24. February 1940" (On the Origin of the Sickle Cut Plan of 24 February 1940), *EWKde* 7, no. 4 (1958): 226–28. Hoth was quite firm when he said: "The guiding idea behind the campaign is Manstein's creative act." The Sickle Cut plan, he noted, was based on the considerations entertained by the army high command "only with regard to details."

38. Manstein, *Lost Victories,* 105; *Verlorene Siege,* 103.
39. Kielmansegg, "Bemerkungen zum Referat von Hauptmann Dr. Frieser [Panzergruppe Kleist] aus der Sicht eines Zeitzeugen" (Comments on the Report of Captain Dr. Frieser [Panzer Group Kleist] as Seen by an Eyewitness), *Operatives Denken und Handeln,* 150; see also Hartmann, *Halder,* 182.
40. Manstein, *Verlorene Siege,* 93.
41. Guderian, *Panzer Leader,* 89; *Erinnerungen,* 79.
42. Tagebuch Jodl, 17.2.1940 (Jodl Diary, 17 February 1940), BA-MA, RW 4/32, 13.
43. See Hoth, "Mansteins Operationsplan," 128.
44. Guderian, *Panzer Leader,* 91; *Erinnerungen,* 81. Concerning the two war games in Koblenz and Mayen, see *Erinnerungen,* 80f.; Halder *KTB,* vol. 1, 185f., 194; Akten HGr A, BA-MA, RH 19 I/25, RH 19 I/35; Akten der 12. Armee, RH 20–12/11, RH 20–12/20.
45. Halder *KTB,* vol. 1, 231; Akten HGr A, BA-MA, RH 19 I/37, 6 March 1940, sheet 22; RH 19 I/38, sheet 160.
46. See, for example, *Denkschrift der Heeresgruppe A vom 31.10.1939* (Memorandum of Army Group A, 31 October 1939), reprinted in: Manstein, *Verlorene Siege,* 625f.; that idea can also be found in the following memorandums printed there.
47. Manstein, *Lost Victories,* 125; *Verlorene Siege,* 123.
48. Tippelskirch, Westfeldzug, vol. 1, pt. 2, Study P–208, 107, BA-MA.
49. Manstein, *Verlorene Siege,* 123, also 101f., 112, 120, 123, 127f.; and in the Document Annex, 626, 629, 632, 634–636, 639, 646f. The most important documents listed here can be found in Akte der HGr A, BA-MA, RH 19 I/26.
50. Clausewitz, *Vom Kriege,* 879.
51. The Army High Command later chose the name *Fall Rot* (Case Red).
52. Manstein, *Lost Victories,* 126; *Verlorene Siege,* 124.
53. Liddell Hart, *History of the Second World War,* 40; *Zweiten Weltkrieges,* 60.
54. Klaus Gerbet, ed., *Generalfeldmarschall Fedor von Bock: The War Diary, 1939–1945* (Atglen, Pa.: Schiffer Military History, 1996), 76 (25 October 1939) (hereafter cited as Gerbet, *Bock: War Diary*), and Bock, KTB pt. 2, 9 (25 October 1939), Study P–210, BA-MA; OKW/WFSt, KTB, Notizen Hptm. Deyle, BA-MA, RW 4/41, 4; see also Jacobsen, *Fall Gelb,* 40.
55. Halder, *Hitler,* 29; *Hitler als Feldherr,* 29.
56. Hoth, "Buchbesprechung," 118; also "Mansteins Operationsplan."
57. Heeresgruppe A, Chef, Vortragsnotiz (19.1.1940) (Army Group A, Chief of Staff, briefing note [19 January 1940]), BA-MA, RH 19 I/26, sheet 101.
58. Halder *KTB,* vol. 1, 166f.; see also OKW/WFSt, KTB, Notizen Hptm. Deyle, BA-MA, RW 4/41, 5ff.
59. Halder, *Hitler als Feldherr,* 28ff.; Hoth, "Mansteins Operationsplan," 130; Manstein, *Verlorene Siege,* 106f.
60. Manstein, *Lost Victories,* 109; *Verlorene Siege,* 106f.
61. See, for example, Halder, *Hitler als Feldherr,* 30f.

62. Generalfeldmarschall Alfred Graf von Schlieffen, *Cannae* (Berlin: Mittler and Sohn, 1925), 262.
63. The following statements are based above all on Günter Roth's essay, "Operatives Denken bei Schlieffen und Manstein" (Operational Thinking in Schlieffen and Manstein), *Entwicklung, Planung und Durchführung operativer Ideen im Ersten und Zweiten Weltkrieg* (Bonn and Herford, 1988), which the author cooperated in drafting.
64. See Horne, *Über die Maas,* 136.
65. Concerning the topic of the Schlieffen Plan and Cannae, there have been two publications with new interpretive approaches most recently: Wolfgang von Groote, "Historische Vorbilder des Feldzugs 1914 im Westen" (Historical Examples of the 1914 Campaign in the West), *MGM* 47, no. 1 (1990): 33–55, and Martin Samuels, "The Reality of Cannae," *MGM* 47, no. 1 (1990): 7–31.
66. Turnbull, *Dunkirk,* 11.
67. This term comes from Jean de Pierrefeu, quoted from J. F. C. Fuller, *Die entartete Kunst Krieg zu führen 1789–1961* [The Degenerate Art of Conducting War, 1789–1961] (Cologne: Verlag Wissenschaft Und Politik, 1964), 171; English-language version, *The Conduct of War, 1798–1961* (New York: Minerva Press, 1968), 156.
68. Shirer, *Collapse,* 122, and *Zusammenbruch,* 82, 123; see also Ferdinand Otto Miksche, *Vom Kriegsbild* (On the Nature of War) (Stuttgart: Verlag Seewald, 1976), 87.
69. In the version that Schlieffen had wanted, the ratio between the mobile attacking wing and the static defensive wing was to be 7:1. Now, 54 divisions were concentrated in the right sector (opposite Belgium and Luxembourg), whereas the left sector (opposite France) was to be screened by only 8 divisions. Of the 8 divisions that in the meantime had been newly organized, however, Schlieffen's successor did not assign a single one to the right wing but rather thus doubled the number of divisions employed on the left wing to 16. In that way—considering qualitative factors—he changed the ratio calculated by Schlieffen from 7:1 to 3:1.
70. Jehuda L. Wallach, *Das Dogma der Vernichtungsschlacht. Die Lehren von Clausewitz und Schlieffen und ihre Wirkungen in zwei Weltkriegen* (The Dogma of the Battle of Annihilation. The Theories of Clausewitz and Schlieffen and Their Effects during Two World Wars) (Frankfurt am Main, 1967), 135; Gerhard Ritter, *Der Schlieffenplan. Kritik eines Mythos* (The Schlieffen Plan: Critique of a Myth) (Munich: R. Oldenbourg, 1956), 19, 38.
71. Concerning the metacriticism in Gerhard Ritter's critique of the Schlieffen Plan, see, for example, Heinz Ludger Borgert, "Grundzüge der Landkriegführung von Schlieffen bis Guderian (Basic Features of Land Warfare from Schlieffen to Guderian)," vol. 5, *Handbuch zur deutschen Militärgeschichte 1648–1939* [Handbook of German Military History, 1648–1939] (Munich, 1979), 455.
72. Ibid.
73. Ritter, *Schlieffenplan,* 56.
74. Wallach, *Dogma,* 145.
75. S. Mette, *Vom Geist deutscher Feldherren. Genie und Technik 1800–1918* (On the Spirit of the German Warlords. Genius and Technology, 1800–1918) (Zürich: Scientia, 1938), 261.
76. Clausewitz, *Vom Kriege,* 1040; Clausewitz, *On War,* 771.
77. Manstein, *Lost Victories,* 99; *Verlorene Siege,* 96.
78. Manstein, *Lost Victories,* 99; *Verlorene Siege,* 97.
79. Liddell Hart, *Jetzt dürfen sie reden,* 197, 208.

80. André Maurois, *Die Tragödie Frankreichs* (The Tragedy of France) (Zürich: Rascher, 1941), 85f; see also Liß, *Westfront,* 119.
81. Umbreit, "Kampf," 241, 277. Particularly informative are the statements by the Generalmajor a.D. Ulrich Liß, who before and during the campaign in the West was the Chief, Foreign Armies West, in the General Staff; see his *Westfront,* 118ff.; "Deutsche Westoffensive," 213ff.; and "Dünkirchen, gesehen mit den Augen des Ic" (Dunkirk as Seen through the Eyes of the Intelligence Officer), *WWR* 8, no. 6 (1958): 325–40. See also Lageberichte West der Abteilung Fremde West des GenstdH (Western Situation Reports of the Foreign Armies West Section, Army General Staff) in: BA-MA, RH 2/1491–1494. The files of the army groups and field armies also indicate that the Wehrmacht was excellently informed about the fact that the Allies were planning to march into Belgium; see, for example, HGr B, RH 19 II/19, 127. From the various memoirs, see, for example, Guderian, *Erinnerungen,* 86.
82. Afterword to Hermann Zimmermann, *Der Griff ins Ungewisse. Die ersten Kriegstage 1940 beim XVI. Panzerkorps im Kampf um die Dylestellung, 10.–17. Mai* (Reaching into the Unknown. The First Days of War for the XVI Panzer Corps at the Dyle Position, 10–17 May) (Neckargemünd: Kurt Vowinckel, 1964), 190.
83. Loßberg, *Im Wehrmachtführungsstab,* 76.
84. Brausch, "Sedan," 65.
85. Oberst Koelitz, "Die Schützen sind drüben" (The Riflemen Are Over)," *Mit den Panzern in Ost und West* (With the Panzers in the East and the West), ed. Heinz Guderian (Berlin, Prague, Vienna, 1942), 134.
86. Kielmansegg, "Scharnier Sedan" (The Hinge at Sedan), pt. 2, *Wehrmacht* 5, no. 12 (1941): 15.
87. Speidel, Der Einsatz, pt. 3, 91, BA-MA, Study Lw 3/2; and apps. 41 and 47, Lw 3/4a.
88. Above all, see Maurice Gamelin, vol. 1, *Servir* (Serving) (Paris: Plon, 1946–47), 89–108.
89. See also doc. 3 (1 September 1939), 22, as well as the facsimile, 170, in *Die Geheimakten des französischen Generalstabs, veröffentl. durch das Auswärtige Amt 1939/41* (The Secret Files of the French General Staff. Published by the Foreign Office, 1939–41), no. 6 (Berlin, 1941).
90. Gaston René Eugène Roton, *Années cruciales: La Course aux armaments (1933–1939). La Campagne (1939–1940)* (Crucial Years: The Arms Race [1933–1939]. The Campaign [1939–1940]) (Paris: Charles-Lavauzelle, 1947), 97; Pierre Lyet, *La bataille de France (mai–juin 1940)* (The Battle of France [May–June 1940]) (Paris: Payot, 1947), 25; Goutard, *1940,* 147.
91. For the discussion on the Dyle-Breda Plan, see Umbreit, "Kampf," 274; Shirer, *Zusammenbruch,* 616ff.; Horne, *Über die Maas,* 116ff.; Jacques Benoist-Méchin, *Der Himmel stürzt ein,* 33f.
92. Miksche, *Kriegsbild,* 86.
93. Horne, *To Lose a Battle,* 215, and *Über die Maas,* 177; Paillat, *La guerre éclair,* 79. On 12 May the French military attaché in London informed Major General Sir Edward Spears, the British liaison officer attached to the French prime minister, that the Germans were making their main effort in the Maastricht-Liège sector. "It seemed to me," Spears commented, "that Georges and Gamelin should be delighted. The Germans were doing exactly what they had expected and hoped." (See Major General Sir Edward Spears, *Prelude to Dunkirk, July 1939-May 1940,* vol. 1, *Assignment to Catastrophe* [London: William Heinemann, Ltd., 1954], 137).

94. Pierre Le Goyet, "Contre-attaques manquées. Sedan 13–15 mai 1940" (Failed Counterattacks. Sedan, 13–15 May 1940), *RHA* 18, no. 4 (1962): 130.
95. "*Jodl Tagebuch,*" printed in: *Prozeß,* vol. 28, 402. Jodl was obviously referring to a metaphor coined by von Clausewitz, see *Vom Kriege,* 230.
96. Horne, *Über die Maas,* 139.
97. Guderian, *Panzer Leader,* 92; *Erinnerungen,* 81f.
98. Guderian, *Panzer Leader,* 91; *Erinnerungen,* 81.
99. This is what Halder wrote on 14 May in a letter to his wife; see also Schall-Riaucour, *Aufstand und Gehorsam,* 151.
100. Heusinger, *Befehl,* 86.
101. Field Marshal the Count von Haeseler probably expressed this parody of the Schlieffen Plan for the first time in 1914; see also Wallach, *Dogma,* 145.
102. Heusinger, *Befehl,* 86.
103. This and preceding quote from Horne, *To Lose a Battle,* 153, and *Über die Maas,* 138; this is found in a more detailed form also in Heusinger, *Befehl,* 85.
104. Manstein, *Lost Victories,* 127–28; *Verlorene Siege,* 126.
105. Field Marshal Paul von Hindenburg, *Aus meinem Leben* (From My Life) (Leipzig: S. Hirzel Verlag, 1927), 118.
106. HGr A, Ia, 16.2.1940 (Army Group A, Operations Officer, 16 February 1940), BA-MA, RH 19 I/26, sheet 237f.
107. Halder *KTB,* vol. 1, 203.
108. Schreiben 22.2.1940 (Anl. 1 zum KTB) (Letter, 22 February 1940 [App. 1, War Diary]), BA-MA, RH 19 I/38, sheet 313.
109. See also HGr A, Chef des Generalstabes vom 5.3.1940 (Army Group A, Chief of the General Staff, 5 March 1940); Schreiben 22.2.1940 (Anl. 1 zum KTB) (Letter, 22 February 1940 [App. 1, War Diary]), sheets 304–12.
110. For Halder's rejoinder to Blumentritt on 22 February 1940, see HGr A, KTB, 22.2.1940 (Army Group A, War Diary, 22 February 1940), BA-MA, RH 19 I/37, sheet 6.
111. Der Chef des Generalstabes des Heeres an den Chef des Generalstabes der HGr A vom 12.3.1940 (Chief of Staff, Army General Staff, to Chief of Staff, Army Group A, 12 March 1940), BA-MA, RH 19 I/38, sheet 156.
112. This figure of speech actually came from World War I but was used to characterize Germany's economic situation after the outbreak of World War II. Dr. C. Krauch, Göring's plenipotentiary-general for special questions of chemical production, already used this metaphor in a report written on 20/21 April 1939; see Dietrich Eichholtz, *Geschichte der deutschen Kriegswirtschaft 1939–1945,* Bd. 1: *1939–1941* (The History of the German War Economy, 1939–1945, vol. 1, 1939–1941) (Berlin: Akademie Verlag, 1969), 59.
113. Hitler was considered to be the "personified revenge" against the Versailles Treaty that was considered to be a big injustice in Germany. The dictator considered France to be the archenemy, who for centuries had ripped one piece of land after the other out of the German Reich to push its eastern border all the way to the Rhine. In his view, there could be no peaceful coexistence with Germany's western neighbor because France's foreign policy allegedly was always geared toward the weakening and Balkanization of Germany. In his very first book, *Mein Kampf* (My Struggle) (Munich: Zentralverlag der NSDAP Franz Eher, 1936), 766, he demanded that "the German nation's will to live" be rallied for a "final active clash with France" and that one would have to go for a "last decisive struggle" (see *Mein Kampf,* 696, 699, 765, as well as

Hitlers Zweites Buch. Ein Dokument aus dem Jahr 1928. Eingeleitet und kommentiert von Gerhard L. Weinberg (Hitler's Second Book: A Document of the Year 1928. An Introduction and Commentary by Gerhard L. Weinberg) (Stuttgart: Deutsches Verlags-Anstalt, 1961), 150. Although Hitler obviously believed that a war was unavoidable in the long run, the campaign in the west was a kind of accident because it came much too early for the German Reich, which was still in the process of rearming.

114. Halder an Sodenstern (12.3.1940), S. 4, HGr A [Halder to Sodenstern (12 March 1940), 4, Army Group A], BA-MA, RH 19 I/38, sheet 159.
115. Heusinger, *Befehl,* 86.
116. Gerbet, *Bock: War Diary,* 140 (13 May 1940), and Bock, KTB, Bd. 1, Teil 3: Tagebuch Westen. Offensive und Besatzungszeit, 10.5.–11.9.1940 [War Diary, vol. 1, pt. 3: Diary West. Offensive and Occupation Period, 10 May–11 September 1940, 9 (13 May 1940), Study P–210, BA-MA.

Chapter 4

1. Ia/Op Nr. 214/40 vom 21.3.1940 (Operations Officer/Operations Order No. 214/40, 21 March 1940), 2, BA-MA, RH 21–1/19.
2. The fact that the Panzer Force was for the first time employed in an independent operational setting during the campaign in the west runs like a red thread through the series of articles by Generaloberst a.D. Kurt Zeitzler titled "Die Panzer-Gruppe v. Kleist im West-Feldzug 1940" (Panzer Group Von Kleist during the 1940 Campaign in the West), pts. 1–4, *EWKde* 8, no. 4 (1959): 182–88; no. 5 (1959): 239–45; no. 6 (1959): 293–98; no. 7 (1959): 366–72. During the campaign in the west, Zeitzler, then a Colonel, was chief of staff of the Panzer Group Kleist. Later on, Halder also declared that "operational use of tanks" was implemented "during the French Campaign, in which full effect was given for the first time to the modern conception of the tank's part in war . . ." (*Hitler as War Lord,* 13; *Hitler als Feldherr,* 16). See also General der Infanterie a.D. Herbert von Boeckmann, "Ansatz der Westoffensive im Mai 1940" (Preparation for the Offensive in the West in May 1940), in: General der Infanterie a.D. Edgar Röhricht, *Große Einkesselungs-Schlachten im 2. Weltkrieg* (Large Encirclement Battles in the Second World War), Study P–209, 22, BA-MA; Karl-Volker Neugebauer, "Operatives Denken zwischen dem Ersten und Zweiten Weltkrieg" (Operational Thinking between the First and Second World Wars), *Operatives Denken und Handeln in deutschen Streitkräften im 19. und 20. Jahrhundert* (Operational Thinking and Action in the German Armed Forces during the 19th and 20th Centuries), vol. 9, *Vorträge zur Militärgeschichte* (Lectures on Military History) (Herford and Bonn: Verlag E. S. Mittler and Sohn, 1988), 120; Jacobsen, *Fall Gelb,* 143. Significantly, this idea turned up in German regulations only after 1940 (see Senff, *Die Entwicklung der Panzerwaffe,* 30).
3. Guderian's letter to Liddell Hart, quoted in Cooper, 174.
4. Zeitzler, "Panzer-Gruppe v. Kleist," *EWKde* 8, no. 4 (1959): 182. The constantly changing organizational setups and strength figures of the Panzer Group are listed exactly in the files of its Abt. Qu (Administrative and Supply Section), BA-MA, RH 21–1/317 and 318.
5. The commanding general of this corps was General der Flakartillerie [Lieutenant General of Antiaircraft Artillery] Hubert Weise; see the latter's report: Organisation der

Luftverteidigung im Felde, erläutert an Beispielen des Flakkorps I (Organization of Air Defense in the Field, Explained with Examples from I Flak Corps), Study D–111, BA-MA; see also Horst-Adalbert Koch, *Flak. Die Geschichte der deutschen Flakartillerie und der Einsatz der Luftwaffenhelfer* (Flak. The History of German Antiaircraft Artillery and the Employment of Air Defense Auxiliaries) (Bad Nauheim: Podzun Verlag, 1965), 92ff.

6. Guderian, *Panzer Leader,* 91; *Erinnerungen,* 81.
7. General von Kleist had commanded the XXII Army Corps (Motorized) until then. On 6 March von Kleist renamed the newly assembled major formation *Group von Kleist* as he officially took command; in the end, it was called Panzer Group Kleist, BA-MA, RH 21–1/18. It was renamed the 1. Panzerarmee (First Panzer Army) in October 1941 during the Russian campaign.
8. Zeitzler, "Panzer-Gruppe v. Kleist," *EWKde* 8, no. 4 (1959): 184.
9. Ibid., 183; in this connection, see Der Erfahrungsbericht der Panzergruppe Kleist aus dem Westfeldzug (After-Action Report of Panzer Group Kleist from the Campaign in the West), BA-MA, RH 21–1/36, sheet 3f.
10. Quoted from Kielmansegg, *Panzer zwischen Warschau und Atlantik* (Panzer Between Warsaw and the Atlantic) (Berlin: Verlag "Die Wehrmacht," 1941), 161.
11. Erfahrungsbericht Quartiermeisterabteilung der PzGr Kleist (After-Action Report, Administrative and Supply Section, Panzer Group Kleist), BA-MA, RH 21–1/320, 3.
12. Zeitzler, "Panzer-Gruppe v. Kleist," *EWKde* 8, no. 7 (1959): 371.
13. Erfahrungsbericht Quartiermeisterabteilung der PzGr Kleist, BA-MA, RH 21–1/320, 11.
14. Ibid., 17.
15. Unless otherwise cited, this section is based on Kielmansegg, "Bemerkungen," 152f; supplemented by verbal communications of Kielmansegg to the author; see also KTB der Abt. Ib (Versorgung) der 1. PzDiv (War Diary, Section Ib [Supply], 1st Panzer Division), BA-MA, RH 27–1/154, 3f.
16. PzGr Kleist, Abt. Qu, KTB (Panzer Group Kleist, Administrative and Supply Section, War Diary), 23, as well as Anh. Logistischer Erfahrungsbericht (Annex, Logistics After-Action Report), 16, BA-MA, RH 21–1/320; Halder *KTB,* vol. 1, 297, 299.
17. Kielmansegg, *Panzer,* 160, 168.
18. Generaloberst a.D. Hans Reinhardt, "Im Schatten Guderians. Das XXXXI. Pz.-Korps und seine Nöte bei dem Vorgehen gegen und über die Maas vom 10. bis 16. Mai 1940" (In Guderian's Shadow. The XXXXI Panzer Corps and Its Troubles during Its Advance to and Across the Meuse from 10 to 16 May 1940), *EWKde* 3, no. 10 (1954): 341.
19. Zeitzler, "Panzer-Gruppe v. Kleist," *EWKde* 8, no. 4 (1959): 185.
20. "Militärgeographischer Überblick über Belgien (Generalstab des Heeres, Januar 1940)" (Military Geography Overview of Belgium [Army General Staff, January 1940]), 16, BA-MA, RHD 21/47. The logistics after-action report of the Panzer Group Kleist also confirms that the roads in Luxembourg and Belgium were "in very excellent condition"; see BA-MA, RH 21–1/320, 14.
21. See also the differing versions of this order in Akten der PzGr Kleist (Files of Panzer Group Kleist), BA-MA, RH 21–1/19.
22. Ausarbeitungen: "Durchbruch der Gruppe v. Kleist über die Maas" (Analysis: "Breakthrough of Group von Kleist across the Meuse River"), BA-MA, RH 21–1/381, 1st pt., 14.
23. Communications from General Graf von Kielmansegg.
24. Ibid.

25. XXXXI.AK, KTB (XXXXI Army Corps, War Diary), BA-MA, RH 24–41/2, 19f. See also the map exercise on 15 April in Idar-Oberstein and the resultant conversations between Reinhardt and Kleist, ibid., 16ff.
26. Reinhardt, "Im Schatten Guderians," 336.
27. As indicated in the KTB des Panzerkorps Reinhardt (War Diary of the Panzer Corps Reinhardt) (BA-MA, RH 24–41/2, 25), the 8th Panzer Division, which was standing by in the Idar-Oberstein area, was able to start moving out only at 2130 on 10 May.
28. PzGr Kleist, KTB, BA-MA, RH 21–1/22 4f.; Durchbruch der Gruppe von Kleist, RH 21–1/381, pt. 1, 5ff.; PzKorps Guderian, KTB (Panzer Corps Guderian, War Diary), RH 21–2/41, 6ff.; 10.PzDiv, KTB, RH 27–10/9, 11/12 May.
29. 12 May 1940, BA-MA, RH 27–6/1D, 9 (sheet 12).
30. Ibid., 11.
31. Kielmansegg, *Panzer,* 103.
32. The French side also assessed that after the war. For example, General Grandsard, Guderian's immediate opponent at Sedan, wrote: "The Ardennes could have been the graveyard of Guderian's divisions"; see General C. Grandsard, *Le 10e Corps d'armée dans la bataille 1939–40* (The X Army Corps in the Battle 1939–40) (Paris: Berger-Levrault, 1949), 316.
33. Communication from General Graf von Kielmansegg.
34. Ibid.
35. With regard to the following text, see the Akten der 1.PzDiv (Files of 1st Panzer Division), BA-MA, RH 27–1/170, 9f., as well as the various Division orders, 110ff.; RH 27–1/14, 16, 173f., 260; Emilie Théodore Melchers, *Kriegsschauplatz Luxemburg August 1914, Mai 1940* (The Luxembourg Theater of War, August 1914, May 1940) (Luxembourg, 1979), 320, 376f.
36. Akten 1.PzDiv, BA-MA, RH 27–1/14, 17, 201, 209; RH 27–1/170, 10f.; Helmut Scheibe, Die Panzeraufklärungs-Abteilung 4 im Westfeldzug (The 4th Armored Reconnaissance Battalion during the Campaign in the West) (private publication), 16f., 23f.; Georges Hautecler, *Le combat de Bodange* (The Fighting at Bodange) (Brussels: Service Historique de l'Armée Belge, 1955), 15ff.
37. Berben and Iselin, *Die Deutschen kommen,* 65.
38. Kielmansegg, *Panzer,* 104.
39. Reference the fight at Bodange, see Akten der 1.PzDiv, BA-MA, RH 27–1/170, 11f.; RH 27–1/14, 17f., 105, 175f., 196, 261ff.; Berben and Iselin, *Die Deutschen kommen,* 65ff.; Robert A. Doughty, *The Breaking Point. Sedan and the Fall of France, 1940* (Hamden, Conn.: Archon Books, 1990), 49ff.; Melchers, *Kriegsschauplatz Luxemburg,* 383ff.; Claude Gounelle, *Sedan. Mai 1940* (Sedan. May 1940) (Paris: Hachette, 1956), 78ff.; Hautecler, *Le combat de Bodange.*
40. Clausewitz, *Vom Kriege,* 261f.; Clausewitz, *On War,* 138.
41. Regarding the Niwi airborne landing mission, see the Akten des PzKorps Guderian: Zusammenfassender Bericht und einzelne Gefechtsberichte über das Unternehmen "Niwi" (Files of the Panzer Corps Guderian: Summary Report and Individual After-Action Reports on Operation "Niwi"), BA-MA, RH 21–2/54; XIX. AK vom 16.4.40, Befehl für den Einsatz der Abteilung Förster-Garski (XIX Army Corps, 16 April 1940, Order for the Employment of the Förster-Garski Detachment), RH 21–2/40; Zeitplan Luftwaffe (Luftwaffe timetable), RH 21–2/852; Akten der PzGr Kleist: Durchbruch der Gruppe von Kleist, RH 21–1/381, pt. 1, 26f.; Akten der 1.PzDiv, RH 27–1/170, 11f.; 2. Kompanie/Sturmpionier-Bataillon 43: Unser Einsatz im Westen vom 10. Mai bis 21.

Juni 1940 (Kriegstagebuch 2. Kompanie/Sturmpionier-Bataillon 43) (2d Company, 43d Assault Engineer Battalion: Our Employment in the West from 10 May to 21 June 1940) (War Diary of the 2d Company, 43d Assault Engineer Battalion), 24f., 36ff. (private document); Halder *KTB,* vol. 1, 209; Guderian, *Erinnerungen,* 88; Helmuth Spaeter, *Die Geschichte des Panzerkorps Großdeutschland* (The History of the Panzer Corps Großdeutschland) (Duisburg-Ruhrort: Selbstverlag Hilfswerk ehem. Soldaten, 1958), sketch on 109; Wolf Durian, *Infanterieregiment Großdeutschland greift an* (Infantry Regiment Großdeutschland Attacks) (Berlin: Scherl, 1942), 14ff.; Melchers, *Kriegsschauplatz Luxemburg,* 380ff.; Hans von Dach, "Panzer durchbrechen eine Armeestellung" (Panzers Break Through an Army Position), *Schweizer Soldat* (Swiss Soldier) 47 (1972): pt. 1, 61f., 66f.; Berben and Iselin, *Die Deutschen kommen,* 60ff.; Hautecler, *Le combat de Bodange,* 31ff.; Doughty, *Breaking Point,* 45, 53ff.; Jean Paul Pallud, *Blitzkrieg in the West: Then and Now* (London: After the Battle, 1991), 88ff. Retired Lieutenant Colonel Bikar, the former chief of the Military History Section of the Belgian Army, developed the most comprehensive description: "10 mai 1940. 'Hedderich' et 'Niwi.' Les deux opérations allemandes aéroportés sur petits avions Fieseler 'Storch' " (10 May 1940, "Hedderich" and "Niwi." The Two German Airborne Operations Using the Little Fieseler "Storch" Aircraft), *RBHM* 20 (1973–74): 411–34, 591–622, 699–723; 21 (1975–76): 48–78, 123–56; see also Bikar, "La 5e division légère de cavalerie française en Ardenne, du 10 au 12 mai" (The French 5th Light Calvary Division in the Ardennes, 10–12 May), *RBHM* 28 (1989–90): 475ff., 491ff.

42. PzKorps Guderian: Zusammenfassender Bericht (Panzer Corps Guderian: Summary Report), BA-MA, RH 21–2/54, 1.
43. The fact that a telephone cable leading to the battalion command post in Fauvillers was cut in the morning by a demolition triggered near Bodange does not have any significance here. Both villages are only two to three kilometers apart and were linked by motorcycle messengers.
44. Bericht Garski vom 19.5.1940, PzKorps Guderian (Report by Garski, 19 May 1940, Panzer Corps Guderian), BA-MA, RH 21–2/54.
45. Kielmansegg, *Panzer,* 105f.
46. See also the detailed combat organization in Bikar, "La 5e division légère de cavalerie," 501ff.
47. Regarding the breakthrough at Neufchâteau, see the Akten der 1.PzDiv, BA-MA, RH 27–1/170, 13f., 120, as well as the after-action reports of the individual units, contained in File RH 27–1/14. See also *Mit den Panzern,* 108; Doughty, *Breaking Point,* 65f., 82ff.; Berben and Iselin, *Die Deutschen kommen,* 54ff., 89ff.; Gounelle, *Sedan,* 89ff.; Grandsard, *Le 10e Corps d'armée,* 102ff.; Edmond Ruby, *Sedan. Terre d'Épreuve. Avec la IIème armée mai–juin 1940* (Sedan. The Testing Ground: With the Second Army, May–June 1940) (Paris: Flammarion, 1948), 73ff. The most detailed study, above all regarding the French side, is Bikar's three-part series in *RBHM,* "La 5e division légère de cavalerie." See also the same author's map series, "La campagne de mai 1940 en Belgique: La 4e division légère de cavalerie française à l'est de la Meuse, les 10, 11, 12 mai 1940" (The May 1940 Campaign in Belgium: The French 4th Light Cavalry Division to the East of the Meuse, 10, 11, 12 May 1940), *RBHM* 25 (1983–84): 529–50, 627–52. The precise route followed by the German Panzer formations during their breakthrough south of Neufchâteau can be traced in the Akten des PzKorps Guderian (Files of Panzer Corps Guderian), BA-MA, RH 21–2/59 (K), Map of 11 May.
48. Gounelle, *Sedan,* 91.

49. Concerning the thrust to Bouillon, see the following files: PzGruppe Kleist (Panzer Group Kleist), BA-MA, RH 21–1/22, 5f.; 1.PzDiv, BA-MA, RH 27–1/170, 14f.; RH 27–1/14, 6, 70–73, 110, 112, 198, 266; KTB Nr. 1 der I.Abt/Panzerregiment 1 (Privatarchiv R. Stoves) (War Diary No. 1, 1st Battalion, 1st Panzer Regiment [private files of R. Stoves]); see also Berben and Iselin, *Die Deutschen kommen,* 97ff.; Bikar, "La 5e division légère de cavalerie," 699ff.; Doughty, *Breaking Point,* 67ff., 88ff.; Pallud, *Blitzkrieg,* 204ff.
50. Before that, Major von Wietersheim had checked with Oberst Keltsch, the commander of the 1st Panzer Brigade, with regard to the possibility of crossing the division boundary line.
51. For the surprise coup against Mouzaive, see the Akten der 1.PzDiv, BA-MA, RH 27–1/170, 14f.; RH 27–1/14, 5f., 22, 99, 113, 178ff., 197; see also Rolf O. G. Stoves, *1. Panzer-Division 1935–1945. Chronik einer der drei Stamm-Divisionen der deutschen Panzerwaffe* (1st Panzer Division, 1939–1945. The Record of One of the Three Parent Divisions of the German Panzer Arm) (Bad Nauheim: Podzun Verlag, 1961), 85f.; Ruby, *Sedan,* 87f.; Doughty, *Breaking Point,* 69ff., 87ff.; Bikar, "La 3e brigade de Spahis dans nos Ardennes, les 10, 11, 12 mai (The 3d Brigade of Spahis in Our Ardennes, 10, 11, 12 May), *RBHM* 25 (1983–84): 395f., and "La 5e division légère de cavalerie," 594f., 691ff.
52. Concerning the push to the Meuse on 12 May, see the Akten der 1.PzDiv (Files of the 1st Panzer Division), BA-MA, RH 27–1/14, 6, 22ff., 73ff., 110, 112ff., 179f., 198, 266f.; RH 27–1/170, 15f., 121f.; RH 27–1/5 (radio messages, 12 May); see also Stoves, *1. Panzer-Division,* 86f.; Bikar, "La 5e division légère de cavalerie," 702ff.; Doughty, *Breaking Point,* 71f., 92.
53. The after-action report of the 8th Company, 1st Panzer Regiment, concerning the fight to take the "La Hatrelle" pillbox, was mistakenly dated as of 13 May (see BA-MA, RH 27–1/14, sheets 74, 76). From the other after-action reports mentioned there (e.g., 23f., 112), one can gather that this episode took place on 12 May. The entries in the Kriegstagebuch der II.Abteilung/PzRgt 1 (War Diary, 2d Battalion, 1st Panzer Regiment) concerning the events of 12 May also confirm this (Rolf Stoves's private archives).
54. Verbal communication to author.
55. Quoted from Shirer, *Collapse,* 185; *Zusammenbruch,* 190.
56. Général André Doumenc, *Histoire de la Neuvième Armée* (History of the Ninth Army) (Paris: B. Arthaud, 1945), 52.
57. Quoted from Shirer, *Collapse,* 631; *Zusammenbruch,* 662.
58. Paillat, *La guerre éclair,* 162.
59. Ruby, *Sedan,* 81.
60. These formulas were repeated over and over again almost like a litany, in which, from time to time, the adjectives "impénétrable" or "impracticable" were used instead of "imperméable"; see also, for example, Pierre Le Goyet, "La percée de Sedan (10–15 mai 940)" (The Breakthrough at Sedan, [10–15 May 1940]), *RHDGM* 15 (1965): 52; Benoist-Méchin, *Soixante jours qui ébranlèrent l'occident. 10 mai–10 juillet 1940* (Sixty Days That Shook the West: 10 May–10 July 1940) (Paris: Éditions Albin Michel, 1956), 42.
61. See also the quote from Pétain at the beginning of this chapter.
62. Brausch, *Sedan 1940,* 82.
63. Regarding the miscalculation concerning the earliest possible time of a German attack, see Liddell Hart, *Jetzt dürfen sie reden,* 189f.; Goutard, *1940,* 140; Robert A. Doughty,

The Seeds of Disaster: The Development of French Army Doctrine, 1919–1939 (Hamden Conn.: Archon Books, 1985), 59; Paillat, *La guerre éclair,* 249f.; Shirer, *Zusammenbruch,* 660, 666; Bikar, "10 mai 1940," pt. 1, 609.

64. See Shirer, *Collapse,* 629; *Zusammenbruch,* 659.
65. Liddell Hart, *Jetzt dürfen sie reden,* 189f.
66. "Travail de reconnaissance de frontière exécuté par le Colonel Bourguignon" (Frontier Reconnaissance Mission Carried Out by Colonel Bourguignon), Service Historique de l'armée de Terre (Historical Service of the French Army, SHAT), Vincennes, 29 N 84: 2ème Armée/Commandant des Chars . . . (Second Army, Commander of Tanks . . .).
67. André Prételat, *Le destin tragique de la ligne Maginot* (The Tragic Destiny of the Maginot Line) (Paris: Berger-Levrault, 1950), 13f.
68. See also the sketch in *Sedan 1940* (Vincennes: SHAT, 1991), 65.
69. Cf. Paillat, *La répétition générale*: *Le désastre de 1940* (The General Repetition, vol. 1, The Disaster of 1940) (Paris: Robert Laffont, 1983), 196. In 1936, Gamelin had directed a similar "war game." It showed that the French Army, even in the case of a successful German thrust across the Meuse, would be very much in a position to resolve the crisis by employing reserves (see Paillat, *La répétition,* 191f.).
70. Cf., for example, Goutard, *1940,* 183, 261. According to the present-day definition of the term "strategic" (see in chap. 1, "The Concept of Blitzkrieg"), it is impossible to speak in terms of "strategic surprise" here. After all, it was the Western powers that declared war on the German Reich and, after that, they had more than eight months for an intensive preparation for the anticipated German offensive. Only the direction of the thrust was a surprise on the operational level.
71. See the rather on-target summary in Doughty, *Breaking Point,* 73f.; see also Paul Paillole, *Notre Espion chez Hitler* (Our Spy with Hitler) (Paris: Laffont, 1985); Jürgen Rohwer, "Der Einfluß der allierten Funkaufklärung auf den Verlauf des Zweiten Weltkrieges" (The Influence of Allied Radio Intelligence on the Course of the Second World War), *Vierteljahrshefte für Zeitgeschichte* (Quarterly Journal of Contemporary History) 27 (1979): 334ff.; Wladislaw Kozaczuk, *Geheimoperation Wicher. Polnische Mathematiker knacken den deutschen Funkschlüssel "Enigma"* (Secret Operation Wicher. A Polish Mathematician Breaks the German Radio Cipher "Enigma") (Koblenz: Bernard and Graefe, 1989), 42ff.
72. F. H. Hinsley with E. F. Thomas, C. F. G. Ransom, and R. C. Knight, *Its Influence on Strategy and Operations.* vol. 1, *British Intelligence in the Second World War* (London: Her Majesty's Stationery Office, 1979), 108f., 136f.
73. See also Shirer, *Zusammenbruch,* 620f.; Benoist-Méchin, *Der Himmel stürzt ein,* 47f.; Horne, *Über die Maas,* 159f.; Jean Vanwelkenhuyzen, "Sicherheitspolitik Belgiens während der Kriegsphase 1939/40" (Belgian's Security Policy during the War's 1939–40 Phase), *ÖMZ* 27, no. 6 (1989): 481; Doughty, *Breaking Point,* 73ff. Brausch (*Sedan,* chap. 5) presented a rather skeptical estimate of actual French reconnaissance findings.
74. Eddy Bauer, *Der Panzerkrieg. Die wichtigsten Panzeroperationen des zweiten Weltkrieges in Europa und Afrika.* Bd. 1: *Vorstoß und Rückzug der deutschen Panzervebände* (The Panzer War. The Most Important Panzer Operations of the Second World War in Europe and Africa. vol.1: Attack and Retreat of the German Panzer Units) (Bonn: Verlag Offene Worte, 1965), 62f.
75. Quoted from Brausch, *Sedan,* 69.
76. This sentence is emphasized in the report concerned by the use of capital letters; see Doughty, *Breaking Point,* 94.

77. Ibid., 95; Shirer, *Zusammenbruch,* 667.
78. Doughty, *Breaking Point,* 97.
79. Herbert Malloy Mason, *The Rise of the Luftwaffe, 1918–1940* (London: Cassell, 1975), 349.
80. Ibid. Concerning the skeptical attitude on the part of the Headquarters of Ninth Army with respect to air reconnaissance reports, see also Max Gelée, "La percée des Ardennes vue d'en haut" (The Ardennes Breakthrough as Seen from Above), *Icare* no. 57 (spring–summer 1971): 68.
81. See the photos reproduced in the essay by Lucien Saint-Genis, "Le début de la poche de Sedan" (The Beginning of the Sedan Pocket), *Icare* no. 59 (autumn–winter 1971): 102ff.
82. Shirer, *Zusammenbruch,* 667.
83. Doughty, *Breaking Point,* 98f.
84. Ibid., 100; see also Brausch, *Sedan,* 77ff.
85. Gunsburg, *Divided,* 184.
86. Mason, *Rise of the Luftwaffe,* 349.
87. André Beaufre, *Le drame de 1940* (The Drama of 1940) (Paris: Plon, 1965), 231f. English-language version, *1940: The Fall of France* (New York: Alfred A. Knopf, 1968).
88. This is also indicated in Hitler's *Weisung Nr. 11* (Directive No. 11) of 14 May. It contains the following statement concerning the enemy situation in Item 1: "The past course of the offensive shows that the enemy did not in time recognize the basic idea behind our operation. He is still moving strong forces toward the Namur-Antwerp Line and seems to neglect the sector in front of Army Group A" (see also Brausch, *Sedan,* 85).

Chapter 5

1. Churchill, *Their Finest Hour,* 42, and *Zweiter Weltkrieg,* vol. 2, bk. 1, 61.
2. Kielmansegg, "Scharnier Sedan," 11.
3. Quoted from Gérard Giuliano, "La 'surprise ardennaise' de mai 1940" (The "Ardennes Surprise" of May 1940), *Terres Ardennaises,* no. 6 (April 1984): 31.
4. In his previously mentioned study, Colonel Bourguignon had referred to the Sedan Sector as a "tank obstacle of the first order" ("une zone anti-char de toute première qualité"); see "Travail de reconnaissance de frontière exécuté par le Colonel Bourguignon," SHAT, 29 N 84: 2ème Armée/Commandant des Chars . . . , section titled "Organisation . . . de Sedan" (Organization . . . of Sedan) (quotation contained in last line).
5. Günther Blumentritt, *Von Rundstedt,* 66.
6. Regarding Taittinger's role, see above all the essay by Martin S. Alexander, "Prophet without Honor? The French High Command and Pierre Taittinger's Report on the Ardennes Defenses, March 1940," *War and Society* 4, no. 1(1986): 52–77, as well as Claude Paillat, *La guerre immobile. Avril 1939–10 mai 1940* (The Immobile War. April 1939–10 May 1940), vol. 2, *Le désastre de 1940* (The Disaster of 1940) (Paris: Robert Laffont, 1986), 329ff.
7. Rapport de M. P. Taittinger (Report by Mr. P. Taittinger), 2, SHAT, 29 N 27:2ème Armée, Historique des opérations . . . (Second Army, History of Operations) (old no. 25).

8. Ibid., 1.
9. The French general Edmund Ruby titled his famous book *Sedan: Terre d'épreuve* (Sedan: The Testing Ground). Several battlefields are laid out on top of each other like geological strata in the earth of Sedan. This city, which again and again was fought over bitterly, originally belonged to the Empire of the German Emperors and in 1642 came into possession of the French kings. It continued to be the scene of military clashes: In 1815, Prussian troops, after the victory at Waterloo, pursued the French Army through the Ardennes and laid siege to the Citadel of Sedan. The latter, however, did not surrender until after Napoleon's final capitulation. In 1870, General von Moltke was able to surround the French Army at Sedan in an encirclement battle and capture Emperor Napoleon III. In 1914, the German Fourth Army crossed the Meuse River at Gaulier along the western edge of Sedan. In 1940, the Panzer Corps Guderian broke through the Meuse River line in the same spot and built a bridge across the Meuse River at Gaulier.
10. See Shirer, *Zusammenbruch,* 630. Later on, as war minister of the Vichy Regime, Huntziger tried to remove the letter in the Military Archives that incriminated him, but that was prevented by an officer from the Army Historical Department (see Shirer, *Zusammenbruch,* 630.).
11. Dach, "Panzer," pt. 1, 54.
12. Ruby, *Sedan,* 49.
13. The statistics pertain to the original overall extent of the Sedan Sector. The sketch on Fortification System only shows the two Villers-sur-Bar and Frénois subsectors but not the Angecourt subsector located to the southeast thereof. As for the completion deadlines of the various bunkers, see the table in the files II Armée, 3 Bureau: Organisation du Secteur de Sedan: Ouvrages terminés et en cours de construction (French Second Army, 3d Bureau [Operations]: Organization of the Sedan Sector: Finished Blockhouses and Those Under Construction), SHAT, 29 N 27: 2ème Armée, Historique des opérations . . . (old no. 25).
14. Koelitz, "Die Schützen sind drüben," in *Mit den Panzern,* 148f.
15. They can be inspected today in the Archives of the French Army Historical Service (SHAT) in Vincennes, near Paris.
16. Only Bunker 306 was planned at the mouth of the Glaire Creek as it flows into the Meuse River. That bunker existed only on paper. This is all the more astonishing because this sector can hardly be observed due to the river's curvature.
17. *Der Marne-Feldzug. Von der Sambre bis zur Marne.* Bd. 3: *Der Weltkrieg 1914 bis 1918. Die militärischen Operationen zu Lande. Bearb. im Reichsarchiv* (The Marne Campaign: From the Sambre to the Marne. Vol. 3: The World War, 1914–1918. The Military Operations on Land. Prepared in The Reich Archives) (Berlin: Verlag Mittler and Sohn, 1926), 14ff.
18. According to Ernst Klink, *Das Gesetz des Handelns. Die Operation "Zitadelle" 1943* (The Law of Initiative. Operation "Citadel"), vol. 7, *Beiträge zur Militärand- und Kriegsgeschichte* (Contributions to Military History and the History of War) (Stuttgart: Deustche Verlags-Anstalt, 1966), 207n.299), the Soviets had put down an average of 1,500 antitank mines and 1,700 antipersonnel mines per kilometer of front line in the Kursk Bulge.
19. Robert A. Doughty, "French Antitank Doctrine, 1940. The Antidote That Failed," *Military Review* 56, no. 5 (May 1976): 48n.53.
20. Ruby, *Sedan,* 49f.

21. Doughty, *Breaking Point,* 119.
22. Berben and Iselin, *Die Deutschen kommen,* 137.
23. Jean Vidalenc, "Les divisions de série 'B' dans l'armée française pendant la campagne de France 1939–1940" (The Series "B" Divisions in the French Army during the Campaign in France, 1939–1940), *RHA* no. 4 (1980): 106ff., 119f.
24. Berben and Iselin, *Die Deutschen kommen,* 138.
25. Hermann Balck, *Ordnung im Chaos. Erinnerungen 1893–1948* (Order in Chaos. Memoirs, 1893–1948) (Osnabrück: Biblio Verlag, 1980), 267.
26. See, for example, Guderian, *Erinnerungen,* 92.
27. Dossier 9a: Rapport capitaine Auzas (20. Dezember 1940) (File 9a: Report of Captain Auzas [20 December 1940]), 1, SHAT, 34 N 174, 295ème Régiment d'Infanterie (295th Infantry Regiment).
28. Capitaine Carribou: Considérations générales (Captain Carribou: General Considerations), 7, SHAT, 34 N 145, 147ème Régiment d'Infanterie de Forteresse (147th Fortress Infantry Regiment), sheet 8.
29. See the various after-action reports prepared by Carribou under the same file number.
30. See also the brilliant analysis that the Israeli military historian Martin van Creveld prepared for the Americans, which is a comparison of the combat effectiveness of the U.S. Army and the German Wehrmacht during World War II: *Kampfkraft. Militärische Organisation und militärische Leistung 1939–1945* (*Fighting Power. Military Organization and Military Performance*) (Freiburg, 1989), 203f., 207. English-language version, *Fighting Power: German and U.S. Army Performance, 1939–1945* (Westport, Conn.: Greenwood Press, 1982).
31. Concerning the insertion of the 71st Infantry Division, see in SHAT, 32 N 251, 55ème Division d'Infanterie (55th Infantry Division), Dossier 1: Chef d'Escadron Labarbarie, "La 55e division d'infanterie à la bataille de Sedan" (File 1: Squadron Commander Labarbarie, "The 55th Infantry Division in the Battle of Sedan"); in SHAT, 32 N 254, 55ème Division d'Infanterie, 4ème bureau (55th Infantry Division, 4th Bureau), Dossier 4: Colonel Chaligne, Rapport d'opérations pour les journées dés 10 au 14 mai 1940 (File 4: Colonel Chaligne, Report on Operations for 10 to 14 May 1940), 9f., and Récit des événements vecus par l'I.D.55 du 10 au 15 mai 1940 (Report on Events Experienced by the 55th Infantry Division, from 10 to 15 May 1940), 10f.; in SHAT, 34 N 145, 147ème Régiment d'Infanterie de Forteresse: Capitaine Joly d'Aussy, Journal de marche (combats de Sedan) (Captain Joly d'Aussy, March Movement Journal [fighting around Sedan]); in SHAT, 34 N 174, 295ème Régiment d'Infanterie: Dossier 9: Rapport de Chef de Bataillon de Réserve Arnoul (File 9: Report of Reserve Battalion Commander Arnoul), 5ff.; Rapport de Commandant de Monferrand (Report of Major de Monferrand), 2f.; Rapport du Lieutenant-Colonel Demay (10 au 14 mai) (Report of Lieutenant Colonel Demay [May 10 to 14]), and Demay, Rapport sur les événements des journées dés 13 et 14 May (Report on the Events of May 13 and 14).
32. Guderian, *Panzer Leader,* 100; *Erinnerungen,* 90.
33. For example, see Deighton, *Blitzkrieg,* 269f.
34. PzKorps Guderian, KTB, BA-MA, RH 21–2/41, 19.
35. Guderian and Loerzer had already initially tested that method during the Polish Campaign at Mlawa on 3 September 1939.
36. Durchbruch der Gruppe von Kleist, BA-MA, RH 21–1/381, pt. 1, 31, and pt. 2, 17f.; Akten des Panzerkorps Guderian, BA-MA, RH 21–2/41, 19; Schreiben an Generalkom-

mando II. Fliegerkorps vom 31.5 (Letter to Headquarters, II Air Corps, 31 May), 1.f., RH 21–2/45; Guderian, *Erinnerungen,* 90; Liddell Hart, *Jetzt dürfen sie reden,* 216.

37. 2.PzDiv, Planübung 30.4.1940 (2d Panzer Division, map exercise, 30 April 1940), BA-MA, RH 27–2/92.
38. Schreiben des Generals v. Kleist an Guderian (XIX.A.K.) vom 18.4.1940 [Letter from General von Kleist to Guderian (XIX Army Corps), 18 April 1940], BA-MA, RH 21–1/20, sheet 26.
39. Paul Deichmann, *Der Chef im Hintergrund* (Chief of Staff in the Background) (Munich and Hamburg, 1979), 100f.; Guderian, *Panzer Leader,* 101f., 104, and *Erinnerungen,* 91f., 94.
40. Akten der PzGruppe Kleist, BA-MA, RH 21–1/22, 7f.; Durchbruch der Gruppe von Kleist, BA-MA, RH 21–1/381, pt. 2, 19f.; see also 45; Gruppenbefehl Nr. 3 (Group Order No. 3), RH 21–1/23, sheet 135; Zeitzler, "Panzer-Gruppe v. Kleist," *EWKde* 8, no. 5 (1959): 240.
41. PzGruppe Kleist, KTB, Eintragung vom 13.4.1940 (Panzer Group Kleist, War Diary, entry of 13 April 1940), BA-MA, RH 21–1/18.
42. BA-MA, RH 21–1/20, sheet 26.
43. The various map exercises can be found above all in Akten des PzKorps Guderian, BA-MA, RH 21–2/32, RH 21–2/33, RH 21–2/34, RH 21–2/36, as well as the 1st, 2d, and 10th Panzer divisions, BA-MA, RH 27–1/5, RH 27–2/92, RH 27–10/4, RH 27–10/7b. The divisions were numbered differently for camouflage reasons; a "2" had been put in front of the particular number. So, for example, the 1st Panzer Division was referred to as "21st Panzer Division."
44. Stoves, *1. Panzer-Division,* 95; see also Dermot Bradley, *Walther Wenck. General der Panzertruppe* (Walther Wenck, General of Panzer Troops) (Osnabrück: Biblio-Verlag, 1981), 139f.; Guderian, *Erinnerungen,* 91; Balck, *Ordnung im Chaos,* 269; 1.PzDiv, BA-MA, RH 27–1/170, 17. The 10th Panzer Division worked the problem the same way and thus fell back on the orders from the last map exercise in Bernkastel, see 10.PzDiv, KTB (10th Panzer Division, War Diary), BA-MA, RH 27–10/9, 13 May 1940, 0230 hours.
45. Quoted from Stoves, *1. Panzer-Division,* 96.
46. 1.PzDiv, KTB (1st Panzer Division, War Diary), BA-MA, RH 27–1/170, 124. The artillery units were assigned as follows: 1st Panzer Division: 73d Artillery Regiment (I./73; II./73; II./56); 49th Artillery Regiment (II./45; II./69; III./74; III./90 [= I./105], 616th Heavy Mortar Battalion). 2d Panzer Division: I./74; II./74. 10th Panzer Division: I./90; II./90. See also 1.PzDiv, BA-MA, RH 27–1/170, 124.
47. Due to its small proportion of active duty personnel, the 55th Infantry Division had been disproportionately reinforced with artillery and had 140 tubes. By 13 May, it received another 34 guns (see Organization Chart, 147); see Doughty, *Breaking Point,* 113.
48. Grandsard, *Le 10e Corps d'armée,* 93ff., 112ff., 124ff.
49. For example, the Nebelwerfer-Abteilung 1 (1st Rocket Launcher Battalion) (multiple-barrel rocket launchers) was also earmarked as a supporting unit but remained stuck in the Ardennes traffic jam and was not employed in action.
50. Akten 1.PzDiv (Files, 1st Panzer Division), BA-MA, RH 27–1/14, 26.
51. Quoted from Liddell Hart, *The German Generals Talk,* 127, and *Jetzt dürfen sie reden,* 215.

52. Ruby, *Sedan,* 127.
53. For example, see Horne, *Über die Maas,* 228.
54. PzGr Kleist, BA-MA, RH 21–1/23, sheet 135.
55. The original files of the Luftwaffe for the raid on Sedan were burned rather extensively; nevertheless, the operational planning and course of this vast mission can be reconstructed for the most part. For example, see the following files of BA-MA: Lageberichte Luftwaffenführungsstab, Ic (Luftwaffe Operations Staff Situation Reports, Intelligence Officer), RM 7/337, sheet 52f. (4.), 59ff.; Hans Seidemann, Einsätze des VIII. Fliegerkorps (Operations of VIII Air Corps), N 406/4, 28ff.; Einsatzbereitschaft der Fliegenden Verbände, 14.5. 1940 (Operational Readiness of Flying Units, 14 May 1940), RL 2 III/736; VIII. Fliegerkorps, Einsatz, 13.5.1940 (VIII Air Corps, Operations, 13 May 1940), RL 8/43; VIII. Fliegerkorps, KTB, 13.5.1940, RL 8/45; I./ Kampfgeschwader 53, KTB (1st Squadron, 53d Bomber Wing, War Diary), 28ff., RL 10/86; Ibel, Jagdgeschwader 27 (27th Fighter Wing), 31ff., RL 10/591; Einsatz des II.Fliegerkorps im Frankreichfeldzug (Employment of II Air Corps during the Campaign against France), 1, ZA 3/44; and Die Bedeutung des Übergangs über die Maas (The Importance of the Crossing of the Meuse River); Sigismund Freiherr von Falkenstein, Die Unterstützung des deutschen Heeres durch die deutsche Luftwaffe im II. Weltkrieg (Entwurf) (German Luftwaffe Support for the German Army during World War II [Draft]), Lw 133/1, sheets 415ff.; HGr A: RH 19 I/37, sheets 102, 108; AOK 12 (Commander in Chief, Twelfth Army), RH 20–12/36, sheet 205; PzGruppe Kleist: RH 21–1/22, 10; Durchbruch der Gruppe von Kleist, BA-MA, RH 21–1/381, pt. 2, 23f.; PzKorps Guderian (Panzer Corps Guderian): RH 21–2/41, 25f., 31; Korpsbefehl Nr. 3 vom 13.5.1940 (mit Anl.) (Corps Order No. 3, 13 May 1940 [with apps.]), RH 21–2/43; Eintragung 13.5.1940 und Schreiben an Generalkommando II.Fliegerkorps vom 31.5.1940 (Entry on 13 May 1940, and letter to Headquarters, II Air Corps, dated 31 May 1940), RH 21–2/45; Funksprüche Fliegerverbindungsoffizier vom 13.5 (Radio messages, Air Liaison Officer, 13 May), RH 21–2/852; 1.PzDiv: RH 27–1/14, 7, 26; RH 27–1/170, 18, 123, 125f.; Speidel, Der Einsatz, pt. 3, 166f., 230f., 233, BA-MA, Study Lw 3/2; and apps. 47, 48, 50, Study Lw 3/4a; General der Flieger a.D. Paul Deichmann, Die Unterstützung des Heeres durch die deutsche Luftwaffe im Zweiten Weltkrieg (The German Luftwaffe Support of the Army in the Second World War), Study Lw, 228 (sheets 232ff.), BA-MA. Additional important details on the firing plan can be found in the previously mentioned map exercises of the Panzer Corps Guderian and the three Panzer divisions.

In the bibliography see: Guderian, *Erinnerungen,* 91f.; Deichmann, *Chef,* 100f.; Stoves, *1. Panzer-Division,* 89, 92; Cajus Bekker, *Angriffshöhe 4000. Ein Kriegstagebuch der deutschen Luftwaffe* (Attack Altitude 4,000: A War Diary of the German Luftwaffe) (Oldenburg: G. Stalling Verlag,1964), 142f.; F. W. von Mellenthin, *Panzerschlachten: Eine Studie über den Einsatz von Panzerverbänden in Zweiten Weltkrieg* (Panzer Battles: A Study in the Employment of Panzer Units during the Second World War) (Neckargemünd: Kurt Vowinckel, 1963), 23, English-language version, *Panzer Battles: A Study of the Employment of Armor in the Second World War* (Norman: University of Oklahoma Press, 1956); Hermann Freter, *Fla nach vorn! Die Fliegerabwehr-Waffe des Heeres und ihre Doppelrolle im Zweiten Weltkrieg* (Light Flak, Forward! The Antiaircraft Arm of the Army and Its Double Role in the Second World War) (Eßlingen, 1971), vol. 1, 143f., 179ff.; Kielmansegg, "Bemerkungen," 153f.; Balke, *Luftkrieg,* vol. 1, 87ff. For the French perspective, see the following: Ruby, *Sedan,*

126ff.; Grandsard, *Le 10e Corps d'armée,* 132ff., 152ff.; Commandant (Major) Rogé, "La Campagne de France. Vue par le Général Guderian" (The Campaign in France, as Seen by General Guderian), *RHA* 3, no. 1 (1947): 116ff. Other authentic descriptions can be found in the Archives of SHAT in Vincennes.

56. Oberst Schwartzkopff survived the triumph of his dive-bombers by just one day. He was shot down on 14 May near Le Chesne (south of Sedan). His grave is located in the military cemetery of Noyers-Pont Maugis at Sedan. Since he was promoted posthumously, the inscription on the tombstone reads "Generalmajor" (Brigadier General).
57. Ulf Balke made the precise calculation on the basis of the Files of BA-MA as well as privately owned documentation.
58. The original documents for the rolling raid on 13 May were burned. A fragment of the target map and the firing plan can be found in the Akten der 2.PzDiv (Files of 2d Panzer Division), BA-MA, RH 27–2/92. It stems from the prior map exercise on 30 April 1940. In the target map, the northern part of the Meuse River loop of Sedan is marked as target area K, whereas the individual target groups are numbered in succession from 1 to 10. In target area L, which adjoins to the south thereof, one can also recognize some bunkers that were reconnoitered by the Luftwaffe and that were marked as individual targets. Thus, the French bunkers 7 ter, 104, and 7 bis are numbered 118, 121, and 122.
59. Loerzer had the job of coordinating the employment of a total of 23 bomber and dive-bomber groups.
60. Balke, *Luftkrieg,* vol. 1, 89.
61. Communication from General Graf von Kielmansegg.
62. Bericht des Unteroffiziers Prümers (Report by Unteroffizier [Sergeant] Prümer), quoted in Stoves, *1. Panzer-Division,* 92.
63. Novak, "Inferno" (Inferno), in *Mit den Panzern,* 121.
64. Quoted from the German translation in Berben and Iselin, *Die Deutschen kommen,* 172f. About a year later, 1st Lieutenant Michard inspected for the French Army Historical Service the battlefield of Sedan, which had hardly changed at all, and systematically investigated the damage to each bunker. He was astonished by the size of the bomb craters, some of which had a diameter of 15 meters and a depth of allegedly 7 meters (see Dossier 4: Renseignements rapportés par M. Michard (File 4: "Information Reported by Mr. Michard"), SHAT, 34 N 145, 147ème Régiment d'Infanterie de Forteresse.
65. Kielmansegg, "Bemerkungen," 154, supplemented by additional communications to the author.
66. Oberstleutnant a.D. Eberhard Wackernagel made written documentation available to the author.
67. Bericht Oberleutnant v. Courbière (6.IRGD), 13.5.1940 [Report by Oberleutnant von Courbière (6th Company, Infantry Regiment Großdeutschland), 13 May 1940], BA-MA, RH 37/6391.
68. Concerning the attack by the Infantry Regiment Großdeutschland, see the after-action reports collected in the Files of BA-MA: 11.Kp/IRGD (11th Company, Infantry Regiment Großdeutschland), 5f., RH 37/6327; II./IRGD (2d Battalion, Infantry Regiment Großdeutschland), 2f., RH 37/6328; Panzerjägerkompanie, 13.5.1940 (Antitank Company, 13 May 1940), RH 37/6332; 6.Kp (Courbière), and 8.Kp (Bethge) (8th Company [Bethge]), RH 37/6391. See also Spaeter, *Großdeutschland,* 111ff. Helmuth Spaeter made numerous documents available to the author from his personal files);

Durian, *Großdeutschland,* 56ff. From the French viewpoint, see Dossier 4: Récit des événements vecus par l'I.D.55 du 10 au 15 mai 1940 (File 4: Report on Events Experienced by the 55th Infantry Division, from 10 to 15 May 1940), 15, in SHAT 32 N 254, 55ème Division d'Infanterie, 4ème bureau; Gounelle, *Sedan,* 148, 170f., 177ff.; Grandsard, *Le 10e Corps d'armée,* 156ff.

69. Only one engineer squad from 2d Company, 43d Assault Engineer Battalion, was subordinated for this mission; using satchel charges, it knocked out several bunkers on Hill 247. See also, Unser Einsatz im Westen vom 10 Mai bis 21. Juni 1940 (KTB 2. Kompanie/Sturmpionier-Bataillon 43) ("Our Employment in the West" [War Diary, 2d Company, 43d Assault Engineer Battalion]), 16f. (in private hands).
70. Bericht Oberleutnant v. Courbière (6.IRGD), 13.5.1940, BA-MA, RH 37/6391, 2.
71. Guderian, *Panzer Leader,* 102; *Erinnerungen,* 92.
72. Akten 1.PzDiv (Files, 1st Panzer Division): BA-MA, RH 27–1/14, sheets 27f., 114ff., 117f.; RH 27–1/170, 18f.; Stoves, 1. Panzer-Division, 93f.; Rapport Capitaine Foucault (Report of Captain Foucault), pt. 1, 1f., pt. 2 (handwritten), 13f., SHAT, 34 N 178, 331ème Régiment d'Infanterie (331st Infantry Regiment); Gounelle, *Sedan,* 145, 177ff.
73. Oberstleutnant a.D. Schütze made Oberleutnant Korthals's after-action report available to the author.
74. The smoke from the smoke candles misled quite a few French soldiers into assuming that the Germans had used flamethrowers. The breakthrough of the extended Maginot Line at Sedan took place so quickly that the flamethrowers that were moved up later were not employed at all. See Arbeitsstab Pioniergeschichte, 1./Sturm-Pionierbataillon 43, Bericht (Engineer History Study Staff, 1st Company, 43d Assault Engineer Battalion, Report), BA-MA, RH 12–5/397, sheet 3, as well as the document of 2.Kompanie: "Unser Einsatz im Westen," 16f. (in private hands). This was confirmed for the author when he questioned eyewitnesses.
75. German and French reports to date about the decisive breakthrough at Bellevue reveal considerable discrepancies as far as the time is concerned. The files of the SHAT in Paris indicate that the attackers crossed the Sedan-Donchery road as early as 1730 (1830 German time) and then attacked the artillery casemate. German files, on the other hand, beyond any doubt show that the 1st Rifle Regiment did not cross that road until 1915. The solution to this riddle is offered by the hitherto missing after-action report by Oberleutnant Korthals. The latter attacked around 1830, sweeping around to the right, across the road, and pushed into the famous "gap."
76. From the French viewpoint, see above all the report by 1st Lieutenant Drapier, the commanding officer of the Centre de résistance "de la Crête." His bunker, with the observation cupola that is still there today, was located right above Bunker 102; see in SHAT, 34 N 145, 147ème Régiment d'Infanterie de Forteresse: Extraits d'une lettre de Lieutenant Drapier (Extracts from a Letter by Lieutenant Drapier) as well as Fiche 340 (Drapier); Chef de Bataillon Crousse, "Les opérations de Sedan 10–14 mai 1940" (Battalion Commander Crousse, "The Operations at Sedan from 10 to 14 May 1940"), 10ff.; see also in SHAT, 32 N 254, 55ème Division d'Infanterie, 4ème: Dossier 4: Colonel Chaligne, Rapport d'opérations, 12ff. As for secondary literature, see Berben and Iselin, *Die Deutschen kommen,* 164, 189f., 200, 226ff., 250; Doughty, *Breaking Point,* 171ff., 185ff.
77. Akten 1.PzDiv (Files, 1st Panzer Division): BA-MA, RH 27–1/14, sheets 28, 114f., 117f.; RH 27–1/170, 19; Stoves, 1. Panzer-Division, 94; Balck, *Ordnung im Chaos,*

270f. Major i.G. a.D. Braune-Krickau, Balck's former aide, gave the author valuable information on the fighting around Sedan. Concerning the fight for Hill 301, from the French viewpoint, see: in SHAT, 34 N 145, 147ème Régiment d'Infanterie de Forteresse: Crousse, "Les opérations de Sedan," 15ff.; in SHAT, 34 N 178, 331ème Régiment d'Infanterie (331st Infantry Regiment): Rapport Capitaine Foucault, pt. 2, 15ff., and Compte rendu du Capitaine Litalien (Report by Captain Litalien), 5f.; Gounelle, *Sedan,* 183f. A keen summary can be found in Doughty, *Breaking Point,* 187ff.

78. Spruch Nr. 417 (Bl.424) vom 13.5., 22.50 Uhr (Radio message no. 417 [sheet 424], 13 May, 2250), BA-MA, RH 27–1/5.
79. 10.PzDiv: KTB, 13.5.1940, BA-MA, RH 27–10/9; Div. Bef., 13.5. (Division Order, 13 May), RH 27–10/107, sheets 8ff.
80. 10.PzDiv: KTB, 13.5.1940, BA-MA, RH 27–10/9; PzPi(mot) 49, KTB, RH 46/743, 5; "Pi 49 im Feldzug in Frankreich" (The 49th Engineers in the Campaign in France), sheet 2 (privately owned); Wolfgang Fischer, *Ohne die Gnade der späten Geburt* (Without the Grace of Late Birth) (Munich: F. A. Herbig, 1990), 58ff.; Hans Lüke, *Die Geschichte des Regiments 69* (The History of Regiment 69) (Hamburg, 1986), 53.
81. 10.SchtzBrig, KTB (10th Rifle Brigade, War Diary), BA-MA, RH 37/1910, 8.
82. Schulze, "Erster Einsatz vor Sedan" (First Action in Front of Sedan), *Militär-Wochenblatt* 125, no. 43 (1941): col. 1738.
83. Written communication from Major i.G. a.D. Sailer.
84. KTB Schützenregiment 86 (War Diary, 86th Rifle Regiment), 6f. (privately owned).
85. The after-action report by Feldwebel Rubarth, cited here in excerpts, is reprinted in Erhard Wittek, *Die Soldatische Tat. Berichte von Mitkämpfern des Heeres im Westfeldzug 1940.* (A Soldierly Deed: Reports from Comrades-in Arms of the Army in the Western Campaign, 1940) (Berlin: Im Deutschen Verlag, 1941), 22ff.; see also Leixner, "Die Bunker bei Sedan fallen" (The Bunkers at Sedan Are Falling), in *Mit den Panzern,* 127ff.; PzPi (mot) 49, KTB, BA-MA, RH 46/743, 5f.; "Pi 49 im Feldzug in Frankreich," 2ff. (privately owned); Robert Brüning and Alex Buchner, *Unteroffiziere entscheiden ein Gefecht* (Sergeants Decide a Combat Action) (Bonn and Herford, 1981), 99ff.; Lucke, "Übergang erzwungen" (Forced Crossing), *Korps Guderian: Berichte und Bilder zur Erinnerung an den Siegeszug vom 10. Mai bis zum 28. Mai unter Führung des Generals der Panzertruppe Guderian* (Corps Guderian: Stories and Pictures towards the Memoir of the Victory March from 10 May to 28 May under Command of General of Panzer Troops Guderian) (Berlin, 1942), 51ff.; Fischer, *Ohne die Gnade der späten Geburt,* 61. The author received important information from Major i.G. a.D. Sailer, who, at that time in his capacity as battalion adjutant of the 49th Panzer Engineer Battalion, had to justify the recommendation for the award of the Knight's Cross to Feldwebel Rubarth. Valuable hints were also received from Mr. Albert Schick, of the Veterans Association of the 10th Panzer Division. He made a series of informative documents available. As for the French viewpoint, see Olivier, "Sedan, mai 40. Le secteur de la gare (Rapport de l'Adjutant-Chief Olivier, 5e Compagnie de mitrailleuses du 147e R.I.F.)" (Sedan, May 40. The Railroad Station Sector [Report of Chief Warrant Officer Olivier, 5th Machine Gun Company, 147th Fortress Infantry Regiment]), *Le Pays Sedanais* 45, n.s., no. 7 (1980); Rapport du Lieutenant Lasson (Report of Lieutenant Lasson) and File 4: After-Action reports, Leflon, Loritte, Thirache, SHAT, 34 N 145, 147ème Régiment d'Infanterie de Fortresse; File 9a: After-Action Reports, Auzas and Gabel, SHAT, 34 N 174, 295ème Régiment d'Infanterie. See also Berben and Iselin, *Die Deutschen kommen,* 165, 197ff., 224; Hans

von Dach, "Panzer durchbrechen eine Armeestellung," *Schweizer Soldat* 47, no. 2 (1972): 79; no. 5 (1972): 50; Doughty, *Breaking Point,* 155ff., 175ff., 181ff.

86. The four bunkers were of the "*abri sous rondins*" (shelter on logs) type, in other words, defensive facilities made of massive logs covered with dirt.
87. Captain Foucault's after-action report (SHAT, 34 N 178, 14) confirms the capture of Bunker "8 ter" by an assault team that advanced from Wadelincourt.
88. A memorial tablet on Bunker 220 (at the railroad crossing north of Wadelincourt) states that the French bunker occupants had been "captured and shot by the Germans." This short description is in error according to the view of the Veterans Association of the 10th Panzer Division. After the bunker occupants had capitulated, one of the previously captured French soldiers pulled Leutnant Hanbauer to the ground by grabbing him from behind. This led to a brawl in which other French prisoners of war also interfered. Thereupon, a German soldier who had come running over opened fire (this version was confirmed by the Gefechtsbericht der 2.Kp/SchtzRgt 86 [After-Action report of 2d Company, 86th Rifle Regiment]: BA-MA, RH 37/138, sheet 25). The behavior of the French prisoners of war was contrary to the provisions of the Hague Rules of Warfare (Convention). Accordingly, a soldier who has surrendered loses his combatant status and no longer has the right to become involved in any combat action.
89. Bericht des I.Btl/SchtzRgt 86 über den Maasübergang bei Sedan (Report of 1st Battalion, 86th Rifle Regiment, on the Meuse River crossing at Sedan) (privately owned); Leutnant Hanbauer, Einsatz der 2.Kompanie bei Sedan (Employment of 2d Company at Sedan) (privately owned); KTB, Schützenregiment 86: 13.5.1940 (War Diary, 86th Rifle Regiment: 13 May 1940), 7 (privately owned); Kronbügel, Kradschützen vor: 7. Kp SchtzRgt 86 im Frankreich (Motorcycle Riflemen, Forward!: 7th Company, 86th Rifle Regiment in France), 4ff. (privately owned); 10.PzDiv, KTB. 13.5.1940, BA-MA, RH 27–10/9; Antrag Ritterkreuz Hanbauer (Recommendation for Award of Knight's Cross for Hanbauer), RH 27–10/68; Gefechtsbericht der 2.Kp/SchtzRgt 86, sheets 21ff., BA-MA, RH 37/138; 10.SchtzBrig, KTB, RH 37/1910, 8f.; Lucke, "Übergang," *Korps Guderian,* 51ff.
90. See also Dossier 4: Renseignements rapportés par M. Michard (File 4: Information Reported by Mr. Michard), SHAT, 34 N 145, 147ème Régiment d'Infanterie de Forteresse.
91. The 2d Panzer Division was also referred to as the Viennese Panzer Division.
92. Concerning the operations of the 2d Panzer Division, see the Akten der 2.PzDiv: BA-MA, RH 27–2/1; 17ff.; RH 27–2/11, 4f.; RH 27–2/92 (map exercises); RH 27–2/93, 3f.; Arbeitsstab Pioniergeschichte (Engineer History Study Staff), RH 12–5/425, 2ff.; RHD 29/8: General der Pioniere und Festungen, "Denkschrift über die Französische Landesbefestigung" (General of Engineers and Fortifications, "Memorandum on French Fortifications"), 260ff.; Gen. d. Inf. a.D. Rudolf Hoffmann, Angriff gegen Befestigungsanlagen. Deutsche Angriffe gegen ständige und verstärkte feldmäßige Befestigungsanlagen im Zweiten Weltkrieg (Attack against Fortifications. German Attacks against Permanent and Reinforced Improvised Fortifications during World War II), Study P–203, 121ff., BA-MA; Koelitz, "Die Schützen sind drüben," in *Mit den Panzern,* 142ff.; Eduard Curt Christophé, *Wir stoßen mit Panzern zum Meer* (We Push to the Sea with Our Panzers) (Berlin: Steiniger Verlag, 1940), 28ff.; Wilhelm Wassung, "Maas-Übergang bei Donchery" (Meuse River Crossing at Donchery), *Mitteilungsblatt der (2.) Wiener Division* (Bulletin of the [2d] Viennese Panzer Division), ser. 39 (1970), no. 2 (May), 3ff.; Gegenbauer, "Im Westen. Mai 1940" (In the West, May 1940), *Mitteilungsblatt der (2.) Wiener Division,* ser. 23, May 1966, 45ff.; Franz-

Joseph Strauß, *Friedensand- und Kriegserlebnisse einer Generation. Ein Kapitel Weltgeschichte aus der Sicht der Panzerjäger-Abteilung 38 (SF) in der ehem. 2. (Wiener) Panzerdivision* (Peacetime and Wartime Experiences of a Generation: A Chapter in World History from the Viewpoint of the 38th Antitank Battalion [Self-Propelled] in the Former 2d [Viennese] Panzer Division) (Kitzingen: desktop publication, 1981), 45ff. Mr. Hans-Christoph Carlowitz, of the Veterans Association of the Former Viennese Panzer Division, made a number of privately owned documents available to the author (e.g., extracts from the war diaries of the 3d and 4th Panzer Regiments). From the French viewpoint, see the following: SHAT, 32 N 254, 55ème Division d'Infanterie, 4ème bureau: Dossier 4: Récit des événements vécus par l'I.D. 55 du 10 au 15 mai 1940, 13ff., and Colonel Chaligne, Rapport d'opérations pour les journées dés 10 au 14 mai 1940, 12ff.; SHAT, 34 N 145, 147ème Régiment d'Infanterie de Fortresse: Extraits d'une lettre du Lieutenant Drapier, 2ff., and Fiche No. 340 (Drapier), and Crousse, Les opérations de Sedan, 9ff. As for secondary literature, see Gounelle, *Sedan,* 145, 167, 177, 183; Berben and Iselin, *Die Deutschen kommen,* 164. 189f., 226ff., 250.

93. Koelitz, "Die Schützen sind drüben," in *Mit den Panzern,* 144.
94. Two battalions crossed the Meuse River at this point during the night. The right-wing attack group was taken out of the line and managed to cross to the other bank at Montimont or at the destroyed railroad bridge, 1,000 meters northwest of Castle Bellevue. The 2d Panzer Brigade also moved into the combat sector of the 1st Panzer Division and, starting at 1113 on 14 May, rolled over the Meuse River on the newly built military bridge at Gaulier. The military bridge of the 2d Panzer Division (500 meters to the east of the destroyed Meuse River bridge of Donchery) was not completed until 0500 on 15 May.
95. Durchbruch der Gruppe von Kleist, BA-MA, RH 21–1/381, pt. 2, 45.
96. Concerning the construction of the military bridge at Gaulier, see the Akten des PzKorps Guderian: Gen.Kdo. XIX A.K., Abt. Ia/Pi, Nr. 472/40, 18.(25.)4.1940, Betr. Überwindung der Semois und Maas (Files of the Panzer Corps Guderian: HQ, XIX Army Corps, Operations/Engineer Section, No. 472/40, 18 [25] April 1940, Concerning the Crossing of the Semois and the Meuse Rivers), BA-MA, RH 21–2/33; RH 21–2/36, sheet 31; RH 21–2/41, 27; RH 21–2/43, sheet 66; from the Akten der 1.PzDiv: RH 27–1/5 (Funksprüche) (radio messages); RH 27–1/14, sheet 269f.; RH 27–1/170, 18ff.; Kurt Grübnau, "Brückenschlag über die Maas westlich Sedan für den Übergang einer Panzerdivision" (Building a Bridge Across the Meuse River west of Sedan for the Crossing of a Panzer Division), *Militär-Wochenblatt* 125, no. 27 (1941). Oberstleutnant a.D. Grübnau, who at that time had the job of organizing the Meuse River crossing, gave the author a series of written and verbal information items on this topic. Particularly valuable was also an unpublished study made available by Oberst-leutnant a.D. Hans-Jürgen Hartung ("Der Angriff über die Maas bei Sedan am 13.Mai 1940" [The Attack Across the Meuse River at Sedan on 13 May 1940]).
97. According to a communication from Oberstleutnant a.D. Grübnau, only a few armored scout cars as well as "one or two assault guns" were put across and that happened so late that they were not able to have any real effect.
98. Before that, only three armored reconnaissance patrols (consisting of one or two Panzer IIs each) had crossed the military bridge since about 0300 in order to reconnoiter to the south at dawn.

99. This is clearly indicated by the order—drafted during the 21 March war game in Koblenz—for the Meuse River crossing by the 1st Panzer Division (BA-MA, RH 27–1/5, sheet 434). In the sequence by which units were to cross the military bridge that was to be built, the two Panzer regiments were positioned relatively far to the rear. Only two companies of Panzer IVs were to be moved up front and were to cross the bridge behind the vehicles carrying the heavy weapons of the Rifle Brigade as well as elements of the artillery. But not even these two Panzer companies were employed in action. Instead, this passage was simply stricken from the order, in longhand.
100. Communication from General Graf von Kielmansegg to the author.
101. Quoted from Mellenthin, *Panzer Battles,* 16; *Panzerschlachten,* 27.
102. This bunker, which is still there today, is located 1,000 meters to the south of Bulson in a former stone quarry along the northeastern edge of the little woods at Fond Dagot.
103. The "Panic of Bulson" is documented in numerous after-action reports on file with SHAT in Paris; see 32 N 251, 55ème division d'Infanterie: Dossier 1: Labarbarie, La 55ème division d'infanterie à la bataille de Sedan 10–14 Mai 1940, 33ff.; SHAT 32 N 254, 55ème Division d'Infanterie, 4ème Bureau, Dossier 4: Colonel Chaligne, Rapport e'opérations pour les journées dès 10 au 14 mai 1940, 15ff., 30f., and Récit des événements vécus par l'I.D. 55 du 10 au 15 mai 1940, 16ff., 30f.; SHAT 32 N 318, 71ème Division d'Infanterie: Dossier 0: 71.D.I. (71st Infantry Division), Intercalaire, No. 2; Dossier 1: Rapport du Général Baudet concernant la 71e division (File 1: Report of General Baudet concerning the 71st Division), 8; Dossier 2: Rapport du Lt-Colonel Regnault (71.I.D.), 30.5.1941 (File 2: Report of Lieutenant Colonel Regnault [71st Infantry Division], dated 30 May 1941), pt. 9, 1; SHAT 34 N 174, 295ème Régiment d'Infanterie: Dossier 9: Rapport du Chef de Bataillon de Réserve Arnoul (File 9: Report of Battalion Commander of Reserve Arnoul), 8ff. See also Doughty, *Breaking Point,* 191ff., 240; Horne, *Über die Maas,* 239ff.; Berben and Iselin, *Die Deutschen kommen,* 232ff., 249f.; Dach, "Panzer," *Schweizer Soldat* 47, no. 5 (1972): 54; Shirer, *Zusammenbruch,* 678f.; Ruby, *Sedan,* 132ff.; Gounelle, *Sedan,* 186ff., 212ff.; Grandsard, *Le 10e Corps d'armée,* 141ff.; Paillat, *La guerre éclair,* 257f., 271ff.; Jean-Louis Crémieux-Brilhac, *Ouvriers et soldats* (Workers and Soldiers), vol. 2, *Les Français de l'an 40* (The French of 1940) (Paris; Robert Laffont, 1990), 575ff.; Paul Huvelin, "Sedan. Mai 1940: l'Armée française coupée en deux" (Sedan. May 1940: The French Army Cut in Two), *Historia,* no. 521 (May 1990), 57f.
104. Ruby, *Sedan,* 132f.
105. The entrance to the command bunker of Lieutenant Colonel Pinaud, who commanded the 147th Fortress Infantry Regiment, in the Frénois subsector, was located just south of Chaumont, in a curve of the road leading to Bulson. This meant that the erroneously reported Panzers would have had to drive directly past his command post. In the evening of 13 May, Pinaud and his staff officers denied several times that German Panzers were attacking from Chaumont and described these "objects" as "*chars fantômes*" (phantom tanks).
106. As stated earlier, the military bridge at Gaulier was not ready until 0010 on 14 May. Starting at 0300, three armored reconnaissance patrols drove across to the other bank. But the 1st Panzer Brigade was late and did not reach the bridge until 0720. The assumption that German Panzers or armored scout cars might already have crossed the Meuse River on ferries in the evening of 13 May and might have attacked through the Bois de la Marfée woods around 1900 cannot be confirmed on the basis of the available files. Oberstleutnant a.D. Grübnau, who at that time supervised the construction

of the military bridge at Gaulier, told the author that, indeed, a few armored vehicles were ferried across, although so late that "there was actually no support for the infantry." He emphasized: "Looking at the time comparison, one must therefore absolutely rule out the possibility that these armored vehicles could have been the real cause of the French Panzer panic."

107. German after-action reports actually mention that French tanks were discovered in the vicinity of Hill 301 (La Boulette). But, as indicated by the description given by Bernard Horen, *Fantassin de 40 ou le conteste contestataire* (The Footslogger of 1940 or The Uneven Fight) [n.p., n.d.], vol. 1, 38), these were not battle tanks but just a few obsolete tanks from World War I that had been used as tractors (possibly of the Renault FT 17 type). In this steep terrain, they carried construction material for the bunkers. In the dark of night, the attacking German soldiers mistakenly considered them to be "captured battle tanks."

108. General Lafontaine maintained later on that his division had fallen victim to the so-called Fifth Column. A search for the men responsible for the Sedan disaster was carried out under the Vichy Regime in the course of the Riom Trials. At that time, mention was made not only of German agents, but also of "communist elements" as causes of that "organized panic." Some officers had trouble providing evidence when they were required to explain who had given them permission to withdraw. Thus was spread the fairy tale of German motorcycle messengers in French uniforms who reportedly drove from command post to command post to drop off retreat orders. In a similar manner, there are also "*parachutistes*"—in other words, German paratroopers—who pop up in French after-action reports and who supposedly caused confusion behind the French lines. But such speculations are certainly false. At that point in time, the German paratroopers were committed in Holland and northern Belgium.

109. Quoted from Prioux, *Souvenirs de guerre 1939–1943* (Memoirs of the War, 1939–1943) (Paris: Flammarion, 1947), 86.

110. The bridge of the 10th Panzer Division along the southern edge of Sedan had, of course, been provisionally completed at around 0700 on 14 May, but regular crossings did not become possible until around 1100. Technical problems necessitated several interruptions on that day. The construction of the military bridge at Donchery on the other hand continued until 0500 on 15 May.

111. François d'Astier de la Vigerie, *Le ciel n'était pas vide. 1940* (The Sky Was Not Empty. 1940) (Paris, 1952), 107.

112. Ibid., 114.

113. Quoted from Philippe de Laubier, "Le bombardement français sur la Meuse. Le 14 mai 1940" (French Bombardment along the Meuse. 14 May 1940), *RHA* no. 160 (1985): 99.

114. See Files in the BA-MA: A.O.K. 12: Kriegsgliederungen (HQ, Twelfth Army: Wartime Organization), RH 20–12/4; Flakkorps I vom 9.4.1940 (I Flak Corps, 9 April 1940), RH 20–12/7; PzGruppe Kleist, Kriegsgliederungen (Panzer Group Kleist: Wartime Organization), RH 21–1/318; PzKorps Guderian: Kriegsgliederungen (Panzer Corps Guderian: Wartime Organization), RH 21–2/54; Decknamenlisten der Divisionen (Lists of Division Code Names), RH 21–2/852; Flakregiment 102, Ia vom 24.5 (102d Flak Regiment, Operations Section, 24 May), RH 21–2/63a; 2.PzDiv: KTB (War Diary), RH 27–2/1, 20; Kriegsgliederungen (Wartime Organization), RH 27–2/11; 10.PzDiv, RH 27–10/107, sheet 10; Auszug aus dem Kriegstagebuch des Flakregiments 102 (14.5.1950) (Extract from war diary of 102d Flak Regiment [14 May 1940]), RL 12/457; I./FlakRgt 18 (1st Battalion, 18th Flak Regiment), RL

12/545; Weise, I Flak Corps, BA-MA, Study D–111, 10ff.; KTB leichte Flakabteilung 83 (War Diary of 83d Light Flak Battalion) (privately owned), 5; Freter, *Fla,* 174ff.; Herman Freter, "Das war unser 'Sedan-Tag.' Die Heeres-Fla im Westfeldzug: 234 Abschüsse" (That Was Our "Day of Sedan": The Army Light Flak during the Campaign in the West: 234 Shot Down), *Neue Feuerwehr* (The New Fire Brigade), May 1986, 18f.; Hugo Novak, *Geschichte der ostpreußischen leichten Flakabteilung 71* (The History of the East Prussian 71st Light Flak Battalion) (Siegen, 1979), 38, 44ff.; Dach, "Panzer," *Schweizer Soldat* 47, no. 2 (1972): 80ff.

115. Some authors inadvertently include Flakabteilung I./38 (1st Battery, 38th Heavy Flak Battalion), that was under the command of III Army Corps during that particular phase.

116. The following were employed: three heavy battalions, each with 12 8.8-cm guns and 33 2-cm guns, as well as four light battalions, each with 9 3.7-cm guns and 24 2-cm guns. One must also consider that each of the light Flak companies of the three Panzer divisions had 12 2-cm antiaircraft guns: 2./Fla 59 (2d Battery, 59th Light Flak Battalion), with 1st Panzer Division; 2./Fla 47 (2d Battery, 47th Light Flak Battalion), with 2d Panzer Division; and 3./Fla 55 (3d Battery, 55th Light Flak Battalion), with 10th Panzer Division. Including those 36 tubes, there was a total of 303 antiaircraft guns. According to Generaloberst a.D. Weise, the Commanding General of I Flak Corps during the 1940 campaign in the west, the reinforced 102d Flak Regiment (Weise inadvertently wrote 101), during its action in the Sedan area, had as many as 321 guns, including 72 heavy ones and 249 medium and light antiaircraft guns (see also BA-MA, Study D 111, 10ff.)

117. Speidel, Der Einsatz, pt. 3, 239f., 246ff., 254f., BA-MA, Study Lw 3/2; Kammhuber, Das Problem der Erringung, BA-MA, Study Lw 12, vol. 2, 19f.; Einsatz des II.Fliegerkorps in Frankreich. Verschiedene Ausarbeitungen (Employment of II Air Corps in the Campaign in France. Miscellaneous Studies), ZA 3/44, BA-MA; Westen 1940, Lageberichte Luftflotten 2 und 3, vom 14.5.1940 (The West 1940, Situation Reports, Second and Third Air Fleets, 14 May 1940), 62f., ZA 3/59, BA-MA; Balke, *Luftkrieg,* vol. 1, 90f.; Bekker, *Angriffshöhe 4000,* 143ff.

118. Denis Richards and Hillary St. George Saunders, *The Fight at Odds,* vol. 1, *The Royal Air Force,* 1939–1945 (London: Her Majesty's Stationery Office, 1953), 120.

119. Kielmansegg, *Panzer,* 115f.

120. Concerning the employment of the Allied air forces and the losses suffered, see also Karl J. Walde, *Guderian* (Guderian) (Frankfurt am Main: Ullstein, 1967), 93; Gérard Giuliano, "Dans le ciel de Sedan, le 14 mai 1940" (In the Sky over Sedan, 14 May 1940), *Terres Ardennaises,* no. 21 (December 1987); J. Sacré, "14 mai 1940. Le Bombardement allié sur la tête de pont de Sedan" (14 May 1940. The Allied Bombing Raids against the Bridgehead at Sedan) and "La chasse au-dessus de Sedan" (The Fight Over Sedan), *Le Pays Sedanais* 55, no. 17 (1990); Laubier, "Le bombardement"; Gunsburg, *Divided,* 201f.; Horne, *Über die Maas,* 268ff.; Berben and Iselin, *Die Deutschen kommen,* 285ff.; Dach, "Panzer," *Schweizer Soldat* 47, no. 5 (1972): 56ff.; d'Astier de la Vigerie, *Le ciel,* 107ff.; Janusz Piekalkiewicz, *Luftkrieg,* 74; Richards, *Fight,* 120f.; *Histoire de l'aviation militaire français,* 376, 380; Robert Jackson, *Air War over France. May–June 1940* (London: Ian Allen, Ltd., 1974), 62ff.; Crémieux-Brilhac, *Ouvriers et soldats,* 659ff.; Danel, "En mai–juin 1940," *Icare* 56f., and "Le bombardement dans la bataille" (Bombardment in Battle), *Icare* no. 57 (spring–summer 1971): 63, 67; Raymond Brohon, "Le groupement de bombardement No 10" (The 10th Bomb Group), *Icare* no. 57 (spring–summer 1971): 88f.; Jean Veron, "Détruire

les ponts de la Meuse" (Destroying the Meuse River Bridges), *Icare* no. 57 (spring–summer 1971); Robert Ankaoua, "Le 14 mai à Sedan" (14 May at Sedan), *Icare* no. 57 (spring–summer 1971): 129ff. The statistics given in German files are considerably higher. This is due to the fact that several antiaircraft guns often simultaneously fired at the same aircraft and the downing of that aircraft, therefore, was reported several times.

121. For example, see Crémieux-Brilhac, *Ouvriers et soldats,* 659.
122. Churchill, *Their Finest Hour,* 41; *Der Zweiten Weltkrieg,* vol. 2, 1st book, 60.
123. Guderian, *Panzer Leader,* 105; *Erinnerungen,* 94f.
124. Quoted from Berben and Iselin, *Die Deutschen kommen,* 134f.
125. Grandsard, *Le 10e Corps d'armée,* 135.
126. Whether Cachou actually approved the way Lieutenant Colonel Labarthe had handled the situation is something that can no longer be reconstructed in view of the conflicting reports.
127. The order for the counterattack (ordre particulier No 32) covered merely half a page of text; see Dossier 6: 10ème Corps d'Armée, 3ème bureau (File 6: X Army Corps, 3d Bureau [Operations]), SHAT, 30 N 92: 10ème Corps d'Armée, 3ème bureau (X Army Corps, 3d Bureau).
128. Grandsard, *Le 10e Corps d'armée,* 165.
129. Lafontaine later on tried to justify himself by arguing that the formations earmarked for the counterattack had been placed under his command too late. But Grandsard unambiguously established that he had clearly regulated the chain of command already at 1900 (German time: 2000) when he ordered the commanding general of the 55th Infantry Division to counterattack; see Grandsard, *Le 10e Corps d'armée,* 143, 161ff.
130. The first elements of the 7th Tank Battalion were already rolling into Chémery when the orders were issued, shortly after 0500.
131. Dossier 4: Colonel Chaligne, 24, SHAT, 32 N 254: 55ème Division d'Infanterie, 4ème bureau.
132. Concerning the above, see above all Grandsard, *Le 10e Corps d'armée*, 134ff., 143f., 146ff., 161ff.; see also SHAT, 30 N 92: 10ème Corps d'Armée, 3ème bureau: Dossier 6: 10ème Corps d'Armée, 3ème bureau (Befehle) (File 6: X Army Corps, 3d Bureau [Operations Section] [orders]); SHAT, 32 N 251: 55ème Division d'Infanterie, Dossier 1: Labarbarie, 35ff.; Rapport du Général Lafontaine sur la bataille dès 13 et 14 mai 1940 (Report of General Lafontaine on the Battle on 13 and 14 May 1940), Dossier 1a: Général Lafontaine, Renseignements sur la 55e division (File 1a: General Lafontaine, "Information on the 55th Division"), SHAT 32 N 254: 55ème Division d'Infanterie, 4ème bureau: Dossier 4: Récit des événements, 22ff.; Colonel Chaligne, 20ff. In the bibliography see: Doughty, *Breaking Point,* 245ff.; see also Berben and Iselin, *Die Deutschen kommen,* 245ff., 261ff; Ruby, *Sedan,* 134ff., 148ff.; Gounelle, *Sedan,* 213ff., 233ff.
133. Grandsard, *Le 10e Corps d'armée,* 147.
134. Krajewski, "Die 'schwarzen Husaren' bei Bulson" (The "Black Hussars" at Bulson), in *Mit den Panzern,* 137.
135. The tanks of the FCM type (Forges et Chantiers de la Méditerranée) were actually among the weaker French models. Nevertheless, the FCM's 40-mm-thick armor gave the German Panzers considerable trouble. The German Panzer IV, with its short-barrel cannon, was able to fire for effect only at close range. The penetration performance of the Panzer III was also inadequate. Major i.G. a.D. von Grolman, who commanded a

Panzer company at that time in the tank battle of Bulson (with the rank of Oberleutnant), wrote the following to the author: "Our caliber (3.7-cm) was effective only between the turret and the chassis." The German Panzer I and Panzer II were completely unfit for tank battles and were kept back at a respectful distance. But the tank fight to some extent took place at very short ranges because the French FCM tanks also only had an obsolete 3.7-cm cannon.

136. Gefechtsbericht des Oberleutnants Beck-Broichsitter, IRGD (14.Mai) (After-Action report by Oberleutnant Beck-Broichsitter, Infantry Regiment Großdeutschland [14 May]), BA-MA, RH 37/6332.

137. The German Panzer battalions were thrown into battle in "zipper fashion": I. Abt/PzRgt2 (1st Battalion, 2d Panzer Regiment), to Bulson (including the Krajewski Company); II. Abt/PzRgt 2 (2d Battalion, 2d Panzer Regiment), to Connage (including von Kleist Company); II. Abt/PzRgt 1 (2d Battalion, 1st Panzer Regiment), to Bulson; I. Abt/PzRgt 1 (1st Battalion, 1st Panzer Regiment), to Connage.

138. Ruby, *Sedan,* 149.

139. Actually, the 213th Infantry Regiment also belonged to the 55th Infantry Division. It had been employed in the left-wing Villers-sur-Bar subsector until 7 May and was then replaced by the 331st Infantry Regiment. During the execution of the counterattack, it was noted as a positive feature that the formations were employed in a compact manner (that is to say, in terms of their original make-up), whereas the rotation principle had completely jumbled up the regiments that had remained in the Sedan Sector.

140. Doughty, *Breaking Point,* 264.

141. Concerning the course of the twin fight at Bulson and Connage, see the files (all BA-MA): Arbeitsstab Pioniergeschichte (Work Staff Engineer History), RH 12–5/397, p. 4; PzKorps Guderian, RH 21–2/41, 35; 1.PzDiv (1st Panzer Division): RH 27–1/14, sheets 7f., 29ff., 79f., 81f., 83f., 99, 120, 205f.; RH 27–1/170, 20ff.; Bericht II.Btl/IRGD, 14.5 (S.3) (Report, 2d Battalion, Infantry Regiment Großdeutschland, 14 May [3]), RH 37/6328; Panzerschlacht südlich Sedan, Pz.Jg.Kp./IRGD, 14 Mai (Panzer Battle South of Sedan, Antitank Gun Company, Infantry Regiment Großdeutschland, 14 May), RH 37/6332; Kriegschronik 15.IRGD (War Chronicle, 15th Company, Infantry Regiment Großdeutschland), RH 37/6335, 21ff.; Beck, Oblt., Amtlicher Bericht über das Gefecht bei Chémery am 14.5 (Oberleutnant Beck, "Official Report on the Action at Chémery on 14 May"), and Bericht Oblt. Beck aus Völk. Beobachter vom 1.1.1941 (Oblt. Beck from the Völk. Beobachter, 1 January 1941), RH 37/6391; 5.PzRgt 1, Tagebuch (5th Company, 1st Panzer Regiment, Diary), RH 39/30, 12f.; SHAT, 32 N 251: 55ème Division d'Infanterie: Général Lafontaine, "Renseignements sur la 55e division," 2f.; Rapport du Général Lafontaine (18.5.1940), 2ff.; Labarbarie, 39ff.; SHAT, 32 N 254: Dossier 4: Récit des événements, 24ff.; SHAT 32 N 254; Colonel Chaligne, 23ff.; SHAT, 34 N 174: 295ème Regiment d'Infanterie: Dossier 9: Rapport du Montferrand (sowie Rapport complementaire) (File 9: Report of Monferrand [as well as Complementary Report]); Rapport du Lieutenant-Colonel Demay (Report of Lieutenant Colonel Demay), 5f.; Guderian, *Erinnerungen,* 94; Balck, *Ordnung im Chaos,* 271ff.; Krajewski, "Die 'schwarzen Husaren' bei Bulson," in *Mit den Panzern,* 136ff.; Durian, *Großdeutschland,* 71ff., 85ff.; Christian von Lucke, *Die Geschichte des Panzer-Regiment 2* (The History of the 2d Panzer Regiment) (Stade, 1953), 31f.; Stoves, *1. Panzer-Division,* 97ff.; Dach, "Panzer," *Schweizer Soldat* 47, no. 2 (1972): 84ff., no. 5 (1972): 58ff.; Berben and Iselin, *Die Deutschen kommen,* 246ff., 261ff.; Doughty, *Breaking Point,* 255ff.; Grandsard, *Le 10e Corps d'armée,*

161ff.; Ruby, *Sedan,* 135ff., 148ff.; Gounelle, *Sedan,* 233ff., 299ff.; Le Goyet, "-Contre-attaques manquées," 111ff.; Paillat, *Le guerre éclair,* 261ff.; Gérard Giuliano, *Les combats du Mont-Dieu,* 14ff.; Yves Buffetaut, *Guderian perce à Sedan* (Guderian Broke Through at Sedan) (Paris, 1992), 40ff. The author received valuable indications from some eyewitnesses, for example, Oberst a.D. Christian von Lucke; Major i.G. a.D. Friedrich von Grolman, as well as Mr. Helmut Beck-Broichsitter, who at that time (with the rank of Oberleutnant) directed the employment of antitank guns near Connage.

Privately owned documents: Scheibe, "Panzer-Aufklärungs-Abteilung 4 im Westfeldzug" (The 4th Armored Reconnaissance Battalion in the Campaign in the West); Lesch, Bericht über ein Unternehmen [eines Panzerspähtrupps] am 14.Mai 1940 bei Chéhéry (Gefechtsbericht 2.Kp/PzRgt 2, abgefaßt 20.5.1940) [Handstreich auf die Brücke von Omicourt] (Report on a Mission [of a Panzer Reconnaissance Patrol] on 14 May 14, 1940, at Chéhéry (After-Action Report, 2d Company, 2d Panzer Regiment, Prepared on 20 May 1940 [Coup de Main on the Bridge at Omicourt]); "Feldzug gegen Frankreich (Sturmpionierbataillon 43), dabei Oberleutnant Korthals, Bericht der 3. Kompanie sowie Oberleutnant Koska, "Tagebuchblätter des Bataillonsadjutanten" (The Campaign against France [43d Assault Engineer Battalion], including Oberleutnant Korthals, "Report of 3d Company," as well as Oberleutnant Koska, "From the Diary of the Battalion Adjutant"); documents from the archives of the 1st and 2d Panzer regiments (via Mr. Rolf Stoves).

142. See also Gesammelte Funkssprüche vom 14. Mai (collected 14 May radio messages) in the Akten des PzKorps Guderian, BA-MA, RH 21–2/47a.
143. Gen. d.Inf a.D. Günther Blumentritt, Westfeldzug, vol. 2, Study P–208, 39f., BA-MA.
144. Schreiben Halders an Sodenstern vom 12.3.1940 (Halder's letter to Sodenstern, 12 March 1940), 5, BA-MA, RH 19 I/38, sheet 160; see also HGr A, KTB, RH 19 I/37, sheet 22.
145. Halder *KTB,* vol. 1, 231.
146. An advance detachment of the 1st Rifle Regiment had already taken the bridge across the Ardennes Canal at Omicourt, located farther to the north, around 0730. The 2d Panzer Division's infantry was able to take the bridge at Hannogne around 1200 and, soon thereafter, also the important bridge across the Ardennes Canal at Pont à Bar, near the place where the canal flows into the Meuse River. The first Panzers rode west cross that bridge, starting at 1430.
147. PzKorps Guderian, BA-MA, RH 21–2/41, 35ff.; 1.PzDiv, RH 27–1/170, 22f.; Guderian, Panzer Leader, 105–106, and Erinnerungen, 95; Walde, Guderian, 93; Bradley, Wenck, 141.
148. Gruppe Guderian Berichte (Group Guderian Reports), Berichte und Bilder zur Erinnerung an den Siegeszug vom 9. Juni bis zum 23. Juni1940 unter Führung des Generals der PzTruppe Guderian (Reports and Illustrations in Memory of the Victorious Campaign from 9 June to 23 June 1940, Under the Command of General of Panzer Troops Guderian) (Berlin, 1940), 7.
149. Quoted from Horne, *To Lose a Battle,* 539; *Über die Maas,* 456.
150. Clausewitz, *Vom Kriege,* 311; Clausewitz, *On War,* 180.
151. Gribble, "Blitzkrieg," 186.
152. The precise statistics can be determined completely only for the 2d Panzer Division (see *KTB,* BA-MA, RH 27–2/1, sheet 62f.). On 13 May, that Division suffered 27 dead, 86 wounded, and two missing. On 14 May, the figure was only seven dead

and 25 wounded. The casualty figures for the 1st and 10th Panzer divisions show up in the files only in fragments but, to the extent that they are there, they point to a lower casualty rate for the individual formations on 13 May than in the case of the 2d Panzer Division. That Division was the only one that did not manage the Meuse River crossing on its own because all attempts at crossing the river were repelled with bloody losses. The estimated figure of about 120 dead and 400 wounded is to that extent perhaps somewhat too high.

153. Quoted from Deighton, *Blitzkrieg,* 180 (226, German edition).
154. See the quantitative balance in the concluding chapter.
155. Pierre Le Goyet, *Le mystère Gamelin* (The Mystery of Gamelin) (Paris: Presses de la Cité, 1975), 316; see also his "La percée de Sedan," 25; Michael Glover, *The Fight for the Channel Ports. Calais to Brest, 1940: A Study in Confusion* (London: Leo Cooper, 1985), 33; Brausch, *Sedan,* 86; Freter, *Fla,* 142; Soldan, "Der Durchbruch über die Maas" (The Breakthrough over the Meuse), *MWR* 5, no. 3 (1940): 309; Uhle-Wettler, *Höhe- und Wendepunkte,* 291. French Supreme Commander Gamelin said that he knew in the afternoon of 15 May that the battle was lost (see his *Servir,* vol. 3, 399, also vol. 1, 342). French prime minister Reynaud appeared to have less illusion because, as far as he was concerned, everything had been decided already on 14 May. On 15 May, he sent Winston Churchill the following telegram: "We lost the battle last night. The route to Paris is open." (See Shirer, *Collapse,* 680; *Zusammenbruch,* 713).

Chapter 6

1. GenKdo XIX. AK, Ia (19.2.1940) (HQ, XIX Corps, Operations Section [19 February 1940]), BA-MA, RH 21–2/31, 4.
2. Jacques Minart, *P.C. Vincennes: Secteur 4* (Command Post, Vincennes: Sector 4), vol. 2 (Paris: Berger-Levrault, 1945), 138; Gounelle, *Sedan,* 225; Horne, *Über die Maas,* 222.
3. Horne, *To Lose a Battle,* 273; *Über die Maas,* 222.
4. See Brausch, "Sedan 1940," 84.
5. Gamelin, *Servir,* vol. 3, 399; vol. 1, 342.
6. Halder an Sodenstern, 12.3.1940 (Halder to Sodenstern, 12 March 1940), BA-MA, RH 19 I/38, sheet 160.
7. Grandsard, *Le 10e Corps d'armée,* 132; Berben and Iselin, *Die Deutschen kommen,* 174.
8. Horne, *To Lose a Battle,* 296, and *Über die Maas,* 239; Gounelle, *Sedan,* 226f.; Grandsard, *Le 10e Corps d'armée,* 137f., Ruby, *Sedan,* 144f.
9. See Doughty, *Breaking Point,* 279. The fighting vehicles of the 7th Tank Battalion, which had been wiped out on 14 May, are not included here.
10. The original strength amounted to 160 battle tanks (see Giuliano, *Les combats du Mont-Dieu,* 32).
11. Historique du 21ème Corps d'Armée du 26 Août 1939 au 22 juin 1940 (History of the XXI Army Corps from 26 August 1939 to 22 June 1940), SHAT, 30 N 225: 21ème Corps d'Armée (XXI Corps), 11. This also indicates that the 5th Light Cavalry Division was again placed under the Army and retained its mission of protecting Flavigny's left flank.
12. Flavigny used the "supporting force" of X Corps—which, within 24 hours, had lost

200 artillery pieces—to put two reconnaissance battalions under his command, as well as the 4th Tank Battalion that had arrived too late for the attack mounted by the Corps reserve. The remaining units were employed to screen the right flank. The 3d North African Infantry Division was placed under XVIII Corps, which was deployed to the right.

13. See Pierre Rocolle, *La défaite (10 mai–25 juin)* (The Defeat [10 May–25 June]), vol. 2, *La guerre de 1940* (The War of 1940) (Paris: Armand Colin, 1990), 370n.36.
14. 1.PzDiv, KTB (1st Panzer Division, War Diary), BA-MA, RH 27–1/170, 22.
15. Giuliano, *Les combats du Mont-Dieu,* 37.
16. Ibid.
17. See Deighton, *Blitzkrieg,* 283; Shirer, *Collapse,* 654, and *Zusammenbruch,* 685.
18. See Le Goyet, "Contre-attaques manquées," 111.
19. Ibid., 110f.
20. Shirer, *Collapse,* 656; *Zusammenbruch,* 687.
21. See Le Goyet, "Contre-attaques manquées," 116.
22. Regarding the two attempted counterattacks by Flavigny on 14 and 15 May, see also: Dossier 1 bis, Rapport du Général Freydenberg sur les opérations executées par la II° Armée, du 10 mai au 25 juin 1940 (Dossier 1 bis, Report of General Freydenberg on operations carried by Second Army, from May 10 to June 25, 1940), SHAT, 29 N 27 (old no. 25); Historique du 21ème Corps d'Armée du 26 Août 1939 au 22 juin 1940, SHAT, 30 N 225; Dossier 2: Rapport sur les opérations de la 3e D.I.M. en Mai et Juin 1940 (Dossier 2: Report on the operations of the 3d Motorized Infantry Division in May and June 1940), SHAT, 32 N 8: 3ème Division d'Infanterie motorisée (3d Motorized Infantry Division); Dossier 3: Documents du Général Bertin-Boussu: 3e division d'infanterie motorisée (Dossier 3: Documents of General Bertin-Boussu: 3d Motorized Infantry Division), SHAT, 32 N 8; Dossier 4/I: Rapport du Colonel Lespinasse Fonsegrive au sujet des opérations du 12 au 25 mai 1940, 31 Mai 1940 (Dossier 4/I: Report of Colonel Lespinasse Fonsegrive on the subject of operations between May 12 and 25, 1940, dated 31 May 1940), SHAT, 32 N 8; Doughty, *Breaking Point,* 271f.; Général Bertin-Boussu, *La 3e division d'infanterie motorisée 1939–1940* (The 3d Motorized Infantry Division 1939–1940); Le Goyet, "Contre-attaques manquées" and "La percée de Sedan," 44ff.; Giuliano, *Les combats du Mont-Dieu,* 26ff.; Ruby, *Sedan,* 161ff., 182ff., 194ff.; Bonotaux and Guerin, *Avec le 3e D.I.M. à Stonne* (With the 3d Motorized Infantry Division at Stonne); d'Ornano, "Après la percée de Sedan" (After the Sedan Breakthrough), *RHDGM* 1 (March 1950): 35ff.; Paillat, *Le guerre éclair,* 251ff., 268ff.; Grandsard, *Le 10e Corps d'armée,* 150, 170ff., Deighton, *Blitzkrieg,* 282ff., Berben and Iselin, *Die Deutschen kommen,* 255f., 282ff.; Horne, *Über die Maas,* 266, 273ff., 290ff., 332ff.; Shirer, *Zusammenbruch,* 683ff.; Hoth, "Das Schicksal," 374f.; Dach, "Panzer," *Schweizer Soldat* 47, no. 2 (1972): 84ff.; no. 5 (1972): 64ff. Claude Lefevre, the mayor of Stonne, made numerous documents available to the author from his own files.
23. Deighton, *Blitzkrieg,* 232 (284, German edition).
24. See Bertin-Boussu, *La 3e division d'infanterie motorisée,* 68.
25. Doughty, *Breaking Point,* 280.
26. Hoth, "Das Schicksal," 375.
27. Stefan Zweig, *Sternstunden der Menschheit. Zwölf historische Miniaturen* (The Tide of Fortune. Twelve Historical Portraits) (Frankfurt am Main, 1988), 108.
28. Uffz. (Corporal) Günter Kruppe, "Stonne," BA-MA, RH 37/6391, 2.
29. Kriegschronik 15.Kp/IRGD, BA-MA, RH 37/6335, 25.

30. This comparison, which is frequently cited by French historians, was actually first made by Generalmajor Paul Wagner who, as commanding officer of the 79th Infantry Regiment, participated in the fighting for Stonne; see also Gounelle, *Sedan,* 372; Bonotaux and Guerin, *Avec la 3e D.I.M. à Stonne,* 50; Bertin-Boussu, *La 3e division d'infanterie motorisée,* 94; Lt. Col. Bouissoux, *Combats des Ardennes. Stonne—Mont-Dieu—Tannay (avec la 3e DCR et la 3e DIM)* (The Battle in the Ardennes. Stonne—Mont-Dieu—Tannay [with the 3d Light Cavalry Division and the 3d Motorized Infantry Division]), 1 (unpublished); Giuliano, *Les combats du Mont-Dieu,* 97.
31. Quoted from Giuliano, *Les combats du Mont-Dieu,* 97.
32. PzKorps Guderian, KTB, BA-MA, RH 21–2/41, 24.
33. Durchbruch der Gruppe von Kleist, BA-MA, RH 21–1/381, pt. 2, 45.
34. Ibid., 35f.; PzKorps Guderian, KTB, BA-MA, RH 21–2/41, 36.
35. Durchbruch der Gruppe von Kleist, BA-MA, RH 21–1/381, pt. 2, 36.
36. Ibid., 39.
37. Ibid.
38. The day before, the 4th Tank Battalion was supposed to have participated in the counterattack launched by X Corps Reserve, but, as stated earlier, had arrived too late.
39. Pz.Jg.Kp./IRGD, 15. Mai 1940 (Antitank Company, Infantry Regiment Großdeutschland, 15 May 1940), BA-MA, RH 37/6332.
40. Ibid.
41. Ibid. Oberfeldwebel (Master Sergeant) Hindelang and his company commander, Oberleutnant (1st Lieutenant) Beck-Broichsitter, who already had stopped a French tank attack (as previously told), received the Knight's Cross of the Iron Cross.
42. Quoted from Le Goyet, "Contre-Attaques manquées," 110.
43. Deighton, *Blitzkrieg,* 284. Also Huntziger's chief of staff, Colonel Lacaille, later testified before the Parliamentary Investigating Committee in Riom that Second Army had "achieved a defensive success"; see also Shirer, *Zusammenbruch,* 689.
44. Spaeter, *Großdeutschland,* 141. The casualties mentioned include 103 dead, 25 missing, and 442 wounded. These statistics cover the period between 10 and 17 May, although almost all of these casualties were inflicted at Stonne.
45. Pz.Jg.Kp./IRGD, 17. Mai 1940 (Antitank Company, Infantry Regiment Großdeutschland, 17 May 1940), BA-MA, RH 37/6332. The casualty figures given here cover the same time interval (see footnote 44). In this case, likewise, almost all casualties occurred during the fighting in Stonne on 15–16 May.
46. The best reports so far, from the French viewpoint, were prepared by Giuliano, *Les combats du Mont-Dieu,* and Horen, *Fantassin de 40.* See also the German files (all in BA-MA): Arbeitsstab Pioniergeschichte (Work Staff Engineer History), RH 12–5/397, 4f.; VI.AK, KTB (VI Corps, War diary), RH 24–6/17, 10ff.; 16.InfDiv (16th Infantry Division), RH 26–16/28, 1ff.; 24.InfDiv (24th Infantry Division), RH 26–24/140, 5; 1.PzDiv, RH 27–1/170, 25; 10.PzDiv, RH 27–10/9 (15–17 May); 10.SchtzBrig, RH 37/1910, 12f; 11./IRGD, RH 37/6327; II./IRGD, RH 37/6328; 14./IRGD (14th Company, IRGD), RH 37/6332; 15./IRGD, RH 37/6335; 6./IRGD, RH 37/6391; Amtl. Bericht über das Gefecht bei Stonne (14.–16.5.) der 14./IRGD (Official Report on the Fight at Stonne (14–16 May) by 14th Company), RH 37/6391; Gen.d.Inf a.D. Günther Blumentritt, Operative und taktische Schulbeispiele aus beiden Weltkriegen Bd. 3, Teil 4: Panzer-Begegnungsgefecht im Westen, Mai 1940, bei Stonne (Operational and Tactical Training Examples from Both World Wars. vol. 3, pt. 4: Panzer Meeting Engagement at Stonne, May 1940), Studies by Historical Divi-

sion, Headquarters, U.S. Army, Europe, Study B–306, 1–3 BA-MA; French files (all SHAT): Dossier 1 bis, Rapport du Général Freydenberg sur les opérations executées par la II° (Armée, du 10 mai au 25 juin, 7ff., 29 N 27 (old no. 25); Historique du 21ème Corps d'Armée du 26 Août 1939 au 22 juin 1940, 11f., 30 N 225; Dossier 2: Rapport sur les opérations de la 3e D.I.M. en mai et juin, 15ff., 32 N 8; Dossier 3; Documents du Général Bertin-Boussu: 3e division d'infanterie motorisée, 32 N 8; Dossier 4/I: Rapport du Colonel Lespinasse Fonsegrive au sujet des opérations du 12 au 25 mai 1940, 31 Mai 1940, 8ff., 32 N 8; Dossier 0/4/II: Général Wagner, Combats du 79ème Régiment d'Infanterie près de Stonne et Mont-Damion (Combat Operations of the 79th Infantry Regiment near Stonne and Mont-Damion), 32 N 8; Dossier O/4/III: Général Schaal, Les combats de la 10 (Panzer Division dans la région de Stonne les 14, 15 et 16 Mai 1940 (Combat actions of the 10th Panzer Division in the region of Stonne on May 14, 15, and 16, 1940), 32 N 8; Spaeter, *Großdeutschland,* 125ff.; Hans von Tettau and Kurt Versock, *Geschichte der 24. Infanterie-Division* (History of the 24th Infantry Division) (Stolberg, 1956), 33ff.; Fritz Memminger, *Die Kriegsgeschichte der Windhund-Division* [16th Infantry Division] (The War History of the Greyhound Division) (Bochum-Langendreer, 1962), sec. T 18/1–53; Wolfgang Werthen, *Geschichte der 16. Panzer Division* (The History of the 16th Panzer Division) (Bad Nauheim, 1958), 12ff.; Hans Lüke, *Auszug aus der Geschichte des Regiments 69* (Extract from the History of the 69th Regiment), 55ff., in private hands; Franz Kurowski and Gottfried Tornau, *Sturmartillerie 1939–1945* (Assault Guns, 1939–1945) (Stuttgart: Motorbuch, 1977), 20ff.; Freter, *Fla,* 181f.; Gerhard von Schwerin, *Souvenirs de guerre. Sedan–Bulson-Stonne de 10 au 15 mai 1940 (recueillis par Michel Baudier)* (Memories of War. Sedan-Bulson-Stonne from 10 to 15 May 1940 [collected by Michel Baudier]) (n.p., 1990), 11f.; Le Goyet, "Contre-attaques manquées," 126ff.; Jean Delmas et al., *Mai-juin 40. Les combattants de l'honneur* (May–June 1940. They Fought for Honor) (Paris, 1980), 94ff.; B. de Susbielle, "Chasseurs à pied, cavaliers et blindés au combat. Canal des Ardennes 16–23 mai 1940" (Chasseurs on Foot, Cavalry and Tanks in Battle. The Ardennes Canal, 16–23 May 1940), *RHA* no. 2 (1972): 76ff.; Bonotaux and Guerin, *Avec la 3e D.I.M. à Stonne;* Bertin-Boussu, *La 3e division d'infanterie motoris*ée, 82ff.; Ruby, *Sedan,* 183ff., 212ff.; Bouissoux, Combat des Ardennes (unpublished); Doughty, *Breaking Point,* 227ff., 290ff.; Pallud, *Blitzkrieg,* 274ff.

In this connection, the author was able to go through a vast volume of private documents that were made available by: Claude Lefevre (Mayor of Stonne), Norbert Di-Fant (Raucourt), Oberstleutnant a.D. Helmut Fleischer (collection of documents and correspondence of Mr. Dietrich Starcke), Albert Schick (Unit Tradition Association, 10th Panzer Division), Oberstleutnant a.D. Gottfried Schütze (documents of Sturmpionier-Bataillon 43), Major i.G. a.D., General Staff (Ret.), Helmut Beck-Broichsitter (former company commander, Panzerjägerkompanie IRGD).

47. For this individual exploit, Captain Billotte later was made a member of the Legion of Honor; see Giuliano, *Les combats du Mont-Dieu,* 511, 107n.15; Pallud, *Blitzkrieg,* 275f.
48. The German infantrymen had found cover along the path between Elevation 339 and the box-shaped section of woods protruding from Bois-du-Mont-Dieu [forest], northwest of Elevation 318 (see also sketch, 261, top).
49. This incident, which, for example, is described by Giuliano (*Les combats du Mont-Dieu,* 61), was the subject of several conversations and exchanges of correspondence many years later between German and French veterans. See also the article in the bul-

letin of the 16th Division, *Unsere 16* (Our 16th), October 1982, 6. Some documents from the files of Dietrich Starcke are particularly informative. The letters collected there also show that a number of soldiers, who had fought so hard at that time, since then became friends. The regular meetings of French and German unit tradition associations in Stonne also played an important role here. After World War II, this village became as important in the reconciliation of former foes as did Verdun after World War I.

50. On 18 May, the French made three more vain attempts to recapture Stonne. They finally withdrew once and for all at 2100.
51. Horne, *Über die Maas,* 514.
52. Concerning the attempts of the French Second, Sixth, and Ninth armies to block Guderian's thrust to the west of the Ardennes Canal, see the files of BA-MA: PzKorps Guderian, KTB, RH 21–2/41, 35ff.; 1.PzDiv, KTB, RH 27–1/170, 22; 2.PzDiv, KTB, RH 27–2/1, 21ff. See also Dossier 1 bis, Rapport du Général Freydenberg sur les opérations executées par la II° Armée, du 10 mai au 25 juin, 6ff., SHAT, 29 N 27 (old no. 25); Ruby, *Sedan,* 156ff; Guderian, *Erinnerungen,* 99ff.; Balck, *Ordnung im Chaos,* 274ff.; Colonel Fox and Chef d'Escadron d'Ornano, "La percée des Ardennes" (Piercing the Ardennes), *RHDGM* 3, no. 10–11 (1953): 105ff.; Georges Le Diberder, "Les spahis dans les combats des Ardennes" (The Spahis in the Fighting in the Ardennes), Maurice Vaïsse, ed., *Ardennes 1940* (Paris: Henri Veyrier, 1990), 154ff.; Bikar, "La 3e brigade de Spahis," 397ff.; Bikar, "La 5e division légère de cavalerie," 703ff.; Ch. Motch, "1939–1940, Le 12e régiment de chasseurs dans la tourmente" (The 12th Light Infantry Regiment in its Travail), *Le Pays Sedanais,* no. 17 (1990): 100; d'Ornano, "Après la percée"; Paillat, *La guerre éclair,* 263, 286ff.; Shirer, *Zusammenbruch,* 704ff.; Horne, *Über die Maas,* 271f., 294ff., 333ff. The most recent investigation was Doughty, *Breaking Point,* 230ff., 273, 294ff.
53. Fox and d'Ornano, "La percée des Ardennes," 108.
54. Shirer, *Zusammenbruch,* 705.
55. See Turnbull, *Dunkirk,* 68.
56. The name is correctly spelled "Marc."
57. Balck, *Ordnung im Chaos,* 276.
58. Ibid., 276f. See also Guderian, *Erinnerungen,* 96f.; Zindler, "Da erscheint plötzlich unser Herr Regimentskommandeur" (Our Regimental Commander Suddenly Showed up in Our Midst), *Mit den Panzer,* 175f.
59. Quoted from Horne, *To Lose a Battle,* 367, and *Über die Maas,* 303; see also Werner Picht, *Das Ende der Illusionen. Der Feldzug im Westen, ein Sieg der Tat über die Täuschung* (The End of Illusions. The Campaign in the West, a Victory of Fact over Deception) (Berlin: Mittler and Sohn, 1941), 39.
60. Denkschrift "Das Wesen des Angriffs" (Study, "The Essence of Attack"), BA-MA, RH 27–6/1D, 3.
61. Reinhardt, "Im Schatten Guderians," 334.
62. Ibid., 337.
63. Paul, *Brennpunkte,* 59.
64. Karl-Heinz Ganns, *Panzer-Artillerie Regiment 76* (1936–1945) (76th Panzer Artillery Regiment [1936–1945]) (Cologne, 1962), 72.
65. Some sources also refer to this regiment as a half-brigade [demi-brigade].
66. BA-MA, RH 21–1/22, 12.

67. Durchbruch der Gruppe von Kleist, BA-MA, RH 21–1/381, pt. 2, 50.
68. Colonel Freiherr [Baron] von Esebeck proved his courage also later when it came to resisting Hitler. He was arrested (with the rank of General der Panzertruppe) after the attempt of 20 July 1944 and, at the end of the war, was liberated in a concentration camp. The leader of that conspiracy was Oberst (General Staff) Count von Stauffenberg who had been with 6th Panzer Division as general staff officer (Ib) during the campaign in the west.
69. Concerning the breakthrough at Monthermé, see the files (all BA-MA): 6.PzDiv (6th Panzer Division), RH 27–6/1D, 10ff.; RH 27–6/4, sheet 78f.; RH 27–6/126, 1–4; II./SchtzRgt 4 (13.–15. Mai sowie Gefechtsberichte) (2d Battalion, 4th Rifle Regiment [13–15 May as well as combat reports]), RH 37/10; I./SchtzRgt 4 (13.–15. Mai) (1st Battalion, 4th Rifle Regiment [15–16 May]), RH 37/11; XXXXI.AK (XXXXI Corps), RH 24–41/2, 31ff.; Ausführungen des Gen.d.PzTr. Reinhardt über den Maasübergang (Statements by Gen. of Panzer Troops Reinhardt concerning the Meuse River crossing), RH 24–41/4; HGr A (13.–15. Mai) (Army Group A [13–15 May]), RH 19 I/37; AOK 12, Armeebefehl Nr. 7 vom 15.5.1940 (HQ, Twelfth Army, Army Order No. 7, 15 May 1940), RH 20–12/33; PzGruppe Kleist, RH 21–1/22, 9ff.; Durchbruch der Gruppe von Kleist, BA-MA, RH 21–1/381, pt. 2, 28f., 40f., 47, 50ff.; Reinhardt, "Im Schatten Guderians," 333ff.; Paul, *Brennpunkte,* 59ff; Ganns, *Panzer-Artillerie Regiment 76,* 72ff.; Zeitzler, "Die Panzer-Gruppe v. Kleist," *EWKde* 8, no. 5 (1959): 241; Berben and Iselin, *Die Deutschen kommen,* 121ff., 160ff., 174f., 179ff., 203ff., 237ff., 253, 278ff., 299ff., 306ff.; Horne, *Über die Maas,* 244ff., 287ff.; Jean Delmas, "Les Ardennes dans les opérations française, rue d'ensemble et cas concret: Monthermé" (The Ardennes during French Operations, Overview and Specific Case: Monthermé), ed. Vaïsse, *Ardennes 1940,* 103ff.; Delmas et al., *Mai-juin 40,* 55ff.; Gounelle, *Sedan,* 195ff.; 320ff.; Lyet, "Mitrailleurs malgaches à Monthermé mai 1940" (Malagasy Machine Gunners at Monthermé, May 1940), *RHA* 19, no. 4 (1963); Paillat, *La guerre éclair,* 278ff.; "Das III.Bataillon Schützenregiment 4 erzwingt am 13.Mai den Maasübergang bei Monthermé (Einzelschilderungen aus dem Kriege an der Westfront)" (The 3d Battalion, 4th Rifle Regiment, Forces the Crossing of the Meuse River at Monthermé on 13 May [Individual Accounts from the War on the Western Front]), *MWR* 5 (1940): 358ff.; "*Kradschützen voran! Verfolgung von der Maas bei Monthermé bis Montcornet durch 1./Kradschützen-Bataillon 6*" (Motorcycle Riflemen, Forward! The Pursuit from the Meuse River and Monthermé all the way to Montcornet by 1st Company, 6th Motorcycle Battalion), *MWR,* 1940, 362ff.; Heinz Maassen, *Über die Maas. Die Erzwingung des Übergangs bei Monthermé* (Over the Meuse River. Forcing the Crossing at Monthermé) (Düsseldorf: Völkischer Verlag, 1941); Dach, "Panzer," *Schweizer Soldat* 47, no. 5 (1972): 73ff.; Pallud, *Blitzkrieg,* 228ff.
70. Lutz Koch, *Rommel. Der "Wüstenfuchs"* (Rommel. The "Desert Fox") (Bielefeld: W. Goldmann, 1978), 23, 24.
71. Hasso von Manteuffel, *Die 7.Panzer-Division im Zweiten Weltkrieg. Einsatz und Kampf der "Gespenster-Division," 1939–1945* (The 7th Panzer Division in the Second World War. Employment and Battles of the "Ghost Division," 1939–1945) (Cologne, 1965), 109f.; Horst Scheibert, *Gespensterdivision. Eine deutsche Panzer-Division (7.) im Zweiten Weltkrieg* (Ghost Division: A German Panzer Division [the 7th] in the Second World War) (Friedberg: Podzun-Pallas-Verlag, 1981), 42f.; Horne,

Über die Maas, 466; David Irving, *Rommel. Eine Biographie* (Rommel. A Biography) (Hamburg: Verlag Hoffmann und Campe, 1978), 75. English-language version, *The Trail of the Fox* (New York: E. P. Dutton, 1977).

72. Bikar, "La 4e division légère de cavalerie française," 647ff.; Berben and Iselin, *Die Deutschen kommen,* 109ff.; Hans von Dach, *Kampfbeispiele* (Combat Action Examples) (Frauenfeld, 1977), 38ff.; Detlev von Plato, *Die Geschichte der 5. Panzerdivision 1938–1945* (The History of the 5th Panzer Division, 1938–1945) (Regensburg, 1978), 46; "An der Maas 1940" (Along the Meuse River in 1940), *MWR* 5, no. 3 (1940): 246ff.; Gounelle, *Sedan,* 112ff.; Pierre Bertin, "Un régiment d'infanterie sur la Meuse en 1940: le 129e R.I. en Belgique" (An Infantry Regiment along the Meuse in 1940: The 129th Infantry Regiment in Belgium), *RHA* no. 4 (1972): 75f.; Paillat, *La guerre éclair,* 172ff.; Buffetaut, *Guderian,* 32; Pallud, *Blitzkrieg,* 188.
73. Paillat, *La guerre éclair,* 176.
74. The author was able to question a number of eyewitnesses on that point; he had gotten their addresses through the Unit Tradition Clubs of the 5th and 7th Panzer Divisions (from Mr. Gutmann and Mr. Penselin). Through these contacts the author obtained several documents that indicate likewise that it was men of the 5th Panzer Division who were the first to reach the west bank of the Meuse River. Particularly indicative here is the private war diary of Generalmajor a.D. Friedrich-Carl von Steinkeller, who at that time (with the rank of Major) commanded the 7th Motorcycle Rifle Battalion. On p. 60f. of his *Erinnerungen (Auszug: Maasübergang des Kradschützen-Bataillons 7 der 7.Panzerdivision am 12./13. Mai 1940*) (Memoirs [Extract: The Meuse Crossing of Motorcycle Battalion 7 of the 7th Panzer Division on 12/13 May 1940]) (privately held), he observes that the famous weir of Houx was not crossed—as is frequently asserted—by motorcycle riflemen of his own battalion but rather by men of the neighboring 5th Panzer Division.

    See also, "An der Maas," 249ff.; Berben and Iselin, *Die Deutschen kommen,* 142; Plato, *5.Panzerdivision,* 48; Alfred Tschimpke, *Die Gespensterdivision. Mit der Panzerwaffe durch Belgien und Frankreich* (The Ghost Division. With the Panzer Force through Belgium and France) (Munich: Zentralverlag der NSDAP, 1941), 56ff.; Paillat, *La guerre éclair,* 175f., 189ff.; Gounelle, *Sedan,* 127ff., 176 (photo); Bertin, "Un régiment d'infanterie," 79ff., 84; Pierre Le Goyet, "Le 11e corps d'armée dans la bataille de la Meuse. 10–15 mai 1940 (The XI Corps in the Battle of the Meuse, 10–15 May 1940)," *RHA* 18, no. 1 (1962): 131ff., 135; Henri Amouroux, *Le peuple du désastre 1939–1940, Tome 1: La grande histoire des Français sous l'occupation* (The People of the Disaster, 1939–1940. vol. 1: The General History of the French under the Occupation) (Paris: Robert Laffont, 1976), 307ff.; Crémieux-Brilhac, *Ouvriers et soldats,* 591ff.
75. Gefechtsbericht des Feldwebels Blunk (3. Kompanie/Schützenregiment 14 [After-Action report by Sergeant] Blunk (3d Company, 14th Rifle Regiment), as cited in Plato, *5.Panzerdivision,* 49.
76. *The Rommel Papers.* ed. B. H. Liddell Hart (New York: Harcourt, Brace, 1953), 9.
77. Ibid., 10.
78. The original of this unfortunate radio message can be found in the Akten des 7.PzDiv (Files of the 7th Panzer Division), BA-MA, RH 27–7/11, 26.
79. *The Rommel Papers,* 12.
80. Plato, *5.Panzerdivision*, 53. Generalleutnant von Plato, the author of this superbly composed divisional history, titled the pertinent chapter "In Rommel's Shadow," and used it to take some ironic sideswipes at Rommel. Nevertheless, he pictured the latter

as a model, in comparison to his own division commander: "The leadership of the (5th Panzer) Division was not what it was with the 7th Panzer Division where the division commander on the first day (13 May) was in the bridgehead twice and inspired all commanders to follow him." (Plato, *5.Panzerdivision*, 51).

81. Minart, *P.C. Vincennes,* vol. 2, 135.
82. Doumenc, *Histoire de la Neuvième Armée,* 86f.
83. Paillat, *La guerre éclair,* 209.
84. Concerning the fighting at Dinant on 13 and 14 May, see the following files (all BA-MA): 7.PzDiv, KTB (7th Panzer Division, War Diary), RH 27–7/3, sheets 38ff.; Meldungen (messages), 13 May, RH 27–7/9; Funksprüche (radio messages), 14 May, RH 27–7/11; Einsatz im Frankreichfeldzug (Employment in the Campaign in France), RH 27–7/215, 5ff.; "Rommelalbum" (Rommel Album), 13, 14 May, RH 27–2/220; 5.PzDiv, KTB (5th Panzer Division, War Diary), RH 27–5/179, 10ff.; PzKorps Hoth (XV.AK) (Panzer Corps Hoth [XV Corps]): Meldungen (messages), RH 21–3/28; KTB (War Diary), RH 21–3/36, 6ff.; Karten (maps), RH 21–3/37; Korpsbefehle (Corps Orders), RH 21–3/38; AOK 4 (HQ, Fourth Army): KTB (War Diary), RH 20–4/54, 32ff.; RH 20–4/62, sheets 28ff.; RH 20–4/64, sheets 20ff.; RH 20–4/68, sheets 81ff.; Kurzer Überblick über die Operationen der 4. Armee (Short overview of the operations of Fourth Army), RH 20–4/81. Additional documents were obtained from private sources through the good services of the Tradition Clubs of the 5th and 7th Panzer Divisions, such as, for example, Kriegstagebuch Nr. 2 (II.Btl/SchtzRgt 7) vom 25.11.1939 bis 7.7.1940 (War Diary Number 2 [2d Battalion, 7th Rifle Regiment] from 25 November 1939 to 7 July 1940) (privately held).

    See also Hilfstudie (XI.AK, Mai) zu P–208 Bd. 2: Generalleutnant a.D. Otto Heidkämper, Die Operationen des XV.AK (zeitweise Gruppe Hoth) in dem Feldzug in Nordfrankreich, 10.–30.5.1940 [Supporting Study (XV Corps, May) to P–208, vol. 2: Generalleutnant a.D. Otto Heidkämper, The Operations of XV Corps (temporarily Group Hoth) during the Campaign in Northern France, 10–30 May 1940], Historical Division, Headquarters, U.S. Army Europe, 16ff., BA-MA; Manteuffel, Die 7.Panzer-Division im Zweiten Weltkrieg, 57ff.; Plato, 5.Panzerdivision, 48ff.; "An der Maas 1940," 246ff.; *The Rommel Papers,* 7ff.; Berben and Iselin, *Die Deutschen kommen,* 146ff., 175ff., 208ff., 240f., 260ff., 271ff., 292ff.; Horne, *Über die Maas,* 213ff., 249ff.; Shirer, *Zusammenbruch,* 690ff.; Kenneth Macksey, *Rommel. Schlachten and Feldzüge* (Rommel: Battles and Campaigns) (Stuttgart, 1982), 44ff.; Deighton, *Blitzkrieg,* 258ff.; Tschimpke, *Gespensterdivision,* 53ff.; Hans von Luck, *Gefangener meiner Zeit. Ein Stück Weges mit Rommel* (Prisoner of My Time. A Piece of the Way with Rommel) (Bonn and Herford, 1991), 56; Rocolle, *La guerre,* vol. 2, 105ff.; Bertin, "Un régiment d'infanterie," 84ff.; Yves Buffetaut, *Rommel. France 1940* (Bayeux: Editions Heimdal, 1985), 29ff., 194; Buffetaut, *Guderian,* 46ff.; Gounelle, *Sedan,* 127ff., 200ff., 267ff.; Pierre Lyet, "La bataille de Belgique et du Nord (La campagne 1939–1940)" (The Battle of Belgium and the North [The Campaign, 1930–1940]), pt. 1, *RHA* 2, no. 2 (1946): 49ff.; Doumenc, *Histoire de la Neuvième Armée,* 83ff.; Le Goyet, "Le 11e corps," *RHA* 18, no. 1 (1962): 131ff.; no. 2 (1961): 83ff.; Paillat, *La guerre éclair,* 178ff., 189ff.; A. Bikar, "La 1ère division légère de cavalerie française à l'est de la Meuse, les 10, 11 et 12 mai" (The French 11th Light Cavalry Division to the East of the Meuse, 10, 11 and 12 May 1940), *RBHM* 26 (1985–86): 205f.; Bikar, "La 4e division légère de cavalerie française," 649ff.; Colin, *Rommel et le franchissement de la Meuse* (Rommel and the Crossing of the Meuse River) (Paris: École Superieure de Guerre, 1971; Crémieux-Brilhac, *Ouvriers et soldats,* 591ff.; Amouroux, *Le peuple du désastre,* 307ff.; Pallud, *Blitzkrieg,* 182f.; Gutzschhahn, "Zum 50. Jahrestag der Kämpfe in Belgien" (On the 50th Anniversary of the Fighting in Belgium), *Rundschreiben 2/1989 des Traditionsverbandes der ehem. 7. Panzerdivision* (Circular 2/1989 of the Unit Tradition Club of the former 7th Panzer Division), 15–19.

85. See Shirer, *Collapse,* 668; *Zusammenbruch,* 701.
86. The 7th Panzer Division had one Panzer regiment with three battalions; the 5th Panzer Division had two Panzer regiments, each with two battalions.
87. At least one company of the 6th Tank Battalion, which belonged to the Ninth Army, was placed under the command of the French 1st Armored Division.
88. Gefechtsbericht des Unteroffiziers Nökel (After-Action report by Corporal Nökel), as quoted in Plato, *5.Panzerdivision,* 57.
89. The same fate also befell the Char B tanks of the 3d Company, 37th Tank Battalion that was trying to push past the 5th Panzer Division to the north and, in the process, penetrated into the combat sector of the German 8th Infantry Division. But the latter formed a blocking position, at the intersection west of Denée, consisting of field artillery, antiaircraft artillery, and antitank guns. Nine Char B tanks were knocked out in a very small area. See also Jean Paul Pallud, "The Road Ends at Denée," *After the Battle,* no. 51 (1986): 47ff.
90. Concerning the tank battle at Flavion, see the following Files (all BA-MA): 7.PzDiv, KTB, RH 27–7/3, sheet 39f.; Funksprüche (radio messages), 15 May, RH 27–7/11; RH 27–7/212, 6ff.; Einsatz im Frankreichfeldzug, RH 27–7/215, 9f.; Rommelalbum (Rommel Album), 15 May, RH 27–7/220; 5.PzDiv, KTB, RH 27–5/179, 14ff.; PzKorps Hoth (XV.AK) (Panzer Corps Hoth [XV Corps]): Meldungen (messages), RH 21–3/28; KTB, RH 21–3/36, 15ff.; Karten (Maps), RH 21–3/37 (K); Korpsbefehle (Corps Orders), RH 21–3/38; AOK 4: KTB, RH 20–4/54, 56ff.; RH 20–4/69, sheet 3ff.; Kurzer Überblick über die Operationen der 4.Armee (A Short Overview of the Operations of the 4th Army), RH 20–4/81; Plato, *5.Panzerdivision,* 53ff.; Manteuffel, *Die 7. Panzer-Division,* 63ff.; Hoth, "Schicksal," 372ff.; Gustav Schrodek, *Ihr Glaube galt dem Vaterland. Geschichte des Panzer-Regiments 15* (They Believed in the Fatherland. The History of the 15th Panzer Regiment) (Munich: Schild, 1976), 70f.; *The Rommel Papers,* 14ff.; Freter, *Fla,* 145f.; Dach, "Panzer," pt. 2, *Schweizer Soldat* 47, no. 5 (1972): 67ff.; Shirer, *Zusammenbruch,* 699ff., 706; Horne, *Über die Maas,* 251ff., 281ff.; Deighton, *Blitzkrieg,* 284f.; Berben and Iselin, *Die Deutschen kommen,* 313f.; Le Goyet, "Le 11e corps," *RHA* 18, no. 2 (1961): 86ff.; Paillat, *La guerre éclair,* 221ff.; Gounelle, *Sedan,* 292ff.; Rocolle, *La guerre,* vol. 2, 115ff.; Buffetaut, *Rommel,* 36ff.; Buffetaut, *Guderian,* 56ff.; Pallud, *Blitzkrieg,* 241ff.
91. Heinrich Bücheler, "Die Panzerschlacht von Hannut. Pfingsten 1940" (The Tank Battle at Hannut, Whitsuntide 1940), *Kampftruppen* 22, no. 3 (1980): 126.
92. The myth according to which the Germans planned a "terror air raid" against Rotterdam has in the meantime been refuted by historiography. Horst Boog, for example, established, "As Rotterdam was no terror raid so Guernica was not one either"; see his "Die Operationen der Luftwaffe gegen die Niederlande vom 10. bis 15. Mai 1940" (The Operations of the German Air Force against the Netherlands from 10 to 15 May 1940), in Hans-Martin Ottmer and Heiger Ostertag, eds., *Ausgewählte Operationen und ihre militärgeschichtlichen Grundlagen* (Selected Operations and Their Basis in Military History) (Herford and Bonn: Verlag E. S. Mittler and Sohn, 1993), 137ff.

93. Both divisions had two regiments, one with 88 Hotchkiss tanks and the other with 88 SOMUA tanks. The 3d Light Mechanized Division had an additional 63 Hotchkiss tanks in the 11th Motorized Dragoon Regiment.
94. In addition to the Hotchkiss 39, the French also used the older Hotchkiss model whose armor amounted to 35 mm, at any rate, thicker than that of the German Panzer IV.
95. See Jeffrey A. Gunsburg, "The Battle of Belgian Plain, 12–14 May 1940: The First Great Tank Battle," *The Journal of Military History* 56, no. 2 (1992): 234f.
96. Geschichte der 4. PzDiv, BA-MA, RH 27–4/199, 50.
97. Concerning Luftwaffe Employment, see Hans Seidemann, Einsätze des VIII. Fliegerkorps, 22ff., 27ff., BA-MA, N 406/4; VIII. Fliegerkorps, Einsatz, BA-MA, RL 8/43, sheet 10f.; VIII. Fliegerkorps, KTB, BA-MA, RL 8/45, 21f.; Ibel, Jagdgeschwader 27, BA-MA, RL 10/591, 26ff.; Lageberichte Luftwaffenführungsstab, Ic (Situation Report, Air Force Operations Staff, Intelligence Section), Nos. 250–253, BA-MA, RM 7/337; Speidel, Der Einsatz, Anlagen 48, 49, Study Lw 3/4a, BA-MA.
98. XVI.(mot.)AK, KTB, BA-MA, RH 21–4/518, 62.
99. 4.PzDiv, KTB (4th Panzer Division, War Diary), BA-MA, RH 27–4/6, 14.
100. Ibid.
101. XVI.(mot.)AK, KTB, BA-MA, RH 21–4/518, 70.
102. Concerning the armor battle at Hannut and the breakthrough at Gembloux see the following Files (all BA-MA): XVI.(mot.)AK, KTB, RH 21–4/518, 48ff.; RH 21–4/527, 42f.; 3.PzDiv (3d Panzer Division): RH 27–3/245, 11ff.; Offener Brief Zimmermann an Görlitz vom 6.5.1976 (Open letter from Zimmermann to Görlitz, 6 May 1976), RH 27–3/251; 4.PzDiv, KTB, RH 27–4/6, 6ff.; Geschichte 4.PzDiv, RH 27–4/199, 45ff.; Speidel, Der Einsatz, pt. 3, 158ff., Study Lw 3/2; Heidkämper, Die Operationen des XV.AK, Mai 1940, 13ff. The following is considered to be the most comprehensive description in the literature on the subject: Hermann Zimmermann, *Der Griff ins Ungewisse;* see also Gunsburg, "The Battle of Belgian Plain," 207ff.; Hoth, "Das Schicksal," 368ff.; Bücheler, "Die Panzerschlacht von Hannut," 125ff; Traditionsverband der Division, *Geschichte der 3.Panzer-Division* (History of 3d Panzer Division) (Berlin, 1976), 44ff.; Joachim Neumann, *Die 4.Panzerdivision 1938–1943* (The 4th Panzer Division, 1938–1943) (Bonn, 1985), pt. 1, 102ff.; Ernst Frhr. von Jungenfeld, *So kämpften Panzer! Erlebnisse eines Panzerregiments im Westen* (That Is How the Panzers Fought! Experiences of a Panzer Regiment in the West) (Berlin: Deutscher Verlag, 1941), 35ff.; Freter, *Fla,* 146f.; Horne, *Über die Maas,* 195, 246f., 278, 361; Shirer, *Zusammenbruch,* 654ff.; Perrett, *Knights,* 56f.; Prioux, *Souvenirs,* 55ff.; Palud, *Blitzkrieg,* 160ff.; Paillat, *La guerre éclair,* 123ff., 320ff.
103. See Josef Marolz, "Die Entwicklung der operativen Führung" (The Development of Operational Command), pt. 3, *ÖMZ* 11, no. 5 (1973): 371.
104. Concerning the deception measures with respect to Switzerland, see above all Janusz Piekalkiewicz, *Ziel Paris. Der Westfeldzug 1940* (Objective: Paris. The 1940 Campaign in the West) (Munich and Berlin, 1986), 88ff., 104, 112f.
105. Liß, *Westfront,* 63f. See also, among other things, from the files of the Army General Staff, Operationsentwurf Tannenbaum (Tannenbaum Operations Draft), BA-MA, RH 2/465, plans for the occupation of Switzerland (with Italian participation) were drawn up only after the Campaign in the West; see also the description by Klaus Urner, *"Die Schweiz muß noch geschluckt werden!" Hitlers Aktiosnpläne gegen die Schweiz* ("Let's Swallow Switzerland, Too!": Hitler's Plans against Switzerland) (Zurich: Verlag Neue Zürcher Zeitung [NZZ], 1990).

106. See Piekalkiewicz, *Ziel Paris,* 164f.
107. Ibid., 167f.
108. Horne, *To Lose a Battle,* 153, and *Über die Maas,* 138; Heusinger, *Befehl im Widerstreit,* 85.
109. See Shirer, *Collapse,* 675; *Zusammenbruch,* 708.
110. In one of the four armored cupolas of Block I, the demolition charges did not have any major effect. The next morning, the machine gun, built into it, opened fire once again. Heavy French artillery fire prevented any approach, so that this armored cupola, likewise, could not be blown until the afternoon.
111. Gérard Giuliano, *Les soldats du beton. La Ligne Maginot dans les Ardennes et en Meuse. 1939–1940* (The Soldiers of Concrete. The Maginot Line in the Ardennes and along the Meuse. 1939–1940) (Charleville-Mézières: Éditions Terres Ardennaises, 1986), 105.
112. Ibid., 73.
113. Concerning the fight for Fort No. 505, see Akte der 71.InfDiv (Files of the 71st Infantry Division): BA-MA, RH 26–71/76, 9ff.; General der Pioniere und Festungen, Denkschrift über die französische Landesbefestigung (General of Engineers and Fortifications, Memorandum on French Fortifications), BA-MA, RHD 29/8, 191ff.; Werner Lahne, *Die Glückhafte Division. Mit den Bezwingern des Panzerwerks 505 nach Verdun und Nancy* (The Lucky Division: With the Conquerors of Fort 505 on to Verdun and Nancy) (n.p., 1940), 9ff.; "Die Einnahme des Panzerwerke 505. Die 71. Infanterie-Division kämpft um den Eckpfeiler der Maginot-Linie" (The Seizure of Fort 505. The 71st Infantry Division Fights at the Cornerstone of the Maginot Line), *Alte Kameraden* 11, no. 5 (1963): 34; Libor Vítez, *Ruhm und Fall der Maginotlinie* (Glory and Fall of the Maginot Line) (Prague: Orbis, 1942), 121ff.; Krumsiek, "Angriff der 71. Infanterie-Division über die Chiers and Durchbruch durch die Maginotlinie (Einnahme des Panzerwerkes 505) vom 15.5.–20.5.1940" [Attack of the 71st Infantry Division across the Chiers and the Breakthrough of the Maginot Line (The Capture of Fort 505) from 15–20 May 1940], *Pioniere* (Engineer), 1959, No. 1; Hans von Dach, "Kampf um ein Festungswerk [La Ferté]. Nach französischen und deutschen Kampfberichten dargestellt" (Fight for a Fortification [La Ferté]: From French and German Combat Reports), *Schweizer Soldat* 43, no. 18 (1967); Giuliano, *Les soldats du beton,* 73ff.; Roger Bruge, *Faites sauter la ligne Maginot, Tome 1: Histoire de la ligne Maginot* (Blow Up the Maginot Line. vol. 1: History of the Maginot Line) (Paris: Fayard, 1973), 209ff.; Rocolle, *La guerre,* vol. 2, 86f.; Hans Nölke, *Die 71. Infanterie-Division im Zweiten Weltkrieg 1939–1945* (The 71st Infantry Division in World War II, 1939–1945) (Hannover: Druckhaus Pinkvoß, 1984), 14ff.; Alain Hohnadel and Michel Truttmann, *Guide de la ligne Maginot: Des Ardennes au Rhin, dans les Alpes* (Guide to the Maginot Line. From the Ardennes to the Rhine [and] into the Alps) (Bayeux: Editions Heimdal, 1988), 31ff.; Pallud, *Blitzkrieg,* 293ff.

Chapter 7

1. Halder, *Halder War Diary,* 145 (16 May 1940); *KTB,* vol. 1, 297.
2. Charles Messenger, *Blitzkrieg. Eine Strategie macht Geschichte* (Blitzkrieg: A Strategy Makes History) (Bergisch Gladbach: Gustav Lübbe Verlag, 1978), 206.

3. Guderian, *Panzer Leader,* 92; *Erinnerungen,* 81f.
4. Guderian, *Panzer Leader,* 92; *Erinnerungen,* 82.
5. Quoted from Walde, *Guderian,* 94.
6. Quoted from Christian Zentner, *Der Frankreichfeldzug—10. May 1940* (The Campaign in France—10 May 1940) (Frankfurt, Berlin, Vienna: Ullstein, 1980), 93.
7. Akten I./FlakRgt 18 (Files, 1st Battalion, 18th Antiaircraft Artillery [Flak] Regiment), BA-MA, RL 12/545, 5 (sheet 6).
8. PzKorps Guderian, KTB, BA-MA, RH 21–2/41, 34.
9. Ibid., 37–39; Blumentritt, Westfeldzug, vol. 2, Study P–208, 39f., BA-MA.
10. Guderian, *Panzer Leader,* 107, and *Erinnerungen,* 96.
11. PzKorps Guderian, KTB, BA-MA, RH 21–2/41, 52.
12. Fischer, *Ohne die Gnade der späten Geburt,* 62f.
13. Churchill, *Their Finest Hour,* vol. 2, *The Second World War,* 59–60, and *Zweiten Weltkrieg,* vol. 2, bk. 1, 80f.
14. Guderian, *Panzer Leader,* 109–10; *Erinnerungen,* 98.
15. PzKorps Guderian, KTB, BA-MA, RH 21–2/41, 59ff. Concerning the "Halt Order" of Montcornet, see also PzGruppe Kleist, KTB (Panzer Group Kleist, War Diary), BA-MA, RH 21–1/22, 19f.; HGr A, KTB, BA-MA, RH 19 I/37, sheets 115ff.; Heeresgruppenbefehle 16. bis 18. Mai (Army Group Orders, 16 to 18 May), BA-MA, RH 19 I/38; Blumentritt, Westfeldzug, vol. 2, Study P–208, 44f., BA-MA; Jacobsen, *Dünkirchen,* 41ff.
16. Paul, *Brennpunkte,* 72.
17. Mellenthin, *Panzerschlachten,* 39f.
18. General Graf von Kielmansegg told the author on 7 June 1993: "Hitler's halt order at Montcornet cost us Dunkirk."
19. Zeitzler, "Panzer-Gruppe v. Kleist," *EWKde* 8, no. 5 (1959): 242.
20. BA-MA, RH 19 I/37, sheet 115.
21. Halder, *Hitler als Feldherr,* 16.
22. Concerning Directive no. 12, already issued by Hitler on 17 May, see the KTB der Operationsabteilung des Generalstabs des Heeres (War Diary of the Operations Section, Army General Staff), BA-MA, RH 2/2972, 28f., as well as *Hitlers Weisungen* (Hitler's Directives), 52f.
23. Liddell Hart, *Jetzt dürfen sie reden,* 221 (Statement by Kleist); Manstein, *Verlorene Siege,* 122, 127; Blumentritt, Westfeldzug, vol. 2, 44f., Study P–208, BA-MA; Heusinger, *Befehl im Widerstreit,* 89.
24. Guderian, *Panzer Leader,* 109; *Erinnerungen,* 98.
25. Heusinger, *Befehl im Widerstreit,* 89.
26. BA-MA, RH 19 I/37, sheet 121.
27. See, for example, Halder, *Hitler als Feldherr,* 16.
28. Blumentritt, *Von Rundstedt,* 71; and Westfeldzug, vol. 2, 46, Study P–208, BA-MA.
29. Halder, *Halder War Diary,* 149 (17 May 1940); Halder, *KTB,* vol. 1, 302.
30. Halder, *Halder War Diary,* 149 (17 May 1940); Halder, *KTB,* vol. 1, 302.
31. Blumentritt, Westfeldzug, vol. 2, 44, Study P–208, BA-MA; Heusinger, *Befehl im Widerstreit,* 89f.
32. Tagebuch Jodl, 18.5.1940 (Jodl Diary, 18 May 1940), BA-MA, RW 4/32, 50.
33. Halder, *Halder War Diary,* 150 (18 May 1940); Halder *KTB,* vol. 1, 303.
34. Quoted from Speidel, Der Einsatz, pt. 3, 278, Study Lw 3/2, BA-MA.
35. Liß, *Westfront,* 165.

36. Ibid., 170; Liß, "Deutsche Westoffensive," 216f.; see also Blumentritt, Westfeldzug, vol. 2, 43, 54f., Study P–208, BA-MA.
37. ADAP, ser. D, vol. 9, 306.
38. Manstein, *Verlorene Siege,* 127.
39. Halder, *Halder War Diary,* 145 (16 May 1940); Halder *KTB,* vol. 1, 297.
40. Halder, *Halder War Diary,* 147 (17 May 1940); Halder *KTB,* vol. 1, 300.
41. Halder, *Halder War Diary,* 147 (17 May 1940); Halder *KTB,* vol. 1, 300; see also Blumentritt, Westfeldzug, vol. 2, Study P–208, 53ff., BA-MA.
42. Halder *KTB,* vol. 1, 302.
43. Manstein, *Verlorene Siege,* 127.
44. Liß, *Westfront,* 167.
45. Manstein, *Verlorene Siege,* 127f.; Liddell Hart, *Jetzt dürfen sie reden,* 220f.; HGr A, KTB, BA-MA, RH 19 I/37, sheet 124.
46. Roderick Macleod and Denis Kelly, eds., *The Ironside Diaries, 1937–1940* (London: Constable, 1962), 317.
47. Beaufre, *1940: The Fall of France,* 183; *Le drame de 1940,* 233.
48. See Shirer, *Collapse,* 679, and *Zusammenbruch,* 712.
49. Churchill, *Their Finest Hour,* 42, and *Zweiten Weltkrieg,* vol. 2, bk. 1, 61.
50. Churchill, *Their Finest Hour,* 42, and *Zweiten Weltkrieg,* vol. 2, bk. 1, 61.
51. Shirer, *Collapse,* 680, and *Zusammenbruch,* 713f.; Amouroux, *Kollabos,* 156; Horne, *To Lose a Battle,* 373, and *Über die Maas,* 307f.; Benoist-Méchin, *Der Himmel stürzt ein,* 83f.
52. Churchill, *Their Finest Hour,* 46, and *Zweiten Weltkrieg,* vol. 2, bk. 1, 65.
53. Churchill, *Their Finest Hour,* 47, and *Zweiten Weltkrieg,* vol. 2, bk. 1, 65f.
54. Minart, *P. C. Vincennes,* vol. 2, 163.
55. Bauer, *Der Panzerkrieg,* 80.
56. See above all Pierre Le Goyet, "L'engagement de la 2e division cuirassée française" (The Commitment of the 2d French Armored Division), *RHA* 20, no. 1 (1964): 147ff. Pallud, *Blitzkrieg,* 280ff.
57. Doughty, *Breaking Point,* 318.
58. Ibid.
59. Quoted from Hoth, "Das Schicksal," 376.
60. Guderian's considerations were confined to the military aspect, but de Gaulle was trying to implement revolutionary military policy concepts with the help of an operational armored force that was to be newly created. He was at the same time trying to introduce a regular, professional army. Characteristically, his attention-getting book bore the title *Vers l'armée de métier* (Toward a Professional Army). That he wanted to tie both these requirements together was later on criticized as being inopportune. In the end, the French Left in the Popular Front accused him of propagating a "coup d'etat army." See Horne, *Über die Maas,* 75; Robert A. Doughty, "De Gaulle's Concept of a Mobile Professional Army: Genesis of French Defeat?" *Parameters* 4, no. 4 (1974): 28f; Wilhelm Deist, "De Gaulle et Guderian. L'influence des expériences militaires de la première guerre mondial en France et en Allemagne" (De Gaulle and Guderian. The Influence of Military Experiences in the First World War in France and Germany), *Etudes Gaulliennes* (Studies on De Gaulle), no. 17 (1977).
61. Charles de Gaulle, *Vers l'armée de métier* (Toward a Professional Army) (Paris, 1944), 2d. ed., 173.

62. Charles de Gaulle, *The Complete War Memoirs of Charles de Gaulle* (New York: Simon and Schuster, 1968), 37, and Charles de Gaulle, *Memoiren* (Memoirs), vol. 1: *Der Ruf 1940–42* (The Call, 1940–42) (Berlin and Frankfurt, 1955), 36f.
63. *The Complete War Memoirs of Charles de Gaulle,* 39, and de Gaulle, *Memoiren,* vol. 1, 37.
64. Kielmansegg, *Panzer,* 164.
65. *The Complete War Memoirs of Charles de Gaulle,* 40, and de Gaulle, *Memoiren,* vol. 1, 38.
66. Concerning the flank attack at Montcornet, see de Gaulle, *Memoiren,* vol. 1, 36ff. See the following files in BA-MA: 1.PzDiv, KTB, RH 27–1/170, 29f.; KTB, Abt. Ib (Versorgung) (War Diary, Section 1b [Supply]), RH 27–1/154, 22; PzKorps Guderian, KTB, RH 21–2/41, 63, 67f.; Kielmansegg, *Panzer,* 164ff.; Horne, *Über die Maas,* 349ff., 390ff.; Shirer, *Zusammenbruch,* 723ff.; Hoth, "Das Schicksal," 376f.; Yves Buffetaut, "De Gaulle. Chef de guerre. 15 mai–6 juin 1940" (De Gaulle: War Leader 15 May–6 June 1940), 39–45; *Guerre contemporaines Magazine,* June 1990, 9ff.; Paillat, *La guerre éclair,* 303ff., 317ff.; P. Huard, *Le Colonel de Gaulle et ses blindés. Laon (15.–20. Mai 1940)* (Colonel De Gaulle and His Tanks. Laon [15–20 May 1940]) (Paris: Plon, 1980), 111ff.; Kirkland, "French Air Force," 114; Pallud, *Blitzkrieg,* 327ff.
67. Kielmansegg, "Bemerkungen," 157.
68. Horne, *Über die Maas,* 74; Michel Forget, "Co-operation between Air Force and Army in the French and German Air Forces during the Second World War," Horst Boog, ed., *The Conduct of the Air War in the Second World War. An International Comparison* (New York: Oxford University Press, 1992), 418f.
69. See David Irving, *Trail,* 50; Irving, *Rommel,* 69.
70. Manteuffel, *Die 7. Panzer-Division,* 109f.; Scheibert, *Gespensterdivision,* 42f.; Horne, *Über die Maas,* 466; Irving, *Rommel,* 75.
71. BA-MA, RH 20–4/69, doc. 44.
72. AOK 4, KTB, BA-MA, RH 20–4/54, 71f., 74ff.
73. Ibid., 90f., 100.
74. Ibid., 101.
75. After the war, Meier-Welcker was the first chief of the Militärgeschichtliches Forschungsamt der Bundeswehr (Military History Research Office of the Federal Armed Forces).
76. See Frontfahrt des Herrn Oberbefehlshabers vom 15.–17.5.1940 sowie Ergänzung (The Ride to the Front of the Commander in Chief, 15–17 May 1940, as well as supplement), BA-MA, RH 20–4/69, sheets 37ff., sheet 41f. See also the essay published anonymously by Meier-Welcker in 1941: "Erlebnisse beim Oberkommando der 4. Armee während der Kämpfe zwischen Maas und Sambre am 15. und 16. Mai" (Experiences at Headquarters, Fourth Army, during the Fighting between the Meuse and Sambre on 15 and 16 May), *MWR* 6, no. 2 (1941), and also his *Aufzeichnungen eines Generalstabsoffiziers 1939–1942* (Notes of a General Staff Officer, 1939–1942) (Freiburg im Breisgau: Rombach Verlag, 1982), 60ff.
77. BA-MA, RH 20–4/69, sheet 41, Ergänzung zum Bericht des Hauptmann i.G. Meier-Welcker (Supplement to the Report of Hauptman i.G. Meier-Welcker).
78. Ibid., Armeebefehl Nr. 3 (Army Order No. 3).
79. 7.PzDiv: Funkspruch 16.5., 14.45 Uhr (7th Panzer Division: Radio message, 16 May, 1445, 7th Panzer Division), BA-MA, RH 27–7/10; *KTB,* RH 27–7/3, sheet 42; RH

27–7/213, sheet 11; *XV. PzKorps, KTB* (XV Panzer Corps, War Diary), BA-MA, RH 21–3/36, 17 (20); *AOK 4,* RH 20–4/69, sheet 39*: Frontfahrt 16.5.* (Front Trip, 16 May)*;* Heidkämper, *Die Operationen des XV.AK,* 23, BA-MA; Hoth, "Der Kampf von Panzerdivisionen in Kampfgruppen in Beispielen der Kriegsgeschichte (Combat Operations of Panzer Divisions in Battle Groups Based on Examples from the History of War)," *EWKde* 8, no. 11 (1959): 581.

80. Dossier 15: 84ème régiment de fortress: compte rendu des événements pour la période comprise entre le 10 et 23 mai 1940 (Dossier 15: 84th Fortress Regiment: Report of Events for the Period Between 10 and 23 May 1940), SHAT, 34 N 95: 84ème Régiment de Fortress.
81. See Horne, *To Lose a Battle,* 402, and *Über die Maas,* 339.
82. Concerning the breakthrough of the extended Maginot Line on 16 May and the push to Landrecies on 17 May, see Akten (Files) (all BA-MA), 7.PzDiv: Tagesberichte 16. und 17. Mai (7th Panzer Division: Daily Situation Reports, 16 and 17 May), RH 27–7/44; RH 27–7/212, 2(sheet 14)ff.; RH 27–7/213, 12ff.; KTB, RH 27–7/3, sheets 43ff.; Rommelalbum, 16./17. Mai (Rommel Album, 16/17 May), RH 27–7/220; XV.PzKorps: KTB, RH 21–3/36, 17(sheet 20)ff.; leichte Flakabteilung 86, Einsatz im Frankreichfeldzug (Schrader, Durchbruch) (86th Light Antiaircraft Artillery [Flak] Battalion, Employment during the Campaign in France [Schrader, Breakthrough]), RL 12/234; Heidkämper, Die Operationen des XV.AK, 24ff.; Manteuffel, *Die 7.Panzer-Division,* 65ff.*; The Rommel Papers,* 17ff.; Tschimpke, *Gespensterdivision,* 89ff.; Irving, *Rommel,* 63ff.; Hoth, "Der Kampf von Panzerdivisionen," 581f.; Buffetaut, *Rommel,* 41ff., 195ff.; Buffetaut, *Guderian,* 71ff.; Pallud, *Blitzkrieg,* 259ff. Additional private documents (e.g., Kriegstagebuch II.Bataillon/Schützenregiment 7 (War Diary, 2d Battalion, 7th Rifle Regiment) were received by the author via the Unit Tradition Association of the 7th Panzer Division.
83. See Horne, *To Lose a Battle,* 403, and *Über die Maas,* 339. See also *The Rommel Papers,* 20. The chapter about the campaign in the west from Rommel's diary was published only in the English edition (*The Rommel Papers*) through Liddell Hart. Manfred Rommel, the Lord Mayor of Stuttgart, sent the author copies of individual documents from his father's possessions (Generalfeldmarschall Rommel, *Dokumente zum Westfeldzug [zur Verfügung gestellt durch seinen Sohn Manfred Rommel]*) (Field Marshal Rommel, Documents on the Campaign in the West [made available by his son Manfred Rommel]).
84. See Irving, *Trail,* 45; *Rommel,* 62f.
85. 7.PzDiv, BA-MA, RH 27–7/212, 3 (sheet 15).
86. See Irving, *Trail,* 49; *Rommel,* 68.
87. Later Hanke in his capacity as Nazi Party Governor (Gauleiter) of Silesia, directed the defenses of Breslau.
88. See Horne, *To Lose a Battle,* 405, and *Über die Maas,* 341.
89. XV.AK, Korpsbefehl für den 17.5 (XV Panzer Corps, Corps order for 17 May), BA-MA, RH 21–3/38; see also 7.PzDiv, KTB, BA-MA, RH 27–7/3, sheet 43; AOK 4, Frontfahrt 16.5. (Fourth Army, Front Trip, 16 May), BA-MA, RH 20–4/69, sheet 39; Heidkämper, Die Operationen des XV.AK, 24f., BA-MA.
90. Regarding the radio messages during the night 16–17 May, see above all the files of 7.PzDiv, KTB, BA-MA, RH 27–7/3, sheets 43ff.; RH 27–7/213, sheets 11ff., 17ff.; Funksprüche, 17. Mai (radio messages, 17 May), RH 27–7/11. See also Funksprüche

Panzerkorps Hoth an 7.Panzerdivision (Radio Messages, Hoth Panzer Corps to 7th Panzer Division), RH 21–3/28.

91. 7.PzDiv, KTB, BA-MA, RH 27–7/3, sheet 43.
92. Ibid., see also XV.AK, KTB, BA-MA, RH 21–3/36, 19 (sheet 22); Heidkämper, Die Operationen des XV.AK, 25, BA-MA.
93. 7.PzDiv, BA-MA, RH 27–7/213, sheet 19.
94. See Manteuffel, *Die 7.Panzer-Division,* 71.
95. 7.PzDiv, BA-MA, RH 27–7/212, 8 (sheet 20).
96. Irving, *Trail,* 47; *Rommel,* 66.
97. The figure of 10,000 prisoners of war (BA-MA, RH 27–7/44), given in the Tagesbericht der 7.PzDiv (Daily Report of 7th Panzer Division) for 17 May, seems too round. The figure of 3,500 is probably more accurate; it is given in the summary statistics of 31 May; see the report Kurzer Gefechtsbericht der 7.Pz.Div. für die Zeit v. 10.–29.5.40 (Short Combat Report of 7th Panzer Division for the Period of 10 to 29 May 1940), BA-MA, RH 27–7/44, sheet 67.
98. 7.PzDiv: Tagesberichte 26. und 17. Mai (Daily Reports, 16 and 17 May), BA-MA, RH 27–7/44.
99. See Liddell Hart, *The German Generals Talk,* 131, and *Jetzt dürfen sie reden,* 227.
100. Halder *KTB,* vol. 1, 301.
101. Ibid., 319.
102. After the arrival of the new formations, the organization of Panzer Group Hoth looked like this—XVI Motorized Corps: 3d Panzer Division, 4th Panzer Division, 20th Infantry Division (Motorized); XXXIX Corps (motorized): 5th Panzer Division, 7th Panzer Division, 11th Rifle Brigade, SS-Totenkopf (Death's Head) Division.
103. Kielmansegg, *Panzer,* 138.
104. *The Rommel Papers,* 30; see also Horne, *Über die Maas,* 418;
105. Even the "light" Mark I infantry tanks had up to 60-mm armor and caused problems for the Germans at Arras.
106. Tagesbericht der 7.PzDiv vom 21.Mai (Daily Report, 7th Panzer Division, 21 May), BA-MA, RH 27–7/44, 20.
107. 7.PzDiv, KTB, BA-MA, RH 27–7/3, sheet 57.
108. Lewin, *Rommel. Eine Biographie* (Rommel. A Biography) (Stuttgart: Kohlhammer, 1969), 297. Thus, his men also said full of respect: "The front is where Rommel is" (Desmond Young, *Rommel* [Wiesbaden: Limes, 1950], 44; Berben and Iselin, *Die Deutschen kommen,* 271).
109. Concerning the battle at Arras (from the German viewpoint), see the following files (all BA-MA): 7.PzDiv, KTB, RH 27–7/3, sheets 56ff.; Tagesbericht 21.5. (Daily Report, 21 May), RH 27–7/44, 20ff.; RH 27–7/212, sheets 38ff.; AOK 4: KTB, RH 20–4/54, 247ff., 262ff.; Meldungen (messages), 21 May, RH 20–4/71; Kurzer Überblick über die Operationen der 4.Armee (Short Overview of the Operations of the Fourth Army), 13ff., RH 20–4/81; XV.AK, KTB (XV Corps, War Diary), RH 21–3/36, 32ff. (sheets 35ff.); XXXIX.PzKorps: KTB (XXXIX Panzer Corps: War Diary), RH 24–39/7, 29 (sheets 31)ff., and Anl. zum KTB (app. to KTB), 21 May, RH 24–39/9; Heidkämper, Die Operationen des XV.AK, 38ff.*; The Rommel Papers,* 29ff.; Manteuffel, *Die 7.Panzer-Division,* 76ff.; Plato, *5.Panzerdivision,* 71; Karl Ullrich, *Wie ein Fels im Meer. Kriegsgeschichte der 3.SS-Panzer-Division "Totenkopf"* (Like a Rock in the Sea: The War History of the 3d SS Panzer Division, "Totenkopf")

(Osnabrück: Munin-Verlag, 1987), 26ff.; Jacobsen, *Dünkirchen,* 54ff.; Macksey, *Rommel,* 51ff.; Lewin, *Rommel,* 28ff.; Horne, *Über die Maas,* 414ff.; Benoist-Méchin, *Der Himmel stürzt ein,* 124ff.; Deighton, *Blitzkrieg,* 304ff.; Brian Bond, *France and Belgium 1939–1940,* 116ff.; Gregory Blaxland, *Destination Dunkirk. The Story of Gort's Army* (London: William Kimber, 1973), 133ff.; Ellis, *The War in France,* 88ff.; Buffetaut, *Rommel,* 63ff., 74ff., 197ff. The Unit Tradition Association of the former 7th Panzer Division supplied the author with additional documents, for example, Kriegstagebuch II.Bataillon/Schützenregiment 7 (War Diary of the 2d Battalion, 7th Rifle Regiment).

110. 7.PzDiv, KTB, BA-MA, RH 27–7/3, sheets 57ff. This file contains almost all radio messages in the division command net during the Battle of Arras.
111. Ibid., sheets 58ff.; Heidkämper, *Die Operationen des XV.AK,* 40, BA-MA; Speidel, *Der Einsatz,* pt. 3, 307ff., BA-MA, Study Lw 3/2.
112. Manteuffel, *Die 7.Panzer-Division,* 78.
113. See Horne, *To Lose a Battle,* n.472, and *Über die Maas,* 523.
114. Clausewitz, *Vom Kriege,* 1158.
115. Horne, *To Lose a Battle,* n.472, and *Über die Maas,* 400; see also Cailloux, "La contre-attaque qui n'eut jamais lieu . . . 19–25 mai (The Counter-attack That Never Took Place . . . 19–25 May)," *RHA* no. 3 (1966): 134ff.
116. Horne, *To Lose a Battle,* n.472, and *Über die Maas,* 400
117. Shirer, *Zusammenbruch,* 750.
118. Klaus-Jürgen Müller, "Dünkirchen 1940. Ein Beitrag zur Vorgeschichte der britischen and französisch Evakuierung" (Dunkirk 1940. A Contribution to the Background of the British and French Evacuation), *Marinerundschau* 57, no. 3 (1960): 142.
119. Churchill, *Their Finest Hour,* 65, and *Zweiten Weltkrieg,* vol. 2, bk. 1, 88.
120. *Ironside Diaries,* 317.
121. Benoist-Méchin, *Der Himmel stürzt ein,* 135.
122. Regarding the planned Weygand offensive, see Maxime Weygand, *Mémoires* (Paris: Flammarion, 1950), vol. 3, 77ff.; Churchill, *Zweiten Weltkrieg,* vol. 2, bk. 1, 77ff.; *Ironside Diaries,* 321ff., 324ff.; Jacobsen, *Dünkirchen,* 66ff., 85ff., 103ff.; Müller, *Dünkirchen,* 140ff.; Horne, *Über die Maas,* 400ff., 409ff., 420ff., 433ff., 440ff., 451ff., 458f.; Shirer, *Zusammenbruch,* 749ff.; Benoist-Méchin, *Der Himmel stürzt ein,* 111ff., 118ff., 124ff., 132ff., 138ff., 141ff., 153ff.; Glover, *The Fight for the Channel Ports,* 104ff.; Deighton, *Blitzkrieg,* 303f.
123. *Ironside Diaries,* 321.
124. Ibid.
125. Shirer, *Zusammenbruch,* 754.
126. Ibid.
127. Detailed Arrangement by Ellis, *The War in France,* 90.
128. Lewin, *Rommel,* 30.
129. Ibid., 32.
130. Concerning the course of the battle of Arras (from the Allied viewpoint): Horne, *Über die Maas,* 414ff.; Blaxland, *Destination Dunkirk,* 136ff.; Perret, *Blitzkrieg,* 97f.; Ellis, *The War in France,* 88f.; Deighton, *Blitzkrieg,* 304ff.; Macksey, *Rommel,* 51ff.; Bond, *France and Belgium,* 116ff.; Buffetaut, *Rommel,* 63ff., 74ff., 197ff.; André Coilliot, *Mai 1940. Un mois pas comme les autres. Le film des événements dans la région d'Arras* (May 1940: A Month Not Like the Others. The Film of Events in the Arras Region) (Arras, 1980), 107ff.; H. C. B. Rogers, "Arras. Mai 1940," *Connaissance de*

l'Histoire (Knowledge of History), no. 48 (September 1982): 46ff.; E. Gillet, "La percée allemande en mai 1940 et la contre-attaque d'Arras," *RBHM* 29 (1992): 607ff.; Pallud, *Blitzkrieg,* 339ff.

131. Blaxland, *Destination Dunkirk,* 143.
132. Ibid.
133. *The Rommel Papers,* 33.
134. AOK 4, KTB, BA-MA RH 20–4/54, 277ff.; PzGruppe Hoth, KTB (Panzer Group Hoth, War Diary), BA-MA, RH 21–3/36, 36f.; Speidel, Der Einsatz, pt. 3, Study Lw 3/2, 188ff., Anlagen, Anl. 54 (app. 54), Lw 3/4a, BA-MA; Shirer, *Zusammenbruch,* 759; Horne, *Über die Maas,* 440.
135. Halder *KTB,* vol. 1, 314.
136. PzGruppe Kleist, KTB, BA-MA, RH 21–1/22, 27.
137. Halder, *Halder War Diary,* 163 (23 May 1940); Halder *KTB,* vol. 1, 316.
138. HGr A, KTB, BA-MA, RH 19 I/37, sheet 134.
139. Plato, *5.Panzerdivision,* 74.
140. Halder *KTB,* vol. 1, 316.
141. Kenneth Macksey, *Guderian: Creator of the Blitzkrieg* (New York: Stein and Day, 1976), 143; *Guderian: Der Panzergeneral,* 185.
142. Guderian, *Panzer Leader,* 114, and *Erinnerungen,* 102; see also PzKorps Guderian, KTB, BA-MA, RH 21–2/41, 109f., 126.
143. Churchill, *Their Finest Hour,* 82, and *Zweiter Weltkrieg,* vol. 2, bk. 1, 107.
144. 7.PzDiv: Gefechtsbericht 21. Mai (7th Panzer Division: After-Action report, 21 May), 20, BA-MA, RH 27–7/44.
145. The so-called Rommelalbum (Rommel Album) is one of the most impressive documents on the campaign in the west. See BA-MA, RH 27–7/220 (in this connection, see also the coverage of the events on 21 May).
146. AOK 4, Kurzer Überblick, BA-MA, RH 20–4/81, 22 May.
147. PzKorps Reinhardt, KTB, BA-MA, RH 24–41/2, 51.
148. AOK 4, BA-MA, RH 20–4/71, sheet 72.
149. AOK 4, Kurzer Überblick, BA-MA, RH 20–4/81, 22 May.
150. Ibid.

Chapter 8

1. *Ironside Diaries,* 333.
2. Gerbet, *Bock: War Diary,* 157 (29 May 1940), and *KTB,* pt. 3, 35 (29 May 1940), Study P–210, vol. 1, BA-MA.
3. HGr A, Anl. 31 b zum KTB (Army Group A, Annex 31 b to War Diary), BA-MA, RH 19 I/38, sheet 104.
4. See also Rundstedt's Heeresgruppenbefehl Nr. 6 (vom 25. Mai) (Army Group Order No. 6 [25 May], Item 1, BA-MA, RH 19 I/38, sheet 88.
5. Gerbet, *Bock: War Diary,* 158 (29 May 1940), and *KTB,* pt. 3, 35 (29 May 1940), Study P–210, vol. 1, BA-MA.
6. Halder, *Halder War Diary,* 161 (23 May 1940), 164 (24 May 1940); Halder *KTB,* vol. 1, 314, 316.
7. Halder, *Halder War Diary,* 164 (24 May 1940); Halder *KTB,* vol. 1, 316, see also 314, 317.

8. HGr A, Anl. 29 zum KTB (Army Group A, app. 29 to War Diary), BA-MA, RH 19 I/38, sheet 116.
9. Halder, *Halder War Diary,* 163 (23 May 1940); Halder *KTB,* vol. 1, 316.
10. AOK 4, KTB, BA-MA, RH 20–4/54, 306.
11. BA-MA, RH 20–4/71, sheet 174; see also ibid., RH 20–4/54, 308, 317.
12. This seems astonishing inasmuch as a precise differentiation was made between the two orders in a monograph already published in 1958 by Hans-Adolf Jacobsen (with the collaboration of Klaus Jürgen Müller), *Dünkirchen* (Dunkirk) (Neckargemünd: 1958), 79ff.
13. XXXXI.PzKorps, KTB (XXXXI Panzer Corps, War Diary), BA-MA, RH 24–41/2, 58.
14. Ibid., 59.
15. BA-MA, RH 21–2/41, 122.
16. Ibid., 125.
17. BA-MA, RH 27–6/1D, 36 (sheet 39).
18. Halder, *Halder War Diary,* 162 (23 May 1940); Halder *KTB,* vol. 1, 314.
19. GenStdH/OpAbt, KTB, BA-MA, RH 2/2972, 45; HGr A, KTB, RH 19 I/37, sheet 138; RH 19 I/38, sheets 107, 114; HGr B, RH 19 II/72, sheet 89.
20. Halder, *Halder War Diary,* 164 (23 May 1940) and Halder *KTB,* vol. 1, 317; HGr A, BA-MA, RH 19 I/38, sheet 107; GenStdH/OpAbt, KTB, RH 2/2972, 45.
21. HGr A, KTB, BA-MA, RH 19 I/37, sheet 140.
22. Tagebuch Jodl, 25.5.1940, BA-MA, RW 4/32, 54.
23. BA-MA, RH 19 I/38, sheet 103.; see also die Meldung an das OKH/Generalstab des Heeres um 17.30 Uhr (Message to Army High Command/Army General Staff at 1730); ibid., sheet 102.
24. In his Bemerkungen zum “Feldzug im Westen” (Comments on “The Campaign in the West”), BA-MA, Study C-053, sheet 4, Rundstedt in fact asserts that it was Hitler alone who issued the “Halt Order.” Here is what he wrote: “*The blame* for this rests only on Hitler and *not on me,* as Mr. Churchill maintains in his Memoirs!! After all, in the end, I *had to obey* Hitler’s order *which he kept repeating over and over again!*”
25. See the statements by General a.D. [Lieutenant General, Ret.] Blumentritt, at that time the Operations Officer of Army Group A, in his Von Rundstedt, 75; see also Blumentritt, Westfeldzug, vol. 2, 86, Study P–208, BA-MA; see also Liddell Hart, *Jetzt dürfen sie reden,* 233ff. In contrast, Hans Meier-Welcker (“Entschluß zum Anhalten der deutschen Panzertruppen in Flandern 1940” [The Decision to Stop the German Panzer troops in Flanders, 1940], *Vierteljahrshefte für Zeitgeschichte* 2 [1954]: 278ff.), as early as 1954 clearly pointed out the agreement between Hitler’s and Rundstedt’s views. Jacobsen writes the following about the decisive scene at noon on 24 May: “Hitler thus approved what Rundstedt had proposed” (*Dünkirchen,* 95, see also 203).
26. *Hitlers Weisungen,* 53; and Trevor-Roper, *Blitzkrieg to Defeat,* 27.
27. Engel, *Heeresadjutant,* 81.
28. Tagebuch Jodl, BA-MA, RW 4/32, 55.
29. BA-MA, RH 19 I/37, sheet 143 (25 May).
30. See Benoist-Méchin, *Der Himmel stürzt ein,* 146.
31. Liß, *Westfront,* 196.
32. Halder, *Halder War Diary,* 165 (25 May 1940); Halder *KTB,* vol. 1, 319. Editor’s note: A comparison of the published German and English versions of the entry for 25 May 1940 revealed a transposition of Army Groups A and B in the first part of the quotation.

The German version had AGp.B holding and AGp.A attacking, while the English version reversed the roles. In the English version, Halder's plans for the Army Groups in the entry's first paragraph contradicted not only his plans for them in the second paragraph but also the actual situation on the ground at the time. This error must have been made in the original English translation of the Halder diaries that was prepared for the postwar International War Crimes Trials at Nürnberg because other English-language versions of the Halder Diary that use that original translation have the same transposition for 25 May 1940. The first part of the quotation cited here uses the Army Group sequence as it appeared in the German version. This brings it into agreement with Halder's plans as laid out in the second part of the quotation, with A as the hammer and B as the anvil, which is from the second paragraph of the entry for 25 May 1940.

33. Heusinger, *Befehl,* 92.
34. Gerbet, *Bock: War Diary,* 153 (26 May 1940), and Halder *KTB,* pt. 3, 28f. (26 May 1940), Study P–210, vol. 1, BA-MA.
35. AOK 4, KTB, BA-MA, RH 20–4/54, 369.
36. Guderian, *Panzer Leader,* 117; *Erinnerungen,* 105.
37. Guderian, *Panzer Leader,* 117; *Erinnerungen,* 104.
38. *Erinnerungen,* 105.
39. Halder, *Halder War Diary,* 165 (24 May 1940); Halder *KTB,* vol. 1, 318.
40. Tagebuch Jodl, BA-MA, RW 4/32, 34.
41. See Jacobsen, *Dünkirchen,* 99f.
42. HGr A, Anl. 37 zum KTB (Army Group A, app. 37, War Diary), BA-MA, RH 19 I/38, sheet 97; see also HGr B, RH 19 II/72, 92.
43. HGr B, KTB, BA-MA, RH 19 II/72, 92.
44. Hans-Adolf Jacobsen and Jürgen Rohwer, eds., *Entscheidungsschlachten des zweiten Weltkrieges* (Decisive Battles of the Second World War) (Frankfurt am Main: Bernard and Graefe, 1960), 42; English-language version, Jacobsen and Rohwer, eds., *Decisive Battles of World War II: The German View* (London: Andre Deutsch, 1965), 58.
45. BA-MA, RH 19, I/37, sheet 143.
46. Both quoted from Charles Messenger, *The Last Prussian: A Biography of Field Marshal Gerd von Rundstedt* (London: Brassey's, 1991), 222.
47. Rundstedt, who was still caught up in the ideas of World War I, had already been retired when he was recalled to active duty shortly before the start of World War II. Dunkirk, where he made the gravest mistake of his career, however, at the same time, was to be at the moment "at which he saw the light." During the second part of the Campaign in France, he suddenly turned out to be a supporter of those very ideas on which he once upon had commented: "This is all nonsense, my dear Guderian, nothing but nonsense!" See Malte Plettenberg, *Guderian. Hintergründe eines deutschen Schicksals, 1918–1945* (Guderian: Background of a German Destiny, 1918–1945) (Düsseldorf: abz-Verlag, 1950), 13.
48. Tagebuch Jodl, BA-MA, RW 4/32, 55.
49. Halder *KTB,* vol. 1, 319.
50. Horne, *Über die Maas,* 460. The approximately five hundred British bombers that kept raiding persistently during the last week of May also achieved a rather considerable effect (see Horne, *Über die Maas,* 527).
51. Speidel, Der Einsatz, pt. 3, Study Lw 3/2, 355, BA-MA.
52. The loss figures of up to 300 German aircraft, which are given in almost all the literature, appear to be much too high. In reality, the Luftwaffe, during the seven days it

was in action against British Operation Dynamo, lost only 174 bombers and fighters (see Akten, Genst der Luftwaffe, Generalquartiermeister, BA-MA, RL 2 III/1173 and 1174). This figure, however, refers to the entire western front, not just to Dunkirk, where the weather made continual sorties impossible.

53. Speidel, Der Einsatz, pt. 3, 352, BA-MA, Study Lw 3/2.
54. Ibid., 366.
55. Concerning the operations of the Luftwaffe, see Jacobsen, *Dünkirchen,* 183ff.; Balke, *Luftkrieg,* vol. 1, 104.
56. VIII.Fliegerkorps, Einsatz, BA-MA, RL 8/43, sheet 21.
57. Loßberg, *Im Wehrmachtführungsstab,* 82.
58. Halder, *Halder War Diary,* 167 (26 May 1940); Halder *KTB,* vol. 1, 320.
59. Halder, *Halder War Diary,* 167 (26 May 1940); Halder *KTB,* vol. 1, 320.
60. Halder, *Halder War Diary,* 167 (26 May 1940); Halder *KTB,* vol. 1, 320; see also Tagebuch Jodl, BA-MA, RW 4/32, 56; HGr A, KTB, RH 19 I/37, sheet 146f.
61. Liß, "Dünkirchen," 337.
62. Müller, *Dünkirchen,* 136, 138.
63. Jacobsen, *Dünkirchen,* 167.
64. Churchill, *Zweiter Weltkrieg,* vol. 2, bk. 1, 129.
65. Ibid., 127.
66. *Ironside Diaries,* 334.
67. For statistics, see Jacobsen, *Dünkirchen,* 182.
68. Walter Lord, *Das Geheimnis von Dünkirchen* (The Secret of Dunkirk) (Bern and Munich: Scherz, 1982), 312; English-language version, *The Miracle of Dunkirk* (New York: The Viking Press, 1982).
69. AOK 18, KTB, Eintragung, 4.Juni (HQ Eighteenth Army, War Diary, Entry 4 June), BA-MA, RH 20–18/35.
70. For statistics according to the Ramsay Report, see Jacobsen, *Dünkirchen,* 182f.; see also Churchill, *Zweiter Weltkrieg,* vol. 2, bk. 1, 145; Ellis, *The War in France,* 246ff.; Lord, *Geheimnis,* 316.
71. The initial assumption—based on the erroneous statement of a French general—pointed to a figure of 40,000 prisoners of war. The exact figure of 80,000 was determined only several days later; see also AOK 18, KTB, Eintragung 4. Juni, BA-MA, RH 20–18/35.
72. Bock, KTB, pt. 3, 43 (2 June 1940), Study P–210, vol. 1, BA-MA.
73. Halder *KTB,* vol. 1, 323.
74. The quotation is from Lord, *Miracle,* 261; Lord, *Geheimnis,* 301.
75. Dahms, *Geschichte des Zweiten Weltkriegs,* 180.
76. Ibid.; see also Ellis, *The War in France,* 246; Williamson Murray, *Strategy for Defeat. The Luftwaffe, 1933–1945* (Maxwell Air Force Base, Ala: Air University Press, 1983), 39.
77. Martin Gilbert, *The Second World War* (London, 1989), 86; Dahms, *Geschichte des Zweiten Weltkriegs,* 180; Lord, *Geheimnis,* 314; Ellis, *The War in France,* 327. General Ironside even mentions 120,000 vehicles that were lost; see *Ironside Diaries,* 354.
78. Gerbet, *Bock: War Diary,* 162 (2 June 1940), and, *KTB,* pt. 3, 41 (2 June 1940), Study P–210, vol. 1, BA-MA.
79. Horne, *Über die Maas,* 445; *To Lose a Battle,* 525.
80. *Ironside Diaries,* 333; see also Lord, *Geheimnis,* 314f.; Liddell Hart, *Jetzt dürfen sie reden,* 172f.; Deighton, *Blitzkrieg,* 323.

81. See Lord, *Miracle,* 273–74; Lord, *Geheimnis,* 314. Original quote is from Arthur Bryant, *The Turn of the Tide, 1939–1943. A Study Based on the Diaries and Autobiographical Notes of Field Marshal the Viscount Alanbrooke, K.G., O.M.* (London: Collins, 1957), 158.
82. A. J. Barker, *Dunkirk: The Great Escape* (New York: David McKay, 1977), 226.
83. Churchill, *Their Finest Hour*, 118; *Zweiter Weltkrieg,* vol. 2, bk. 1, 141.
84. Deighton, *Blitzkrieg,* 315, 323.
85. This is particularly clear in Barker, *Dunkirk,* 226f.
86. Norman Gelb, *Dunkirk: The Complete Story of the First Step in the Defeat of Hitler* (New York: William Morrow, 1989), 316–17.
87. Liddell Hart, *History of the Second World War,* 75; *Zweiten Weltkrieges,* 104.
88. Rundstedt, "Bemerkungen zum 'Feldzug im Westen,' " 4, BA-MA, Study C-053.
89. Loßberg, *Im Wehrmachtführungsstab,* 81.
90. Concerning the criticism of this theory, see Walde, *Guderian,* 95ff.; Macksey, *Guderian: Der Panzergeneral,* 186ff.
91. PzKorps Guderian, KTB, BA-MA, RH 21–2/41, 163 (28 May 1940).
92. This emerges already from an entry in the war diary on 22 May, when Guderian—in an effort to run right over "the enemy while he was building up his defenses" at Dunkirk—even wanted to ignore the orders given by von Kleist: "For the same reasons, the Corps Commander (Guderian) ordered the 1st Panzer Division, contrary to the preliminary order from the (Kleist) Group, to move not only up to the St. Momelin—Gravelines line on 23 May, but also on ahead *to Dunkirk,* were presumably strong elements of the British Expeditionary Corps will try to escape the encirclement." (PzKorps Guderian, KTB, BA-MA, RH 21–2/41, (28 May 1940), 117; see also Guderian's almost identical situation estimate on the evening of 23 May, ibid., 125).
93. Guderian, *Panzer Leader,* 119; *Erinnerungen,* 107.
94. Halder, *Hitler,* 13; *Hitler als Feldherr,* 16; see also Blumentritt, *Von Rundstedt,* 76.
95. HGr A, KTB, BA-MA, RH 19 I/37, sheet 140; see also Rundstedt, "Bemerkungen zum 'Feldzug im Westen,' " Study C-053, 4, BA-MA; Blumentritt, Westfeldzug, vol. 2, 86, Study P–208, vol. 2, BA-MA.
96. HGr A, BA-MA, RH 19 I/38, sheet 116.
97. Irving, *Hitlers Krieg,* 174.
98. PzGruppe Kleist, KTB, BA-MA, RH 21–1/22, 29f.
99. During the campaign in the east, the German Panzer Arm had to get along with considerably more unfavorable operational statistics and was still astonishingly successful in operational terms. For example, the First Panzer Army, led by Kleist, early in December 1941 only had 59 operational battle tanks but were still able to beat off a counteroffensive by four Soviet armies [= corps] at Rostov; see also Gen.d. Art. a.D (general of artillery, retired) Friedrich Wilhelm Hauck, Die Abwehrkämpfe am Donetz und auf der Krim und das Wiedergewinnen der Initiative, Dezember 1941 bis Juni 1942 (Die Operationen der deutschen Heeresgruppen an der Ostfront 1941–1945, Südliches Gebiet, Zweiter Teil) (The Defense Battles along the Donets and in the Crimea and the Seizure of the Initiative, December 1941 to June 1942) (in the Operations of the German Army Groups on the Eastern Front, 1941–1945, Southern Region, pt. 2), app., 71, table 2, study P–114c, pt. 2, BA-MA.
100. Stoves, *1. Panzer-Division,* 124.
101. Halder, *Halder War Diary,* 163 (23 May 1940); Halder *KTB,* vol. 1, 316.
102. By 24 May, the total loss figure was relatively small. The 10-day summaries, prepared

by the Wehrwirtschaftsand- und Rüstungsamt (Defense Economy and Armament Office), reported only 125 Panzer losses for the period of 10–20 May. The number rose increasingly only at the end of May; Wehrwirtschaftsand- und Rüstungsamt (Wehrwirtschaftsamt) (Defense Economy and Armament Office [Defense Economy Office]), BA-MA, RW 19/1938, sheet 1.

103. See also Meier-Welcker, "Entschluß zum Anhalten," 276n.6; Blumentritt, *Von Rundstedt,* 76. There was merely a brief bottleneck in the supply of certain spare parts, which was resolved by means of air transport; see PzGruppe Kleist, BA-MA, RH 21–1/317, 39f.
104. See Irving, *Hitler's War,* 125; *Hitlers Krieg.* 178. See also Jacobsen, *Dünkirchen,* 221 (communication from Salmuth along these lines).
105. Loßberg, *Im Wehrmachtführungsstab,* 81.
106. Rundstedt, "*Bemerkungen zum 'Feldzug im Westen,'*" BA-MA, Study C-053, 4.
107. Halder, *Halder War Diary,* 171 (29 May 1940); Halder *KTB,* vol. 1, 325.
108. See Halder *KTB,* vol. 1, 315. On 23 May, Halder had already noted (*KTB,* vol. 1, 315) an initial cautious estimate that indicated 45 encircled Allied divisions.
109. Liß, "Dünkirchen," 337, 340; also, *Westfront,* 211ff.
110. See Hans-Adolf Jacobsen, ed., *Dokumente zum Westfeldzug 1940* (Documents on the Campaign in the West, 1940) (Göttingen, Berlin, and Frankfurt am Main: Musterschmidt, 1960), 135.
111. See, for example, Deighton, *Blitzkrieg,* 322. It must be pointed out that originally not even the British Admiralty believed in the possibility of a complete evacuation. Its pessimistic forecast indicated that 45,000 men could be saved at best. But this statement must be seen in the proper context. As Churchill stated in *Zweiten Weltkrieg,* vol. 2, bk. 1, 127, this estimate covers only a period of "two days." The British figured that the German leadership would behave in a rational way and believed that they would do everything possible to seize Dunkirk as quickly as possible. And so, they hoped they might be able to hold the port city perhaps for another two days, which, at best, would have meant an evacuation rate of 45,000 men.
112. Liß, "Dünkirchen," 335.
113. Ibid., 336.
114. Ibid., 335.
115. Ibid., 336.
116. Trevor-Roper, *Hitler's War Directives,* 27; *Hitlers Weisungen,* 53f.
117. Walter Ansel, *Hitler Confronts England* (Durham, N.C.: Duke University Press, 1960), 75; see also Walter Warlimont, *Im Hauptquartier der deutschen Wehrmacht 1939–1945* (In the Headquarters of the German Wehrmacht, 1939–1945) (Frankfurt am Main: Bernard and Graefe, 1962), 113. See the report of an eyewitness, Schmid (later: Generalleutnant), quoted in Speidel, Der Einsatz, pt. 3, 329f., Study Lw 3/2, BA-MA; Irving, *Tragödie,* 150f.; Jacobsen, *Dünkirchen,* 90.
118. Speidel, Der Einsatz, pt. 3, 334, Study Lw 3/2, BA-MA.
119. See Horne, *Über die Maas,* 447. See also the statements made by Jodl and Keitel in Loßberg, *Im Wehrmachtführungsstab,* 81; Halder, *KTB,* vol. 1, 318; Engel, *Heeresadjutant,* 80; Meier-Welcker, "Entschluß zum Anhalten," 288.
120. Engel, *Heeresadjutant,* 80.
121. Seidemann, "Bericht," 2, BA-MA, ZA 3/44.
122. VIII. FliegerKorps, Einsatz, BA-MA, RL 8/43, sheet 18.

123. Blumentritt, *Von Rundstedt,* 77.
124. Albert Kesselring, *Soldat bis zum letzten Tag* (Soldier to the Last Day) (Bonn: Athenäum, 1953), 77; English-language version, Albert Kesselring, *Kesselring: A Soldier's Record* (New York: William Morrow, 1954), 58.
125. Kesselring, *A Soldier's Record,* 58, and, *Soldat,* 77f.; see also Deichmann, *Chef,* 101.
126. See the statistics of Generalstab der Luftwaffe (Gen.Qu.6. Abt.) (Luftwaffe General Staff, Deputy Chief of Staff, Administration and Supply, 6th Department), in *Akten,* BA-MA, RL 2 III/1173.
127. *Hitlers politisches Testament. Die Bormann Diktate vom Febr. und April 1945* (Hitler's Political Testament. Bormann's Dictation, February and April 1945) (Hamburg, 1981), 113.
128. Irving, *Hitlers Krieg,* 130.
129. Ibid., 178; see also Bernd Martin, "Das 'Dritte Reich' und die 'Friedens'-Frage in Zweiten Weltkrieg" (The "Third Reich" and the "Peace Issue" during the Second World War), *Nationalsozialistische Außenpolitik,* 532.
130. See also Blumentritt, *Von Rundstedt,* 74f.
131. See Halder, *Halder War Diary,* 156 (22 May 1940); Halder *KTB,* vol. 1, 308.
132. See Irving, *Hitler's War,* 82; *Hitlers Krieg,* 130.
133. Tagebuch Jodl, BA-MA, RW 4/32, 52.
134. Otto Abetz, *Das offene Problem. Ein Rückblick auf zwei Jahrzehnte deutscher Frankreichpolitik* (The Unresolved Problem: A Review of Two Centuries of German Policy toward France) (Cologne: Greven Verlag, 1951), 129.
135. Leeb, *Tagebuchaufzeichnungen,* 233.
136. Liddell Hart, *The German Generals Talk,* 134–135, as quoted in Liddell Hart, *Zweiten Weltkrieges,* 114f., and *History of the Second World War,* 83; see also Blumentritt, *Von Rundstedt,* 78.
137. Liddell Hart, *Jetzt dürfen sie reden,* 248, and *The German Generals Talk,* 135; see also Blumentritt, *Von Rundstedt,* 78.
138. Rundstedt, "Bemerkungen zum 'Feldzug im Westen,' " 4, BA-MA, Study C-053; see also Warlimont, *Im Hauptquartier,* 114n.9.
139. Seidemann, "Bericht," 2, ZA 3/44, BA-MA.
140. See Liddell Hart, *History of the Second World War,* 83; *Zweiten Weltkrieges,* 115.
141. Trevor-Roper, *Blitzkrieg to Defeat,* 27; *Hitlers Weisungen,* 53; see also Engel, *Heeresadjutant,* 80.
142. Halder, *KTB,* vol. 1, 327.
143. See Meier-Welcker, "Entschluß zum Anhalten," 286.
144. See Irving, *Rise and Fall of the Luftwaffe,* 90; *Die Tragödie,* 151.
145. Halder, *KTB,* vol. 1, 319.
146. Tagebuch Jodl, BA-MA, RW 4/32, 54.
147. Ibid. The Generalfeldmarschall (field marshal) (meaning Göring) argued that, in issuing his disputed order, Brauchitsch did "not in any way wish to push" Army Group B. Concerning Hitler's aversion against the conservative Army and the predominantly Prussian military aristocracy, see Heusinger, *Befehl,* 93; Warlimont, *Im Hauptquartier,* 106; Engel, *Heeresadjutant,* 41, 80.
148. At that time, people talked in terms of the "Imperial Navy," that had been built up under Wilhelm II, the "Royal Army" in the tradition of Frederick the Great, and the "National Socialist Luftwaffe."

149. Halder, *Hitler,* 30; *Hitler als Feldherr,* 30.
150. This quotation can be found hidden away in a footnote in: Meier-Welcker, "Entschluss zum Anhalten," 289n.56.
151. See Albert Zoller, *Hitler privat. Erlebnisbericht seiner Geheimsekretärin* (The Private Hitler: The Account of His Personal Secretary) (Düsseldorf: Droste Verlag, 1949), 141.

Chapter 9

1. The Campaign's subdivision into two successive major operations goes back to Manstein's idea. Of course, the terms *Fall Gelb* (Case Yellow) and *Fall Rot* (Case Red) came from the Army High Command.
2. Ploetz, *Geschichte des Zweiten Weltkrieges,* pt. 1, 23.
3. Müller-Hillebrand, *Das Heer,* vol. 2, 48f.
4. Gerbet, *Bock: War Diary,* 166 (6 June 1940), and KTB, pt. 3, 47 (6 June 1940), Study P 210, vol. 1, BA-MA.
5. Manstein, *Lost Victories,* 130; Manstein, *Verlorene Siege,* 127.
6. Manstein, *Lost Victories,* 130; Manstein, *Verlorene Siege,* 128.
7. See Borgert, *Grundzüge,* 520f.
8. BA-MA, RH 27–7/215, 50.
9. Manstein, *Verlorene Siege,* 124.
10. Ibid.; Manstein, *Lost Victories,* 126.
11. *The Halder War Diary,* 194 (10 June 1940); Halder *KTB,* 194 (10 June 1940), vol. 1, 346.
12. Guderian, *Panzer Leader,* 130; *Erinnerungen,* 108.
13. Dach, *Kampfbeispiele* (Examples of Combat Operations), 60ff.
14. Wallach, *Dogma,* 379.
15. See Dahms, *Geschichte des zweiten Weltkrieges,* 185.
16. Umbreit, "Kampf um die Vormachtstellung," 310; see also Gerhard Schreiber, "Die politische und militärische Entwicklung im Mittelmeerraum 1939/40" (Political and Military Developments in the Mediterranean Area), Gerhard Schreiber, Bernd Stegemann, and Detlef Vogel, *Der Mittelmeerraum und Südosteuropa* (The Mediterranean Area and Southeastern Europe), vol. 3, *Das Deutsche Reich und der Zweiten Weltkrieg* (Stuttgart: Deutsche Verlags-Anstalt,1984), 33ff.
17. At the start of the western campaign, the Dutch forces numbered 400,000 men.
18. Belgium had 650,000 soldiers.
19. *Zusammenfassender Bericht des OKW* (Summarizing Report of Wehrmacht High Command), see *Dokumente zum Westfeldzug,* 150.
20. See the speech of French prime minister Reynaud on 7 June (Generalstab des Heeres [Army General Staff], BA-MA, RH 2/1556, 20).
21. Testimony by General Weygand during the subsequent trial of Marshal Pétain (see Benoist-Méchin, *Der Himmel stürzt ein,* 239; *Sixty Days that Shook the West,* 222).
22. HGr Süd, KTB (Army Group South, War Diary), BA-MA, RH 19 I/73, sheet 132. (26 September 1941).
23. Rüdiger Overmans, "Das andere Gesicht des Krieges: Leben und Sterben der 6.Armee" (The Other Face of War: Life and Death of the Sixth Army), Jürgen Förster, ed., *Stalingrad: Ereignis-Wirkung-Symbol* (Stalingrad: Event-Effect-Symbol) (Munich: Piper Verlag, 1992), 446.

24. See the statistics in Akten: OKW/Allgemeines Wehrmachtamt/Wehrmachtverlustwesen (Files: Wehrmacht High Command/General Wehrmacht Office/Wehrmacht Casualty Section), BA-MA, RW 6/180; WiRüAmt, Personelle Verluste (Defense Economy and Armament Office, Personnel Losses), RW 19/1381; OKW/Wehrmachtverlustwesen, Allgemeines Marinehauptamt (Wehrmacht High Command/Wehrmacht Casualty Section, General Navy Main Office), BA-MA, RM 7/807 and RM 7/808. One must also consider here about 52,000 wounded.
25. 1.PzDiv (1st Panzer Division), BA-MA, RH 27–1/14, sheet 343f.
26. See the tables in: BA-MA, RW 6/180; RW 19/1381; RM 7/807; RM 7/808 (such as n.24). In addition, there were about 111,000 wounded; see Zusammenfassender Bericht des OKW, Dokumente zum Westfeldzug [Summary Report of Wehrmacht High Command (Documents from the Campaign in the West), 287]; see the tables in Files BA-MA, RW 4/170 (Verluste im 1. Kriegsjahr) (Losses during the 1st year of the War), as well as RW 6/180.
27. Raymond Cartier, *Der Zweiten Weltkrieg* (The Second World War) vol. 1 (Munich: Piper Verlag, 1967), 190; Gunsburg, *Divided,* 275.
28. Gunsburg, *Divided,* 275; Dahms, *Geschichte des zweiten Weltkrieges,* 178.
29. Gunsburg, *Divided,* 275.
30. Horne, *Über die Maas,* 482; Perrett, *Knights,* 67; Ellis, *The War in France,* 326; Gunsburg, *Divided,* 273; Pallud, *Blitzkrieg,* 609.
31. Müller, "Mobilisierung der deutschen Wirtschaft," 636.
32. Akten Genst der Luftwaffe (Generalquartiermeister) (Files, Luftwaffe General Staff, Deputy Chief of Staff, Administration and Supply), BA-MA, RL 2/III/1173 and 1174 (these figures were calculated by Ulf Balke). The statistics fluctuate just about 900: Cot, *En 40,* 42; Buffotot and Ogier, *L'armeé de l'air,* 111.
33. Harvey, "The French Armeé de l'Air," 455; *Histoire le l'aviation militaire française,* 390; Kirkland, "French Air Force," 117n.4.
34. Harvey, 455; Kirkland, 117n.4.

Chapter 10

1. PzRgt7, BA-MA, RH 39/103 (Bericht von Oberst Straub) (7th Panzer Regiment. Report by Oberst Straub), 12.
2. Franz Knipping, "*Frankreich in der Zeit der Weltkriege (1914–1945)*" (France in the Time of the World Wars, 1914–1945), Karl Ploetz, *Geschichte der Weltkriege. Mächte,* Ereignisse, Entwicklungen 1900–1945 (History of the World Wars. Powers, Events, Developments, 1900–1945) (Freiburg and Würzburg: Ploetz Verlag, 1981), ed. Andreas Hillgruber and Jost Dülffer, pt. 1, 243; Porch, "Why Did France Fall?," *Quarterly Journal of Military History* 2, no. 3 (spring 1990): 34.
3. Daniel Cordier, *Jean Moulin. L'inconnu du Panthéon, Tome 2: Le choix d'un destin, juin 1936-novembre 1940* (Jean Moulin: The Unknown Man of the Panthéon, vol. 2: The Choice of Fate, June 1936-November 1940) (Paris: Lattès, 1989), 207, 552f.
4. Regarding French pacifism and German peace propaganda aimed at it, see above all the following: Wilhelm von Schramm, . . . *Sprich vom Frieden, wenn du den Krieg willst. Die psychologischen Offensiven Hitlers gegen die Franzosen 1933 bis 1939* (. . . Talk of Peace If You Want War: Hitler's Psychological Offensives against the French, 1933 to 1939) (Mainz: Hase and Köhler Verlag, 1973); Piekalkiewicz, *Ziel Paris,* 7, 22ff., 91ff.,

185ff.; Horne, *Über die Maas,* 59ff.; Franz Herre, *Deutsche und Franzosen: Der lange Weg zur Freundschaft* (Germans and Frenchmen: The Long Way to Friendship) (Bergisch-Gladbach: Lübbe Verlag, 1988), 240ff.; Shirer, *Zusammenbruch,* 505f., 540f.; Hans Habe, *Ob tausend fallen—Ein Bericht* (Regardless of Whether Thousands Fall—A Report) (Freiburg i. Breisgau, 1974), 54ff.; Jean-Louis Crémieux-Brilhac, *La guerre oui ou non?, Tome. 1, Les Français de l'an 40* (The War, Yes or No?, Vol. 1: The French of 1940) (Paris: Robert Laffont, 1990), 84ff., 423 ff.; Norman Ingram, *Politics of Dissent. Pacific's in France, 1919–1939* (Oxford: Oxford University Press, 1991); Ortwin Buchbender and Reinhard Hauschild, *Geheimsender gegen Frankreich—Die Täuschungsoperation "Radio Humanité" 1940* (Secret Radio Station against France—The Deception Operation "Radio Humanity" 1940) (Bonn and Herford: Verlag E. S. Mittler and Sohn, 1984).

5. Piekalkiewicz, *Ziel Paris,* 33f.
6. Ibid., 35.
7. Wolfram Wette, "*Ideologien, Propaganda und Innenpolitik als Voraussetzungen der Kriegspolitik des Dritten Reiches*" (Ideology, Propaganda, and Internal Politics as Preconditions of the War Policy of the Third Reich), *Ursachen und Voraussetzungen der deutschen Kriegspolitik,* 113.
8. Mellenthin, *Schach dem Schicksal,* 79.
9. Piekalkiewicz, *Ziel Paris,* 82ff.
10. Buchbender and Hauschild, 52; see also Piekalkiewicz, *Ziel Paris,* 45, 166.
11. Leendert Johann Hartog, *Und morgen die ganze Welt. Der deutsche Angriff im Westen. 10. Mai bis 17. September 1940* (And Tomorrow the Whole World: The German Offensive in the West, 10 May to 17 September 1940) (Gütersloh: Mohn, 1961), 57.
12. Lord, *Geheimnis,* 17f.
13. See Buchbender and Hauschild.
14. Alfred Fabre-Luce, *Französisches Tagebuch August 1939-Juni 1940* (French Diary, August 1939-June 1940) (Hamburg: Hanseatische Verlagsanstalt, 1942), 216f.
15. Marc Bloch, *Die Seltsame Niederlage: Frankreich 1940. Der Historiker als Zeuge* (The Strange Defeat: France, 1940. The Historian as Witness) (Frankfurt am Main, 1992), 81; Marc Bloch, *Strange Defeat: A Statement of Evidence Written in 1940* (New York: W. W. Norton, 1968), 36.
16. See Fuller, *Conduct,* 246, and *Entartete Kunst,* 270; see also Shirer, *Zusammenbruch,* 191.
17. Churchill, *The Gathering Storm,* vol. 1, *The Second World War* (Boston: Houghton Mifflin, 1948), 474; *Der Zweiten Weltkrieg,* vol. 2, bk. 2, 94f.
18. Clausewitz, *Vom Kriege,* 615; Clausewitz, *On War,* 428.
19. Clausewitz, *Vom Kriege,* 634; Clausewitz, *On War,* 443.
20. Schramm, 14.
21. See also Hans-Jürgen Heimsoeth, *Der Zusammenbruch der Dritten Französischen Republik. Frankreich während der "Drôle de Guerre" 1939/1940* (The Collapse of the Third French Republic—France during the "Phony War" of 1939–1940) (Bonn: Bouvier, 1990). Accordingly, the decay phenomena in French society were noticed only after the start of the war—during the "Phony War" that was felt to be meaningless.
22. For example, this was reported by von Leeb whose Army Group at that time was positioned along the Maginot Line; see his *Tagebuchaufzeichnungen,* 174; see also Ortwin Buchbender and Horst Schuh, *Die Waffe, die auf die Seele zielt. Psychologische Kriegführung, 1939–1945* (The Weapon that Aims at the Soul: Psychological Warfare, 1939–1945) (Stuttgart: Motorbuch Verlag, 1983), 75.

23. Piekalkiewicz, *Ziel Paris,* 74.
24. Ibid., 90f.
25. Abetz, 113.
26. Quoted from Shirer, *Collapse,* 17; *Zusammenbruch,* 15.
27. Blumentritt, Westfeldzug, vol. 2, 10, Study P–208, BA-MA.
28. Bloch, *Strange Defeat,* 36; *Die Seltsame Niederlage,* 81.
29. Bloch, *Strange Defeat,* 37; *Die Seltsame Niederlage,* 82.
30. See Shirer, *Collapse,* 173; *Zusammenbruch,* 178.
31. See De Gaulle, *Memoiren,* vol. 1, 10.
32. Horne, *Über die Maas,* 148; see also 107ff.
33. Shirer, *Collapse,* 621; *Zusammenbruch,* 652.
34. Dach, "Panzer," pt. 3, 65.
35. See Shirer, *Collapse,* 621; *Zusammenbruch,* 652.
36. Shirer, *Collapse,* 622; *Zusammenbruch,* 653.
37. Piekalkiewicz, *Ziel Paris,* 209.
38. Bloch, *Strange Defeat,* 43; *Die Seltsame Niederlage,* 89.
39. Doughty, *Breaking Point,* 295.
40. *Entscheidung im Westen. Der Feldzug der sechs Wochen. Die Berichte des Oberkommandos der Wehrmacht vom 10. Mai bis 25. Juni 1940 mit den täglichen militärischen und politischen Erläuterungen der Kölnischen Zeitung (von Dr. J. Schäfer)* (Decision in the West: The Six-Week Campaign. The Report of the Wehrmacht High Command from 10 May to 25 June 1940, with the Daily Military and Political Explanations by the Cologne Journal [Dr. J. Schäfer]) (Cologne: Verlag M. DuMont Schauberg, 1940), 46f.
41. Wilhelm Weiß, "*Zeitenwende: Betrachtungen zum Jahreswechsel 1940/41*" (Changing Times: Reflections on the Year of Change, 1940–41), Wilhelm Weiß, ed., *Triumph der Kriegskunst. Das Kriegsjahr 1940 in der Darstellung des "Völkischen Beobachters"* (Triumph of the Art of War. The War Year of 1940 as Described by the "People's Observer") (Munich: Eher, 1941), 14.
42. Rabenau, "Revolution der Kriegsführung," OKW/WPr (Revolution of Warfare, Wehrmacht High Command/Wehrmacht Propaganda), BA-MA, RW 4/414, sheets 36–41. See Wallach, *Dogma,* 380ff.; Neugebauer, *Operatives Denken,* 97f.
43. Rabenau, BA-MA, RW 4/414, 1 (sheet 36).
44. Ibid., 5 (sheet 40).
45. Ibid., 2 (sheet 37).
46. Ibid., 6 (sheet 41).
47. Later on, Rabenau also came into conflict with the Nazi regime. After the 20 July 1944 plot against Hitler, he was arrested and killed in a concentration camp.
48. Rabenau, BA-MA, RW 4/414, sheet 32.
49. Ibid., sheet 33.
50. Konstantin Hierl, "Die deutsche Oberste Führung im Westfeldzug und der Schlieffen-Plan" (The German Supreme Command during the Campaign in the West and the Schlieffen Plan), in *Triumph der Kriegskunst,* 74. Reichsleiter Hierl, Reich Labor Leader, had been an instructor in military history and the theory of operations at the Bavarian War Academy before 1914 and was on duty as the chief of staff of an army corps during World War I.
51. See Schall-Riaucour, *Aufstand und Gehorsam,* 151 (14 May 1940).
52. See Senff, *Die Entwicklung der Panzerwaffe,* 28ff.
53. Heinemann, "Development," 57; Cooper, 151.
54. Erich von Manstein, *Aus einem Soldatenleben 1887–1939* (From a Soldier's Life,

1887–1939) (Bonn, 1958), 238f.; see also Walter K. Nehring, *Die Geschichte der deutschen Panzerwaffe 1916–1945* (The History of the German Panzer Force, 1916–1945) (Berlin: Propylöen Verlag, 1969), 75.

55. Karl Wahl, *. . . es ist das deutsche Herz. Erlebnisse und Erkenntnisse eines ehemaligen Gauleiters* (. . . It is the German Heart. Experiences and Realizations of a Former Gauleiter) (Augsburg: Karl Wahl, 1954), 246. For example, this observation was confirmed by Field Marshal von Leeb, in his *Tagebuchaufzeichnungen,* 184.
56. Abetz, 108.
57. See also the term "efficiency mania" in Florian K. Rothbrust, *Guderian's XIXth Panzer Corps and the Battle of France. Breakthrough in the Ardennes, May 1940* (Westport, Conn. and London: Greenwood Press, 1990), 90; see also the basic presentation by T. N. Dupuy, *A Genius for War: The German Army and General Staff, 1807–1945* (Fairfax, Va., 1984).
58. Creveld, *Kampfkraft,* 4, 102, 107, 203f.
59. Ibid., 207.
60. Ibid., 204*; Fighting Power,* 163.
61. Wehrwirtschaftsand- und Rüstungsamt, Stab, KTB (Staff, Defense Economy and Armament Office, War Diary), BA-MA, RW 19/173, sheet 276 (2).
62. Clausewitz, *Vom Kriege,* 221, 227ff.
63. Ibid., 453.
64. See John F. C. Fuller, *Der Zweiten Weltkrieg. Darstellung seiner Strategie und Taktik* (The Second World War. An Account of its Strategy and Tactics) (Vienna and Stuttgart: Humboldt Verlag, 1950), 29f.
65. Quoted from Kroener, "Personellen Ressourcen," 693.
66. See the title of the book by Wallach, *Das Dogma der Vernichtungsschlacht* (The Dogma of the Battle of Annihilation).
67. Kroener, "Personellen Ressourcen," 693f.
68. Quoted from Jehuda Wallach, *Kriegstheorien. Ihre Entwicklung im 19. und 20. Jahrhundert* (Theories of War. Their Development in the 19th and 20th Centuries) (Frankfurt am Main: Bernard and Graefe, 1972), 175.
69. Hans-Henning von Sandrart, "*Operative Führung über die Gefechtstaktik hinaus*" (Operational Command above and beyond Combat Tactics), *Europäische EWKde* 36, no. 9 (1987): 504. The definition of the term "operational" was covered in the introductory chapter. See also Dieter Brand, "*Grundsätze operativer Führung*" (Basic Principles of Operational Command), *Denkschriften zu Fragen der operativen Führung, hrsg. vom Inspekteur des Heeres* (Reports on the Question of Operational Leadership, Collected by the Inspector General of the Army) (Bonn, 1987), 29ff., 43ff.; Neugebauer, 99; Hanno Kielmansegg, *Plädoyer für operative Führung. Forderung nach der Fähigkeit, die Abwehrschlacht zu schlagen* (Plea for Operational Command. Requirement for the Ability to Fight Defensive Battles)," *EWKde* 34, no. 11 (1985); Clayton R. Newell, *The Framework of Operational Warfare* (London and New York: Routledge, 1991), foreword, XIf.
70. Quoted from Hanno Kielmansegg, 614.
71. Brand, 56.
72. See also Rolf-Josef Eibicht, *Schlieffen. Strategie und Politik. Aus der Unterlegenheit zum Sieg* (Schlieffen: Strategy and Policy. From Inferiority to Victory) (Lünen, 1991).
73. See Ludendorff's explanation: "Tactics had to be placed above pure strategy." See Borgert, 521.

74. Ibid.
75. Manstein, *Lost Victories,* 63; *Verlorene Siege,* 56f.
76. Liddell Hart, *The German Generals Talk,* 14.
77. Hans von Seeckt, *Gedanken eines Soldaten* (Thoughts of a Soldier) (Berlin: Verlag für Kulturpolitik, 1929), 86.
78. Ibid., 95.
79. See the recently published account by James S. Corum, *The Roots of Blitzkrieg: Hans von Seeckt and German Military Reform* (Lawrence: University Press of Kansas, 1992).
80. Neugebauer, 120.
81. Quoted from Seeckt, *Bemerkungen des Chefs der Heeresleitung, Generaloberst von Seeckt bei Besichtigungen und Manövern aus den Jahren 1920 bis 1926 (Bes.Bem.)* (Comments of the Chief of the Army Command, General von Seeckt, during Inspections and Maneuvers from the Years 1920 to 1926 (Special Comments) (Berlin: Reichswehrministerium, 1927), 33.
82. Horne, *Über die Maas,* 107.
83. See Hartog, 99f.
84. See Pallud, *Blitzkrieg,* 64.
85. Schlieffen, *Cannae,* 3f.
86. Ibid., 254.
87. Ibid., 263.
88. Waldemar Erfurth, *Der Vernichtungssieg. Eine Studie über das Zusammenwirken getrennter Heeresteile* (The Annihilation Victory: A Study of the Cooperation of Separate Army Components) (Berlin, 1939), 102.
89. Cajus Bekker, *The Luftwaffe War Diaries* (New York: Ballantine, 1969), 195; and *Angriffshöhe 4000,* 177.
90. Konrad Krafft von Dellmensingen, *Der Durchbruch. Studie an Hand der Vorgänge des Weltkrieges 1914–1918* (The Breakthrough: A Study Based on the Events of the World War, 1914–1918) (Hamburg: Hanseatische Verlagsanstalt, 1937), 11f.
91. See Horst Scheibert, *Das war Guderian. Ein Lebensbericht im Bildern* (That Was Guderian: A Report on his Life in Pictures) (Friedberg: Podzun-Pallas Verlag, 1980), 173; see also GenKdo XIX.AK/Ia vom 12.1.1940 (Headquarters, XIX Corps, Operations Section, 12 January 1940), BA-MA, RH 21–2/30, sheet 21.
92. B. H. Liddell Hart, *The Memoirs of Captain Liddell Hart,* vol. 1 (London: Cassell, 1965), 49.
93. For an account of such attacks, see Bruce Gudmundson, *Stormtroop Tactics. Innovation in the German Army, 1914–1918* (New York, 1989); see also Borgert, 523ff.
94. According to Wilhelm Meier-Dörnberg, the failure of the German offensive is also due to the rather unclear formation of the German main effort. Accordingly, Ludendorff supposedly wanted to achieve too much all at once so that the attack was broken up. "Die große deutsche Frühjahrsoffensive 1918 zwischen Strategie und Taktik" (The Great German 1918 Spring Offensive between Strategy and Tactics), *Operatives Denken und Handeln,* 93f.
95. Written communication from Oberst a.D. Günther von Below to the author.
96. Manstein, *Lost Victories,* 63; *Verlorene Siege,* 57 and 314f., 413ff.
97. See, for example, Dupuy, *A Genius for War,* 7.
98. Erwin Rommel, *Krieg ohne Haß* (War without Hate) (Heidenheim: Heidenheimer Zeitung, 1950), ed. Lucie-Marie Rommel and Generalleutnant Fritz Bayerlein, 102.
99. Creveld, *Kampfkraft,* 42f.; see also the basic investigations by Dirk W. Oetting, *Auf-*

tragstaktik. Geschichte und Gegenwart einer Führungskonzeption (Mission Tactics. History and Presence of a Command Concept) (Frankfurt a.M. and others, 1993).

100. Moltke, for instance, said: "There are many situations in which the officer must act as he sees fit. It would be very wrong if he were to wait for orders at moments when orders often cannot be issued." (*Moltkes Militärische Werke* [Moltke's Military Works] [Berlin: E. S. Mittler, 1900], vol. 2, pt. 2, 174.) See also: Hans Peter Stein, "Führen durch Auftrag" (Command through Mission), in *Truppenpraxis,* Supplement 1, 1985, 4f.; Wallach, *Kriegstheorien,* 80ff.; Carl-Gero von Ilsemann, "Das operative Denken des Älteren Moltke" (The Operative Thought of Moltke the Elder), *Operatives Denken und Handeln,* 22ff.
101. Seeckt defined mission tactics as follows: "By that, we mean, in contrast to the order that interferes in details of practical execution, the designation of the objective to be attained, with allocation of resources, but with full freedom for the accomplishment of the mission. This was based on the sound idea that he who bears responsibility for success must also pick the way to get there." (Seeckt, *Gedanken,* 64).
102. Rothbrust, *Guderian's XIXth Panzer Corps,* 89f.
103. For a comparison between the French and German command systems, see Doughty, *Breaking Point,* 29f., 32, 325.
104. See Irving, *Rommel,* 68.
105. Dach, "Panzer," *Schweizer Soldat* 47, no. 8 (1972): 62.
106. Addington, *The Blitzkrieg Era,* 32.
107. Borgert, 577f.
108. "Blitzkriegmethoden" (Blitzkrieg Methods), *Weltwoche* (World Week), 4 July 1941.
109. Zeitzler, "Panzer Gruppe v. Kleist," *EWKde* 8, no. 7 (1959): 369.
110. Quoted from Scheibert, *Guderian,* 173.
111. Guderian, however, was not the sole founder of the German Panzer Force; see, for example, Corum, *The Roots of Blitzkrieg,* 122ff.
112. Heinz Guderian, *Die Panzerwaffe, ihre Entwicklung, ihre Kampftaktik und ihre operativen Möglichkeiten bis zum Beginn des großdeutschen Freiheitskampfes* (The Panzer Arm, Its Development, Its Fighting Tactics, and Its Operational Possibilities, Up to the Start of the Greater German Freedom Struggle) (Stuttgart, 1943), 178.
113. See overview *Sturmpanzerwagen A 7 V. Vom Urpanzer zum Leopard 2* (The A 7 V Armored Assault Vehicle: From the Original Panzer to the Leopard 2) (Herford, 1990).
114. Bradley, *Guderian,* 152, 179ff.; John J. Mearsheimer, *Liddell Hart and the Weight of History* (Ithaca, New York: Cornell University Press, 1988), 37ff., 87, 160ff.; Jeffery A. Gunsburg, "Liddell Hart and Blitzkrieg," *Armor 2,* no. 83 (1974): 26–30; Corum, *The Roots of Blitzkrieg,* 141f.
115. Volker Wieland, "Pigeaud versus Velpry. Zur Diskussion über Motorisierung und Mechanisierung, Panzertechnik und Panzertaktik in Frankreich nach dem Ersten Weltkrieg" (Pigeaud versus Velpry. A Discussion of Motorization and Mechanization, Tank Technology and Tank Tactics in France after the First World War), *MGM* 17, no. 1 (1975): 49; Nehring, *Geschichte,* 85.
116. Addington, *The Blitzkrieg Era,* 34; Rolak, "Fathers of Blitzkrieg," 76; Gunsburg, "Liddell Hart and Blitzkrieg," 27.
117. Heinemann, "Development," 68f.; Cooper, 166, 219.
118. See, for example, Grandsard, *Le 10e Corps de armée,* 154, 317.
119. Dossier 4: Colonel Chaligne, Rapport d'opérations pour les journées dès 10 au 14 mai 1940 (File 4: Colonel Chaligne, Report of Operations for the Days of 10–14 May

1940), 29, SHAT 32 N 254. This phrase is found almost verbatim also in: Dossier 4: Récit des événements vécus par l'I.D. 55 au 10 au 15 mai 1940 (File 4: Report on Events Experienced by the 55th Infantry Division, from 10 to 15 May 1940), 29, SHAT 32 N 254; Compte-rendu du Lieutenant Michard (Report of Lieutenant Michard), 1, SHAT 34 N 145; Foucault, Quartier Bellevue—Frénois (The Sector Bellevue-Frénois), 12, SHAT 34 N 178.

120. Compte rendu du Capitaine Litalien (Report of Captain Litalien), 4, SHAT 34 N 178; almost the same phrasing can be found in: Colonel Chaligne (see n.119), 13, 29; Récit des événements vécus par l'I.D. 55 (see n.119), 14; Battalion Commander Crousse, Les opérations de Sedan (10–14 mai 1940) (The Operations at Sedan [10–14 May 1940]), 7, 34 N 145.
121. Dossier 1: Chef d'Escadron Labarbarie, La 55e division d'infanterie à la bataille de Sedan 10–14 Mai 1940 (File 1: Squadron Commander Labarbarie, 55th Infantry Division in the Battle of Sedan, 10–14 May 1940), 29, SHAT 32 N 251.
122. Kirkland, "French Air Strength," 33.
123. See also: Speidel, Der Einsatz, pt. 3, 46, BA-MA, Study Lw 3/2.
124. This number also includes 170 transport aircraft that were lost mostly during airborne landing missions; see Genst der Luftwaffe (Generalquartiermeister), BA-MA, RL 2 III/1173, 10 May 1940.
125. Robineau, "French Air Policy in the Inter-War Period and the Conduct of the Air War against Germany from September 1939 to June 1940," in Horst Boog, *The Conduct of the Air War in the Second World War,* 647.
126. Ibid., 645.
127. Ibid.
128. Ibid., 650ff., 653.
129. Deighton, *Blitzkrieg,* 297; Dach, "Panzer," *Schweizer Soldat* 47, no. 8 (1972): 39; Messenger, *Blitzkrieg,* 192.
130. Piekalkiewicz, *Luftkrieg,* 83.
131. Ibid.
132. Boog, "Führungsdenken in der Luftwaffe" (Command Thinking in the Luftwaffe), *Operatives Denken und Handeln,* 189–91; Boog, *Die deutsche Luftwaffenführung 1935–1945. Führungsprobleme–Spitzengliederung–Generalstabsausbildung* (The German Luftwaffe Command, 1935–1945. Command Problems—Top Echelon Organization—General Staff Training), vol. 21, *Beiträge zur Militärand- und Kriegsgeschichte* (Contributions to Military History and the History of War) (Stuttgart, 1981), 151ff., 157. See Speidel, Der Einsatz, pt. 3, 37ff., 210, BA-MA, Study Lw 3/2; General der Flieger a.D. Paul Deichmann, Die Unterstützung des Heeres, BA-MA, Study Lw 10, 205f.; Klaus A. Maier, "Totaler Krieg und operativer Luftkrieg" (Total War and Operational Air Warfare), *Die Errichtung der Hegemonie auf dem europäischen Kontinent;* Ekkehart Guth, "Vom Nahkampfgedanken zu Close Air Support. Der Taktische Luftkrieg der Luftwaffe im zweiten Weltkrieg" (From the Idea of Close-Quarter Combat to Close Air Support. The Tactical Air War of the German Air Force during World War II), *Truppenpraxis* 31, no. 2 (1987): 148ff.
133. Three different phases emerged during Operation Sickle Cut: (1) During the first three days (10–12 May), priority went to the effort to subdue the enemy air forces and their ground organization. (2) On 13 and 14 May, the Luftwaffe was employed mostly in a tactical setting for "close air support." The major main effort consisted of an attack against the French positions at Sedan. (3) Operational missions predominated during

the third phase, until the time the Channel coast was reached, that is to say, the effort was aimed at sealing off the exposed flanks. That was done mainly indirectly, by raids against railroad stations and important traffic junctions to prevent the enemy from moving up reserves. But there were also tactical sorties against dangerous flank attacks by Allied tank units. The latter were smashed, in some cases, for example, at Cambrai, from the air alone by bombers and dive-bombers.

134. See also the graphics in Michel Forget, "Co-operation between the Air Force and Army in the French and German Air Forces during the Second World War," Horst Boog, ed., *The Conduct of the Air War in the Second World War,* 450ff. (Annexes 4–6).
135. Speidel, Der Einsatz, 180ff., BA-MA, Study Lw 3/2.
136. Ibid., 181.
137. Richard P. Hallion, *Strike from the Sky: A History of Battlefield Air Attack, 1911–1945* (Washington. D.C.: Smithsonian Institution Press, 1989), 144. For the French bombers, the figure was as little as 0.28 to 0.38 mission per day; see also Kirkland, "French Air Strength," 32.
138. Fuller, *Conduct,* 256; *Entartete Kunst,* 282.
139. Guderian, *Erinnerungen,* 95.
140. Walter A. Raleigh and H. A. Jones, *The War in the Air* (Oxford: Oxford University Press, 1922–37), vol. 6, 135f.
141. Bloch, *Strange Defeat,* 47–48; *Die Seltsame Niederlage,* 93.
142. Stephen W. Richey, "The Philosophical Basis of Air Land Battle," *Military Review* 64, no. 5 (May 1984): 52.

Chapter 11

1. Clausewitz, "Notes from 1803 to 1809," printed in Hans Rothfels, *Carl von Clausewitz. Politik und Krieg. Eine ideengeschichtliche Studie* (Carl von Clausewitz. Politics and War. A Study on the History of Ideas) (Berlin, 1920), 212.
2. Seeckt, *Gedanken,* 17.
3. Clausewitz, *Vom Kriege,* 738f; Clausewitz, *On War,* 528.
4. See Lev Besymenskiy, *Die Schlacht um Moskau 1941* (The Battle for Moscow, 1941) (Cologne, 1981), 46 (Speer is given as the source).
5. See Halder's lecture note, quoted at the beginning of the introduction, for the Versailles Conference scheduled for 28 June 1940 (HGr C, BA-MA, RH 19 III/141, sheet 44).
6. Kroener, "Personellen Ressourcen," 695, 999, 1014.
7. Rolf-Dieter Müller, "Von der Wirtschaftsallianz zum kolonialen Ausbeutungskrieg" (From Economic Alliance to Colonial War of Exploitation), 185, and Joachim Hoffmann, "Die Sowjetunion bis zum Vorabend des deutschen Angriffs" (The Soviet Union on the Eve of the German Attack), 62, both in Horst Boog, Jürgen Förster, Joachim Hoffmann, Ernst Klink, Rolf-Dieter Müller, and Gerd R. Ueberschär, *Der Angriff auf die Sowjetunion* (The Attack on the Soviet Union), vol. 4, *Das Deutsche Reich und der Zweiten Weltkrieg* (Stuttgart: Deutsche Verlags-Anstalt, 1983).
8. According to the table prepared by Schustereit (*Vabanque,* 73), the figure was 3,906,765 prisoners of war.
9. Halder, *Halder War Diary,* 446 (3 July 1941); Halder *KTB,* vol. 3, 38.
10. Halder, *Halder War Diary,* 447 (3 July 1941), and Halder, *KTB,* vol. 3, 39; see also *Hitlers Weisungen,* 129ff.

11. Andreas Hillgruber, "Der Faktor Amerika in Hitlers Strategie 1938–1941" (The American Factor in Hitler's Strategy, 1938–1941), *Nationalsozialistische Außenpolitik,* 513.
12. Such a Japanese thrust had been discussed in February and March 1941 between Hitler and the Japanese ambassador and Lt. Gen. Oshima Hiroshi. However, Germany did not reveal its own intentions, which called for an attack on the Soviet Union. The Japanese adopted a wait-and-see attitude, concentrating their forces for a strike against the United States. See Hillgruber, Faktor Amerika, 514ff.; Hillgruber, *Hitlers Strategie,* 731ff.
13. Foss, *Panzer,* 7.
14. Roland G. Foerster, "Die Ardennenoffensive 1944. Politische-strategische Überlegungen und operative Konzepte auf deutscher Seite" (The Ardennes Offensive, 1944. The Political-Strategic Background and Operational Concepts on the German Side), *Entwicklung, Planung und Durchführung,* 82.
15. Horst Rohde, "Die operativen Grundlagen der Ardennenoffensive: Wirtschaft und Logistik auf deutscher Seite" (The Operational Fundamentals of the Ardennes Offensive: Economy and Logistics on the German Side), *Entwicklung, Planung und Durchführung,* 104.
16. Karl Marx and Friedrich Engels, *Werke* (Works) (East Berlin, 1956), vol. 8, 115.
17. Bericht Oberleutnant Beck-Broichsitter (14.Kp/IRGD): "Panzerschlacht südlich Sedan" (14.5.1940) (Report of Oberleutnant Beck-Broichsitter [14th Company, Infanterie Regiment Großdeutschland]: "Panzer Battle South of Sedan" [14 May 1940]), BA-MA, RH 37/6332; *see also* Durian, *Großdeutschland,* 75. The cavalry patrol most probably consisted of troopers from the 3d Spahi Brigade; see Bikar, *La 3e Brigade de Spahis,* 397f.; Le Diberder, *Les spahis,* 155; Paillat, *La guerre éclair,* 263.
18. See Horne, *To Lose a Battle,* 539; *Über die Maas,* 456.

Bibliography

In general, only the sources and publications given in the footnotes are included here for reasons of space.

Unprinted Sources

1. Bundesarchiv-Militärarchiv (Federal Military Archives) Freiburg im Breisgau, Germany (BA-MA)

(a) Oberkommando der Wehrmacht (OKW) (Wehrmacht High Command)

Wehrmachtführungsstab (Wehrmachtführungsamt) (Wehrmacht Operations Staff [Wehrmacht Operations Office]): RW 4/32, 35, 41, 170, 414, 611

Allgemeines Wehrmachtamt (General Wehrmacht Office): RW 6/180

Wehrwirtschafts- und Rüstungsamt (Wehrwirtschaftsamt) (Defense Industry and Armament Office [Defense Industry Office]): RW 19/173, 261, 1022, 1381, 1792, 1938

(b) Oberkommando des Heeres (OKH) (Army High Command)

Generalstab des Heeres (Army General Staff): RH 2/181, 182, 465, 768, 1491–94, 1556, 2972

Chef Heeresnachrichtenwesen (Chief, Army Signal Service): RH 6/1–3

Heereswaffenamt (Army Ordnance Office): RH 8/1012, 1023

Chef der Schnellen Truppen (Chief, Mobile Forces): RH 10/1

Inspektion der Pioniere (hier: Arbeitsstab Pioniergeschichte) (Inspector of Engineers [Specifically: Engineer History Working Staff]): RH 12–5/397, 425

(c) Heeresgruppenkommandos (Army Group Headquarters)

Heeresgruppe A (Army Group A): RH 19 I/25, 26, 35, 37, 38, 41, 73

Heeresgruppe B (Army Group B): RH 19 II/19, 21, 72

Heeresgruppe C (Army Group C): RH 19 III/92, 141

(d) Armeeoberkommandos (Field Army Headquarters)

4. Armee (Fourth Army): RH 20–4/54, 62, 64, 68, 69, 71, 81

12. Armee (Twelfth Army): RH 20–12/4, 7, 11, 20, 33, 36

18. Armee (Eighteenth Army): RH 20–18/35

(e) Panzerkorps/Panzergruppen (Panzer Corps/Panzer Groups)

Gruppe v. Kleist (Group Von Kleist): RH 21–1/18, 19, 20, 22, 23, 36, 317, 318, 320, 381

Panzerkorps Guderian (ehem. XIX.Armeekorps, ab 28.5. Panzergruppe Guderian) (Panzer Corps Guderian [formerly XIX Army Corps, as of 28 May, Panzer Group Guderian]): RH 21–2/30, 31, 32–34, 36, 40–43, 45, 47, 48, 54, 59(K). 63, 852

Gruppe Hoth (ehem. XV.mot.Armeekorps, ab 20.5. Gruppe Hoth) (Group Hoth [formerly XV Motorized Corps, as of 20 May, Group Hoth]): RH 21–3/28, 36–38

Panzerkorps Hoepner (XVI.mot.Armeekorps) (Panzer Corps Hoepner [XVI Motorized Army Corps]): RH 21–4/518, 527

Panzerkorps Reinhardt (XXXXI.mot.Armeekorps) (Panzer Corps Reinhardt [XXXXI Motorized Army Corps]: RH 24–41/2, 4

(f) Armeekorps (Corps)

VI. Armeekorps (VI Corps): RH 24–6/17

XXXIX.(mot.) Armeekorps (XXXIX Corps [Motorized]): RH 24–39/7, 9

(g) Infanteriedivisionen (Infantry Divisions)

16. InfDiv (16th Infantry Division): RH 26–16/28

24. InfDiv (24th Infantry Division): RH 26–24/140

71. InfDiv (71st Infantry Division): RH 26–71/76

(h) Panzerdivisionen (Panzer Divisions)

1. PzDiv (1st Panzer Division): RH 27–1/5, 14, 154, 170

2. PzDiv (2d Panzer Division): RH 27–2/1, 11, 92, 93

3. PzDiv (3d Panzer Division): RH 27–3/245, 251

4. PzDiv (4th Panzer Division): RH 27–4/6, 199

5. PzDiv (5th Panzer Division): RH 27–5/179

6. PzDiv (6th Panzer Division): RH 27–6/1D, 4, 126

7. PzDiv (7th Panzer Division): RH 27–7/3, 9–11, 44, 212, 213, 215, 220

10. PzDiv (10th Panzer Division): RH 27–10/4, 7b, 9, 68, 107

(i) Infanterieverbände (Infantry Units)

Schützenregiment 4 (4th Rifle Regiment): RH 37/10, 11

Schützenregiment 10 (10th Rifle Brigade): RH 37/138, 1910

Infanterieregiment Großdeutschland (Infantry Regiment *Großdeutschland*): RH 37/6327, 6328, 6332, 6335, 6391

(j) Panzerverbände (Panzer Units)

Panzerregiment 1 (1st Panzer Regiment): RH 39/30
Panzerregiment 7 (7th Panzer Regiment): RH 39/103

(k) Pionierverbände (Engineer Units)

Panzer-Pionierbataillon 49 (49th Panzer Engineer Battalion): RH 46/743

(l) Druckschriften u.ä (Publications and the Like)

RHD 21/47 Militärgeographischer Überblick über Belgien und angrenzende Gebiete, hrsg. vom Generalstab des Heeres, Chef Kriegskarten und Vermessungswesen (Military-Geographical Overview of Belgium and Adjoining Regions, published by the Army General Staff, Chief, War Maps and Surveying, Berlin, 1940)

RHD 21/152–155 Militärgeographische Beschreibung von Frankreich, Teil I, Nordostfrankreich (Military-Geographical Description of France, part 1, Northeastern France). Berlin, 1940

RHD 29/8 General der Pioniere und Festungen, "Denkschrift über die französische Landesbefestigung" (General of Engineers and Fortifications, "Memorandum on French Land Fortifications"). 1 October 1941

(m) Generalstab der Luftwaffe (Luftwaffe General Staff)

Generalquartiermeister (Deputy Chief of Staff, Supply and Administration): RL 2 III/707, 736, 1173, 1174

(n) Kommandobehörden (etc.) der Fliegertruppe [Command Authorities (etc.) of Air Units]

VIII. Fliegerkorps (VIII Air Corps): RL 8/43, 45

(o) Fliegende Verbände (Flying Units)

I./Kampfgeschwader 53 (1st Squadron, 53d Ground-Attack Wing): RL 10/86
Jagdgeschwader 27 (27th Fighter Wing): RL 10/591

(p) Verbände und Einheiten der Flakartillerie (Major and Minor Antiaircraft Artillery Units)

Leichte Flakabteilung 86 (86th Light Flak Battalion): RL 12/234
Flakregiment 102 (102d Flak Regiment): RL 12/457
I./Flakregiment 18 (1st Battalion, 18th Flak Regiment): RL 12/545

(q) Oberkommando der Kriegsmarine (Navy High Command)

Seekriegsleitung (Office of the Chief of Naval Operations): RM 7/337
Allgemeines Marinehauptamt (General Navy Main Office): RM 7/807, 808
Kriegswissenschftl. Abteilung (Military Science Department): RM 8/1491

(r) Nachlässe (Bequests)

N 406 Hans Seidemann

(s) Studies by Historical Division, Headquarters, U.S. Army, Europe

B-306 Günther Blumentritt, Gen.d.Inf. a.D., Operative und taktische Schulbeispiele aus beiden Weltkriegen. III. Teil, 4.: Panzer-Begegnungsgefecht im Westen, Mai 1940, bei Stonne (Operational and Tactical Training Examples from the Two World Wars. Part 3, 4.: Panzer Meeting Engagement in the West at Stonne, May 1940)

C-053 Gerd v. Rundstedt, Gen.Feldm., Bemerkungen zum "Feldzug im Westen" (Comments on "Campaign in the West")

D-111 Hubert Weise, Gen.Oberst a.D., Organisation der Luftverteidigung im Felde, erläutert an Beispielen des Flakkorps I (Organization of Air Defense in the Field, Explained with the Help of the Examples of I Flak Corps)

P-114c Part 2: Friedrich Wilhelm Hauck, Gen.d.Art. a.D., Die Abwehrkämpfe am Donets und auf der Krim und das Wiedergewinnen der Initiative, Dezember 1941 bis Juni 1942 (Die Operationen der deutschen Heeresgruppen an der Ostfront 1941–1945. Südliches Gebiet, Zweiter Teil) (Defensive Fighting along the Donets and in the Crimea and Recovery of Initiative, December 1941 to June 1942 [The Operations of the German Army Groups on the Eastern Front, 1941–1945. Southern Sector, Second Part])

P–203 Rudolf Hofmann, Gen.d.Inf. a.D., Angriff gegen Befestigungsanlagen. Deutsche Angriffe gegen ständige und verstärkte feldmäßige Befestigungsanlagen im Zweiten Weltkrieg (Attack against Fortifications. German Attacks against Permanent and Reinforced Improvised Fortifications during World War II)

P-208 Der Westfeldzug 1940 (The 1940 Campaign in the West) Vol. 1, Kurt von Tippelskirch, Gen.d.Inf. a.D., Die Vorgeschichte, Teile I und II (Early History, Parts 1 and 2). Vol. 2, Günther Blumentritt, Gen.d.Inf. a.D., Darstellung der Operationen (Description of Operations)

Zu P-208 Vol. 2, Chapter E: Günther Blumentritt, Gen.d.Inf. a.D., Kritik (1. Fassung des Bandes 2, Abschnitt E) (Critique [1st Version of vol. 2, Chapter E])

Hilfstudie (Supporting Study) (XI Army Corps, May) for P–208, Vol. 2, Otto Heidkämper, Gen.Lt. a.D., Die Operationen des XV.AK (zeitweise Gruppe Hoth) in dem Feldzug in Nordfrankreich, 10.-30.5.1940 (The Operations of XV Corps [temporarily, Group Hoth] during the Campaign in Northern France, 10–30 May 1940)

P-209 Edgar Röhricht, Gen.d.Inf. a.D., Grosse Einkesselungs-Schlachten im 2. Weltkrieg (Large Encirclement Battles during World War II); including pp. 22–36; Herbert von Boeckmann, Gen.d.Inf. a.D., Ansatz der Westoffensive im May 1940 (Operations for the Western Offensive in May 1940)

P-210, Vol. 1, Fedor von Bock, Gen.Feldm. Kriegstagebuch (War Diary) (3 Parts) Tagebuch-Notizen zum Polen-Feldzug Mai–Juni 1939–3. Oktober 1939 (Diary Entries on the Polish Campaign, May–June 1939–3 October 1939); Tagebuchnotizen Westen. Vorbereitungszeit, 4.10.1939–9.5.1940 (Diary Entries West, Preparatory Period, 4 October 1939–9 May 1940); Tagebuch Westen. Offensive und Besatzungszeit, 10.5.1940–11.9.1940 (Diary West. Offensive and Occupation Period, 10 May–11 September 1940)

(t) Studies and Collections of Materials of the Luftwaffe Study Group of the U.S. Air Force Historical Division

Lw 3 Wilhelm Speidel, Gen.d.Fl. a.D., Der Einsatz der operativen Luftwaffe im Westfeldzug 1939/40. “Studie West” (The Employment of the Operational Luftwaffe during the 1939–1940 Campaign in the West, “West Study”). 5 vols.

Lw 10 Paul Deichmann, Gen.d.Fl. a.D., Die Unterstützung des Heeres durch die deutsche Luftwaffe im Zweiten Weltkrieg (Luftwaffe Support for the Army during World War II)

Lw 12 Joseph Kammhuber, Gen.d.Fl. a.D., Das Problem der Erringung der Luftherrschaft durch Gegenmaßnahmen der Luftwaffe (The Problem of Winning Control of the Air by Luftwaffe Countermeasures). 2 vols.

Lw 106/7 Materialsammlung: Stärken (Ist-Stärken und Einsatzbereitschaft) der Fliegenden Verbände der Luftwaffe 1938–1945 (Collection of Materials: Strength Figures [Actual Strength Figures and Operational Readiness] of Luftwaffe Flying Formations, 1938–1945)

Lw 133/1 Sigismund Frhr. von Falkenstein, Gen.M. a.D., Die Unterstützung des deutschen Heeres durch die deutsche Luftwaffe im II. Weltkrieg (Entwurf) (Luftwaffe Support for the German Army during World War II) (Draft)

ZA 3/44 Arbeitsmaterialien: Einsatz des II.Fliegerkorps in Frankreich. Verschiedene Ausarbeitungen (Working Materials: Employment of II Air Crops in France. Miscellaneous Studies)

ZA 3/59 Arbeitsmaterialien: Westen 1940, Lageberichte Luftflotten 2 und 3 (Working Materials: West 1940, Situation Reports, Air Fleets 2 and 3)

2. Service Historique de l'Armée de Terre (French Army Historical Service [SHAT]) Vincennes (The inventory contains war diaries, orders, after-action reports, survey documents, etc.)

29 N 27 2ème Armée, Historique des opérations . . .
(Second Army, History of Operations . . .)
29 N 84 2ème Armée/Commandement des Chars . . .
(Second Army, Commander of Tanks . . .)
30 N 92 10ème Corps d' Armée, 3ème bureau
(X Army Corps, Operations Section)
30 N 225 21ème Corps d' Armée (XXI Army Corps)
32 N 8 3ème Division d'Infanterie motorisée
(3d Motorized Infantry Division)
32 N 251 55ème Division d'Infanterie
(55th Infantry Division)
32 N 254 55ème Division d'Infanterie, 4éme bureau
(55th Infantry Division, Supply Section)
32 N 318 71ème Division d'Infanterie
(71st Infantry Division)
34 N 95 84ème Régiment de Fortresse
(84th Fortress Regiment)
34 N 145 147ème Régiment d'Infanterie de Fortresse
(147th Fortress Infantry Regiment)
34 N 174 295ème Régiment d'Infanterie
(295th Infantry Regiment)
34 N 178 331ème Régiment d'Infanterie
(331st Infantry Regiment)

3. Berichte von Zeitzeugen (Eyewitness Reports)

Written or verbal communications on the campaign in the west were received from the following individuals (rank not given):

Helmut Beck-Broichsitter
Joachim Beinlich
Walter Brandt
Andreas Braune-Krickau
Hans-Christoph Carlowitz
Norbert Di-Fant
Heinrich Draeger
Alois Ehrmann
Rudolf Fasbender
Helmut Fleischer
Friedrich Försterling
Peter Frantz
Friedrich von Grolman
Kurt Grübnau
W. Gutmann
Helmut Gutzschhahn
Hans-Jürgen Hartung
Hans von Hirschfeld

Gerhard Hohensee
Bernard Horen
Peter Otto Kruse
Willy Lesch
Dr. Henning Mahler
Rolf Penselin
Max Sauder
Günter Schmitz
Gottfried Schütze
Rolf O. G. Stoves
Werner Trippe
Eberhard Wackernagel
Rudolf Wulff
H.J. von Hopffgarten
Johann Adolf Graf von Kielmansegg
Claude Lefevre
Christian von Lucke
Fabian von Ostau-Bonin
Gerd Sailer
Albert Schick
Bruno Schulze
Helmuth Spaeter
Walter Trieps
Siegfried Unger
August Weber

4. Dokumente in Privatbesitz (Auswahl) (Privately Owned Documents [Selection])

Below, Günther von (Oberst a.D.). Gedanken-Splitter (Fragments of Thoughts).

Bericht über den Maasübergang bei Sedan (Gefechtsbericht I. Btl/SchtzRgt 86) [Report on the Crossing of the Meuse River at Sedan [After-Action Report, 1st Battalion, 86th Rifle Regiment]).

Hanbauer (Leutnant u. Kompanieführer) (2d Lieutenant and Company Commander). Einsatz der 2. Kompanie bei Sedan (Gefechtsbericht 2. Kp/SchtzRgt 86) (Employment of 2d Company at Sedan [After-Action Report, 2d Company, 86th Rifle Regiment]).

Korthals (Oberleutnant) (1st Lieutenant). Feldzug gegen Frankreich (Kriegstagebuch 3.Kompanie/Sturmpionier-Bataillon 43) (The Campaign against France [War Diary, 3d Company, 43d Assault Engineer Battalion]).

Koska (Oberleutnant) (1st Lieutenant). Der Feldzug gegen Frankreich 1940 (Tagebuchblätter des Bataillonsadjutanten Sturmpionier-Bataillon 43) (The 1940 Campaign against France [Pages from the Diary of the Battalion Adjutant, 43d Assault Engineer Battalion]).

Kriegstagebuch leichte Flakabtlg. 83 (Westfeldzug) (War Diary, 83d Light Flak Battalion [Campaign in the West]).

Kriegstagebuch Nr. 2 (II.Btl/SchtzRgt 7) vom 25.11.1939 bis 7.7.1940 (War Diary No. 2 [2d Battalion, 7th Rifle Regiment] from 25 November 1939 to 7 July 1940).

Kriegstagebuch Schützenregiment 86 (War Diary, 86th Rifle Regiment).

Kriegstagebuch Nr. 1 der I.Abteilung/Panzerregiment 1 (War Diary No. 1, 1st Battalion, 1st Panzer Regiment).

Kriegstagebücher Nr. 2 und 3 der II.Abteilung/Panzerregiment 1 (War Diaries Nos. 2 and 3, 2d Battalion, 1st Panzer Regiment).

Kriegstagebuch Panzerregiment 4 (Westfeldzug) (War Diary, 4th Panzer Regiment [Campaign in the West]).

Kronbügel (Unteroffizier) (Sergeant). "Kradschützen vor" (Kriegstagebuch 7.Kp/ SchtzRgt86) [Motorcycle Riflemen, Forward!] (War Diary, 7th Company, 86th Rifle Regiment).

Lesch, Willy. Bericht über Unternehmen [eines Panzerspähtrupps] am 14.Mai 1940 bei Chéhéry (Gefechtsbericht 2.Kp/PzRgt 2, abreact 20.5.1940) (Report on a Mission [of a Panzer Reconnaissance Patrol] on May 14, 1940, at Chéhéry [After-Action Report, 2d Company, 2d Panzer Regiment, Prepared on 20 May 1940]).

Lüke, Hans. Auszug aus der Geschichte des Regiments 69 (Extract from the History of the 69th Regiment).

Pi 49 im Feldzug in Frankreich (Kriegstagebuch Panzerpionierbatalion 49) (49th Engineers in the Campaign in France [War Diary, 49th Panzer Engineer Battalion]).

Regimentsgeschichte des Panzerregiments 3 (Regimental History of 3d Panzer Regiment).

Rommel, Generalfeldmarschall (Field Marshal). Dokumente zum Westfeldzug (zur Verfügung gestellt durch seinen Sohn Manfred Rommel) (Documents on the Campaign in the West [made available by his son Manfred Rommel]).

Scheibe, Helmut (Leutnant). Die Panzer-Aufklärungs-Abteilung 4 im Westfeldzug (The 4th Panzer Reconnaissance Battalion during the Campaign in the West).

Steinkeller, Friedrich-Carl von. Erinnerungen (Auszug: Maasübergang des Kradschützen Bataillons 7 der 7. Panzerdivision am 12./13. Mai 1940) (Memoirs [Excerpt: The Maas River Crossing by the 7th Motorcycle Rifle Battalion, 7th Panzer Division, on 12–13 May 1940]).

Unser Einsatz im Westen vom 10.Mai bis 21.Juni 1940 (Kriegstagebuch 2.Kompanie/ Sturmpionier-Batallion 43) (Our Employment in the West Between 10 May and 21 June 1940 [War Diary, 2d Company, 43d Assault Engineer Battalion]).

5. Unveröffentliche Darstellungen (Unpublished Accounts)

Bouissoux (Lt-Col.). Combats des Ardennes. Stonne-Mont-Dieu-Tannay (avec la 3e DCR et la 3e DIM) (Fighting in the Ardennes. Stonne-Mont-Dieu-Tannay [with the 3d French Armored Division and the 3d Motorized Infantry Division]).

Denkschriften zu Fragen der operativen Führung, hrsg. durch den Inspekteur des Heeres (Memorandum on Questions of Operational Command, Published through the Office of the Inspector General of the Army). Bonn: July 1987.

Hartung, Hans-Jürgen. Der Angriff über die Maas bei Sedan am 13. Mai 1940 (The Attack Across the Maas River at Sedan on 13 May 1940).

Sarholz, Thomas. Überraschung und Wahl des Schwerpunktes als Elemente operativen Führens-Lehren aus der Frankreich-Offensive 1940 und Folgerungen für den modernen militärischen Führer (Jahresarbeit an der Führungsakademie der Bundeswehr) (Surprise and Selection of Main Effort as Element in Operational Command—Lessons Learned during the 1940 Offensive in France and Conclusions for the Modern Military Commander [Academic-Year Study at the Command Academy of the Federal Armed Forces]). Hamburg, 1989.

Schwerin, General Gerhard Graf von. Souvenirs de Guerre. Sedan-Bulson-Stonne du 10 au 15 Mai 1940 (recueillis par Michael Baudier) (Memories of War. Sedan-Bulson-Stonne, from 10 to 15 May 1940 [Collected by Michael Baudier]).

Sedan 1940. Historische Geländebesprechung der 5.Panzerdivision (Historical Staff Ride of the 5th Panzer Division). Diez/Lahn, 1987.

Bibliography

Abetz, Otto. *Das offene Problem. Ein Rückblick auf zwei Jahrzehnte deutscher Frankreichpolitik* (The Unresolved Problem: A Review of Two Centuries of German Policy toward France). Cologne: Greven Verlag, 1951.

ADAP (Akten zur deutschen auswärtigen Politik, 1918–1945. Aus dem Archiv des Deutschen Auswärtigen Amts. Serie D, 1937–1941, Bd. 1–13.) (Files on German Foreign Policy, 1918–1945. From the Archives of the German Foreign Office. Ser. D, 1937–1941, vols. 1–13). Baden-Baden, 1950–70.

Addington, Larry H. *The Blitzkrieg Era and the German General Staff, 1865–1941.* New Brunswick, N.J.: Rutgers University Press, 1971.

Alexander, Martin S. "Prophet without Honour? The French High Command and Pierre Taittinger's Report on the Ardennes Defenses, March 1940." *War and Society* 4, no. 1 (1986): 52–77.

———. *The Republic in Danger: General Maurice Gamelin and the Politics of French Defense, 1933–1940.* Cambridge: Cambridge University Press, 1992.

Alfoldi, Laszlo M. "The Hutier Legend." *Parameters* 5, no. 2 (1976): 69–74.

Amouroux, Henri. *Le peuple du désastre 1939–1940.* Tome 1: *La grande histiore des Français sous l'occupation* (The People of the Disaster, 1939–1940. Vol. 1, The General History of the French under the Occupation). Paris: Robert Laffont, 1976.

———. "Kollabos, Helden und Verräter. Die Franzosen unter deutscher Besetzung" (Collaborators, Heroes, and Traitors: The French under German Occupation). Part 1. *Der Spiegel* (the Mirror) 44, no. 20 (1990): 150–63.

"An der Maas 1940" (*Einzelschilderungen aus dem Kriege an der Westfront*) (On the Meuse River in 1940 [Individual Accounts from the War on the Western Front]). *MWR* 5 no. 3 (1940): 246–54.

Ankaoua, Robert. "Le 14 mai à Sedan" (14 May at Sedan). *Icare: Revue de l'aviation française* no. 57 (spring–summer 1971): 128–32.

Ansel, Walter. *Hitler Confronts England.* Durham, N.C.: University of North Carolina Press, 1960.

Ardennes 1940. Ed. Maurice Vaïsse. Paris: Henri Veyrier, 1991.

d'Astier de la Vigerie, François. *Le ciel n'était pas vide. 1940* (The Sky Was Not Empty. 1940). Paris: René Julliard, 1952.

Ausgewählte Operationen und ihre militärhistorischen Grundlagen (Selected Operations and Their Bases in Military History). Vol. 4, *Operatives Denken und Handeln in deutschen Streitkräften* (Operational Thinking and Action in the German Armed Forces). Ed. Hans-Martin Ottmer and Heiger Ostertag, by direction of the Military History Research Office. Herford and Bonn: Verlag E. S. Mittler and Sohn, 1993.

Balck, Hermann. *Ordnung im Chaos. Erinnerungen, 1893–1948* (Order in Chaos: Memoirs, 1893–1948). Osnabrück: Biblio Verlag, 1980.

Balke, Ulf. *Der Luftkrieg in Europa. Die operativen Einsätze des Kampfgeschwaders 2 im Zweiten Weltkrieg* (The Air War in Europe. The Operational Missions of the 2d Bomber Wing during World War II). 2 vols. Koblenz: Bernard and Graefe, 1989.

Barker, Arthur J. *Dunkirk: The Great Escape*. London: Dent, 1977.

Bauer, Eddy. *Der Panzerkrieg. Die wichtigsten Panzeroperationen des zweiten Weltkrieges in Europa und Afrika*. Bd. 1: *Vorstoß und Rückzug der deutschen Panzervebände* (The Panzer War. The Most Important Panzer Operations of the Second World War in Europe and Africa. Vol. 1, Attack and Retreat of the German Panzer Units). Bonn: Verlag Offene Worte, 1965.

Beaufre, André. *Le drame de 1940* (The Drama of 1940). Paris: Plon, 1965. English language version: *1940: The Fall of France*. Trans. by Desmond Flower. New York: Alfred A. Knopf, 1968.

Bekker, Cajus. *Angriffshöhe 4000. Ein Kriegstagebuch der deutschen Luftwaffe* (Attack Altitude 4000: A War Diary of the German Luftwaffe). Oldenburg: G. Stalling Verlag, 1964. English language version, *The Luftwaffe War Diaries*. New York: Ballantine Books, 1969.

Below, Nicolaus von. *Als Hitlers Adjutant, 1937–1945* (As Hitler's Military Aide, 1937–1945). Mainz: Hase und Koehler, 1980.

Benoist-Méchin, Jacques. *Der Himmel stürzt ein. Frankreichs Tragödie 1940* (The Sky Is Falling: France's Tragedy in 1940). Düsseldorf: Droste Verlag, 1958.

———. *Soixante jours qui ébranlèrent l'occident. 10 mai–10 juliet 1940* (Sixty Days That Shook the West: 10 May–10 July 1940). Paris: Éditions Albin Michel, 1956. English language version: *Sixty Days That Shook the West: The Fall of France, 1940*. New York: G. P. Putnam's Sons, 1963.

Berben, Paul, and Bernard Iselin. *Die Deutschen kommen. Mai 1940. Der Überfall auf Westeuropa* (The Germans Are Coming. May 1940. The Surprise Attack on Western Europe). Hamburg: Christian Wegner, 1969.

Bertin, Pierre. "Un régiment d'infanterie sur a la Meuse en 1940: le 129e R.I. en Belgique" (An Infantry Regiment on the Meuse in 1940: The 129th Infantry Regiment in Belgium). *RHA* no. 4 (1972): 75–103.

Bertin-Boussu, General. *La 3e division d'infanterie motorisée 1939–1940* (The 3d Motorized Infantry Division, 1939–1940). Aurillac: N.p., n.d.

Besymenskiy, Lev. *Die Schlacht um Moskau 1941* (The Battle for Moscow). Cologne, 1981.

Bikar, A. "10 mai 1940. 'Hedderich' et 'Niwi.' Les deux opérations allemandes aéroportées sur petits avions Fieseler 'Storch' (10 May 1940)" ("Hedderich" and "Niwi": The Two German Airborne Operations Using the Small Fieseler "Stork" Aircraft [10 May 1940]). *RBHM* 20 (1973–74): 411–34, 591–622, 699–723; 21 (1975–76): 48–78, 123–56.

———. "La campagne de mai 1940 en Belgique: La 4e division légère de cavalerie français à l'est de la Meuse, les 10, 11, et 12 mai 1940" (The May 1940 Campaign in Belgium: The French 4th Light Cavalry Division to the East of the Meuse on 10, 11, and 12 May 1940). *RBHM* 25 (1983–84): 519–50, 627–52.

———. "La 1ère légère division de cavalerie français à l'est de la Meuse, les 10, 11, et 12 mai 1940" (The French 1st Light Cavalry Division to the East of the Meuse on 10, 11, and 12 May). *RBHM* 26 (1985–86): 137–59, 175–210.

———. "La 3e brigade de Spahis dans nos Ardennes, les 10, 11, et 12 mai" (The 3d Brigade of Spahis in Our Ardennes on 10, 11, and 12 May). *RBHM* 26 (1985–86): 387–402.

———. "Les événements dans le sud de la province du Luxembourg: Le repli des chasseurs ardennais le 10 mai et la 2e division légère de cavalerie français (2e DLC) les 10, 11 et 12 mai 1940 (The Events in the Southern Part of the Province of Luxembourg: The Withdrawal of the Ardennes Light Infantry on 10 May and the French 2d Light Cavalry Division [2d DLC] on 10, 11, and 12 May). *RBHM* 27 (1987–88): 437–74, 537–73, 613–48.

———. "La 5e division légère de cavalerie français en Ardenne, du 10 au 12 mai (The French 5th Light Cavalry Division in the Ardennes between 10 and 12 May). *RBHM* 28 (1989–90): 467–508, 589–613, 691–714.

Bitzel, Uwe. *Die Konzeption des Blitzkrieges bei der deutschen Wehrmacht* (The German Wehrmacht's Blitzkrieg Concept). Frankfurt am Main: Peter Lang, 1991.

Blaxland, Gregory. *Destination Dunkirk: The Story of Gort's Army.* London: William Kimber, 1973.

Der Blitzkrieg in Polen. 18 Tage Krieg in Polen in Berichten des Oberkommandos der Wehrmacht (The Blitzkrieg in Poland: 18 Days of War in Poland as Covered in the Reports of the Wehrmacht High Command). Essen, 1939.

"Blitzkriegmethoden (von Dr. F. K.). Erfolge und Gefahren einer neuen Kriegführung" [Blitzkrieg Methods (by Dr. F. K.). Successes and Dangers of a New Method of Warfare], *Weltwoche,* 4 July 1941.

"Blitzkrieg und Panzerdivisionen" (Blitzkrieg and the Panzer Divisions). *Ostasiatischer Beobachter* (30 November 1940): 11–13.

"Blixtanfallet" (ed.). *1939 års Färsvarsförbund.* Stockholm, 1940.

"Blixkriget och sprängberedskapen." *Tidskrift i fortifikation* no. 3 (1943): 121–37.

" 'Blixtkrig' och försvar mot 'blixtkrig.' " Kungl. Krigsvetenskaps-Akadem. *Handlingar och Tidskrift* no. 3 (1942): 56–80.

Bloch, Marc. *Die seltsame Niederlage: Frankreich 1940. Der Historiker als Zeuge* (The Strange Defeat: France, 1940—The Historian as Witness). Frankfurt am Main, 1992. English language version: *Strange Defeat: A Statement of Evidence Written in 1940.* New York: W. W. Norton, 1968.

Blumentritt, Günther. *Von Rundstedt: The Soldier and the Man.* London: Odhams Press Limited, 1952.

Bond, Brian. *France and Belgium, 1939–1940.* London, 1975.

Bonotaux and Guerin. "Avec la 3e D.I.M. à Stonne" (With the 3d Motorized Infantry Division at Stonne). *RHA* 6, no. 2 (1950): 47–50.

Boog, Horst. *Die deutsche Luftwaffenführung 1935–1945. Führungsprobleme-Spitzengliederung-Generalstabsausbildung* (The German Luftwaffe Command, 1935–1945. Command Problems—Top Echelon Organization—General Staff Training). Vol. 21, *Beiträge zur Militär- und Kriegsgeschichte* (Contributions to Military History and the History of War). Stuttgart: Deutsche Verlags-Anstalt, 1981.

———. "Die Operationen der Luftwaffe gegen die Niederlande vom 10. bis 15. Mai 1940" (The Operations of the Luftwaffe against the Netherlands Between 10 and 15 May 1940). *Ausgewählte Operationen und ihre militärhistorischen Grundlagen.* 347–67.

———. "Führungsdenken in der Luftwaffe im Zweiten Weltkrieg" (Command Thinking in the Luftwaffe during World War II). *Operatives Denken und Handeln in deutschen Streitkräften im 19. und 20. Jahrhundert.* 183–206.

Borgert, Heinz Ludger. "Grundzüge der Landkriegführung von Schlieffen bis Guderian" (Basic Features of Land Warfare from Schlieffen to Guderian). Vol. 5, *Handbuch zur deutschen Militärgeschichte 1648 bis 1939.* 427–584.

Botelho, A. "O commando e a guerra relâmpago" (Command and the Lightning War). *Revista militar* (Military Review) [Lisbon] no. 9 (1942): 522–33.

Bradley, Dermot. *Generaloberst Heinz Guderian und die Entstehungsgeschichte des modernen Blitzkrieges* (General Heinz Guderian and the Origin of the Modern Blitzkrieg). Osnabrück: Biblio-Verlag, 1978.

———. *Walther Wenck. General der Panzertruppe* (Walther Wenck: General of Panzer Forces). Osnabrück: Biblio-Verlag, 1981.

Brand, Dieter. "Grundsätze operativer Führung" (Principles of Operational Command). In *Denkschriften zu Fragen der operativen Führung* (Memorandum on Questions of Operational Command). Ed. Inspekteur des Heeres (Inspector General of the Army). Bonn, 1987.

Braun. "Der strategische Überfall" (The Strategic Surprise Attack). *Militär-Wochenblatt* no. 18 (1938): cols. 1134–36.

Brausch, Gerd. "Sedan 1940. Deuxième Bureau and strategische Überraschung" (Sedan 1940: French Army Intelligence and the Strategic Surprise). *MGM* no. 2 (1967): 15–93.

Brohon, Raymond. "Le groupement de bombardement No 10" (The 10th Bombardment Group). *Icare* no. 57 (spring-summer 1971): 80–92.

Bruge, Roger. *Histoire de la ligne Maginot* (History of the Maginot Line). Vol. 1, *Faites sauter la ligne Maginot* (Blow Up the Maginot Line). Paris: Fayard, 1973. Vol. 2, *On a livré la ligne Maginot* (The Maginot Line Was Betrayed). Paris: Fayard, 1975. Vol. 3, *Offensive sur le Rhin* (Offensive on the Rhine). Paris: Fayard, 1977.

Brüning, Robert, and Alex Buchner. *Unteroffiziere entscheiden ein Gefecht* (Noncommissioned Officers Decide a Combat Operation). Herford, 1981.

Bryant, Arthur. *The Turn of the Tide 1939–1943. A Study Based on the Diaries and Autobiographical Notes of Field Marshal the Viscount Alanbrooke, K.G., O.M.* London: Collins, 1957.

Buchbender, Ortwin, and Reinhard Hauschild. *Geheimsender gegen Frankreich: Die Täuschungsoperation "Radio Humanité" 1940* (Secret Radio Transmitter against France: The Deception Operation "Radio Humanity" 1940). Bonn and Herford: Verlag E. S. Mittler and Sohn, 1984.

Buchbender, Ortwin, and Horst Schuh. *Die Waffe, die auf die Seele zielt. Psychologische Kriegführung 1939–1945* (The Weapon That Aims at the Soul: Psychological Warfare, 1939–1945). Stuttgart: Motorbuch Verlag, 1983.

Bücheler, Heinrich. *Carl-Heinrich von Stülpnagel. Soldat, Philosoph, Verschwörer* (Carl-Heinrich von Stülpnagel—Soldier, Philosopher, Conspirator). Berlin and Frankfurt am Main: Ullstein, 1989.

———. "Die Panzerschlacht von Hannut. Pfingsten 1940" (The Panzer Battle of Hannut. Whitsuntide 1940). *Kampftruppen* 22, no. 3 (1980): 125–27.

Buffetaut, Yves. "De Gaulle. Chef de guerre. 15 mai–6 juin 1940" (De Gaulle: War Leader, 15 May–6 June 1940). 39–45. *Guerre contemporaines Magazine* (June 1990): 9–37.

———. *Guderian perce à Sedan* (Guderian Broke Through at Sedan). Paris, 1992.

———. *Rommel. France 1940* (Rommel. France 1940). Bayeux: Éditions Heimdal, 1985.

Buffotot, Patrice, and Jacques Ogier. "L'armée de l'air française dans la campagne de France (10 mai–25 juin 1940)" (The French Air Force in the Campaign in France [10 May–25 June 1940]). *RHA* no. 3 (1975): 88–117.

Cabiati, Aldo. *La guerra lampo. Polonia-Norvegia-Francia* (The Lightning War: Poland-Norway-France). Milan, 1940.

Cailloux. "La contre-attaque qui n'eut jamais lieu . . . 19–25 mai" (The Counterattack That Never Took Place . . . 19–25 May). *RHA* no. 3 (1966): 133–47.

Carr, William. "Rüstung, Wirtschaft und Politik am Vorabend des Zweiten Weltkrieges" (Armament, Economy, and Politics on the Eve of World War II). *Nationalsozialistische Außenpolitik.* 437–54.

Cartier, Raymond. *Der Zweiten Weltkrieg* (The Second World War). Vol. 1. Munich: Piper, 1967.

Christophé, Eduard Curt. *Wir stoßen mit Panzern zum Meer* (We Are Pushing to the Sea with Our Panzers). Berlin: Steiniger Verlag, 1940.

Churchill, Winston S. *His Complete Speeches, 1897–1963.* Ed. Robert Rhodes James. Vol. 6, *1935–1942.* New York and London: Bowker, 1974.

———. *Der Zweiten Weltkrieg* (The Second World War). Vols. 1 and 2, Stuttgart: 1948–49. English language version: *The Second World War.* Vol. 1, *The Gathering Storm.* Boston: Houghton Mifflin Company, 1948; Vol. 2, *Their Finest Hour.* Boston: Houghton Mifflin Company, 1949.

Clausewitz, Carl von. *Vom Kriege* (On War). 19th ed. Bonn, 1980.

———. *On War: Carl von Clausewitz.* Ed. and trans. by Michael Howard and Peter Paret. New York: Everyman's Library, 1993.

Cohen, Eliot A., and John Gooch. *Military Misfortunes. The Anatomy of Failure in War.* New York: Vintage Books, 1990.

Coilliot, André. Mai 1940. *Un mois pas comme les autres. Le film des événements dans la région d'Arras* (May 1940: A Month Not Like the Others. The Film of Events in the Arras Region). Arras, 1980.

Colin. *Rommel et le franchissement de la Meuse* (Rommel and the Crossing of the Meuse River). Paris: École Superieure de Guerre (War College). 1971.

The Conduct of the Air War in the Second World War. An International Comparison. Proceedings of the International Conference of Historians in Freiburg i.Br., Federal Republic of Germany, from 29 August to 2 September 1988. Ed. Horst Boog. New York and Oxford: Berg Publishers, 1992. German version: *Luftkriegführung im Zweiten Weltkrieg. Ein internationaler Vergleich* (The Conduct of the Air War in the Second World War: An International Comparison). Vol. 12, *Vorträge zur Militärgeschichte* (Lectures on Military History), by direction of the Military History Research Office. Herford and Bonn: Verlag E. S. Mittler and Sohn, 1993.

Cooper, Matthew. *The German Army, 1933–1945: Its Political and Military Failure.* London: Macdonald and Janes, 1978.

Cordier, Daniel. *Jean Moulin. L'inconnu du Panthéon.* Tome 2, *Le choix d'un destin, juin 1936–novembre 1940* (Jean Moulin. The Unknown Man of the Panthéon, Vol. 2, The Choice of Fate, June 1936–November 1940) (Paris: Lattès, 1989)

Corum, James S. *The Roots of Blitzkrieg: Hans von Seeckt and German Military Reform.* Lawrence, Kansas: University Press of Kansas, 1992.

Cot, Pierre. "En 40 où etaient nos avions?" (Where Were Our Aircraft in 1940?). *Icare* no. 57 (spring-summer 1971): 35–57.

Crémieux-Brilhac, Jean-Louis. *Les Français de l'an 40* (The French of 1940). Vol. 1, *La guerre oui ou non?* (The War, Yes or No?); Vol. 2, *Ouvriers et soldats* (Workers and Soldiers). Paris: Robert Laffont, 1990.

Creveld, Martin van. *Kampfkraft. Militärische Organisation und militärische Leistung 1939–1945* (Combat Efficiency: Military Organization and Military Achievement, 1939–1945). Freiburg, 1989. English language version: *Fighting Power: German and U.S. Army Performance, 1939–1945.* Westport, Conn.: Greenwood Press, 1982.

Dach, Hans von. *Kampfbeispiele* (Examples of Combat Operations). Frauenfeld, 1977.

———. "Kampf um ein Festungswerk (La Ferté). Nach französischen und deutschen Kampfberichten dargestellt" (Fight to Take a Fortress [La Ferté]. Described on the basis of French and German combat reports). *Schweizer Soldat* 43, no. 18 (1967): 408–29.

———. "Panzer durchbrechen eine Armeestellung" (Panzers Break Through an Army Position). 3 parts, *Schweizer Soldat* 47, no. 2 (1972): 47–88; no. 5 (1972): 45–91; no. 8 (1972): 38–72.

Dahms, Hellmuth Günther. *Die Geschichte des Zweiten Weltkriegs* (The History of the Second World War). Munich and Berlin: F. A. Herbig, 1983.

Danel, Raymond. "Le bombardement dans la bataille" (Bombardment in Battle). *Icare* no. 57 (spring-summer 1971): 58–69.

———. "La conquête de la Hollande: Opération secondaire?" (The Conquest of Holland: A Secondary Operation?). *Icare* no. 79 (winter 1976–77): 13–57.

———. "En mai–juin 1940: Ils étaient les plus forts" (In May–June 1940: They Were Stronger). *Icare* no. 54 (summer 1970): 48–73.

Davis, Clyde R. *Von Kleist: From Hussar to Panzer Marshal.* Houston, Tex., 1979.

Deichmann, Paul. *Der Chef im Hintergrund* (The Chief of Staff in the Background). Munich and Hamburg: Oldenburg, 1979.

Deighton, Len. *Blitzkrieg. Von Hitlers Triumphen bis zum Fall von Dünkirchen* (Blitzkrieg: About Hitler's Triumph up to the Fall of Dunkirk). Munich: Heyne, 1983. English language version: *Blitzkrieg: From the Rise of Hitler to the Fall of Dunkirk.* New York: Alfred A. Knopf, 1980.

Deist, Wilhelm. "Die Aufrüstung der Wehrmacht" (The Rearmament of the Wehrmacht). *Das Deutsche Reich und der Zweiten Weltkrieg.* Vol. 1, *Ursachen und Voraussetzungen der deutschen Kriegpolitik* (Causes and Conditions of German War Policy). 369–532.

———. "De Gaulle et Guderian. L'influence des expériences militaries de la première guerre mondiale en France et en Allemagne" (De Gaulle and Guderian: The Influence of Military Experiences during World War I in France and Germany). *Etudes Gaulliennes* no. 17 (1977): 47–57.

Delmas, Jean. "Les Ardennes dans les opérations françaises, rue d'ensemble et cas concret: Monthermé" (The Ardennes during French Operations, Overview and Specific Case: Monthermé). *Ardennes 1940.* 97–114.

Delmas, Jean, Paul Devautour, and Eric Lefèvre. *Mai–juin 40. Les combattants de l'honneur* (May–June 1940. They Fought for Honor). Paris: Copernic, 1980.

Denkschriften zu Fragen der operativen Führung (Memorandum on Questions of Operational Command). Ed. Inspekteur des Heeres (inspector-general of the army). Bonn: 1987.

"Deutsche Blitzkriegsstrategen" (German Blitzkrieg Strategists). *Weltwoche* (4 July 1941).

Das Deutsche Reich und der Zweiten Weltkrieg (The German Reich and the Second

World War). 7 vols. Stuttgart: Deutsche Verlags-Anstalt, 1979–. Vol. 1, Wilhelm Deist, Manfred Messerschmidt, Hans-Erich Volkmann, and Wolfram Wette. *Ursachen und Voraussetzungen der deutschen Kriegspolitik* (Causes and Conditions of German War Policy). Stuttgart: Deutsche Verlags-Anstalt, 1979. Vol. 2, Klaus A. Meier, Horst Rohde, Bernd Stegemann, and Hans Umbreit. *Die Errichtung der Hegemonie auf dem europäischen Kontinent* (The Establishment of Hegemony on the European Continent). Stuttgart: Deutsche Verlags-Anstalt, 1979. Vol. 3, Gerhard Schreiber, Bernd Stegemann, and Detlef Vogel. *Der Mittelmeerraum und Südosteuropa* (The Mediterranean Area and Southeastern Europe). Stuttgart: Deutsche Verlags-Anstalt, 1984. Vol. 4, Horst Boog, Jürgen Förster, Joachim Hoffmann, Ernst Klink, Rolf-Dieter Müller, and Gerd R. Ueberschär. *Der Angriff auf die Sowjetunion* (The Attack on the Soviet Union). Stuttgart: Deutsche Verlags-Anstalt, 1983. Vol. 5, part 1, Bernard R. Kroener, Rolf-Dieter Müller, and Hans Umbreit. *Organisation und Mobilisierung des deutschen Machtbereichs. Kriegsverwaltung, Wirtschaft und personelle Ressourcen 1939 bis 1941* (Organization and Mobilization of the German Sphere of Power. Wartime Administration, Economy and Personnel Resources). Stuttgart: Deutsche Verlags-Anstalt, 1988.

Deutsch, Harold C. *Verschwörung gegen den Krieg. Der Widerstand in den Jahren 1939–1940* (Conspiracy against War: Resistance during the Years from 1939–1940). Munich: Beck, 1969.

"Diskussiya o 'molnienosnoy voyne.' " *Voennyy Zarubeẑnik* no. 10 (1940): 13–31.

Dokumente zum Westfeldzug 1940 (Documents on the 1940 Campaign in the West). Ed. Hans-Adolf Jacobsen. Göttingen, Berlin, and Frankfurt am Main: Musterschmidt, 1960.

Dokumente zur Vorgeschichte des Westfeldzuges 1939–1940 (Documents on the Background of the 1939–1940 Campaign in the West). Ed. Hans-Adolf Jacobsen. Göttingen, Berlin, and Frankfurt am Main: Musterschmidt, 1956.

Domarus, Max, ed. *Hitler. Reden und Proklamationen 1932–1945* (Hitler: Speeches and Proclamations, 1932–1945). 2 vols. Würzburg, 1962–1963.

Dönitz, Karl. *Zehn Jahre und zwanzig Tage* (Ten Years and Twenty Days). Munich, 1977.

Doughty, Robert Allan. *The Breaking Point: Sedan and the Fall of France, 1940.* Hamden, Conn.: Archon Books, 1990.

———. "De Gaulle's Concept of a Mobile Professional Army: Genesis of French Defeat?" *Parameters* 4, no. 4 (1974): 23–34.

———. "The Enigma of French Armored Doctrine 1940." *Armor* (September/October 1974): 39–44.

———. "French Antitank Doctrine, 1940. The Antidote That Failed." *Military Review* 56, no. 5 (May 1976): 36–48.

———. *The Seeds of Disaster: The Development of French Army Doctrine, 1919–1939.* Hamden, Conn.: Archon Books, 1985.

Doumenc, A. *Histoire de la Neuvième Armée* (History of the Ninth Army). Paris: B. Arthaud, 1945.

"Das III.Bataillon Schützenregiment 4 erzwingt am 13.Mai den Maasübergang bei Monthermé (Einzelschilderungen aus dem Kriege an der Westfront)" (The 3d Battalion, 4th Rifle Regiment, Forces the Crossing of the Meuse River at Monthermé on 13 May [Individual Accounts from the War on the Western Front]). *MWR* 5 (1940): 358–62.

Dupuy, Trevor N. *A Genius for War: The German Army and General Staff, 1807–1945.* Fairfax, Va.: HERO Books, 1984.

———. *Numbers, Predictions, and War: Using History to Evaluate Combat Factors and Predict the Outcome of Battles.* London: Macmillan, 1979.

Durian, Wolf. *Infanterieregiment Großdeutschland greift an* (Infantry Regiment Großdeutschland Attacks). Berlin: Scherl, 1942.

Ehrensvaerd, Carl August. *Hårt mot hårt, Blixtanfallet och Blixförsvar.* Stockholm, n.p., 1943.

Eibicht, Rolf-Josef. *Schlieffen. Strategie und Politik. Aus der Unterlegenheit zum Sieg* (Schlieffen: Strategy and Policy. From Inferiority to Victory). Lünen, 1991.

Eichholtz, Dietrich. *Geschichte der deutschen Kriegswirtschaft 1939–1945.* Bd. 1, *1939–1941* (History of the German War Economy, 1939–1945. Vol. 1, 1939–1941). Berlin: Akademie Verlag, 1969.

"Ein Überblick über die Operationen des belgischen Heeres im Mai 1940. Dargestellt nach belgischen Quellen" (An Overview of the Operations of the Belgian Army in May 1940, Described according to Belgian Sources). *MWR* 6, no. 3 (1941): 274–85.

Die Einnahme des Panzerwerks 505. Die 71.Infanterie-Division kämpft um den Eckpfeiler der Maginot-Linie (Capture of Armored Fort 505. The 71st Infantry Division Fights to Capture the Cornerstone of the Maginot Line). *Alte Kameraden* 11, no. 5 (1963): 34.

Ellis, L. F. *The War in France and Flanders, 1939–1940.* London: Her Majesty's Stationery Office, 1953.

Enfer, Jacques. *10 mai–25 juin 1940. La campagne de France* (10 May–25 June 1940. The Campaign in France). Paris: Barré & Dayez, 1990.

Engel, Gerhard. *Heeresadjutant bei Hitler 1938–1943. Aufzeichnungen des Majors Engel* (Hitler's Army Aide, 1938–1943. Notes of Major Engel). Ed. Hildegard von Kotze. Stuttgart: Deutsche Verlags-Anstalt, 1974.

Engelmann, Joachim. *Manstein. Stratege und Truppenführer. Ein Lebensbericht in Bildern* (Manstein: Strategist and Troop Leader: A Report on His Life in Pictures). Friedberg: Podzun-Pallas Verlag, 1981.

Entscheidung im Westen. Der Feldzug der sechs Wochen. Die Berichte des Oberkommandos der Wehrmacht vom 10.Mai bis 25.Juni 1940 mit den täglichen militärischen und politischen Erläuterungen der Kölnischen Zeitung (von Dr.

J. Schäefer) (Decision in the West—The Six-Week Campaign. The Reports of the Armed Forces High Command from May 10 to June 25, 1940, with the daily military and political explanations by Cologne Journal [by Dr. J. Schäefer]). Cologne: Verlag M. DuMont Schauberg, 1940.

Entscheidungsschlachten des zweiten Weltkrieges (Decisive Battles of World War II). Ed. Hans-Adolf Jacobsen and Jürgen Rohwer. Frankfurt am Main: Bernard and Graefe, 1960. English language version: *Decisive Battles of World War II: The German View*. London: Andre Deutsch, 1965.

Entwicklung, Planung und Durchführung opeativer Ideen im Ersten und Zweiten Weltkrieg (Development, Planning, and Execution of Operational Ideas during World War I and World War II). Vol. 2, *Operatives Denken und Handeln in deutschen Streitkräften* (Operational Thinking and Action in the German Armed Forces). Herford and Bonn: Verlag E. S. Mittler and Sohn, 1989.

Erdmann, Karl-Dietrich. *Deutschland unter der Herrschaft des Nationalsozialismus 1933–1939* (Germany under the Rule of National Socialism, 1933–1939). Vol. 20, Gebhardt, Handbuch der deutschen Geschichte (Handbook of German History). Munich: Deutscher Taschenbuch Verlag, 1980.

Erfurth, Waldemar. *Der Vernichtungssieg. Eine Studie über das Zusammenwirken getrennter Heeresteile* (The Annihilation Victory: A Study on the Cooperation of Separate Army Components). Berlin: Mittler Verlag, 1939.

Fabre-Luce, Alfred. *Französisches Tagebuch August 1939–Juni 1940* (French Diary, August 1939–June 1940). Hamburg: Hanseatische Verlagsanstalt, 1942.

Facon, Patrick. "Chasseurs et bombardiers dans la bataille" (Fighters and Bombers in Battle). *Historia Spécial* no. 5 (1990): 34–40.

Der Feldzug in Frankreich vom 10. Mai bis 25. Juni 1940 (Lagenatlas) (The Campaign in France from 10 May to 25 June 1940 [Situation Atlas]). (1949, reproduction).

Fischer, Fritz. *Griff nach der Weltmacht. Die Kriegspolitik des kaiserlichen Deutschland 1914/18* (The Grasp for World Power. The War Policy of Imperial Germany, 1914–18). Düsseldorf: Droste Verlag und Druckerei GmbH, 1961.

Fischer, Wolfgang. *Ohne die Gnade der späten Geburt* (Without the Mercy of Late Birth). Munich: F. A. Herbig, 1990.

Förster, Gerhard. *Totaler Krieg und Blitzkrieg* (Total War and Blitzkrieg). East Berlin: Deutscher Militärverlag, 1967.

Foerster, Roland G. "Die Ardennenoffensive 1944. Politisch-strategisch Überlegungen und operative Konzepte auf deutscher Seite" (The 1944 Ardennes Offensive. Political-Strategic Considerations and Operational Concepts on the German Side). *Entwicklung, Planung und Durchführung operativer Ideen.* 73–91.

Foerster, Wolfgang. *Generaloberst Ludwig Beck. Sein Kampf gegen den Krieg* (General Ludwig Beck. His Fight against the War). Munich: Isar Verlag, 1952.

Forget, Michel. "Co-operation between Air Force and Army in the French and German Air Forces during the Second World War." *The Conduct of the Air War in the Second World War.* 415–57.

Forty, George, and John Duncan. *The Fall of France: Disaster in the West, 1939–1940.* Tunbridge Wells, Kent, England: Nutshell, 1980.

Foss, Christopher F. *Die Panzer des Zweiten Weltkrieges* (The Panzers of World War II). Friedberg: Podzun-Pallas, 1988.

Fox (Colonel) and d'Ornano. "La percée des Ardennes" (The Breakthrough in the Ardennes.) *RHDGM* 3, nos. 10–11 (1953): 77–118.

Freter, Hermann. *Fla nach vorn! Die Fliegerabwehr-Waffe des Heeres und ihre Doppelrolle im Zweiten Weltkrieg* (Light Antiaircraft Artillery, Forward! The Antiaircraft Arm of the Army and Its Twin Role during World War II). Vol. 1, Eßlingen: Eigenverlag der Fla-Kamerad-Schaft (Self-published by the Union of Former Antiaircraft Soldiers), 1971.

———. "Das war unser 'Sedan-Tag.' Die Heeres-Fla im Westfeldzug: 234 Abschüsse" (That Was Our "Day of Sedan": Army Light Antiaircraft Artillery during the Campaign in the West: 234 Enemy Planes Shot Down). *Die Neue Feuerwehr* (May 1986): 18f. Eßlingen: Eigenverlag der Fla-Kamerad-Schaft (Self-published by the Union of Former Antiaircraft Soldiers).

Fuller, John F. C. *Die entartete Kunst Krieg zu führen 1789–1961* (The Degenerate Art of Conducting Warfare, 1789–1961). Cologne: Verlag Wissenschaft und Politik, 1964. English language version: *The Conduct of War, 1789–1961.* New York: Minerva Press, 1968.

———. *Der Zweiten Weltkrieg. Darstellung seiner Strategie und Taktik* (World War II. An Account of Its Strategy and Tactics). Vienna and Stuttgart: Humboldt Verlag, 1950.

Galland, Adolf. *Die Ersten und die Letzten. Die Jagdflieger im zweiten Weltkrieg* (The First and the Last: The Fighters in World War II). Darmstadt: Schneekluth, 1953.

Gamelin, Maurice. *Servir* (To Serve). 3 vols. Paris: Plon, 1946–47.

Ganns, Karl-Heinz. *Panzer-Artillerie Regiment 76 (1936–1945)* (76th Panzer Artillery Regiment [1936–1945]). Cologne: Stemmler Verlag, 1962.

Gaul. "Der Blitzkrieg in Frankreich" (The Blitzkrieg in France). *Militär-Wochenblatt* 125, no. 35 (1941): cols. 1513–16.

Gaulle, Charles de. *Memoiren* (Memoirs). Vol. 1, *Der Ruf. 1940–42* (The Call, 1940–42). Berlin, Frankfurt am Main, 1955. English language version: Charles de Gaulle, *The Complete War Memoirs of Charles de Gaulle.* New York: Simon and Schuster, 1968.

———. *Vers l'armée de métier* (Toward a Professional Army). 2d ed. Paris, 1944.

Gegenbauer. "Im Westen. Mai 1940" (In the West. May 1940). *Mitteilungsblatt der (2.) Wiener Panzerdivision* (Bulletin of the [2d] Viennese Panzer Division) ser. 23 (May 1966): 3–10.

Die Geheimakten des französischen Generalstabes, veröffentl. durch das Auswärtige Amt 1939/41 (The Secret Files of the French General Staff, Published by the Foreign Office, 1939–41). No. 6. Berlin, 1941.

Gelb, Norman. *Dunkirk: The Complete Story of the First Step in the Defeat of Hitler.* New York: William Morrow, 1989.

Gelée, Max. "La percée des Ardennes vue d'en haut" (The Ardennes Breakthrough Seen from Above). *Icare* no. 57 (spring–summer 1971): 68–71.

Gemzell, Carl-Axel. *Raeder, Hitler und Skandinavien. Der Kampf für einen maritimen Operationsplan* (Raeder, Hitler, and Scandinavia. The Fight for a Maritime Operations Plan). Lund: C. W. K. Glerrup, 1965.

Generalfeldmarschall Keitel-Verbrecher oder Offizier. Erinnerungen, Briefe, Dokumente des Chefs OKW (Field Marshal Keitel: Criminal or Officer? Memoirs, Letters, and Documents of the Chief of the Wehrmacht High Command). Ed. Walter Görlitz. Göttingen, Berlin, and Frankfurt am Main: Musterschmidt, 1961. English language version: *The Memoirs of Field Marshal Keitel.* Ed. Walter Görlitz; Trans. David Irving. New York: Stein and Day, 1966.

Gerbet, Klaus, ed., *Generalfeldmarschall Fedor von Bock: The War Diary, 1939–1945.* Atglen, Pa.: Schiffer Military History, 1996.

German Nationalism and the European Response, 1890–1945. Ed. Carole Fink, Isabel V. Hull, and MacGregor Knox. London: University of Oklahoma Press, 1985.

Geschichte der 3. Panzer-Division (History of the 3d Panzer Division). Published by the Tradition Club of the Division. Berlin: Richter, 1967.

Geyer, Michael. "German Strategy in the Age of Machine Warfare, 1914–1945." *Makers of Modern Strategy.* Ed. Peter Paret. Princeton, New Jersey: Princeton University Press, 1986. 527–97.

Gibson, Hugh, ed. *The Ciano Diaries, 1939–1943.* New York: Doubleday, 1946.

Gilbert, Martin. *The Second World War.* London: Weidenfeld and Nicolson, 1989.

Gillet, E. "La percée allemande en mai 1940 et la contre-attaque d'Arras" (The German Breakthrough in May 1940 and the Arras Counterattack). *RBHM* 29 (1992): 593–619.

Gisevius, Hans Bernd. *Bis zum bitteren Ende. Vom Reichstagsbrand bis zum Juli 1944* (To the Bitter End: From the Reichstag Fire to July 1944). Hamburg: Claassen & Goverts, 1947.

Giuliano, Gérard. *Les combats du Mont-Dieu. Mai 1940* (The Fighting at Mont-Dieu. May 1940). Charleville-Mézières: Éditions Terres Ardennaises, 1990.

———. "Dans le ciel de Sedan, le 14 mai 1940" (In the Sky Over Sedan on 14 May 1940). *Terres Ardennaises* no. 21 (December 1987): 45–52; no. 22 (March 1988): 41–51.

———. *Les soldats du beton. La Ligne Maginot dans les Ardennes et en Meuse. 1939–1940* (The Concrete Soldiers. The Maginot Line in the Ardennes and along the Meuse. 1939–1940). Charleville-Mézières: Éditions Terres Ardennaises, 1986.

———. "La 'surprise ardennaise' de mai 1940" (The "Ardennes Surprise" of May 1940). *Terres Ardennaises* no. 6 (April 1984): 23–32.

Glover, Michael. *The Fight for the Channel Ports. Calais to Brest 1940: A Study in Confusion.* London: Leo Cooper, 1985.

Goethe, Johann Wolfgang von. *Faust.* Munich: Deutscher Taschenbuch Verlag, 1962.

Gounelle, Claude. *Sedan. Mai 1940* (Sedan. May 1940). Paris: Presses de la Cité, 1965.

Goutard, Adolphe. *1940: La guerre des occasions perdues* (1940: The War of Lost Opportunities). Paris: Hachette, 1956.

Les Grandes Unités Françaises. Campagne 1939–1940. Cartes des situation journalières (The Major French Units during the 1939–1940 Campaign. Daily Situation Maps). Paris: n.p., 1967.

Grandsard, C. Le *10ème corps d'armée dans la bataille 1939–1940* (The X Army Corps in the Battle, 1939–1940). Paris: Berger-Levrault, 1949.

Gribble, Philip. "Blitzkrieg." *Die Auslese* 41, no. 3 (1941): 185–190; no. 4 (1941): 307–312. First published in the *Saturday Evening Post,* Philadelphia, 7 December 1940.

Groote, Wolfgang von. "Historische Vorbilder des Feldzugs 1914 im Westen" (Historical Models of the 1914 Campaign in the West). *MGM* 47, no. 1 (1990): 33–55.

Groscurth, Helmuth. *Tagebücher eines Abwehroffiziers 1938–1940. Hrsg. von Helmut Krausnick und Harold C. Deutsch unter Mitarbeit von Hildegard von Kotze* (Diaries of a Counter-Intelligence Officer, 1938–1940, ed. Helmut Krausnick and Harold C. Deutsch with the cooperation of Hildegard von Kotze). Stuttgart: Deutsche Verlags-Anstalt, 1970.

Grübnau, Kurt. "Brückenschlag über die Maas westlich Sedan für den Übergang einer Panzerdivision" (Building the Bridge Across the Meuse River to the West of Sedan for the Crossing of a Panzer Division). *Militär-Wochenblatt* 125, no. 27 (1941): cols. 1291–93.

Gruppe Guderian. Berichte und Bilder zur Erinnerung an den Siegeszug vom 9. Juni bis zum 23. Juni 1940 unter Führung des Generals der PzTruppe Guderian (Group Guderian Reports and Illustrations in Memory of the Victorious Campaign from 9 June to 23 June 1940, Under the Command of General of Panzer Troops Guderian). Berlin, 1940.

Guadegnini, Ulisse. *La guerra futura* (The War of the Future). Rome: n.p., 1925.

Guderian, Heinz. *Achtung—Panzer! Die Entwicklung der Panzerwaffe, ihre Kampftaktik und ihre operativen Möglichkeiten* (Attention—Panzers! The Development of the Panzer Arm, Its Combat Tactics, and Its Operational Possibilities). Stuttgart: Union Deutsch Verlagsgesellschaft, 1937.

———. "Blitzkrieg 1940." In *Decisive Battles of the Second World War.* Ed. Peter Young. London: Arthur Barker, 1967. 15–48.

———. *Erinnerungen eines Soldaten* (Memoirs of a Soldier). Stuttgart: Motorbuch Verlag, 1986. English language version: *Panzer Leader.* New York: De Capo Press, 1996.

———. *Panzer-Marsch! Aus dem Nachlass des Schöpfers der deutschen Panzerwaffe* (Panzer, Forward March! From the Estate of the Creator of the German Panzer Arm). Munich: Schild-Verlag, 1956.

———. "Die Panzertruppen und ihr Zusammenwirken mit den anderen Waffen" (The Panzer Troops and Their Cooperation with the Other Arms). *MWR* 1 (1936): 607–26.

———. *Die Panzerwaffe, ihre Entwicklung, ihre Kampftaktik und ihre operativen Möglichkeiten bis zum Beginn des großdeutschen Freiheitskampfes* (The Panzer Arm, Its Development, Its Fighting Tactics, and Its Operational Possibilities, Up to the Start of the Greater German Freedom Struggle). Stuttgart: Union Deutsche Verlagsgesellschaft, 1943.

Gudmundsson, Bruce I. *Stormtroop Tactics: Innovation in the German Army, 1914–1918.* New York: Praeger, 1989.

Gunsburg, Jeffrey A. "The Battle of Belgian Plain, 12–14 May 1940: The First Great Tank Battle." *Journal of Military History* 56, no. 2 (April 1992): 207–44.

———. *Divided and Conquered: The French High Command and the Defeat of the West, 1940.* London: Greenwood Press, 1979.

———. "Liddell Hart and Blitzkrieg." *Armor* 2, no. 83 (1974): 26–30.

Guth, Ekkehart. "Vom Nahkampfgedanken zu Close Air Support. Der taktische Luftkrieg der Luftwaffe im zweiten Weltkrieg" (From the Close Quarter Combat to Close Air Support. The Tactical Air War of the German Air Force during World War II). *Truppenpraxis* 31, no. 2 (1987): 146–55.

Gutzschhahn. "Zum 50. Jahrestag der Kämpfe in Belgien" (On the 50th Anniversary of the Fighting in Belgium). Rundschreiben 2/1989 des Traditionsverbandes der ehem. 7. *Panzerdivision* (Circular Letter, 2/1989, of the Tradition Club of the former 7th Panzer Division). 15–19.

Habe, Hans. *Ob tausend fallen—Ein Bericht* (Let Thousands Fall—A Report). Freiburg im Breisgau: Walter, 1974.

Hadamovsky, Eugen. *Blitzmarsch nach Warschau* (Lightning March to Warsaw). Munich: Zentralverlag der NSDAP Franz Eher, 1941.

Halder, Franz. *Hitler als Feldherr* (Hitler as Warlord). Munich: Münchener Dom-Verlag, 1949. English language version: *Hitler as War Lord.* London: Putnam, 1949.

———. *Kriegstagebuch. Tägliche Aufzeichnungen des Chefs des Generalstabes des Heeres 1939 bis 1942* (War Diary: Daily Entries of the Army Chief of Staff, 1939 to 1942). Ed. Hans-Adolf Jacobsen. 3 vols. Stuttgart: Kohlhammer, 1962–64. English language version: *The Halder War Diary, 1939–1942.* Ed. Charles Burdick and Hans-Adolf Jacobsen. Novato, Calif.: Presidio Press, 1988.

Hallion, Richard P. *Strike from the Sky: The History of Battlefield Air Attack, 1911–1945.* Washington, London: Smithsonian Institution Press, 1989.

Handbuch zur deutschen Militärgeschichte 1648 bis 1939 (Handbook of German Military History, 1648–1939). 5 vols. Ed. Militärgeschichtliches Forschungsamt (Military History Research Office). Munich: Bernard and Graefe Verlag, 1979–81.

Hargreaves, R. "Blitzkrieg. Illegitimate Son of Mars." *Cavalry Journal* no. 5 (1940): 386–91.

Hart, B. H. Liddell, ed. *The Rommel Papers.* London: Collins, 1953.

Hartmann, Christian. *Halder. Generalstabschef Hitlers* (Halder—Hitler's Chief of the General Staff). Paderborn: Verlag Ferdinand Schöningh, 1991.

Hartog, Leendert Johann. *Und morgen die ganze Welt. Der deutsche Angriff im Westen. 10. Mai bis 17. September 1940* (And Tomorrow the Whole World. The German Offensive in the West: 10 May to 17 September 1940). Gütersloh: Mohn, 1961.

Harvey, A. D. "The French Armée de l'Air in May–June 1940: A Failure of Conception." *Journal of Contemporary History* 25, no. 4 (1990): 447–65.

Hassell, Ulrich von. *Die Hassell-Tagebücher 1938–1944. Aufzeichnungen vom Andern Deutschland* (The Hassell Diaries, 1938–1944: Diary Entries About the Other Germany). Ed. Friederich Freiherr Hiller von Gaetringen. Berlin: Siedler Verlag, 1989.

Haupt, Werner. *Sieg ohne Lorbeer: Der Westfeldzug 1940* (Victory without Laurels: The 1940 Campaign in the West). Preetz Holstein: E. Geerdes, 1965.

Hautecler, Georges. *Le combat de Bodange. 10 mai 1940* (The Fighting at Bodange, 10 May 1940). Brussels: Service Historique de l'Armée Belge (Historical Service of the Belgian Army). 1955.

Heider, Paul, and Richard Lakowski. "Theorie vom totalen Krieg. Blitzkriegskonzeption und Wehrmacht in Vorbereitung des zweiten Weltkrieges (Theory of Total War. Blitzkrieg Concept and the German Armed Forces in Preparation of World War II). *Militärgeschichte* 28, no. 4 (1989): 291–300.

Heimsoeth, Hans-Jürgen. *Der Zusammenbruch der Dritten Französischen Republik: Frankreich während der "Drôle de Guerre" 1939/1940* (The Collapse of the Third French Republic: France during the "Phony War" of 1939–1940). Bonn: Bouvier, 1990.

Heinemann, Winfried. "The Development of German Armoured Forces 1918–40." *Armoured Warfare*. Ed. J. P. Harris and F. H. Toase. London: B. T. Batsford Limited, 1990. 51–69.

Herbst, Ludolf. *Der totale Krieg und die Ordnung der Wirtschaft. Die Kriegswirtschaft im Spannungsfeld von Politik, Ideologie und Propaganda 1939–1945* (Total War and the Organization of the Economy. The War Economy in the Context of Politics, Ideology, and Propaganda, 1939–1945). Stuttgart: Deutsche Verlags-Anstalt, 1982.

Herre, Franz. *Deutsche und Franzosen. Der lange Weg zur Freundschaft* (Germans and Frenchmen: The Long Road to Friendship). Bergisch-Gladbach: Lübbe, 1988.

———. *Moltke. Der Mann und sein Jahrhundert* (Moltke: The Man and His Century). Stuttgart: Deutsche Verlags-Anstalt, 1984.

Heusinger, Adolf. *Befehl im Widerstreit. Schicksalsstunden der deutschen Armee 1923–1945* (Conflicting Orders: The Fateful Hours of the German Army, 1923–1945). Tübingen: Rainer Wunderlich, 1957.

Hierl, Konstantin. "Die deutsche Oberste Führung im Westfeldzug und der Schlieffen-Plan" (The German Supreme Command during the Campaign in the West and the Schlieffen Plan). *Triumph der Kriegskunst*. Ed. Wilhelm Weiß. Munich: Zentralverlag der NSDAP Franz Eher, 1941. 67–74.

Hillgruber, Andreas. "Der Faktor Amerika in Hitlers Strategie 1938–1941" (America, A Factor in Hitler's Strategy, 1938–1941). *Nationalsozialistische Aussenpolitik.* 493–525.

———. *Hitlers Strategie: Politik und Kriegführung 1940–1941* (Hitler's Strategy: Politics and Warfare, 1940–1941). 2d ed. Munich: Bernard and Graefe Verlag, 1982.

Hillgruber, Andreas, ed. *Probleme des Zweiten Weltkrieges* (Problems of the Second World War). Cologne: Kiepenheuer and Witsch, 1967.

Hindenburg, Field Marshal Paul von. *Aus meinem Leben* (From My Life). Leipzig: S. Hirzel Verlag, 1927.

Hinsley, F. H., with E. F. Thomas, C. F. G. Ransom, and R. C. Knight. *Its Influence on Strategy and Operations.* Vol. 1, *British Intelligence in the Second World War.* London: Her Majesty's Stationery Office, 1979.

Histoire de l'aviation militaire française (History of French Military Aviation). Paris: Limoges, 1980.

Hitler, Adolf. *Mein Kampf* (My Struggle). Munich: Zentralverlag der NSDAP Franz Eher, 1936.

———. *Monologe im Führerhauptquartier 1941–1944. Die Aufzeichnungen Heinrich Heims* (Monologues at Führer Headquarters, 1941–1944: The Notes Taken by Heinrich Heims). Ed. Werner Jochmann. Hamburg: Albrecht Knaus, 1980.

Hitlers Politisches Testament. Die Bormann Diktate vom Febr. und April 1945 (Hitler's Political Testament: The Bormann Dictation of February and April 1945). Hamburg: A. Knaus, 1981.

Hitlers Weisungen für die Kriegführung 1939–1945. Dokumente des Oberkommandos der Wehrmacht (Hitler's Directives for the Conduct of War, 1939–1945: Documents of the Armed Forces High Command). Ed. Walther Hubatsch. 2d rev. ed. Koblenz: Bernard and Grafe, 1983. English language version: *Blitzkrieg to Defeat: Hitler's War Directives 1939–1945*, ed. H. R. Trevor-Roper. New York: Holt, Rinehart and Winston, 1964.

Hitlers Zweites Buch. Ein Dokument aus dem Jahr 1928 (Hitler's Second Book: A Document from the Year 1928). With an introduction and comments by Gerhard L. Weinberg. Stuttgart: Deutsche Verlags-Anstalt, 1961.

Hoffmann, Joachim. "Die Sowjetunion bis zum Vorabend des deutschen Angriffs" (The Soviet Union Up to the Eve of the German Offensive). *Das Deutsche Reich und der Zweiten Weltkrieg.* Vol. 4, *Der Angriff auf die Sowjetunion* (The Attack on the Soviet Union). Stuttgart: Deutsche Verlag-Anstalt, 1983. 38–97.

Hoffmann, Peter. *Widerstand-Staatsstreich-Attentat. Der Kampf der Opposition gegen Hitler* (Resistance-Coup Detat-Attempt on His Life. The Opposition's Fight against Hitler). Munich: R. Piper, 1969.

Hohnadel, Alain, and Michel Truttmann. *Guide de la Ligne Maginot: Des Ardennes au Rhin, dans les Alpes* (Guide to the Maginot Line: From the Ardennes to the Rhine [and] into the Alps). Bayeux: Éditions Heimdal, 1988.

Horen, Bernard. *Fantassin de 40 ou le conteste contestataire* (The Footslogger of 1940 or the Uneven Fight). Vol. 1, N.p., n.d.

Horne, Alistair. *Über die Maas, über Schelde und Rhein. Frankreichs Niederlage 1940* (Across the Meuse River, the Schelde and the Rhine. France's Defeat in 1940). Vienna, Munich, and Zürich: Molden Verlag, 1969. English language version: *To Lose a Battle: France 1940.* Boston: Little, Brown, 1969.

Hoth, Herman. "Buchbesprechung zu: Jacobsen 'Fall Gelb' " (Book Review for: Jacobsen, "Case Yellow"). *Wehrkunde* 7, no. 2 (1958): 118f.

———. "Der Kampf von Panzerdivisionen in Kampfgruppen in Beispielen der Kriegsgeschichte" (The Combat Operations of the Panzer Divisions in Battle Groups, Citing Examples from the History of War). *Wehrkunde* 8, no. 11 (1959): 576–84.

———. "Mansteins Operationsplan für den Westfeldzug 1940 und die Aufmarschanweisung des OKH vom 27.2.40" (Manstein's Operations Plan for the 1940 Campaign in the West and the Deployment Directive of the Army High Command, 27 February 1940). *Wehrkunde* 7, no. 3 (1958): 127–30.

———. "Das Schicksal der französischen Panzerwaffe im 1. Teil des Westfeldzuges 1940" (The Fate of French Armor during the First Part of the 1940 Campaign in the West). *Wehrkunde* 7, no. 7 (1958): 367–77.

———. "Zu 'Mansteins' Operationsplan für den Westfeldzug 1940 und die Aufmarschanweisung des OKH von 27.2.40" (On Manstein's Operations Plan for the 1940 Campaign in the West and the Deployment Directive of the Army High Command, 27 February 1940). *Wehrkunde* 7, no. 8 (1958): 459.

Huard, P. *Le Colonel de Gaulle et ses blindés. Laon (15.–20. mai 1940)* (The Colonel de Gaulle and His Tanks. Laon [15–20 May 1940]). Paris: Plon, 1980.

Hughes, Daniel J. "Blitzkrieg." *International Military and Defense Encyclopedia.* Vol. 1, *A–B.* Ed. Trevor N. Dupuy and others. Washington, D.C., New York, 1993. 377–81.

———. "Preparations of the German Army." Annual Meeting of the American Military Institute, Washington, D.C., 30 March 1990.

Huvelin, Paul. "Sedan. Mai 1940: l'Armée française coupée en Deux" (Sedan, May 1940: The French Army Cut in Two). *Historia* No. 521 (May 1990): 50–60.

Ilsemann, Carl-Gero von. "Das operative Denken des Älteren Moltke" (Operational Thinking on the Part of Moltke the Elder). *Operatives Denken und Handeln in deutschen Streitkräften im 19. und 20. Jahrhundert.* Herford and Bonn: Verlag E. S. Mittler and Sohn, 1993. 17–44

Ingram, Norman. *The Politics of Dissent: Pacifism in France, 1919–1939.* Oxford: Oxford University Press, 1991.

The Ironside Diaries, 1937–1940. Ed. Roderick Macleod and Denis Kelly. London: Constable, 1962.

Irving, David. *Hitlers Krieg. Die Siege 1939–1942* (Hitler's War. The Victories of 1939–1942). Munich and Berlin: F. A. Herbig, 1983. English language version: *Hitler's War.* New York: Viking Press, 1977.

———. *Die Tragödie der deutschen Luftwaffe. Aus den Akten und Erinnerungen von Feldmarschall Milch* (The Tragedy of the Luftwaffe: From the Files and Memoirs of Field Marshal Milch). Frankfurt am Main: Ullstein, 1970. English language version: *The Rise and Fall of the Luftwaffe: The Life of Field Marshal Erhard Milch.* Boston: Little, Brown, 1973.

———. *Rommel. Eine Biographie* (Rommel. A Biography). Hamburg: Verlag Hoffmann und Campe, 1978. English language version: *The Trail of the Fox.* New York: E. P. Dutton, 1977.

Jackson, Robert. *Air War over France, May–June 1940.* London: Ian Allen, Ltd., 1974.

Jacobsen, Hans-Adolf. *Dünkirchen* (Dunkirk). Neckargemünd: Kurt Vowinckel, 1958.

———. "Zur Entstehung des Sichelschnittplanes vom 24. February 1940" (On the Origin of the Sickle Cut Plan of 24 February 1940). *Wehrkunde* 7, no. 4 (1958): 226–28.

———. *Fall Gelb. Der Kampf um den deutschen Operationsplan zur Westoffensive 1940* (Case Yellow. The Fight over the German Operations Plan for the 1940 Offensive in the West). Wiesbaden: Franz Steiner Verlag, 1957.

Jacobsen, Hans-Adolf, and Jürgen Rohwer. "Planung und Operationen der deutschen Kriegsmarine in Zusammenhang mit dem Fall 'Gelb' " (Planning and Operations of the German Navy in Conjunction with Case "Yellow"). *Marinerundschau* 57, no. 2 (1960): 65–78.

Jünger, Ernst. *Gärten und Straßen. Aus den Tagebüchern von 1939 und 1940* (Gardens and Streets: From the Diaries of 1939 and 1940). Berlin: Verlag E. S. Mittler, 1942.

———. *In Stahlgewittern. Aus dem Tagebuch eines Stoßtruppführers* (Storm of Steel: From the Diary of an Assault Team Leader). Berlin: Mittler and Sohn, 1929.

Jungenfeld, Ernst Freiherr von. *So kämpften Panzer! Erlebnisse eines Panzerregiments im Westen* (This Is How the Panzers Fought! Experiences of a Panzer Regiment in the West). Berlin: Deutscher Verlag, 1941.

Kesselring, Albert. *Soldat bis zum letzen Tag* (Soldier to the Very Last Day). Bonn: Athenäum, 1953. English language version: Albert Kesselring, *Kesselring: A Soldier's Record.* New York: William Morrow, 1954.

Kielmansegg, Hanno, Graf von. "Plädoyer für operative Führung. Forderung nach der Fähigkeit, die Abwehrschlacht zu schlagen" (A Plea for Operational Command: Requirement for the Ability to Fight the Defensive Battle). *EWKde* 34, no. 11 (1985): 614–18.

Kielmansegg, Johann Adolf, Graf von. "Bemerkungen zum Referat von Hauptmann Dr. Frieser (Panzergruppe Kleist) aus der Sicht eines Zeitzeugen" (Comments on the Report by Captain Dr. Frieser [Panzer Group Kleist] as Seen by an Eyewitness).

Operatives Denken und Handeln in deutschen Streitkräften im 19. und 20. Jahrhundert. 149–59

———. *Panzer zwischen Warschau und Atlantik* (Panzers between Warsaw and the Atlantic). Berlin: Verlag "Die Wehrmacht," 1941.

———. "Scharnier Sedan" (Sedan: The Hinge). *Wehrmacht* 5, no. 11 (21 May 1941): 11–14; no. 12 (4 June 1941): 15–19.

Kirkland, Faris R. "The French Air Force in 1940. Was It Defeated by the Luftwaffe or by Politics?" *Air University Review* 36, no. 6 (1985): 101–18.

———. "French Air Strength in May 1940." *Air Power History* 40, no. 1 (1993): 22–34.

Klein, Burton H. *Germany's Economic Preparation for War.* Cambridge, Mass.: Harvard University Press, 1959.

Klink, Ernst. "Das Gesetz des Handelns. Die Operation 'Zitadelle' 1943" (The Law of Initiative: Operation "Citadel" in 1943). Vol. 7, *Beiträge zur Militär- und Kriegsgeschichte* (Contributions to Military History and the History of War). Stuttgart: Deutsche Verlags-Anstalt, 1966.

Knipping, Franz. "Frankreich in der Zeit der Weltkriege (1914–1945)" (France during the Time of the World Wars [1914–1945]). Karl Ploetz, *Geschichte der Weltkriege.* 237–47.

Koch, Horst-Adalbert. *Flak. Die Geschichte der deutschen Flakartillerie und der Einsatz der Luftwaffenhelfer* (Flak: The History of the German Antiaircraft Artillery and Employment of Auxiliaries). Bad Nauheim: Podzun, 1965.

Koch-Kent, Henri. *10 mai 1940 en Luxembourg* (10 May 1940 in Luxembourg). Luxembourg: Anciens combattants, 1971.

Koch, Lutz. *Rommel. Der "Wüstenfuchs"* (Rommel: The "Desert Fox"). Bielefeld: W. Goldmann, 1978.

Köhn. "Die Infanterie im 'Blitzkrieg' " (The Infantry during the "Blitzkrieg"). *Militär-Wochenblatt* 125, no. 5 (1940): 165f.

Korps Guderian. Berichte und Bilder zur Erinnerung an den Siegeszug vom 10. Mai bis zum 28. Mai unter Führung des Generals der Panzertruppen Guderian (Corps Guderian: Stories and Pictures towards the Memoir of the Victory March from 10 May to 28 May under Command of General of Panzer Troops Guderian). Berlin: Oberkommando der Wehrmacht, 1942.

Kosthorst, Erich. "Die deutsche Opposition gegen Hitler zwischen Polen- und Frankreichfeldzug" (The German Opposition against Hitler between the Polish Campaign and the French Campaign). Erich Kosthorst, *Zeitgeschichte und Zeitperspektive* (Contemporary History and Contemporary Perspectives). Paderborn: Ferdinand Schöningh, 1981. 23–46.

Kozaczuk, Wladislaw. *Geheimoperation Wicher. Polnische Mathematiker knacken den deutschen Funkschlüssel "Enigma"* (Secret Operation Wicher: A Polish Mathematician Breaks the German Radio Cipher "Enigma"). Koblenz: Bernard & Graefe, 1989.

"Kradschützen voran! Verfolgung von der Maas bei Monthermé bis Montcornet durch 1./ Kraftradschützen-Bataillon 6" (Motorcycle Riflemen, Forward! Pursuit from the Meuse River and Monthermé all the way to Montcornet by 1st Company, 6th Motorcycle Rifle Battalion). *MWR,* 1940: 362ff.

Krafft von Dellmensingen, Konrad. *Der Durchbruch. Studie an Hand der Vorgänge des Weltkrieges 1914–1918* (The Breakthrough: Study Based on the Events of the World War, 1914–1918). Hamburg: Hanseatische Verlagsanstalt, 1937.

Kroener, Bernhard R. "Der Kampf um den 'Sparstoff Mensch.' Forschungskontroversen über die Mobilisierung der deutschen Kriegswirtschaft 1939–1945" (The Struggle for Manpower, "the Scarce Resource." Research Controversies Concerning the Mobilization of the German War Economy, 1939–1942). *Der Zweiten Weltkrieg.* 402–17.

———. "Die personellen Ressourcen des Dritten Reiches im Spannungsfeld zwischen Wehrmacht, Bürokratie und Kriegswirtschaft 1939–1942" (The Manpower Resources of the Third Reich in the Context of the Wehrmacht, the Bureaucracy, and the War Economy). *Das Deutsche Reich und der Zweiten Weltkrieg.* Vol. 5, pt. 1, *Organisation und Mobilisierung des deutschen Machtsbereiches* (Organization and Mobilization in the German Sphere of Power). 691–1001.

———. "Squaring the Circle. Blitzkrieg Strategy and Manpower." *The German Military in the Age of the Total War.* Ed. Wilhelm Deist. Leamington Spa, 1985. 282–303.

Krumpelt, Ihno. *Das Material und die Kriegführung* (Matériel and Warfare). Frankfurt am Main: Mittler and Sohn, 1968.

Krumsiek. "Angriff der 71. Infanterie-Division über die Chiers und Durchbruch durch die Maginotlinie (Einnahme des Panzerwerkes 505) vom 15.5.–20.5.1940" (Attack of the 71st Infantry Division across the Chiers and the Breakthrough of the Maginot Line [The Capture of Fort 505] from 15–20 May 1940). *Pioniere* (Engineer) no. 1 (1959): 17–25.

KTB OKW (Kriegstagebuch des Oberkommmandos der Wehrmacht) (Wehrmachtführungsstab) Bd. 1: *1.8.1940–31.12.1941* (War Diary of the Wehrmacht High Command [Wehrmacht Operations] Staff. Vol. 1: 1 August 1940–31 December 1941). Comp. and ed. Hans-Adolf Jacobsen. Munich: Pawlak Verlag, 1982.

Kurowski, Franz, and Gottfried Tornau. *Sturmartillerie 1939–1945* (Assault Artillery, 1939–1945). Stuttgart: Motorbuch, 1977.

Lahne, Werner. *Die glückhafte Division. Mit den Bezwingern des Panzerwerks 505 nach Verdun und Nancy* (The Lucky Division: With the Conquerors of Armored Fort 505 on to Verdun and Nancy) [71st Infantry Division]. Berlin: Maximilian-Gesellschaft, 1942.

Langer, William L. *Our Vichy Gamble.* New York: Alfred A. Knopf, 1947.

Laubier, Philippe de. "Le bombardement française sur la Meuse. Le 14 mai 1940" (The French Bombardment along the Meuse on 14 May 1940). *RHA* no. 160 (1985): 96–109.

Le Diberder, Georges. "Les spahis dans les combats des Ardennes" (The Spahis during the Fighting in the Ardennes). *Ardennes, 1940.* 149–62.

Leeb, Wilhelm Ritter von. *Tagebuchaufzeichnungen und Lagebeurteilungen aus zwei Weltkriegen. Aus dem Nachlaß hrsg. und mit einem Lebensabriß versehen von Georg Meyer* (Diary Entries and Situation Estimates from Two World Wars: From the Estate, edited and with a brief biographical sketch by Georg Meyer). Vol. 16, *Beiträge zur Militär- und Kriegsgeschichte* (Contributions to Military and War History). Stuttgart: Deutsche Verlags-Anstalt, 1976.

Le Goyet, Pierre. "Contre-attaques manquées: Sedan—13–15 mai 1940" (Failed Counterattacks: Sedan, 13–15 May 1940). *RHA* 18, no. 4 (1962): 110–30.

———. "Le 11e corps d'armée dans la bataille de la Meuse. 10–15 mai 1940" (The XI Corps in the Battle of the Meuse, 10–15 May 1940). 2 parts, *RHA* 18, no. 1 (1962): 125–38; no. 2 (1962): 83–94.

———. "L'engagement de la 2e division cuirassée française" (The Commitment of the French 2d Armored Division). *RHA* 20, no. 1 (1964): 147–67.

———. *Le mystère Gamelin* (The Gamelin Mystery). Paris: Presses de la Cité, 1975.

———. "La percée de Sedan (10–15 mai 1940) (The Breakthrough at Sedan [10–15 May 1940]). *RHDGM* 15, no. 59 (1965): 25–52.

Lewin, Ronald. *Rommel. Eine Biographie* (Rommel: A Biography). Stuttgart: Kohlhammer, 1969.

Liddell Hart, Basil Henry. *Geschichte des Zweiten Weltkrieges* (History of World War II). Wiesbaden: Fourier Verlag, 1970. English language version: *History of the Second World War.* New York: G. P. Putnam's Sons, 1970.

———. *Jetzt dürfen sie reden. Hitlers Generale berichten* (Now They Can Speak Out: Hitler's Generals Report). Stuttgart: Stuttgarter Verlag, 1950. This is the German edition of *The Other Side of the Hill.* The American edition, *The German Generals Talk.*

———. *The Memoirs of Captain Liddell Hart.* Vol. 1. London: Cassell, 1965.

———. *The Other Side of the Hill. Germany's Generals: Their Rise and Fall, with their own Account of Military Events, 1939–1945.* London: Cassell, 1948. The American edition, *The German Generals Talk.* New York: William Morrow, 1948.

Lipcsey-Magyar, S. "Villámharcászat-zsakhadászat." *Magyar szemle* 11, no. 11 (1941): 257–67.

Liß, Ulrich. "Die deutsche Westoffensive 1940 vom Blickpunkt des Ic" (The German Offensive in the West in 1940 from the Viewpoint of the Intelligence Officer). *WWR* 8, no. 4 (1958): 208–19.

———. "Dünkirchen, gesehen mit den Augen des Ic" (Dunkirkas Seen through the Eyes of the Intelligence Officer). *WWR* 8, no. 6 (1958): 325–40.

———. *Westfront 1939/40: Erinnerungen des Feindbearbiters im O.K.H.* (Western Front, 1939–1940: Memoirs of an Intelligence Officer in the OKH). Neckargemünd: Kurt Vowinckel, 1959.

Lord, Walter. *Das Geheimnis von Dünkirchen* (The Secret of Dunkirk). Bern and Munich: Scherz, 1982. English language version: *The Miracle of Dunkirk.* New York: The Viking Press, 1982.

Loritte, Pierre. "Comment en est-on arrive au 13 mai 1940?" (How Did We Get to 13 May 1940?). *Le Pays Sedanais* 55, no. 17 (1990): 109–28.

———. "Le 13 mai 1940, au bloc du passage à niveau de Wadelincourt" (13 May 1940—Bunker at Railroad Level Crossing near Wadelincourt). *Le Pays Sedanais* 45, no. 7 (1980): 20–24.

Loßberg, Bernhard von. *Im Wehrmachtführungsstab. Bericht eines Generalstabsoffiziers* (In the Wehrmacht Operations Staff. Report of a General Staff Officer). Hamburg: Nölke, 1950.

Luck, Hans von. *Gefangener meiner Zeit. Ein Stück Weges mit Rommel* (Prisoner of My Time: A Piece of the Way with Rommel). Herford and Bonn: Mittler Verlag, 1991.

Lucke, Christian von. *Die Geschichte des Panzer-Regiments 2* (The History of the 2d Panzer Regiment). Stade: Boss-Druck und Verlag, 1953.

Lucke, Fritz. "Übergang erzwungen!" (Forced Crossing). *Korps Guderian.* Berlin: Oberkommando der Wehrmacht, 1942. 51–58.

Lüke, Hans. Die Geschichte des Regiment 69 (The History of the 69th Regiment). Hamburg, 1986.

Lupfer, Timothy T. "Die Dynamik der Kriegslehre. Der Wandel der taktischen Grundsätze des deutschen Heeres im Ersten Weltkrieg" (The Dynamics of the Theory of War: The Change in Tactical Principles in the German Army during World War I). *Militärgeschichtliches Beiheft zur Europäischen Wehrkunde* (Military History Supplement to European Military Science), no. 5 (October 1988).

Lyet, Pierre. "À-propos de Sedan 1940" (Concerning Sedan in 1940). *RHA* 18, no. 4 (1962): 89–109.

———. *La bataille de France (mai–juin 1940)* (The Battle of France, May–June 1940). Paris: Payot, 1947.

———. "La bataille de Belgique et du nord (la campagne 1939–1940)" (The Battle of Belgium and the North [The 1939–1940 Campaign]). *RHA* 2, no. 2 (1946): 41–75; no. 3 (1946): 59–91.

———. "Mitrailleurs malgaches à Monthermé mai 1940" (Malagasy Machine-Gunners at Monthermé, May 1940). *RHA* 19, no. 4 (1963): 130–32.

Maassen, Heinz. *Über die Maas. Die Erzwingung des Übergangs bei Monthermé* (Across the Meuse River: Forcing the Crossing at Monthermé). Düsseldorf: Völkischer Verlag, 1941.

Macksey, Kenneth John. *Deutsche Panzertruppen* (German Panzer Forces). Vienna and Munich: Moewig, 1985.

———. *Guderian der Panzergeneral* (Guderian, the Panzer General). Düsseldorf and Vienna: Econ Verlag, 1976. English language version: *Guderian: Creator of the Blitzkrieg.* New York: Stein and Day, 1976.

———. *Military Errors of World War II.* London: Arms and Armour Press, 1987.

———. *Panzer Division: The Mailed Fist.* New York: Ballantine Books, 1968.

———. *Rommel. Schlachten und Feldzüge* (Rommel: Battles and Campaigns). Stuttgart: Motorbuch Verlag, 1982.

Maier, Klaus A. "Der operative Luftkrieg bis zur Luftschlacht um England" (The Operational Air War up to the Air Battle for England). *Das Deutsche Reich und der Zweiten Weltkrieg.* Vol. 2, *Die Errichtung der Hegemonie auf dem europäischen Kontinent* (The Establishment of Hegemony on the European Continent). Stuttgart: Deutsche Verlags-Anstalt, 1988. 329–41.

———. "Totaler Krieg und operativer Luftkrieg" (Total War and the Operational Air War). *Das Deutsche Reich und der Zweiten Weltkrieg.* Vol. 2, *Die Errichtung der Hegemonie auf dem europäischen Kontinent* (The Establishment of Hegemony on the European Continent). Stuttgart: Deutsche Verlags-Anstalt, 1988. 43–69.

Mann, Golo. *Deutsche Geschichte des 19. und 20. Jahrhunderts* (German History of the 19th and 20th Centuries). Stuttgart and Hamburg, 1958. English language version: *The History of Germany since 1789.* Trans. Marian Jackson. New York: Frederick A. Praeger, 1968.

Manstein, Erich von. *Aus einem Soldatenleben 1887–1939* (From a Soldier's Life). Bonn: Athenäum, 1958.

———. *Verlorene Siege* (Lost Victories). Koblenz: Bernard and Graefe, 1987. English language version: *Lost Victories.* Chicago: Henry Regnery, 1958.

Manteuffel, Hasso von. *Die 7. Panzer-Division 1935–1945. Die Gespenster-Division* (The 7th Panzer Division, 1935–1945. The Ghost Division). Friedberg: Podzun-Pallas Verlag, 1978.

———. *Die 7. Panzer-Division im Zweiten Weltkrieg. Einsatz und Kampf der "Gespenster-Division" 1939–1945* (The 7th Panzer Division during World War II: Employment and Combat Actions of the "Ghost Division," 1939–1945). Cologne: Buchdruckerei Josef Broich, 1965.

Marolz, Josef. "Die Entwicklung der operativen Führung" (The Development of Operational Command). Part 3, *ÖMZ* 11, no. 5 (1973): 369–76.

Marshall, S. L. A. *Blitzkrieg. Its History, Strategy, Economics, and the Challenge to America.* New York: William Morrow, 1940.

Martin, Bernd. "Das 'Dritte Reich' und die 'Friedens'-Frage im Zweiten Weltkrieg" (The "Third Reich" and the "Peace Issue" during World War II). *Nationalsozialistische Aussenpolitik.* Darmstadt: Wissenschafliche Buchgesellschaft, 1978. 526–49.

Marx, Karl, and Friedrich Engels. *Werke* (Works). Vol. 8. East Berlin, 1956.

Mason, Herbert Molloy. *The Rise of the Luftwaffe, 1918–1940.* London: Cassell, 1975.

Mason, Timothy W. "Innere Krise und Angriffskrieg 1938/1939" (Domestic Crisis and War of Aggression, 1938/1939). *Wirtschaft und Rüstung.* 158–88.

Maurois, André. *Die Tragödie Frankreich* (France's Tragedy). Zürich: Rascher, 1941.

Mearsheimer, John J. *Liddell Hart and the Weight of History.* Ithaca, N.Y.: Cornell University Press, 1988.

Meier-Dörnberg, Wilhelm. "Der große deutsche Frühjahrsoffensive 1918 zwischen Strategie und Taktik" (The Great German Spring Offensive in 1918 between Strategy and Tactics). *Operatives Denken und Handeln.* 73–95.

Meier-Welcker, Hans. *Aufzeichnungen eines Generalstabsoffiziers, 1939–1942* (Notes of a General Staff Officer, 1939–1942). Vol. 26, *Einzelschriften zur Militärgeschichte* (Monographs on Military History). Freiburg im Breisgau: Rombach Verlag, 1982.

———. "Der Entschluß zum Anhalten der deutschen Panzertruppen in Flandern 1940" (The Decision to Stop the German Armored Units in Flanders, 1940). *Vierteljahrshefte für Zeitgeschichte* (Journal of Contemporary History) 2 (1954): 274–90.

———(anonymous). "Erlebnisse beim Oberkommando der 4.Armee während der Kämpfe zwischen Maas und Sambre am 15. und 16. Mai" (Experiences with Headquarters, Fourth Army, during the Fighting between the Sambre Rivers on 15 and 16 May). *MWR* 6, no. 2 (1941): 132–39.

Melchers, Emilie Théodore. *Kriegsschauplatz Luxemburg, August 1914, Mai 1940* (The Luxembourg Theater of War, August 1914, May 1940). Luxembourg: St. Paulus Druck, 1979.

Meldungen aus dem Reich 1938–1945. Die geheimen Lageberichte des Sicherheitsdienstes der SS (Messages from the Reich, 1938–1945: The Secret Situation Reports of the Security Service of the SS). Vol. 4, ed. Heinz Boberach. Herrsching: Pawlak, 1984.

Mellenthin, Friedrich Wilhelm von. *Panzerschlachten. Eine Studie über den Einsatz von Panzerverbänden im Zweiten Weltkrieg* (Panzer Battles: A Study on the Employment of Panzer Units in the Second World War). Neckargemünd: Kurt Vowinckel, 1963. English language version: *Panzer Battles: A Study of the Employment of Armor in the Second World War.* Norman: University of Oklahoma Press, 1956.

———. *Schach dem Schicksal* (Checkmating Destiny). Osnabrück: Biblio Verlag, 1989.

Memminger, Fritz. *Die Kriegsgeschichte der Windhund-Division* (The War History of the Greyhound Division). Bochum-Langendreer: Druck und Verlag H. Pöppinghaus, 1962.

Menke, Erich. "Militärtheoretische Überlegungen im deutschen Generalstab vor dem zweiten Weltkrieg" (Military Theory Considerations in the German General Staff before World War II Regarding the Employment of Panzers). *Revue Internationale d'Histoire Militaire* no. 71 (1989): 151–63.

Messenger, Charles. *Blitzkrieg. Eine Strategie macht Geschichte* (Blitzkrieg War: A Strategy Makes History). Bergisch Gladbach: Gustav Lübbe Verlag, 1978.

———. *The Last Prussian. A Biography of Field Marshal Gerd von Rundstedt.* London: Brassey's, 1991.

Mette, S. *Vom Geist deutscher Feldherren. Genie und Technik 1800–1918* (About the Spirit of German Warlords: Genius and Technology, 1800–1918). Zürich: Scientia, 1938.

Miksche, Ferdinand Otto. *Atom-Waffen und Streitkräfte* (Atomic Weapons and Armed Forces). Bonn: Westunion/Offene Worte, 1955.

———. *Blitzkrieg*. London: Faber and Faber, 1942.

———. *Vom Kriegsbild* (About the Image of War). Stuttgart: Verlag Seewald, 1976.

Milward, Alan S. *Die deutsche Kriegswirtschaft 1939–1945* (The German War Economy, 1939–1945). Stuttgart: Deutsche Verlags-Anstalt, 1966.

———. "Hitlers Konzept des Blitzkrieges" (Hitler's Concept of Blitzkrieg). *Probleme des Zweiten Weltkrieges* (Problems of the Second World War). Ed. Andreas Hillgruber. Cologne: Kiepenheuer and Witsch, 1967. 19–40.

———. "The Influence of Economic and Non-Economic Factors on the Strategy of Lightning War." *Wirtschaft und Rüstung*. Düsseldorf: Droste Verlag, 1975. 189–201.

———. *Der Zweiten Weltkrieg. Krieg, Wirtschaft und Gesellschaft 1939–1945* (The Second World War: War, Economy, and Society, 1939–1945). Vol. 5, *Geschichte der Weltwirtschaft im 20. Jahrhundert* (The History of the World Economy in the Twentieth Century). Munich: Deutscher Taschenbuch Verlag, 1977.

Minart, Jacques. *P. C. Vincennes: Secteur 4* (Command Post, Vincennes: Sector 4). Vol. 2. Paris: Berger-Levrault, 1945.

Mit den Panzern in Ost und West (With the Panzers in East and West). Ed. Heinz Guderian. Berlin, Prague, and Vienna: Volk und Reich Verlag, 1942.

Moltke, Helmuth von. *Gesammelte Schriften und Denkwürdigkeiten des General-Feldmarschalls Grafen Helmuth von Moltke* (Collected Works and Memorabilia of Field Marshal Count von Moltke). 8 vols. Berlin: Mittler and Sohn, 1891–93.

Moltkes Militärische Werke (Moltke's Military Works). Vol. 2, pt. 2. Berlin: E. S. Mittler, 1900. Vol. 4, pt. 3. Berlin: E. S. Mittler, 1912.

Motch, Ch. "1939–1940: The 12th Regiment of Chasseurs in its Travail." *Le Pays Sedanais* no. 17 (1990): 95–106.

Müller, Klaus-Jürgen. "Dünkirchen 1940. Ein Beitrag zur Vorgeschichte der britischen und französichen Evakuierung" (Dunkirk 1940: A Contribution to the Background of the British and French Evacuation). *Marinerundschau* 57, no. 3 (1960): 133–68.

———. *Das Heer und Hitler. Armee und nationalsozialistisches Regime 1939–1940* (The Army and Hitler: The Army and the National Socialist Regime, 1939–1940). Vol. 10, *Beiträge zur Militär- und Kriegsgeschichte* (Contributions to Military and War History). Stuttgart: Deutsche Verlags-Anstalt, 1969.

———. "Witzleben-Stülpnagel-Speidel: Offiziere im Widerstand" (Witzleben, Stülpnagel, Speidel: Officers in the Resistance). No. 7, *Beiträge zum Widerstand 1933–1945* (Contributions to the Resistance, 1933–1945). Berlin: Landeszentrale für politische Bildungsarbeit, 1988.

Müller, Rolf-Dieter. "Die Mobilisierung der Deutschen Wirtschaft für Hitlers Kriegsführung" (The Mobilization of the German Economy for Hitler's Warfare). *Das Deutsche Reich und der Zweiten Weltkrieg.* Vol. 5, Pt. 1, *Organisation und Mobilisierung des Deutschen Machtbereichs* (Organization and Mobilization in the German Sphere of Power). 347–689.

———. "Die Mobilisierung der Deutschen Wirtschaft für den Krieg—eine Aufgabe der Armee? Wehrmacht und Wirtschaft 1939–1942" (The Mobilization of the Economy for the War—A Task for the Army? Armed Forces and Economy, 1933–1942). *Das Deutsche Reich und der Zweiten Weltkrieg.* Vol. 5, Pt. 1, *Organisation und Mobilisierung des Deutschen Machtbereichs* (Organization and Mobilization in the German Sphere of Power). 349–62.

———. "Von der Wirtschaftsallianz zum kolonialen Ausbeutungskrieg" (From Economic Alliance to Colonial War of Exploitation). *Das Deutsche Reich und der Zweiten Weltkrieg.* Vol. 4, *Der Angriff auf die Sowjetunion* (The Attack on the Soviet Union), 8–189.

Müller-Hillebrand, Burkhart. *Das Heer 1933–1945. Entwicklung des organisatorischen Aufbaus* (The Army, 1933–1945: Development of Organizational Build-Up). Vol. 1, *Das Heer bis zum Kriegsbeginn* (The Army to the Start of the War). Darmstadt, 1954. Vol. 2, *Die Blitzfeldzüge 1939–1941* (The Lightning Campaigns, 1939–1941). Frankfurt am Main: Verlag E. S. Mittler and Sohn, 1956.

Murray, Williamson. "The German Army Doctrine, 1918–1939, and the Post–1945 Theory of 'Blitzkrieg Strategy.' " *German Nationalism.* London: University of Oklahoma Press, 1985. 71–94.

———. *Strategy for Defeat. The Luftwaffe, 1933–1945.* Maxwell Air Force Base, Ala.: Air University Press, 1983.

Mußhoff, H. "Blitzkriegpsychose" (Blitzkrieg Psychosis). *Ostasiatischer Beobachter* 8, Ser. 86, 31 August 1940: 3–7.

Nationalsozialistiche Aussenpolitik (National Socialist Foreign Policy). Ed. Wolfgang Michalka. Darmstadt: Wissenschaftliche Buchgesellschaft, 1978.

Nehring, Walther K. *Die Geschichte der deutschen Panzerwaffe 1916–1945* (The History of the German Panzer Arm, 1916–1945). Berlin: Propylöen Verlag, 1969.

Neugebauer, Karl-Volker. "Operatives Denken zwischen dem Ersten und Zweiten Weltkrieg" (Operational Thinking between the First and Second World Wars). *Operatives Denken und Handeln in deutschen Streitkräften im 19. und 20. Jahrhundert.* Herford and Bonn: Verlag E. S. Mittler and Sohn, 1988. 97–122.

Neumann, Joachim. *Die 4.Panzerdivision 1938–1943* (The 4th Panzer Division, 1938–1943). 2 vols. Bonn: self-published, 1985.

Newell, Clayton R. *The Framework of Operational Warfare.* London and New York: Routledge, 1991.

Nölke, Hans. *Die 71. Infanterie-Division in Zweiten Weltkrieg 1939–1945* (The 71st Infantry Division in World War II, 1939–1945). Hannover: Druckhaus Pinkvoß, 1984.

Novak, Hugo. *Geschichte der ostpreußischen leichten Flakabteilung 71* (The History of the 71st East Prussian Light Antiaircraft Artillery Battalion). Siegen: n.p., 1979.

Oetting, Dirk W. *Auftragstaktik. Geschichte und Gegenwart einer Führungskonzeption* (Mission Tactics: History and Presence of a Command Concept). Frankfurt am Main and others: Report Verlag, 1993.

Olivier. "Sedan, mai 40. Le secteur de la gare (Rapport de l'Adjutant-Chef Olivier, 5e Compagnie de mitrailleuses du 147e R.I.F.)" (Sedan, May '40. The Railroad Station Sector [Report of Chief Warrant Officer Olivier, 5th Machine Gun Company, 147th Fortress Infantry Regiment]). *Le Pays Sedanais* 45, n.s., no. 7 (1980): 26–29.

Operatives Denken und Handeln in deutschen Streitkräften im 19. und 20. Jahrhundert (Operational Thinking and Action in the German Armed Forces during the 19th and 20th Centuries). Vol. 9, *Vorträge zur Militärgeschichte* (Lectures on Military History). Herford and Bonn: Verlag E. S. Mittler and Sohn, 1988.

d'Ornano. "Après la percée de Sedan" (After the Breakthrough at Sedan). *RHDGM* 1 (March 1950): 35ff.

Otto, Helmut. "Entstehung und Wesen der Blitzkriegsstrategie des deutschen Imperialismus vor dem ersten Weltkrieg" (Origin and Essence of Blitzkrieg Strategy of German Imperialism before World War I). *Zeitschrift für Militärgeschichte* 6, no. 4 (1967): 400–414.

———. "Illusion und Fiasko der Blitzkriegsstrategie gegen Frankreich, 1914" (Illusion and Failure of Blitzkrieg Strategy against France, 1914). *Militärgeschichte* 28, no. 4 (1989): 301–8.

"Out-Blitz the Blitzkrieg." *Army and Navy Journal* no. 38 (1940): 885f.

Overmans, Rüdiger. "Das andere Gesicht des Krieges: Leben und Sterben der 6.Armee" (The Other Face of War: Life and Death of the Sixth Army). Stalingrad. Ereignis—Wirkung—Symbol (Stalingrad: Event—Effect—Symbol). Ed. Jürgen Förster, by direction of the MGFA. Munich: Piper Verlag, 1992. 419–55.

Overy, Richard James. *The Air War, 1939–1945.* London: Europa Publications, 1980.

———. " 'Blitzkriegswirtschaft?' Finanzpolitik, Lebensstandard und Arbeitseinsatz in Deutschland 1939–1942 ("Blitzkrieg Economy"? Financial Policy, Living Standard, and Labor Employment in Germany, 1939–1942). *Vierteljahrshefte für Zeitgeschichte* (Journal of Contemporary History) 36 (1988): 379–435.

Paget, Reginald T. Manstein. *Seine Feldzüge und sein Prozeß* (Manstein: His Campaigns and His Methods). Wiesbaden: Limes Verlag, 1952.

Paillat, Claude. *Le désastre de 1940* (The Disaster of 1940). 3 vols. *Dossiers secrets de la France contemporaine* (Secret Files of Contemporary France). Paris: Robert Laffont, 1983–86. Vol. 1, *La répétition générale* (The General Repetition). 1983. Vol. 2, *La guerre immobile. Avril 1939–10 mai 1940* (The Immobile War: April 1939–10 May 1940). 1986. Vol. 3. *La guerre éclair. 10 mai–24 juin 1940* (The Lightning War: 10 May–24 June 1940). 1985.

Paillole, Paul. *Notre espion chez Hitler* (Our Spy with Hitler). Paris, 1985.

Pallud, Jean Paul. *Blitzkrieg in the West: Then and Now.* London: After the Battle, 1991.

———. "The Road Ends at Denée." *After the Battle* no. 51 (1986): 46–54.

Paul, Wolfgang. *Brennpunkte. Die Geschichte der 6.Panzerdivision (1. leichte)* (Focal Points: The History of the 6th Panzer Division [1st Light Division]). Osnabrück: Biblio Verlag, 1984.

Perrett, Bryan. *A History of Blitzkrieg.* New York: Stein and Day, 1983.

———. *Knights of the Black Cross: Hitler's Panzerwaffe and Its Leaders.* New York: St. Martins Press, 1986.

Picht, Werner. *Das Ende der Illusionen. Der Feldzug im Westen, ein Sieg der Tat über die Täuschung* (The End of Illusions: The Campaign in the West, a Victory of Fact over Deception). Berlin: Mittler and Sohn, 1941.

Piekalkiewicz, Janusz. *Krieg der Panzer 1939–1945* (The War of the Panzers, 1939–1945). Gütersloh: Bertelsmann, n.d.

———. *Luftkrieg 1939–1945* (Air War, 1939–1945). Munich: Südwest-Verlag, 1978.

———. *Ziel Paris. Der Westfeldzug 1940* (Target Paris. The 1940 Campaign in the West). Munich and Berlin: F. A. Herbig, 1986.

Plato, Detlev von. *Die Geschichte der 5. Panzerdivision 1938–1945* (The History of the 5th Panzer Division, 1938–1945). Regensburg: Selbstverlag-Gemeinschaft der Angehörigen der ehemaligen 5. Panzerdivision (Self-published by the Union of the Members of the Former 5th Panzer Division), 1978.

Plettenberg, Malte. *Guderian. Hintergründe eines deutschen Schicksals, 1918–1945* (Guderian: Background of a German Destiny, 1918–1945). Düsseldorf: abz-Verlag, 1950.

Ploetz, Karl. *Auszug aus der Geschichte* (Extracts from History). Würzburg: Ploetz Verlag, 1960.

———. *Geschichte der Weltkriege. Mächte, Ereignisse, Entwicklungen 1900–1945* (History of the World Wars: Powers, Events, Developments, 1900–1945). Ed. Andreas Hillgruber and Jost Dülffer. Freiburg and Würzburg: Ploetz Verlag, 1981.

———. *Geschichte des Zweiten Weltkrieges* (History of the Second World War). Prepared by Percy Ernst Schramm and Hans O. H. Stange. 2d expanded ed. Würzburg: Ploetz Verlag, 1960.

Porch, Douglas. "Why Did France Fall?" *Quarterly Journal of Military History* 2 (spring 1990): 30–41.

Possony, Stefan T. *Die Wehrwirtschaft des totalen Krieges* (The War Economy of Total War). Vienna: Gerold, 1938.

Prételat, André. *Le destin tragique de la ligne Maginot* (The Tragic Destiny of the Maginot Line). Paris: Berger-Levrault, 1950.

Prioux, René Jacques. *Souvenirs de guerre 1939–1943* (Memories of the War, 1939–1943). Paris: Flammarion, 1947.

Der Prozeß gegen die Hauptkriegsverbrecher vor dem internationalen Militärgerichtshof. Nürnberg, 14 November 1945–1 October 1946. 42 vols. Nürnberg, 1947–49. English language version: *The Trial of the Major War Criminals before the International Military Court. Nuremberg, 14 November 1945–1 October 1946.* Nürnberg, 1947–49.

Raleigh, Walter Alexander, and H. A. Jones. *The War in the Air.* 6 vols. Oxford: Oxford University Press, 1922–37.

Raudzens, George. "Blitzkrieg Ambiguities: Doubtful Usage of a Famous Word." *War and Society* 7, no. 2 (1989): 77–94.

Reichsarchiv (Bearbeitet im) (Reichs Archives [Prepared in]). *Der Weltkrieg 1914 bis 1918. Die militärischen Operationen zu Lande.* Bd. 3: *Der Marne-Feldzug. Von der Sambre bis zur Marne* (The World War, 1914–1918. The Military Operations on Land. Vol. 3, The Marne Campaign: From the Sambre to the Marne). Berlin: Verlag Mittler and Sohn, 1926.

Reilly, Henry J. "Bliksemoorlog." *De Kern* 10 (1940): 161–64.

———. "Blitzkrieg." *Foreign Affairs* 18, no. 2 (1940): 254–65.

———. "Can 'Blitzkrieg' Be Stopped?" *Illustrated London News* no. 5282 (1940): 50.

———. "Na fone molnienosnoy voyny." *Voenny Zarubeẑnik* no. 9 (1940): 36–44.

Reinhardt, Hans. "Im Schatten Guderians. Das XXXXI.Pz.-Korps und seine Nöte bei dem Vorgehen gegen und über die Maas vom 10. bis 16. Mai 1940" (In Guderian's Shadow: The XXXXI Panzer Corps and Its Troubles during Its Advance to and Across the Meuse River from 10 to 16 May 1940). *Wehrkunde* 3, no. 10 (1954): 333–41.

Richards, Denis, and Hilary St. George Saunders. *Royal Air Force, 1939–1945.* Vol. 1, *The Fight at Odds.* London: Her Majesty's Stationery Office, 1953.

Richey, Stephen W. "The Philosophical Basis of the Air Land Battle. Auftragstaktik, Schwerpunkt, Aufrollen." *Military Review* 64, no. 5 (May 1984): 48–53.

Ritter, Gerhard. *Der Schlieffenplan. Kritik eines Mythos* (The Schlieffen Plan. Critique of a Myth) Munich: R. Oldenbourg, 1956. English language version: *The Schlieffen Plan: Critique of a Myth.* London: Oswold Wolff, 1958.

———. *Staatskunst und Kriegshandwerk. Das Problem des "Militarismus" in Deutschland* (Statecraft and the Profession of Arms: The Problem of "Militarism" in Germany). 4 vols. Munich: R. Oldenbourg, 1954–68. English language version: *The Sword and the Scepter: The Problem of Militarism in Germany.* Coral Gables: University of Miami Press, 1969–73.

Robineau, Lucien. "La conduite de la guerre aérienne contre l'Allemagne, de septembre 1939 à juin 1940" (The Conduct of the Air War against Germany from September 1939 to June 1940). *RHA* no. 176 (September 1989): 102–12.

———. "French Air Policy in the Inter-War period and the Conduct of the Air War against Germany from September 1939 to June 1940." *The Conduct of the Air War in the Second World War.* Herford and Bonn: Verlag E. S. Mittler and Sohn, 1993. 627–57.

Rocolle, Pierre. *La guerre de 1940* (The War of 1940). Vol. 1, *Les Illusions (novembre 1918–mai 1940)* (The Illusions [November 1918–May 1940]); Vol. 2, *La défaite (10 mai–25 juin)* (The Defeat [10 May–25 June]). Paris: Armand Colin, 1990.

Rogé. "La Campagne de France. Vue par le Général Guderian" (The Campaign in France: As Seen by General Guderian). *RHA* 3, no. 1 (1947): 109–19.

Rogers, H. C. B. "Arras. Mai 1940" (Arras, May 1940). *Connaissance de l'Histoire* (Knowledge of History) no. 48 (September 1982): 46–51.

Rohde, Horst. "Hitlers erster 'Blitzkrieg' und seine Auswirkungen auf Nordosteuropa" (Hitler's First "Blitzkrieg" and Its Effects on Northeastern Europe). *Das Deutsche Reich und der Zweiten Weltkrieg.* Vol. 2, *Die Errichtung der Hegemonie auf dem europäischen Kontinent* (The Establishment of Hegemony on the European Continent). 77–156.

———. "Die operativen Grundlagen der Ardennenoffensive: Wirtschaft und Logistik auf deutscher Seite" (The Operational Fundamentals of the Ardennes Offensive—Economy and Logistics on the German Side). *Entwicklung, Planung und Durchführung operativer Ideen im Ersten und Zweiten Weltkrieg.* 93–141.

Rohwer, Jürgen. "Der Einfluß der alliierten Funkaufklärung auf den Verlauf des Zweiten Weltkrieges" (The Influence of Allied Radio Intelligence on the Course of the Second World War). *Vierteljahrshefte für Zeitgeschichte* 27 (1979): 325–69.

Rolak, B. J. "Fathers of the Blitzkrieg." *Military Review* 49, no. 5 (May 1969): 73–76.

Rommel, Erwin. *Krieg ohne Haß* (War without Hate). Ed. Lucie-Marie Rommel and Generalleutnant Fritz Bayerlein. Heidenheim: Heidenheimer Zeitung, 1950.

Rothbrust, Florian K. *Guderian's XIXth Panzer Corps and the Battle of France: Breakthrough in the Ardennes, May 1940.* Westport, Conn., and London: Greenwood Press, 1990.

Rothfels, Hans. *Carl von Clausewitz. Politik und Krieg. Eine ideengeschichtliche Studie* (Carl von Clausewitz. Politics and War: A Study on the History of Ideas). Berlin: F. Dümmler, 1920.

Roth, Günter. "Operatives Denken bei Schlieffen und Manstein" (Operational Thinking of Schlieffen and Manstein). *Entwicklung, Planung und Durchführung operativer Ideen im Ersten und Zweiten Weltkrieg.* 7–46.

Roton, Gaston René Eugène. *Années cruciales: La Course aux armaments (1933–1939). La Campagne (1939–1940)* (Crucial Years: The Arms Race [1933–1939]. The Campaign [1939–1940]). Paris: Charles-Lavauzelle, 1947.

Rottgardt, Dirk. "Die deutsche Panzertruppe am 10.5.1940" (The German Panzer Arm on 10 May 1940). *Zeitschrift für Heerskunde* 49, no. 319 (May–June 1985): 61–67.

Ruby, Edmond. *Sedan: Terre d'Épreuve. Avec la IIème armée mai–juin 1940* (Sedan. The Testing Ground: With the Second Army, May–June, 1940). Paris: Flammarion, 1948.

Sacré, J. "La chasse au-dessus de Sedan" (The Fighters above Sedan). *Le pays Sedanais* 55, no. 17 (1990): 155–70.

———. "14 mai 1940. Le bombardement allié sur la tête de pont de Sedan" (14 May 1940. The Allied Bombing Raids against the Bridgehead at Sedan). *Le pays Sedanais* 55, no. 17 (1990): 129–54.

Saint-Genis, Lucien. "Le début de la poche de Sedan" (The Start of the Sedan Pocket). *Icare* no. 59 (autumn–winter 1971): 102–13.

Salewski, Michael. *Die deutsche Seekriegsleitung, 1935–1945* (The German Supreme Naval War Staff, 1935–1945). 2 vols. Munich: Bernard and Graefe, 1970–75.

———. "Knotenpunkt der Weltgeschichte? Die Raison des deutsch–französischen Waffenstillstands vom 22.Juni 1940" (Crucial Junctures in World History? The Rationale behind the German-French Armistice of 22 June 1940). *La France et l'Allemagne en guerre. Septembre 1939–Novembre 1942* (France and Germany at War. September 1939–November 1942). Ed. Claude Carlier and Stefan Martens. Paris: I.H.A.P.-I.H.C.C, 1990. 115–29.

Samuels, Martin. "The Reality of Cannae." *MGM* 47, no. 1 (1990): 7–31.

Sandrart, Hans-Henning von. "Operative Führung über die Gefechtstaktik hinaus" (Operational Command above and beyond Combat Tactics). *EWKde* 36, no. 9 (1987): 503–5.

Schall-Riaucour, Heidemarie. *Aufstand und Gehorsam. Offizierstum und Generalstab im Umbruch. Leben und Wirken von Generaloberst Franz Halder, Generalstabschef 1938–1942* (Insurrection and Obedience. Commissioned Officers and General Staff in Revolution: Life and Work of General Franz Halder, Chief of Staff, 1938–1942). Wiesbaden: Limes Verlag, 1972.

Scheibert, Horst. *Die Gespensterdivision. Eine deutsche Panzer-Division (7.) im Zweiten Weltkrieg* (The Ghost Division: A German Panzer Division [7th] during World War II). Friedberg: Podzun-Pallas-Verlag, 1981.

———. *Das war Guderian. Ein Lebensbericht im Bildern* (That Was Guderian: A Report on his Life in Pictures) Friedberg: Podzun-Pallas-Verlag, 1980.

Schlieffen, Alfred von. *Cannae.* Berlin: Mittler and Sohn, 1925.

Schmidt, Paul. *Statist auf diplomatischer Bühne 1923–45. Erlebnisse des Chefdolmetschers im Auswärtigen Amt mit den Staatsmännern Europas* (An Extra on the Diplomatic Stage, 1923–45: Experiences of the Chief Interpreter in the Foreign Office in Dealing with Europe's Statesmen). Bonn: Athenäum, 1954.

Schramm, Wilhelm von. *. . . sprich vom Frieden, wenn du den Krieg willst. Die psychologischen Offensiven Hitlers gegen die Franzosen 1933 bis 1939* (. . . Talk Peace If You Want War: Hitler's Psychological Offensives against the French, 1933 to 1939). Mainz: Hase and Köhler, 1973.

Schreiber, Gerhard. "Die politische und militärische Entwicklung im Mittelmeerraum 1939/40" (Political and Military Developments in the Mediterranean Area, 1939–1940). *Das Deutsche Reich und der Zweiten Weltkrieg.* Vol. 3, *Der Mittelmeerraum und Südosteuropa* (The Mediterranean and Southeast Europe). 4–271.

Schrodek, Gustav. *Ihr Glaube galt dem Vaterland. Geschichte des Panzer-Regiments 15* (They Believed in the Fatherland: History of the 15th Panzer Regiment). Munich: Schild, 1976.

Schulze. "Erster Einsatz vor Sedan" (First Action before Sedan). *Militär-Wochenblatt* 125, no. 43 (1941): cols. 1736–40.

Schustereit, Hartmut. "Heeresrüstung und 'Blitzkriegskonzept.' Fakten zur Materiallage im Herbst 1939" (Army Armament and the "Blitzkrieg" Concept: Facts Regarding the Matériel Situation in the Autumn of 1939). *Soldat und Technik* 33 (1990): 126–32.

———. *Vabanque. Hitlers Angriff auf die Sowjetunion 1941 als Versuch, durch den Sieg im Osten den Westen zu bezwingen* (Go-for-Broke Gamble: Hitler's Attack on the Soviet Union in 1941 as an Attempt to Defeat the West by Winning in the East). Bonn and Herford: E. S. Mittler and Sohn, 1988.

Schwichow, von. "Die Ernährungswirtschaft als Wehrproblem" (The Food Economy as a National Defense Problem). *Deutsche Wehr* 39, no. 18 (1935): 257–60.

Seeckt, Hans von. *Bemerkungen des Chefs der Heeresleitung, Generaloberst von Seeckt bei Besichtigungen und Manövern aus den Jahren 1920 bis 1926 (Bes. Bem.)* (Comments of the Chief of the Army Command, General von Seeckt, during Inspections and Maneuvers from the Years 1920 to 1926 [Special Comments]). Berlin: Reichswehr Ministry, 1927.

———. *Gedanken eines Soldaten* (Thoughts of a Soldier). Berlin: Verlag für Kulturpolitik, 1929.

Sendtner, Kurt. "Die deutsche Militäropposition im ersten Kriegsjahr" (The German Military Opposition during the First Year of the War). *Die Vollmacht des Gewissens.* Bd. 1: *Probleme des militärischen Widerstandes gegen Hitler* (The Power of Conscience. Vol. 1: The Problems of the Military Resistance against Hitler). Frankfurt am Main and Berlin: Alfred Metzner Verlag, 1960. 385–532.

Senff, Hubertus. *Die Entwicklung der Panzerwaffe im deutschen Heer zwischen den beiden Weltkriegen* (The Development of the Panzer Arm in the German Army between the Two World Wars). Frankfurt: Mittler and Sohn, 1969.

Service Historique de l'Armée de Terre (French Army Historical Service, ed). *Sedan 1940.* Vincennes, 1991.

Shepperd, Alan. *France, 1940: Blitzkrieg in the West.* London: Osprey, 1990.

Shirer, William L. *Aufstieg und Fall des Dritten Reiches* (The Rise and Fall of the Third Reich). Cologne and Berlin: Kiepenheuer and Witsch, 1961. English language version: *The Rise and Fall of the Third Reich: A History of Nazi Germany.* New York: Simon and Schuster, 1960.

———. *Der Zusammenbruch Frankreichs. Aufstieg und Fall der Dritten Republik* (The Collapse of France: The Rise and Fall of the Third Republic). Munich and Zürich: Droemersche Verlagsanstalt, 1970. English language version: *The Collapse of The Third Republic: An Inquiry into the Fall of France in 1940.* New York: Simon and Schuster, 1969.

Soldan. "Der Durchbruch über die Maas am 13.Mai 1940" (The Breakthrough across the Meuse River on 13 May 1940). *MWR* 5, no. 3 (1940): 296–309.

Sormail, Isabelle. "Le haut commandement aérien français et la participation de la RAF à la bataille de France: Une note du Général Vuillemin du 8 juillet 1940" (The French Air Force High Command and Participation of the Royal Air Force in the Battle of France: A Note by General Vuillemin on 8 July 1940). *RHA* no. 168 (1987): 2–8.

Spaeter, Helmuth. *Die Geschichte des Panzerkorps Großdeutschland* (The History of the Panzer Corps Großdeutschland). Duisburg-Ruhrort: Selbstverlag Hilfswerk ehem. Soldaten, 1958.

Spears, Edward L. *Assignment to Catastrophe.* Vol. 1, *Prelude to Dunkirk, July 1939–May 1940.* London: William Heinemann, 1954.

Stalingrad. Ereignis—Wirkung—Symbol (Stalingrad: Event—Effect—Symbol). Ed. Jürgen Förster, by direction of the MGFA. Munich: Piper Verlag, 1992.

Stegemann, Bernd. "Hitlers 'Stufenplan' und die Marine" (Hitler's "Step-by-Step Plan" and the Navy). *Historische Studien zu Politik, Verfassung und Gesellschaft (Festschrift für Richard Dietrich zum 65. Geburtstag)* (Historical Studies on Politics, Constitution and Society [Festschrift for Richard Dietrich on His 65th Birthday]). Frankfurt am Main: Peter Lang, 1976. 301–16.

———. "Hitlers Ziele im ersten Kriegsjahr 1939/40. Ein Beitrag zur Quellenkritik" (Hitler's Objectives during the First Year of the War, 1939–1940: A Contribution to Source Critique). *MGM* 27, no. 1 (1980): 93–105.

Stein, Hans Peter. "Führen durch Auftrag" (Leading through Mission). *Truppenpraxis,* supp. 1 (1985): 1–15.

Sternberg, Fritz. *Die deutsche kriegsstärke. Wie lange kann Hitler Krieg führen?* (Germany's Wartime Strength: How Long Can Hitler Fight the War?). Paris: Éditions Sebastian Brant, 1939 [copyright 1938].

———. *Germany and a Lightning War.* London: Faber and Faber, 1938.

Stolfi, R. H. S. "Equipment for Victory in France in 1940." *History* 55, no. 183 (February 1970): 1–20.

Stoves, Rolf O. G. *1. Panzer-Division 1935–1945. Chronik einer der drei Stamm-Divisionen der deutschen Panzerwaffe* (1st Panzer Division, 1935–1945: Record of One of the Three Parent Divisions of the German Panzer Arm). Bad Nauheim: Podzun Verlag, 1961.

———. *Die 1. Panzer-Division 1935–1945. Ihre Aufstellung—die Bewaffnung—der Einsatz—ihre Männer* (The 1st Panzer Division, 1935–1945: Its Organization, Armament, Employment, and Personnel). Dorheim (Friedberg): Podzun Verlag, 1975.

Strachan, Hew. *European Armies and the Conduct of War.* London: George Allen and Unwin, 1983.

Strauß, Franz Joseph. *Friedens- und Kriegserlebnisse einer Generation. Ein Kapitel Weltgeschichte aus der Sicht der Panzerjäger-Abteilung 38 (SF) in der ehem. 2. (Wiener) Panzerdivision* (Peacetime and Wartime Experiences of a Generation: A Chapter in World History from the Viewpoint of the 38th Antitank Battalion [Self-

Propelled] in the Former 2d [Viennese] Panzer Division). Kitzingen. Desktop publication, 1981.

Sturmpanzerwagen A 7 V. Vom Urpanzer zum Leopard 2 (The A 7 V Assault Panzer: From the Original Panzer to the Leopard 2). Herford: E. S. Mittler and Sohn, 1990.

Susbielle, B. de. "Chasseurs à pied, cavaliers et blindés au combat. Canal des Ardennes 16–23 mai 1940" (Chasseurs on Foot, Cavalry, and Tanks in Combat: The Ardennes Canal, 16–23 May 1940). *RHA* no. 2 (1972): 75–99.

Teiß. "Der Blitzkrieg" (The Blitzkrieg). *Rheinisch Westfälische Zeitung,* 1 October 1942.

Tettau, Hans von, and Kurt Versock. *Geschichte der 24. Infanterie-Division* (History of the 24th Infantry Division). Stolberg: n.p., 1956.

Thomas, Georg. *Geschichte der deutschen Wehr- und Rüstungswirtschaft (1918–1945)* (History of the German Defense and Armament Industry [1918–1945]). Boppard am Rhein: Boldt, 1966.

———. "Operatives und wirtschaftliches Denken" (Operational and Economic Thinking). *Kriegswirtschaftliche Jahresberichte* (War Industry Annual Reports). Hamburg: Hanseatische Verlags-Anstalt, 1937, 11–18.

Thompson, P. W. "Inûenernye vojska v molnienosnoj vojne," Zarubeẑnik no. 11/12 (1940). 72–79.

Tournoux, Paul-Émile. "Pouvait-on prévoir l'attaque allemande des Ardennes de mai 1940? Un général avait dit 'oui' " (Could We Have Foreseen the German Attack in the Ardennes in May 1940? A General Said, "Yes"). *RHA* no. 2 (1971): 130–41.

Trials of War Criminals before the Nuernberg Military Tribunals under Council Law No. 10. Nuernberg, October 1946–April 1949. Washington, D.C.: U.S. Government Printing Office, 1950.

Tschimpke, Alfred. *Die Gespensterdivision. Mit der Panzerwaffe durch Belgien und Frankreich* (The Ghost Division: With the Panzer Arm through Belgium and France). Munich: Zentralverlag der NSDAP Franz Eher, 1941.

Turnbull, Patrick. *Dunkirk: Anatomy of Disaster.* New York: Holmes and Meier Publishers, 1978.

Ueberschär, Gerd R. *Franz Halder. Generalstabschef, Gegner und Gefangener Hitlers* (General Franz Halder: Chief of the General Staff, Opponent and Prisoner of Hitler). Göttingen: Musterschmidt, 1991.

———. "Generaloberst Halder im militärischen Widerstand 1938–1940" (General Halder in the Military Resistance, 1938–1940). *Wehrforschung* 2, no. 1 (1973): 20–31.

Uhle-Wettler, Franz. *Höhe- und Wendepunkte Deutscher Militärgeschichte* (High Points and Turning Points of German Military History). Mainz: v. Hase & Koehler, 1984.

Ullrich, Karl. *Wie ein Fels im Meer. Kriegsgeschichte der 3. SS-Panzerdivision "Totenkopf"* (Like a Rock in the Sea: Wartime History of the 3d SS Panzer Division "Death's Head"). Osnabrück: Munin-Verlag, 1987.

Umbreit, Hans. "Der Kampf um die Vormachtstellung in Westeuropa" (The Struggle to Achieve Predominance in Europe). *Das Deutsche Reich und der Zweiten Weltkrieg.* Vol. 2, *Die Errichtung der Hegemonie auf dem europäischen Kontinent.* 233–327.

Urner, Klaus. *"Die Schweiz muß noch geschluckt werden!" Hitlers Aktiosnpläne gegen die Schweiz* (Let's Swallow Switzerland, Too! Hitler's Plans against Switzerland) Zurich: Verlag Neue Zürcher Zeitung (NZZ), 1990.

Vanwelkenhuyzen, Jean. "Die Sicherheitspolitik Belgiens während der Kriegsphase 1939/40" (Belgium's Security Policy during the 1939–1940 Phase of the War). *ÖMZ* 27, no. 6 (1989): 477ff.

Veron, Jean. "Detruire les ponts de la Meuse" (Destroying the Bridges over the Meuse). *Icare* no. 57 (spring-summer 1971): 122–27.

Vidalenc, Jean. "Les divisions de série 'B' dans l'armée française pendant la campagne de France 1939–1940" (The "B" Series Divisions in the French Army during the French Campaign, 1939–1940). *RHA* no. 4 (1980): 106–26.

Vítěz, Libor. *Ruhm und Fall der Maginotlinie* (Glory and Fall of the Maginot Line). Prague: Orbis, 1942.

Vogel, Rudolf. *Grenzerjunge im Blitzkrieg. Eine Erzählung aus dem Polenfeldzug* (Border Youth during the Blitzkrieg: Tales from the Polish Campaign). Stuttgart: Union Deutsche Verlagsgesellschaft, 1940.

Volkmann, Hans-Erich. "Die NS-Wirtschaft in Vorbereitung des Krieges" (The Nazi Economy in Preparation for the War). *Das Deutsche Reich and der Zweiten Weltkrieg.* Vol. 1, *Ursachen und Voraussetzungen der deutschen Kriegspolitik.* 175–368.

Wahl, Karl. . . . *es ist das deutsche Herz. Erlebnisse und Erkenntnisse eines ehemaligen Gauleiters* (. . . It Is the German Heart: Experiences and Realizations of a Former Gauleiter) Augsburg: Karl Wahl, 1954.

Walde, Karl J. *Guderian* (Guderian). Frankfurt am Main: Ullstein, 1976.

Wallach, Jehuda L. *Das Dogma der Vernichtungsschlacht. Die Lehren von Clausewitz und Schlieffen und ihre Wirkungen in zwei Weltkriegen* (The Dogma of the Battle of Annihilation: The Theories of Clausewitz and Schlieffen and their Effects during Two World Wars). Frankfurt am Main: Bernard & Graefe, 1967.

———. *Kriegstheorien. Ihre Entwicklung im 19. und 20. Jahrhundert* (Theories of War: Their Development during the 19th and 20th Centuries). Frankfurt am Main: Bernhard and Graefe, 1972.

Walle, Heinrich. "Krampnitz. Von der Kavallerieschule zur Panzertruppenschule II 1937–1945" (Krampnitz: From the Cavalry School to the Panzer Force School, II, 1937–1945." *Potsdam. Staat, Armee, Residenz in der preußisch-deutschen Militär-geschichte* (Potsdam: State, Army, Residence in Prussian-German Military History). Ed. Bernhard R. Kroener, with the cooperation of Heiger Ostertag, by direction of the MGFA. Frankfurt am Main and Berlin: Propyläen Verlag, 1993.

Warlimont, Walter. *Im Hauptquartier der deutschen Wehrmacht 1939–1945* (In the Headquarters of the German Wehrmacht, 1939–1945). Frankfurt am Main: Bernard and Graefe, 1962.

Wassung, Wilhelm. "Der Maas-Übergang bei Donchery" (The Meuse River Crossing at Donchery). *Mitteilungsblatt der (10.) Wiener Panzer Division* (Bulletin of the [10th] Viennese Panzer Division), ser. 39 (1970), no. 2 (May): 3–6.

Weiß, Wilhelm, ed. *Triumph der Kriegskunst. Das Kriegsjahr 1940 in der Darstellung des "Völkischen Beobachters"* (Triumph of the Art of War: The War Year of 1940 as Described by the "Völkischer Beobachter"). Munich: Zentralverlag der NSDAP Franz Eher, 1941.

———. "Zeitenwende. Betrachtungen zum Jahreswechsel 1940/41" (Changing Times: Reflections on the Year of Change, 1940–41). *Triumph der Kriegskunst.* 11–52.

Wernick, Robert. *Der Blitzkrieg* (The Blitzkrieg). Amsterdam: Time-Life Books, 1979.

Werthen, Wolfgang. *Geschichte des 16. Panzer-Division* (History of the 16th Panzer Division). Bad Nauheim: Podzun Verlag, 1958.

Wette, Wolfram. "Ideologien, Propaganda und Innenpolitik als Voraussetzungen der Kriegspolitik des Dritten Reiches und der Zweiten Weltkrieg" (Ideology, Propaganda, and Internal Politics as Preconditions of the War Policy of the Third Reich). *Das Deutsche Reich und der Zweiten Weltkrieg.* Vol. 1, *Ursachen und Voraussetzungen der deutschen Kriegspolitik.* Stuttgart: Deutsche Verlags-Anstalt, 1988. 23–173.

Weygand, Maxime. *Mémoires* (Memoirs). Vol. 3. Paris: Flammarion, 1950.

Wieland, Volker. "Pigeaud versus Velpry. Zur Diskussion über Motorisierung und Mechanisierung, Panzertechnik und Panzertaktik in Frankreich nach dem Ersten Weltkrieg" (Pigeaud versus Velpry. A Discussion of Motorization and Mechanization, Tank Technology and Tank Tactics in France after the First World War). *MGM* 17, no. 1 (1975): 49–66.

Wirtschaft und Rüstung am Vorabend des Zweiten Weltkrieges (The Economy and Armaments on the Eve of the Second World War). Ed. Friedrich Forstmeier and Hans-Erich Volkmann. Düsseldorf: Droste Verlag, 1975.

Wittek, Erhard. *Die Soldatische Tat: Berichte von Mitkämpfern des Heeres im Westfeldzug 1940.* (A Soldierly Deed: Reports from Comrades in Arms of the Army in the Western Campaign, 1940). Vol. 1. Berlin: Im Deutschen Verlag, 1941.

Wörterbuch zur deutschen Militärgeschichte (Schriften des Militärgeschichtlichen Instituts der DDR) (Dictionary of German Military History [Works of the Military History Institute of the DDR]). 4 vols. East Berlin: Militärvelag der DDR, 1985–87.

Young, Desmond. *Rommel.* Wiesbaden: Limes Verlag, 1950.

Zaloga, Steven J. Blitzkrieg. *Armor, Camouflage, and Markings, 1939–1940.* Carrollton, Tex.: Squadron/Signal Publications, 1980.

Zeitgeschichte und Zeitperspektive (Contemporary History and Contemporary Perspectives). Paderborn: Ferdinand Schöningh, 1981.

Zeitzler, Kurt. "Die Panzer-Gruppe v. Kleist im West-Feldzug 1940" (The Panzer Group Kleist in the Campaign in the West, 1940). Parts 1–4, *Wehrkunde* 8 (1959): 182–88, 239–45, 293–98, 366–72.

Zentner, Christian. *Der Frankreichfeldzug—10. Mai 1940* (The Campaign in France—10 May 1940). Frankfurt am Main, Berlin, and Vienna: Ullstein, 1980.

Zimmermann, Hermann. *Der Griff ins Ungewisse. Die ersten Kriegstage 1940 beim XVI.Panzerkorps im Kampf um die Dylestellung, 10.–17. Mai* (Reaching into the Unknown. The First Days of War for the XVI Panzer Corps at the Dyle Position, 10–17 May). Neckargemünd: Kurt Vowinckel, 1964.

Zoller, Albert. *Hitler Privat. Erlebnisbericht seiner Geheimsekretärin* (The Private Hitler: The Account of His Personal Secretary). Düsseldorf: Droste Verlag, 1949.

Zweig, Stefan. *Sternstunden der Menschheit. Zwölf historische Miniaturen* (The Tide of Fortune: Twelve Historical Portraits). Frankfurt am Main: Fischer-Taschenbuch-Verlag, 1988.

Der Zweiten Weltkrieg. Analysen, Grundzüge, Forschungsbilanz (The Second World War: Analyses, Characteristics, and Research Balance). Ed. Wolfgang Michalka, by direction of the MGFA. Munich and Zürich: Piper Verlag, 1989.

Index of Personalities

Page numbers in italics refer to photographs. Page numbers followed by *n,* plus a number, refer to endnotes.

Index

Page numbers in italics refer to charts and photographs. Page numbers followed by *n,* plus a number, refer to endnotes.

About the Author

Colonel Dr. Karl-Heinz Frieser was born in Pressath, Germany. He joined the Bundeswehr as an officer candidate in 1970. After completing the regular training of an infantry officer, he was assigned to the Combat Arms School at Hammelburg. As a special award, he was selected in 1978 to study politics and history at Würzburg University where he received a doctorate degree in 1981. He later returned to a troop assignment to serve as commander of an armoured infantry company for three years. In 1985, he was assigned to the Military History Research Institute of the Bundeswehr where he is now head of the Department of World Wars I and II. His most successful book, *Blitzkrieg-Legende* (The Blitzkrieg Legend), was first published in 1995 and has been translated into several languages, including Japanese, French, and now English. For the French edition, the *Institute de France* awarded him the *Prix Edmond Fréville* (Edmond Fréville Prize) in December 2004. He was the first foreign historian to receive that award. As a supplement to this book, he wrote the military-historical battlefield guide *Ardennen-Sedan* (Ardennes-Sedan) (Frankfurt: Report Verlag, 2000). His current research focuses on the German-Soviet war. Soon, his comprehensive article "German Military Operations on the Eastern Front, 1943–44" will be published in the official series *Germany and the Second World War.*

About the Editor

Dr. John T. Greenwood received his undergraduate degree in history from the University of Colorado in 1964 and his master's degree from the University of Wisconsin-Madison in 1966. He completed his doctorate in military and aviation history in 1971 at Kansas State University where he worked under Professor Robin Higham. He was a historian with the U.S. Air Force from 1970 to 1978 and later became Chief Historian of the U.S. Army Corps of Engineers (1978–88) in Washington, D.C. He then served as Chief, Field Programs and Historical Services Division, U.S. Army Center of Military History (1988–98). Since October 1998 he has been Chief Historian for the Office of The Surgeon General, U.S. Army, in Falls Church, Virginia. He has published on U.S. and Soviet military aviation and history, military engineering, amphibious warfare, and military medicine, and on the impact of disease on military operations. His most recent work, *Medics at War: Military Medicine from Colonial Times to the 21st Century,* which he coauthored with F. Clifton Berry Jr., was published by the Naval Institute Press in the summer of 2005.

The Naval Institute Press is the book-publishing arm of the U.S. Naval Institute, a private, nonprofit membership society for sea service professionals and others who share an interest in naval and maritime affairs. Established in 1873 at the U.S. Naval Academy in Annapolis, Maryland, where its offices remain today, the Naval Institute has members worldwide.

Members of the Naval Institute support the education programs of the society and receive the influential monthly magazine *Proceedings* and discounts on fine nautical prints and on ship and aircraft photos. They also have access to the transcripts of the Institute's Oral History Program and get discounted admission to any of the Institute-sponsored seminars offered around the country. Discounts are also available to the colorful bimonthly magazine *Naval History*.

The Naval Institute's book-publishing program, begun in 1898 with basic guides to naval practices, has broadened its scope to include books of more general interest. Now the Naval Institute Press publishes about one hundred titles each year, ranging from how-to books on boating and navigation to battle histories, biographies, ship and aircraft guides, and novels. Institute members receive significant discounts on the Press's more than eight hundred books in print.

Full-time students are eligible for special half-price membership rates. Life memberships are also available.

For a free catalog describing Naval Institute Press books currently available, and for further information about joining the U.S. Naval Institute, please write to:

Customer Service
U.S. Naval Institute
291 Wood Road
Annapolis, MD 21402-5034
Telephone: (800) 233-8764
Fax: (410) 269-7940
Web address: www.navalinstitute.org